LIVES OF THE ENGLISH POETS

LIVES OF THE ENGLISH POETS

SAMUEL JOHNSON

EDITED BY

GEORGE BIRKBECK HILL

IN THREE VOLUMES

VOL. I

COWLEY—DRYDEN

ff

faber and faber

This edition first published in 2009
by Faber and Faber Ltd
Bloomsbury House, 74–77 Great Russell Street
London WC1B 3DA

Printed by CPI Antony Rowe, Eastbourne

A CIP record for this book is available from the British Library

ISBN 978-0-571-25517-7

CONTENTS OF VOLUME I

LIVES OF THE POETS

CONTENTS OF VOLUME II

CONTENTS OF VOLUME III

LIVES OF THE ENGLISH POETS

IN ALPHABETICAL ORDER

PREFATORY NOTE TO THE PRESENT EDITION

THE text and notes of this edition of *The Lives of the Poets* are, with a few necessary exceptions, scrupulously printed as my uncle, the late Dr. Birkbeck Hill, left them. Whatever changes or additions I have made are enclosed within square brackets.

The Text is based on that of the four-volumed octavo edition of 1783—the last edition published in Johnson's lifetime. The spelling has been retained, save in a few places where obvious typographical errors have been corrected; but Johnson's punctuation, which seems to rest on no system, has been altered in accordance with modern usage, and with Dr. Birkbeck Hill's express directions.

A posthumous edition of a work must always suffer from lack of that care in revision, as it passes through the press, which the editor himself alone can bestow. Yet it has been my constant endeavour to strive, so far as was within my powers, to carry out the work as my uncle would have wished it done. There is, I believe, scarcely a quotation or a reference in the notes which has not been verified in the proofs by a comparison with the original authority.

In his work Dr. Birkbeck Hill received the assistance which happily scholars are ever ready to give to one another. I think that, in most instances, acknowledgement has been made in the notes; yet where this has not been done, as he is no longer with us to remedy the omission, I wish to express here, in his name, the sense of gratitude which he entertained to all who gave him aid. In my own portion of the work I have received the greatest help and kindness from my uncle's friends, among whom I would particularly express my gratitude to Mr. C. E. Doble, M.A., of the Clarendon Press; Mr. G. K. Fortescue, Keeper of the Printed Books, British Museum; and Mr. Thomas Seccombe, M.A.

HAROLD SPENCER SCOTT.

18 Church Row, Hampstead,
October, 1905.

ADDENDA AND CORRIGENDA

vol. i, p. 163, l. 16, 'Where there is,' &c., *delete* quotation marks.

vol. i, p. 249 *n.* 2, Waller was born on March 3, 1606 : *Amersham Parish Reg.*, quoted in *Waller's Poems*, ed. G. T. Drury, 1893, Pref. xv. *n.*

vol. i, p. 410 *n.* 7, *for* 1859 *read* 1589.

vol. i, p. 412 *n.* 1, for *Essay of English Poesy* read *Essay of Dramatic Poesy.*

vol. ii, p. 87 *n.* 5, *Ante* ADDISON, 22 *n.* 7 read 22 *n.* 6.

vol. ii, p. 287, l. 1, comma *after* ' imitated.'

vol. iii, p. 43 *n.* 2, *for* Lyons *read* Lyon.

vol. iii, p. 161 *n.* 4. For a detailed account of the early editions of Pope's *Essay on Man* see Mr. G. A. Aitken's communication to the *Athenaeum*, Jan. 28, 1905.

vol. iii, p. 228 *n.* 4. There is an error here. The comparison is with Dryden's second *Ode for St. Cecilia's Day, Alexander's Feast,* the last stanza of which ends :—

> ' He rais'd a mortal to the skies ;
> She drew an angel down.'

vol. iii, p. 237 *n.* 2, *for* 1523 *read* 1723.

vol. iii, p. 337 *n.* 2, for *The Poetical Character* read *The Poetical Calendar.*

vol. iii, p. 359, app. T, last line but one, *for* Whitfield *read* Whitefield.

In the Notes, all cross-references to passages in the *Lives* give the number of the paragraph of the *Life* to which allusion is made, e. g. *Ante* or *Post* MILTON 274. The paragraph numbers are printed throughout in bold italic on the outer margin of each page of the text.

In the Index, the roman numerals refer to the Volumes; the arabic figures to the Pages.

BRIEF MEMOIR OF
DR. BIRKBECK HILL

GEORGE BIRKBECK NORMAN HILL, second son of Arthur Hill and Ellen Tilt, daughter of Joseph Maurice, was born on June 7, 1835, at Bruce Castle, Tottenham, in Middlesex, at that time a quiet and picturesque village. His father was one of a band of brothers, sons of Thomas Wright Hill, of Birmingham, who, one and all treading in the footsteps of their father, a disciple of Priestley and an ardent Reformer, not only threw themselves with enthusiasm into the political movement towards Reform, of which Birmingham became the centre, but took an active part in furthering the cause of truth, justice, freedom, and social welfare according to their lights. They were free traders, condemners of the harsh penal code, haters of all religious inequality and intolerance, and earnest supporters of the anti-slavery cause. Withal they were thorough Englishmen. Never did they desire the victory of the French in the long war.

At the time of Birkbeck Hill's birth, Thomas Wright Hill and his sons were chiefly known as the founders of the Hazelwood [1] system of education, which with its reliance on love as the principle to which all trainers of the young should chiefly trust, its elaborate constitution of government by the boys, and its endeavour to discover each pupil's natural bent, attracted much attention in the early part of the last century, and greatly influenced general education. The other brothers, notably Rowland Hill, the Postal Reformer, and Matthew Davenport Hill, afterwards Recorder of Birmingham, had left the school before the birth of Birkbeck Hill, to devote themselves to a more public career; but Arthur Hill found his absorbing interest in education, and in 1833 became head master of the new school established at Bruce Castle to carry on the system originally founded at Birmingham. Birkbeck Hill's mother, Ellen Tilt Maurice, who died when he was only four years old, was on

---

[1] After the name of the house in the Hagley Road, Birmingham, where the school was carried on from 1819 to 1833.

her father's side related to Frederic Denison Maurice; on the mother's side she was of Huguenot ancestry. All who knew her bear witness to the singular charm and brightness of her nature.

Birkbeck Hill used to say that he had been brought up as a utilitarian; yet there were other influences present in his childhood and youth which served to cultivate the imaginative and literary side of his nature. The old Jacobean mansion which had inherited from far earlier times the name of Bruce Castle was destined to be his home, with a short break on his marriage, for more than forty years. 'The park,' to quote his own words, 'was but small, yet so thick was the foliage of the stately trees, and so luxuriant the undergrowth of the shrubberies, that its boundaries failed to reach the eye. Hard by the main building stood an ancient tower which was standing when Queen Elizabeth visited the mansion, and when Henry VIII met there his sister, Queen Margaret of Scotland[1].' Furthermore his father, though deeply interested in reform in common with the rest of the 'Hill brothers,' had in his nature a strong literary bent. Injury to sight which had befallen him when still a young man, from earnest study under unfavourable conditions as he thought, raised a barrier to so full a cultivation of this side of his character as he would otherwise have enjoyed. Even with this impediment, which did much to cut him off from entering on new fields of literature, so great was his love of Shakespeare that he had stored in his retentive memory at least eight plays, which when close on eighty he could still recite by heart; while at a still greater age he was able to translate Horace's *Ars Poetica* into blank verse almost entirely from his recollection of the original.

Moreover, though Birkbeck Hill would sometimes regret the excessive influence of the utilitarianism with which he was surrounded in childhood and early youth, yet to much of the faith of his fathers he clung tenaciously throughout his life. From his father he inherited, in addition to a strong moral rectitude, a love of justice, a hatred of tyrannies and shams, and a sympathy with the oppressed. 'Beg of Arthur not to get over-intoxicated with the Greek news,' had been written of his father in 1829 on the tidings of the battle of Navarino. Of

[1] *Life of Sir Rowland Hill*, i. 181.

Birkbeck Hill himself it is told that, after he had succeeded to the head mastership of Bruce Castle, he was once asked to receive into the school the son of a planter whose wealth was raised in great part by slave labour. With his detestation of slavery the first thought was to refuse; but afterwards reflecting that the boy might receive good from the school, he determined to take him, resolving at the same time to devote all the fees to charitable objects. Like Dr. Johnson he might have given as his toast, 'Here's to the next insurrection of the negroes in the West Indies.'

It was in his father's school that Birkbeck Hill was educated until he matriculated at Oxford. The teaching was excellent, so far as it went. Thoroughness and good discipline were achieved: individuality and intelligence were encouraged. Yet, as he himself admits, the scholastic attainments of the founders of the new system were not equal to their ingenuity and enthusiasm. He was wont to mention with regret the fact that he did not begin Greek until he was sixteen. From Bruce Castle School Birkbeck Hill went up to Oxford, matriculating from Pembroke College on March 1, 1855. Here he passed into a new world. 'I was brought up,' he writes, 'among those whose canon of taste was contained in the *Edinburgh Review*. I sat, as it were, at the feet of Jeffrey and Macaulay. Not a doubt did I ever hear cast on their infallibility. In them was contained all the law and the prophets. Byron's *English Bards and Scotch Reviewers* was constantly in the hands and on the tongues of my young associates. . . . Wordsworth was our scoff. . . . I entered Oxford as ignorant of the new School of Poetry as any one well could be. I do not think that I had ever seen a single poem of Keats or Shelley. Mr. Browning's name was, I believe, unknown to me. Of Wordsworth and Tennyson I had read only a very few poems. Tennyson I had heard treated with the same scorn as his great forerunners [1].' It was for him a happy day when he became acquainted with Mr. William Fulford, a member of his college and editor of the short-lived *Oxford and Cambridge Magazine*, to which Rossetti and William Morris were contributors. Fulford introduced him to the little fraternity, of which Burne-Jones and William Morris were the leaders. 'It was,' to quote his own words, '"a nest of

[1] *Writers and Readers*, p. 99.

singing birds," who night after night were found in the neighbourhood of Dr. Johnson's old college, often in the college itself. . . .
The subjects which I had always heard discussed were never
discussed here, while matters on which I had never heard any
one speak formed here the staple of the talk. I recall how one
evening the nineteenth century was denounced for its utter want
of poetry. This was more than I could bear, for the nineteenth
century was almost an object of adoration in my father's house.
I ventured to assert that it could boast at all events of one piece
of poetry—the steam engine. The roar of laughter which burst
forth nearly overwhelmed me. The author of *The Earthly
Paradise* almost overturned his chair as he flung himself back-
wards overpowered with mirth. I was too much abashed to
explain that I was recalling the sight I had once had of an
engine rushing through the darkness along a high embankment,
drawing after it a cloud of flame and fiery steam [1].' In this
fraternity Birkbeck Hill was not unfrequently in the company of
Rossetti, who, 'with a friendly band of young pre-Raphaelite
painters,' was covering with frescoes the walls of the new Debating Room of the Oxford Union Society [2]. Of Swinburne, too,
he was a contemporary and friend.

So ardently did Birkbeck Hill drink in the new knowledge
that, when he had scarcely taken his degree, he dared to give
a lecture at the Mechanics' Institute of the very village in which
he had been brought up, wherein he challenged a place for
Tennyson among the great poets. For a time he even went to
the opposite extreme, and learnt to speak as contemptuously of
Pope as he had before spoken of Wordsworth and Tennyson.

Other friends he had, not of this set, like Professor Dicey, and,
perhaps above all others, George Rankine Luke of Balliol, afterwards Senior Student of Christ Church, a man of singular ability,
high character, and enthusiastic energy, whose untimely death by
drowning in the Isis in 1862 robbed the University of 'a great
and beneficent influence,' to quote the late Master of Balliol, and
was lamented in an eloquent tribute by Stanley in a farewell
sermon to the University [3]. The sudden loss of one so dear to him
and so honoured was perhaps Birkbeck Hill's first great grief.

[1] *Letters of D. G. Rossetti to W. Allingham*, p. 177.
[2] Now the Library.
[3] For a brief account of Mr. Luke, and a testimony to his influence, the

Ill health, the result of a severe attack of typhoid, proved a bar to any attempt at honours, and he was obliged to be content with an 'honorary fourth class' *In Literis Humanioribus.* He took his B.A. degree in the Michaelmas Term of 1858, but never proceeded to an M.A. through dislike of the religious tests then imposed. In 1866 he took the degree of B.C.L., and in 1871 that of D.C.L., availing himself of the University Tests Act passed in that year.

On leaving Oxford in 1858 Birkbeck Hill joined his father in the school, though he did not take orders as he had originally intended when he went up to Oxford. In the January of the next year he was married to Annie Scott, the daughter of Edward Scott, a solicitor of Wigan in Lancashire. They had become engaged before Birkbeck Hill went up to Oxford, when they were still boy and girl.

At Bruce Castle School, first in partnership with his father, but from 1868 as sole head master, Birkbeck Hill remained until 1877. At Tottenham all his seven children were born. The school continued to enjoy fair prosperity and success. Some changes were introduced, chiefly in the direction of bringing up the teaching to modern requirements, but on the whole the old principles were maintained to the end. Yet it may be said here that the profession was not one suited to Birkbeck Hill's sensitive nature—unsupported, as he at any rate came to be, by enthusiasm or even confidence in his calling; while many of the duties incumbent on the master of a private school, though always performed with that conscientiousness which was a characteristic of his work, grew more and more irksome to him as years went on.

It may be of interest to some of Birkbeck Hill's friends who are aware of his denunciation of the tyranny of over-organized athleticism in our schools and universities, to hear that while at Bruce Castle he was a keen cricketer, taking part as a regular member of the school eleven in the matches of the boys. He was always a vigorous walker. In earlier manhood a holiday passed amid the Lake mountains was one of his greatest pleasures; nor in his later years did this source of health and happiness desert him. I well remember the long mountain rambles we took

reader is referred to the *Life and Letters of Benjamin Jowett,* i. 331, where a portion of the late Master's obituary notice of him, contributed to the *Times,* is given.

together day after day during one winter I passed with him at
Alassio. Often did it fall to my lot in Hampstead, where he
chiefly passed the last years of his life, to be his companion in
the brisk walks which he regularly took on the Heath or round
Golder's Hill.

Through his enduring friendship with Charles Joseph Faulkner [1], 'the pleasantest of companions as he was always the truest
of friends,' who was the third member in the art firm of Morris,
Marshall, Faulkner & Co. (now Morris & Co.), Birkbeck Hill
kept in touch with many of the men in whose company he
had entered upon the new world of art and literature. Yet it
was not until 1869 that Birkbeck Hill began regularly to write.
In that year he became a contributor to the *Saturday Review*,
then under the editorship of his friend Philip Harwood, in its
palmy days when it numbered among the contributors E. A.
Freeman, J. R. Green, Sir Henry Maine, Lord Justice Bowen,
Sir James Stephen, Sir Leslie Stephen, and Professor Owen. As
Matthew Arnold once said to Birkbeck Hill, it was easy to see
that every subject was entrusted to a writer who was master of it.
For many years he was a regular contributor, his last review,
I believe, appearing in 1884, in the year after Harwood ceased to
be editor. With the political part of the journal he had, of course,
nothing whatever to do. 'The editor,' as he himself tells us, 'discovered in me a certain vein of humour, and for the most part
sent me books to review which deserved little more than ridicule.
What havoc I made among the novelists and minor poets! I
amused my readers because I was first amused myself by the
absurdities which I everywhere found in these writers, and by the
odd fancies which rose in my mind as I read their works.' At
last the minor poets overwhelmed him. Dejection took the place
of amusement as he read. At his entreaty they were entrusted
to a fresher hand. The time too came when the novelists ceased
to amuse him, and he became aware that he could no longer raise
a natural laugh. 'One result of all this novel-reading,' he tells
us, 'was a total incapacity, lasting for many years, of reading
any novels except those which were the favourites of my younger
days. To read a novel became so inseparably connected in my
mind with three pounds ten shillings, the usual payment for a
Saturday Review article, that without the one I could not under-

[1] Scholar of Pembroke and Fellow of University College, Oxford.

take the other. All in vain have friends urged me to read the works of Black, Blackmore, Hardy, Howells, Henry James, Stevenson, and Kipling. Not a single story of any one of these writers have I ever read or am I ever likely to read[1].' In addition to his work as a Saturday Reviewer he contributed also to the *Cornhill Magazine*, the *Pall Mall Gazette*, and the *Times*.

It was not until 1878 that his first book, *Dr. Johnson: His Friends and His Critics*, was published. This was the first outcome of those Johnsonian studies which were to be the main pursuit of his life.

In the Preface to his edition of Boswell, Birkbeck Hill has described the happy day in 1869 when, 'in an old book-shop, almost under the shadow of a great cathedral,' he bought a second-hand copy of an early edition of the *Life*. For though when he entered Pembroke College he loved to think that Johnson had been there before him, he had scarcely opened the pages of Boswell since his boyhood until that day. Yet Addison had attracted him in his undergraduate days, and with him and the other great writers of his and the succeeding age he had become familiar. 'The volumes,' he writes, 'became my inseparable companions. Before long I began to note the parallel passages and allusions.' In his reviewing it fell to his lot to criticize works that bore both on Boswell and Johnson, and his love and knowledge of the subject increased; but it was not until 1875 that he first definitely resolved to prepare a new edition of the *Life*. From that time he began steadily to collect materials. Unfortunately ill health came upon him, and the work of preparation had to be carried on amid many interruptions and disadvantages. More than once his health seemed almost hopelessly broken down. One hindrance to his literary work was, however, removed in 1877, for a complete and alarming breakdown, accompanied by distressing asthma, made him finally resolve to give up the school and devote himself henceforth to literature. A few months passed at Mentone, the first of many winters to be spent abroad, did much to remove the worst symptoms of his illness; but he never possessed the same physical vigour again. A removal to the country was determined on, and the autumn of 1877 saw him settled at Burghfield, near Reading, where he lived until 1886. With the rest from the ever-increasing burden which the school had come

[1] *Talks about Autographs*, p. 79.

to be to him and his wife, Birkbeck Hill felt immediate relief, and the quiet and beauty of the country were a never-failing source of pleasure to him. Freedom from duties to other people's children allowed him to take a greater share in the companionship and education of his own. His way of life was one of great simplicity, and regular hours of work and exercise marked his day. Withal, he was never a silent scholar rooted to his study. He depended much on the love and sympathy of those around him. The society of children, and indeed of all young people, was a special delight to him; and with them, even in times of illness and depression, the natural gaiety of his nature would reassert itself, while his wise sympathy was freely given to them in their hopes and fears. Soon after settling at Burghfield he began to take an interest in the public affairs of the neighbourhood, and became a Poor Law Guardian of the Bradfield Union. For some time also he was president of the South Berkshire Liberal Association. During several years of comparative health he was able to try his strength as a critic and an editor, besides still regularly contributing to the *Saturday Review*. In the spring after his settlement at Burghfield appeared his first book, *Dr. Johnson: His Friends and His Critics*, wherein he reviewed the judgements passed on Johnson and Boswell by Lord Macaulay and Mr. Carlyle, and described Oxford as it was known to Johnson. The next year he edited Boswell's *Journal of a Tour to Corsica*. Twice was he drawn away from the task which he had set before himself, a new edition of Boswell's *Life of Johnson*. On the death of his uncle, Sir Rowland Hill, he was called upon to edit his *History of Penny Postage*, and to write his *Life*. In 1880 also, General Gordon's brother, Sir Henry Gordon, entrusted him with the duty of editing the letters which General Gordon had written to his sister during the six years of his government of the Soudan. For this task Birkbeck Hill had one qualification apart from all others. Of Egyptian affairs he had of late heard much from his brother-in-law, Sir John Scott, at that time Vice-President of the International Court at Alexandria. It had, indeed, at first been intended that Sir John Scott, a personal friend of Colonel Gordon, as he then was, should undertake the work; and it was on his recommendation that it was entrusted to Birkbeck Hill.

The book appeared under somewhat unusual conditions, for though General Gordon had given his consent to the publication of the letters he refused to take any direct part in it. Whatever information was needed had to be obtained through Sir Henry Gordon, his brother. Birkbeck Hill's admiration for the 'rare genius, the wise and pure enthusiasm, and the exalted beneficence of that great man' was conspicuous. The strong religious utterances occurring in the letters expressed thoughts which were not Birkbeck Hill's, but he saw in Gordon—it may be with longing—one who 'by manifold struggles feels his feet on the Everlasting Rock.' The labour given to these works, as regards the main purpose, was not thrown away. He would often say that he was trained by it in the duties of an editor, and strengthened in his hatred of carelessness and error.

Yet again he was forced to turn aside from his purpose, and this time by a great sorrow. The loss of a beloved son, a boy of singular sweetness and promise, who died in 1882 after a painful illness, for the time wellnigh took from him every kind of hope. A second serious illness closely followed, compelling him to spend three winters on the shores of the Mediterranean. 'During two of them my malady and my distress,' he writes, 'allowed of no rival, and my work made scarcely any advance.' It was not until the third winter spent at San Remo that his strength began to return and he could again resume his work. With all these interruptions the summer of 1885 was upon him before the printing of the book could begin. At last, in 1887, Boswell's *Life* was published by the Clarendon Press. Twelve years had he been engaged on it. Five years had passed since his proposal was accepted by the Delegates.

The year of the publication of *Boswell* found Birkbeck Hill removed from his country home and settled at Oxford. For close on six years his home was here in a small house near 'The Parks.' Though he missed the country, he enjoyed Oxford life to the full. Amid new scenes and change of life his health improved. The society of men of like tastes, who could appreciate his scholarship and take pleasure in that vein of humour and anecdotal power of which he was possessed, made the period of his residence in Oxford, on the whole, a happy one. Nor was his intercourse confined to men engaged in similar studies to his own, as is shown by the mention of Professor Morfill, Professor Burdon Sanderson, and the Rev. C. W. Boase [1] among

[1] Fellow of Exeter, and University Reader in Foreign History.

the friends made during this Oxford time. He availed himself of his residential qualification to become a member of Congregation, while his election in 1892 to an honorary fellowship of his old college gave him very great pleasure. With quickened life and a ready access to books, which the Bodleian afforded, his power of work increased. Though the connexion with the *Saturday Review* had ceased, he still sent occasional articles, chiefly on Johnsonian subjects, to the *Cornhill Magazine* or *Macmillan's*, and when the *Speaker* was founded as a Liberal weekly he became a fairly frequent contributor. In 1888 he was able to put before the world a series of hitherto unpublished letters written by David Hume to Strahan, which in the summer of the preceding year he had had the opportunity of examining when in the possession of a dealer in autographs. He at once set about the work of saving the series from dispersion; but for some weeks he almost despaired of finding a purchaser. In his trouble he consulted the late Master of Balliol, to whom as 'Johnsonianissimus' the edition of *Boswell* had been dedicated, in grateful acknowledgement of the interest he had taken in its publication when his term of Vice-Chancellorship brought him into close connexion with the Clarendon Press. It was by his happy suggestion that application was made to the Earl of Rosebery, who at once consented to buy the whole collection. The Clarendon Press were the publishers. In the Preface he shows us the principle which guided all his editing. 'In my notes,' he writes, 'my aim has been not only to make every letter clear, but also to bring before my readers the thoughts and the feelings of Hume's contemporaries in regard to the subject which he discusses.' He quotes with approval Hume's rule: 'Every book should be as complete as possible within itself, and should never refer for anything material to other books.'

In this year also he brought out an edition of Goldsmith's *Traveller*, for the use of schools, in the Clarendon Press Series. *Rasselas* had been edited by him in the preceding year for the same series. These were followed by a selection under the title of *Wit and Wisdom of Samuel Johnson*.

With his next work, *The Footsteps of Dr. Johnson*, published in 1890, Birkbeck Hill entered upon a new field of writing, though the great study of his life was still the subject. In this book he traces Johnson's journey through Scotland; but he does more than merely weave together the three accounts that we have of it. It was his chief aim to bring before his readers 'the Scotland which Johnson saw, the Scotland which he had come to study.' The 'wild objects' he left rather to his artist colleague, Mr. Lancelot Speed, in whose company he visited very many of the scenes of Johnson's wanderings. '" The peculiar manners" which interested Johnson far more than natural objects' were Birkbeck Hill's special study.

With the severe winter of 1890-1 the comparative freedom from ill health which he had for some time enjoyed was broken by a severe attack of bronchitis complicated by asthma, his old and constant enemy. He was forced reluctantly to the conclusion that the climate of Oxford was not sufficiently suited to his health to suffer him to continue to make a home there. Five successive winters he and his wife passed abroad—1892-3, 1893-4, 1894-5 near Clarens, and 1895-6, 1896-7 at Alassio; during the summer months they made their home chiefly at Hampstead with their second daughter, Mrs. Crump.

In 1891 he made a selection for the Clarendon Press of Lord Chesterfield's *Worldly Wisdom*, a volume similar to the selection of Johnson's *Wit and Wisdom*, three years before.

Meanwhile he had not lost sight of his main work. For some time he had been engaged in editing Johnson's *Letters*, and the year 1892 saw the completion of his task. He again found a publisher in the Clarendon Press. This collection includes about ninety letters published by him for the first time.

The same year appeared *Writers and Readers*, embodying a series of six lectures which, under the titles of 'Revolutions in Literary Taste' and 'The Study of Literature as a part of Education,' he had read in the Hall of New College before the members of the Teachers' University Association who were in residence in Oxford during part of the Long Vacation of the preceding year. In these lectures Birkbeck Hill spoke to his audience almost as he talked to his friends, taking them into his confidence, and no book of his has more of the personal element than this. Pleasant old memories of his undergraduate days and early life occur here and there. A similar strain of recollections runs through his *Talks about Autographs*, the *Rossetti Letters*, and his book on Harvard.

In 1893 he and his wife crossed the Atlantic on a visit to their

eldest daughter and her husband, Mr. W. J. Ashley, then
Professor of Economic History at Harvard (now Professor of
Commerce in the University of Birmingham). With them he
passed the summer and early autumn, partly at Cambridge,
Massachusetts, and partly in a pleasant village on Cape Cod.
A result of this visit was *Harvard College by an Oxonian,*
published in 1894. The summer of 1896 again found him in
America, renewing pleasant intercourse with the friends he had
made in his first visit. It was during this second visit that the
honorary degree granted him by Williams College in 1892 was
actually conferred. That same year he brought out *Talks about
Autographs,* which had appeared originally in the *Atlantic
Monthly.* The following year saw the publication of the last
piece of Johnsonian work which he lived to complete. At the
suggestion of Sir Leslie Stephen he edited all those writings
which have long been included under the general title of
'Johnsoniana.' In the Preface to the *Letters of Samuel Johnson*
he had spoken of his hope of completing the main work of his
life as a scholar by a new edition of the *Lives of the Poets.* Of
this he had already laid the foundations as far back as 1892 ;
but he now put the work aside for a time in order to turn to this
new task. The result was the two volumes of *Johnsonian
Miscellanies* published by the Clarendon Press in 1897. Their
publication had been delayed by three years of ill health, and by
the necessity of passing his winters abroad. 'In the six volumes
of the *Life* there is,' he tells us, 'scarcely a quotation or a
reference in the notes which I did not verify in the proof by
a comparison with the original authority. The labour was great,
but it was not more than a man should be ready to undergo who
ventures to edit an English classic.' On the banks of the Lake
of Geneva or on the shores of the Mediterranean he could no
longer do this. Often he cast 'a long look' towards the Bodleian
and the British Museum. His next book, *Letters of Dante
Gabriel Rossetti to William Allingham,* 1897, was a new
departure. Yet the letters brought back to him his undergraduate days, when he was not seldom in Rossetti's company,
or memories of the old house in Red Lion Square where
Burne-Jones and William Morris had their rooms. One hot
morning he recalls when he had watched Burne-Jones painting
a cluster of crown lilies in the square garden, perhaps the first

time that the painter ever worked in oils. He was, moreover, able to draw on the reminiscences of his old friend, Mr. Arthur Hughes, who, though not one of the Pre-Raphaelite Brothers, lived in great intimacy with them. A considerable portion of these letters had already appeared under his editing in four papers contributed to the *Atlantic Monthly* during the preceding year.

In 1898 he published nothing, with the exception of a small selection from the letters of Johnson and Lord Chesterfield, which formed a volume in a series entitled *Eighteenth Century Letters* under the general editorship of Mr. Brimley Johnson. For some time, however, he had been engaged in preparing a series of unpublished letters written by Swift to Knightley Chetwode between 1714 and 1731. The book appeared in 1899. The knowledge gained in the editing of these letters doubtless did much to prepare the way for the view which he takes of the Dean's character in his notes to Johnson's life of Swift.

In 1899 two articles by him, *Boswell's Proof Sheets*[1] and *The Boswell Centenary*, were included in a collection of papers on Dr. Johnson written by members of the Johnson Club[2], and published in book form under the title of *Johnson Club Papers by Various Hands*. Since Birkbeck Hill had been a member of the Johnson Club, serving as Prior in 1891 and 1892, the meetings at the Cheshire Cheese and elsewhere were a source of much pleasure to him; he especially enjoyed the visits he made to Lichfield, Bath, Ashbourne, Stratford, or other places associated with Johnson, in company with the members of the Club.

In 1900 his last work was published—an edition of Gibbon's *Autobiography* under the title of *The Memoirs of the Life of Edward Gibbon*, a title found by him in Gibbon's handwriting on the manuscript of the various sketches of the Autobiography now preserved in the British Museum. In this edition one of his chief aims was to throw light on Gibbon's character from his own writings and correspondence. For the text he made use of both the first and the second editions of Lord Sheffield's version Respect for Mr. Murray's copyright checked emendations; but, as is the case with all Birkbeck Hill's work, the *Memoirs* are enriched with copious footnotes and appendices.

During the last three years of his life he gave his time and

---

[1] *Boswell's Proof Sheets* first appeared in the *Atlantic Monthly.*
[2] Founded Dec. 13, 1884.

strength to completing the edition of Johnson's *Lives of the Poets*. His own increasing ill health and that of his wife often compelled him to lay the work aside ; but after every check he resolutely returned to his labours, with the result that on his death the work was almost ready for the printer's hands. A few additions and some research, rendered comparatively easy by the precision with which he worked and the good order in which his papers were kept, were alone needed.

In the spring of 1902 the health of his wife, which had been for some years previously the cause of much anxiety to him, began rapidly to fail. She was a woman of marked intellectual ability, and, with the aid of her rare forethought, courage, and firmness of character, he had weathered many of the troubles of life. It was a source of comfort to him, during the brief span of life left, that his own failing strength had permitted him to tend and watch over her till the last. She died in their pleasant little country home at Aspley Guise on Oct. 30, 1902. The blow fell heavily on Birkbeck Hill. Yet it was hoped that there were, in spite of his own infirmities, some years of quiet work before him. It was not to be. Hardly four months did he survive her. He died at Hampstead, in his daughter's home, on Feb. 27, 1903, at the age of sixty-seven.

BIBLIOGRAPHY

Dr. Johnson: His Friends and His Critics. London, 1878.

Boswell's Correspondence with the Honourable Andrew Erskine and His Journal of a Tour to Corsica, edited with a Preface, Introduction, and Notes. London, 1879.

The Life of Sir Rowland Hill and the History of Penny Postage, by Sir Rowland Hill and his nephew, George Birkbeck Hill, 2 vols. London, 1880.

Colonel Gordon in Central Africa, 1874-9. From original Letters and Documents. Edited by George Birkbeck Hill. London, 1881. Second edition, 1884.

Boswell's Life of Johnson, including Boswell's Journal of a Tour to the Hebrides and Johnson's Diary of a Journey into North Wales, edited by George Birkbeck Hill, D.C.L., Pembroke College, Oxford. 6 vols. Oxford, at the Clarendon Press, 1887.

Johnson: History of Rasselas, Prince of Abyssinia, edited with Introduction and Notes by George Birkbeck Hill. Clarendon Press Series. Oxford, 1887.

Goldsmith: The Traveller, edited with Introduction and Notes. Clarendon Press Series. Oxford, 1888.

Letters of David Hume to William Strahan, now first edited with Notes, Index, &c. By G. Birkbeck Hill, D.C.L., Pembroke College. Oxford, at the Clarendon Press, 1888.

Wit and Wisdom of Samuel Johnson, selected and arranged by George Birkbeck Hill. Oxford, at the Clarendon Press, 1888.

Footsteps of Dr. Johnson (Scotland), by George Birkbeck Hill, with Illustrations by Lancelot Speed. London, 1890.

Lord Chesterfield's Worldly Wisdom. Selections from his Letters and Characters, arranged and edited by George Birkbeck Hill. Oxford, at the Clarendon Press, 1891.

Letters of Samuel Johnson, LL.D., collected and edited by George Birkbeck Hill, D.C.L., Pembroke College, Oxford. 2 vols. Oxford, at the Clarendon Press, 1892.

Writers and Readers. London, 1892.

Harvard College by an Oxonian. New York and London, 1894.

Talks about Autographs. Boston and New York, 1896.

Johnsonian Miscellanies, arranged and edited by George Birkbeck Hill, D.C.L., LL.D., Honorary Fellow of Pembroke College, Oxford. 2 vols. Oxford, at the Clarendon Press, 1897.

Letters of Dante Gabriel Rossetti to William Allingham, 1854-70. London, 1897.

Eighteenth Century Letters. Johnson: Lord Chesterfield. London, 1898.

Unpublished Letters of Dean Swift, edited by George Birkbeck Hill, D.C.L., LL.D., Hon. Fellow of Pembroke College, Oxford. London, 1899.

Boswell's Proof Sheets. The Boswell Centenary. Included in *Johnson Club Papers by Various Hands.* London, 1899.

The Memoirs of the Life of Edward Gibbon, with Various Observations and Excursions by Himself, edited by George Birkbeck Hill, D.C.L., LL.D., Honorary Fellow of Pembroke College, Oxford. London, 1900.

Letters written by a Grandfather, selected by Lucy Crump. London, 1903.

Contributed articles and reviews to the following magazines and news-papers:—*Macmillan, Cornhill, Contemporary, Atlantic Monthly, Times, Saturday Review, Pall Mall Gazette*, and *Speaker.*

THE AUTHOR'S ADVERTISEMENT
TO THE THIRD EDITION [1]

THE Booksellers having determined to publish a Body of English Poetry [2] I was persuaded to promise them

[1] In the first edition (PREFACES BIOGRAPHICAL AND CRITICAL TO THE WORKS OF THE ENGLISH POETS. BY SAMUEL JOHNSON. London. 1779–81, 12mo. 10 vols.) the advertisement is dated March 15, 1779.

[2] [Mr. Edward Dilly, the bookseller, writing to Boswell on Sept. 26, 1777, gives the following account of 'this plan so happily conceived' in the early part of that year—'The first cause that gave rise to this undertaking, I believe, was owing to the little trifling edition of *The Poets*, printing by the Martins, at Edinburgh, and to be sold by Bell, in London. Upon examining the volumes which were printed, the type was found so extremely small, that many persons could not read them; not only this inconvenience attended it, but the inaccuracy of the press was very conspicuous. These reasons, as well as the idea of an invasion of what we call our Literary Property, induced the London Booksellers to print an elegant and accurate edition of all the English Poets of reputation, from Chaucer to the present time.

'Accordingly a select number of the most respectable booksellers met on the occasion; and, on consulting together, agreed that all the proprietors of copy-right in the various Poets should be summoned together; and when their opinions were given, to proceed immediately on the business. Accordingly a meeting was held, consisting of about forty of the most respectable booksellers of London, when it was agreed that an elegant and uniform edition of *The English Poets* should be immediately printed, with a concise account of the life of each authour, by Dr. Samuel Johnson; and that three persons should be deputed to wait upon Dr. Johnson, to solicit him to undertake the Lives, *viz.*, T. Davies, Strahan, and Cadell. The Doctor very politely undertook it, and seemed exceedingly pleased with the proposal. As to the terms, it was left entirely to the Doctor to name his own: he mentioned two hundred guineas: it was immediately agreed to; and a farther compliment, I believe, will be made him. A committee was likewise appointed to engage the best engravers, *viz.*, Bartolozzi, Sherwin, Hall, etc. Likewise another committee for giving directions about the paper, printing, etc., so that the whole will be conducted with spirit, and in the best manner, with respect to authourship, editorship, engravings, etc., etc. My brother will give you a list of the Poets we mean to give, many of which are within the time of the Act of Queen Anne, which Martin and Bell cannot give, as they have no property in them; the proprietors are almost all the booksellers in London, of consequence.' Boswell's *Life of Johnson*, ed. by G. Birkbeck Hill, iii. 110.

Johnson 'had bargained for two hundred guineas, and the book-a Preface to the Works of each Author; an undertaking, as it was then presented to my mind, not very extensive[1] or difficult.

My purpose was only to have allotted to every Poet an Advertisement, like those which we find in the French Miscellanies, containing a few dates and a general character[2]; but I have been led beyond my intention, I hope, by the honest desire of giving useful pleasure.

In this minute kind of History the succession of facts is not easily discovered, and I am not without suspicion that some of Dryden's works are placed in wrong years[3]. I have followed Langbaine, as the best authority for his plays; and if I shall hereafter obtain a more correct chronology will publish it, but I do not yet know that my account is erroneous[4].

Dryden's *Remarks on Rymer* have been somewhere printed[5]

---

sellers spontaneously added a third hundred; on this occasion Dr. Johnson observed to me—"Sir, I have always said the booksellers were a generous set of men. Nor, in the present instance, have I reason to complain. The fact is, not that they have paid me too little, but that I have written too much." The *Lives* were soon published in a separate edition; when, for a few corrections, he was presented with another hundred guineas.' Nichols's *Lit. Anec.* viii. 416. In Mr. Morrison's *Collection of Autographs*, &c., vol. ii, 'is Johnson's receipt for £100 from the proprietors of *The Lives of the Poets* for revising the last edition of that work.' It is dated Feb. 19, 1783. 'Underneath, in Johnson's autograph, are these words : " It is great impudence to put *Johnson's Poets* on the back of books which Johnson neither recommended nor revised. He recommended only Blackmore on the Creation, and Watts. How then are they Johnson's? This is indecent."' Boswell's *Johnson*, iv. 35.

The poets whom Johnson recommended were Blackmore, Watts, Pomfret, and Yalden. *Post*, WATTS, i.]

Mrs. Boscawen wrote to Mrs. Delany on Nov. 16, 1779: ' I hope you will get Dr. Johnson's *Prefaces to*

the *Lives, &c., of the Poets*, which however is not easy, because they are not to be bought unless you buy also a perfect litter of poets in fillagree (that is very small print, whereas one already possesses said poets in large letter) therefore I could not possibly give ten guineas for this smaller edition, but a friend of mine, to whom Dr. Johnson presented them, was so kind as to lend them to me.' Mrs. Delany's *Auto. and Corres.* v. 493.

[1] In the first edition,—' tedious.'

[2] [Johnson on May 3, 1777, wrote to Boswell, who had seen the forthcoming work advertised, ' I am engaged to write little Lives, and little Prefaces to a little edition of *The English Poets.*' Boswell's *Johnson*, iii. 109.]

[3] Johnson does not always give Dryden's plays in their chronological order. See *post*, DRYDEN, 64 *n.* 4.

[4] In the first edition a passage follows here relating to Dryden's funeral. See *post*, DRYDEN, 154 *n.* 2, where this passage is given and the subject discussed.

[5] [In Colman's *Beaumont and Fletcher*, 1778. *Eng. Poets*, 1790, vol. i. p. 4 *n.* In the first edition of the *Lives* the sentence runs—' I have been told that Dryden's *Remarks*,' &c.]

before. The former edition I have not seen. This was transcribed for the press from his own manuscript [1].

As this undertaking was occasional and unforeseen I must be
supposed to have engaged in it with less provision of materials
than might have been accumulated by longer premeditation [2].
Of the later writers at least I might, by attention and enquiry,
have gleaned many particulars, which would have diversified
and enlivened my Biography. These omissions, which it is now
useless to lament, have been often supplied by the kindness of
Mr. STEEVENS and other friends; and great assistance has been
given me by Mr. SPENCE's *Collections*, of which I consider the
communication as a favour worthy of publick acknowledgement [3].

[1] The Advertisement of the first
edition ends here.

[2] Malone writing of the *Lives* says,
' Dr. Johnson having, as he himself
told me, made no preparation for
that difficult and extensive undertaking, not being in the habit of
extracting from books and committing to paper those facts on which
the accuracy of literary history in
a great measure depends, and being
still less inclined to go through the
tedious and often unsatisfactory process of examining ancient registers,
&c. ; he was under the necessity of
trusting much to his own most
retentive memory,' &c. Malone's
Dryden, i. 2.
The errors Johnson often makes
in quoting verses and other passages
are those of a man who had such
a stock of words at his command
that in copying he substituted one
for another—sometimes for the better.
They show that vast as were the
powers of his memory, they were not
always strictly accurate.

[3] 'This valuable collection is the
property of the Duke of Newcastle,
who, upon the application of Sir
Lucas Pepys, was pleased to permit
it to be put into the hands of Dr.
Johnson, who I am sorry to think
made but an awkward return.' Johnson did not own 'to whom he was
obliged; so that the acknowledgement is unappropriated to his Grace.'
Boswell's *Johnson*, iv. 63.

COWLEY [1]

THE Life of Cowley, notwithstanding the penury of English [1]
biography [2], has been written by Dr. Sprat, an author whose
pregnancy of imagination and elegance of language have deservedly
set him high in the ranks of literature ; but his zeal of friendship,
or ambition of eloquence, has produced a funeral oration rather
than a history : he has given the character, not the life of Cowley ;
for he writes with so little detail that scarcely any thing is
distinctly known, but all is shewn confused and enlarged through
the mist of panegyrick [3].

ABRAHAM COWLEY was born in the year one thousand [2]
six hundred and eighteen. His father was a grocer, whose
condition Dr. Sprat conceals under the general appellation of
a citizen [4] ; and, what would probably not have been less carefully

[1] On July 27, 1778, Johnson wrote
to John Nichols, the printer of the
Lives :—' You have now all Cowley.
I have been drawn to a great length,
but Cowley or Waller never had any
critical examination before.' *Letters
of Johnson*, ii. 68.
   ' The *Life of Cowley* Johnson himself considered as the best of the
whole, on account of the dissertation
which it contains on the *Metaphysical
Poets*.' Boswell's *Johnson*, iv. 38.

[2] ' Talking of biography, Dr. Johnson said he did not think that the
life of any literary man in England
had been well written.' Boswell's
Johnson, v. 240. See also *ib.* ii. 40.

[3] *Post*, SPRAT, 7, 21. Sprat's *Life
of Cowley* is given in Hurd's *Select
Works of Cowley*, i. 1.
   Addison, in an early poem, ab-
surdly praises Sprat. Addressing
Cowley he says :—
' Blest man ! who now shalt be for
      ever known
   In Sprat's successful labours and thy
      own.' Addison's *Works*, i. 24.

' What literary man has not regretted the prudery of Sprat, in
refusing to let his friend Cowley
appear in his slippers and dressing-
gown?' COLERIDGE, *Biog. Lit.* 1847,
i. 59 ; *post*, COWLEY, 45 *n.*

[4] ' His parents were citizens of a
virtuous life and sufficient estate.'
SPRAT, Hurd's *Cowley*, i. 4. ' He
was borne in Fleet-street, near
Chancery-lane ; his father a grocer.'
AUBREY, *Brief Lives*, i. 189. See
also Wood's *Fasti Oxon.* ii. 209.
   ' His father, Thomas Cowley, was
a citizen and stationer of the parish
of St. Michael at Querne, a church
in Cheapside, destroyed in the Great
Fire, and not rebuilt. He died in
Aug. 1618, and left £140 apiece to
his six living children and his posthumous child.' *Lives of the Poets*,
ed. Cunningham, i. 3. ' There is no
reason why Cowley's father should
not have been a grocer, and yet have
held the freedom of the Stationers'
Company. James I was a cloth-
worker.' *N. & Q.* 7 S. iii. 438.

suppressed, the omission of his name in the register of St. Dunstan's parish [1] gives reason to suspect that his father was a sectary. Whoever he was, he died before the birth of his son, and consequently left him to the care of his mother, whom Wood represents as struggling earnestly to procure him a literary education [2], and who, as she lived to the age of eighty, had her solicitude rewarded by seeing her son eminent, and, I hope, by seeing him fortunate, and partaking his prosperity. We know at least, from Sprat's account, that he always acknowledged her care, and justly paid the dues of filial gratitude [3].

3 In the window of his mother's apartment lay Spenser's *Fairy Queen,* in which he very early took delight to read, till, by feeling the charms of verse, he became, as he relates, irrecoverably a poet [4]. Such are the accidents, which, sometimes remembered, and perhaps sometimes forgotten, produce that particular designation of mind and propensity for some certain science or employment, which is commonly called Genius. The true Genius is a mind of large general powers, accidentally determined to some particular direction [5]. Sir Joshua Reynolds, the great Painter of the present age, had the first fondness for his art excited by the perusal of Richardson's treatise [6].

[1] St. Dunstan's is in Fleet Street.

[2] *Fasti Oxon.* ii. 209.

[3] Hurd's *Cowley,* i. 45.

[4] ' I believe I can tell the particular little chance that filled my head first with such chimes of verse as have never since left ringing there ; for I remember, when I began to read and to take some pleasure in it, there was wont to lie in my mother's parlour . . . Spenser's works ; this I happened to fall upon, and was infinitely delighted with the stories of the knights, and giants, and monsters, and brave houses, which I found everywhere there ; . . . and by degrees, with the tinkling of the rhyme and dance of the numbers ; so that I think I had read him all over before I was twelve years old, and was thus made a poet as immediately as a child is made an eunuch.' *Eng. Poets,* ix. 122.

Lamb, describing ' an old great house ' in which part of his childhood was spent, mentions ' the cheerful store-room, in whose hot window-seat I used to sit and read Cowley.' *Essays of Elia,* p. 206.

Cowley, according to Dryden, looked upon Chaucer as ' a dry old-fashioned wit, not worth reviving. Having read him over at the Earl of Leicester's request, he declared he had no taste of him.' Dryden's *Works,* xi. 232.

[5] ' Every age has a kind of universal genius which inclines those that live in it to some particular studies.' DRYDEN, *ib.* xv. 293.

' I am persuaded,' wrote Cowper (*Works,* vi. 94), ' that Milton did not write his *Paradise Lost,* nor Homer his *Iliad,* nor Newton his *Principia,* without immense labour. Nature gave them a bias to their respective pursuits, and that strong propensity, I suppose, is what we mean by Genius. The rest they gave themselves.' See also Boswell's *Johnson,* ii. 437 ; *John. Misc.* i. 314 ; ii. 287 ; and Gibbon's *Memoirs,* pp. 143, 303.

[6] *Two Discourses on the Art of Criticism as it relates to Painting,*

By his mother's solicitation he was admitted into West- 4
minster school[1], where he was soon distinguished. 'He was
wont,' says Sprat, 'to relate that he had this defect in his
memory at that time, that his teachers never could bring it
to retain the ordinary rules of grammar[2].'

This is an instance of the natural desire of man to propagate 5
a wonder[3]. It is surely very difficult to tell any thing as it
was heard, when Sprat could not refrain from amplifying a commodious incident, though the book to which he prefixed his
narrative contained its confutation. A memory admitting some
things and rejecting others, an intellectual digestion that concocted
the pulp of learning, but refused the husks, had the appearance
of an instinctive elegance, of a particular provision made by
Nature for literary politeness. But in the author's own honest
relation, the marvel vanishes: he was, he says, such 'an enemy
to all constraint, that his master never could prevail on him to
learn the rules without book[4].' He does not tell that he could
not learn the rules, but that, being able to perform his exercises
without them, and being an 'enemy to constraint,' he spared
himself the labour.

Among the English poets, Cowley, Milton, and Pope might 6
be said 'to lisp in numbers[5],' and have given such early
proofs, not only of powers of language, but of comprehension
of things, as to more tardy minds seems scarcely credible. But
of the learned puerilities of Cowley there is no doubt, since
a volume of his poems was not only written but printed in his
thirteenth year[6], containing, with other poetical compositions,

&c., 1719. By Jonathan Richardson.
See Northcote's *Reynolds*, i. 14, and
Leslie and Taylor's *Reynolds*, i. 9.
Reynolds told Malone that 'the first
book that gave him a turn for painting
was the *Jesuit's Perspective*, a book
which happened to be in the parlour
window in the house of his father.'
Prior's *Malone*, p. 389. Johnson,
who must have heard Reynolds tell
the same story, transferred 'the parlour window' to the house of Cowley's
mother. In the first edition of the
Lives Reynolds's name is not given.

[1] *Fasti Oxon.* ii. 209.
[2] Hurd's *Cowley*, i. 6.
[3] 'Wonders are willingly told and
willingly heard.' *Post*, POPE, 199.

See also Boswell's *Johnson*, iii. 229 ;
John. Misc. i. 241-4.
[4] See Appendix A.
[5] POPE, *Prol. Sat.* l. 128 ; *post*,
POPE, 8.
[6] Johnson here follows Sprat,
Hurd's *Cowley*, i. 5. Cowley, mentioning an ode, continues :—'which
I made when I was but thirteen
years old and which was then printed
with many other verses.' *Eng. Poets*,
ix. 120. In 1656 he writes that 'the
poems he wrote at school from the
age of ten till after fifteen have already
past through several editions.' *Ib.*
vii. 15. They were published in
1633, when he was fifteen. He
quotes (*ib.* ix. 121) three stanzas of

The tragical History of Pyramus and Thisbe, written when he was ten years old, and *Constantia and Philetus*, written two years after[1].

7   While he was yet at school he produced a comedy called *Love's Riddle*, though it was not published till he had been some time at Cambridge. This comedy is of the pastoral kind, which requires no acquaintance with the living world[2], and therefore the time at which it was composed adds little to the wonders of Cowley's minority.

8   In 1636, he was removed to Cambridge, where he continued his studies with great intenseness; for he is said to have written, while he was yet a young student, the greater part of his *Davideis*[3], a work of which the materials could not have been collected without the study of many years but by a mind of the greatest vigour and activity.

9   Two years after his settlement at Cambridge he published *Love's Riddle*[4], with a poetical dedication to Sir Kenelm Digby[5], of whose acquaintance all his contemporaries seem to have been ambitious[6], and *Naufragium Joculare*[7], a comedy written in Latin, but without due attention to the ancient models: for it is not loose verse, but mere prose. It was printed with a dedication in verse to Dr. Comber, master of the college[8], but having neither the facility of a popular nor the accuracy of a learned work, it seems to be now universally neglected.

---

the ode written at thirteen. The title of the poems was *Poeticall Blossomes*.

[1] *Eng. Poets*, vii. 31, 33, 56. In the third edition of *Poeticall Blossomes*, 1637, Cowley says of *Pyramus and Thisbe*:—'I hope a pardon may easily be gotten for the errors of ten years old. My *Constantia and Philetus* confesseth me two years older when I writ it.'

[2] *Post*, MILTON, 181; POPE, 313.

[3] Hurd's *Cowley*, i. 29; *post*, COWLEY, 145.

[4] *Loues Riddle. A Pastoral Comaedie*. Written at the time of his being Kings Scholler in Westminster Schoole by A. Cowley. London, 1638. The frontispiece is a portrait of Cowley, with a cherub hovering over him, holding a pen in its right hand, and a laurel chaplet in its left. There is an inscription, *Aetatis suae* 13.

[5] The Dedication ends:—

'And if it please your tast my Muse will say,
The Birch which crown'd her then is growne a Bay.'

[6] Jonson celebrated him in *Underwoods*, No. xcvi. Evelyn (*Diary*, i. 284) calls him 'an arrant mountebank.'

[7] It was acted before the College in Feb.1638-9. The Dedication ends:—
'Collegii nam qui nostri dedit ista Scholaris,
Si Socius tandem sit, meliora dabit.'

'Feb. 18, 1660-1. Spent the evening in reading of a Latin play, the *Naufragium Joculare*.' PEPYS, *Diary*, i. 193.

[8] He was Master of Trinity College 1631-1644, when he was ejected for sending the College plate to the King. As Vice-Chancellor he admitted Milton to the M.A. degree. Masson's *Milton*, i. 257.

At the beginning of the civil war, as the Prince passed 10 through Cambridge in his way to York, he was entertained with the representation of *The Guardian*, a comedy which Cowley says was neither written nor acted, but rough-drawn by him, and repeated by the scholars [1]. That this comedy was printed during his absence from his country, he appears to have considered as injurious to his reputation ; though during the suppression of the theatres, it was sometimes privately acted with sufficient approbation [2].

In 1643, being now master of arts, he was, by the prevalence 11 of the parliament, ejected from Cambridge [3], and sheltered himself at St. John's College in Oxford, where, as is said by Wood [4], he published a satire called *The Puritan and Papist*, which was only inserted in the last collection of his works ; and so distinguished himself by the warmth of his loyalty, and the elegance of his conversation, that he gained the kindness and confidence of those who attended the King, and amongst others of Lord

[1] 'It was printed in 1650. . . . It was neither made nor acted, but rough-drawn only, and repeated.' Hurd's *Cowley*, i. 65. In the Prologue he says : —
'Accept our hasty zeal ; a thing that's play'd
Ere 'tis a play, and acted ere 'tis made.' *Eng. Poets*, vii. 128.
In March, 1641-2, the Prince of Wales [Charles II], in his twelfth year, visited Cambridge. A letter-writer tells how 'he went to Trinity College, where, after dinner, he saw a comedy in English, and gave all sighnes of great acceptance which he could, and more than the University dared expect.' Cooper's *Annals of Cambridge*, iii. 321. In 'the Extraordinaries' in the Senior Bursar's book for 1642 is the following :—'To Mr. Willis for Ds. [Dominus] Cooley's Comedy. lxv*li*. xvi *s*. [£65 16*s*.].' The spelling seems to show that Cowley was pronounced Cooley, as the poet Cowper's name was pronounced Cooper. The name also appears as 'Cooley' in the books, as Mr. W. Aldis Wright informs me.
[2] Cowley states this in the Preface to *Cutter of Coleman Street* (*post*, COWLEY, 36). Hurd's *Cowley*, i. 91.

[3] For the facts in the following note I am obliged to Mr. W. Aldis Wright : Cowley was admitted Minor Fellow on Oct. 30, 1640, when there was no vacancy. He received his stipend as a Scholar up to Michaelmas, 1643, in which year he took his M.A. degree. By the statutes he could have retained his Fellowship, without taking orders, for seven years from this degree ; but as he was at once ejected the King, on the Restoration, got the College to allow him to count his seven years from his reinstatement as Fellow. He lived long enough nearly to exhaust his seven years.
[4] *Fasti Oxon*. ii. 210, where it is stated that Cowley published this satire 'under the name of a Scholar of Oxford.'
'In the first edition of this *Life* Dr. Johnson wrote, "which was never inserted in any collection of his works," but he altered the expression when the *Lives* were collected into volumes. The satire was added to Cowley's works by the particular direction of Dr. Johnson.' NICHOLS, Johnson's *Works*, vii. 4. See *Eng. Poets*, vii. 171.

Falkland, whose notice cast a lustre on all to whom it was extended [1].

12   About the time when Oxford was surrendered to the parliament, he followed the Queen to Paris [2], where he became secretary to the Lord Jermin, afterwards Earl of St. Albans [3], and was employed in such correspondence as the royal cause required, and particularly in cyphering and decyphering the letters that passed between the King and Queen; an employment of the highest confidence and honour. So wide was his province of intelligence that for several years it filled all his days and two or three nights in the week [4].

13   In the year 1647 his *Mistress* was published; for he imagined, as he declared in his preface to a subsequent edition [5], that 'poets are scarce thought freemen of their company without paying some duties, or obliging themselves to be true to Love [6].'

14   This obligation to amorous ditties owes, I believe, its original to the fame of Petrarch, who, in an age rude and uncultivated, by his tuneful homage to his Laura, refined the manners of the lettered world, and filled Europe with love and poetry. But the basis of all excellence is truth: he that professes love ought to feel its power [7]. Petrarch was a real lover, and Laura doubtless deserved his tenderness. Of Cowley we are told by Barnes, who had means enough of information, that, whatever he may talk of his own inflammability and the variety of characters by which his heart was divided, he in reality was in love but once, and then never had resolution to tell his passion [8].

[1] Hurd's *Cowley*, i. 9; *post*, COWLEY, 106.
[2] In 1646. *Dict. Nat. Biog.*
[3] Created Baron Jermyn in 1643, and Earl of St. Albans in 1660. He was suspected of being the Queen's lover at this time, and her husband after the King's death. Masson's *Milton*, iii. 495; Clarendon's *Hist.* vii. 622, 633. Cowley, in his will, described him as 'my Lord and once kind Master.' Cunningham, *Lives of the Poets*, i. 63. See *post*, WALLER, 23, 63 *n*., 104.
[4] Hurd's *Cowley*, i. 10; *post*, DENHAM, 13.
[5] The folio of 1656.
[6] He continues:—'Sooner or later they must all pass through that trial,

like some Mahometan monks that are bound by their order, once at least in their life, to make a pilgrimage to Mecca:—
"In furias ignemque ruunt: amor omnibus idem" [VIRGIL, *Geor.* iii. 244].' *Eng. Poets*, vii. 16.
[7] 'Mais pour bien exprimer ces caprices heureux,
C'est peu d'être poëte, il faut être amoureux.'
BOILEAU, *L'Art poétique*, ii. 43.
[8] 'V. Barnesii *Anacreontem*.' JOHNSON.
'Ita Anacreon scripsit *Oden* xxxii, εἰς τοὺς ἑαυτοῦ ἔρωτας, in qua innumeras ex omnibus Asiae et Europae gentibus puellas sibi charas commemorat; quem locum Couleius noster

This consideration cannot but abate in some measure the 15 reader's esteem for the work and the author. To love excellence is natural; it is natural likewise for the lover to solicit reciprocal regard by an elaborate display of his own qualifications. The desire of pleasing has in different men produced actions of heroism and effusions of wit; but it seems as reasonable to appear the champion as the poet of an 'airy nothing,' and to quarrel as to write for what Cowley might have learned from his master Pindar to call the 'dream of a shadow[1].'

It is surely not difficult, in the solitude of a college or in the 16 bustle of the world, to find useful studies and serious employment. No man needs to be so burthened with life as to squander it in voluntary dreams of fictitious occurrences. The man that sits down to suppose himself charged with treason or peculation, and heats his mind to an elaborate purgation of his character from crimes which he was never within the possibility of committing, differs only by the infrequency of his folly from him who praises beauty which he never saw, complains of jealousy which he never felt, supposes himself sometimes invited and sometimes forsaken, fatigues his fancy, and ransacks his memory, for images which may exhibit the gaiety of hope or the gloominess of despair, and dresses his imaginary Chloris or

imitatur in *Oda* cui titulus, *The Chronicle* [*Eng. Poets*, vii. 137], ubi plus centum amicas enumerat; qui revera, quum unicam tantum haberet, prae nimia tamen verecundia, nunquam illam, licet in iisdem aedibus manentem, de amore compellare ausus est; quod ex certa relatione accepimus.' Barnes's *Anacreon*, 1705, Preface, p. 32.

'Poesy is not the picture of the poet, but of things and persons imagined by him. He may be in his own practice and disposition a philosopher, nay a Stoic, and yet sometimes speak with the softness of an amorous Sappho:—
"ferat et rubus asper amomum"
[VIRGIL, *Ecl.* iii. 89].'
COWLEY, *Eng. Poets*, vii. 17.
In his *Essay of Greatness*, Cowley says:—'If I were ever to fall in love again (which is a great passion, and therefore I hope I have done with it) it would be, I think, with prettiness

rather than with majestical beauty.' *Eng. Poets*, ix. 80.
According to Pope 'he was much in love with his Leonora [Heleonora], who is mentioned at the end of that good ballad of his on his different mistresses [*The Chronicle, ib.* vii. 140]. She was married to Dean Sprat's brother, and Cowley never was in love with anybody after.' Spence's *Anecdotes*, p. 286.

[1] Cowley, in his *Life and Fame*, says to Life:—
'Dream of a shadow! a reflection made
From the false glories of the gay reflected bow
Is a more solid thing than thou.'
Eng. Poets, viii. 147.
In a note on this in *Pindarick Odes*, 1674, p. 39, he writes:—'Τί δέ τις, τί δ' οὔ τις; σκιᾶς ὄναρ ἄνθρωπος. PINDAR. Quid est aliquis, aut quid est nemo? Somnium umbrae homo est.' See Pindar, *P.* viii. 136.

Phyllis sometimes in flowers fading as her beauty, and sometimes in gems lasting as her virtues.

17   At Paris, as secretary to Lord Jermin, he was engaged in transacting things of real importance with real men and real women [1], and at that time did not much employ his thoughts upon phantoms of gallantry [2].   Some of his letters to Mr. Bennet, afterwards Earl of Arlington, from April to December in 1650, are preserved in *Miscellanea Aulica*, a collection of papers published by Brown [3].   These letters, being written like those of other men whose mind is more on things than words, contribute no otherwise to his reputation than as they shew him to have been above the affectation of unseasonable elegance, and to have known that the business of a statesman can be little forwarded by flowers of rhetorick.

18   One passage, however, seems not unworthy of some notice. Speaking of the Scotch treaty then in agitation :

19   'The Scotch treaty,' says he, 'is the only thing now in which we are vitally concerned ; I am one of the last hopers, and yet cannot now abstain from believing, that an [the] agreement will be made : all people upon the place incline to that of union [to that opinion].   The Scotch will moderate something [somewhat] of the rigour of their demands ; the mutual necessity of an accord is visible, the King is persuaded of it [, and all mankind but two or three mighty tender consciences about him].   And to tell you the truth (which I take to be an argument above all the rest), Virgil has told the same thing [me something] to that purpose [4].'

20   This expression from a secretary of the present time would be considered as merely ludicrous, or at most as an ostentatious

---

[1] In his *Complaint* he makes the Muse reproach him with this part of his life (*Eng. Poets*, vii. 249) :—
'Thou would'st, forsooth, be some-
        thing in a state,
And business thou would'st find, and
        would'st create ;
    Business ! the frivolous pretence
Of human lusts to shake off inno-
        cence ;
    Business ! the grave impertinence ;
Business ! the thing which I of all
        things hate ;
Business ! the contradiction of thy
        fate.'
[2] 'Though I was in a crowd of as good company as could be found any-
where; though I was in business of great and honourable trust ; though I ate at the best table ... yet I could not abstain from renewing my old school-boy's wish, in a copy of verses to the same effect :—
"Well then ; I now do plainly see
    This busy world and I shall ne'er
        agree," &c.'
Ib. ix. 123 ; viii. 29.
[3] *Miscellanea Aulica; or a Collection of State Treatises, never before publish'd.*   Faithfully collected from their Originals by Mr. T. Brown. 1702.   One of Cowley's letters bears date Sept. 13, 1653, p. 158.
[4] *Ib.* p. 130.

display of scholarship; but the manners of that time were so tinged with superstition, that I cannot but suspect Cowley of having consulted on this great occasion the Virgilian lots [1], and to have given some credit to the answer of his oracle.

Some years afterwards, 'business,' says Sprat, 'passed of 21 course into other hands'; and Cowley, being no longer useful at Paris, was in 1656 sent back into England that, 'under pretence of privacy and retirement, he might take occasion of giving notice of the posture of things in this nation [2].'

Soon after his return to London he was seized by some mes- 22 sengers of the usurping powers, who were sent out in quest of another man; and, being examined, was put into confinement, from which he was not dismissed without the security of a thousand pounds given by Dr. Scarborow [3].

This year he published his poems with a preface, in which 23 he seems to have inserted something, suppressed in subsequent editions, which was interpreted to denote some relaxation of his loyalty [4]. In this preface he declares, that 'his desire had been

[1] 'Consulting the Virgilian lots, *Sortes Virgilianae*, is a method of divination by the opening of Virgil, and applying to the circumstances of the peruser the first passage in either of the two pages that he accidentally fixes his eyes on.' For Charles I and Falkland thus turning up in the Bodleian, as it was reported, the *Aeneid*, iv. 615; xi. 152 see Johnson's *Works*, vii. 6 n. See also *Diary of Dr. Edward Lake*, under Jan. 29, 1677–8, quoted by Cunningham, *Lives of the Poets*, i. 9.

[2] Hurd's *Cowley*, i. 11.

[3] *Ib.* In an ode addressed to him he says, 'with enormous and disgusting hyperbole' (*post*, COWLEY, 80):—
'Scarce could the sword dispatch
   more to the grave
Than thou didst save;
By wondrous art, and by successful
   care,
The ruins of a civil war thou dost
   alone repair.'
          Eng. Poets, viii. 143.
Aubrey tells how 'at Oxford Harvey grew acquainted with Dr. Charles Scarborough, then a young physitian; and whereas before he marched up and downe with the army, he tooke him to him, and made him ly in his chamber and said to him: —" Prithee leave off thy gunning and stay here; I will bring thee into practice."' *Brief Lives*, i. 299. See *post*, WALLER, 86.

[4] Sprat writes :—'Some have endeavoured to bring his loyalty in question upon occasion of a few lines in the preface to one of his books.... Seeing his good intentions were so ill interpreted he told me, the last time that ever I saw him, that he would have them omitted in the next impression.' Hurd's *Cowley*, i. 12, 14.

Hearne, writing about a copy given by Cowley to the Bodleian, remarks how strongly 'he speaks for the republicans and Oliverians.' Hearne's *Remains*, i. 260; where, in a note, the suppressed passage is quoted. Among other things Cowley says :—'When the event of battle and the unaccountable will of God has determined the controversy, and that we have submitted to the conditions of the conqueror, we must lay down our pens as well as arms, we must march out of our cause itself, and dismantle *that*, as well as our towns and castles, of all the works and fortifications of wit and reason by which we defended it.'

for some days [years] past, and did still very vehemently continue, to retire himself to some of the American plantations, and to forsake this world for ever [1].'

24   From the obloquy, which the appearance of submission to the usurpers brought upon him, his biographer has been very diligent to clear him, and indeed it does not seem to have lessened his reputation. His wish for retirement we can easily believe to be undissembled ; a man harassed in one kingdom and persecuted in another who, after a course of business that employed all his days and half his nights in cyphering and decyphering, comes to his own country and steps into a prison, will be willing enough to retire to some place of quiet, and of safety [2]. Yet let neither our reverence for a genius, nor our pity for a sufferer, dispose us to forget that, if his activity was virtue, his retreat was cowardice [3].

25   He then took upon himself the character of Physician, still, according to Sprat, with intention 'to dissemble the main design [intention] of his coming over [4],' and, as Mr. Wood relates, 'complying with the men then in power (which was much taken notice of by the royal party), he obtained an order to be created Doctor of Physick, which being done to his mind (whereby he gained the ill-will of some of his friends), he went into France again, having made a copy of verses on Oliver's death [5].'

26   This is no favourable representation, yet even in this not much wrong can be discovered. How far he complied with the men in power is to be enquired before he can be blamed. It is not said that he told them any secrets, or assisted them by intelligence, or any other act. If he only promised to be quiet, that they in whose hands he was might free him from confinement, he did what no law of society prohibits.

27   The man whose miscarriage in a just cause has put him in

[1] *Eng. Poets*, vii. 13.

[2] In the Preface Cowley says that no one ought 'to envy poets the imaginary happiness' of posthumous fame, 'since they find commonly so little in present that it may be truly applied to them, which St. Paul speaks of the first Christians, "If their reward be in this life, they are of all men the most miserable."' *Ib.* vii. 11.

[3] Johnson ends his sixth *Rambler*, entitled *Happiness not local*, with reflections on Cowley's desire 'to retire himself.'

[4] Hurd's *Cowley*, i. 34. Cowley himself says :—'For to make myself absolutely dead in a poetical capacity, my resolution at present is never to exercise any more that faculty. It is, I confess, but seldom seen that the poet dies before the man.' *Eng. Poets*, vii. 11.

[5] *Fasti Oxon.* ii. 210.

the power of his enemy may, without any violation of his integrity, regain his liberty, or preserve his life, by a promise of neutrality: for the stipulation gives the enemy nothing which he had not before; the neutrality of a captive may be always secured by his imprisonment or death. He that is at the disposal of another may not promise to aid him in any injurious act, because no power can compel active obedience. He may engage to do nothing, but not to do ill.

There is reason to think that Cowley promised little. It 28 does not appear that his compliance gained him confidence enough to be trusted without security, for the bond of his bail was never cancelled; nor that it made him think himself secure, for at that dissolution of government, which followed the death of Oliver, he returned into France, where he resumed his former station, and staid till the Restoration [1].

'He continued,' says his biographer, 'under these bonds till 29 the general deliverance [2]'; it is therefore to be supposed that he did not go to France, and act again for the King, without the consent of his bondsman: that he did not shew his loyalty at the hazard of his friend, but by his friend's permission.

Of the verses on Oliver's death, in which Wood's narrative 30 seems to imply something encomiastick, there has been no appearance. There is a discourse concerning his government, indeed, with verses intermixed, but such as certainly gained its author no friends among the abettors of usurpation [3].

A doctor of physick, however, he was made at Oxford, in 31 December 1657; and in the commencement of the Royal Society, of which an account has been published by Dr. Birch, he appears

---

[1] 'Till near the time of the King's return.' Hurd's *Cowley*, i. 12.

[2] Sprat wrote, 'till the general redemption.'

[3] In Cowley's *Discourse by Way of Vision concerning the Government of Oliver Cromwell* is a copy of verses written, he says, 'on the funeral day of the late man who made himself to be called Protector.' *Eng. Poets*, viii. 325, 7. In the same *Discourse* there are three other poems on Cromwell. *Ib.* pp. 338, 372, 375. Milton's 'Cromwell, our chief of men,' was bespattered by Cowley with such abuse as the following:—'They say he invented (O Antichrist! Πονηρόν and ὁ πονηρός!) to sell St. Paul's to the Jews for a synagogue, if their purses and devotions could have reached to the purchase. And this indeed, if he had done only to reward that nation which had given the first noble example of crucifying their King, it might have had some appearance of gratitude: but he did it only for love of their mammon; and would have sold afterwards, for as much more, St. Peter's (even at his own Westminster) to the Turks for a *mosquito*.' *Ib.* p. 364.

Hume quotes this *Discourse*. *Hist. of Engl.* vii. 287.

busy among the experimental philosophers with the title of
Doctor Cowley[1].

32   There is no reason for supposing that he ever attempted
practice, but his preparatory studies have contributed something
to the honour of his country.   Considering botany as necessary
to a physician, he retired into Kent to gather plants; and as the
predominance of a favourite study affects all subordinate operations
of the intellect, botany in the mind of Cowley turned into poetry[2].
He composed in Latin several books on plants, of which the first
and second display the qualities of herbs, in elegiac verse; the
third and fourth the beauties of flowers in various measures; and
in the fifth and sixth, the uses of trees in heroick numbers.

33   At the same time were produced from the same university the
two great Poets, Cowley and Milton[3], of dissimilar genius, of
opposite principles, but concurring in the cultivation of Latin
poetry, in which the English, till their works and May's poem
appeared, seemed unable to contest the palm with any other of
the lettered nations[4].

[1] He was elected on March 6,
1660-1. Birch's *Hist. of the Royal Soc.*
ed. 1756, i. 17. I do not find him
entered as taking any part in the
proceedings. He is not in the list
of Fellows drawn up on May 20,
1663. *Ib.* p. 239.

In his *Proposition for the Advancement of Experimental Philosophy* he
sets forth a plan for 'a philosophical
college' with an endowment of £4,000
a year. In his *Of Agriculture* he
anticipated our agricultural colleges
by nearly 250 years. *Eng. Poets,*
ix. 46, 133.

Johnson in 1756 reviewed Birch's
History.

[2] Hurd's *Cowley,* i. 34. Gibbon,
in *The Decline and Fall,* iii. 249,
after quoting from Claudian the
description of the old man's trees,
'his old *contemporary* trees,' adds in
a note :—

'"Ingentem meminit parvo qui ger-
   mine quercum
Aequaevumque videt consenuisse
   nemus."

"A neighbouring wood born with
   himself he sees,
And loves his old contemporary
   trees." [*Eng. Poets,* ix. 108.]
In this passage Cowley is perhaps

superior to his original; and the
English poet, who was a good bota-
mist, has concealed the oaks under
a more general expression.'

In his poem *Of the Garden* Cowley
writes (*Eng. Poets,* ix. 72) :—
'God the first garden made, and the
   first city Cain.'
With this we may compare Cowper's
line (*The Task,* i. 749) :—
'God made the country, and man
   made the town.'

[3] They were not contemporaries.
Milton entered the University in
1624, and graduated as M.A. in 1632
(*post,* MILTON, 14 *n.*); Cowley entered in 1636. *Ante,* COWLEY, 8, and
Appendix A.

[4] *Post,* COWLEY, 197. 'The Latin
poetry of *Deliciae Poetarum Sco-
torum* would have done honour to
any nation ; at least, till the publication of May's *Supplement,* the English
had very little to oppose.' JOHNSON,
Works, ix. 23.

Thomas May published in 1640
Supplementum Lucani. He translated also Lucan and his own *Supplementum* into English verse. For
his character see *Life of Clarendon,*
i. 39 and Marvell's *Tom May's Death.*
On his tomb in Westminster Abbey

If the Latin performances of Cowley and Milton be com- 34 pared, for May I hold to be superior to both, the advantage seems to lie on the side of Cowley. Milton is generally content to express the thoughts of the ancients in their language; Cowley, without much loss of purity or elegance, accommodates the diction of Rome to his own conceptions[1].

At the Restoration, after all the diligence of his long service, 35 and with consciousness not only of the merit of fidelity, but of the dignity of great abilities, he naturally expected ample preferments; and, that he might not be forgotten by his own fault, wrote a Song of Triumph[2]. But this was a time of such general hope that great numbers were inevitably disappointed, and Cowley found his reward very tediously delayed[3]. He had been promised by both Charles the first and second the Mastership of the Savoy, but 'he lost it,' says Wood, 'by certain persons, enemies to the Muses[4].'

The neglect of the court was not his only mortification: 36 having, by such alteration as he thought proper, fitted his old

he was described as a man 'quem Anglicana Respublica habuit vindicem,' and as dying 'A° Libertatis ⎱ Humanae ⎰ Restitutae ⎱ MDCL° ' ⎰ ⎱ Angliae ⎰ ⎱ II° ⎰ At the Restoration his body was ejected, and 'his monument throw'd aside.' Crull's *Antiquities of St. Peter's*, ii. App. 24.

[1] See Appendix B.

[2] *Eng. Poets*, vii. 228. It was out on May 31, 1660, two days after Restoration Day. Waller anticipated him by a day. Masson's *Milton*, vi. 12, 13; *post*, WALLER, 68.

[3] In the Preface to *Cutter of Coleman Street*, first acted in 1661, he says:—'This I do affirm, that from all which I have written I never received the least benefit; but, on the contrary, have felt sometimes the effects of malice and misfortune.' Hurd's *Cowley*, i. 105.

[4] 'He was by the most generous endeavours of the Earl of St. Albans designed to be master of the Savoy; which, though granted to his merit by both the Charles's 1 and 2, yet by certain persons, enemies to the Muses, he lost that place.' WOOD, *Fasti Oxon.* ii. 210.

[According to a statement of

Cowley's case (*Cal. State Papers Dom.* 1661–2, p. 210) both Charles I and Charles II had promised him the mastership 'under their hands'; but it was claimed by another on a promise of Charles I. The fact that Cowley was not in orders was raised as an objection, as the statement alleges that the place might be held 'by a person not a divine.']

According to Hurd the mastership was the Rachel in Cowley's *Complaint (Eng. Poets*, vii. 251):—

'The Rachel, for which twice seven years and more
Thou didst with faith and labour serve,
And didst (if faith and labour can) deserve,
Though she contracted was to thee
Giv'n to another,' &c.
Hurd's *Cowley*, i. 187.

Oldham, speaking of the neglect of men of genius, continues :—
'Great Cowley's Muse the same illtreatment had,
Whose verse shall live for ever to upbraid
Th' ungrateful world that left such worth unpaid.'
Oldham's *Works*, 1703, p. 420.

Comedy of *The Guardian* for the stage, he produced it to the publick under the title of *The Cutter of Coleman-street*[1]. It was treated on the stage with great severity, and was afterwards censured as a satire on the king's party.

37   Mr. Dryden, who went with Mr. Sprat to the first exhibition, related to Mr. Dennis, 'that when they told Cowley how little favour had been shewn him, he received the news of his ill success, not with so much firmness as might have been expected from so great a man.'

38   What firmness they expected or what weakness Cowley discovered cannot be known. He that misses his end will never be as much pleased as he that attains it, even when he can impute no part of his failure to himself; and when the end is to please the multitude, no man perhaps has a right, in things admitting of gradation and comparison, to throw the whole blame upon his judges, and totally to exclude diffidence and shame by a haughty consciousness of his own excellence[2].

39   For the rejection of this play it is difficult now to find the reason ; it certainly has, in a very great degree, the power of fixing attention and exciting merriment. From the charge of disaffection he exculpates himself in his preface by observing how unlikely it is that, having followed the royal family through all their distresses, 'he should chuse the time of their restoration [restitution] to begin a quarrel with them[3].' It appears, however, from the *Theatrical Register* of Downes the prompter, to have been popularly considered as a satire on the Royalists[4].

40   That he might shorten this tedious suspense he published his pretensions and his discontent in an ode called *The Complaint*, in which he styles himself the *melancholy* Cowley[5].

---

[1] See Appendix C.

[2] In the Preface Cowley asks :— 'What can be more ridiculous than to labour to give men delight, whilst they labour on their part more earnestly to take offence? To expose one's self voluntarily and frankly to all the dangers of that narrow passage to unprofitable fame which is defended by rude multitudes of the ignorant, and by armed troops of the malicious?' Hurd's *Cowley*, i. 103. See also *post*, DRYDEN, 28.

[3] Hurd's *Cowley*, i. 93. He was accused too of profaneness.

'Profane, to deride the hypocrisy of those men whose skulls are not yet bare upon the gates since the public and just punishment of it?' *Ib.* p. 98.

[4] 'This comedy being acted so perfectly well and exact, it was performed a whole week with a full audience. *Note*, This play was not a little injurious to the Cavalier indigent officers; especially the characters of Cutter and Worms.' Downes's *Roscius Anglicanus*, ed. 1789, p. 35.

[5] 'In a deep vision's intellectual scene,
    Beneath a bower for sorrow made,

This met with the usual fortune of complaints, and seems to have excited more contempt than pity.

These unlucky incidents are brought, maliciously enough, 41 together in some stanzas, written about that time, on the choice of a laureat; a mode of satire by which, since it was first introduced by Suckling [1], perhaps every generation of poets has been teazed:

'Savoy-missing Cowley came into the court,
  Making apologies for his bad play;
Every one gave him so good a report,
  That Apollo gave heed to all he could say;
Nor would he have had, 'tis thought, a rebuke,
  Unless he had done some notable folly;
Writ verses unjustly in praise of Sam Tuke [2],
  Or printed his pitiful Melancholy.'

His vehement desire of retirement now came again upon 42 him. 'Not finding,' says the morose Wood, 'that preferment conferred upon him which he expected, while others for their money carried away most places, he retired discontented into Surrey [3].'

'He was now,' says the courtly Sprat, 'weary of the vexations 43 and formalities of an active condition. He had been perplexed with a long compliance to foreign manners. He was satiated with the arts of a court, which sort of life, though his virtue made it innocent to him, yet nothing could make it quiet. Those were the reasons that moved him to [forego all public employments and to] follow the violent inclination of his own mind, which, in the greatest throng of his former business, had still called upon him, and represented to him the true delights of solitary studies, of temperate pleasures, and [of] a moderate revenue below the malice and flatteries of fortune [4].'

So differently are things seen and so differently are they 44 shown; but actions are visible, though motives are secret. Cowley

---

Th' uncomfortable shade
Of the black yew's unlucky green,
Mixt with the mourning willow's
  careful grey,
Where reverend Cam cuts out his
  famous way,
The melancholy Cowley lay.'
        Eng. Poets, vii. 248.
[1] In *A Session of the Poets*, Suckling's *Fragmenta Aurea*, ed. 1648, p. 7.
[2] On Colonel Tuke's *Tragi-Comedy of the Adventures of Five Hours,*

Eng. Poets, vii. 254. Pepys, on Jan. 8, 1662-3, described it as 'the famous new play acted the first time to-day.' *Diary*, ii. 94. On Feb. 15, 1688-9, he recorded:—'I do find Sir Samuel Tuke, I think, a little conceited, but a man of very fine discourse as any I ever heard almost, which I was mighty glad of.' *Ib.* v. 113. Tuke was Evelyn's cousin. Evelyn's *Diary*, ii. 37.
[3] *Fasti Oxon.* ii. 210.
[4] Hurd's *Cowley*, i. 16.

certainly retired ; first to Barn-elms [1], and afterwards to Chertsey, in Surrey. He seems, however, to have lost part of his dread of the 'hum of men [2].' He thought himself now safe enough from intrusion, without the defence of mountains and oceans ; and, instead of seeking shelter in America, wisely went only so far from the bustle of life as that he might easily find his way back, when solitude should grow tedious. His retreat was at first but slenderly accommodated ; yet he soon obtained, by the interest of the Earl of St. Albans and the duke of Buckingham, such a lease of the Queen's lands as afforded him an ample income [3].

45   By the lover of virtue and of wit it will be solicitously asked, if he now was happy. Let them peruse one of his letters accidentally preserved by Peck [4], which I recommend to the consideration of all that may hereafter pant for solitude [5].

To Dr. THOMAS SPRAT.

' Chertsey, 21 May, 1665.

The first night that I came hither I caught so great a cold, with a defluxion of rheum, as made me keep my chamber ten days [6]. And, two after, had such a bruise on my ribs with a fall,

---

[1] Hurd's *Cowley*, i. 52. Evelyn recorded on May 14, 1663 :—' To Barnes, to visit my excellent and ingenious friend, Abraham Cowley.' *Diary*, i. 396. Pepys, who rowed up the river to ' Barne Elmes ' on May 26, 1667, recorded in his *Diary*, iv. 53 :—' I walked the length of the Elmes, and with great pleasure saw some gallant ladies and people come with their bottles, and basket, and chairs, and form, to sup under the trees by the water-side, which was mighty pleasant.'

[2] *L'Allegro* of Milton [l. 118]. JOHNSON.

[3] See Appendix D.

[4] In *Memoir of Oliver Cromwell*, &c. by Francis Peck, 1740, Part ii. p. 81. Sprat, addressing Clifford (*post*, DRYDEN, 94), says :—' In his letters to his private friends he always expressed the native tenderness and innocent gaiety of his mind. I think, Sir, you and I have the greatest collection of this sort. But I know you agree with me that nothing of this nature should be published.' Hurd's *Cowley*, i. 37 ; *ante*, COWLEY, 1 *n.*

[5] In his Essay *Of Solitude* he writes :—
' Oh Solitude, first state of human-
   kind !
Which blest remain'd till man did
   find
Ev'n his own helper's company.
As soon as two, alas ! together
   join'd,
The serpent made up three.'
Eng. Poets, ix. 32. See also *ib.* p. 106.
   Atterbury wrote to Pope from Bromley :—' I generally keep here what Mr. Cowley calls the worst of company in the world, my own.' *Atterbury Corres.* i. 81. He refers, perhaps, to the following :—' And yet our dear self is so wearisome to us that we can scarcely support its conversation for an hour together.' *Eng. Poets*, ix. 28.

[6] In *The Garden* he had written :—
' Here health itself does live,
That salt of life which does to all a
   relish give.' *Ib.* ix. 75.
   In his Essay *Of Myself* he writes : —' God laughs at a man who says to his soul, *Take thy ease*. I meet presently . . . with so much sickness

that I am yet unable to move or turn myself in my bed. This is my personal fortune here to begin with. And, besides, I can get no money from my tenants[1], and have my meadows eaten up every night by cattle put in by my neighbours. What this signifies, or may come to in time, God knows ; if it be ominous, it can end in nothing less than hanging[2]. Another misfortune has been, and stranger than all the rest, that you have broke your word with me, and failed to come, even though you told Mr. Bois[3] that you would. This is what they call *Monstri simile*[4]. I do hope to recover my late hurt so farre within five or six days (though it be uncertain yet whether I shall ever recover it) as to walk about again. And then, methinks, you and I and *the Dean* might be very merry upon St. Anne's Hill[5]. You might very conveniently come hither the way of Hampton Town, lying there one night. I write this in pain and can say no more: *Verbum sapienti*[6].'

He did not long enjoy the pleasure or suffer the uneasiness 46 of solitude, for he died at the Porch-house in Chertsey in 1667, in the 49th year of his age[7].

He was buried with great pomp near Chaucer and Spenser[8]; 47 and king Charles pronounced 'That Mr. Cowley had not left

(a new misfortune to me) as would have spoiled the happiness of an emperor as well as mine.' *Ib*. ix. 125.

[1] In his Essay *Of Agriculture* he asserted that 'the means of improving estates is as easy and certain in agriculture as in any other track of commerce.' *Ib*. ix. 41.

[2] In his will, written four months later, he says of his estate, 'which it has pleased God to bestow upon me much above my deserts.' Cunningham, *Lives of the Poets*, i. 62.

[3] Pepys mentions Mr. Bois, whose house in Cheapside was burnt down in Aug. 1664. *Diary*, ii. 368.

[4] 'Eho, nonne hoc monstri simile est ?' TERENCE, *Eun*. ii. 3. 43.

[5] At St. Anne's Hill was Fox's last home.

[6] 'Dictum sapienti sat est.' TERENCE, *Phor*. iii. 3. 8.

[7] 'He died at a house called the Porch house, towards the west end of the town of Chertsey, on July 28, aged 49 years.' WOOD, *Fasti Oxon*. ii. 212. Johnson says in a note that the house is 'now in the possession of Mr. Clarke, Alderman of London.' See *post*, MILTON, 97 n. Clarke be-

longed to Johnson's Essex Head Club. Boswell's *Johnson*, iv. 258.

Pope asks :—

'Who now shall charm the shades where Cowley strung
His living harp, and lofty Denham sung?'

In a note he adds :—'Mr. Cowley died at Chertsey, on the borders of the Forest.' *Windsor Forest*, l. 279.

For an improbable account of his death see Spence's *Anecdotes*, p. 13, and *Dict. Nat. Biog*. xii. 381, and for his will see Cunningham, *Lives of the Poets*, i. 62.

[8] Evelyn recorded on Aug. 3 :— 'Went to Mr. Cowley's funeral, whose corpse was conveyed to Westminster Abbey in a hearse with six horses and all funeral decency, near a hundred coaches of noblemen and persons of quality following ; among these all the wits of the town, divers bishops and clergymen.' *Diary*, ii. 30.

Pepys did not hear of his death till Aug. 10, when he recorded :—'To the New Exchange, to the bookseller's there. . . . Cowley, he tells me, is dead ; who, it seems, was a mighty civil, serious man ; which I did not

a better man behind him in England ¹.' He is represented by Dr. Sprat as the most amiable of mankind, and this posthumous praise may be safely credited as it has never been contradicted by envy or by faction.

48 Such are the remarks and memorials which I have been able to add to the narrative of Dr. Sprat, who, writing when the feuds of the civil war were yet recent and the minds of either party easily irritated, was obliged to pass over many transactions in general expressions, and to leave curiosity often unsatisfied. What he did not tell cannot, however, now be known. I must therefore recommend the perusal of his work, to which my narration can be considered only as a slender supplement.

49 COWLEY, like other poets who have written with narrow views and, instead of tracing intellectual pleasure to its natural sources in the mind of man, paid their court to temporary prejudices, has been at one time too much praised and too much neglected at another ².

50 Wit, like all other things subject by their nature to the choice of man, has its changes and fashions, and at different times takes different forms. About the beginning of the seventeenth century

---

know before.' *Diary*, iv. 153. 'The New Exchange was at the western end of the Strand.' *N. & Q.* 4 S. x. 73.

On his monument we read how he was 'honorifica pompa elatus ex Aedibus Buckinghamianis.' Aubrey adds :—'His Grace the Duke of Bucks held a tassell of the pall.' *Brief Lives*, i. 190.

Of his epitaph in Latin verse Johnson writes :—'It is always with indignation or contempt that I read it. ... I condemn them [the expressions in it] as uninstructive and unaffecting, as too ludicrous for reverence and grief, for Christianity and a temple.' Johnson's *Works*, v. 262. *Post*, POPE, 410.

¹ Hurd's *Cowley*, i. 55.

² Wood describes Cowley as 'Anglorum Pindarus, Flaccus, Maro, deliciae, decus et desiderium aevi sui.' *Fasti Oxon.* ii. 209. Dryden wrote of him in 1699 :—'One of our late great poets is sunk in his reputation because he could never forego any conceit which came in his way, but swept, like a drag-net, great and

small. ... For this reason, though he must always be thought a great poet, he is no longer esteemed a good writer ; and for ten impressions which his works have had in so many successive years, yet at present a hundred books are scarcely purchased once a twelve month : for, as my last Lord Rochester said, though somewhat profanely, "Not being of God he could not stand."' Dryden's *Works*, xi. 223.

Pope, in 1737, in *Imit. Hor.* 2 *Epis.* i. 75 asks :—
'Who now reads Cowley? if he
    pleases yet,   [wit.'
His moral pleases, not his pointed

Richardson (*Corres.* ii. 229), in 1750, wonders 'why Cowley is so absolutely neglected.' In the eighteenth century only two complete editions of his works (exclusive of those in *English Poets*) were published. Malone's *Dryden*, iii. 611. Hurd's *Select Works in Verse and Prose of Cowley*, published in 1772 in two small octavo volumes, reached a third edition in five years.

appeared a race of writers that may be termed the metaphysical poets, of whom in a criticism on the works of Cowley it is not improper to give some account [1].

The metaphysical poets were men of learning, and to shew 51 their learning was their whole endeavour ; but, unluckily resolving to shew it in rhyme, instead of writing poetry they only wrote verses, and very often such verses as stood the trial of the finger better than of the ear ; for the modulation was so imperfect that they were only found to be verses by counting the syllables.

If the father of criticism has rightly denominated poetry 52 τέχνη μιμητική [2], *an imitative art*, these writers will without great wrong lose their right to the name of poets, for they cannot be said to have imitated any thing : they neither copied nature nor life ; neither painted the forms of matter nor represented the operations of intellect.

Those however who deny them to be poets allow them to be 53 wits. Dryden confesses of himself and his contemporaries that they fall below Donne in wit, but maintains that they surpass him in poetry [3].

If Wit be well described by Pope as being 'that which has 54 been often thought, but was never before so well expressed [4],' they certainly never attained nor ever sought it, for they endeavoured to be singular in their thoughts, and were careless of their diction. But Pope's account of wit is undoubtedly erroneous ; he depresses it below its natural dignity, and reduces it from strength of thought to happiness of language.

If by a more noble [5] and more adequate conception that 55

---

[1] See Appendix E.

[2] An Aristotelian scholar informs me that he does not think ' Aristotle uses the phrase τέχνη μιμητική, *totidem verbis*, of poetry. It is no doubt contained by implication in *Poetics*, ch. viii, but the prevailing mode of expression is to speak of poetry as a form of μίμησις (μίμησίς τις), or of the several kinds of poetry as so many μιμήσεις (cf. *Poet.* ch. i) ; ἡ μιμητική or ἡ μιμητικὴ τέχνη, as a whole, would cover many other arts besides poetry, and so Plato uses the phrase ἡ τῆς ποιήσεως μιμητική, *ex. gr.* in *Rep.* p. 603 c, substituting for it ἡ μιμητική a few lines lower down.'

[3] ' Doctor Donne, the greatest wit, though not the best poet of our nation.' DRYDEN, *Works*, xi. 123. ' If we are not so great wits as Donne, yet certainly we are better poets.' *Ib.* xiii. 109.

'Donne had no imagination, but as much wit, I think, as any writer can possibly have.' POPE, Spence's *Anec.* p. 136.

[4] See Appendix F.

[5] ' When the poet writes humour he makes folly ridiculous ; when wit, he moves you, if not always to laughter, yet to a pleasure that is more noble.' DRYDEN, *Works*, iii. 248.

be considered as Wit which is at once natural and new, that
which though not obvious is, upon its first production, acknowledged to be just; if it be that, which he that never found it,
wonders how he missed; to wit of this kind the metaphysical
poets have seldom risen. Their thoughts are often new, but seldom
natural; they are not obvious, but neither are they just; and the
reader, far from wondering that he missed them, wonders more
frequently by what perverseness of industry they were ever found.

56   But Wit, abstracted from its effects upon the hearer, may
be more rigorously and philosophically considered as a kind of
discordia concors[1]; a combination of dissimilar images, or
discovery of occult resemblances in things apparently unlike.
Of wit, thus defined, they have more than enough. The most
heterogeneous ideas are yoked by violence together; nature and
art are ransacked for illustrations, comparisons, and allusions;
their learning instructs, and their subtilty surprises; but the
reader commonly thinks his improvement dearly bought, and,
though he sometimes admires, is seldom pleased.

57   From this account of their compositions it will be readily
inferred that they were not successful in representing or moving
the affections. As they were wholly employed on something unexpected and surprising they had no regard to that uniformity
of sentiment, which enables us to conceive and to excite the pains
and the pleasure of other minds: they never enquired what on
any occasion they should have said or done, but wrote rather as
beholders than partakers of human nature; as beings looking
upon good and evil, impassive and at leisure; as Epicurean
deities making remarks on the actions of men and the vicissitudes
of life, without interest and without emotion. Their courtship
was void of fondness and their lamentation of sorrow. Their
wish was only to say what they hoped had been never said before[2].

58   Nor was the sublime more within their reach than the pathetick; for they never attempted that comprehension and expanse

[1] [Manilius, *Astron.* i. 142.]

[2] 'Donne and Cowley, by happen-
ing to possess more wit, and faculty
of illustration, than other men, are
supposed to have been incapable of
nature or feeling: they are usually
opposed to such writers as Shenstone
and Parnell; whereas, in the very
thickest of their conceits,—in the
bewildering mazes of tropes and
figures,—a warmth of soul and generous feeling shines through, the "sum"
of which, "forty thousand" of those
natural poets, as they are called,
"with all their quantity," could not
make up.' LAMB, *Mrs. Leicester's
School, and Other Writings*, ed. 1885,
p. 358. Lamb's quotation is from
Hamlet, v. 1. 292.

of thought which at once fills the whole mind, and of which the first effect is sudden astonishment, and the second rational admiration. Sublimity is produced by aggregation, and littleness by dispersion. Great thoughts are always general, and consist in positions not limited by exceptions, and in descriptions not descending to minuteness. It is with great propriety that subtlety[1], which in its original import means exility of particles, is taken in its metaphorical meaning for nicety of distinction. Those writers who lay on the watch for novelty could have little hope of greatness; for great things cannot have escaped former observation. Their attempts were always analytick: they broke every image into fragments, and could no more represent by their slender conceits and laboured particularities the prospects of nature or the scenes of life, than he who dissects a sun-beam with a prism can exhibit the wide effulgence of a summer noon.

What they wanted however of the sublime they endeavoured 59 to supply by hyperbole; their amplification had no limits: they left not only reason but fancy behind them, and produced combinations of confused magnificence that not only could not be credited, but could not be imagined.

Yet great labour directed by great abilities is never wholly 60 lost: if they frequently threw away their wit upon false conceits, they likewise sometimes struck out unexpected truth[2]: if their conceits were far-fetched, they were often worth the carriage. To write on their plan it was at least necessary to read and think. No man could be born a metaphysical poet, nor assume the dignity of a writer by descriptions copied from descriptions, by imitations borrowed from imitations, by traditional imagery and hereditary similes, by readiness of rhyme and volubility of syllables[3].

[1] Johnson defines *subtlety* (he spells it *subtilty*) as 'thinness; fineness; exility of parts.' *Exility* he does not give in his *Dictionary*.

[2] 'Some to *Conceit* alone their taste confine,
And glitt'ring thoughts struck out at every line;
Pleas'd with a work where nothing's just or fit; [of wit.'
One glaring Chaos and wild heap
POPE, *Essay on Criticism*, l. 289.

[3] Southey, quoting this passage, says:—'Justly as Johnson condemned the metaphysical poets, he saw how superior they were to those who were trained up in the school of Dryden.' Southey's *Cowper*, ii. 136.
'In the elder poets, from Donne to Cowley, we find the most fantastic out-of-the-way thoughts, but in the most pure and genuine mother English; in the modern poets the most obvious thoughts in language the

61 In perusing the works of this race of authors the mind is exercised either by recollection or inquiry; either something already learned is to be retrieved, or something new is to be examined. If their greatness seldom elevates their acuteness often surprises; if the imagination is not always gratified, at least the powers of reflection and comparison are employed; and in the mass of materials, which ingenious absurdity has thrown together, genuine wit and useful knowledge may be sometimes found, buried perhaps in grossness of expression, but useful to those who know their value, and such as, when they are expanded to perspicuity and polished to elegance, may give lustre to works which have more propriety though less copiousness of sentiment.

62 This kind of writing, which was, I believe, borrowed from Marino [1] and his followers, had been recommended by the example of Donne, a man of very extensive and various knowledge, and by Jonson, whose manner resembled that of Donne more in the ruggedness of his lines than in the cast of his sentiments [2].

63 When their reputation was high they had undoubtedly more imitators than time has left behind. Their immediate successors, of whom any remembrance can be said to remain, were Suckling, Waller, Denham, Cowley, Cleiveland [3], and Milton [4]. Denham and Waller sought another way to fame, by improving the harmony of our numbers [5]. Milton tried the metaphysick style only in his lines upon Hobson the Carrier [6]. Cowley adopted it, and excelled his predecessors; having as much sentiment and more musick. Suckling neither improved versification nor abounded in conceits. The fashionable style remained chiefly with Cowley: Suckling could not reach it, and Milton disdained it [7].

64 CRITICAL REMARKS are not easily understood without ex-

most fantastic and arbitrary.' COLERIDGE, *Biog. Lit.* i. 22.

'I always said about Cowley, Donne, &c., whom Johnson calls the metaphysical poets, that their very quibbles of fancy showed a power of logic which could follow fancy through such remote analogies.' *Letters of Edward FitzGerald*, ii. 26.

[1] See Appendix G.

[2] Ben Jonson said that 'Done, for not keeping of accent, deserved hanging.' Jonson's *Works*, ed. Cunningham, ix. 367.

[3] Dryden defines *Cleivelandism* as 'wresting and torturing a word into another meaning.' *Works*, xv. 287.

[4] Johnson omits Sprat (*post*, SPRAT, 22). Cunningham points out (i. 22) the omission of Crashaw and Herbert.

[5] *Post*, DENHAM, 21; WALLER, 5, 142.

[6] Milton's *Poetical Works* (ed. W. Aldis Wright), p. 23.

[7] 'Wit,' said Gray, 'had gone entirely out of fashion since the reign of Charles II.' Mitford's *Gray*, v. 39.

amples, and I have therefore collected instances of the modes of writing by which this species of poets, for poets they were called by themselves and their admirers, was eminently distinguished.

As the authors of this race were perhaps more desirous of being admired than understood they sometimes drew their conceits from recesses of learning not very much frequented by common readers of poetry. Thus Cowley on *Knowledge*:

> 'The sacred tree midst the fair orchard grew;
>   The phœnix Truth did on it rest,
>   And built his perfum'd nest,
> That right Porphyrian tree which did true logick shew.
>   Each leaf did learned notions give,
>   And th' apples were demonstrative:
>   So clear their colour and divine,
> The very shade they cast did other lights outshine[1].'

On Anacreon continuing a lover in his old age:

> 'Love was with thy life entwin'd,
>   Close as heat with fire is join'd;
>   A powerful brand prescrib'd the date
>   Of thine, like Meleager's fate.
>   Th' antiperistasis of age
>   More enflam'd thy amorous rage[2].'

In the following verses we have an allusion to a Rabbinical opinion concerning Manna:

> 'Variety I ask not: give me one
>   To live perpetually upon.
>   The person Love does to us fit,
>   Like manna, has the taste of all in it[3].'

Thus *Donne* shews his medicinal knowledge in some encomiastick verses:

> 'In every thing there naturally grows
>   A balsamum to keep it fresh and new,
>   If 'twere not injur'd by extrinsique blows;
>   Your youth [birth] and beauty are this balm in you.

65

66

67

68

---

[1] *Eng. Poets*, vii. 144.

[2] *Ib.* vii. 197. 'This hard word [antiperistasis] only means *compression*. The word is used by naturalists to express the power which one quality has by pressing on all sides to augment its contrary; as here the cold with which old age is surrounded increases heat. He expresses this quaint idea more plainly in two verses of *The Mistress* [*Eng. Poets*, viii. 3], where he says:—
'Flames their most vigorous heat do hold,
  And purest light, if compass'd round with cold.'
          Hurd's *Cowley*, i. 155.

[3] *Eng. Poets*, viii. 39.

> But you, of learning and religion,
> And virtue and such ingredients, have made
> A mithridate, whose operation
> Keeps off or cures what can be done or said [1].'

69   Though the following lines of Donne, on the last night of the year, have something in them too scholastick, they are not inelegant:

> 'This twilight of two years, not past nor next,
> Some emblem is of me, or I of this,
> Who, meteor-like, of stuff and form perplext,
> Whose what and where in disputation is,
> If I should call me any thing, should miss.
>
> I sum the years and me, and find me not
> Debtor to th' old nor creditor to th' new;
> That cannot say my thanks I have forgot,
> Nor trust I this with hopes; and yet scarce true
> This bravery is, since these times shew'd me you [2].'
>
> DONNE.

70   Yet more abstruse and profound is *Donne's* reflection upon Man as a Microcosm:

> 'If men be worlds, there is in every one
> Something to answer in some proportion
> All the world's riches: and in good men this
> Virtue, our form's form, and our soul's soul is [3].'

71   Of thoughts so far-fetched as to be not only unexpected but unnatural, all their books are full.

> To a lady, who wrote [made] poesies for rings:
>
> 'They, who above do various circles find,
> Say, like a ring th' æquator heaven does bind.
> When heaven shall be adorn'd by thee
> (Which then more heaven than 'tis, will be),
> 'Tis thou must write the poesy there,
> For it wanteth one as yet,
> Though the sun pass through't twice a year,
> The sun, which [who] is esteem'd the god of wit.'
>
> COWLEY [4].

72   The difficulties which have been raised about identity in philosophy are by Cowley with still more perplexity applied to Love:

> 'Five years ago (says story) I lov'd you,
> For which you call me most inconstant now;

---

[1] Grosart's *Donne*, ii. 30.   [3] *Ib.* ii. 79.
[2] *Ib.* ii. 42.   [4] *Eng. Poets*, vii. 127.

Pardon me, madam, you mistake the man;
For I am not the same that I was then;
No flesh is now the same 'twas then in me,
And that my mind is chang'd yourself may see.
The same thoughts to retain still, and intents,
Were more inconstant far; for accidents
Must of all things most strangely inconstant prove,
If from one subject they t' another move:
My members then, the father members were
From whence these take their birth, which now are here.
If then this body love what th' other did,
'Twere incest, which by nature is forbid [1].'

The love of different women is, in geographical poetry, compared 73
to travels through different countries:

' Hast thou not found, each woman's breast
  (The land [lands] where thou hast travelled)
Either by savages possest,
  Or wild, and uninhabited?
What joy could'st take, or what repose,
In countries so uncivilis'd as those?

Lust, the scorching dog star, here
  Rages with immoderate heat;
Whilst Pride, the rugged Northern Bear,
  In others makes the cold too great.
And where these are temperate known,
The soil's all barren sand, or rocky stone.'
                                    COWLEY [2].

A lover burnt up by his affection is compared to Egypt: 74

' The fate of Egypt I sustain,
  And never feel the dew of rain,
From clouds which in the head appear;
  But all my too much moisture owe
  To overflowings of the heart below.'—COWLEY [3].

The lover supposes his lady acquainted with the ancient laws 75
of augury and rites of sacrifice:

' And yet this death of mine, I fear,
  Will ominous to her appear:
When found in every other part,
  Her sacrifice is found without an heart.
  For the last tempest of my death
  Shall sigh out that too, with my breath [4].'

[1] *Eng. Poets*, viii. 13.
[2] *Ib.* viii. 48. In the edition of Cowley's *Poems*, 1674, the last line runs:—
' The soyls are,' &c.   [3] *Ib.* viii. 61.   [4] *Ib.* viii. 66.

76   That the chaos was harmonised has been recited of old[1]; but
whence the different sounds arose remained for a modern to
discover:

> 'Th' ungovern'd parts no correspondent knew,
> An artless war from thwarting motions grew;
> Till they to number and fixt rules were brought
> [By the Eternal Mind's poetick thought].
> Water and air he for the tenor chose,
> Earth made the base, the treble flame arose.'
>
>   COWLEY[2].

77   The tears of lovers are always of great poetical account, but
Donne has extended them into worlds.   If the lines are not easily
understood they may be read again.

> 'On a round ball
> A workman, that hath copies by, can lay
> An Europe, Afric, and an Asia,
> And quickly make that, which was nothing, all.
> So doth each tear,
> Which thee doth wear,
> A globe, yea world, by that impression grow,
> Till thy tears mixt with mine do overflow
> This world, by waters sent from thee my [by] heaven dis-
> solved so[3].'

On reading the following lines the reader may perhaps cry
out, 'Confusion worse confounded[4].'

> 'Here lies a she sun, and a he moon here,
> She gives the best light to his sphere,
> Or each is both, and all, and so
> They unto one another nothing owe[5].'
>
>   DONNE.

78   Who but Donne would have thought that a good man is a
telescope?

> 'Though God be our true glass, through which we see
> All, since the being of all things is he,
> Yet are the trunks, which do to us derive
> Things in proportion fit by perspective,

---

[1] By Plato in *Politicus*, 273 c, d,
and in *Timaeus*, 69 c; by Ovid in
Metamor. bk. 1.
'From harmony, from heavenly har-
    mony
  This universal frame began.'
      DRYDEN, *St. Cecilia*, l. 1.

[2] *Eng. Poets*, viii. 194. 'Cowley
appears by these lines to have been
but little skilled in music.' HAW-
KINS, Johnson's *Works*, 1787, ii. 30.
[3] Grosart's *Donne*, ii. 198.
[4] *Paradise Lost*, ii. 996.
[5] Grosart's *Donne*, i. 258.

Deeds of good men; for by their living [being] here,
Virtues, indeed remote, seem to be near [1].'

Who would imagine it possible that in a very few lines so many 79
remote ideas could be brought together?

'Since 'tis my doom, Love's undershrieve,
    Why this reprieve?
Why doth my She Advowson fly
    Incumbency [2]?
To sell thyself dost thou intend
    By candle's end,
And hold the contrast [contract] thus in doubt,
    Life's taper out?
Think but how soon the market fails,
Your sex lives faster than the males;
As if to measure age's span,
The sober Julian were th' acount of man,
Whilst you live by the fleet Gregorian.'
                                    CLEIVELAND [3].

Of enormous and disgusting hyberboles these may be ex- 80
amples:

'By every wind, that comes this way,
Send me at least a sigh or two,
Such and so many I'll repay
As shall themselves make winds to get to you.'
                                    COWLEY [4].

'In tears I'll waste these eyes,
    By Love so vainly fed;
So lust of old the Deluge punished.'—COWLEY [5].

'All arm'd in brass the richest dress of war
(A dismal glorious sight) he shone afar.
The sun himself started with sudden fright,
To see his beams return so dismal bright.'
                                    COWLEY [6].

---

[1] Grosart's *Donne*, ii. 115.
[2] Here follow five lines omitted by Johnson.
[3] *Works*, ed. 1687, p. 6. On the titlepage the name is printed Cleveland, but underneath his portrait which faces it—Cleaveland. Johnson gives a third spelling. Another variety is Clevland. Cleveland's executors in their *Epistle Dedicatory* aim at rivalling his wit. 'Whilst Randolph and Cowley,' they write, 'lie embalmed in their own native wax, how is the name and memory of Cleveland equally prophaned by those that usurp and those that blaspheme it! By those that are ambitious to lay their Cuckow's Eggs in his Nest; and those that think to raise up Phenixes of Wit by firing his spicy Bed about him!'
[4] *Eng. Poets*, vii. 123.
[5] *Ib.* viii. 28.
[6] *Ib.* viii. 258.

An universal consternation:

> ' His bloody eyes he hurls round, his sharp paws
> Tear up the ground; then runs he wild about,
> Lashing his angry tail and roaring out.
> Beasts creep into their dens, and tremble there;
> Trees, though no wind is stirring, shake with fear;
> Silence and horror fill the place around:
> Echo itself dares scarce repeat the sound.'—COWLEY [1].

81   Their fictions were often violent and unnatural.

Of his Mistress bathing:

> 'The fish around her crouded, as they do
> To the false light that treacherous fishers shew,
> And all with as much ease might taken be,
>   As she at first took me:
>   For ne'er did light so clear
>   Among the waves appear,
> Though every night the sun himself set there.'
> COWLEY [2].

82   The poetical effect of a Lover's name upon glass:

> ' My name engrav'd herein
> Doth contribute my firmness to this glass;
>   Which, ever since that charm, hath been
> As hard as that which grav'd it was.'—DONNE [3].

83   Their conceits were sometimes slight and trifling.

On an inconstant woman :

> ' He enjoys thy calmy sunshine now,
>   And no breath stirring hears;
> In the clear heaven of thy brow,
>   No smallest cloud appears.
> He sees thee gentle, fair and gay,
> And trusts the faithless April of thy May.'
> COWLEY [4].

84   Upon a paper written with the juice of lemon, and read by
the fire:

> ' Nothing [So nothing] yet in thee is seen;
> But when a genial heat warms thee within,
> A new-born wood of various lines there grows;
> Here buds an L [A], and there a B,

[1] *Eng. Poets*, viii. 201.
[2] *Ib.* viii. 100.
[3] Grosart's *Donne*, ii. 182.
[4] *Eng. Poets*, vii. 136.

Here sprouts a V, and there a T,
And all the flourishing letters stand in rows.'
                                        COWLEY [1].'

As they sought only for novelty they did not much enquire 85
whether their allusions were to things high or low, elegant
or gross; whether they compared the little to the great, or the
great to the little.

Physick and Chirurgery for a Lover :

'Gently, ah gently, madam, touch
    The wound, which you yourself have made;
That pain must needs be very much,
    Which makes me of your hand afraid.
Cordials of pity give me now,
For I too weak for purgings grow.'—COWLEY [2].

The World and a Clock :

' Mahol th' inferior world's fantastic face
Through all the turns of matter's maze did trace;
Great Nature's well-set clock in pieces took;
On all the springs and smallest wheels did look
Of life and motion; and with equal art
Made up again the whole of every part.'—COWLEY [3].

A coal-pit has not often found its poet; but, that it may 86
not want its due honour Cleiveland has paralleled it with the
Sun :

'The moderate value of our guiltless ore
Makes no man atheist, and no woman whore;
Yet why should hallow'd vestal's sacred shrine
Deserve more honour than a flaming mine?
These pregnant wombs of heat would fitter be
Than a few embers, for a deity.
    Had he our pits, the Persian would admire
No sun, but warm's devotion at our fire :
He'd leave the trotting whipster, and prefer
Our profound Vulcan 'bove that waggoner.
For wants he heat, or light? or would have store
Of both? 'tis here: and what can suns give more?
Nay, what's the sun but, in a different name,
A coal-pit rampant, or a mine on flame!
Then let this truth reciprocally run,
The sun's heaven's coalery, and coals our sun [4].'

[1] *Eng. Poets*, viii. 12.   [3] *Ib.* viii. 204; 1 *Kings* iv. 31.
[2] *Ib.* viii. 37.   [4] Cleveland's *Works*, p. 287.

Death, a Voyage:

> 'No family
> Ere rigg'd a soul for heaven's discovery,
> With whom more venturers might boldly dare
> Venture their stakes, with him in joy to share.'
>
> DONNE [1].

87 Their thoughts and expressions were sometimes grossly absurd, and such as no figures or licence can reconcile to the understanding.

A Lover neither dead nor alive:

> 'Then down I laid my head,
> Down on cold earth; and for a while was dead,
> And my freed soul to a strange somewhere fled:
> Ah, sottish soul, said I,
> When back to its cage again I saw it fly:
> Fool to resume her broken chain,
> And row her galley here again!
> Fool, to that body to return
> Where it condemn'd and destin'd is to burn!
> Once dead, how can it be,
> Death should a thing so pleasant seem to thee,
> That thou should'st come to live it o'er again in me?'
>
> COWLEY [2].

A Lover's heart, a hand grenado:

> 'Wo to her stubborn heart, if once mine come
> Into the self-same room,
> 'Twill tear and blow up all within,
> Like a grenado shot into a magazin.
> Then shall Love keep the ashes and torn parts
> Of both our broken hearts:
> Shall out of both one new one make;
> From her's th' allay, from mine the metal, take.'
>
> COWLEY [3].

The poetical Propagation of Light:

> 'The Prince's favour is diffus'd o'er all,
> From which all fortunes, names, and natures fall;
> Then from those wombs of stars, the Bride's bright eyes,
> At every glance a constellation flies,
> And sows the court with stars, and doth prevent,
> In light and power, the all-ey'd firmament:

---

[1] Grosart's *Donne*, ii. 143. The third line runs:—'With whom adventurers more boldly dare.'   [2] *Eng. Poets*, viii. 28.   [3] *Ib.* viii. 44.

First her eye kindles [eyes kindle] other ladies' eyes,
Then from their beams their jewels' lustres rise ;
And from their jewels torches do take fire,
And all is warmth, and light, and good desire.'—DONNE [1].

They were in very little care to clothe their notions with 88
elegance of dress, and therefore miss the notice and the praise
which are often gained by those who think less, but are more
diligent to adorn their thoughts.

That a mistress beloved is fairer in idea than in reality is by 89
Cowley thus expressed :

'Thou in my fancy dost much higher stand,
  Than women can be plac'd by Nature's hand ;
  And I must needs, I'm sure, a loser be,
  To change thee, as thou'rt there, for very thee [2].'

That prayer and labour should co-operate are thus taught 90
by Donne :

'In none but us, are such mixt engines found,
  As hands of double office : for the ground
  We till with them ; and them to heaven we raise ;
  Who prayerless labours, or without this prays,
  Doth but one half, that's none [3].'

By the same author a common topick, the danger of procrasti- 91
nation, is thus illustrated :

'—That which I should have begun
  In my youth's morning, now late must be done ;
  And I, as giddy travellers must do,
  Which stray or sleep all day, and having lost
  Light and strength, dark and tir'd must then ride post [4].'

All that Man has to do is to live and die ; the sum of humanity 92
is comprehended by Donne in the following lines :

'Think in how poor a prison thou didst lie
  After, enabled but to suck and cry.
  Think, when 'twas grown to most, 'twas a poor inn,
  A province pack'd up in two yards of skin,
  And that usurp'd, or threaten'd with a [the] rage
  Of sicknesses, or their true mother, age.
  But think that death hath now enfranchis'd thee ;
  Thou hast thy expansion now, and liberty ;
  Think, that a rusty piece discharg'd is flown
  In pieces, and the bullet is his own,

[1] Grosart's *Donne*, i. 262.   [3] Grosart's *Donne*, ii. 38.
[2] *Eng. Poets*, viii. 42.   [4] *Ib.* ii. 15.

And freely flies: this to thy soul allow,
Think thy shell broke, think thy soul hatch'd but now[1].'

93   They were sometimes indelicate and disgusting. Cowley thus
apostrophises beauty:

'—Thou tyrant, which leav'st no man free!
Thou subtle thief, from whom nought safe can be!
Thou murtherer, which hast kill'd, and devil, which would'st
    damn me[2]!'

Thus he addresses his Mistress:

'Thou who, in many a propriety,
    So truly art the sun to me,
Add one more likeness, which I'm sure you can,
And let me and my sun beget a man[3].'

94   Thus he represents the meditations of a Lover:

'Though in thy thoughts scarce any tracts have been
        So much as of original sin,
    Such charms thy beauty wears as might
    Desires in dying confest saints excite.
        Thou with strange adultery
    Dost in each breast a brothel keep;
        Awake, all men do lust for thee,
    And some enjoy thee when they sleep[4].'

The true taste of Tears:

'Hither with crystal vials, lovers, come,
    And take my tears, which are Love's wine,
And try your mistress' tears at home;
    For all are false that taste not just like mine.'
                                        DONNE[5].

95   This is yet more indelicate:

'As the sweet sweat of roses in a still,
As that which from chaf'd musk-cat's pores doth trill,
As the almighty balm of th' early East,
Such are the sweet drops of [on] my mistress' breast.
And on her neck her skin such lustre sets,
They seem no sweat-drops, but pearl coronets [carkanets]:
Rank sweaty froth thy mistress' brow defiles.'—DONNE[6].

96   Their expressions sometimes raise horror, when they intend
perhaps to be pathetick:

'As men in hell are from diseases free,
        So from all other ills am I,

---

[1] Grosart's *Donne*, i. 137.   [4] *Ib.* viii. 95.
[2] *Eng. Poets*, viii. 63.   [5] Grosart's *Donne*, ii. 186.
[3] *Ib.* viii. 64.   [6] *Ib.* i. 183.

Free from their known formality :
But all pains eminently lie in thee.'—COWLEY [1].

THEY were not always strictly curious whether the opinions **97**
from which they drew their illustrations were true ; it was enough
that they were popular. Bacon remarks that some falsehoods
are continued by tradition, because they supply commodious
allusions [2].

'It gave a piteous groan, and so it broke ;
In vain it something would have spoke :
The love within too strong for 't was,
Like poison put into a Venice-glass.'—COWLEY [3].

IN forming descriptions they looked out not for images, but **98**
for conceits. Night has been a common subject, which poets
have contended to adorn. Dryden's *Night* is well known [4];
Donne's is as follows :

'Thou seest me here at midnight ; now all rest,
Time's dead low-water ; when all minds divest
To-morrow's business ; when the labourers have
Such rest in bed, that their last church-yard grave,
Subject to change, will scarce be a type of this.
Now when the client, whose last hearing is
To-morrow, sleeps ; when the condemned man—
Who when he opes his eyes must shut them then
Again by death—although sad watch he keep,
Doth practise dying by a little sleep ;
Thou at this midnight seest me [5].'

IT must be however confessed of these writers that if they **99**
are upon common subjects often unnecessarily and unpoetically
subtle, yet where scholastick speculation can be properly admitted, their copiousness and acuteness may justly be admired.
What Cowley has written upon Hope shews an unequalled
fertility of invention :

'Hope, whose weak being ruin'd is,
Alike if it succeed, and if it miss ;
Whom good or ill does equally confound,
And both the horns of Fate's dilemma wound ;

[1] *Eng. Poets*, viii. 75.
[2] 'As things now are, if an untruth
in nature be once on foot, what by
reason of the neglect of examination
and countenance of antiquity, and
what by reason of the use of the
opinion in similitudes and ornaments
of speech, it is never called down.'
Advancement of Learning, bk. ii.
Works, 1803, i. 77.
[3] *Eng. Poets*, viii. 73.
[4] *Post*, DRYDEN, 19.
[5] Grosart's *Donne*, ii. 115.

Vain shadow, which dost vanish quite,
Both at full noon and perfect night!
The stars have not a possibility
Of blessing thee;
If things then from their end we happy call,
'Tis Hope is the most hopeless thing of all.

Hope, thou bold taster of delight,
Who, whilst thou should'st but taste, devour'st it quite!
Thou bring'st us an estate, yet leav'st us poor,
By clogging it with legacies before!
The joys which we entire should wed,
Come deflower'd virgins to our bed;
Good fortunes without gain imported be,
Such mighty custom's paid to thee:
For joy, like wine, kept close does better taste:
If it take air before, its spirits waste[1].'

100   To the following comparison of a man that travels and his
wife that stays at home with a pair of compasses, it may be
doubted whether absurdity or ingenuity has the better claim:

'Our two souls therefore, which are one,
Though I must go, endure not yet
A breach, but an expansion,
Like gold to airy thinness beat.

If they be two, they are two so
As stiff twin-compasses are two:
Thy soul, the fixt foot, makes no show
To move, but doth, if th' other do.

And though it in the centre sit,
Yet when the other far doth roam,
It leans, and hearkens after it,
And grows erect, as that comes home.

Such wilt thou be to me, who must,
Like th' other foot, obliquely run;
Thy firmness makes my circle just,
And makes me end where I begun.'

DONNE[2].

[1] *Eng. Poets*, viii. 54.
[2] Grosart's *Donne*, ii. 211, where the poem is entitled *Upon Partinge from his Mistris*. Walton, quoting the whole poem (*A Valediction, Forbidding to Mourn*), says 'they were given by Mr. Donne to his wife at the time he parted from her,' when he accompanied the English ambassador to Paris. Walton's *Lives*, 1838, p. 28.
'A curious mathematical quatrain of Omar's has been pointed out to me; the more curious because almost exactly paralleled by some verses of Dr. Donne's. Here is Omar:—
"You and I are the image of a pair of compasses, though we have two

In all these examples it is apparent that whatever is im- 101 proper or vicious is produced by a voluntary deviation from nature in pursuit of something new and strange, and that the writers fail to give delight by their desire of exciting admiration.

HAVING thus endeavoured to exhibit a general representation 102 of the style and sentiments of the metaphysical poets, it is now proper to examine particularly the works of Cowley, who was almost the last of that race and undoubtedly the best.

His Miscellanies contain a collection of short compositions, 103 written some as they were dictated by a mind at leisure, and some as they were called forth by different occasions; with great variety of style and sentiment, from burlesque levity to awful grandeur. Such an assemblage of diversified excellence no other poet has hitherto afforded. To choose the best among many good is one of the most hazardous attempts of criticism. I know not whether Scaliger himself has persuaded many readers to join with him in his preference of the two favourite odes, which he estimates in his raptures at the value of a kingdom [1]. I will however venture to recommend Cowley's first piece, which ought to be inscribed *To my Muse*, for want of which the second couplet is without reference [2]. When the title is added, there will still remain a defect; for every piece ought to contain in itself whatever is necessary to make it

heads (sc. our *feet*) we have one body; when we have fixed the centre for our circle we bring our heads (sc. feet) together at the end." ' E. FITZ-GERALD, *Omar Khayyám*, 1898, p. 67.
'Tennyson would quote the last four stanzas of this poem, praising its wonderful ingenuity.' *Life of Tennyson*, ii. 503.
[1] [My friend Mr. John Marshall of Lewes informs me that the reference is to the elder Scaliger, who is writing of Horace's *Odes*. The passage runs: ' Omnes inquam tantae sunt venustatis ut et mihi et aliis prudentioribus omnem ademerint spem talium studiorum. Inter caeteras vero, duas animadverti quibus ne ambrosiam quidem aut nectar dulciora putem. Altera est tertia quarti libri : " Quem tu Melpomene . . . " Altera nona ex tertio : " Donec gratus eram . . . " Quarum similes a me compositas malim quam Pythionicarum multas

Pindari et Nemeonicarum, quarum similes malim composuisse quam esse totius Tarraconensis Rex.' Iul. Caesaris Scaligeri *Poetices* libri septem. Apud Antonium Vincentium. M.D.LXI. libr. vi. p. 339 A,B. The passage is quoted in the Delphine *Horace* (1776), p. 344.]
[2] It is inscribed *The Motto*. It begins :—
' What shall I do to be for ever known,
  And make the age to come my own ?
I shall like beasts or common people die,
  Unless you write my elegy.'
  Eng. Poets, vii. 107.
' We have had in our language,' wrote Gray, ' no other odes of the sublime kind than that of Dryden *On St. Cecilia's Day*; for Cowley, who had his merit, yet wanted judgment, style and harmony for such a task.' Mitford's *Gray*, i. 36 *n*.

intelligible. Pope has some epitaphs without names; which are therefore epitaphs to be let, occupied indeed for the present, but hardly appropriated [1].

104 The ode on Wit is almost without a rival. It was about the time of Cowley that *Wit*, which had been till then used for *Intellection* in contradistinction to *Will*, took the meaning whatever it be which it now bears [2].

105 Of all the passages in which poets have exemplified their own precepts none will easily be found of greater excellence than that in which Cowley condemns exuberance of Wit:

> ' Yet 'tis not to adorn and gild each part;
>   That shews more cost than art.
> Jewels at nose and lips but ill appear;
> Rather than all things wit, let none be there.
>   Several lights will not be seen,
>   If there be nothing else between.
> Men doubt, because they stand so thick i' th' sky,
> If those be stars which paint the galaxy [3].'

106 In his verses to lord Falkland [4], whom every man of his time was proud to praise [5], there are, as there must be in all Cowley's compositions, some striking thoughts; but they are not well wrought. His elegy on Sir Henry Wotton is vigorous and happy, the series of thoughts is easy and natural, and the conclusion, though a little weakened by the intrusion of Alexander, is elegant and forcible [6].

107 It may be remarked that in this Elegy, and in most of his encomiastick poems, he has forgotten or neglected to name his heroes [7].

108 In his poem on the death of Hervey [8] there is much praise,

[1] *Post*, COWLEY, 107; POPE, 396.

[2] *Ante*, COWLEY, 54. Johnson defines *wit* in its original sense as 'the powers of the mind; the mental faculties; the intellects.'

Mackintosh (*Life*, ii. 93) says :— 'What was the first instance of the limitation of the term wit to the modern sense of ludicrous fancy I cannot tell. It must have been after Pope's definition.'

[3] *Eng. Poets*, vii. 110.

[4] *Ib.* vii. 111; *ante*, COWLEY, 11.

[5] For Waller's verses to him see *Eng. Poets*, xvi. 82.

' There never was a stronger instance of what the magic of words and the art of an historian can effect than in the character of this lord, who seems to have been a virtuous, well-meaning man with a moderate understanding; who got knocked on the head early in the Civil War because it boded ill; and yet, by the happy solemnity of my Lord Clarendon's diction, Lord Falkland is the favourite personage of that noble work.' HORACE WALPOLE, *Works*, i. 501. See Clarendon's *Hist.* (1826), iv. 240.

[6] *Post*, COWLEY, 176 *n*.

[7] *Ante*, COWLEY, 103.

[8] *Eng. Poets*, vii. 129; *post*, MILTON, 181. 'This elegy,' writes

but little passion, a very just and ample delineation of such virtues as a studious privacy admits, and such intellectual excellence as a mind not yet called forth to action can display[1]. He knew how to distinguish and how to commend the qualities of his companion, but when he wishes to make us weep he forgets to weep himself, and diverts his sorrow by imagining how his crown of bays, if he had it, would *crackle* in the *fire*[2]. It is the odd fate of this thought to be worse for being true. The bay-leaf crackles remarkably as it burns; as therefore this property was not assigned it by chance, the mind must be thought sufficiently at ease that could attend to such minuteness of physiology. But the power of Cowley is not so much to move the affections, as to exercise the understanding[3].

The Chronicle is a composition unrivalled and alone[4]: such 109 gaiety of fancy, such facility of expression, such varied similitude, such a succession of images, and such a dance of words, it is vain to expect except from Cowley. His strength always appears in his agility; his volatility is not the flutter of a light, but the bound of an elastick mind. His levity never leaves his learning behind it; the moralist, the politician, and the critick, mingle their influence even in this airy frolick of genius.

Sprat, 'was the first occasion of his entering into business. It brought him into the acquaintance of Mr. John Hervey, the brother of his friend; by his means he came into the service of my Lord St. Albans.' Hurd's *Cowley*, i. 7. Hervey was Lord St. Albans' first cousin. Cunningham's *Lives of the Poets*, i. 63.

[1] 'Say, for you saw us, ye immortal lights,
How oft unweary'd have we spent the nights,
Till the Ledaean stars, so fam'd for love,
Wonder'd at us from above.
We spent them not in toys, in lusts, or wine;
But search of deep philosophy,
Wit, eloquence, and poetry,
Arts which I lov'd, for they, my friend, were thine.'
Eng. Poets, vii. 130.

[2] 'Had I a wreath of bays above my brow
I should contemn that flourishing honour now,

Condemn it to the fire, and joy to hear
It rage and crackle there.'
Ib. p. 132.

[3] Lamb, writing of one of his own Sonnets, in which are the lines:—
'The time has been
We two did love each other's company;
Time was, we two had wept to have been apart';
continues: — 'Cowley's exquisite Elegy on the death of his friend Hervey suggested the phrase of "we two."
"Was there a tree that did not know
The love betwixt us two?"'
Lamb's *Letters*, i. 6.
The first line runs:—
'Was there a tree about which did not know.' *Eng. Poets*, vii. 131.

[4] *Ib.* vii. 137. Of this poem Hurd wrote in 1772:—'Nothing is more famous even in our days than Cowley's *mistresses*.' Hurd's *Cowley*, i. 128.

To such a performance Suckling could have brought the gaiety, but not the knowledge; Dryden could have supplied the knowledge, but not the gaiety.

110 The verses to Davenant[1], which are vigorously begun and happily concluded, contain some hints of criticism very justly conceived and happily expressed. Cowley's critical abilities have not been sufficiently observed: the few decisions and remarks which his prefaces and his notes[2] on the *Davideis* supply were at that time accessions to English literature, and shew such skill as raises our wish for more examples.

111 The lines from Jersey[3] are a very curious and pleasing specimen of the familiar descending to the burlesque.

112 His two metrical disquisitions *for* and *against* Reason[4] are no mean specimens of metaphysical poetry. The stanzas against knowledge produce little conviction. In those which are intended to exalt the human faculties, Reason has its proper task assigned it: that of judging, not of things revealed, but of the reality of revelation. In the verses *for* Reason is a passage which Bentley, in the only English verses which he is known to have written, seems to have copied, though with the inferiority of an imitator[5].

> 'The holy Book like the eighth sphere does shine
>   With thousand lights of truth divine,
> So numberless the stars that to our [the] eye
>   It makes all but [but all] one galaxy:
> Yet Reason must assist too; for in seas
>   So vast and dangerous as these,
> Our course by stars above we cannot know
>   Without the compass too below[6].'

113 After this says Bentley:

> 'Who travels in religious jars,
>   Truth mix'd with error, clouds [shades] with rays,
> With [Like] Whiston wanting pyx and [or] stars,
>   In the wide ocean [In ocean wide or] sinks or strays.'

[1] *Eng. Poets*, vii. 141.
[2] These notes are suppressed in *Eng. Poets*.
[3] *Ib.* vii. 142. [4] *Ib.* vii. 144-7.
[5] 'Johnson one day gave high praise to Dr. Bentley's verses, which he recited with his usual energy. Dr. Adam Smith, who was present, observed in his decisive professorial manner, "Very well—Very well." Johnson however added, "Yes, they *are* very well, Sir; but you may observe in what manner they are well. They are the forcible verses of a man of a strong mind, but not accustomed to write verse; for there is some uncouthness in the expression."' Boswell's *Johnson*, iv. 23, where the verses are given.
[6] *Eng. Poets*, vii. 147.

Cowley seems to have had, what Milton is believed to have 114
wanted[1], the skill to rate his own performances by their just
value, and has therefore closed his *Miscellanies* with the verses
upon Crashaw, which apparently excel all that have gone before
them, and in which there are beauties which common authors may
justly think not only above their attainment, but above their
ambition[2].

To the *Miscellanies* succeed the *Anacreontiques,* or para- 115
phrastical translations of some little poems, which pass, however justly, under the name of Anacreon. Of those songs
dedicated to festivity and gaiety, in which even the morality is
voluptuous, and which teach nothing but the enjoyment of the
present day, he has given rather a pleasing than a faithful
representation, having retained their spriteliness, but lost their
simplicity. The Anacreon of Cowley, like the Homer of Pope[3],
has admitted the decoration of some modern graces, by which
he is undoubtedly made more amiable to common readers, and
perhaps, if they would honestly declare their own perceptions, to
far the greater part of those whom courtesy and ignorance are
content to style the Learned.

These little pieces will be found more finished in their kind 116
than any other of Cowley's works. The diction shews nothing
of the mould of time, and the sentiments are at no great
distance from our present habitudes of thought[4]. Real mirth

---

[1] *Post,* MILTON, 146.
[2] *Eng. Poets,* vii. 148. The verses
begin :—
'Poet and Saint! to thee alone are
        given
The two most sacred names of Earth
        and Heaven.'
For 'Poet and Saint' see *post,*
WEST, 5.
    The following couplet :—
'His faith, perhaps, in some nice
        tenets might
Be wrong; his life, I'm sure was in
        the right'
has been imitated by Pope :
'For modes of faith let graceless
        zealots fight;
His can't be wrong whose life is in the
        right.' *Essay on Man,* iii. 305.
[3] *Post,* POPE, 352.
[4] Crabbe's son tells how when a
child he was taken by his father to
hear John Wesley, 'on one of the
last of his peregrinations,' preach at
Lowestoff, who quoted in his sermon
Cowley's translation from Anacreon's
Age [*Eng. Poets,* vii. 189] :—
'Oft am I by the women told,
Poor Anacreon! thou growest old;
Look how thy hairs are falling all;
Poor Anacreon, how they fall!
Whether I grow old or no,
By th' effects I do not know;
This I know, without being told,
'Tis time to live if I grow old.'
    'My father,' the son adds, 'was
much struck by Wesley's reverend
appearance and his cheerful air, and
the beautiful cadence he gave to
these lines.' Crabbe's *Works,* 1834,
i. 148. This is said to have happened
in Sept. 1791 (*ib.* p. 141); but Wesley
died on March 2 of that year.

must be always natural, and nature is uniform. Men have been wise in very different modes; but they have always laughed the same way.

117 Levity of thought naturally produced familiarity of language, and the familiar part of language continues long the same : the dialogue of comedy, when it is transcribed from popular manners and real life, is read from age to age with equal pleasure[1]. The artifice of inversion, by which the established order of words is changed, or of innovation, by which new words or new meanings of words are introduced, is practised, not by those who talk to be understood, but by those who write to be admired.

118 The *Anacreontiques* therefore of Cowley give now all the pleasure which they ever gave. If he was formed by nature for one kind of writing more than for another, his power seems to have been greatest in the familiar and the festive.

119 The next class of his poems is called *The Mistress*, of which it is not necessary to select any particular pieces for praise or censure. They have all the same beauties and faults, and nearly in the same proportion. They are written with exuberance of wit, and with copiousness of learning; and it is truly asserted by Sprat that the plenitude of the writer's knowledge flows in upon his page, so that the reader is commonly surprised into some improvement[2]. But, considered as the verses of a lover, no man that has ever loved will much commend them. They are neither courtly nor pathetick, have neither gallantry nor fondness. His praises are too far-sought and too hyperbolical, either to express love or to excite it : every stanza is crouded with darts and flames, with wounds and death, with mingled souls, and with broken hearts[3].

[1] 'The polite are always catching modish innovations, and the learned depart from established forms of speech, in hope of finding or making better; those who wish for distinction forsake the vulgar, when the vulgar is right; but there is a conversation above grossness and below refinement, where propriety resides, and where this poet [Shakespeare] seems to have gathered his comick dialogue. He is therefore more agreeable to the ears of the present age than any other author equally remote.'
JOHNSON, *Works*, v. 114.

[2] Hurd's *Cowley*, i. 26.
'I mentioned Shenstone's saying of Pope that he had the art of condensing sense more than any body. Dr. Johnson said, "It is not true, Sir. There is more sense in a line of Cowley than in a page (or a sentence, or ten lines,—I am not quite certain of the very phrase) of Pope."'
Boswell's *Johnson*, v. 345. For Shenstone's saying see *ib. n.* 2.
[3] 'The goddess soon began to see,
  Things were not ripe for a decree;
  And said she must consult her
    books,

The principal artifice by which *The Mistress* is filled with 120 conceits is very copiously displayed by Addison[1]. Love is by Cowley as by other poets expressed metaphorically by flame and fire; and that which is true of real fire is said of love, or figurative fire, the same word in the same sentence retaining both significations. Thus, 'observing the cold regard of his mistress's eyes, and at the same time their power of producing love in him, he considers them as burning-glasses made of ice[2]. Finding himself able to live in the greatest extremities of love he concludes the torrid zone to be habitable[3]. Upon the dying of a tree, on which he had cut his loves, he observes that his flames had burnt up and withered the tree[4].'

These conceits Addison calls mixed wit, that is, wit which 121 consists of thoughts true in one sense of the expression, and false in the other. Addison's representation is sufficiently indulgent[5]: that confusion of images may entertain for a moment, but being unnatural it soon grows wearisome. Cowley delighted in it, as much as if he had invented it; but, not to mention the ancients, he might have found it full-blown in modern Italy[6].

The Lovers' Fletas, Bractons, Cokes.
.   .   .   .   .   .
As for Tibullus's reports,
They never pass'd for law in courts;
For Cowley's briefs, and pleas of Waller,
Still their authority was smaller.'
SWIFT, *Cadenus and Vanessa, Works,* xiv. 432.

In *The Battle of the Books,* when Cowley is cleft in twain by Pindar, one half of him is turned into a dove by Venus, and harnessed to her chariot. *Ib.* x. 238. See also *post,* PRIOR, 56.

[1] *The Spectator,* No. 62.
[2] *Eng. Poets,* viii. 21.
[3] *Ib.* viii. 4.   [4] *Ib.* viii. 89.
[5] 'As true wit consists in the resemblance of ideas, and false wit in the resemblance of words, there is another kind of wit, which consists partly in the resemblance of ideas, and partly in the resemblance of words; which, for distinction' sake, I shall call mixed wit. This kind of wit is that which abounds in Cowley more than in any author that ever

wrote. Mr. Waller has likewise a great deal of it. Mr. Dryden is very sparing in it.' *The Spectator,* No.62. See also Addison's *Works,* i. 151.

Addison, in his *English Poets,* after saying of Cowley:—
'His turns too closely on the readers press;
He more had pleased us had he pleased us less';
adds:—
'Pardon, great poet, that I dare to name
The unnumbered beauties of thy verse with blame;
Thy fault is only wit in its excess,
But wit like thine in any shape will please.' *Eng. Poets,* xxx. 35.

[6] 'The Italians, even in their epic poetry, are full of it. . . . We find a great deal of it in Ovid, and scarce anything else in Martial.' *Spectator,* No. 62.

In the first edition of *The Lives* after 'Italy' followed:—'Thus Sannazaro.' The quotation is from his *Epigrammata,* i. 64—*Ad Vesbiam.* In Johnson's first edition Vesbia [formed from Vesbius, contracted collateral form of Vesuvius] is correctly printed

'Aspice quam variis distringar, Lesbia, [Vesbia] curis,
  Uror, et heu! nostro manat ab igne liquor;
Sum Nilus, sumque Ætna simul; restringite flammas [flammam]
  O lacrimæ, aut lacrimas ebibe flamma meas.'

122   One of the severe theologians of that time censured him as
having published 'a book of profane and lascivious Verses [1].'
From the charge of profaneness the constant tenour of his life,
which seems to have been eminently virtuous, and the general
tendency of his opinions, which discover no irreverence of religion,
must defend him; but that the accusation of lasciviousness is
unjust, the perusal of his works will sufficiently evince [2].

123   Cowley's *Mistress* has no power of seduction [3]; she 'plays
round the head, but comes not at [to] the heart [4].' Her beauty
and absence, her kindness and cruelty, her disdain and inconstancy, produce no correspondence of emotion. His poetical
account of the virtues of plants and colours of flowers is not
perused with more sluggish frigidity. The compositions are such
as might have been written for penance by a hermit, or for hire
by a philosophical rhymer who had only heard of another sex; for
they turn the mind only on the writer, whom, without thinking
on a woman but as the subject for his talk, we sometimes esteem
as learned and sometimes despise as trifling, always admire as
ingenious, and always condemn as unnatural.

124   The *Pindarique Odes* are now to be considered, a species of
composition which Cowley thinks Pancirolus might have counted

in the first line. The last line in the
original runs:—'O lacrimae, lacrimas,'
&c.
    Howell (*Letters*, Aug. 12, 1621)
quotes Sannazaro's 'famous hexastic'
on Venice, 'for every one verse of
which he had given him by St. Mark
a hundred zecchins, which amounts
to about £300.' See also *post*,
A. PHILIPS, 16; *John. Misc.* i. 366.
    [1] 'The pious Mr. Edmund Elys, of
Exeter College, Oxford, taking um-
brage at some passages in it [Sprat's
Life of Cowley], published, *An Exclamation to all those that love the
Lord Jesus in sincerity against an
Apology, written by an ingenious
person, for Mr. Abraham Cowley's
lascivious and profane verses.*' *Biog.
Brit.* p. 3816. Elys removed from
Exeter College to Balliol. *Athenae
Oxon.* iv. 470.

[2] 'I am not ashamed,' writes Sprat,
'to commend Mr. Cowley's *Mistress*.
I only except one or two expressions,
which I wish I could have prevailed
with those that had the right of the
other edition to have left out.' Hurd's
Cowley, i. 25.
    There are a few gross passages in
Cowley's *Cutter of Coleman Street*.
Elys might justly have reproached
Donne with lasciviousness.
    [3] *Ante*, COWLEY, 14. See also
Eng. Poets, xvii. 335, for the same
criticism in Walsh's *Preface upon
Amorous Poetry* (*post*, WALSH, 11).
    [4] POPE, *Essay on Man*, iv. 254.
    Coleridge, comparing Cowley and
his school with the modern poets,
says:—'The one sacrificed the heart
to the head; the other both heart
and head to point and drapery.'
Biog. Lit. 1847, i. 23.

'in his list of the lost inventions of antiquity[1],' and which he has made a bold and vigorous attempt to recover.

The purpose with which he has paraphrased an *Olympick* 125 and *Nemeæan Ode* is by himself sufficiently explained. His endeavour was not to shew 'precisely what Pindar spoke, but his manner of speaking[2].' He was therefore not at all restrained to his expressions, nor much to his sentiments; nothing was required of him, but not to write as Pindar would not have written.

Of the *Olympick Ode* the beginning is, I think, above the 126 original in elegance, and the conclusion below it in strength. The connection is supplied with great perspicuity, and the thoughts, which to a reader of less skill seem thrown together by chance, are concatenated without any abruption. Though the English ode cannot be called a translation, it may be very properly consulted as a commentary.

The spirit of Pindar is indeed not every where equally pre- 127 served. The following pretty lines are not such as his 'deep mouth[3]' was used to pour:

'Great Rhea's son,
If in Olympus' top where thou
Sitt'st to behold thy sacred show,
If in Alpheus' silver flight,
If in my verse thou take [dost] delight,
My verse, great [O] Rhea's son, which is
Lofty as that, and smooth as this[4].'

In the *Nemeæan Ode* the reader must, in mere justice to 128 Pindar, observe that whatever is said of 'the original new moon, her tender forehead and her horns[5],' is superadded by his para-

---

[1] In 1599 was published *Rerum memorabilium iam olim deperditarum &c. libri duo*, a translation by H. Salmuth of an Italian treatise by Guido Panciroli. It went through many editions; an English version appeared in 1715 (*British Museum Catalogue*).

[2] *Eng. Poets*, viii. 111. For 'imitation' see *post*, DENHAM, 32; ROCHESTER, 19; DRYDEN, 107, 223, and Dryden's *Works*, xii. 16, 18.

[3] 'Fervet, immensusque ruit profundo
Pindarus ore.'
HORACE, *Odes*, iv. 2. 7.

[4] *Eng. Poets*, viii. 114. The passage begins:—
'To which, great son of Rhea, say
The firm word which forbids things to decay.
If in Olympus' top,' &c.

[5] 'Beauteous Ortygia! the first breathing-place
Of great Alpheus' close and amorous race!
Fair Delos' sister, the child-bed
Of bright Latona, where she bred
Th' original new moon!
Who saw'st her tender forehead ere the horns were grown.'
Ib. viii. 121.

phrast. who has many other plays of words and fancy unsuitable
to the original, as

> ' The table, [which is] free for every guest,
>   No doubt will thee admit,
>   And feast more upon thee, than thou on it[1].'

129   He sometimes extends his author's thoughts without improving them.   In the *Olympionick* an oath is mentioned in a single
word, and Cowley spends three lines in swearing by the 'Casta-
lian Stream[2].'   We are told of Theron's bounty, with a hint
that he had enemies, which Cowley thus enlarges in rhyming
prose :

> 'But in this thankless world the giver [givers]
>   Is [Are] envied even by the receiver [receivers] ;
>   'Tis now the cheap and frugal fashion
>   Rather to hide than own [pay] the obligation :
>   Nay, 'tis much worse than so ;
>   It now an artifice does grow
>   Wrongs and injuries [outrages] to do,
>   Lest men should think we owe[3].'

130   It is hard to conceive that a man of the first rank in learning
and wit, when he was dealing out such minute morality in such
feeble diction, could imagine, either waking or dreaming, that he
imitated Pindar.

131   In the following odes, where Cowley chooses his own subjects,
he sometimes rises to dignity truly Pindarick, and, if some
deficiencies of language be forgiven, his strains are such as those
of the Theban bard were to his contemporaries :

> ' Begin the song, and strike the living lyre :
> Lo how the years to come, a numerous and well-fitted quire,
>   All hand in hand do decently advance,
> And to my song with smooth and equal measure [measures]
>   dance ;
> While [Whilst] the dance lasts, how long soe'er it be,
> My musick's voice shall bear it company ;
>   Till all gentle notes be drown'd
>   In the last trumpet's dreadful sound[4].'

132   After such enthusiasm who will not lament to find the poet
conclude with lines like these !

---

[1] *Eng. Poets*, viii. 123.
[2] *Ib.* viii. 119. [Pindar had written αὐδάσομαι ἐνόρκιον λόγον ἀλαθεῖ νόῳ,
O. 2. 165.]   [3] *Ib.* viii. 120.   [4] *Ib.* viii. 129.

'But stop, [Stop, stop] my Muse . . .
Hold thy Pindarick Pegasus closely in,
    Which does to rage begin . . .
'Tis an unruly and a hard mouth'd horse . . .
    'Twill no unskilful touch endure,
But flings writer and reader too that sits not sure [1].'

The fault of Cowley, and perhaps of all the writers of the 133
metaphysical race, is that of pursuing his thoughts to their
last ramifications, by which he loses the grandeur of generality,
for of the greatest things the parts are little ; what is little
can be but pretty, and by claiming dignity becomes ridiculous [2].
Thus all the power of description is destroyed by a scrupulous
enumeration ; and the force of metaphors is lost when the mind
by the mention of particulars is turned more upon the original
than the secondary sense, more upon that from which the illustration is drawn than that to which it is applied.

Of this we have a very eminent example in the ode intituled 134
The Muse, who goes to 'take the air' in an intellectual chariot, to
which he harnesses Fancy and Judgement, Wit and Eloquence,
Memory and Invention : how he distinguished Wit from Fancy,
or how Memory could properly contribute to Motion, he has not
explained ; we are however content to suppose that he could
have justified his own fiction, and wish to see the Muse begin
her career ; but there is yet more to be done.

'Let the *postilion* Nature mount, and let
The *coachman* Art be set ;
And let the airy *footmen*, running all beside,
Make a long row of goodly pride,
Figures, conceits. raptures, and sentences,
In a well-worded dress,
And innocent loves, and pleasant truths, and useful lies,
In all their gaudy *liveries* [3].'

Every mind is now disgusted with this cumber of magnificence ; 135
yet I cannot refuse myself the four next lines :

'Mount, glorious queen, thy travelling throne,
    And bid it to put on ;
For long though cheerful is the way,
And life alas ! allows but one ill winter's day.'

---

[1] *Eng. Poets*, viii. 130. [Johnson
might have said with more exactness
*conclude with a stanza containing
lines like these*, for out of thirteen
lines he does not quote six in entirety,
nor do these follow each other con-
secutively.]

[2] Johnson had said much the same
in *The Rambler*, No. 36.

[3] *Eng. Poets*, viii. 131.

136   In the same ode, celebrating the power of the Muse, he gives her prescience or, in poetical language, the foresight of events hatching in futurity; but having once an egg in his mind he cannot forbear to shew us that he knows what an egg contains:

> 'Thou [There] into the close nests of Time dost peep,
>   And there with piercing eye
> Through the firm shell and the thick white dost spy
>   Years to come a-forming lie,
> Close in their sacred fecundine asleep.'

137   The same thought is more generally, and therefore more poetically, expressed by Casimir[1], a writer who has many of the beauties and faults of Cowley:

> 'Omnibus mundi Dominator horis
> Aptat urgendas per inane pennas,
> Pars adhuc nido latet, et futuros
>   Crescit in annos[2].'

138   Cowley, whatever was his subject, seems to have been carried by a kind of destiny to the light and the familiar, or to conceits which require still more ignoble epithets. A slaughter in the Red Sea 'new dies [paints] the waters name[3]'; and England during the Civil War was 'Albion no more, nor to be named from white[4].' It is surely by some fascination not easily surmounted that a writer professing to revive 'the noblest and highest [kind of] writing in verse[5],' makes this address to the new year:

> 'Nay, if thou lov'st me, gentle year,
>   Let not so much as love be there,
> Vain fruitless love I mean; for, gentle year,
>   Although I fear,
> There's of this caution little need,
>   Yet, gentle year, take heed
>   How thou dost make
>   Such a mistake;
> Such love I mean alone
> As by thy cruel predecessors has been shewn;

[1] 'Casimir Sarbiewski, whose name has been Latinised into Sarbievius (1646). His contemporaries considered him as the greatest rival of Horace that had appeared, and he received a gold medal from the Pope, who made him his laureate.' Morfill's *Poland*, p. 278.

Dr. Watts, who imitated some of his odes (*Eng. Poets*, lv. 116, 126, 127), described him (*ib.* p. 35) as 'that noblest Latin poet of modern ages.'

[2] *Odes*, i. 4.
[3] *Eng. Poets*, viii. 173.
[4] *Ib.* viii. 143.
[5] *Ib.* viii. 111.

For, though I have too much cause to doubt it,
I fain would try, for once, if life can live without it[1].'

The reader of this will be inclined to cry out with Prior— 139

—'Ye Criticks, say,
How poor to this was Pindar's style[2]!'

Even those who cannot perhaps find in the Isthmian or Nemeæan songs what Antiquity has disposed them to expect, will at least see that they are ill represented by such puny poetry; and all will determine that if this be the old Theban strain it is not worthy of revival.

To the disproportion and incongruity of Cowley's sentiments 140 must be added the uncertainty and looseness of his measures. He takes the liberty of using in any place a verse of any length, from two syllables to twelve. The verses of Pindar have, as he observes, very little harmony to a modern ear[3]; yet by examining the syllables we perceive them to be regular, and have reason enough for supposing that the ancient audiences were delighted with the sound. The imitator ought therefore to have adopted what he found, and to have added what was wanting: to have preserved a constant return of the same numbers, and to have supplied smoothness of transition and continuity of thought[4].

It is urged by Dr. Sprat, that the '*irregularity of numbers* 141 *is the very thing* which makes *that kind of poesy fit for all manner of subjects*[5].' But he should have remembered that what is fit for every thing can fit nothing well. The great pleasure of verse arises from the known measure of the lines and uniform structure of the stanzas, by which the voice is regulated and the memory relieved[6].

[1] *Eng. Poets*, viii. 153.
[2] *On the Taking of Namur. Ib.* xxxii. 221.
[3] 'In effect they are little better than prose to our ears.' *Ib.* viii. 110. See also *ib.* vii. 18; viii. 130.
[4] 'Mr. Cowley has brought it as near perfection as was possible in so short a time. But, if I may be allowed to speak my mind modestly, and without injury to his sacred ashes, somewhat of the purity of English, somewhat of more equal thoughts, somewhat of sweetness in the num-

bers, in one word, somewhat of a finer turn and more lyrical verse is yet wanting.' DRYDEN, *Works*, xii. 300.
[5] Hurd's *Cowley*, i. 27.
[6] *Post*, DRYDEN, 275, 349; PRIOR, 77; CONGREVE, 44; POPE, 321; AKENSIDE, 23.
Ruskin, in 1861, wrote to D. G. Rossetti of Miss Rossetti's poems:—
'Irregular measure (introduced, to my great regret, in its chief wilfulness by Coleridge) is the calamity of modern poetry.' *Ruskin: Rossetti: Preraphaelitism*, 1889, p. 258.

142   If the Pindarick style be what Cowley thinks it, 'the highest and noblest [noblest and highest] kind of writing in verse¹,' it can be adapted only to high and noble subjects; and it will not be easy to reconcile the poet with the critick, or to conceive how that can be the highest kind of writing in verse which, according to Sprat, 'is chiefly to be preferred for its near affinity to [with] prose².'

143   This lax and lawless versification so much concealed the deficiencies of the barren and flattered the laziness of the idle, that it immediately overspread our books of poetry; all the boys and girls caught the pleasing fashion, and they that could do nothing else could write like Pindar³. The rights of antiquity were invaded, and disorder tried to break into the Latin : a poem on the Sheldonian Theatre, in which all kinds of verse are shaken together, is unhappily inserted in the *Musæ Anglicanæ*⁴. Pindarism prevailed above half a century, but at last died gradually away, and other imitations supply its place⁵.

144   The *Pindarique Odes* have so long enjoyed the highest degree of poetical reputation that I am not willing to dismiss them with unabated censure; and surely, though the mode of their composition be erroneous, yet many parts deserve at least that admiration which is due to great comprehension of knowledge and great fertility of fancy. The thoughts are often new and often striking, but the greatness of one part is disgraced by the littleness of another; and total negligence of language gives the noblest conceptions the appearance of a fabric, august in the plan, but mean in the materials. Yet surely those verses are not without a just claim to praise; of which it may be said with truth, that no one but Cowley could have written them.

145   The *Davideis* now remains to be considered; a poem

---

¹ *Ante*, COWLEY, 138.
² Hurd's *Cowley*, i. 27.
³ 'The seeming easiness of it,' wrote Dryden, 'has made it spread.' He adds that he sees 'a noble sort of poetry, so happily restored by one man and so grossly copied by almost all the rest.' *Works*, xii. 300, 302. One of these copiers was Dryden's cousin, Swift. *Post*, SWIFT, 18.
Addison ridiculed the Pindaric writers in *The Spectator*, No. 58, and in No. 160, where he speaks of 'men following irregularities by rule.'

⁴ *Musae Anglicanae*, 1761, i. 75. The poem, by Corbett Owen, was published in 1669—*Carmen Pindaricum in Theatrum Sheldonianum in Solemnibus Magnifici Operis Encaeniis*. Evelyn heard the 'Pindarics' recited on this occasion. The Encaenia 'lasted from eleven in the morning till seven at night.' *Diary*, ii. 44.
⁵ *Post*, PRIOR, 77; CONGREVE, 44; YALDEN, 15; SWIFT, 18; POPE, 321; WATTS, 6.
'Wordsworth said he thought of

which the author designed to have extended to twelve books, merely, as he makes no scruple of declaring, because the *Æneid* had that number [1]; but he had leisure or perseverance only to write the third part [2]. Epick poems have been left unfinished by Virgil, Statius, Spenser, and Cowley. That we have not the whole *Davideis* is, however, not much to be regretted, for in this undertaking Cowley is, tacitly at least, confessed to have miscarried. There are not many examples of so great a work produced by an author generally read and generally praised that has crept through a century with so little regard. Whatever is said of Cowley, is meant of his other works. Of the *Davideis* no mention is made; it never appears in books, nor emerges in conversation. By the *Spectator* it has once been quoted [3], by Rymer it has once been praised [4], and by Dryden, in *Mac Flecknoe* [5], it has once been imitated; nor do I recollect much other notice from its publication till now in the whole succession of English literature.

Of this silence [6] and neglect, if the reason be inquired, it will 146 be found partly in the choice of the subject, and partly in the performance of the work.

Sacred History has been always read with submissive reverence, 147 and an imagination over-awed and controlled. We have been accustomed to acquiesce in the nakedness and simplicity of the authentick narrative, and to repose on its veracity with such humble confidence as suppresses curiosity. We go with the historian as he goes, and stop with him when he stops. All amplification is frivolous and vain: all addition to that which

writing an essay on "Why bad poetry pleases." He never wrote it—a loss to our literature.' H. C. Robinson's *Diary*, i. 265.

[1] Cowley describes it as 'an heroical poem of the troubles of David; which I designed into twelve books; not for the tribes' sake, but after the pattern of our master Virgil.' *Eng. Poets*, vii. 19.

[2] He finished four books. *Post*, COWLEY, 165.

[3] *Spectator*, No. 590, by Addison, where is quoted :—
'Nothing is there to come, and nothing past,
But an eternal Now does always last.' *Eng. Poets*, viii. 191.

[4] 'The epick poems of Spenser, Cowley, and such names as will ever be sacred to me.' *The Tragedies of the Last Age*, p. 10. For Rymer see *post*, DRYDEN, 200.

[5] 'Where their vast courts the mother-strumpets keep,
And undisturb'd by watch in silence sleep.'
Mac Flecknoe, l. 72.
'Where their vast court the mother-waters keep,
And undisturb'd by moons in silence sleep.'
Eng. Poets, viii. 181.

[6] In the first edition, 'Of this obscurity.'

is already sufficient for the purposes of religion seems not only useless, but in some degree profane[1].

148 Such events as were produced by the visible interposition of Divine Power are above the power of human genius to dignify. The miracle of Creation, however it may teem with images, is best described with little diffusion of language : 'He spake the word, and they were made[2].'

149 We are told that Saul 'was troubled with an evil spirit[3]'; from this Cowley takes an opportunity of describing hell and telling the history of Lucifer, who was, he says,

> 'Once general of a gilded host of sprites,
> Like Hesper leading forth the spangled nights;
> But down like lightning, which him struck, he came,
> And roar'd at his first plunge into the flame[4].'

150 Lucifer makes a speech to the inferior agents of mischief, in which there is something of heathenism, and therefore of impropriety; and, to give efficacy to his words, concludes by lashing 'his breast with his long tail[5].' Envy after a pause steps out, and among other declarations of her zeal utters these lines:

> 'Do thou but threat, loud storms shall make reply,
> And thunder echo [echo 't] to the trembling sky;
> Whilst raging seas swell to so bold an height,
> As shall the fire's proud element affright.
> Th' old drudging Sun, from his long-beaten way,
> Shall at thy voice start, and misguide the day.
> The jocund orbs shall break their measur'd pace,
> And stubborn Poles change their allotted place.

[1] Johnson is perhaps answering Cowley, who, in the Preface to his Poems (1656), justifies sacred poetry by such arguments as the following :— 'Amongst all holy and consecrated things which the devil ever stole and alienated from the service of the Deity . . . there is none that he so universally and so long usurp as poetry. . . . It is time to baptize it in Jordan, for it will never become clean by bathing in the waters of Damascus. There wants, methinks, but the conversion of that and the Jews for the accomplishment of the Kingdom of Christ.' Eng. Poets, vii. 21.

In the Davideis he writes :—
'Too long the Muses' land hath heathen been;

Their gods too long were Devils, and virtues Sin;
But thou, Eternal Word, hast call'd forth me,
Th' apostle to convert that world to thee;
T' unbind the charms that in slight fables lie,
And teach that Truth is truest poesy.' Ib. viii. 180.
See also post, DENHAM, 18; MILTON, 246; WALLER, 135; FENTON, 23; WATTS, 33; YOUNG, 155.
[2] Psalms cxlviii. 5.
[3] 'An evil spirit from the Lord troubled him.' 1 Samuel xvi. 14.
[4] Eng. Poets, viii. 182.
[5] 'With his long tail he lash'd his breast.' Ib. viii. 184.

Heaven's gilded troops shall flutter here and there,
Leaving their boasting songs tun'd to a sphere[1].'

Every reader feels himself weary with this useless talk of an 151
allegorical Being.

It is not only when the events are confessedly miraculous 152
that fancy and fiction lose their effect: the whole system of life,
while the Theocracy was yet visible, has an appearance so
different from all other scenes of human action that the reader
of the Sacred Volume habitually considers it as the peculiar
mode of existence of a distinct species of mankind, that lived
and acted with manners uncommunicable; so that it is difficult
even for imagination to place us in the state of them whose
story is related, and by consequence their joys and griefs are
not easily adopted, nor can the attention be often interested in
any thing that befals them.

To the subject, thus originally indisposed to the reception 153
of poetical embellishments, the writer brought little that could
reconcile impatience or attract curiosity. Nothing can be more
disgusting than a narrative spangled with conceits, and conceits
are all that the *Davideis* supplies.

One of the great sources of poetical delight is description, 154
or the power of presenting pictures to the mind. Cowley gives
inferences instead of images, and shews not what may be supposed
to have been seen, but what thoughts the sight might have
suggested. When Virgil describes the stone which Turnus lifted
against Æneas, he fixes the attention on its bulk and weight:

'Saxum circumspicit ingens,
Saxum antiquum, ingens, campo quod forte jacebat,
Limes agro positus, litem ut discerneret arvis[2].'

Cowley says of the stone with which Cain slew his brother,

'I saw him fling the stone, as if he meant
At once his murther and his monument[3].'

Of the sword taken from Goliah he says,

'A sword so great, that it was only fit
To cut off [take off] his great head that [who] came with it[4].'

[1] *Eng. Poets*, viii. 185.
[2] *Aeneid*, xii. 896.
[3] 'The warrior said, and cast his fiery
eyes
Where an huge stone, a rocky
fragment lies;
Black, rough, prodigious, vast!—the
common bound
For ages past, and barrier of the
ground.' PITT, *Eng. Poets*, liii. 377.
[3] *Eng. Poets*, viii. 186.
[4] *Ib*. p. 245.

155　Other poets describe death by some of its common appearances; Cowley says, with a learned allusion to sepulchral lamps real or fabulous,

> ''Twixt his right ribs deep pierc'd the furious blade,
> And open'd wide those secret vessels where
> Life's light goes out, when first they let in air[1].'

156　But he has allusions vulgar as well as learned. In a visionary succession of kings:

> 'Joas at first does bright and glorious show,
> In life's fresh morn his fame does [did] early crow[2].'

157　Describing an undisciplined army, after having said with elegance,

> 'His forces seem'd no army, but a crowd
> Heartless, unarm'd, disorderly, and loud';

he gives them a fit of the ague[3].

158　The allusions however are not always to vulgar things: he offends by exaggeration as much as by diminution:

> 'The king was plac'd alone, and o'er his head
> A well-wrought heaven of silk and gold was spread[4].'

159　Whatever he writes is always polluted with some conceit:

> 'Where the sun's fruitful beams give metals birth,
> Where he the growth of fatal gold does see,
> Gold, which alone [above] more influence has than he[5].'

160　In one passage he starts a sudden question, to the confusion of philosophy:

> 'Ye learned heads, whom ivy garlands grace,
> Why does that twining plant the oak embrace?
> The oak, for courtship most of all unfit,
> And rough as are the winds that fight with it[6].'

161　His expressions have sometimes a degree of meanness that surpasses expectation:

> 'Nay, gentle guests [guest], he cries [said he], since now
>   you're in,
> The story of your gallant friend begin[7].'

In a simile descriptive of the Morning:

[1] *Eng. Poets*, viii. 303.
[2] *Ib.* p. 233.
[3] 'The quick contagion, Fear, ran swift through all,
And into trembling fits th' infected fall.' *Ib.* p. 308.
[4] *Ib.* p. 225.
[5] *Ib.* p. 181.
[6] *Ib.* p. 215.
[7] *Ib.* p. 255.

'As glimmering stars just at th' approach of day,
    Cashier'd by troops, at last drop all away[1].'

The dress of Gabriel deserves attention :   162

'He took for skin a cloud most soft and bright,
    That e'er the midday sun pierc'd through with light;
    Upon his cheeks a lively blush he spread,
    Wash'd from the morning beauties' deepest red;
    An harmless flattering [flaming] meteor shone for hair,
    And fell adown his shoulders with loose care;
    He cuts out a silk mantle from the skies,
    Where the most sprightly azure pleas'd the eyes;
    This he with starry vapours sprinkles [spangles] all,
    Took in their prime ere they grow ripe and fall;
    Of a new rainbow, ere it fret or fade,
    The choicest piece cut [took] out, a scarfe is made[2].'

This is a just specimen of Cowley's imagery : what might 163
in general expressions be great and forcible he weakens and
makes ridiculous by branching it into small parts. That Gabriel
was invested with the softest or brightest colours of the sky
we might have been told, and been dismissed to improve the
idea in our different proportions of conception ; but Cowley could
not let us go till he had related where Gabriel got first his skin,
and then his mantle, then his lace, and then his scarfe, and
related it in the terms of the mercer and taylor.

Sometimes he indulges himself in a digression, always con- 164
ceived with his natural exuberance, and commonly, even where
it is not long, continued till it is tedious :

'I' th' library a few choice authors stood ;
    Yet 'twas well stor'd, for that small store was good ;
    Writing, man's spiritual physic, was not then
    Itself, as now, grown a disease of men.
    Learning (young virgin) but few suitors knew ;
    The common prostitute she lately grew,
    And with the spurious brood loads now the press ;
    Laborious effects of idleness[3].'

As the *Davideis* affords only four books, though intended to 165
consist of twelve, there is no opportunity for such criticisms as
Epick poems commonly supply. The plan of the whole work
is very imperfectly shewn by the third part : the duration of
an unfinished action cannot be known[4]. Of characters either

---

[1] *Eng. Poets*, viii. 297.
[2] *Ib.* p. 240.   [3] *Ib.* p. 203.

[4] 'I intended,' Cowley wrote, 'to
close all with that most poetical and

not yet introduced, or shewn but upon few occasions, the full extent and the nice discriminations cannot be ascertained. The fable is plainly implex [1], formed rather from the *Odyssey* than the *Iliad*; and many artifices of diversification are employed, with the skill of a man acquainted with the best models. The past is recalled by narration, and the future anticipated by vision; but he has been so lavish of his poetical art that it is difficult to imagine how he could fill eight books more without practising again the same modes of disposing his matter; and perhaps the perception of this growing incumbrance inclined him to stop. By this abruption posterity lost more instruction than delight. If the continuation of the *Davideis* can be missed, it is for the learning that had been diffused over it, and the notes in which it had been explained [2].

166　Had not his characters been depraved like every other part by improper decorations, they would have deserved uncommon praise. He gives Saul both the body and mind of a hero:

'His way once chose, he forward thrust outright,
　Nor turn'd [step'd] aside for danger [dangers] or delight [3].'

excellent elegy of David on the death of Saul and Jonathan; for I had no mind to carry him quite on to his anointing at Hebron, because it is the custom of heroic poets (as we see by the examples of Homer and Virgil, whom we should do ill to forsake to imitate others) never to come to the full end of their story; but only so near that every one may see it; as men commonly play not out the game, when it is evident that they can win it, but lay down their cards, and take up what they have won.' *Eng. Poets*, vii. 19.

[1] 'The fable of every poem is, according to Aristotle's division, either simple or implex. It is called simple when there is no change of fortune in it; implex, when the fortune of the chief actor changes from bad to good, or from good to bad.' ADDISON, *Spectator*, No. 297.

[2] *Ante*, COWLEY, 110. The learning and the notes are sometimes curious. Thus in *Davideis* (*Eng. Poets*, viii. 181) he writes:—

'Beneath the dens where unfletch'd tempests lie,
And infant winds their tender voices try,
Beneath the mighty ocean's wealthy caves,
Beneath th' eternal fountain of all waves,
Where their vast court the mother-waters keep,
And, undisturb'd by moons, in silence sleep,' &c.

He thus explains this:—' To give a problematical reason of the perpetual supply of water to fountains and rivers it is necessary to establish an abyss, or deep gulf of waters, into which the sea discharges itself, as rivers do into the sea. . . . For to refer the original of all fountains to condensation, and afterwards to dissolution of vapours under the earth, is one of the most unphilosophical opinions in all Aristotle.' Cowley's *Works*, 1674, *Davideis*, p. 26. See also *ib.* p. 116 for thunder as 'an exhalation hot and dry.'

[3] *Eng. Poets*, viii. 295.

And the different beauties of the lofty Merab and the gentle Michal are very justly conceived and strongly painted [1].

Rymer has declared the *Davideis* superior to the *Jerusalem* 167 of Tasso, 'which,' says he, 'the poet, with all his care, has not totally purged from pedantry [2].' If by pedantry is meant that minute knowledge which is derived from particular sciences and studies, in opposition to the general notions supplied by a wide survey of life and nature, Cowley certainly errs by introducing pedantry far more frequently than Tasso. I know not, indeed, why they should be compared; for the resemblance of Cowley's work to Tasso's is only that they both exhibit the agency of celestial and infernal spirits, in which however they differ widely: for Cowley supposes them commonly to operate upon the mind by suggestion; Tasso represents them as promoting or obstructing events by external agency.

Of particular passages that can be properly compared I re- 168 member only the description of Heaven [3], in which the different manner of the two writers is sufficiently discernible. Cowley's is scarcely description, unless it be possible to describe by negatives; for he tells us only what there is not in heaven. Tasso endeavours to represent the splendours and pleasures of the regions of happiness. Tasso affords images, and Cowley sentiments. It happens, however, that Tasso's description affords some reason for Rymer's censure. He says of the Supreme Being,

'Hà sotto i piedi e [il] fato e la natura,
    Ministri humili, e 'l moto, e ch' il [chi 'l] misura [4].'

The second line has in it more of pedantry than perhaps can 169 be found in any other stanza of the poem.

In the perusal of the *Davideis*, as of all Cowley's works, we 170 find wit and learning unprofitably squandered. Attention has no relief; the affections are never moved; we are sometimes surprised, but never delighted, and find much to admire, but little to approve. Still, however, it is the work of Cowley, of a mind capacious by nature, and replenished by study.

In the general review of Cowley's poetry it will be found 171 that he wrote with abundant fertility, but negligent or unskilful selection; with much thought, but with little imagery; that he

[1] *Eng. Poets*, viii. 267.
[2] *Translation of Rapin's Reflections on Aristotle's Treatise of Poesie,*

Preface, p. 19. See *ante*, COWLEY, 145.
[3] *Eng. Poets*, viii. 190.
[4] *La Gerusalemme Liberata*, ix. 56.

is never pathetick, and rarely sublime, but always either ingenious or learned, either acute or profound[1].

172   It is said by Denham in his elegy:

> ' To him no author was unknown;
> Yet what he writ was all his own[2].'

This wide position requires less limitation when it is affirmed of Cowley than perhaps of any other poet[3]: He read much, and yet borrowed little.

173   His character of writing was indeed not his own: he unhappily adopted that which was predominant[4].   He saw a certain way to present praise; and not sufficiently enquiring by what means the ancients have continued to delight through all the changes of human manners he contented himself with a deciduous laurel, of which the verdure in its spring was bright and gay, but which time has been continually stealing from his brows[5].

174   He was in his own time considered as of unrivalled excellence. Clarendon represents him as having taken a flight beyond all that went before him[6]; and Milton is said to have declared that the three greatest English poets were Spenser, Shakespeare, and Cowley[7].

175   His manner he had in common with others; but his sentiments were his own.   Upon every subject he thought for himself, and such was his copiousness of knowledge that something at once remote and applicable rushed into his mind; yet it

[1] ' Cowley seems to have possessed the power of writing easily beyond any other of our poets; yet his pursuit of remote thought led him often into harshness of expression.' JOHNSON, *The Idler*, No. 77.
    Coleridge distinguishes between the ' very fanciful mind' of Cowley and the ' highly imaginative mind' of Milton. *Biog. Lit.* 1847, i. 81.
[2] *Post*, DENHAM, 20, 34.
[3] Much the same was said of Swift. *Post*, SWIFT, 141.
[4] Sprat writes:—' If any shall think that he was not wonderfully curious in the choice and elegance of all his words, I will affirm with more truth on the other side, that he had no manner of affectation in them; he took them as he found them made to his hands; he neither went before, nor came after the use of the age.   He forsook the conversation, but never the language of the City and Court.' Hurd's *Cowley*, i. 21.
[5] *Ante*, COWLEY, 49.
[6] *Post*, COWLEY, 179 *n.*   In the same passage Clarendon says that ' Ben Jonson very much reformed the stage, and indeed the English poetry itself. . . . He was the best judge of, and fittest to prescribe rules to poetry and poets of any man who had lived with, or before him, or since.' *Life of Clarendon*, ed. 1827, i. 34.   Shakespeare he passes over in silence.   What is stranger, he never mentions Milton in the *Life*, nor even in his *History*. [Clarendon's letter to Gauden, March 13, 1661, affords one instance at least of a mention by him of Milton.   The letter is quoted by Todd in his *Letter to the Archbishop of Canterbury concerning the Authorship of Icôn Basiliké*, p. 21.]
[7] *Post*, MILTON, 164.

is not likely that he always rejected a commodious idea merely because another had used it; his known wealth was so great, that he might have borrowed without loss of credit.

In his elegy on Sir Henry Wotton the last lines have such resemblance to the noble epigram of Grotius upon the death of Scaliger that I cannot but think them copied from it, though they are copied by no servile hand [1]. **176**

One passage in his *Mistress* is so apparently borrowed from Donne that he probably would not have written it, had it not mingled with his own thoughts, so as that he did not perceive himself taking it from another : **177**

> ' Although I think thou never found wilt be,
> Yet I'm resolv'd to search for thee ;
> The search itself rewards the pains.
> So, though the chymic his great secret miss
> (For neither it in Art nor Nature is),
> Yet things well worth his toil he gains :
> And does his charge and labour pay
> With good unsought experiments by the way [2].'
>
> COWLEY.

> ' Some that have deeper digg'd Love's mine than I,
> Say, where his centric happiness doth lie :
> I have lov'd, and got, and told ;
> But should I love, get, tell, till I were old,
> I should not find that hidden mystery ;
> Oh, 'tis imposture all :
> And as no chymic yet th' elixir got,
> But glorifies his pregnant pot,
> If by the way to him befal
> Some odoriferous thing, or medicinal ;

[1] *Ante*, COWLEY, 106.
' We say that learning 's endless, and blame Fate
For not allowing life a longer date :
He did the utmost bounds of knowledge find,
He found them not so large as was his mind ;
But like the brave Pellaean youth did moan
Because that art had no more worlds than one ;
And when he saw that he through all had past
He died, lest he should idle grow at last.' *Eng. Poets*, vii. 114.
Grotius's epigram thus ends :—

' Omnia dum retro mundi vestigia quaerit,
Quaerentem retro destituere dies.
Emensus populos et dissona gentibus ora
Ambierat quantum lumine Phoebus obit.
Testamur, natura, tibi non defuit ille ;
Tu gentes alias, saecula plura dares.
Ultra Scaligerum nihil est ; nec Scaliger ultra.
Ille tui finem repperit, ille sui.'
Grotii *Poemata*, 1670, p. 248.
[2] *Eng. Poets*, viii. 76.

So lovers dream a rich and long delight,
But get a winter-seeming summer's night[1].'

178   Jonson and Donne, as Dr. Hurd remarks, were then in the highest esteem[2].

179   It is related by Clarendon that Cowley always acknowledged his obligation to the learning and industry of Jonson[3], but I have found no traces of Jonson in his works: to emulate Donne appears to have been his purpose; and from Donne he may have learned that familiarity with religious images, and that light allusion to sacred things, by which readers far short of sanctity are frequently offended; and which would not be borne in the present age, when devotion, perhaps not more fervent is more delicate.

180   Having produced one passage taken by Cowley from Donne I will recompense him by another, which Milton seems to have borrowed from him.   He says of Goliah[4],

'His spear, the trunk was of a lofty tree,
Which Nature meant some tall ship's mast should be.'

Milton of Satan,

'His spear, to equal which the tallest pine
Hewn on Norwegian hills, to be the mast
Of some great admiral, were but a wand,
He walk'd with[5].'

181   His diction was in his own time censured as negligent[6]. He seems not to have known, or not to have considered, that words being arbitrary must owe their power to association, and have the influence, and that only, which custom has given them. Language is the dress of thought; and as the noblest mien or most graceful action would be degraded and obscured by a garb appropriated to the gross employments of rusticks or mechanicks, so the most heroick sentiments will lose their efficacy, and the most splendid ideas drop their magnificence, if they are conveyed

[1] Grosart's *Donne*, ii. 199.
[2] This paragraph is not in the first edition. 'Donne and Jonson were the favourite poets of the time, and therefore the models on which our poet was ambitious to form himself.' Hurd's *Cowley*, i. 163.
[3] Clarendon, who knew both poets, after saying that Cowley 'had made a flight beyond all men' [*ante*, COWLEY, 174], added, 'with that modesty yet to ascribe much of this to the example and learning of Ben Jonson.' *Life of Clarendon*, 1827, i. 34.
[4] *Eng. Poets*, viii. 258.
[5] *Paradise Lost*, i. 292.
[6] Dryden wrote in 1697:—'Cowley's language is not always pure.' *Works*, xiv. 222. See *ante*, COWLEY, 60 *n*.

by words used commonly upon low and trivial occasions, debased by vulgar mouths, and contaminated by inelegant applications.

Truth indeed is always truth, and reason is always reason; 182 they have an intrinsick and unalterable value, and constitute that intellectual gold which defies destruction: but gold may be so concealed in baser matter that only a chymist can recover it; sense may be so hidden in unrefined and plebeian words that none but philosophers can distinguish it; and both may be so buried in impurities as not to pay the cost of their extraction.

The diction, being the vehicle of the thoughts, first presents 183 itself to the intellectual eye; and if the first appearance offends, a further knowledge is not often sought. Whatever professes to benefit by pleasing must please at once. The pleasures of the mind imply something sudden and unexpected; that which elevates must always surprise. What is perceived by slow degrees may gratify us with the consciousness of improvement, but will never strike with the sense of pleasure.

Of all this Cowley appears to have been without knowledge 184 or without care. He makes no selection of words, nor seeks any neatness of phrase; he has no elegances either lucky or elaborate: as his endeavours were rather to impress sentences upon the understanding than images on the fancy he has few epithets, and those scattered without peculiar propriety or nice adaptation. It seems to follow from the necessity of the subject, rather than the care of the writer, that the diction of his heroick poem is less familiar than that of his slightest writings. He has given not the same numbers, but the same diction, to the gentle Anacreon and the tempestuous Pindar.

His versification seems to have had very little of his care; 185 and if what he thinks be true, that his numbers are un-musical only when they are ill read, the art of reading them is at present lost; for they are commonly harsh to modern ears[1]. He has indeed many noble lines, such as the feeble

---

[1] Cowley wrote of his *Pindaric Odes*:—'The numbers are various and irregular, and sometimes (especially some of the long ones) seem harsh and uncouth, if the just measures and cadences be not observed in the pronunciation. So that almost all their sweetness and numerosity (which is to be found, if I mistake not, in the roughest, if rightly repeated) lies, in a manner, wholly at the mercy of the reader.' *Eng. Poets*, vii. 18.

'If his verses,' writes Sprat, 'in some places seem not as soft and flowing as some would have them, it

care of Waller never could produce[1]. The bulk of his thoughts sometimes swelled his verse to unexpected and inevitable grandeur, but his excellence of this kind is merely fortuitous[2]; he sinks willingly down to his general carelessness, and avoids with very little care either meanness or asperity.

186   His contractions are often rugged and harsh:

> 'One flings a mountain, and its rivers [river] too
> Torn up with 't[3].'

187   His rhymes are very often made by pronouns or particles, or the like unimportant words, which disappoint the ear and destroy the energy of the line[4].

188   His combination of different measures is sometimes dissonant and unpleasing; he joins verses together, of which the former does not slide easily into the latter.

189   The words *do* and *did*, which so much degrade in present estimation the line that admits them, were in the time of Cowley little censured or avoided[5]; how often he used them and with how bad an effect, at least to our ears, will appear by a passage, in which every reader will lament to see just and noble thoughts defrauded of their praise by inelegance of language:

> 'Where honour or where conscience *does* not bind,
>   No other law shall shackle me;
>   Slave to myself I ne'er will [will not] be;
> Nor shall my future actions be confin'd
>   By my own present mind.
> Who by resolves and vows engag'd *does* stand
>   For days, that yet belong to fate,
> *Does* like an unthrift mortgage his estate,
>   Before it falls into his hand;
>   The bondman of the cloister so,
> All that he *does* receive *does* always owe.

was his choice, not his fault. . . . Where the matter required it, he was as gentle as any man.' Hurd's *Cowley*, i. 21.

'Cowley had no ear for harmony, and his verses are only known to be such by the rhyme which terminates them. In his rugged untuneable numbers are conveyed sentiments the most strained and distorted; long spun allegories, distant allusions and forced conceits. Great ingenuity, however, and vigour of thought sometimes break out amidst these unnatural conceptions.' HUME, *Hist. of Eng.* vii. 345. See also *The Rambler*, No. 86, and *post*, DRYDEN, 222.

[1] *Post*, WALLER, 144.
[2] 'If Cowley had sometimes a finished line, he had it by chance.' *Post*, DRYDEN, 343.
[3] *Eng. Poets*, viii. 258.
[4] *Post*, POPE, 398.
[5] *Post*, WALLER, 145.

And still as Time comes in, it goes away,
  Not to enjoy, but debts to pay.
Unhappy slave, and pupil to a bell,
Which his hours' work as well as hours *does* tell!
Unhappy till the last, the kind releasing knell[1].'

His heroick lines are often formed of monosyllables, but yet 190
they are sometimes sweet and sonorous[2].

He says of the Messiah, 191

  'Round the whole earth his dreaded name shall sound,
    And reach to worlds that must not yet be found[3].'

In another place, of David, 192

  'Yet bid him go securely, when he sends;
  'Tis Saul that is his foe, and we his friends.
  The man who has his God, no aid can lack;
  And we who bid him go, will bring him back[4].'

Yet amidst his negligence he sometimes attempted an im- 193
proved and scientifick versification; of which it will be best to
give his own account subjoined to this line,

  'Nor can the glory contain itself in th' endless space[5].'

'I am sorry that it is necessary to admonish the most part of
readers that it is not by negligence that this verse is so loose,
long, and, as it were, vast; it is to paint in the number the nature
of the thing which it describes, which I would have observed in
divers other places of this poem that else will pass for very
careless verses: as before,

"And over-runs the neighb'ring fields with violent course[6]."

---

[1] *Eng. Poets*, ix. 24. For Johnson's dislike of vows see Johnson's *Shakespeare*, vi. 12, 399; *Johnson's Letters*, i. 217; and Boswell's *Johnson*, iii. 357.

[2] 'It is pronounced by Dryden that a line of monosyllables is almost always harsh. This, with regard to our language, is evidently true, not because monosyllables cannot compose harmony, but because our monosyllables, being of Teutonick original, or formed by contraction, commonly begin and end with consonants.' *Rambler*, No. 88.

Dryden, in the Dedication of *Troilus and Cressida*, says:—'We are full of monosyllables, and those clogged with consonants, and our pronunciation is effeminate; all which are enemies to a sounding language.' *Works*, vi. 252. In the Dedication of

the *Aeneis* he speaks of 'the monosyllables, and those clogged with consonants, which are the dead weight of our mother-tongue. It is possible, I confess, though it rarely happens, that a verse of monosyllables may sound harmoniously.... My first line of the *Aeneis* is not harsh—"Arms and the man I sing who, forced by fate."' *Ib.* xiv. 218.

He describes how a certain poet 'creeps along with ten little words in every line.' *Ib.* xv. 288.
'And ten low words oft creep in one dull line.'
POPE, *Essay on Criticism*, l. 347. See also *J. Hughes' Corres.* ii. 22.

[3] *Eng. Poets*, viii. 241.
[4] *Ib.* p. 192.
[5] *Ib.* p. 191.
[6] *Ib.* p. 181.

'In the second book,

    "Down a precipice deep, down he casts them all[1]."

'And,

    "And fell a-down his shoulders with loose care[2]."

'In the third,

    "Brass was his helmet, his boots brass, and o'er
    His breast a thick plate of strong brass he wore[3]."

'In the fourth,

    "Like some fair pine o'er-looking all th' ignobler wood[4]."

'And,

    "Some from the rocks cast themselves down headlong[5]."

'And many more: but it is enough to instance in a few. The thing is, that the disposition of words and numbers should be such as that, out of the order and sound of them, the things themselves may be represented. This the Greeks were not so accurate as to bind themselves to; neither have our English poets observed it, for aught I can find. The Latins (*qui musas colunt severiores*[6]) sometimes did it, and their prince, Virgil, always; in whom the examples are innumerable, and taken notice of by all judicious men, so that it is superfluous to collect them[7].'

194   I know not whether he has in many of these instances attained the representation or resemblance that he purposes. Verse can imitate only sound and motion. A *boundless* verse, a *headlong* verse, and a verse of *brass* or of *strong brass*, seem to comprise very incongruous and unsociable ideas. What there is peculiar in the sound of the line expressing *loose care* I cannot discover; nor why the *pine* is *taller* in an Alexandrine than in ten syllables[8].

195   But, not to defraud him of his due praise, he has given one example of representative versification, which perhaps no other English line can equal:

    'Begin, be bold, and venture to be wise.
    He who defers this work from day to day,
    Does on a river's bank expecting stay

[1] *Eng. Poets*, viii. 233.
[2] *Ib.* p. 240.
[3] *Ib.* p. 258.
[4] *Ib.* p. 295.
[5] *Ib.* p. 316.
[6] 'Nobis non licet esse tam disertis

Qui Musas colimus severiores.'
    MARTIAL, *Epig.* ix. 12, 15.
[7] Cowley's *Works*, ed. 1674, *Davideis*, p. 32.
[8] *Post*, POPE, 331.

Till the whole stream that [which] stopp'd him shall [should]
  be gone,
Which [That] runs, and as it runs, for ever shall [will] run on[1].'

Cowley was, I believe, the first poet that mingled Alexandrines 196
at pleasure with the common heroick of ten syllables, and from
him Dryden borrowed the practice, whether ornamental or
licentious[2].' He considered the verse of twelve syllables as
elevated and majestick, and has therefore deviated into that measure when he supposes the voice heard of the Supreme Being.

The Author of the *Davideis* is commended by Dryden for 197
having written it in couplets, because he discovered that any
staff was too lyrical for an heroick poem[3]; but this seems to have
been known before by May[4] and Sandys[5], the translators of the
Pharsalia and the *Metamorphoses*.

In the *Davideis* are some hemistichs, or verses left im- 198
perfect by the author, in imitation of Virgil, whom he supposes
not to have intended to complete them[6]: that this opinion is
erroneous may be probably concluded, because this truncation
is imitated by no subsequent Roman poet; because Virgil himself
filled up one broken line in the heat of recitation[7]; because in
one the sense is now unfinished[8]; and because all that can be
done by a broken verse, a line intersected by a *cæsura* and a full
stop will equally effect.

Of triplets[9] in his *Davideis* he makes no use, and perhaps 199
did not at first think them allowable; but he appears afterwards
to have changed his mind, for in the *Verses on the government of
Cromwell* he inserts them liberally[10] with great happiness.

[1] *Eng. Poets*, ix. 116. Cf. HORACE, *Epis.* i. 2. 40.
[2] *Post*, DRYDEN, 344, 348; POPE, 376.
[3] 'Mr. Cowley had found out that no kind of staff [stanza] is proper for a heroic poem, as being all too lyrical.' DRYDEN, *Works*, xiv. 222.
[4] *Ante*, COWLEY, 33.
[5] *Post*, DRYDEN, 223; GARTH, 14 *n.*; POPE, 5.
[6] Cowley's *Works*, 1674, *Davideis*, p. 28. *Post*, ADDISON, 158.
[7] 'Erotem librarium et libertum eius . . . tradunt referre solitum, quondam in recitando eum duos dimidiatos versus complesse extempore, et huic, *Misenum Aeoliden*,

adiecisse, *quo non praestantior alter.* Item huic, *Aere ciere viros*, simili calore iactatum subiunxisse, *Martemque accendere cantu* [*Aeneid*, vi. 164–5].' *Life* attributed to Donatus. Preface to *Delphin Virgil*.
[8] *Aeneid*, iii. 340. *Post*, PRIOR, 71; YOUNG, 167.
'Cowley frequently affects half verses, . . . and there is no question but he thought he had Virgil's authority for that license.' DRYDEN, *Works*, xiv. 222.
[9] *Post*, DRYDEN, 344, 349; POPE, 376.
[10] Twice in a poem of fifty-four lines. *Eng. Poets*, viii. 372.

200   After so much criticism on his Poems, the Essays which accompany them must not be forgotten. What is said by Sprat of his conversation, that no man could draw from it any suspicion of his excellence in poetry [1], may be applied to these compositions. No author ever kept his verse and his prose at a greater distance from each other. His thoughts are natural, and his style has a smooth and placid equability, which has never yet obtained its due commendation [2]. Nothing is far-sought, or hard-laboured ; but all is easy without feebleness, and familiar without grossness.

201   It has been observed by Felton, in his *Essay on the Classicks*, that Cowley was beloved by every Muse that he courted, and that he has rivalled the Ancients in every kind of poetry but tragedy [3].

202   It may be affirmed without any encomiastick fervour that he brought to his poetick labours a mind replete with learning [4], and that his pages are embellished with all the ornaments which books could supply ; that he was the first who imparted to English numbers the enthusiasm of the greater ode, and the gaiety of the less ; that he was equally qualified for spritely sallies and for lofty flights ; that he was among those who freed translation from servility [5], and, instead of following

[1] 'He never willingly recited any of his own writings. None but his intimate friends ever discovered he was a great poet by his discourse.' Hurd's *Cowley*, i. 44.
'There is not methinks an handsomer thing said of Mr. Cowley in his whole life than that none but his intimate friends ever discovered he was a great poet by his discourse.' *The Guardian*, No. 24.
According to Aubrey 'he discoursed very ill and with hesitation.' *Brief Lives*, i. 190.
For the conversation of other poets see *post*, DRYDEN, 168 ; ADDISON, 106, 117 ; POPE, 264.

[2] 'Tell me,' wrote Lamb to Coleridge, 'if Cowley's prose essays, in particular, as well as no inconsiderable part of his verse, be not delicious. I prefer the graceful rambling of his essays even to the courtly elegance and ease of Addison ; abstracting from this the latter's exquisite humour.' Lamb's *Letters*, i. 64. Francis Horner 'resolved to read the *Essays*

over again three or four times, till (he wrote) I fix some of those beauties in my memory, and accustom my ear to the tune.' *Memoirs*, 1843, i. 197. For these *Essays* see *Eng. Poets*, vii. 7 ; viii. 109, 325 ; ix. 3, and Hurd's *Cowley*. For Addison's prose see *post*, ADDISON, 168.

[3] *A Dissertation on Reading the Classics*, by Henry Felton, D.D., 4th ed. 1730, p. 27.
The Bishop of Asaph wrote to Jones the year of the publication of the *Lives* :—' I don't know whether I can assent to your criticism on the word *replete*, that it is never used in a good sense. . . . It was never naturalized in conversation or in prose.' *Life of Sir William Jones*, p. 256. The four instances given in Johnson's *Dict.* are all in a bad sense. He himself uses it in a good sense here, and so does Fielding in *Tom Jones*, bk. i. ch. 4—'a human being replete with benevolence.'

[5] *Ante*, COWLEY, 125 ; *post*, DRYDEN, 107, 223.

his author at a distance, walked by his side ; and that if he left versification yet improvable, he left likewise from time to time such specimens of excellence as enabled succeeding poets to improve it.

APPENDIX A (Page 3)

'Even when I was a very young boy at school, instead of running about on holy-days and playing with my fellows, I was wont to steal from them, and walk into the fields, either alone with a book, or with some one companion, if I could find any of the same temper. I was then, too, so much an enemy to all constraint, that my masters could never prevail on me, by any persuasions or encouragements, to learn without book the common rules of grammar ; in which they dispensed with me alone, because they found I made a shift to do the usual exercise out of my own reading and observation.' *Eng. Poets*, ix. 120.

Mr. Sargeaunt, in his *Annals of Westminster School*, p. 30, speaking of the elections of the boys to scholarships at the universities (*post*, SMITH, 4), says :—' There was one point on which the Electors for many years showed great strictness. They would allow no genius to atone for ignorance of the rules of grammar. This Cowley found to his cost in 1636. He was rejected by Trinity in favour of four boys, no one of whom afterwards made any figure.'

Mr. Aldis Wright has kindly sent me the following from the records of Trinity College :—

'March 30th, 1636.
'It is ordered by the Master and Seniors in the Chappel the 30th of March 1636, that Abraham Cowley was chosen into a drie Chorister's place in reversion, and that the Colledge shal allowe him the benefit thereof till it fall, or that he be chosen Scholler att the Election of Schollers next following.

'June 14, 1637.
'Cowley chosen and admitted Scholler by the Kinges letters dispensatory.'

Mr. Wright conjectures 'that "a drie Chorister" was a Chorister who did not sing.' He entered Trinity on April 21, 1636. In his poem on young Hervey's death (see COWLEY, 108) he thus mentions his university :—

'Ye fields of Cambridge, our dear Cambridge, say,
Have ye not seen us walking every day ?'
Eng. Poets, vii. 131.

Dryden was of the same College. 'Six of the translators of James the First's Bible were found among the resident Fellows.' Monk's *Bentley*, i. 141.

APPENDIX B (PAGE 13)

'Cowley's taste was false and unclassical. In his six books on plants he imitates Martial rather than Virgil, and has given us more epigrams than descriptions. He had a most happy manner of imitating the easy manner of Horace's epistles.' J. WARTON, Pope's *Works*, ii. 268.

'May is certainly a sonorous dactylist. His skill is in parody. . . . Milton's Latin poems may be justly considered as legitimate classical compositions. Cowley's Latinity presents a mode of diction half Latin and half English. Milton was a more perfect scholar.' T. WARTON, Milton's *Poems*, 1791, Preface, pp. 17–21.

'Casimir's style and diction are really classical; while Cowley, who resembles Casimir in many respects, completely barbarizes his Latinity, and even his metre, by the heterogeneous nature of his thoughts.' COLERIDGE, *Biog. Lit.* ii. 295.

'There is no Latin verse of Cowley worth preservation. May, indeed, is an admirable imitator of Lucan; so good a one that, if in Lucan you find little poetry, in May you find none. But his verses sound well on the anvil.' LANDOR, *Imag. Conv.* iv. 291. 'Small as is the portion of glory which accrues to Milton from his Latin poetry, there are single sentences in it, ay, single images, worth all that our island had produced before.' *Ib.* p. 299. See COWLEY, 137; *post*, MILTON, 8, 10.

APPENDIX C (PAGE 14)

The title of the play is *Cutter of Coleman Street*. Cutter is described as 'a merry sharking Fellow about the Town, pretending to have been a Colonel in the King's Army.' To win a rich wife 'o' the Fifth Monarchy Faith' he talks in the following fashion :—'I am to return [after death] upon a Purple Dromedary, which signifies Magistracy, with an Axe in my Hand that is call'd Reformation, and I am to strike with that Axe upon the Gate of Westminster-Hall, and cry *Down* Babylon, and the Building call'd Westminster-Hall is to run away, and cast itself into the River, and then Major-General Harrison is to come in green Sleeves from the North upon a Sky-colour'd Mule, which signifies heavenly Instruction.' Cowley's *Works*, 1707, ii. 802, 851. In the Epilogue mention is made of 'The Fifth Monarch's Court in Coleman Street.' Neal, in his *History of the Puritans*, 1822, iv. 278, mentions 'the little conventicle in Coleman Street, where Venner warmed his admirers with passionate expectations of a fifth universal monarchy, under the personal reign of King Jesus upon earth.'

'Dec. 16, 1661. After dinner to the Opera, where there was a new play (*Cutter of Coleman Street*) made in the year 1658, with reflections much upon the late times; and it being the first time, the pay was doubled. . . . A very good play it is—it seems of Cowley's making.' PEPYS, *Diary*, i. 305.

Cowley had a share in the Duke of York's Theatre, where the play was acted. Cunningham, *Lives of the Poets*, i. 63. 'It was revived about 1730 at the theatre in Lincoln's Inn Fields.' *Biog. Dram.* ii. 148.

APPENDIX D (Page 16)

Cowley, speaking of his desire to be 'master of a small house and large garden,' and of his 'abandoning all ambitions and hopes in this world,' continues :—'I am gone out from Sodom, but I am not yet arrived at my little Zoar. *O let me escape thither (is it not a little one?), and my soul shall live* [*Genesis* xix. 20].' *Eng. Poets*, ix. 68.

In *The Wish* he writes :

'Ah yet, ere I descend to th' grave,
May I a small house and large garden have,
And a few friends, and many books, both true,
Both wise, and both delightful too !'—*Ib*. viii. 29.

Johnson's authority for Cowley's lease of the Queen's lands is Wood, *Fasti Oxon.* ii. 210. Aubrey tells how 'George, duke of Bucks, came to the earl of St. Albans, and told him he would buy such a lease in Chertsey, belonging to the queen mother. Said the earle to him, "that is beneath your grace to take a lease." "That is all one," qd he, " I desire to have the favour to buy it for my money." He bought it, and then freely bestowed it on his beloved Cowley.' *Brief Lives*, i. 190.

Cowley writes in his Essay *Of Greatness* :—'When you have pared away all the vanity, what solid and natural contentment does there remain which may not be had with £500 a year?' *Eng. Poets*, ix. 84.

'He who would . . . discover his acquaintance with splendour and magnificence may talk, like Cowley, of . . . the paucity of nature's wants, and the inconveniencies of superfluity, and at last, like him, limit his desires to £500 a year.' Johnson, *The Rambler*, No. 202. In Cowley's time £500 a year would perhaps be equal to £2,000 a year now.

See *Eng. Poets*, ix. 129, for Cowley's *Epitaphium vivi Auctoris*, and Addison's *Works*, vi. 536, for Addison's translation.

APPENDIX E (Page 19)

Wordsworth writes of 'that class of curious thinkers whom Johnson has strangely styled metaphysical poets.' Wordsworth's *Works*, ed. 1859, vi. 365. 'The designation,' says Southey, 'is not fortunate, but so much respect is due to Johnson that it would be unbecoming to substitute, even if it were easy to propose, one which might be unexceptionable.' Southey's *Cowper*, ii. 127. In what sense did Johnson use the term? In his *Dictionary* he defines *metaphysical*, ' 1. versed in metaphysicks ; relating to metaphysicks ; 2. In Shakespeare it means *supernatural* or *preternatural*.' *Metaphysicks* he defines, ' Ontology ; the doctrine of the general affections of substances existing.' These definitions do not help us much. We are more helped by his saying that 'he hated to hear people whine about metaphysical distresses, when there was so much want and hunger in the world.' H. More's *Memoirs*, i. 249. Swift, replying in his youth to a charge that he was forming an imprudent attachment with a girl, wrote :—' If you knew how metaphysical I am

that way you would little fear I should venture on one who has
given so much occasion to tongues.' Swift's *Works*, xv. 241. 'Those,'
wrote South, 'who neither do good turns, nor give good looks, nor
speak good words, have a love strangely subtile and metaphysical.'
Sermons, ed. 1823, ii. 304. *Metaphysical* in these passages means not
so much *supernatural* or *preternatural* as *unnatural, unreal, fantastic.*
These poets, says Johnson, 'neither copied nature nor life.' See
COWLEY, 52. Dr. Warton speaks of 'Johnson's dissertation on Cowley
and his fantastic style,' and of 'his discussion on false and unnatural
thoughts.' Warton's Pope's *Works*, i. 267.

Johnson may have borrowed the word from Dryden, who wrote :—
'Donne affects the metaphysics, not only in his satires, but in his
amorous verses, where nature only should reign ; and perplexes the
minds of the fair sex with nice speculations of philosophy,' &c. Dryden's
Works, xiii. 6. If we could be sure that Johnson had seen Spence's *Anecdotes* before he finished the *Life of Cowley* (in July, 1778. *John. Letters*,
ii. 68), he might have borrowed the word from Pope, who said :—
'Cowley, as well as Davenant, borrowed his metaphysical style from
Donne.' Spence's *Anec.* p. 173.

Cowley, after mentioning 'metaphysic, physic, morality, mathematics,
logic, rhetoric,' continues :—'which are all, I grant, good and useful
faculties (except only metaphysic, which I do not know whether it be any
thing or no).' *Eng. Poets*, ix. 44.

Warburton applies *metaphysical* to the machinery (*post*, MILTON, 222)
of an epic. He says of *The Rape of the Lock* :—'As the *civil* part is
intentionally debased by the choice of an insignificant action, so
should the *metaphysical* by the use of some very extravagant system.'
Warburton's *Pope*, i. 169. Burke calls Don Quixote 'the metaphysic
Knight of the sorrowful countenance.' *Works*, 1808, v. 36.

'The "metaphysical poets"' (writes Sir Leslie Stephen) are courtier
pedants. They represent the intrusion into poetry of the love of
dialectical subtlety encouraged by the still prevalent system of scholastic
disputation.' *Dict. Nat. Biog.* xii. 382.

In the first edition of the *Lives*, after the words 'the works of Cowley,'
followed, 'the last of the race.' Gray, classifying the English poets,
writes :—'A third Italian school, full of conceit, began in Queen
Elizabeth's reign, continued under James and Charles I by Donne,
Crashaw, Cleveland ; carried to its height by Cowley, and ending
perhaps in Sprat.' Mitford's *Gray*, Preface, p. 112. For Sprat's imitation of Cowley see *post*, SPRAT, 22.

APPENDIX F (PAGE 19)

'True wit is nature to advantage dress'd ;
   What oft was thought, but ne'er so well express'd.'
                                        Essay on Criticism, l. 297.

'"That, Sir," cried Dr. Johnson, "is a definition both false and
foolish. Let wit be dressed how it will, it will equally be wit, and
neither the more nor the less for any advantage dress can give it.'
Mme. d'Arblay's *Diary*, ii. 164.

Pope follows Boileau, of whom Addison writes:—'Give me leave to mention what he has so very well enlarged upon in the preface to his works, that wit and fine writing doth not consist so much in advancing things that are new, as in giving things that are known an agreeable turn.' *Spectator*, No. 253.

'Un bon mot n'est bon mot qu'en ce qu'il dit une chose que chacun pensait, et qu'il la dit d'une manière vive, fine et nouvelle.' BOILEAU, *Œuvres*, 1747, i. Preface, p. 61.

South, in 1660, said:—'Wit in divinity is nothing else but sacred truths suitably expressed.' *Sermons*, iii. 33.

Dryden, in 1675, defined wit as 'a propriety of thoughts and words, or, in other terms, thoughts and words elegantly adapted to the subject.' *Works*, v. 124. See also *ib.* vii. 228.

Addison, in *The Spectator*, No. 62, says of this definition:—'If this be a true definition of wit I am apt to think that Euclid was the greatest wit that ever set pen to paper. . . . If it be a true one, I am sure Mr. Dryden was not only a better poet but a greater wit than Mr. Cowley.'

Johnson, in his *Dictionary*, defines wit as 'sentiments produced by quickness of fancy.' Peter Cunningham examines the question in *N. & Q.* 3 S. v. 30.

APPENDIX G (PAGE 22)

Giovanni Battista Marini, or Marino, was born in 1569 and died in 1625.

Pope wrote of Crashaw:—'He formed himself upon Petrarch, or rather upon Marino. His thoughts . . . are oftentimes far-fetched, and too often strained and stiffened to make them appear the greater.' Pope's *Works* (Elwin and Courthope), vi. 117.

'The seductive faults, the *dulcia vitia* of Cowley, Marini, or Darwin, might reasonably be thought capable of corrupting the public judgment for half a century.' COLERIDGE, *Biog. Lit.* 1847, i. 72.

'No one has ever denied genius to Marino, who corrupted not merely the taste of Italy, but that of all Europe, for nearly a century.' BYRON, *Works*, 1854, ix. 79.

'Johnson has mistaken the character of Marino. Marino abounds in puerile conceits; but they are not far-fetched, like those of Donne or Cowley; they generally lie on the surface, and often consist of nothing more than a mere play upon words; so that, if to be a punster is to be a metaphysician, Marino is a poetical Heraclitus.' CARY, *English Poets*, 1846, p. 86.

In Pope's *Works* (Elwin and Courthope), v. 52, is an interesting criticism by Mr. Courthope of Johnson's account of the rise of the metaphysical poets, and 'an explanation of the extraordinary outburst of the witty or "metaphysical" writing between the middle of the sixteenth and the middle of the seventeenth centuries.'

DENHAM

1 OF Sir JOHN DENHAM very little is known but what is related of him by Wood[1] or by himself[2].

2 He was born at Dublin in 1615, the only son of Sir John Denham, of Little Horsely in Essex, then chief baron of the Exchequer in Ireland[3], and of Eleanor, daughter of Sir Garret Moore, baron of Mellefont[4].

3 Two years afterwards his father, being made one of the barons of the Exchequer in England[5], brought him away from his native country, and educated him in London.

4 In 1631 he was sent to Oxford[6], where he was considered 'as a dreaming young man, given more to dice and cards than study'; and therefore gave no prognosticks of his future eminence, nor was suspected to conceal under sluggishness and laxity a genius born to improve the literature of his country[7].

5 When he was three years afterwards removed to Lincoln's Inn[8] he prosecuted the common law with sufficient appearance

---

[1] *Ath. Oxon.* iii. 823. 'His eie was a kind of light goose-gray, not big, but it had a strange piercingness, not as to shining and glory, but (like a Momus) when he conversed with you he look't into your very thoughts.' AUBREY, *Brief Lives*, i. 220.

[2] In the dedication of his poems to Charles II. *Eng. Poets*, ix. 155.

[3] [In 1609 he was made Chief Baron, and in 1612 Chief Justice of the King's Bench in Ireland. Foss's *Judges*, 1870, p. 215. Little Horkesley is the correct name of the place.]

[4] [Sir Gerald or Garret Moore, Kt., first Baron Mellefont (Co. Louth) and Viscount Moore of Drogheda. Cokayne's *Complete Peerage*.]

[5] For Bacon's speech to him on his appointment see Bacon's *Works*, 1803, iv. 504. He lived long enough to give judgement in Hampden's favour in the Ship-Money Case.

Gardiner's *Hist. of Eng.* iii. 81 ; viii. 279.

[6] To Trinity College. He entered on Nov. 18, 1631. Aubrey's *Brief Lives*, i. 217; *N. & Q.* 4 S. x. 250.

[7] 'Being looked upon as a slow and dreaming young man by his seniors and contemporaries, and given more to cards and dice than his study, they could never then in the least imagine that he could ever enrich the world with his fancy, or issue of his brain, as he afterwards did.' *Athenae Oxon.* iii. 823.

'He was the dreamingst young fellow. . . . When he had played away all his money he would play away his father's wrought rich gold cappes.' AUBREY, *Brief Lives*, i. 217.

[8] 'He was admitted into the Society of that Inn on April 26, in the seventh year of the reign of King Charles [1631].' *N. & Q.* 4 S. x.

of application [1], yet did not lose his propensity to cards and dice, but was very often plundered by gamesters.

Being severely reproved for this folly he professed, and perhaps 6 believed, himself reclaimed, and, to testify the sincerity of his repentance, wrote and published *An Essay upon Gaming* [2].

He seems to have divided his studies between law and poetry, for in 1636 he translated the second book of the *Æneid* [3].

Two years after his father died [4]; and then, notwithstanding 8 his resolutions and professions, he returned again to the vice of gaming, and lost several thousand pounds that had been left him [5].

In 1631 [6] he published *The Sophy*. This seems to have 9 given him his first hold of the publick attention, for Waller remarked 'that he broke out like the Irish rebellion threescore thousand strong, when nobody was aware, or in the least suspected it [7]'—an observation which could have had no propriety, had his poetical abilities been known before.

He was after that pricked for sheriff of Surrey, and made 10 governor of Farnham Castle for the king; but he soon resigned

---

250. [*Records of Lincoln's Inn. Admissions*, i. 213. He was called to the Bar, Jan. 29, 1639. *Black Books of Lincoln's Inn*, ii. 350.]

[1] 'He was generally temperate as to drinking, but one time, when he was a student of Lincolne's inne, having been merry at ye taverne with his camerades late at night, a frolick came into his head to gett a playsterer's brush and a pott of inke, and blott out all the signes between Temple barre and Charing crosse, w[ch] made a strange confusion the next day, and 'twas in terme time. But it happened that they were discovered, and it cost him and them some moneys. This I had from R. Estcott esq. that carried the inke pot.' AUBREY, *MS. Lives*, quoted in *Athenae Oxon*. iii. 824; *Brief Lives*, i. 220.

[2] It was not published till 1651, and then without the author's consent, under the title of ' *The Anatomy of Play*, Written by a Worthy and Learned Gent. Dedicated to his Father to shew his Detestation of it.' See also *Brief Lives*, i. 217.

[3] *The Destruction of Troy. An Essay upon the Second Book of Virgil's Æneis*. Written in the year 1636. London, 1656. *Post*, DENHAM, 33; *Eng. Poets*, ix. 172. For *Essay* see *post*, ROSCOMMON, 25. According to Aubrey 'he also burlesqued Virgil, and burnt it, sayeing that 'twas not fitt that the best poet should be so abused.' *Brief Lives*, i. 218.

[4] On Jan. 6, 1638-9. *N. & Q.* 4 S. i. 552.

[5] '2000 or 1500 *li.* in ready money, 2 houses well furnished and much plate.' Aubrey's *Brief Lives*, i. 217.

[6] A slip for 1641. According to Masson's *Milton*, iii. 447, *The Sophy* was published in Aug. 1642.

[7] *Athenae Oxon*. iii. 824. Dryden makes this said, not by Waller, but of Waller. *Works*, xviii. 5. It suits Denham, for at the same time he and the Irish rebellion 'broke out.'

' *The Sophy* was acted at the private house in Black Friars with great applause.' *Biog. Brit.* ed. 1750, p. 1646.

that charge[1], and retreated to Oxford, where, in 1643, he published *Cooper's Hill*[2].

11 This poem had such reputation as to excite the common artifice by which envy degrades excellence. A report was spread that the performance was not his own, but that he had bought it of a vicar for forty pounds[3]. The same attempt was made to rob Addison of his *Cato*[4], and Pope of his *Essay on Criticism*[5].

12 In 1647 the distresses of the royal family required him to engage in more dangerous employments. He was entrusted by the queen with a message to the king; and, by whatever means, so far softened the ferocity of Hugh Peters that by his intercession admission was procured. Of the king's condescension he has given an account in the dedication of his works[6].

[1] ['He was but a young soldier, and did not keepe it.' Aubrey's *Brief Lives*, i. 218. Farnham Castle was captured by Sir William Waller Dec. 1, 1642, and Denham sent a prisoner to London. Rushworth's *Collections*, v. 82. It was at this time probably that he 'contracted a great familiarity' with Hugh Peters which was of service to him five years later. *Memoirs of Sir John Berkeley, Harl. Misc.* ix. 470. See *post*, DENHAM, 12. Denham was soon set at liberty and retired to Oxford. *Dict. Nat. Biog.*]

[2] *Eng. Poets*, ix. 159. 'This hill is in the parish of Egham in Surrey above Runey Mead, and hath a very noble prospect.' *Athenae Oxon.* iii. 824.

'In 1642-3, after Edgehill fight, his poeme was printed at Oxford in a sort of browne paper, for then they could gett no better.' Aubrey's *Brief Lives*, i. 218. The fight was on Oct. 23, 1642. '*Cooper's Hill* was published in Aug. 1642, the very month in which the King raised his standard.' Masson's *Milton*, iii. 447. See also *N. & Q.* 7 S. iii. 137.

[3] 'Then in came Denham, that limping old bard,
    Whose fame on the *Sophy* and *Cooper's Hill* stands;
And brought many stationers who swore very hard,
    That nothing sold better, except 'twere his lands.

But Apollo advised him to write something more,
    To clear a suspicion which possessed the Court,
That *Cooper's Hill*, so much bragg'd before,
    Was writ by a Vicar, who had forty pound for 't.'
Sessions of Poets, *Poems on Affairs of State*, 1697, i. 222; *Biog. Brit.* 1750, p. 1646.
Butler (*Genuine Remains*, i. 156), addressing Denham, said how some 'now expect far greater matters of ye,
Than the bought *Cooper's Hill* or borrow'd *Sophy*.'

[4] Perhaps this refers to the composition of the fifth act. *Post*, ADDISON, 56.

[5] 'The story told was that Wycherley sent the *Essay* to Pope for his revision, and that Pope published it as his own.' *Pope* (E. & C.), ii. 72.

[6] *Eng. Poets*, ix. 155. [Sir John Berkeley mentions in 1647 meeting 'Mr. Denham, who during his imprisonment had contracted a great familiarity with Mr. Peters, a preacher and a powerful person in the army.' *Memoirs of Sir John Berkeley, Harl. Misc.* ix. 470.] See *ante*, DENHAM, 10 *n*. 'The ferocity of Hugh Peters' strangely contrasts with the character drawn of him by Dr. S. R. Gardiner, who says that 'his love of liberty sprang from the kindliness of a man

He was afterwards employed in carrying on the king's 13 correspondence[1], and, as he says, discharged this office with great safety to the royalists; and being accidentally discovered by the adverse party's knowledge of Mr. Cowley's hand[2] he escaped, happily both for himself and his friends.

He was yet engaged in a greater undertaking. In April, 14 1648, he conveyed James the duke of York from London into France, and delivered him there to the Queen and prince of Wales[3]. This year he published his translation of *Cato Major*[4].

He now resided in France as one of the followers of the 15 exiled King; and, to divert the melancholy of their condition, was sometimes enjoined by his master to write occasional verses[5]: one of which amusements was probably his ode or song upon the Embassy to Poland[6], by which he and lord Crofts procured a contribution of ten thousand pounds from the Scotch, that wandered over that kingdom[7]. Poland was at that time very

of genial temper . . . who, without disguising his own opinions, preferred goodness of heart to rigidity of doctrine.' *The Great Civil War*, ii. 325.

[1] 'I was furnished with nine several cyphers in order to it.' *Eng. Poets*, ix. 156.

[2] *Ante*, COWLEY, 12.

[3] Wood is Johnson's authority for this. *Athenae Oxon.* iii. 824. But Aubrey (*Brief Lives*, i. 218), who was Wood's authority, introduces the statement with *quaere*. According to Clarendon (*Hist. Rebel.* vi. 19) the Duke escaped 'with Colonel Bamfield only.' Carte (*Hist. of Eng.* iv. 579) makes Bamfield (sometimes called Bamford) the leader; among those who helped he does not mention Denham.

[4] *Post*, DENHAM, 33.

[5] *Eng. Poets*, ix. 156.

[6] *On my Lord Crofts and my Journey into Poland, from whence we brought* 10,000*l. for His Majesty by the Decimation of his Scottish subjects there. Ib.* ix. 196. The contribution was forced. The poet tells how the Scots would

'Not assist our affairs
With their monies nor their wares,
As their answer now declares,
But only with their prayers.'
The Diet was appealed to:

'For when
It was moved there and then
They should pay one in ten,
The Diet said, Amen.'

Milton, on Feb. 6, 1649–50, in the name of the Council of State, wrote to the Senate of Dantzig:—'Many letters are brought us from our merchants trading upon the coast of Borussia, wherein they complain of a grievous tribute imposed upon them in the grand council of the Polanders, enforcing them to pay the tenth part of all their goods for the relief of the King of Scots, our enemy.' *Works*, iv. 337. Borussia is the mediaeval name of Prussia. The Czar Alexis also sent the exiled king money. Morfill's *Russia*, 1890, p. 126. For Crofts see *post*, WALLER, 8.

[7] 'I can remember when every pedlar was called a Scotchman by servants,' &c. MRS. PIOZZI, *Auto.* 1861, ii. 134.

[In the Parliament of 1606, one of the arguments used against union with Scotland was the danger that England would be overrun with 'the multiplicities of the Scots' as Poland had been. It is suggested that 'the special accident of time and place that draws the Scots to Poland,' mentioned by Bacon in these debates, was that large bodies had been levied

much frequented by itinerant traders, who, in a country of very little commerce and of great extent, where every man resided on his own estate, contributed very much to the accommodation of life, by bringing to every man's house those little necessaries which it was very inconvenient to want and very troublesome to fetch. I have formerly read without much reflection of the multitude of Scotchmen that travelled with their wares in Poland ; and that their numbers were not small the success of this negotiation gives sufficient evidence.

16 About this time what estate the war and the gamesters had left him was sold by order of the parliament ; and when, in 1652, he returned to England he was entertained by the earl of Pembroke[1].

17 Of the next years of his life there is no account[2]. At the Restoration he obtained, that which many missed, the reward of his loyalty, being made surveyor of the king's buildings[3] and dignified with the order of the Bath[4]. He seems now to have learned some attention to money, for Wood says that he got by his place seven thousand pounds[5].

18 After the Restoration he wrote the poem *On* [*Of*] *Prudence*[6] and *Justice*[7], and perhaps some of his other pieces ; and as he appears, whenever any serious question comes before him, to have

in Scotland during the latter half of the sixteenth century for the service of Sweden and employed in Polish wars. *N. & Q.* I S. vii. 600.]

[1] Philip Herbert, fourth Earl. For Clarendon's character of him see *Hist. Rebel.* iii. 553. 'At Wilton [the Earl's mansion],' writes Aubrey, 'I had the honour to contract an acquaintance with Sir John Denham.' *Brief Lives*, i. 218.

[2] Mr. C. H. Firth has printed in *N. & Q.* 7 S. x. 41 an order by the Council, dated June 9, 1655, for Denham's arrest ; also some unpublished verses, almost certainly the poet's, on the Cavaliers imprisoned that year.

[3] 'The patent dated June 13, 1660.' Cunningham, *Lives of the Poets*, i. 70.

According to Wood, 'Charles I did grant to him the reversion of the place after the decease of Inigo Jones.' *Ath. Oxon.* iii. 825.

Denham says that Charles II conferred it upon him freely. *Eng. Poets*, ix. 156.

Evelyn, consulting with Denham 'about the placing of the palace at Greenwich, came away, knowing Sir John to be a better poet than architect.' *Diary*, i. 377.

[4] On April 19, 1661, Evelyn recorded :—'To London, and saw the bath-ing and rest of the ceremonies of the Knights of the Bath, preparatory to the Coronation. I might have received this honour, but declined it.' *Ib.* i. 366.

[5] 'He got seven thousand pounds, as Sir Christopher Wren told me of, to his owne knowledge. Sir Christopher was his deputie.' Aubrey's *Brief Lives*, i. 219.

Butler, in sixteen verses, accuses him of making money by 'little tricks.' *Genuine Remains*, i. 158 ; *Eng. Poets*, xiv. 201.

[6] *Ib.* ix. 243.

[7] *Ib.* p. 253.

been a man of piety, he consecrated his poetical powers to religion, and made a metrical version of the psalms of David [1]. In this attempt he has failed; but in sacred poetry who has succeeded [2]?

It might be hoped that the favour of his master and esteem of the publick would now make him happy. But human felicity is short and uncertain: a second marriage brought upon him so much disquiet as for a time disordered his understanding; and Butler lampooned him for his lunacy. I know not whether the malignant lines were then made publick, nor what provocation incited Butler to do that which no provocation can excuse.

His frenzy lasted not long [3]; and he seems to have regained his full force of mind, for he wrote afterwards his excellent poem upon the death of Cowley [4], whom he was not long to survive; for on the 19th of March, 1668, he was buried by his side [5].

DENHAM is deservedly considered as one of the fathers of English poetry. 'Denham and Waller,' says Prior, 'improved our versification, and Dryden perfected it [6].' He has given specimens of various composition, descriptive, ludicrous, didactick, and sublime.

He appears to have had, in common with almost all mankind, the ambition of being upon proper occcasions *a merry fellow* [7], and in common with most of them to have been by

[1] They were first published in 1714. In the Preface (p. 20) Denham, after speaking of his age and infirmities, continues:—' I advise no man to dishearten himself by the sense of age or decay of strength.'

[2] *Ante*, COWLEY, 147.

[3] See Appendix H.

[4] *Eng. Poets*, ix. 210; *ante*, COWLEY, 172.

[5] He died on March 19, 1668-9, and was buried on March 23. Aubrey's *Brief Lives*, i. 219; *N. & Q.* 4 S. x. 13, 250.

[6] Prior, in the Preface to *Solomon*, says of the heroic verse:—'As Davenant and Waller corrected, and Dryden perfected it, it is too confined.' *Eng. Poets*, xxxiii. 206. Johnson, it seems, mistook Davenant for Denham. 'We must be children before we grow men. . . . Even after Chaucer there was a Spenser, a Harrington, a Fairfax, before Waller and Denham were in being; and our numbers were in their nonage till these last appeared.' DRYDEN, *Works*, xi. 226.

Cowper, writing of 'the breaks and pauses' in Milton's blank verse, continues:—'But these are graces to which rhyme is not competent; so broken, it loses all its music; of which any person may convince himself by reading a page only of any of our poets anterior to Denham, Waller and Dryden.' Southey's *Cowper*, xi. Preface, p. 13. See also *ib.* ii. 130; *ante*, COWLEY, 63; *post*, WALLER, 5, 142; DRYDEN, 343.

[7] Johnson perhaps prints 'merry fellow' in italics to show that he is thinking of the Clown in *Twelfth Night*, iii. 1. 30, of whom Viola says:—

nature or by early habits debarred from it. Nothing is less exhilarating than the ludicrousness of Denham. He does not fail for want of efforts: he is familiar, he is gross; but he is never merry, unless *The Speech against peace in the close Committee* be excepted [1]. For grave burlesque however his imitation of Davenant shews him to have been well qualified [2].

23 Of his more elevated occasional poems there is perhaps none that does not deserve commendation. In the verses to Fletcher we have an image that has since been often adopted:

> ' But whither am I stray'd? I need not raise
> Trophies to thee from other men's dispraise;
> Nor is thy fame on lesser ruins built,
> Nor need thy juster title the foul guilt
> Of eastern kings, who, to secure their reign,
> Must have their brothers, sons, and kindred slain [3].'

After Denham, Orrery in one of his prologues—

> ' Poets are sultans, if they had their will;
> For every author would his brother kill [4].'

And Pope,

> ' Should such a man, too fond to rule alone,
> Bear like the Turk no brother near the throne [5].'

' I warrant thou art a merry fellow and carest for nothing.' See *post*, DRYDEN, 130, for another *merry fellow.*

[1] *Eng. Poets*, ix. 214. The committee is described as

> ' That invisible Committee,
> The wheel that governs all.'

It sat, as one line shows, in Haberdashers' Hall. In that Hall sat the Committee for Advance of Money. Gardiner's *Great Civil War*, 1897, i. 74. Mr. C. H. Firth thinks Denham meant the Committee of Safety, for which see Gardiner's *Hist. of Eng.* x. 209.

[2] *Eng. Poets*, ix. 233. For Davenant see *post*, MILTON, 102; DRYDEN, 26, 97.

[3] *Eng. Poets*, ix. 227.

[4] '' 'Tis the wits' nature, or at best their fate,

> Others to scorn, and one another hate.
> They would be sultans, if they had their will;

For each of them would all his brothers kill.'
Prologue to Tryphon, Dramatic Works of Roger Boyle, Earl of Orrery, 1739, i. 132. *Post*, DRYDEN, 16.

[5] *Prol. Sat.* l. 198.

' Aristoteles, more Ottomanorum, regnare se haud tuto posse putabat, nisi fratres suos omnes contrucidasset.' BACON, *De Aug. Sci.* iii. 4; *Works*, 1803, vii. 191.

' In our own country a man seldom sets up for a poet without attacking the reputation of all his brothers in the art. The ignorance of the moderns, the scribblers of the age, the decay of poetry, are the topics of detractation with which he makes his entrance into the world; but how much more noble is the fame that is built on candour and ingenuity, according to those beautiful lines of Sir John Denham, in his poem on Fletcher's works!' ADDISON, *The Spectator*, No. 253.

But this is not the best of his little pieces; it is excelled by 24
his poem to Fanshaw, and his elegy on Cowley.

His praise of Fanshaw's version of Guarini contains a very 25
spritely and judicious character of a good translator [1].

'That servile path thou nobly dost decline,
Of tracing word by word, and line by line.
Those are the labour'd births of slavish brains,
Not the effect of poetry, but pains ;
Cheap vulgar arts, whose narrowness affords
No flight for thoughts, but poorly stick [sticks] at words.
A new and nobler way thou dost pursue,
To make translations and translators too.
They but preserve the ashes, thou the flame,
True to his sense, but truer to his fame [2].'

The excellence of these lines is greater, as the truth which
they contain was not at that time generally known.

His poem on the death of Cowley was his last, and among his 26
shorter works his best performance [3] : the numbers are musical,
and the thoughts are just.

Cooper's Hill is the work that confers upon him the rank 27
and dignity of an original author [4].   He seems to have been, at
least among us, the author of a species of composition that may
be denominated *local poetry*, of which the fundamental subject is
some particular landscape to be poetically described, with the
addition of such embellishments as may be supplied by historical
retrospection or incidental meditation.

To trace a new scheme of poetry has in itself a very high 28
claim to praise, and its praise is yet more when it is apparently

[1] Sir Richard Fanshaw's version
of Guarini's *Pastor Fido* was published in 1648. For translation see
ante, COWLEY, 125, 202 ; *post*, DRY-
DEN, 107, 223.

[2] *Eng. Poets*, ix. 229. See *post*,
ROSCOMMON, 36.

[3] *Ante*, DENHAM, 20.

[4] *Ante*, DENHAM, 10. 'This poem
was first printed, without the author's
name, in 1643. In that edition a
great number of verses are to be
found since entirely omitted ; and
very many others since corrected
and improved. Some few the author
afterwards added ; and in particular
the four celebrated lines on the
Thames, all with admirable judgment ; and the whole read together
is a very strong proof of what Mr.
Waller says :—
"Poets lose half the praise they
    should have got,
Could it be known what they dis-
    creetly blot."
                    [*Eng. Poets*, xvi. 175.]'
POPE, Spence's *Anec.*, p. 282.
'*Cooper's Hill*, for the majesty of
the style, is and ever will be, the
exact standard of good writing.'
DRYDEN, *Works*, ii. 137. On this
Southey remarks :—'Adulation was
so common in Dryden's days that
probably he never thought himself
degraded by using it.' Southey's
Cowper, ii. 133.

copied by Garth and Pope[1]; after whose names little will be gained by an enumeration of smaller poets, that have left scarce a corner of the island not dignified either by rhyme or blank verse.

29 *Cooper's Hill* if it be maliciously inspected will not be found without its faults. The digressions are too long, the morality too frequent, and the sentiments sometimes such as will not bear a rigorous enquiry[2].

30 The four verses, which, since Dryden has commended them[3], almost every writer for a century past has imitated[4], are generally known:

> 'O could I flow like thee, and make thy stream
> My great example, as it is my theme!
> Though deep, yet clear; though gentle, yet not dull;
> Strong without rage, without o'erflowing full[5].'

31 The lines are in themselves not perfect, for most of the words thus artfully opposed are to be understood simply on one side of the comparison, and metaphorically on the other; and if there be any language which does not express intellectual operations by material images, into that language they cannot

---

[1] 'The design of *Windsor Forest* is evidently derived from *Cooper's Hill*, with some attention to Waller's poem on *The Park.*' *Post*, POPE, 315. For Pope's praise of *Cooper's Hill* see *Windsor Forest*, ll. 259-272.

Campbell gives the following imitations of *Cooper's Hill* as 'alone meriting notice':—'Waller's *St. James' Park* [*Eng. Poets*, xvi. 152]; Pope's *Windsor Castle*; Garth's *Claremont* [*Ib.* xxviii. 91]; Tickell's *Kensington Gardens* [*Ib.* xxxix. 258; *post*, TICKELL, 17]; Dyer's *Grongar Hill* [*Ib.* lviii. 109; *post*, DYER, 9]; Jago's *Edge-Hill* [*post*, SHENSTONE, 3 *n.*]; John Scott's *Amwell*; Michael Bruce's *Lochleven*, and Kirke White's *Clifton Grove.*' *British Poets*, p. 242.

[2] Pope, in his *Iliad*, xvi. 466 *n*, after praising Homer's 'indirect and oblique manner of introducing moral sentences and instructions,' continues:—'It is this particular art that is the very distinguishing excellence of *Cooper's Hill.*'

[3] 'I am sure there are few who make verses have observed the sweetness of these two lines in *Cooper's Hill*—"Though deep, &c.";

and there are yet fewer who can find the reason of that sweetness.' DRYDEN, *Works*, xiv. 207.

[4] 'Nor let my votaries show their skill
In aping lines from *Cooper's Hill*;
For know I cannot bear to hear
The mimicry of deep, yet clear.'
SWIFT, *Apollo's Edict*, *Works*, xiv. 129.

'Flow, Welsted, flow! like thine inspirer, Beer,
Though stale, not ripe; though thin, yet never clear;
So sweetly mawkish and so smoothly dull;
Heady, not strong; o'erflowing, though not full.'
POPE, *The Dunciad*, iii. 169.

For Denham's lines see *Eng. Poets*, ix. 165. They first appeared in the published edition of the poem in 1655. *N. & Q.* 7 S. iii. 137.

[5] In *N. & Q.* 4 S. xii. 493, is quoted from Ascham's *Epistolae*, 1590, p. 254, a passage probably imitated by Denham. Ascham describes Osorius in his style as 'sic fluens ut nunquam redundet, sic sonans ut nunquam perstrepat, sic plenus ut nunquam turgescat.'

be translated. But so much meaning is comprised in so few words; the particulars of resemblance are so perspicaciously collected, and every mode of excellence separated from its adjacent fault by so nice a line of limitation; the different parts of the sentence are so accurately adjusted; and the flow of the last couplet is so smooth and sweet—that the passage however celebrated has not been praised above its merit. It has beauty peculiar to itself, and must be numbered among those felicities which cannot be produced at will by wit and labour, but must arise unexpectedly in some hour propitious to poetry [1].

He appears to have been one of the first that understood 32 the necessity of emancipating translation from the drudgery of counting lines and interpreting single words [2]. How much this servile practice obscured the clearest and deformed the most beautiful parts of the ancient authors may be discovered by a perusal of our earlier versions; some of them the works of men well qualified, not only by critical knowledge, but by poetical genius, who yet by a mistaken ambition of exactness degraded at once their originals and themselves.

Denham saw the better way, but has not pursued it with 33 great success [3]. His versions of Virgil [4] are not pleasing, but they taught Dryden to please better [5]. His poetical imitation of Tully on *Old Age* [6] has neither the clearness of prose, nor the spriteliness of poetry.

The 'strength of Denham,' which Pope so emphatically 34 mentions [7], is to be found in many lines and couplets, which

---

[1] *Post*, ADDISON, 135; POPE, 402.

[2] Denham, in the Preface to his *Aeneid* (*ante*, DENHAM, 7), says of the translator :—'It is not his business alone to translate language into language, but poesy into poesy.'

[3] *Ante*, COWLEY, 125; *post*, DRYDEN, 223. 'Denham and Cowley contrived another way of turning authors into our tongue, called, by the latter of them, imitation.... Denham advised more liberty than he took himself.' DRYDEN, *Works*, xii. 18, 21. See also *The Guardian*, No. 164.

In *The Battle of the Books* we read how 'with a long spear Homer slew Denham, a stout modern, who from his father's side derived his lineage from Apollo, but his mother was of mortal race. He fell, and bit the

earth. The celestial part Apollo took, and made it a star; but the terrestrial lay wallowing upon the ground.' SWIFT, *Works*, x. 235.

[4] *Ante*, DENHAM, 7; *Eng. Poets*, ix. 172.

[5] Pope, in his *Iliad*, xii. 387 *n.*, says :—'This speech of Sarpedon is excellently translated by Denham, and, if I have done it with any spirit, it is partly owing to him.' For the translation see *Eng. Poets*, ix. 203.

[6] *Ib.* ix. 266.

[7] 'And praise the easy vigour of a line
Where Denham's strength and Waller's sweetness join.'
Essay on Criticism, l. 360. See *post*, WALLER, 144.

Dryden says of the earlier writers : 'They can produce nothing . . . so

convey much meaning in few words, and exhibit the sentiment
with more weight than bulk.

On the Thames[1].

'Though with those streams he no resemblance hold,
Whose foam is amber, and their gravel gold;
His genuine and less guilty wealth t' explore,
Search not his bottom, but survey his shore.'

On Strafford[2].

'His wisdom such, at once it did appear
Three kingdoms' wonder, and three kingdoms' fear;
While single he stood forth, and seem'd, although
Each had an army, as an equal foe.
Such was his force of eloquence, to make
The hearers more concern'd than he that spake;
Each seem'd to act that part he came to see,
And none was more a looker on than he:
So did he move our passions; some were known
To wish, for the defence, the crime their own.
Now private pity strove with publick hate,
Reason with rage, and eloquence with fate.'

On Cowley.

'To him no author was unknown,
Yet what he wrote was all his own[3];
Horace's wit, and Virgil's state,
He did not steal, but emulate!
And when he would like them appear,
Their garb, but not their cloaths, did wear.'

35   As one of Denham's principal claims to the regard of posterity
arises from his improvement of our numbers[4], his versification
ought to be considered. It will afford that pleasure which
arises from the observation of a man of judgement naturally right
forsaking bad copies by degrees and advancing towards a better
practice, as he gains more confidence in himself.

majestic, so correct as Sir John
Denham.' *Works*, xv. 291. See
also *post*, DRYDEN, 292.
    Pope follows Dryden in praising
Denham's majesty:—
'Here his first lays majestic Denham
    sung.' *Windsor Forest*, l. 271.
    Dryden, in his lines on Milton,
speaks of the 'majesty' of Virgil.
    [1] From *Cooper's Hill. Eng. Poets*,
ix. 165.

[2] *Ib*. p. 191.
    [3] Johnson omits after the first
couplet the following lines:—
'He melted not the ancient gold,
    Nor with Ben Jonson did make
    bold
To plunder all the Roman stores
Of poets and of orators.'
Ib. p. 211; *ante*, COWLEY, 172.
    [4] *Ante*, DENHAM, 21.

In his translation of Virgil, written when he was about **36**
twenty-one years old, may be still found the old manner of
continuing the sense ungracefully from verse to verse.

> 'Then all those
> Who in the dark our fury did escape,
> Returning, know our borrow'd arms, and shape,
> And differing dialect : then their numbers swell
> And grow upon us ; first Chorœbus fell
> Before Minerva's altar ; next did bleed ⎫
> Just Ripheus, whom no Trojan did exceed ⎬
> In virtue, yet the Gods his fate decreed. ⎭
> Then Hypanis and Dymas, wounded by
> Their friends ; nor thee, Pantheus, thy piety,
> Nor consecrated mitre, from the same
> Ill fate could save ; my country's funeral flame
> And Troy's cold ashes I attest, and call
> To witness for myself, that in their fall
> No foes, no death, nor danger I declin'd,
> Did, and deserv'd no less, my fate to find [1].'

From this kind of concatenated metre he afterwards refrained, **37**
and taught his followers the art of concluding their sense in
couplets[2]; which has perhaps been with rather too much constancy
pursued.

This passage exhibits one of those triplets which are not **38**
infrequent in this first essay, but which it is to be supposed his
maturer judgement disapproved, since in his latter works he has
totally forborne them.

His rhymes are such as seem found without difficulty by **39**
following the sense ; and are for the most part as exact at

---

[1] *Eng. Poets*, ix. 186.

[2] *Post*, DRYDEN, 217, 290. 'The
excellence and dignity of rhyme were
never fully known till Mr. Waller
taught it ; he first made writing easily
an art ; first showed us to conclude
the sense, most commonly, in distichs, which, in the verse of those
before him, runs on for so many
lines together that the reader is out
of breath to overtake it. This sweetness of Mr. Waller's lyrick poesy
was afterwards followed in the epick
by Sir John Denham in his *Cooper's
Hill.* . . . But if we owe the invention
of it to Mr. Waller, we are acknowledging for the noblest use of it to
Sir William Davenant, who at once

made it perfect in the *Siege of
Rhodes.*' DRYDEN, *Works*, ii. 137.

Churchill, in *The Apology* (*Works*,
1766, i. 72), says that Waller
'In couplets first taught straggling
sense to close.'

'When once,' writes Mr. Elwin,
'the change had commenced, there
was a constant movement towards
uniformity till the utmost verge was
reached, and a fresh reaction began.'
Pope's *Works* (Elwin and Courthope),
i. 337.

For Young's 'style sometimes concatenated,' see *post*, YOUNG, 154,
and for 'the concatenation of Akenside's verses,' see *post*, AKENSIDE,
17.

least as those of other poets, though now and then the reader is shifted off with what he can get.

> 'O how *transform'd!*
> How much unlike that Hector, who *return'd*
> Clad in Achilles' spoils[1]!'

And again:

> 'From thence a thousand lesser poets *sprung,*
> Like petty princes from the fall of *Rome*[2].'

40   Sometimes the weight of rhyme is laid upon a word too feeble to sustain it:

> 'Troy confounded falls
> From all her glories: if it might have stood
> By any power, by this right hand it *shou'd*[3].'

> '—And though my outward state misfortune *hath*
> Deprest thus low, it cannot reach my faith[4].'

> '—Thus by his fraud and our own faith o'ercome,
> A feigned tear destroys us, against *whom*
> Tydides nor Achilles could prevail,
> Nor ten years' conflict, nor a thousand sail[5].'

41   He is not very careful to vary the ends of his verses; in one passage the word *die* rhymes three couplets in six[6].

42   Most of these petty faults are in his first productions, when he was less skilful or, at least, less dexterous in the use of words, and though they had been more frequent they could only have lessened the grace, not the strength of his composition. He is one of the writers that improved our taste and advanced our language, and whom we ought therefore to read with gratitude, though having done much he left much to do.

APPENDIX H (PAGE 75)

He was married on May 25, 1665. Cunningham, *Lives of the Poets,* i. 71. 'Upon some discontent arising from a second match he became crazed for a time, and so consequently contemptible among vain fops.' *Ath. Oxon.* iii. 825; Aubrey's *Brief Lives,* i. 219.
'June 10, 1666. He [Pierce] tells me how the Duke of York is wholly given up to his new mistress, my Lady Denham, going at noonday with all his gentlemen with him to visit her in Scotland Yard; she

---

[1] *Eng. Poets,* ix. 181.
[2] *Ib.* p. 228.   [3] *Ib.* p. 181.
[4] *Ib.* p. 175.   [5] *Ib.* p. 179.
[6] In *Of Justice.* In the second couplet after the last of these six, *dies* rhymes with *flies. Ib.* p. 256. In *Cooper's Hill, die* rhymes two couplets in three. *Ib.* p. 170.

declaring she will not be his mistress, as Mrs. Price, to go up and down the Privy-stairs, but will be owned publickly, and so she is.' PEPYS, *Diary*, iii. 208.

'Jan. 7, 1666–7. Lord Brouncker tells me that my Lady Denham is at last dead. Some suspect her poisoned.' *Ib.* p. 372.

In the *Memoirs of Grammont*, 1876, p. 207, Denham is accused of poisoning his wife. According to Aubrey, she was 'poysoned by the Co. of Roc. [Countess of Rochester] with chocolatte.' *Brief Lives*, i. 219.

Butler, after charging him with fraud in his surveyorship, continues :—

> ' All this was done before those days began
> In which you were a wise and happy man.
> For who e'er liv'd in such a Paradise,
> Until fresh straw and darkness op'd your eyes ? '
> > Butler's *Genuine Remains*, i. 159, *Eng. Poets*, xiv. 202.

Lord Lisle wrote to Temple on Sept. 26, 1667 :—' If Sir John Denham had not the name of being mad, I believe in most companies he would be thought wittier than ever he was.' Temple's *Works*, 1757, i. 484.

MILTON[1]

1 THE Life of Milton has been already written in so many forms[2] and with such minute enquiry that I might perhaps more properly have contented myself with the addition of a few notes to Mr. Fenton's elegant Abridgement[3], but that a new narrative was thought necessary to the uniformity of this edition.

2 JOHN MILTON was by birth a gentleman[4], descended from the proprietors of Milton near Thame in Oxfordshire, one of whom forfeited his estate in the times of York and Lancaster[5].

---

[1] 'Milton's *Life* was begun in January 1779, and finished in six weeks.' *Gent. Mag.* 1785, p. 9.

Malone wrote on April 5, 1779:— 'Johnson told me, "we have had too many honeysuckle lives of Milton, and that his should be in another strain."' *Hist. MSS. Com.* Report xii. App. x. 345.

'Johnson's treatment of Milton,' wrote Cowper, 'is unmerciful to the last degree. A pensioner is not likely to spare a republican; and the Doctor, in order, I suppose, to convince his royal patron of the sincerity of his monarchical principles, has belaboured that great poet's character with the most industrious cruelty.' Southey's *Cowper's Works*, iii. 313.

Pattison after calling Johnson 'a literary bandit,' 'who conspired with one Lauder to stamp out Milton's credit' [Boswell's *Johnson*, i. 228], continues:—'He afterwards took ample revenge for the mortification of this exposure [of the conspiracy], in his *Lives of the Poets*, in which he employed all his vigorous powers and consummate skill to write down Milton. He undoubtedly dealt a heavy blow at the poet's reputation.' Pattison's *Milton*, pp. 217-9.

Landor, on the other hand, wrote: —'In Johnson's estimate [of Milton] I do not perceive the unfairness of which many have complained.' *Imag. Conver.* (Crump), iv. 243.

[2] The following list of the Lives of Milton used by Johnson I have taken from Mr. C. H. Firth's edition of Johnson's *Milton*, Clarendon Press, 1888, p. 83:—Wood's *Ath. Oxon.* 1691-2 [*Fasti Oxon.* 1815, i. 479]; *Letters of State written by Milton, with Life*, by Edward Phillips, 1694; *Life*, by John Toland, 1698; *Explanatory Notes, &c., on Paradise Lost, with Life*, by Jonathan Richardson, 1734; *Milton's Prose Works, with Life*, by Thomas Birch, 1738; *Milton's Poems, with Life*, by Thomas Newton, Bishop of Bristol, 1749-52.

Johnson might also have seen Francis Peck's *New Memoirs of Milton*, 1740, and *Biog. Brit.* p. 3106. On Aubrey's *Brief Lives*, ii. 60, Wood's account was based, whose *Life of Milton*, writes T. Warton, 'is the groundwork of all the *Lives.*' *Milton's Poems*, ed. T. Warton, 1791, p. 422.

[3] *Post*, FENTON, 14.

[4] 'The arms that John Milton did use and seal his letters with were, Argent a spread eagle with two heads gules, legg'd and beak'd sable.' WOOD, *Fasti Oxon.* i. 480 n.

[5] Johnson's authorities are Phillips (*Milton's Letters of State, with Life*, p. 5), and Wood (*Fasti Oxon.* i. 480), whose informant was Aubrey, who had his account from Milton and his relations. Milton's grandfather, writes Wood, 'was descended from

Which side he took I know not; his descendant inherited no veneration for the White Rose.

His grandfather John was keeper of the forest of Shotover, 3 a zealous papist who disinherited his son, because he had forsaken the religion of his ancestors.

His father, John, who was the son disinherited, had recourse 4 for his support to the profession of a scrivener. He was a man eminent for his skill in musick, many of his compositions being still to be found [1]; and his reputation in his profession was such that he grew rich, and retired to an estate. He had probably more than common literature, as his son addresses him in one of his most elaborate Latin poems [2]. He married a gentlewoman of the name of Caston [3], a Welsh family, by whom he had two sons, John the poet, and Christopher who studied the law, and adhered, as the law taught him, to the King's party, for which he was awhile persecuted; but having, by his brother's interest, obtained permission to live in quiet [4], he supported himself so honourably by chamber-practice, that soon after the accession of King James, he was knighted and made a Judge [5]; but his constitution being too weak for business, he retired before any disreputable compliances became necessary.

He had likewise a daughter Anne, whom he married with 5

those of this name who had lived beyond all record at Milton.' Bliss adds in a note that 'the name as a surname does not occur in any part of the register.' Professor Masson calls them 'the legendary Miltons of Milton.' The poet's great-grand-father and great-grandmother seem to have belonged to 'the small-farming class.' Masson's *Milton*, i. 11, 15.

[1] See Appendix I.

[2] *Sylvarum Liber*, vi. For Cowper's translation of it see Southey's *Cowper*, x. 164.

[3] 'His wife, Sarah, was of the family of Caston, derived originally from Wales.' Phillips' *Milton*, p. 4. Her name was Sarah Jeffrey. 'There were Castons among her progenitors.' Masson's *Milton*, i. 31.

[4] He had been 'one of the King's Commissioners for sequestrating the estates of Parliamentarians.' In 1646 he petitions for leave to com-

pound for his property now sequestered in turn... His case was protracted for five years.' *Ib.* iii. 485, 632.

[5] Phillips' *Milton*, p. 6. 'June 2, 1686. New judges, among which was Milton, a Papist (brother to that Milton who wrote for the Regicides), who presumed to take his place without passing the Test.' EVELYN, *Diary*, ii. 265.

He was appointed in April 1686, on the dismissal of four judges, 'all violent Tories,' for refusing to support the King's pretensions to the dispensing power. [*Post*, ROWE, 1.] 'It does not appear that he was ever formally reconciled to the Church of Rome.' MACAULAY, *History*, ii. 337.

'Not a single dictum of his is recorded in any report book of his time.' HAWKINS, Johnson's *Works*, 1787, i. 83. See also *post*, MILTON, 172.

a considerable fortune to Edward Philips, who came from
Shrewsbury, and rose in the Crown-office to be secondary[1];
by him she had two sons, John and Edward, who were
educated by the poet[2], and from whom is derived the only
authentick account of his domestick manners[3].

6   John, the poet, was born in his father's house, at the Spread-
Eagle in Bread-street Dec. 9, 1608, between six and seven in
the morning[4]. His father appears to have been very solicitous
about his education[5]; for he was instructed at first by private
tuition under the care of Thomas Young, who was afterwards
chaplain to the English merchants at Hamburgh, and of whom
we have reason to think well, since his scholar considered him
as worthy of an epistolary Elegy[6].

7   He was then sent to St. Paul's School, under the care of Mr. Gill[7],
and removed, in the beginning of his sixteenth year, to Christ's
College in Cambridge, where he entered a sizar, Feb. 12, 1624[8].

[1] Phillips' *Milton*, p. 7. He was
in the Crown Office of the Court of
Chancery. Johnson's *Works*, 1787,
ii. 144. He died in 1631. Masson's
Milton, i. 104 ; ii. 98. For her second
husband see *post*, MILTON, 171.
[2] *Post*, MILTON, 35, 42, 171.
[3] See Appendix J.
[4] Wood's *Fasti Oxon.* i. 480 ;
Aubrey's *Brief Lives*, ii. 62. For
a description of Bread Street see
Masson's *Milton*, i. 41.
   Milton's Bible, with the entries,
mostly in his own hand, of the birth
of himself and others of his family,
&c., is in the British Museum (Add.
MS. 32,310). *N. & Q.* 7 S. vi. 253.
[5] 'After I had for my first years,
by the ceaseless diligence and care
of my father (whom God recompense), been exercised to the tongues
and some sciences, as my age would
suffer,' &c. MILTON, *Works*, i. 118.
'Pater me puerulum humaniorum
literarum studiis destinavit.' *Ib.* v.
230.
'When I was yet a child, no childish
   play
To me was pleasing: all my mind
   was set
Serious to learn and know.'
            Paradise Regained, i. 201.
[6] Cowper thus translates ll. 29–
32 :—

'First led by him through sweet
   Aonian shade,
Each sacred haunt of Pindus I
   surveyed ;
And, favoured by the Muse whom
   I implored,
Thrice on my lip the hallowed
   stream I poured.'
            Southey's *Cowper*, x. 138.
   See also Masson's *Milton*, i. 68 ;
post, MILTON, 46 *n.*
[7] Alexander Gill, 'a noted Latinist,
critic and divine.' *Ath. Oxon.* ii.
597. For 'his whipping-fitts' see
Aubrey's *Brief Lives*, i. 262. In
1628 his son, an usher in the school,
for saying in Oxford, among other
things, 'that our King was fitter to
stand in a Cheapside shop, with an
apron before him, and say *What
lack you ?* than to govern the kingdom,' was sentenced in the Star
Chamber ' to lose one ear at London,
and the other at Oxford, and to be
fined at 2,000 *lib.*' On the father's
petition the fine was mitigated, and
the ears spared. *Ath. Oxon.* iii. 43.
For Milton's praise of the son's
'carmina sane grandia' see *Works*,
vi. 110. See also Masson's *Milton*,
i. 78–85.
[8] Feb. 12, 1625 N.S. A sizar at
Cambridge, like a servitor at Oxford,
was supported and educated in return

He was at this time eminently skilled in the Latin tongue ; 8
and he himself by annexing the dates to his first compositions,
a boast of which the learned Politian had given him an
example, seems to commend the earliness of his own proficiency to the notice of posterity[1]; but the products of his
vernal fertility have been surpassed by many, and particularly
by his contemporary Cowley[2]. Of the powers of the mind
it is difficult to form an estimate ; many have excelled Milton
in their first essays who never rose to works like *Paradise Lost*.

At fifteen, a date which he uses till he is sixteen, he translated 9
or versified two Psalms, 114 and 136[3], which he thought worthy
of the publick eye, but they raise no great expectations ; they
would in any numerous school have obtained praise, but not
excited wonder.

Many of his elegies appear to have been written in his 10
eighteenth year, by which it appears that he had then read
the Roman authors with very nice discernment. I once heard
Mr. Hampton, the translator of Polybius[4], remark, what I think
is true, that Milton was the first Englishman who, after the
revival of letters, wrote Latin verses with classick elegance[5].
If any exceptions can be made they are very few ; Haddon[6]
and Ascham[7], the pride of Elizabeth's reign, however they
may have succeeded in prose, no sooner attempt verses than
they provoke derision. If we produced anything worthy of

---

for menial services. 'There is nothing of eminent and illustrious,' wrote
Cowley, 'to be expected from a
low, sordid and hospital-like education.' *Eng. Poets*, ix. 148. See also
Boswell's *Johnson*, v. 122, and *John.
Misc.* ii. 88.

Milton was not a sizar. ' He went,
at his owne chardge only, to Christ's
College.' Aubrey's *Brief Lives*, ii.
63. He entered as 'pensionarius
minor'—a commoner. *Pensionarius
maior* was a fellow commoner. See
Masson's *Milton*, i. 111 ; *post*,
HALIFAX, 4 *n*.

[1] *Post*, MILTON, 153.

[2] *Ante*, COWLEY, 6 ; *post*, POPE,
25.

[3] 'Metrical psalmody was much
cultivated in this age of fanaticism.'
T. Warton's *Milton's Poems*, p. 370.
Of Milton's version of *Psalm* 136

Miss Martineau wrote (*Auto.* i. 34) :
—' It is the very hymn for children,
set to its own simple tune.'

[4] *Post*, ROWE, 35 *n*. Johnson
reviewed this translation in 1756.
Johnson's *Works*, vi. 77. 'The
translator has preserved the admirable sense, and improved the coarse
style of his Arcadian original.'
GIBBON, *Misc. Works*, v. 588.

[5] *Ante*, COWLEY, 33 ; *post*, MIL-
TON, 176.

[6] 'Haddon had certainly laboured
at an imitation of Cicero, but without
catching his manner, or getting rid of
the florid, semi-poetical tone of the
fourth century.' HALLAM, *Literature
of Europe*, 1855, ii. 32, where a specimen of his oratory is given. See also
John. Misc. i. 110.

[7] For Johnson's *Life of Roger
Ascham* see Johnson's *Works*, vi. 503.

notice before the elegies of Milton it was perhaps Alabaster's *Roxana*[1].

11   Of these exercises which the rules of the University required, some were published by him in his maturer years[2]. They had been undoubtedly applauded, for they were such as few can perform: yet there is reason to suspect that he was regarded in his college with no great fondness[3]. That he obtained no fellowship is certain[4]; but the unkindness with which he was treated was not merely negative: I am ashamed to relate what I fear is true, that Milton was one of the last students in either university that suffered the publick indignity of corporal correction[5].

12   It was, in the violence of controversial hostility, objected to him that he was expelled[6]; this he steadily denies, and it was apparently not true; but it seems plain from his own verses to Diodati that he had incurred *Rustication*, a temporary dismission into the country, with perhaps the loss of a term:

> 'Me tenet urbs refluâ quam Thamesis alluit undâ,
> Meque nec invitum patria dulcis habet.
> Jam nec arundiferum mihi cura revisere Camum,
> Nec dudum *vetiti* me *laris* angit amor.—

[1] William Alabaster's *Roxana*, 'in the style of the turgid Seneca, written in 1592, was first published in 1632.' T. WARTON, *Milton's Poems*, p. 430. For a mystical sermon of his see *The Spectator*, No. 221. Cromwell, in his first speech in parliament, accused him of 'preaching flat Popery at Paul's Cross.' Carlyle's *Cromwell*, ed. 1857, i. 50.

Warton (*Milton's Poems*, Preface, p. 16) adds Leland to Milton's predecessors 'who wrote with classic elegance.'

[2] *Post*, MILTON, 176.

[3] He was unpopular in his College in his early career, but 'he passed through a final stage of triumph.' Masson's *Milton*, i. 270, 307.

[4] In one election Charles I 'willed and required' the Master and Fellows to choose a youth five years his junior—Edward King, whose death he was to lament in *Lycidas*. *Ib*. i. 238. See also *ib*. p. 239 *n*. for the interference of the Secretary of State in another election. For Dryden's

not obtaining a fellowship see *post*, DRYDEN, 6.

[5] In the first edition, 'was the last student,' &c. Aubrey, after stating that Milton 'received some unkindnesse from his first tutor, Mr. Chappell,' adds in the margin:—'whip't him.' *Brief Lives*, ii. 63. Johnson's authority was Aubrey's *MS.*, says Masson (i. 159), who shows that, if there is any truth in the story, there is more exaggeration. For whipping at both universities see T. Warton's *Milton's Poems*, p. 421, and for a threatened whipping at Queen's College, Oxford, in 1680 see *Hist. MSS. Com.* Report xii. App. 7, pp. 166, 168.

[6] *Post*, MILTON, 48. 'Aiunt hominem Cantabrigiensi Academia ob flagitia pulsum dedecus et patriam fugisse, et in Italiam commigrasse.' *Regii Sanguinis Clamor*, &c., 1652, p. 9.

'He left the university of his own accord, and was not expelled for misdemeanours, as his adversaries have said.' WOOD, *Fasti Oxon.* i. 480.

Nec duri libet usque minas perferre magistri
Cæteraque ingenio non subeunda meo.
Si sit hoc *exilium* patrios adiisse penates,
Et vacuum curis otia grata sequi,
Non ego vel *profugi* nomen sortemve recuso,
Lætus et *exilii* conditione fruor [1].

I cannot find any meaning but this, which even kindness [13] and reverence can give to the term *vetiti laris*, 'a habitation from which he is excluded,' or how *exile* can be otherwise interpreted. He declares yet more, that he is weary of enduring 'the threats of a rigorous master, and something else, which a temper like his cannot undergo [2].' What was more than threat was probably punishment. This poem, which mentions his *exile*, proves likewise that it was not perpetual, for it concludes with a resolution of returning some time to Cambridge [3]. And it may be conjectured from the willingness with which he has perpetuated the memory of his exile, that its cause was such as gave him no shame [4].

He took both the usual degrees, that of Batchelor in 1628, [14] and that of Master in 1632 [5]; but he left the university with no kindness for its institution [6], alienated either by the injudicious

---

[1] *Eleg. Liber.* i. 9. Thus translated by Cowper :—
'I well content, where Thames with influent tide
My native city laves, meantime reside,
Nor zeal nor duty now my steps impel
To ready Cam, and my forbidden cell.
. . . .
'Tis time that I a pedant's threats disdain,
And fly from wrongs my soul will ne'er sustain.
If peaceful days, in letter'd leisure spent
Beneath my father's roof, be banishment,
Then call me banish'd, I will ne'er refuse
A name expressive of the lot I choose.'
Southey's *Cowper*, x. 130.

[2] 'Here, indeed,' writes Dr. Symmons, 'Johnson translates with sufficient correctness; but in the following sentence this "something else" is changed into "something more," and we are told that what was *more* than threat was evidently punishment ! ! !' Milton's *Works*, vii. 32.

[3] 'Stat quoque iuncosas Cami remeare paludes,
Atque iterum raucae murmur adire Scholae.' *Eleg. Liber*, i. 89.
'And I will even repass Cam's reedy pools,
To face once more the warfare of the schools.'
Southey's *Cowper*, x. 133.

[4] This sentence is not in the first edition.

[5] 'He kept every term at Cambridge until he graduated as M.A. on July 3, 1632.' LESLIE STEPHEN, *Dict. Nat. Biog.* xxxviii. 25.
'Magistri quem vocant gradum cum laude etiam adeptus.' *Works*, v. 230.

[6] In his *Apology for Smectymnuus* (1642) he says of his university :—
'which, as in the time of her better health and mine own younger judgment, I never greatly admired, so now much less.' *Ib.* i. 220.

severity of his governors, or his own captious perverseness[1]. The cause cannot now be known, but the effect appears in his writings. His scheme of education, inscribed to Hartlib[2], supersedes all academical instruction ; being intended to comprise the whole time which men usually spend in literature, from their entrance upon grammar, 'till they proceed, as it is called, masters of arts[3].' And in his Discourse *On the likeliest Way* [*Means*] *to remove Hirelings out of the Church*, he ingeniously proposes that 'the profits of the lands forfeited by the act for superstitious uses should be applied to such academies all over the land, where languages and arts may be taught together; so that youth may be at once brought up to a competency of learning and an honest trade, by which means such of them as had the gift, being enabled to support themselves (without tithes) by the latter, may, by the help of the former, become worthy preachers[4].'

15   One of his objections to academical education as it was then conducted is that men designed for orders in the Church were permitted to act plays, 'writhing and unboning their clergy limbs to all the antick and dishonest gestures of Trincalos[5], buffoons and bawds, prostituting the shame of that ministry which [either] they had or were near [nigh] having to the eyes of courtiers and court-ladies, [with] their grooms and mademoiselles[6].'

16   This is sufficiently peevish in a man who, when he mentions his exile from the college, relates with great luxuriance the compensation which the pleasures of the theatre afford him[7]. Plays were therefore only criminal when they were acted by academicks.

17   He went to the university with a design of entering into

---

[1] Wood describes him as 'a great reproacher of the universities, scholastical degrees, decency and uniformity in the Church.' *Fasti Oxon.* i. 482. See also *Works*, i. 55, 275.

[2] See Appendix K.

[3] 'Commencing, as they term it, master of art.' *Works*, i. 277.

[4] This is an abstract of Milton's words. *Ib.* iii. 376-7.

[5] A character in Tomkis's *Albumazar*, first acted at Cambridge in 1614. Pepys, who saw it acted on Feb. 22, 1667-8, recorded :—'The king here, and, indeed, all of us pretty merry at the mimique tricks of Trinkilo.' *Diary*, iv. 366.

[6] From *An Apology for Smectymnuus*, *Works*, i. 221. He continues :—'There, while they acted and overacted, among other young scholars I was a spectator; they thought themselves gallant men and I thought them fools.'

[7] *Eleg. Liber*, i. 27-46.
Cowper's translation begins :—
'Here too I visit, or to smile or weep,
The winding theatre's majestic sweep.'
Southey's *Cowper*, x. 131.

the church[1], but in time altered his mind; for he declared that
whoever became a clergyman must 'subscribe slave and take an
oath withal, which, unless he took with a conscience that could
[would] retch, he must [either] straight perjure himself [or split
his faith]. He [I] thought it better to prefer a blameless silence
before the [sacred] office of speaking, bought and begun with
servitude and forswearing[2].'

These expressions are I find applied to the subscription of 18
the Articles[3], but it seems more probable that they relate to
canonical obedience. I know not any of the Articles which
seem to thwart his opinions[4]; but the thoughts of obedience,
whether canonical or civil, raised his indignation.

His unwillingness to engage in the ministry, perhaps not 19
yet advanced to a settled resolution of declining it, appears in
a letter to one of his friends who had reproved his suspended
and dilatory life, which he seems to have imputed to an insatiable
curiosity and fantastick luxury of various knowledge[5]. To this
he writes a cool and plausible answer, in which he endeavors to
persuade him that the delay proceeds not from the delights of
desultory study, but from the desire of obtaining more fitness
for his task; and that he goes on 'not taking thought of being
late, so it give advantage to be more fit[6].'

When he left the university he returned to his father, then 20
residing at Horton in Buckinghamshire[7], with whom he lived
five years[8]; in which time he is said to have read all the
Greek and Latin writers[9]. With what limitations this universality
is to be understood who shall inform us?

---

[1] 'To whose service, by the intentions of my parents and friends, I was destined of a child, and in mine own resolutions.' *Works*, i. 123.

[2] *Ib.*

[3] 'Subscribing to the Articles was in his opinion subscribing slave.' *Milton's Poems, with Life*, ed. Newton, 1770, Preface, p. 5.

[4] *Post*, MILTON, 149, 166. He had already, as Professor Masson points out, twice subscribed the Articles in taking his University degrees. It was 'the general condition of the Church of England' under Laud that he disliked. 'He was "Church-outed by the Prelates"' [*Works*, i. 124] is his own emphatic phrase.' Masson's *Milton*, i. 326.

[5] Milton in his answer speaks of 'a poor, regardless, and unprofitable sin of curiosity'; 'the empty and fantastic chase of shadows and notions'; and 'the endless delight of speculation.' *Works*, vii. 48-9.

[6] *Ib.* vii. 49.

[7] At Horton he wrote among other poems *L'Allegro, Il Penseroso, Comus*, and *Lycidas*. There his mother died. For the village and his life there see Masson's *Milton*, i. 552-663.

[8] 'Exacto in hunc modum quinquennio,' &c. *Works*, v. 230.

[9] Newton's *Milton*, Preface, p. 5. Milton wrote to Diodati on Sept. 23, 1637, that he had read the whole of

21   It might be supposed that he who read so much should
have done nothing else; but Milton found time to write the
Masque of *Comus* [1], which was presented at Ludlow, then the
residence of the Lord President of Wales [2], in 1634, and had
the honour of being acted by the Earl of Bridgewater's sons [3]
and daughter. The fiction is derived from Homer's *Circe* [4];
but we never can refuse to any modern the liberty of borrowing
from Homer:

'—a quo ceu fonte perenni
Vatum Pieriis ora rigantur aquis [5].'

22   His next production was *Lycidas*, an elegy written in 1637
on the death of Mr. King [6], the son of Sir John King, secretary
for Ireland in the time of Elizabeth, James, and Charles. King
was much a favourite at Cambridge, and many of the wits
joined to do honour to his memory [7]. Milton's acquaintance
with the Italian writers [8] may be discovered by a mixture of
longer and shorter verses, according to the rules of Tuscan
poetry, and his malignity to the Church by some lines which
are interpreted as threatening its extermination [9].

Greek history, and the history of the Italians under the Lombards, Franks, and Germans down to Rudolf who granted the Italians their liberty. *Works*, vi. 116. In *Defensio Secunda* he writes:—'Paterno rure . . . evolvendis Graecis Latinisque scriptoribus summum per otium totus vacavi.' *Ib.* v. 230.

'Milton's Greek Poetry,' wrote C. Burney, 'is abominably bad.' Parr's *Works*, vii. 408. For Burney's *Remarks on the Greek Verses of Milton* see T. Warton's *Milton's Poems*, p. 591.

[1] Published in 1637. *Post*, MILTON, 175, 194.

[2] *Post*, BUTLER, 9; Masson's *Milton*, i. 587, 604.

[3] The elder of the sons, nearly twenty years later, wrote on a copy of Milton's *Defensio* [*post*, MILTON, 67]:—'Liber igni, Author furca, dignissimi (Book richly deserving the fire, Author the gallows).' Masson's *Milton*, iv. 531.

[4] *Odyssey*, x. 133–end. 'It was rather taken from the *Comus* of Erycius Puteanus, published at Louvain in 1611.' HAWKINS, Johnson's *Works*, 1787, i. 90. For other modern pieces it resembled see T.

Warton's *Milton's Poems*, p. 135; Masson's *Milton*, i. 622.

'Lawes' music to *Comus* was never printed; but by a MS. in his own hand it appears that the two songs *Sweet Echo* and *Sabrina Fair*, together with three other passages, "Back, shepherds, back"; "To the ocean now I fly"; "Now my task is smoothly done," were the whole of the original music, and that the rest was uttered as blank verse.' HAWKINS, *Hist. of Music*, iv. 52, where the music to *Sweet Echo* is given. See Milton's *Sonnet to Lawes* (No. xiii). For masques see Masson's *Milton*, i. 578; Pattison's *Milton*, p. 21.

[5] OVID, *Amores*, iii. 9. 25.

[6] *Ante*, MILTON, 11 n.

[7] They honoured it in three Greek, nineteen Latin, and thirteen English poems, printed at Cambridge in 1638. T. Warton's *Milton's Poems*, p. 37.

[8] *Post*, MILTON, 271.

[9] *Lycidas*, ll. 108–31. 'This passage raises in us a thrill of awe-struck expectation which I can only compare with that excited by the Cassandra of Aeschylus's *Agamemnon*.' PATTISON, *Milton*, p. 29. *Post*, MILTON, 180.

He is supposed about this time to have written his *Arcades* ; 23
for while he lived at Horton he used sometimes to steal from
his studies a few days, which he spent at Harefield, the house of
the countess dowager of Derby [1], where the *Arcades* made part
of a dramatick entertainment.

He began now to grow weary of the country, and had 24
some purpose of taking chambers in the Inns of Court [2], when
the death of his mother [3] set him at liberty to travel, for
which he obtained his father's consent and Sir Henry Wotton's
directions [4], with the celebrated precept of prudence, *i pensieri
stretti, ed il viso sciolto*, 'thoughts close, and looks loose [5].'

In 1638 he left England, and went first to Paris, where, 25
by the favour of Lord Scudamore, he had the opportunity of
visiting Grotius [6], then residing at the French court as ambassador
from Christina of Sweden. From Paris he hasted into Italy,
of which he had with particular diligence studied the language
and literature ; and, though he seems to have intended a very
quick perambulation of the country, staid two months at
Florence ; where he found his way into the academies [7], and

---

[1] Her cousin, Edmund Spenser, had dedicated to her his *Tears of the Muses*, and now Milton wrote *Part of an Entertainment presented to the Countess by some Noble Persons of her Family*. There is no evidence that he was her guest. Masson's *Milton*, i. 598 *n*.

[2] On Sept. 23, 1637, he wrote to Diodati from London:—'Dicam iam nunc serio quid cogitem, in hospitium iuridicorum aliquod immigrare, sicubi amoena et umbrosa ambulatio est . . . ; ubi nunc sum, ut nosti, obscure et anguste sum.' *Works*, vi. 116.

[3] She died on April 3, 1637. *Gent. Mag.* 1787, p. 779 ; Masson's *Milton*, i. 632. Milton described her as 'mater probatissima, et eleemosynis per viciniam potissimum nota.' *Works*, v. 230.

[4] Johnson's authority is Milton's *Defensio Secunda. Ib.* v. 231. For Wotton's letter to Milton see *ib.* vii. 85, and for his *Life* see Walton's *Lives*. Horton is within an easy walk of Eton College, of which Wotton was Provost.

[5] Wotton says that he got this advice from ' an old Roman courtier

in dangerous times, having been steward to the Duca di Pagliano, who, with all his family, were [*sic*] strangled, save this only man, that escaped by foresight of the tempest.' Milton's *Works*, vii. 87.

It was a favourite maxim of Chesterfield's. ' The height of abilities,' he wrote, ' is to have *volto sciolto*, and *pensieri stretti* ; that is, a frank, open, and ingenuous exterior, with a prudent and reserved interior : to be upon your own guard, and yet, by a seeming natural openness, to put people off of theirs.' *Letters to his Son*, ii. 90.

[6] Scudamore was the English ambassador at Paris. *Works*, v. 231. Johnson described Grotius as a scholar ' from whom perhaps every man of learning has learnt something.' Boswell's *Johnson*, iii. 125.

[7] ' The academies in Italy corresponded to what are now called clubs, or to our literary and debating societies. . . . A list has been drawn up of more than 500 known to have existed before 1729.' Masson's *Milton*, i. 764. In the minutes of one of these, the *Apatisti*, preserved in the Magliabecchian Library at Florence, it is

produced his compositions with such applause as appears to have exalted him in his own opinion, and confirmed him in the hope, that 'by labour and intense study, which,' says he, 'I take to be my portion in this life, joined with a [the] strong propensity of nature,' he might '[perhaps] leave something so written to after-times, as they should not willingly let it die[1].'

26 It appears in all his writings that he had the usual concomitant of great abilities, a lofty and steady confidence in himself, perhaps not without some contempt of others[2]; for scarcely any man ever wrote so much and praised so few[3]. Of his praise he was very frugal, as he set its value high; and considered his mention of a name as a security against the waste of time and a certain preservative from oblivion[4].

27 At Florence he could not indeed complain that his merit wanted distinction. Carlo Dati presented him with an encomiastick inscription, in the tumid lapidary style[5]; and Francini wrote him an ode, of which the first stanza is only empty noise, the rest are perhaps too diffuse on common topicks, but the last is natural and beautiful.

28 From Florence he went to Sienna, and from Sienna to Rome, where he was again received with kindness by the Learned and the Great. Holstenius, the keeper of the Vatican Library, who had resided three years at Oxford[6], introduced him to Cardinal Barberini; and he at a musical entertainment waited

recorded that on Sept. 16, 1638:—'Il Giovanni Miltone, Inglese, lesse una poesia latina di versi esametri molto erudita.' Masson's *Milton*, i. 782.

For the foundation of these academies by the pastoral versifiers see Baretti's *Account of the Manners, &c., of Italy*, 1768, i. 254.

[1] *Works*, i. 119, 224; v. 231. *Post*, MILTON, 47.

[2] *Post*, MILTON, 138, 231, 277. See also the last lines of his *Ad Patrem*. *Sylvarum Liber*, vi. 115. Johnson had this 'lofty and steady confidence in himself'; also Dryden (*post*, DRYDEN, 161), Addison (*post*, ADDISON, 109), and Pope (*post*, POPE, 20).

[3] 'In his sonnets, and in his *Defensio Secunda*, he liberally praises all the leading men of the republican party.' Firth's *Milton*, p. 90.

[4] 'He can requite thee, for he knows the charms

That call fame on such gentle acts as these,

And he can spread thy name o'er lands and seas,

Whatever clime the sun's bright circle warms.' *Sonnets*, No. viii.

[5] *Lapidary*, as an adjective, is not in Johnson's *Dictionary*. See *post*, MILTON, 275, where Johnson writes:— 'Blank verse makes some approach to that which is called the *lapidary style*.' 'In lapidary inscriptions,' he said, 'a man is not upon oath.' Boswell's *Johnson*, ii. 407. For Dati's inscription and Francini's ode see Milton's *Poetical Works* (ed. W. Aldis Wright), pp. 493-5, and for translations of them see Masson's *Milton*, i. 783-5. Dati was but eighteen. *Ib.* i. 775. Milton mentions them in his *Epitaphium Damonis*, l. 136.

[6] *Works*, vi. 120; Masson's *Milton*, i. 798.

for him at the door, and led him by the hand into the assembly [1]. Here Selvaggi praised him in a distich [2] and Salsilli in a tetrastick [3]; neither of them of much value. The Italians were gainers by this literary commerce: for the encomiums with which Milton repaid Salsilli, though not secure against a stern grammarian [4], turn the balance indisputably in Milton's favour [5].

Of these Italian testimonies, poor as they are [6], he was proud 29 enough to publish them before his poems; though he says, he cannot be suspected but to have known that they were said *non tam de se, quam supra se* [7].

At Rome, as at Florence, he staid only two months; a time 30 indeed sufficient if he desired only to ramble with an explainer of its antiquities or to view palaces and count pictures, but certainly too short for the contemplation of learning, policy, or manners [8].

---

[1] 'Ipse me tanta in turba quaesitum ad fores expectans, et pene manu prehensum persane honorifice intro admisit.' *Works*, vi. 120.

Evelyn, in 1644, wrote that 'Francisco Barberini styled himself Protector of the English, to whom he was indeed very courteous.' *Diary*, i. 130. Barberini was nephew of the Pope, Urban VIII. Masson's *Milton*, i. 798.

According to Ménage, Holstein, by publicly styling Barberini *Eminentissimus*, so provoked the jealousy of the Cardinals, that the Pope decreed that they should all be addressed as *Eminence* and *Eminentissime*. *Menagiana*, iii. 289.

[2] Milton's *Poetical Works* (ed. W. Aldis Wright), p. 492. Dryden's inscription under Milton's picture is an amplification of this distich. *Works*, xi. 162. Cowper turned Dryden's lines into Latin verse. Southey's *Cowper*, x. 237. 'Who Selvaggi was I have not been able to ascertain.' Masson's *Milton*, i. 805.

[3] Milton's *Poetical Works* (ed. W. A. Wright), p. 492. 'Giovanni Salzilli is a poet not mentioned in any of the histories of Italian literature.' Masson's *Milton*, i. 806.

[4] Bishop Wordsworth, in an article *On some Faults in Milton's Latin Poetry*, after writing:—'I admire Milton's Latin verses upon the whole very much,' adds that Johnson's re-

mark 'must not be confined to this one production.' *Classical Review*, i. 48.

[5] T. Warton (*Milton's Poems*, p. 534) says of this poem:—'I know not any finer modern Latin lyric poetry than from this verse [23] to the end. The close is perfectly antique.'

'The scazons to Salsilli are a just and equitable return for his quatrain; for they are full of false quantities, without an iota of poetry.' LANDOR, *Imag. Conver.* iv. 297. For Cowper's translation of them see Southey's *Cowper*, x. 169.

[6] Milton, in his *Speech for the Liberty of Unlicensed Printing*, says that 'the learned men' of Italy 'did nothing but bemoan the servile condition into which learning amongst them was brought; ... that nothing had been written there now these many years but flattery and fustian.' *Works*, i. 313.

[7] The preface to the Latin poems thus begins:—'Haec quae sequuntur de Authore testimonia, tametsi ipse intelligebat non tam de se quam supra se esse dicta,' &c. 'Though these following testimonies concerning the Author,' he says, 'were understood by himself to be pronounced not so much *about* him as *over* him, by way of subject or occasion.' Masson's *Milton*, iii. 454.

[8] 'Postquam illius urbis antiquitas

31   From Rome he passed on to Naples, in company of a hermit;
a companion from whom little could be expected, yet to him
Milton owed his introduction to Manso, marquis of Villa, who
had been before the patron of Tasso[1]. Manso was enough
delighted with his accomplishments to honour him with a sorry
distich, in which he commends him for every thing but his
religion[2]; and Milton in return addressed him in a Latin
poem, which must have raised an high opinion of English
elegance and literature[3].

32   His purpose was now to have visited Sicily and Greece, but
hearing of the differences between the king and parliament,
he thought it proper to hasten home rather than pass his life in
foreign amusements while his countrymen were contending for
their rights[4]. He therefore came back to Rome, though the
merchants informed him of plots laid against him by the
Jesuits, for the liberty of his conversations on religion. He
had sense enough to judge that there was no danger, and therefore kept on his way, and acted as before, neither obtruding nor
shunning controversy[5]. He had perhaps given some offence by
visiting Galileo, then a prisoner in the Inquisition for philosophical

et prisca fama me ad bimestre fere
spatium tenuisset, Neapolim perrexi.'
Works, v. 231.

Gibbon gave 'the daily labour of
eighteen weeks' to 'a cool and minute
investigation' of Rome, under the
guidance of an antiquary, 'till,' he
continues, ' I was myself qualified, in
a last review, to select and study the
capital works of ancient and modern
art.' Gibbon's *Memoirs*, p. 163.
Matthew Arnold wrote:—'I think
three days will do what is indispensable at Rome.' *Letters*, 1895, i. 272.

[1] Milton thus writes of Manso in the
Preface to his Latin poem *Mansus*:—
'Ad quem Torquati Tassi dialogus
extat de Amicitia scriptus; erat
enim Tassi amicissimus; ab quo
etiam inter Campaniae principes cele-
bratur in illo poemate cui titulus
Gerusalemme Conquistata, lib. 20.
" Fra cavalier magnanimi e cortesi
    Risplende il Manso."'
In his *Epitaphium Damonis*, l. 182,
he describes him as
' Mansus Chalcidicae non ultima
    gloria ripae.'

See also *Works*, v. 231; Pattison's
Milton, p. 38, and Masson's *Milton*,
i. 808.

[2] ' Ut mens, forma, decor, facies, mos,
    si pietas sic,
    Non *Anglus*, verum hercle *An-
        gelus* ipse, fores.'
Milton's *Poetical Works* (ed. W. A.
Wright, p. 492).

[3] *Ib.* pp. 534-7. 'How gloriously he
bursts forth again in all his splendour
for Manso. . . . What a glorious verse
[84] is—
" Frangam Saxonicas Britonum sub
    Marte phalanges"!'
    LANDOR, *Imag. Conver.* iv. 297.

[4] *Works*, v. 231.

[5] ' Sic enim mecum statueram, de
religione quidem iis in locis sermones
ultro non inferre; interrogatus de
fide, quicquid essem passurus, nihil
dissimulare.' *Ib.* p. 232.

Evelyn, visiting Milan in 1646, says
that ' English travellers but rarely
would be known to pass through that
city for fear of the Inquisition.' *Diary*,
i. 237. See also Masson's *Milton*, i.
821; iv. 475.

heresy[1]; and at Naples he was told by Manso that, by his declarations on religious questions, he had excluded himself from some distinctions which he should otherwise have paid him[2]. But such conduct, though it did not please, was yet sufficiently safe; and Milton staid two months more at Rome, and went on to Florence without molestation.

From Florence he visited Lucca[3]. He afterwards went to **33** Venice[4], and having sent away a collection of musick and other books travelled to Geneva, which he probably considered as the metropolis of orthodoxy[5]. Here he reposed as in a congenial element, and became acquainted with John Diodati[6] and Frederick Spanheim[7], two learned professors of Divinity. From Geneva he passed through France, and came home after an absence of a year and three months.

At his return he heard of the death of his friend Charles **34** Diodati[8]; a man whom it is reasonable to suppose of great merit, since he was thought by Milton worthy of a poem, intituled *Epitaphium Damonis*, written with the common but childish imitation of pastoral life[9].

[1] 'There it was that I found and visited the famous Galileo grown old, a prisoner to the Inquisition, for thinking in astronomy otherwise than the Franciscan and Dominican licensers thought.' *Works*, i. 313. Galileo is 'the Tuscan artist' of *Paradise Lost*, i. 288. See also *ib.* v. 262.

He was living in his villa at Arcetri, 'just beyond the walls of Florence,' but 'under certain restrictions on his liberty imposed by the Holy Office.' At Rome he had been confined in a prison. Masson's *Milton*, i. 766, 788.

[2] *Works*, v. 231.

[3] The native place of the family of his friend Charles Diodati. Milton's *Epit. Damonis*, Argumentum.

[4] 'Cui urbi lustrandae quum mensem unum impendissem,' &c. *Works*, v. 232. 'The spectacle of Venice,' wrote Gibbon, 'afforded some hours of astonishment and some days of disgust.' *Auto.* ed. Murray, p. 268.

[5] Evelyn wrote of Geneva in 1646:— 'The Church Government is severely Presbyterian ... but nothing so rigid as either our Scots or English sectaries of that denomination.' *Diary*, i. 249.

[6] 'Genevae cum Ioanne Deodato, theologiae professore doctissimo, quotidianus versabar.' *Works*, v. 232.

Evelyn, who visited him in 1646, describes him as 'the famous Italian minister and translator of the Bible into that language.' *Diary*, i. 246. See also Masson's *Milton*, i. 99.

[7] 'Vir sane doctus et pastor integerrimus.' *Works*, v. 206. He was the father of Ezechiel Spanheim, whose 'great work *De Praestantia et Usu Numismatum*' Gibbon read. Gibbon's *Memoirs*, p. 160.

[8] His father, John Diodati's brother, had settled in England as a physician. Charles was Milton's school fellow at St. Paul's. He died in Aug. 1638. The name is pronounced Diodăti. Masson's *Milton*, i. 98, 102, 829.

[9] For Johnson's contempt of pastoral poetry see *post*, MILTON, 181.

'I am now,' wrote Cowper, 'translating Milton's *Epitaphium Damonis*, a pastoral in my judgment equal to any of Virgil's *Bucolics*, but of which Dr. Johnson (so it pleased him) speaks contemptuously. But he who never saw any beauty in a rural scene was not likely to have much taste for a

35   He now hired a lodging at the house of one Russel, a taylor in St. Bride's Churchyard, and undertook the education of John and Edward Philips, his sister's sons [1]. Finding his rooms too little he took a house and garden in Aldersgate street [2], which was not then so much out of the world as it is now, and chose his dwelling at the upper end of a passage that he might avoid the noise of the street. Here he received more boys, to be boarded and instructed.

36   Let not our veneration for Milton forbid us to look with some degree of merriment on great promises and small performance, on the man who hastens home because his countrymen are contending for their liberty, and, when he reaches the scene of action, vapours away his patriotism in a private boarding-school [3]. This is the period of his life from which all his biographers seem inclined to shrink. They are unwilling that Milton should be degraded to a schoolmaster [4]; but, since it cannot be denied that he taught boys, one finds out that he taught for nothing, and another that his motive was only zeal for the propagation of learning and virtue [5]; and all tell what they do not know to be true, only to excuse an act which no wise man will consider as in itself disgraceful [6]. His father was alive, his allowance was not ample, and he supplied its deficiencies by an honest and useful employment.

pastoral.' Southey's *Cowper*, vii. 69. For the translation see *ib*. x. 175 ; also Masson's *Milton*, ii. 85.

T. Warton, criticizing Johnson's criticism, says (*Milton's Poems*, p. 562) :—' Milton cannot be a shepherd long. His own native powers often break forth, and cannot bear the assumed disguise.'

' In it [the *Epitaphium*] there are many beautiful verses ; for instance—

"Ovium quoque taedet, at illae Moerent, inque suum convertunt ora magistrum" [l. 66].

The pause at *moerent*, and the word also, show the great master.' LANDOR, *Imag. Conver.* iv. 298.

[1] *Ante*, MILTON, 5 ; Phillips' *Milton*, p. 16. Aubrey adds :—' He made his nephews songsters, and sing from the time they were with him.' *Brief Lives*, ii. 64.

[2] ' He took a pretty garden-house in Aldersgate Street, at the end of an entry. There are few streets in London more free from noise than that.' Phillips' *Milton*, p. 20.

' A garden-house is a house situate in a garden. The term is technical.' HAWKINS, Johnson's *Works*, 1787, i. 94.

[3] Milton wrote of his house :—' Ibi ad intermissa studia beatulus me recepi ; rerum exitu Deo imprimis, et quibus id muneris populus dabat, facile permisso.' *Works*, v. 232.

[4] *Post*, BLACKMORE, 3.

[5] *Post*, MILTON, 60 ; Toland's *Life of Milton*, p. 25 ; Richardson's *Explanatory Notes, &c., on Paradise Lost, with Life*, p. 70 ; *Milton's Poems, with Life*, ed. Newton, Preface, p. 17.

[6] Johnson, who had himself been a schoolmaster (Boswell's *Johnson*, i. 97), quotes Peacham as observing that ' the schoolmaster has long been one of the ridiculous personages in the farces of Italy.' Johnson's *Shakespeare*, ii. 156.

It is told that in the art of education he performed wonders, 37
and a formidable list is given of the authors, Greek and Latin,
that were read in Aldersgate-street by youth between ten and
fifteen or sixteen years of age [1]. Those who tell or receive
these stories should consider that nobody can be taught faster
than he can learn. The speed of the horseman must be limited
by the power of his horse. Every man that has ever undertaken
to instruct others can tell what slow advances he has been able
to make, and how much patience it requires to recall vagrant
inattention, to stimulate sluggish indifference, and to rectify absurd
misapprehension.

The purpose of Milton, as it seems, was to teach something 38
more solid than the common literature of schools, by reading
those authors that treat of physical subjects; such as the
Georgick, and astronomical treatises of the ancients [2]. This was
a scheme of improvement which seems to have busied many
literary projectors of that age. Cowley, who had more means
than Milton of knowing what was wanting to the embellishments
of life, formed the same plan of education in his imaginary College [3].

But the truth is that the knowledge of external nature, and the 39
sciences which that knowledge requires or includes, are not the
great or the frequent business of the human mind. Whether we
provide for action or conversation, whether we wish to be useful
or pleasing, the first requisite is the religious and moral knowledge of right and wrong [4]; the next is an acquaintance with the

---

[1] Phillips' *Milton*, p. 17; Masson's
Milton, iii. 253. 'We do amiss to
spend seven or eight years merely
in scraping together so much miserable Latin and Greek as might be
learned otherwise easily and delight-
fully in one year.' *Works*, i. 275.
Aubrey says that Milton made his
two nephews, boys of nine and ten,
'in a year's time capable of interpreting a Latin author at sight. And
within three years they went through
the best of Latin and Greek poetts.'
Brief Lives, ii. 64.
That great linguist, Sir W. Jones,
in studying modern languages, 'followed in all respects Milton's plan of
education, which he had by heart.'
Teignmouth's *Life of Jones*, p. 42.
See also Ascham's *Scholemaster*, ed.
Arber, p. 90.

[2] *Works*, i. 278.
[3] Cowley, after stating that 'it is
deplorable to consider the loss which
children make of their time at most
schools, employing, or rather casting
away, six or seven years in the learning of words only, and that too very
imperfectly,' sketches a method for
the school of his College 'for the
infusing knowledge and language at
the same time into them.' *Eng.
Poets*, ix. 145. In the *Davideis* he
describes a College
'By Samuel built, and moderately
endow'd.' *Ib*. viii. 201.
See also Pattison's *Milton*, p. 47.
'JOHNSON. Education in England
has been in danger of being hurt by
two of its greatest men, Milton and
Locke.' Boswell's *Johnson*, iii. 358.
[4] 'The end of learning is to repair

history of mankind, and with those examples which may be said to embody truth and prove by events the reasonableness of opinions. Prudence and Justice are virtues and excellences of all times and of all places ; we are perpetually moralists, but we are geometricians only by chance. Our intercourse with intellectual nature is necessary ; our speculations upon matter are voluntary and at leisure. Physiological [1] learning is of such rare emergence that one man may know another half his life without being able to estimate his skill in hydrostaticks or astronomy, but his moral and prudential character immediately appears.

40　　Those authors, therefore, are to be read at schools that supply most axioms of prudence, most principles of moral truth, and most materials for conversation ; and these purposes are best served by poets, orators, and historians.

41　　Let me not be censured for this digression as pedantick or paradoxical, for if I have Milton against me I have Socrates on my side. It was his labour to turn philosophy from the study of nature to speculations upon life, but the innovators whom I oppose are turning off attention from life to nature. They seem to think that we are placed here to watch the growth of plants, or the motions of the stars. Socrates was rather of opinion that what we had to learn was, how to do good and avoid evil.

Ὅττι τοι ἐν μεγάροισι κακόν τ' ἀγαθόν τε τέτυκται [2].

the ruins of our first parents by regaining to know God aright. . . . I call a complete and generous education that which fits a man to perform justly, skilfully, and magnanimously all the offices, both private and public, of peace and war.' *Works*, i. 274, 277. See also *ib.* i. 280, where he describes how 'their young and pliant affections are led through all the moral works of Plato, Xenophon, Cicero,' &c.

[1] *Physiology*, which is now defined as 'the science of the functions of living beings,' was defined by Johnson as 'the doctrine of the constitution of the works of nature.' See *post*, MILTON, 208, for 'physiology.'

[2] *Odyssey*, iv. 392.
　　'What good, what ill
Hath in thine house befallen.'
　　　　Southey's *Cowper*, xiii. 87.
　　Johnson might have quoted from *Paradise Lost*, viii. 191 :—

'That not to know at large of things
　　remote
From use, obscure and subtle, but to
　　know
That which before us lies in daily
　　life
Is the prime wisdom.'

　　Swift makes Gulliver, when among the Houyhnhnms, say:—'When I used to explain to my master our several systems of natural philosophy he would laugh, "that a creature pretending to reason should value itself upon the knowledge of other people's conjectures, and in things where that knowledge, if it were certain, could be of no use." Wherein he agreed entirely with the sentiments of Socrates as Plato delivers them.' *Gulliver's Travels*, Part iv, ch. 8.
　　See also *Rasselas*, ch. 46; *The Rambler*, Nos. 24, 180; and Boswell's *Johnson*, iii. 358.

Of institutions we may judge by their effects. From this **42**
wonder-working academy I do not know that there ever proceeded any man very eminent for knowledge ; its only genuine
product, I believe, is a small *History of Poetry*, written in Latin
by his nephew Philips, of which perhaps none of my readers
has ever heard [1].

That in his school, as in every thing else which he under- **43**
took, he laboured with great diligence, there is no reason for
doubting. One part of his method deserves general imitation :
he was careful to instruct his scholars in religion. Every Sunday was spent upon theology, of which he dictated a short
system, gathered from the writers that were then fashionable in
the Dutch universities [2].

He set his pupils an example of hard study and spare diet [3] ; **44**
only now and then he allowed himself to pass a day of festivity
and indulgence with some gay gentlemen of Gray's Inn [4].

He now began to engage in the controversies of the times, and **45**
lent his breath to blow the flames of contention [5]. In 1641 he
published a treatise of *Reformation* [6], in two books, against the

---

[1] Not in E. Phillips' *Theatrum
Poetarum*, but (as Johnson told Ma-
lone) his *Tractatulus* [*Tractatus*] *de
Carmine Dramatico*,&c.,1679. JAMES
BOSWELL, JUN., Johnson's *Works*,
vii. 77 *n*. For Milton's pupils see
Masson's *Milton*, iii. 656.

[2] Phillips says (*Milton*, p. 19) that
part 'of the Sunday's work was the
writing from his own dictation some
part, from time to time, of a Tractate
which he thought fit to collect from
the ablest of divines, . . . a perfect
System of Divinity.' See *post*, MIL-
TON, 83 *n*., 166 *n*.

[3] 'He gave an example to those
under him of hard study and spare
diet.' Phillips' *Milton*, p. 20.

The diet in an academy 'should
be plain, healthful, and moderate.'
MILTON, *Works*, i. 285.

'Plain living and high thinking.'
WORDSWORTH, *Sonnet written in
London*.

[4] 'Once in three weeks or a month
he would drop into the society of some
young sparks of his acquaintance, the
chief of whom were Mr. Alphry and
Mr. Miller, two gentlemen of Gray's
Inn, the Beaus of those times, but

nothing near so bad as those now-a-
days ; with these gentlemen he would
so far make bold with his body as
now and then to keep a Gawdy-day.'
Phillips' *Milton*, p. 20.
'To-day deep thoughts resolve with
me to drench
In mirth that after no repenting
draws ;
Let Euclid rest and Archimedes
pause.'
    MILTON, *Sonnets*, No. xxi.

[5] T. Warton (*Milton's Poems*, Preface, p. 13) lamented that 'those years
of his life in which imagination is on
the wing were wasted on temporary
topics. . . . Smit with the deplorable
polemics of puritanism he suddenly
ceased to gaze on "such sights as
youthful poets dream" [*L'Allegro*,
l. 129].' For Pattison's expansion of
this passage see his *Milton*, pp. 65,
88, and for John Morley's defence of
the poet see *Crit. Misc.* ed. 1886, iii.
160, and for Goldwin Smith's see
his Review of Pattison's *Milton* in
Lectures and Essays, 1881.

[6] *Of Reformation in England, and
the Causes that hitherto have hin-
dered it*, *Works*, i. 1.

established Church ; being willing to help the Puritans, who were, he says, 'inferior to the Prelates in learning[1].'

46   Hall[2], bishop of Norwich, had published an *Humble Remonstrance* in defence of Episcopacy, to which in 1641 six ministers, of whose names the first letters made the celebrated word *Smectymnuus*[3], gave their Answer. Of this answer a Confutation was attempted by the learned Usher[4]; and to the Confutation Milton published a Reply, intituled *Of Prelatical Episcopacy, and whether it may be deduced from the Apostolical Times, by virtue of those testimonies which are alledged to that purpose in some late treatises, one whereof goes under the name of James, Lord Bishop of Armagh*[5].

47   I have transcribed this title to shew, by his contemptuous mention of Usher, that he had now adopted the puritanical savageness of manners[6]. His next work was *The Reason of Church Government urged against Prelacy* [*Prelaty*], by Mr. John Milton, 1642[7]. In this book he discovers, not with ostentatious exultation, but with calm confidence, his high opinion of his own powers ; and promises to undertake something, he yet knows not what, that may be of use and honour to his country[8].

'This,' says he, 'is not to be obtained but by devout prayer to that Eternal Spirit that [who] can enrich with all utterance and knowledge, and sends out his Seraphim with the hallowed fire of his altar to touch and purify the lips of whom he pleases. To this must be added industrious and select reading, steady

---

[1] 'Ministris, facundiam hominis, ut ferebatur, aegre sustinentibus, suppetias tuli.' *Works*, v. 233. See also Newton's *Milton*, Preface, p. 19.

[2] *Post*, DRYDEN, 344 ; POPE, 380. He was at this time Bishop of Exeter ; he was translated to Norwich the same year. Gardiner's *Hist. Eng.* ix. 107, 274. For 'the significance of the very title' of his work see *ib.* x. 41 ; also Masson's *Milton*, ii. 123, 214.

[3] The five (not six) ministers were Stephen Marshall, Edmund Calamy, Thomas Young, Matthew Newcomen, and William Spurstow. *W* was represented by *uu*. Young was Milton's old tutor. *Ante*, MILTON, 6. 'There is something like proof that Milton had a hand in the pamphlet.' The postscript was written, in whole or in part, by him. Masson's *Milton*, ii. 238, 260. It is to be hoped that he had nothing to do with the passage where the Copernican theory is cited as a delusion. *Ib.* ii. 221. For the title of the book, too long to quote, see *ib.* ii. 219.

[4] *The Judgment of Dr. Rainoldes touching the originall of Episcopacy more largely confirmed out of Antiquity.* London, 1641. 'Usher, Johnson said, was the great luminary of the Irish Church ; and a greater, he added, no Church could boast of, at least in modern times.' Boswell's *Johnson*, ii. 132.

[5] *Works*, i. 60.

[6] For 'Milton's savageness' see *post*, ADDISON, 83.

[7] *Works*, i. 78.

[8] *Ante*, MILTON, 25.

observation, and [*deleted*] insight into all seemly and generous arts
and affairs ; till which in some measure be compast, [at mine own
peril and cost,] I refuse not to sustain this expectation [1].

From a promise like this, at once fervid, pious, and rational,
might be expected the *Paradise Lost* [2].

He published the same year two more pamphlets upon the 48
same question [3]. To one of his antagonists, who affirms that he
was 'vomited out of the university [4],' he answers in general terms :

' The Fellows of the College wherein I spent some years, at my
parting, after I had taken two degrees, as the manner is, signified
many times [ways] how much better it would content them that
I should [would] stay.—As for the common approbation or dislike of that place as now it is, that I should esteem or disesteem
myself the more for that, too simple [and too credulous] is the
answerer [confuter], if he think to obtain with me [or any right
discerner]. Of small practice were the [that] physician who could
not judge, by what [both] she and [or] her sister have of long time
vomited, that the worser stuff she strongly keeps in her stomach,
but the better she is ever kecking at, and is queasy : she vomits
now out of sickness ; but before it be well with her she must
vomit by strong physick. The university in the time of her
better health, and my [mine own] younger judgement, I never
greatly admired, but [so] now much less [5].'

This is surely the language of a man who thinks that he has 49
been injured. He proceeds to describe the course of his conduct,

---

[1] *Works*, i. 122. 'It is not neces-
sary to turn to the grander poetry of
Milton for verses more harmonious
than those adduced ; we find them
even in the midst of his prose. . . .
"When God commands to take the
  trumpet
And blow a shriller and a louder
  blast,
It rests not in Man's will what he
  shall do,
Or what he shall forbear."
This sentence in his *Treatise on
Prelaty* is printed in prose ; it sounds
like inspiration.' LANDOR, *Longer
Prose Works*, ii. 207.
The sentence runs in the original :
'But when God commands to take
the trumpet, and blow a dolorous or
a jarring blast, it lies not in man's
will what he shall say, or what he
shall conceal.' *Works*, i. 115.
[2] Professor Masson believes that

Milton had in view a poem on King
Arthur. Masson's *Milton*, ii. 95 ;
post, MILTON, 86.
[3] *Animadversions upon the Remonstrant's Defence against Smectymnuus*, 1641, and *An Apology
against a Pamphlet call'd A Modest
Confutation of the Animadversions
of the Remonstrant against Smectymnuus*, 1642, *Works*, i. 152, 207 ;
Masson's *Milton*, ii. 257, 398.
[4] ' Thus being grown to an impost-
hume in the breast of the University,
he was at length vomited out thence
into a suburb sink about London,
which, since his coming up, hath
groaned under two ills, Him and the
Plague.' Preface to *A Modest Confutation of a Slanderous and Scurrilous Libel*, &c., 1642, attributed to
Bishop Hall. See *ante*, MILTON,
12.
[5] *Works*, i. 219.

and the train of his thoughts ; and, because he has been suspected of incontinence, gives an account of his own purity : ' That if I be justly charged [have been justly taxed],' says he, ' with this crime, it may come upon me, [after all this my confession,] with [a] tenfold shame [1].'

50   The style of his piece is rough, and such perhaps was that of his antagonist.   This roughness he justifies, by great examples, in a long digression.   Sometimes he tries to be humorous :

'Lest I should take him for some chaplain in [at] hand, some squire of the body to his prelate, one who [that] serves not at the altar only, but at the Court-cupboard, he will bestow on us a pretty model of himself; and sets [sobs] me out half a dozen ptisical mottos, wherever he had them, hopping short in the measure of convulsion fits ; in which labour the agony of his wit having scaped narrowly, instead of well-sized periods, he greets us with a quantity of thumb-ring posies.'—And thus ends this section, or rather dissection, of himself [2].

Such is the controversial merriment of Milton; his gloomy seriousness is yet more offensive [3].   Such is his malignity *that hell grows darker at his frown* [4].

51   His father, after Reading was taken by Essex, came to reside in his house [5] ; and his school increased.   At Whitsuntide, in his thirty-fifth year, he married Mary, the daughter of Mr. Powel, a justice of the Peace in Oxfordshire [6].   He brought her to town

---

[1] *Works*, i. 226.   [2] *Ib.* pp. 237-9.
[3] Mr. C. H. Firth (*Milton*, p. 94) quotes the following remark from Coleridge (*Misc. Aesthetic and Literary*, ed. Ashe, p. 310) on this passage :—'The man who reads a work meant for immediate effect on one age with the notions and feelings of another may be a refined gentleman, but must be a sorry critic.   He who possesses imagination enough to live with his forefathers, and, leaving comparative reflection for an after moment, to give himself up during the first perusal to the feelings of a contemporary, if not a partisan, will, I dare aver, rarely find any part of Milton's prose works disgusting.'
For instances of the roughness of Milton's style see Masson's *Milton*, iii. 320.
[4]
        ' that hell
Grew darker at their frown.'
            Paradise Lost, ii. 719.

[5] Reading was taken on April 26, 1643.   Gardiner's *Civil War*, i. 129. Milton's father had been living in that town with his younger son.   The rest of his life he spent in his elder son's house.   Phillips' *Milton*, p. 21.
[6] 'About Whitsuntide [1643] he took a journey into the country . . . After a month's stay, home he returns a married man that went out a bachelor.' *Ib.* p. 20.
His wife was seventeen.   Her father 'was worth at least £310 a year'—equivalent, say, to £1,000, at the present day.' So early as 1627, he owed Milton's father £312, who transferred the claim to his son. The debt was still owing.   Milton must have run some risk in going to Forest Hill, so close to the king's head quarters at Oxford.   A month later Hampden fell at Chalgrove hard by. Masson's *Milton*, ii.493-505. Sir William Jones wrote of Forest

with him, and expected all the advantages of a conjugal life. The lady, however, seems not much to have delighted in the pleasures of spare diet and hard study; for, as Philips relates, 'having for a month led a philosophical life, after having been used at home to a great house, and much company and joviality, her friends, possibly by her own desire, made earnest suit to have her company the remaining part of the summer; which was granted, upon a promise of her return at Michaelmas [1].'

Milton was too busy to much miss his wife; he pursued his **52** studies, and now and then visited the Lady Margaret Leigh, whom he has mentioned in one of his sonnets [2]. At last Michaelmas arrived; but the lady had no inclination to return to the sullen gloom of her husband's habitation [3], and therefore very willingly forgot her promise. He sent her a letter, but had no answer; he sent more with the same success. It could be alleged that letters miscarry; he therefore dispatched a messenger, being by this time too angry to go himself. His messenger was sent back with some contempt. The family of the lady were Cavaliers [4].

In a man whose opinion of his own merit was like Milton's, less **53** provocation than this might have raised violent resentment. Milton soon determined to repudiate her for disobedience [5]; and, being one of those who could easily find arguments to justify inclination [6], published (in 1644) *The Doctrine and Discipline of Divorce*, which was followed by *The Judgement of Martin Bucer, concerning Divorce*; and the next year his Tetrachordon, *Expositions upon*

Hill in 1769:—'The tradition of Milton having lived there is current among the villagers; one of them showed us a ruinous wall that made part of his chamber, and another, who had forgotten the name of Milton, recollected him by the title of The Poet.' Teignmouth's *Jones*, p. 86.

[1] Phillips' *Milton*, p. 21.

[2] *Sonnets*, No. x; Phillips' *Milton*, p. 23. She was daughter of the Earl of Marlborough. Masson's *Milton*, iii. 57.

[3] 'She found it very solitary; no company came to her; oftentimes heard his nephews beaten and cry.' AUBREY, *Brief Lives*, ii. 65.

[4] Phillips' *Milton*, p. 23. 'Two opinions doe not well on the same

boulster. She was a royalist.' AUBREY, *Brief Lives*, ii. 65.

[5] Phillips' *Milton*, p. 24. He tells how a man 'shall find himself bound fast to an uncomplying discord of nature, or, as it oft happens, to an image of earth and phlegm, with whom he looked to be the copartner of a sweet and gladsome society.' *Works*, i. 356.

[6] 'When Milton writ his book of divorces, it was presently rejected as an occasional treatise, because everybody knew he had a wife. ... It is a piece of logic which will hardly pass on the world, that, because one man has a sore nose, therefore all the town should put plasters upon theirs.' SWIFT, *Works*, viii. 109.

the four chief Places of Scripture which treat of Marriage [or nullities in Marriage] [1].

54   This innovation was opposed, as might be expected, by the clergy, who, then holding their famous assembly at Westminster, procured that the author should be called before the Lords ; 'but that House,' says Wood, 'whether approving the doctrine, or not favouring his accusers, did soon dismiss him [2].'

55   There seems not to have been much written against him, nor any thing by any writer of eminence [3]. The antagonist that appeared is styled by him, 'a Serving man turned Solicitor [4].' Howel in his letters mentions the new doctrine with contempt [5]; and it was, I suppose, thought more worthy of derision than of confutation. He complains of this neglect in two sonnets, of which the first is contemptible [6], and the second not excellent [7].

56   From this time it is observed that he became an enemy to the Presbyterians, whom he had favoured before [8]. He that changes his party by his humour is not more virtuous than he that changes it by his interest ; he loves himself rather than truth [9].

---

[1] See Appendix L.

[2] *Fasti Oxon.* i. 483. The Assembly did not proceed directly, but 'stirred up the Stationers' Company to activity in the matter.' Milton had openly violated the *Ordinance for Printing* of the Long Parliament, dated June 14, 1643. His *Doctrine and Discipline* he had neither licensed, nor registered by the Stationers' Company, to their loss of fees. 'There was a trade-feeling behind the petition' presented by the Company to Parliament on Aug. 24, 1644, against unlicensed pamphlets generally and Milton's particularly. A few days earlier he had been attacked in a sermon before both Houses by a divine of the Assembly. The petition was referred to a Committee, which 'let Milton alone.' On Dec. 9, 1644, five weeks after the publication of *Areopagitica* (also unlicensed and unregistered), the Company renewed the attack, this time before the Lords. Two justices were ordered to examine him. There is not a word in the *Journals* to show that any action was taken against him on their report, or that he appeared before the Lords. Masson's *Milton*, iii. 164, 264–5, 270–4, 291, 295.

On July 2 of this year the battle of Marston Moor had been fought, and Milton's friends, the Independents, with their doctrine of toleration, were becoming 'lords of the ascendant.'

[3] Milton mentions this in *Colasterion*, *Works*, ii. 240. 'It was animadverted upon, but without any mention of Milton's name, by Bishop Hall, in his *Cases of Conscience*, Decade 4, case 2.' JAMES BOSWELL, JUN., Johnson's *Works*, vii. 81 *n.* For other writers (of whom the most eminent was Prynne) see Masson's *Milton*, iii. 262, 298, 466.

[4] *Works*, ii. 243.

[5] 'That opinion of a poor shallow-brain'd Puppy . . . deserves to be hiss'd at rather than confuted.' *Letters*, 1892, p. 569.

[6] No. xi. Johnson, in his *Dictionary*, under *Sonnet*, after saying that 'it has not been used by any man of eminence since Milton,' quotes this sonnet in full. For his *Sonnets* see *post*, MILTON, 206.

[7] No. xii.

[8] *Biog. Brit.* p. 3112 ; Newton's *Milton*, Preface, p. 24.

[9] He had changed with many of

His wife and her relations now found that Milton was not an 57
unresisting sufferer of injuries; and perceiving that he had begun
to put his doctrine in practice, by courting a young woman of
great accomplishments, the daughter of one Doctor Davis, who
was however not ready to comply [1], they resolved to endeavour a
reunion. He went sometimes to the house of one Blackborough,
his relation, in the lane of St. Martin's-le-Grand [2], and at one of
his usual visits was surprised to see his wife come from another
room, and implore forgiveness on her knees [3]. He resisted her
intreaties for a while; 'but partly,' says Philips, 'his own generous nature, more inclinable to reconciliation than to perseverance
in anger or revenge, and partly the strong intercession of friends
on both sides, soon brought him to an act of oblivion and a firm
league of peace [4].' It were injurious to omit, that Milton
afterwards received her father and her brothers in his own house,
when they were distressed, with other Royalists [5].

He published about the same time his *Areopagitica, a Speech* 58
of Mr. John Milton for the liberty of unlicensed Printing [6]. The

the best men in England, when it
was seen that
'New Presbyter is but Old Priest
writ large.'

[1] Phillips' *Milton*, p. 26.

[2] *Ib.* p. 28. 'The lane was that
bend of Aldersgate Street where now
the General Post Office stands.'
Masson's *Milton*, iii. 440.

[3] This interview was about July or
August, 1645. Their first child was
born on July 29, 1646. The submission was probably due to the defeat
of the king at Naseby on June 14,
1645. Her father was weighed down
with debt, and the sequestrations and
fines for delinquency, which followed
the surrender of Oxford on June 24,
1646, were threatening him. *Ib.* iii.
439, 473, 483, 632 ; *N. & Q.* 2 S. viii.
142. Fenton thinks that from this
interview sprung 'that pathetic scene
in *Paradise Lost* (x. 940), in which
Eve addresseth herself to Adam for
pardon and peace.' *Paradise Lost*,
1727, ed. Fenton, Preface, p. 13.
Compare also *Samson Agonistes*, ll.
710–1060, where Dalila is spurned
by Samson.

[4] Phillips' *Milton*, p. 27.

[5] 'She had a great resort of her

kindred with her in her house, viz.
her father and mother, and several
of her brothers and sisters, which
were in all pretty numerous.' *Ib.*
See also Masson's *Milton*, iii. 652 ;
Works, vi. 122.

[6] It appeared Nov. 24, 1644, with
this title :—' *Areopagitica ; A Speech
of Mr. John Milton for the Liberty
of Unlicens'd Printing to the Parlament of England.*' Masson's *Milton*,
iii. 277 ; *Works*, i. 286.

On June 14, 1643, Parliament had
appointed eight sets of licensers of
the press. 'For Books of Philosophy, History, Poetry, Morality and
Arts,' two of the three licensers were
' the three School-Masters of Paul's.'
Rushworth's *Hist. Collections*, v. 336.
For the Licensing Act and its aboli-
tion in 1695 see Macaulay's *Hist.* vi.
360; vii. 167. After describing 'the
reasons which determined the Lower
House not to renew the Act' Macaulay
concludes :—'Such were the arguments which did what Milton's *Areopagitica* had failed to do.' *Ib.* vii.169.

For a reprint of *Areopagitica* in
1738, when the Act was passed for
licensing plays, see *post*, THOMSON,
31 *n.*

danger of such unbounded liberty and the danger of bounding it have produced a problem in the science of Government, which human understanding seems hitherto unable to solve. If nothing may be published but what civil authority shall have previously approved, power must always be the standard of truth[1]; if every dreamer of innovations[2] may propagate his projects, there can be no settlement; if every murmurer at government may diffuse discontent, there can be no peace; and if every sceptick in theology may teach his follies, there can be no religion. The remedy against these evils is to punish the authors; for it is yet allowed that every society may punish, though not prevent, the publication of opinions, which that society shall think pernicious[3]: but this punishment, though it may crush the author, promotes the book[4]; and it seems not more reasonable to leave the right of printing unrestrained, because writers may be afterwards censured, than it would be to sleep with doors unbolted, because by our laws we can hang a thief[5].

59 But whatever were his engagements, civil or domestick, poetry was never long out of his thoughts. About this time (1645) a collection of his Latin and English poems appeared[6], in which the *Allegro* and *Penseroso*[7], with some others, were first published.

60 He had taken a larger house in Barbican[8] for the reception of

[1] 'JOHNSON. In short, Sir, I have got no further than this: Every man has a right to utter what he thinks truth, and every other man has a right to knock him down for it.' Boswell's *Johnson*, iv. 12. See also *post*, SAVAGE, 107.

[2] For 'the fury of innovation,' from which 'Tyburn itself was not safe,' see *ib.* iv. 188.

[3] 'JOHNSON. No member of a society has a right to *teach* any doctrine contrary to what the society holds to be true.' *Ib.* ii. 249.

[4] 'As burning a book by the common hangman is a known expedient to make it sell, so to write a book that deserves such treatment is another.' SWIFT, *Works*, viii. 112. Hume explains how, 'though late, there arose the paradoxical principle and salutary practice of toleration.' *Hist. Eng.* vi. 165.

[5] 'The only plausible argument heretofore used for restraining the just freedom of the press, "that it

was necessary, to prevent the daily abuse of it," will entirely lose its force, when it is shown (by a seasonable exertion of the laws) that the press cannot be abused to any bad purpose without incurring a suitable punishment: whereas it never can be used to any good one when under the control of an inspector.' BLACKSTONE, *Comm.* iv. 153.

[6] On Jan. 2, 1645-6. Masson's *Milton*, iii. 451. See *post*, MILTON, 152, 177.
'I do not recollect that for seventy years afterwards these poems are once mentioned in the whole succession of English literature.' T. WARTON, *Milton's Poems*, Preface, p. 5. Warton points out how, in the latter half of the eighteenth century, 'the school of Milton rose in emulation of the school of Pope.' *Ib.* p. 12. For Pope's discovery of Milton's minor poems see *post*, POPE, 344 *n.*

[7] *Post*, MILTON, 185.

[8] Phillips' *Milton*, p. 28; Masson's *Milton*, iii. 443. Bridgewater House

scholars, but the numerous relations of his wife, to whom he generously granted refuge for a while, occupied his rooms. In time, however, they went away; 'and the house again,' says Philips, 'now looked like a house of the Muses only, though the accession of scholars was not great. Possibly his having proceeded so far in the education of youth may have been the occasion of [some of] his adversaries calling him pedagogue and school-master; whereas it is well known he never set up for a publick school to teach all the young fry of a parish, but only was willing to impart his learning and knowledge to relations and the sons of gentlemen who were his intimate friends, and that neither his writings nor his way of teaching ever savoured in the least of pedantry [1].'

Thus laboriously does his nephew extenuate what cannot be 61 denied, and what might be confessed without disgrace. Milton was not a man who could become mean by a mean employment [2]. This, however, his warmest friends seem not to have found; they therefore shift and palliate. He did not sell literature to all comers at an open shop; he was a chamber-milliner, and measured his commodities only to his friends.

Philips, evidently impatient of viewing him in this state of 62 degradation, tells us that it was not long continued; and, to raise his character again, has a mind to invest him with military splendour: 'He is much mistaken,' he says, 'if there was not about this time a design of making him an adjutant-general in Sir William Waller's army [3]. But the new modelling of the army proved an obstruction to the design [4].' An event cannot be set at a much greater distance than by having been only *designed, about some time*, if a man *be not much mistaken*. Milton shall be a pedagogue

in the Barbican, Aldersgate Street, in the seventeenth century, says Pennant (on the authority of Evelyn's *Fumifugium*, p. 18), 'was celebrated for its orchards.' Pennant's *London*, 1790, p. 225. In Bridgewater Gardens the memory lingers of the Earl of Bridgewater and *Comus*. *Ante*, MILTON, 21.

[1] Phillips' *Milton*, p. 28; *ante*, MILTON, 36.

[2] *Post*, MILTON, 147.

[3] The 'William the Conqueror' of the citizens of London. Clarendon's *Hist.* iv. 114. Johnson praised his

Directory as 'a pious rational book, but in any except a very regular life difficult to practise.' *John. Misc.* i. 103.

[4] Phillips' *Milton*, p. 28. For the New Model, by which the command of the army passed from the Presbyterians to the Independents, from the lukewarm to the thorough-goers, from Essex, Manchester, and Waller to Fairfax, Cromwell, and Skippon, see Clarendon's *Hist.* v. 88, 130, and Gardiner's *Civil War*, ii. 5, 79, 116.

no longer; for, if Philips be not much mistaken, somebody at some time designed him for a soldier [1].

63 About the time that the army was new-modelled (1645) he removed to a smaller house in Holbourn, which opened backward into Lincoln's-Inn-Fields [2]. He is not known to have published any thing afterwards till the King's death, when, finding his murderers condemned by the Presbyterians, he wrote a treatise to justify it, and 'to compose the minds of the people [3].'

64 He made some *Remarks on the Articles of Peace between Ormond and the Irish Rebels* [4]. While he contented himself to write, he perhaps did only what his conscience dictated; and if he did not very vigilantly watch the influence of his own passions, and the gradual prevalence of opinions, first willingly admitted and then habitually indulged, if objections by being overlooked were forgotten, and desire superinduced conviction, he yet shared only the common weakness of mankind, and might be no less sincere than his opponents. But as faction seldom leaves a man honest, however it might find him, Milton is suspected of having interpolated the book called *Icon Basilike* [5], which the Council of State, to whom he was now made Latin secretary [6], employed him to censure, by inserting a prayer taken from Sidney's *Arcadia*, and

[1] In *Defensio Secunda*, Milton says that it was not through want of courage or zeal that he had never borne arms. His training fitted him for different, though not less dangerous services. *Works*, v. 199.

[2] Phillips' *Milton*, p. 28. He removed in 1647. Masson's *Milton*, iv. 104.

[3] *The Tenure of Kings and Magistrates, Works*, ii. 271. 'It was published a fortnight after the King's death,' and only a few days after *Eikon Basilike*. 'It was written mainly' while the king was alive. Masson's *Milton*, iv. 65, 76.
'Liber iste non nisi post mortem regis prodiit, ad componendos potius hominum animos factus quam ad statuendum de Carolo quicquam.' *Works*, v. 235.

[4] *Observations upon the Articles of Peace with the Irish Rebels, on the Letter of Ormond to Col. Jones, and the Representation of the Presbytery at Belfast, Works*, ii. 360; Masson's *Milton*, iv. 98.

Ormond having 'coupled' Cromwell with John of Leyden, Milton replied :—'Cromwell, whom he couples with a name of scorn, hath done in few years more eminent and remarkable deeds whereon to found nobility in his house, though it were wanting, and perpetual renown to posterity, than Ormond and all his ancestors put together can show from any record of their Irish exploits, the widest scene of their glory.' *Works*, ii. 367.

[5] See Appendix M.

[6] On March 15, 1648-9. Masson's *Milton*, iv. 82. See also *ib.* v. 396, 570, 623, 674, and *post*, MILTON, 162.
'They [the Commonwealth] stuck to this noble and generous resolution not to write to any Princes and States, or receive answers from any, but in a language most proper to maintain a correspondence among the learned of all nations; scorning to carry on their affairs in the wheedling lisping jargon of the cringing French.' Phillips' *Milton*, p. 30.

imputing it to the King; whom he charges, in his *Iconoclastes*[1], with the use of this prayer as with a heavy crime, in the indecent language with which prosperity had emboldened the advocates for rebellion to insult all that is venerable or great: 'Who would have imagined so little fear in him of the true all-seeing Deity . . . as, immediately before his death, to pop into the hands of the [that] grave bishop that [who] attended him, as [for] a special relique of his saintly exercises, a prayer stolen word for word from the mouth of a heathen woman praying to a heathen god[2]?'

The papers which the King gave to Dr. Juxon on the scaffold 65 the regicides took away, so that they were at least the publishers of this prayer; and Dr. Birch, who had examined the question with great care[3], was inclined to think them the forgers. The use of it by adaptation was innocent; and they who could so noisily censure it, with a little extension of their malice could contrive what they wanted to accuse[4].

King Charles the Second, being now sheltered in Holland, 66 employed Salmasius, professor of Polite Learning at Leyden, to write a defence of his father and of monarchy; and, to excite his industry, gave him, as was reported, a hundred Jacobuses[5]. Salmasius was a man of skill in languages, knowledge of antiquity, and sagacity of emendatory criticism, almost exceeding all hope of human attainment; and having by excessive praises

---

[1] 'Huic respondere iussus, Iconi Iconoclasten opposui, non "regiis manibus insultans," ut insimulor, sed reginam veritatem regi Carolo anteponendam arbitratus.' *Works*, v. 235. He entitled his book *Iconoclastes*, the surname of the Greek emperors who broke the images in the churches, as it was an answer to Εἰκὼν βασιλική, that is to say *The King's Image. Ib.* ii. 395.
The emperors were Leo the Isaurian (A.D. 726) and his successors to A.D. 840. Gibbon's *Decline and Fall*, v. 251.
Iconoclastes was published in Oct. 1649; a second edition in 1650, and a French translation in 1652. Masson's *Milton*, iv. 95, 246, 448.
[2] *Works*, ii. 408.
[3] In the Appendix to the *Life of Milton* in Milton's *Works*, 1738. In the edition of 1753, Preface, p. 33,

Birch disbelieves in the forgery.
[4] The original prayer is in Book iii of the *Arcadia*. The two prayers are printed in parallel columns in Masson's *Milton*, iv. 139. 'The prayer is not in the *Eikon Basilike* proper, but is one of a few that were appended to some of the earlier and more expensive editions.' *Ib.* The slander that it was interpolated by Milton was started early, and soon formed part of 'that strange stream of Restoration tradition, which seems to have choked all high honour out of the English literary conscience for some generations.' *Ib.* iv. 249. See also Newton's *Milton*, Preface, p. 30.
[5] Milton describes the *Defensio* as 'centenis Iacobis empta, ingenti pretio ab egentissimo rege.' *Works*, v. 40. A Jacobus was a twenty-shilling piece. See also *post*, ADDISON, 83.

been confirmed in great confidence of himself, though he probably had not much considered the principles of society or the rights of government, undertook the employment without distrust of his own qualifications [1]; and, as his expedition in writing was wonderful, in 1649 published *Defensio Regis* [2].

67   To this Milton was required to write a sufficient answer [3], which he performed (1651) in such a manner that Hobbes declared himself unable to decide whose language was best, or whose arguments were worst [4]. In my opinion, Milton's periods are smoother, neater,

---

[1] Balzac said of him :—'Non homini, sed scientiae, deest quod nescivit Salmasius.' *Ménagiana*, iii. 257.

'Salmasius one day meeting two of his brethren, Messrs. Gaulmin and Maussac, in the Royal Library at Paris, Gaulmin told the other two that he believed they three could make head against all the learned in Europe. To which the great Salmasius fiercely replied :—"Do you and Mr. Maussac join yourselves to all that is learned in the world, and you shall find that I alone am a match for you all."' WARBURTON, quoted in Pope's *Works* (Elwin and Courthope), ii. 99.

'Salmasius had read as much as Grotius, perhaps more. But their different modes of reading made the one an enlightened philosopher, and the other, to speak plainly, a pedant puffed up with an useless erudition.' GIBBON, *Misc. Works*, v. 209.

'Salmasius too often involves himself in the web of his disorderly erudition.' *Decline and Fall*, v. 465. See also Masson's *Milton*, iv. 162.

Fox pointed out 'the coincidence between the arguments, declamations, and even the very expressions of Salmasius against Milton and Burke upon the French Revolution.' *Memoirs of F. Horner*, 1843, i. 324.

[2] *Defensio Regia pro Carolo I.* Masson's *Milton*, iv. 150.

[3] On Jan. 8, 1649-50, the Council of State ordered 'that Mr. Milton do prepare something in answer to the Book of Salmasius.' *Ib.* iv. 151. On Dec. 23, 1650, he was ordered to print it. It was published about March 1650-1. No English translation

appeared before 1692. *Ib.* iv. 230, 251, 258 *n.*, 312 ; *Works*, iii. 103 ; v. 37. Want of health (failing sight no doubt) had made Milton long over his task. *Ib.* v. 39.

'*The Defence of the English People* is stolen from Buchanan, *De Iure Regni apud Scotos.*' DRYDEN, *Works*, ix. 425. It was *The Tenure of Kings and Magistrates* (*ante*, 63 *n.*) that 'may have been taken from Buchanan.' Masson's *Milton*, iv. 66.

Malone saw a copy of Milton's book 'in which the former possessor says in Latin, that Milton's brother told him that with all the *legal* arguments Milton was furnished by Bradshaw.' Prior's *Malone*, p. 395.

For the burning of the *Defensio* by the hangman see *post*, MILTON, 99.

[4] 'They are very good Latin both, and hardly to be judged which is better, and both very ill reasoning, hardly to be judged which is worse.' *Behemoth*, 1682, p. 369.

South, in a sermon on Jan. 30, 1662-3, described Milton as 'the Latin advocate who, like a blind adder, has spit so much poison upon the King's person and cause.' *Sermons*, iii. 439.

The French ambassador, writing to Lewis XIV in 1663, speaks of 'un nommé Miltonius, qui s'est rendu plus infame par ses dangereux escrits que les bourreaux et les assassins de leur Roi.' Pepys' *Diary*, v. 430, App.

'Milton . . . le réfuta comme une bête féroce combat un sauvage.' VOLTAIRE, *Œuvres*, xvii. 162.

Lamb describes Milton's work as 'uniformly great, and such as is befitting the very mouth of a great

and more pointed; but he delights himself with teasing his adversary as much as with confuting him. He makes a foolish allusion of Salmasius, whose doctrine he considers as servile and unmanly, to the stream of Salmacis, which whoever entered left half his virility behind him [1]. Salmasius was a Frenchman, and was unhappily married to a scold [2]. 'Tu es Gallus,' says Milton, 'et, ut aiunt, nimium gallinaceus [3].' But his supreme pleasure is to tax his adversary, so renowned for criticism, with vitious Latin. He opens his book with telling that he has used *Persona*, which, according to Milton, signifies only a *Mask*, in a sense not known to the Romans, by applying it as we apply *Person* [4]. But as Nemesis is always on the watch, it is memorable that he has enforced the charge of a solecism by an expression in itself grossly solecistical [5], when, for one of those supposed blunders, he says, as Ker, and I think some one before him, has remarked, 'propino te grammatistis tuis *vapulandum* [6].' From *vapulo*, which has a passive sense, *vapulandus* can never be derived. No man forgets his original trade: the rights of nations and of kings sink into questions of grammar, if grammarians discuss them [7].

nation, speaking for itself.' *Letters*, i. 191.

See Masson's *Milton*, iv. 263, for Milton's 'Latin Billingsgate.'

Atterbury (*Corres.* iii. 452) said of Sir Thomas More's answer to Luther that 'the author had the best knack of any man in Europe at calling bad names in good Latin.'

[1] *Works*, v. 42; Ovid's *Metam.* iv. 285.

[2] 'The fashion of aspersing the birth and condition of an adversary seems to have lasted from the time of the Greek orators to the learned grammarians of the last age.' GIBBON, *Decline and Fall*, i. 139 *n.*

[2] 'Parmi tout le bruit que lui faisaient sa femme, ses enfans et ses domestiques, il ne laissait pas de composer dans un coin de sa chambre, aussi tranquillement que s'il eût été seul dans son cabinet.' *Ménagiana*, v. 386. See also *ib.* p. 408.

[3] *Works*, v. 118.

[4] *Ib.* v. 41.

[5] *Solecistical* is not in Johnson's *Dictionary*.

[6] '. . . non tam mihi, neque enim est otium, quam ipsis tuis grammati-

stis poenas dabis; quibus ego te deridendum et vapulandum propino.' *Works*, v. 41.

'Pinguis soloecismus Miltono excidit, ubi Salmasium ob soloecismum exagitavit. Eum notavit Vavassor, *De Epig.* 22, 302 [*De Epigrammate Liber*, by Francis Vavasseur, 1678, p. 301].' *Selectarum de Lingua Latina Observationum Libri Duo*. John Ker. 1708-9, vol. ii, under *Vapulandum*.

'Milton, in his fifth Elegy, wrote in the first edition, 1645, "quotannis," with the last syllable short. For this Salmasius did not spare him. In the second edition of 1673 the line (30) was altered by the substitution of "perennis," as it now stands.' BISHOP WORDSWORTH, *Classical Review*, i. 47.

[7] 'So some polemics use to draw their swords
Against the language only and the words:
As he who fought at barriers with Salmasius
Engaged with nothing but the style and phrases;

. . . .

68   Milton when he undertook this answer was weak of body
and dim of sight[1]; but his will was forward, and what was
wanting of health was supplied by zeal[2].   He was rewarded with
a thousand pounds[3], and his book was much read[4]; for paradox,
recommended by spirit and elegance, easily gains attention : and
he who told every man that he was equal to his King could
hardly want an audience.

69   That the performance of Salmasius was not dispersed with
equal rapidity or read with equal eagerness, is very credible.   He
taught only the stale doctrine of authority and the unpleasing
duty of submission; and he had been so long not only the
monarch but the tyrant of literature that almost all mankind
were delighted to find him defied and insulted by a new name,
not yet considered as any one's rival.   If Christina[5], as is said,
commended the *Defence of the people*, her purpose must be
to torment Salmasius, who was then at her Court[6]; for neither
her civil station nor her natural character could dispose her to
favour the doctrine, who was by birth a queen and by temper
despotick[7].

And counted breaking Priscian's
    head a thing
More capital than to behead a King.'
BUTLER, *Genuine Remains*, 1759, i.
220.
  [1] In 1654 Milton wrote that his
sight began to fail about ten years
earlier, and that the left eye became
useless some years before the right.
Works, vi. 128.   By the spring of
1652 he was blind.   Masson's *Milton*,
iv. 427.
  [2] See *Works*, v. 215, for the fine
passage in which he says that,
though he was warned that to persist
in his 'noble task' would make him
blind, he went on ; and *Sonnets*, No.
xxii ; also Morley's *Crit. Misc.* iii.
160; *post*, MILTON, 159 *n*.; GRAY, 39.
  [3] Toland (p. 102) is the authority
for this.   Milton describes himself
as 'nulla ambitione, lucro, aut gloria
ductus.'   *Works*, v. 215.   See also
ib. vii. 336.
In the Council Order Book a
scored-out entry of June 18, 1651,
shows that the Council voted its
thanks and a reward to Milton.   In
the substituted entry the reward is
omitted, but the thanks are enlarged.

Milton, no doubt, refused to accept
the money.   Masson's *Milton*, iv.
321.   See *post*, MILTON, 162.
  [4] 'Of which all Europe rings from
        side to side.'   *Sonnets*, No. xxii.
On May 18 Heinsius wrote from
Leyden :—'We have seen already
four editions of the book, besides the
English one ; moreover a fifth edition,
as Elzevir tells me, is being hurried
through the press at the Hague.   I
see also a Dutch translation hawked
about.'   Masson's *Milton*, iv. 318.
For its widespread reputation, see
ib. iv. 637 and *Works*, v. 200.
  [5] Queen of Sweden, daughter of
Gustavus Adolphus.   She gathered
scholars from all parts to her Court.
Masson's *Milton*, iv. 268.
  [6] Isaac Vossius wrote from Stock-
holm that 'in the presence of many
she spoke highly of the genius of the
man [Milton], and his manner of
writing.'   *Ib*. iv. 317.
  [7] Milton, addressing her, wrote :—
' Quod enim erat in tyrannos dictum,
negabas id ad te ullo modo pertinere.'
Works, v. 225 ; vi. 395 ; Masson's
Milton, iv. 345.
The lines *Ad Christinam*, &c., in-

That Salmasius was, from the appearance of Milton's book, 70
treated with neglect, there is not much proof [1]; but to a man so
long accustomed to admiration, a little praise of his antagonist
would be sufficiently offensive, and might incline him to leave
Sweden; from which, however, he was dismissed, not with any
mark of contempt, but with a train of attendance scarce less than
regal [2].

He prepared a reply, which, left as it was imperfect, was 71
published by his son in the year of the Restauration [3]. In the
beginning, being probably most in pain for his Latinity, he
endeavours to defend his use of the word *persona*; but, if I
remember right, he misses a better authority than any that he
has found, that of Juvenal in his fourth satire;

> '—Quid agis [agas] cum dira & fœdior omni
> Crimine *Persona* est [4]?'

As Salmasius reproached Milton with losing his eyes in the 72
quarrel, Milton delighted himself with the belief that he had
shortened Salmasius's life; and both perhaps with more malignity
than reason. Salmasius died at the Spa, Sept. 3, 1653 [5]; and, as
controvertists are commonly said to be killed by their last dispute,
Milton was flattered with the credit of destroying him [6].

Cromwell had now dismissed the parliament by the authority 73
of which he had destroyed monarchy, and commenced monarch
himself under the title of protector, but with kingly and more

cluded in almost all the editions of
Milton's *Poems* (*Epig.* xiii), are, in
Professor Masson's opinion, by Mar-
vell. Masson's *Milton*, iv. 624.

[1] Milton, speaking of the effect of
his *Defensio* on the queen, says that
Salmasius departing 'hoc unum in
dubio permultis relinqueret, hono-
ratiorne advenerit an contemptior
abierit.' *Works*, v. 201; vi. 366.
Symmons quotes Needham's *Mer-
curius Politicus* as stating that 'the
Queen cashiered Salmasius her
favour as a pernicious parasite and a
promoter of tyranny.' *Ib.* vii. 338.

[2] In the first edition the sentence
ends with 'Sweden.' In the addition Johnson is answering Phillips,
who (p. 32) says that Salmasius 'was
dismissed with so cold and slight an
adieu that, after a faint dying reply,
he was glad to have recourse to death.'

See also Toland's *Life of Milton*, p.
104. For his treatment in Sweden
see Masson's *Milton*, iv. 344.

[3] *Ib.* vi. 203.

[4] JUVENAL, *Sat.* iv. 14. Salmasius does not quote Juvenal. See his
Ad Ioannem Miltonum Responsio,
1660, p. 31.

[5] Masson's *Milton*, iv. 539.

[6] 'Non enim, ut ille mihi caecita-
tem, sic ego illi mortem vitio vertam.
Quanquam sunt qui nos etiam necis
eius reos faciunt, illosque nostros
nimis acriter strictos aculeos.' *Works*,
v. 202; vi. 367; Masson's *Milton*,
iv. 585.
'If any one thinks that classical
studies of themselves cultivate the
taste and the sentiments, let him look
into Salmasius's *Responsio*.' Pattison's *Milton*, p. 108.

than kingly power. That his authority was lawful, never was pretended; he himself founded his right only in necessity: but Milton, having now tasted the honey of publick employment, would not return to hunger[1] and philosophy, but, continuing to exercise his office under a manifest usurpation, betrayed to his power that liberty which he had defended. Nothing can be more just than that rebellion should end in slavery: that he, who had justified the murder of his king, for some acts which to him seemed unlawful, should now sell his services and his flatteries to a tyrant, of whom it was evident that he could do nothing lawful[2].

74 He had now been blind for some years; but his vigour of intellect was such that he was not disabled to discharge his office of Latin secretary, or continue his controversies: his mind was too eager to be diverted, and too strong to be subdued.

75 About this time his first wife died in childbed, having left him three daughters[3]. As he probably did not much love her he did not long continue the appearance of lamenting her, but after a short time married Catherine, the daughter of one captain Woodcock of Hackney[4]; a woman doubtless educated in opinions like his own[5]. She died within a year of childbirth, or some distemper that followed it[6]; and her husband has honoured her memory with a poor sonnet.

76 The first Reply to Milton's *Defensio Populi* was published in 1651, called *Apologia pro Rege et Populo Anglicano, contra Johannis Polypragmatici (alias Miltoni [Angli]) defensionem*

---

[1] Milton had private means of his own, as Johnson knew. *Post*, MILTON, 104, 162.

[2] The Whig Addison attacks Milton scarcely less severely than the Tory Johnson—

'Oh! had the poet ne'er profaned his pen
To varnish o'er the guilt of faithless men,' &c.
                    Addison's *Works*, i. 25.
  Milton, though 'an ardent Oliverian,' nevertheless, in his *Defensio Secunda*, 'praised most heartily after Cromwell,' men who, as republicans, were opposed to the Protector. Masson's *Milton*, iv. 605. See also *ib.* iv. 608-15; *Works*, v. 259; vi. 436, for his 'appeals to Cromwell not to use

his power to the detriment of liberty,' and his exhortations to his countrymen to remember that true liberty is neither won nor lost by arms, but is the fruit of piety, of justice, of temperance, and of unadulterated virtue.

[3] She, and a son born on March 16, 1650-1, died between May and October, 1652. Masson's *Milton*, iv. 335, 468.

[4] Toland's *Milton*, p. 105. They were married on Nov. 12, 1656. Masson's *Milton*, v. 281.

[5] Johnson perhaps infers this from Milton's describing her as 'my late espoused saint.' *Sonnets*, No. xxiii.

[6] She was buried in St. Margaret's, Westminster, on Feb. 10, 1657-8. *Fasti Oxon.* i. 486 *n.*

destructivam Regis et Populi [*Anglicani*]. Of this the author was
not known[1]; but Milton and his nephew Philips, under whose
name he published an answer so much corrected by him that it
might be called his own[2], imputed it to Bramhal[3], and, knowing
him no friend to regicides, thought themselves at liberty to treat
him as if they had known what they only suspected.

Next year appeared *Regii Sanguinis clamor ad Cœlum*[4]. Of 77
this the author was Peter du Moulin, who was afterwards preben-
dary of Canterbury[5]; but Morus, or More, a French minister[6],
having the care of its publication, was treated as the writer by
Milton in his *Defensio Secunda*[7], and overwhelmed by such
violence of invective that he began to shrink under the tempest,
and gave his persecutors the means of knowing the true author[8].
Du Moulin was now in great danger[9], but Milton's pride operated
against his malignity[10]; and both he and his friends were more
willing that Du Moulin should escape than that he should be
convicted of mistake[11].

[1] For the book see Masson's *Milton*, iv. 347, and for John Rowland, the author, see *ib*. p. 536.

[2] Phillips' *Milton*, p. 32. The book is entitled *Ioannis Philippi Angli Responsio ad Apologiam Anonymi cuiusdam Tenebrionis pro Rege et Populo Anglicano Infantissimam*. *Works*, v. 351. Phillips was nineteen. *Ib*. vii. 341. It was published on Dec. 24, 1652. Masson's *Milton*, iv. 470.

[3] Evelyn recorded on July 28, 1660:—'I saluted my old friend, the Archbishop of Armagh, formerly of Londonderry [Dr. Bramhall].' *Diary*, i. 358. Bramhall complained of 'that silly book' being ascribed to him. Masson's *Milton*, iv. 348, 536 *n*.
He is described as 'ab ineunte aetate homo discinctus et ebriosus; ... inedia pressus et latrantis stomachi instinctu, nihil sibi utilius esse duxit quam ut, sacerdotis munere indutus, Ecclesiam, tunc quidem lupis omnibus patentem, invaderet.' *Works*, v. 353.

[4] 'It was probably published in Aug. 1652.' Masson's *Milton*, iv. 453.

[5] He was the son of a French Protestant theologian. *Ib*. v. 215; vi. 213. See also *ib*. v. 220, where he writes:—'I looked on in silence, and not without a soft chuckle, at seeing my bantling laid at another man's door, and the blind and furious Milton fighting and slashing the air, like the hoodwinked horse-combatants in the old circus, not knowing by whom he was struck and whom he struck in return.'

[6] Alexander More or Moir, the son of a Presbyterian Scot the Principal of a French Protestant College, had held professorships at Geneva and Middelburg, and now held one at Amsterdam. *Ib*. iv. 459, 627.

[7] *Ioannis Miltoni Angli pro Populo Anglicano Defensio Secunda: Contra Infamem Libellum Anonymum cui titulus Regii Sanguinis Clamor ad Coelum adversus Parricidas Anglicanos*. It was published on May 30, 1654. *Ib*. iv. 467, 580; *Works*, v. 197. For Morus's reply in October see Masson's *Milton*, v. 150, and for his *Supplementum* in 1655 see *ib*. p. 192.

[8] 'Morus was almost chivalrously reticent' about the author's name. *Ib*. v. 222.

[9] See his *Poematum Libelli Tres*, p. 141, quoted *ib*. v. 219.

[10] 'It was hard for Milton ever to admit he was wrong, even in a trifle.' *Ib*. v. 209.

[11] 'His sharp writing against Alex-

78   In this second Defence he shews that his eloquence is not merely satirical; the rudeness of his invective is equalled by the grossness of his flattery.

'Deserimur, Cromuelle; tu solus superes, ad te summa nostrarum rerum [rerum summa nostrarum] rediit, in te solo consistit, insuperabili tuæ virtuti cedimus cuncti, nemine vel obloquente, nisi qui [aut] æquales inæqualis ipse honores sibi quærit, aut digniori concessos invidet, aut non intelligit nihil esse in societate hominum magis vel Deo gratum, vel rationi consentaneum, esse in civitate nihil æquius, nihil utilius, quam potiri rerum dignissimum. Eum te agnoscunt omnes, Cromuelle, ea tu civis maximus et * gloriosissimus, dux publici consilii, fortissimorum exercituum imperator, pater patriæ gessisti. Sic tu spontanea bonorum omnium et animitus missa voce salutaris [1].'

79   Cæsar when he assumed the perpetual dictatorship had not more servile or more elegant flattery. A translation may shew its servility, but its elegance is less attainable. Having exposed the unskilfulness or selfishness of the former government

'We were left,' says Milton, 'to ourselves; the whole national interest fell into your hands, and subsists only in your abilities. To your virtue, overpowering and resistless, every man gives way, except some who without equal qualifications aspire to equal honours, who envy the distinctions of merit greater than their own, or who have yet to learn that in the coalition of human society nothing is more pleasing to God or more agreeable to reason than that the highest mind should have the sovereign power. Such, Sir, are you by general confession; such are the things atchieved

ander More, of Holland, upon a mistake, notwithstanding he had given him by the ambassador all satisfaction to the contrary: viz. that the booke called *Clamor* was writt by Peter du Moulin. Well, that was all one; he having writt it, it shuld goe into the world; one of them was as bad as the other.' AUBREY, *Brief Lives*, ii. 69.

Professor Masson thinks it possible that it was not till after the Restoration that Milton discovered the secret. Morus had done more than 'care for the publication' of the book. He had written the Dedicatory Epistle with its 'malignant notice of Milton.' Masson's *Milton*, v. 214, 222.

[1] *Works*, v. 258; vi. 435; Masson's *Milton*, iv. 605.

'The second *Defence*,' wrote Lamb to Coleridge, 'which is but a succession of splendid episodes, slightly tied together, has one passage, which, if you have not read, I conjure you to lose no time, but read it: it is his consolations in his blindness, which had been made a reproach to him. ... It gives so rational, so true an enumeration of his comforts, so human, that it cannot be read without the deepest interest.' Lamb quotes the passage (*Works*, v. 217; vi. 385). Lamb's *Letters*, i. 192.

[* It may be doubted whether *gloriosissimus* be here used with Milton's boasted purity. *Res gloriosa* is an *illustrious thing*; but *vir gloriosus* is commonly a *braggart*, as in *miles gloriosus*. JOHNSON.]

by you, the greatest and most glorious of our countrymen, the
director of our publick councils, the leader of unconquered armies,
the father of your country: for by that title does every good man
hail you, with sincere and voluntary praise.'

Next year, having defended all that wanted defence, he found 80
leisure to defend himself: he undertook his own vindication
against More, whom he declares in his title to be justly called the
author of the *Regii Sanguinis clamor*[1]. In this there is no want
of vehemence nor eloquence, nor does he forget his wonted wit,
'Morus es? an Momus? an uterque idem est[2]?' He then remembers that *Morus* is Latin for a Mulberry-tree, and hints at the
known transformation:

'Poma alba ferebat
Quæ post nigra tulit Morus[3].'

With this piece ended his controversies[4]; and he from this time 81
gave himself up to his private studies and his civil employment.

As secretary to the Protector[5] he is supposed to have written 82
the Declaration of the reasons for a war with Spain[6]. His agency
was considered as of great importance; for when a treaty with
Sweden was artfully suspended, the delay was publickly imputed
to Mr. Milton's indisposition; and the Swedish agent was provoked to express his wonder, that only one man in England
could write Latin, and that man blind[7].

[1] *Ioannis Miltoni, Angli, Pro Se
Defensio contra Alexandrum Morum, Ecclesiasten, Libelli famosi cui
titulus 'Regii Sanguinis Clamor ad
Coelum adversus Parricidas Anglicanos,' Authorem recte dictum*, 1655;
Works, v. 269; Masson's *Milton*, v. 198.

[2] *Works*, v. 315.

[3] *Ib.* p. 325.
'quae poma alba ferebat,
Ut nunc nigra ferat contactu san-
guinis arbor.'
OVID, *Metam.* iv. 51.
For his defence in this work of his
abuse see *Works*, v. 329; Masson's
Milton, v. 210.

[4] He had entered on them unwillingly. Following the fine passage
quoted *ante*, MILTON, 47, he wrote:—
'I leave a calm and pleasing solitari-
ness, fed with cheerful and confident
thoughts, to embark in a troubled sea
of noises and hoarse disputes.' *Works*,
i. 123.

His controversies did not wholly
end. In 1658 he published a revised
edition of his *Defensio Prima*. Masson's *Milton*, v. 572. See also *post*, MIL-
TON, 95, for his attack on Dr. Griffith.

[5] Under date of Sept. 1654, Pro-
fessor Masson writes (iv. 642):—
'Milton was to be Cromwell's Foreign
Secretary more and more distinctly
to the very end of the Protectorate.'
See also *ib.* v. 623, 674.

[6] *Works*, vi. 90. For an English
version see *ib.* v. 12. See Masson's
Milton, v. 243, for an examination
of the question how far Milton was
helped in it.

[7] On April 8, 1656, the Swedish
ambassador asked to have the treaty
drawn up in Latin. On May 3, he
complained that 'it was fourteen
days they made him stay for that
translation, and sent it to one Mr.
Milton, a blind man, to put the articles into Latin.... It seemed strange

83   Being now forty-seven years old, and seeing himself disencumbered from external interruptions, he seems to have recollected his former purposes [1], and to have resumed three great works which he had planned for his future employment [2]: an epick poem [3], the history of his country, and a dictionary of the Latin tongue [4].

84   To collect a dictionary seems a work of all others least practicable in a state of blindness, because it depends upon perpetual and minute inspection and collation.   Nor would Milton probably have begun it after he had lost his eyes, but, having had it always before him, he continued it, says Philips, 'almost to his dying-day; but the papers were so discomposed and deficient, that they could not be fitted for the press [5].'   The compilers of the Latin dictionary printed at Cambridge had the use of those collections in three folios [6]; but what was their fate afterwards is not known.

85   To compile a history from various authors, when they can only be consulted by other eyes, is not easy nor possible, but with more skilful and attentive help than can be commonly obtained [7]; and it was probably the difficulty of consulting and comparing

to him, there should be none but a blind man capable of putting a few articles into Latin.' Whitelocke's *Memorials of the English Affairs*, 1732, pp. 640, 645.

[1] *Ante*, MILTON, 47.

[2] Phillips' *Milton*, p. 34.

[3] 'Milton did not write his *Paradise Lost* till he had outlived his politics. With all his parts, and noble sentiments of liberty, who would remember him for his barbarous prose?' HORACE WALPOLE, *Letters*, v. 203.

Hume describes his prose writings as 'disagreeable, though not altogether defective in genius.' In another edition he had written, 'devoid of genius.' *Hist. of Engl.* vii. 343.

[4] 'He wrote likewise a *System of Divinity*. It was in the hands of Cyriack Skinner, and where at present is uncertain.' Toland's *Milton*, p. 148.

Aubrey (ii. 71) recorded in the catalogue of Milton's writings:—'*Idea Theologiae* in MS. in the hands of Mr. Skinner.' *Ante*, MILTON, 43. For its publication see *post*, MILTON, 166 *n*.

[5] 'Even very near to his dying

day; but the papers after his death were so discomposed and deficient that it could not be made fit for the press.' Phillips' *Milton*, p. 34.

[6] *Ib*.; Aubrey's *Brief Lives*, ii. 66; Toland's *Milton*, p. 148. The editors of *Linguae Romanae Dictionarium*, &c., Cambridge, 1693, write:—'We had by us, and made use of, a manuscript collection in three large folios, digested into an alphabetical order, which the learned Mr. John Milton had made,' &c.   *N. & Q.* 2 S. iv. 183.

[7] Prescott recorded, when he was nearly blind:—'Johnson says that no man can compile a history who is blind.   But although I should lose the use of my vision altogether, by the blessing of God, if my ears are spared me, I will disprove the assertion, and my chronicle shall not be wanting in accuracy and research.' Ticknor's *Life of Prescott*, 1864, p. 74.   In the Preface to *Ferdinand and Isabella* he says:—'This remark of the great critic, which first engaged my attention in the midst of my embarrassments, although discouraging at first, in the end stimulated my desire to overcome them.'

that stopped Milton's narrative at the Conquest [1]; a period at which affairs were not yet very intricate nor authors very numerous.

For the subject of his epick poem, after much deliberation, 86 'long chusing, and beginning late [2],' he fixed upon *Paradise Lost*; a design so comprehensive that it could be justified only by success. He had once designed to celebrate King Arthur, as he hints in his verses to Mansus [3]; but 'Arthur was reserved,' says Fenton, 'to another destiny [4].'

It appears by some sketches of poetical projects left in manu- 87 script, and to be seen in a library at Cambridge [5], that he had digested his thoughts on this subject into one of those wild dramas which were anciently called Mysteries [6]; and Philips had seen what he terms part of a tragedy, beginning with the first ten lines of Satan's address to the Sun [7]. These Mysteries consist of

[1] Phillips' *Milton*, pp. 28, 39; *Works*, iv. 1; *post*, MILTON, 142.

Milton says that it was his appointment as Latin Secretary (*ante*, MILTON, 64) which took him off from his task. 'Quatuor iam libros absolveram, quum ecce nihil tale cogitantem me . . . Concilium Status, quod dicitur, . . . ad se vocat.' *Works*, v. 235.

His MS. notes (*post*, MILTON, 87) show that in 1639–40, in preparing for his projected epic on King Arthur, he had studied the history before the Conquest. Masson's *Milton*, ii. 105. See also *ib.* iii. 670.

[2] *Paradise Lost*, ix. 26; *post*, MILTON, 110.

[3] *Sylvarum Liber. Mansus*, l. 80. See also *Epitaphium Damonis*, l. 162. In *Paradise Lost*, ix. 27, he describes himself as

'Not sedulous by nature to indite
Wars, hitherto the only argument
Heroic deem'd, chief mast'ry to
    dissect
With long and tedious havock fa-
    bled knights
In battels feign'd.'

[4] '*Id est*, to be the subject of an heroic poem by Blackmore.' Johnson's *Works*, vii. 90 *n*. See *post*, BLACKMORE, 11. For Dryden's projected epic see *post*, DRYDEN, 140, and for Pope's, *post*, POPE, 241.

[5] Trinity College. See *Facsimile of the MS. of Milton's Minor Poems*, &c., 1899, pp. 33, 38, for a facsimile

of all these sketches. In Dr. Aldis Wright's opinion (Pref. p. 3) they were written in 1640–2. See also Masson's *Milton*, ii. 106, 117, 121 *n*.

[6] See Spence's *Anec.* p. 397, for an extraordinary Mystery which he saw in Turin in 1739.

[7] *Paradise Lost*, iv. 32. 'In the 4th booke of *Paradise Lost*, there are about six verses of Satan's exclamation to the sun, which Mr. E. Philips remembers about 15 or 16 yeares before ever his poem was thought of. Which verses were intended for the beginning of a tragoedie which he had designed, but was diverted from it by other businesse.' AUBREY, *Brief Lives*, ii. 69.

Phillips (p. 35) says that ten verses (iv, 32–41) were shown to him.

Milton, in his *Animadversions* (*ante*, MILTON, 48), seems to allude to some great poem, when, addressing 'the ever-begotten Light,' he says :—
'When thou hast settled peace in the Church, and righteous judgment in the Kingdom, then shall all thy saints address their voices of joy and triumph to thee, standing on the shore of that Red Sea into which our enemies had almost driven us. And he that now for haste snatches up a plain ungarnished present as a thank-offering to thee, . . . may then perhaps take up a harp, and sing thee an elaborate song to generations.' *Works*, i. 184.

allegorical persons, such as *Justice, Mercy, Faith*[1]. Of the tragedy or mystery of *Paradise Lost* there are two plans:

'The Persons.	The Persons.
Michael.	Moses.
Chorus of Angels.	Divine Justice, Wisdom,
Heavenly Love.	[Mercy], Heavenly Love.
Lucifer.	The Evening Star, Hes-
Adam, ⎱ with the	perus.
Eve, ⎰ Serpent.	Chorus of Angels.
Conscience.	Lucifer.
Death.	Adam.
Labour, ⎫	Eve.
Sickness, ⎪	Conscience.
Discontent, ⎬ Mutes.	Labour, ⎫
Ignorance, ⎪	Sickness, ⎪
with others; ⎭	Discontent, ⎬ Mutes.
Faith.	Ignorance, ⎪
Hope.	Fear, ⎪
Charity.	Death; ⎭
	Faith.
	Hope.
	Charity.

Paradise Lost.

The Persons.

88   'Moses προλογίζει, recounting how he assumed his true body: that it corrupts not, because it is [of his being] with God in the mount; declares the like of Enoch and Elijah [Eliah]; besides the purity of the place, that certain pure winds, dews, and clouds preserve it from corruption; whence exhorts to the sight of God; tells they cannot see Adam in the state of innocence, by reason of their sin.

Justice, ⎫
Mercy, ⎬ debating what should become of man, if he fall.
Wisdom, ⎭
Chorus of Angels singing [sing] a hymn of the Creation.

ACT II.

Heavenly Love.
Evening Star.
Chorus sing the marriage-song and describe Paradise.

[1] 'The dramas in which Justice, Mercy, Faith, &c. were introduced were moralities, not mysteries.' MA-LONE, Johnson's *Works*, vii. 91 *n*.

ACT III.

Lucifer, contriving Adam's ruin.
Chorus fears for Adam, and relates Lucifer's rebellion and fall.

ACT IV.

Adam, } fallen.
Eve,
Conscience cites them to God's examination.
Chorus bewails, and tells the good Adam has [hath] lost.

ACT V.

Adam and Eve driven out of Paradise.
     ,,   ,,   presented by an angel with
Labour, Grief, Hatred, Envy, War,)
   Famine, Pestilence, Sickness, Dis- } Mutes.
   content, Ignorance, Fear, Death,)
To whom he gives their names. Likewise Winter, Heat,
   Tempest, &c.[1]
Faith,)
Hope, } comfort him and instruct him.
Charity,)
Chorus briefly concludes.'

Such was his first design, which could have produced only an 89
allegory or mystery. The following sketch seems to have attained
more maturity.

' Adam unparadised :

'The angel Gabriel, either descending or entering ; shewing, since 90
this globe was created, his frequency as much on earth as in heaven;
describes Paradise. Next, the Chorus, shewing the reason of his
coming—to keep his watch in Paradise, after Lucifer's rebellion,
by command from God ; and withal expressing his desire to see
and know more concerning this excellent new creature, man. The
angel Gabriel, as by his name signifying a prince of power, tracing
Paradise with a more free office, passes by the station of the Chorus,
and, desired by them, relates what he knew of man; as the creation
of Eve, with their love and marriage. After this, Lucifer appears [2] ;
after his overthrow, bemoans himself, seeks revenge on man. The
Chorus prepare resistance at his first approach. At last, after discourse of enmity on either side, he departs : whereat the Chorus
sings of the battle and victory in heaven, against him and his

---

[1] After '&c.' follows :—'enter'd
into yᵉ world.' *Facsimile of MS. of
Milton's Minor Poems*, p. 35.
[2] In the first edition there is a
comma after 'appears.' The facsimile omits both comma and semi-
colon. *Ib.*

accomplices : as before, after the first act, was sung a hymn of the creation. Here again may appear Lucifer, relating and insulting [1] in what he had done to the destruction of man. Man next, and Eve having by this time been seduced by the Serpent, appears confusedly covered with leaves. Conscience, in a shape, accuses him ; Justice cites him to the place whither Jehovah called for him. In the mean while the Chorus entertains the stage, and is informed by some angel the manner of the [his] Fall. Here the Chorus bewails Adam's fall ; Adam then and Eve return ; [and] accuse one another ; but especially Adam lays the blame to his wife ; is stubborn in his offence. Justice appears, reasons with him, convinces him. The Chorus admonisheth Adam, and bids him beware [by] Lucifer's example of impenitence. The angel is sent to banish them out of Paradise ; but before causes to pass before his eyes, in shapes, a mask of all the evils of this life and world. He is humbled, relents, despairs : at last appears Mercy, comforts him, promises the Messiah ; then calls in Faith, Hope, and Charity ; instructs him ; he repents, gives God the glory, submits to his penalty. The Chorus briefly concludes. Compare this with the former draught.'

91   These are very imperfect rudiments of *Paradise Lost*, but it is pleasant to see great works in their seminal state pregnant with latent possibilities of excellence ; nor could there be any more delightful entertainment than to trace their gradual growth and expansion, and to observe how they are sometimes suddenly advanced by accidental hints, and sometimes slowly improved by steady meditation.

92   Invention is almost the only literary labour which blindness cannot obstruct, and therefore he naturally solaced his solitude by the indulgence of his fancy and the melody of his numbers. He had done what he knew to be necessarily previous to poetical excellence : he had made himself acquainted with ' seemly arts and affairs [2],' his comprehension was extended by various knowledge, and his memory stored with intellectual treasures. He was skilful in many languages, and had by reading and composition attained the full mastery of his own. He would have wanted little help from books, had he retained the power of perusing them.

93   But while his greater designs were advancing, having now, like many other authors, caught the love of publication, he amused

---

[1] [' Exulting in,' &c. *Lives of the Poets, a new edition, corrected,* 1806 ; and subsequent editions ; but Johnson's ' insulting in ' appears in Milton's own MS. *Facsimile,* &c., p. 38.]

[2] ' Seemly and generous arts and affairs.' *Ante,* MILTON, 47.

himself as he could with little productions. He sent to the press (1658) a manuscript of Raleigh, called *The Cabinet Council*[1], and next year gratified his malevolence to the clergy by a *Treatise of Civil Power in Ecclesiastical Cases*[2], and *The Means of removing Hirelings out of the Church*[3].

Oliver was now dead; Richard was constrained to resign: the **94** system of extempory government, which had been held together only by force, naturally fell into fragments when that force was taken away; and Milton saw himself and his cause in equal danger. But he had still hope of doing something. He wrote letters, which Toland has published, to such men as he thought friends to the new commonwealth[4]; and even in the year of the Restoration he 'bated no jot of heart or hope[5],' but was fantastical enough to think that the nation, agitated as it was, might be settled by a pamphlet, called *A [The] ready and easy way to establish a Free Commonwealth*, which was, however, enough considered to be both seriously and ludicrously answered[6].

The obstinate enthusiasm of the commonwealthmen was very **95** remarkable. When the king was apparently returning, Harrington, with a few associates as fanatical as himself, used to meet, with

[1] See Masson's *Milton*, v. 404, for the full title, and for Milton's Address 'To the Reader,' which begins:— 'Having had the manuscript of this Treatise, written by Sir Walter Raleigh, many years in my hands, and finding it lately by chance among other books and papers.'

[2] *A Treatise of Civil Power in Ecclesiastical Causes: shewing that it is not lawfull for any power on Earth to compell in matters of Religion*, 1659, *Works*, iii. 317; Masson's *Milton*, v. 581.

[3] *Considerations touching the likeliest means to remove Hirelings out of the Church*, *Works*, iii. 348; Masson's *Milton*, v. 605.

[4] See Toland's *Milton*, p. 118. In the former of these letters, dated Oct. 20, 1659, upholding 'the good old cause,' he says:—'The terms to be stood on are liberty of conscience to all professing Scripture to be the rule of their faith and worship, and the abjuration of a single person [as King].' *Works*, iii. 395. In the second, addressed to Monk, he advo-

cates a kind of Home Rule—'a standing council in every city and great town . . . with a competent territory adjoined.' A Grand or General Council of the Nation, 'not without assent of the standing council in each city,' shall govern the country as a whole. *Ib.* p. 398.

[5] 'nor bate a jot
Of heart or hope.' *Sonnets*, No. xxii.

[6] *Works*, iii. 401. The pamphlet was published about March 1, 1659–60; 'a second and enlarged edition' more than a month later. Of this edition not a single copy is known to exist. Masson's *Milton*, v. 677–8, 689 *n.* For the daring of the peroration see *ib.* p. 655. 'Not one of Milton's pamphlets provoked a more rapid fury of criticism.' *Ib.* p. 657. The ludicrous answer—*The Censure of the Rota* [*post*, MILTON, 95 *n.*] *upon Mr. Milton's Book*, &c.—appeared on March 30. *Ib.* p. 659. The serious answer—*The Dignity of Kingship Asserted*, &c.—appeared about the end of April. *Ib.* p. 691.

all the gravity of political importance, to settle an equal government by rotation[1]; and Milton, kicking when he could strike no longer, was foolish enough to publish, a few weeks before the Restoration, *Notes* upon a sermon preached by one Griffiths[2], intituled *The Fear of God and the King*. To these notes an answer was written by L'Estrange[3], in a pamphlet petulantly called *No blind Guides*[4].

96   But whatever Milton could write or men of greater activity could do the king was now about to be restored[5] with the irresistible approbation of the people. He was therefore no longer secretary, and was consequently obliged to quit the house which he held by his office[6]; and, proportioning his sense of danger to his opinion of the importance of his writings, thought

[1] James Harrington, author of *Oceana*. 'He had every night a meeting at the Turke's head in the New Pallace-yard, . . . at one Miles's, where was made purposely a large ovall-table, with a passage in the middle for Miles to deliver his coffee. About it sat his disciples and the virtuosi. The discourses in this kind were the most ingeniose and smart that ever I heard, or expect to heare, and bandied with great eagernesse.' AUBREY, *Brief Lives*, i. 289. The Club was called The Rota. Aubrey adds:—'The greatest part of the Parliament-men perfectly hated this designe of *rotation by ballotting*.' *Ib.* p. 291.

Pepys heard 'admirable discourse' there in January, 1659-60. *Diary*, i. 9, 11.

'Great men have been among us; hands that penned
And tongues that uttered wisdom—better none:
The later Sidney, Marvel, Harrington,
Young Vane, and others who called Milton friend.'
WORDSWORTH, *Poet. Works*, 1870, iii. 69.

[2] Matthew Griffith (not Griffiths) 'shewing himself a grand episcoparian' suffered many imprisonments. In a sermon preached in London on March 25, 1660, 'shewing himself too zealous for the royal cause, before Monk durst own it, [he] was, to please and blind the fanatical party, im-

prison'd in Newgate, but soon after released.' *Ath. Oxon.* iii. 711. See also Masson's *Milton*, v. 667, and Milton's *Works*, iii. 438, for a fine passage in which he maintains that a Protector like Monk is better than a Stuart king.

[3] *Post*, ADDISON, 42. Burnet describes L'Estrange as having 'an unexhausted copiousness in writing.' *Hist. of his own Time*, ii. 72. 'His nature, at once ferocious and ignoble, showed itself in every line that he penned.' MACAULAY, *History*, i. 407. See also Masson's *Milton*, v. 689.

[4] *No Blinde Guides, in answer to a Seditious Pamphlet of J. Milton's*. 1660.

[5] In the first edition, 'the king was now evidently approaching.'

[6] Early in 1649 Milton moved from Holborn (*ante*, MILTON, 63) to lodgings at Spring Gardens, Charing Cross. On Nov. 19, 1649, the Council of State assigned him rooms in Whitehall. At the end of 1651 he moved to 'a pretty garden-house in Petty France, opening into St. James's Park,' afterwards known as 19 York Street. It stood till 1876, bearing the inscription put up by Jeremy Bentham:—'Sacred to Milton, Prince of Poets.' Masson's *Milton*, iv. 104, 150, 153, 418; Phillips' *Milton*, p. 33.

'There was a sort of rivalry between Clarke, who bought Cowley's house [*ante*, COWLEY, 46 *n*.], and Bentham's father, who had bought Milton's.' Bentham's *Works*, x. 51.

it convenient to seek some shelter, and hid himself for a time in Bartholomew-Close by West Smithfield [1].

I cannot but remark a kind of respect, perhaps unconsciously, 97 paid to this great man by his biographers: every house in which he resided is historically mentioned, as if it were an injury to neglect naming any place that he honoured by his presence [2].

The King, with lenity of which the world has had perhaps no 98 other example [3], declined to be the judge or avenger of his own or his father's wrongs, and promised to admit into the Act of Oblivion all, except those whom the parliament should except; and the parliament doomed none to capital punishment but the wretches who had immediately co-operated in the murder of the King. Milton was certainly not one of them; he had only justified what they had done [4].

This justification was indeed sufficiently offensive; and (June 16) 99 an order was issued to seize Milton's *Defence*, and Goodwin's *Obstructors of Justice*, another book of the same tendency, and burn them by the common hangman [5]. The attorney-general was

[1] Phillips' *Milton*, p. 37.

[2] Boswell quotes this passage when giving the list of Johnson's habitations. *Johnson*, iii. 405. See also *ib.* i. 111.

[3] Johnson might be borrowing Hume's words, who speaks of 'an unexampled lenity.' *Hist. of Eng.* vii. 358.

South, on May 29, 1670, preaching about loving one's enemies, said that the king 'brought with him the greatest, the brightest and most stupendous instance of this virtue that, next to what has been observed of our Saviour, was ever yet shown by man.' *Sermons*, ii. 320.

Dryden wrote three years later :—
'Neither the French history, nor our own, could have supplied me, nor Plutarch himself, were he now alive, could have found a Greek or Roman to have compared to him in that eminent virtue of his clemency.' *Works*, vii. 158.

Sir Walter Scott magnifies this unexampled lenity by reducing the number put to a cruel death from thirteen to nine. Dryden's *Works*, ed. 1821, ix. 59.

[4] Vane, who had not co-operated, was judicially murdered. Peters had not co-operated more than Milton,

and yet he was put to a cruel death. Professor Masson shows that had Milton been sent to trial, Chief Justice Bridgman would have easily brought his case within the statute of Edward III on treason. The danger he ran was very great. Masson's *Milton*, v. 658, 674; vi. 168-193.

[5] 'Neque in ipsos modo auctores, sed in libros quoque eorum saevitum, delegato triumviris ministerio ut monumenta clarissimorum ingeniorum in comitio ac foro urerentur.' TACITUS, *Agricola*, ch. 2.

Iconoclastes also was burnt: '"They were solemnly burnt at the Session House in the Old Bailey."' *Masson*, vi. 39, 181, 193. Goodwin had a narrow escape from death. *Ib.* pp. 176, 184, 190. Wood calls him 'that infamous and black-mouthed independent.' *Ath. Oxon.* iii. 964.

'On July 21, 1683, twenty-seven propositions gathered from the writings of Milton and others, were ordered by the University of Oxford to be burnt in the court of the Schools [under the Bodleian]. See Somers's *Tracts*, iii. 223.' *Milton's Poems*, ed. T. Warton, p. 358; *post*, SMITH, 9 *n*.

Warton goes on to quote from

ordered to prosecute the authors; but Milton was not seized, nor perhaps very diligently pursued [1].

100 Not long after (August 19) the flutter of innumerable bosoms was stilled by an act, which the King, that his mercy might want no recommendation of elegance, rather called an *act of oblivion* than of grace [2]. Goodwin was named, with nineteen more, as incapacitated for any publick trust [3]; but of Milton there was no exception.

101 Of this tenderness shewn to Milton the curiosity of mankind has not forborne to enquire the reason. Burnet thinks he was forgotten [4]; but this is another instance which may confirm Dalrymple's observation, who says, 'that whenever Burnet's narrations are examined, he appears to be mistaken [5].'

Decretum Oxoniense, 1683 (*Musae Anglicanae*, ed. 1714, ii. 180), the following lines :—
'Quanquam O, si simili quicunque haec scripserit auctor
Fato succubuisset, eodemque arserit igne ;
In medio videas flamma crepitante cremari
Miltonum, coelo terrisque inamabile nomen.'
Milton's *Defensio* was burnt also at Paris and Toulouse. Toland's *Milton*, p. 104. In 1698 his prose works were published ; but 'the publication was even then deemed somewhat venturesome ; though printed in London, they purported to have been printed at Amsterdam.' Masson's *Milton*, vi. 814.
In 1710 the decree of the University, together with Sacheverell's sermon, was burnt by the common hangman by order of the House of Lords. *Parl. Hist.* vi. 885.
[1] In a Proclamation by the King (preserved in the British Museum) on Aug. 13, 1660, for the suppression of two books by Milton and one by Goodwin, we read :—'Whereas the said John Milton and John Goodwin are both fled, or so obscure themselves that no endeavours used for their apprehension can take effect whereby they might . . . receive condign punishment for their treasons and offences,' &c.
[2] It was on Aug. 29 that the 'Act of Free and General Pardon, In-

demnity and Oblivion' was passed. Masson's *Milton*, vi. 53.
[3] *Ib.* vi. 55.
[4] Burnet does not say he was forgotten ; but that 'it was thought a strange omission if he was forgot, and an odd strain of clemency if it was intended he should be forgiven.' *History*, i. 179.
[5] 'I have never tried Burnet's facts by the tests of dates and of original papers without finding them wrong.' DALRYMPLE, *Memoirs of Great Britain*, &c., 1790, i. 49. For Johnson's contempt of these *Memoirs* see Boswell's *Johnson*, ii. 210 ; v. 403.
'JOHNSON. I do not believe that Burnet intentionally lied ; but he was so much prejudiced that he took no pains to find out the truth.' *Ib.* ii. 213.
Hume, on Dec. 4, 1756, wrote of some fact :—'It stands only on Burnet's authority, who is very careless and inaccurate.' *MSS. Royal Society of Edinburgh*.
'Burnet's credulity is great, but his simplicity is equally great ; and he never deceives you for a moment.' COLERIDGE, *Table Talk*, 1884, p. 101.
Macaulay described him 'as honest, though careless.' Trevelyan's *Macaulay*, i. 335. In his *History*, ii. 433 *n*., he writes :—'It is usual to censure Burnet as a singularly inaccurate historian ; but I believe the charge to be altogether unjust.' See also *post*, GRANVILLE, 19.

Forgotten he was not, for his prosecution was ordered[1]; it 102 must be therefore by design that he was included in the general oblivion. He is said to have had friends in the House, such as Marvel[2], Morrice, and Sir Thomas Clarges[3]; and undoubtedly a man like him must have had influence. A very particular story of his escape is told by Richardson in his Memoirs, which he received from Pope, as delivered by Betterton, who might have heard it from Davenant[4]. In the war between the King and Parliament, Davenant was made prisoner and condemned to die, but was spared at the request of Milton[5]. When the turn of success brought Milton into the like danger, Davenant repaid the benefit by appearing in his favour. Here is a reciprocation of generosity and gratitude so pleasing that the tale makes its own way to credit. But if help were wanted, I know not where to find it. The danger of Davenant is certain from his own relation[6]; but of his escape there is no account. Betterton's narration can be traced no higher; it is not known that he had it from

[1] On the same day that the House of Commons ordered the burning of Milton's books the Attorney-General was instructed to proceed against him for his defence of the regicide, and the Serjeant-at-Arms was ordered to arrest him. Masson's *Milton*, vi. 39.

For an interesting examination 'How did Milton escape?' see *ib.* vi. 184.

[2] 'Marvel acted very vigorously in his behalf.' Phillips' *Milton*, p. 38. Aubrey mentions him among his 'familiar learned acquaintance.' *Brief Lives*, ii. 72. According to Toland (p. 123) 'he used to frequent him the oftenest of any body.' For his lines on *Paradise Lost* see Marvell's *Poems*, 1870, p. 75.

[3] 'I have heard that Secretary Morrice and Sir Thomas Clarges were his friends.' Richardson's *Explanatory Notes, &c., on Paradise Lost, with Life*, Preface, p. 89. 'Morrice was the person that had prevailed with Monk to declare for the King.' Burnet's *Hist.* i. 106. Clarges was Monk's brother-in-law. For the probable assistance of Annesley, afterwards Earl of Anglesey, see *post*, MILTON, 143 *n*.

[4] ''Twas Sir William Davenant obtained his remission, in return for his own life procured by Milton's interest, when himself was under condemnation, Anno 1650. . . . What authority have I for this story? My first answer is Mr. Pope told it me. Whence had he it? from Mr. Betterton.' Richardson's *Explanatory Notes*, &c., Pref. p. 89. '"I believe this story was first retailed in print by Wood. *Ath. Oxon.* [1691, ii. 292]." MALONE, *Shakespeare*, ed. Boswell, iii. 282.' Cunningham, *Lives of the Poets*, i. 113. For Davenant see *ante*, DENHAM, 22 ; *post*, DRYDEN, 26, 97.

[5] According to Wood, Davenant, when carrying some artisans from France to Virginia in 1650, was stopped on the main ocean, and sent to the Tower to be tried for his life; 'but upon the mediation of Milton and others'—among them two aldermen of York—he was saved. *Ath. Oxon.* iii. 805. Aubrey, who told Wood of the aldermen, says nothing of Milton's intervention. *Brief Lives*, i. 207.

[6] In the Postscript to the Reader, dated Cowes Castle, Oct. 22, 1650: he says:—'I am here arrived at the middle of the third book [of *Gondibert*]. . . . But 'tis high time to strike sail and cast anchor (though I have run but half my course) when

Davenant. We are told that the benefit exchanged was life for life, but it seems not certain that Milton's life ever was in danger. Goodwin, who had committed the same kind of crime, escaped with incapacitation; and as exclusion from publick trust is a punishment which the power of government can commonly inflict without the help of a particular law, it required no great interest to exempt Milton from a censure little more than verbal. Something may be reasonably ascribed to veneration and compassion— to veneration of his abilities, and compassion for his distresses, which made it fit to forgive his malice for his learning. He was now poor and blind; and who would pursue with violence an illustrious enemy, depressed by fortune, and disarmed by nature[1]?

103   The publication of the act of oblivion put him in the same condition with his fellow-subjects. He was however, upon some pretence not now known, in the custody of the serjeant in December[2]; and when he was released, upon his refusal of the fees demanded, he and the serjeant were called before the House. He was now safe within the shade of oblivion, and knew himself to be as much out of the power of a griping officer as any other man. How the question was determined is not known. Milton would hardly have contended, but that he knew himself to have right on his side[3].

at the helm I am threatened with death.' *Gondibert*, 1651, p. 243.

[1] 'The mercy which induced the worst of a bad race to spare him was so capricious, and apparently so motiveless, that it may almost be considered as providential.' SOUTHEY, *Specimens*, Preface, p. 26.

Milton, in his *Defensio Secunda*, says of the blind:—'Nos ab iniuriis hominum non modo incolumes, sed paene sacros, divina lux reddidit, divinus favor.' *Works*, v. 217. His blindness most probably saved him. Charles II and Hyde might well have shrunk from exposing the blind scholar and poet to the brutal hands of the hangman.

[2] For the order for his prosecution on June 16 see *ante*, MILTON, 99. He lived in 'a place of retirement and abscondence till the Act of Oblivion came forth' on Aug. 29. Phillips' *Milton*, p. 37. The Serjeant-at-Arms, who received large fees from his prisoners, would not admit that this Act cancelled

the order of the House of Commons. Masson's *Milton*, vi. 193.

[3] 'Saturday, xvth December, 1660. Ordered that Mr. Milton, now in custody of the Serjeant at Arms attending this House, be forthwith released, paying his fees.' *Journals of the House of Commons*, viii. 208.

'Monday, xviith December, 1660. A complaint being made that the Serjeant at Arms had demanded excessive fees for the imprisonment of Mr. Milton; Ordered, that it be referred to the Committee for Privileges to examine this business; and to call Mr. Milton and the Serjeant before them; and to determine what is fit to be given to the Serjeant for his fees in this case.' *Ib.* p. 209.

'Soon after [Dec. 17] Mr. Andrew Marvel complained that the Serjeant had exacted £150 fees of Mr. Milton. Sir Heneage Finch observed that Milton was Latin Secretary to Cromwell, and deserved hanging.' *Parl. Hist.* iv. 162.

He then removed to Jewin-street, near Aldersgate-street [1] ; and 104 being blind, and by no means wealthy, wanted a domestick companion and attendant, and therefore, by the recommendation of Dr. Paget, married Elizabeth Minshul, of a gentleman's family in Cheshire, probably without a fortune [2]. All his wives were virgins, for he has declared that he thought it gross and indelicate to be a second husband [3]: upon what other principles his choice was made cannot now be known, but marriage afforded not much of his happiness. The first wife left him in disgust, and was brought back only by terror ; the second, indeed, seems to have been more a favourite [4], but her life was short ; the third, as Philips relates, oppressed his children in his life-time, and cheated them at his death [5].

Soon after his marriage, according to an obscure story, he was 105 offered the continuance of his employment, and, being pressed by his wife to accept it, answered, 'You, like other women, want to ride in your coach ; my wish is to live and die an honest man [6].'

[1] He had first taken 'a house in Holborn, near Red Lyon Fields.' Phillips' *Milton*, p. 38.

[2] *Ib.* Aubrey mentions Dr. Nathan Paget among Milton's 'familiar learned acquaintance.' *Brief Lives*, ii. 72. It was through him that Ellwood 'was admitted to come to Milton.' *Life of Ellwood*, ed. Crump, p. 88. Under the Commonwealth he was Physician to the Tower. Masson's *Milton*, vi. 454. He was a cousin of Elizabeth Minshul. Her father was a yeoman. The marriage took place on Feb. 24, 1662-3. She was twenty-four. In Masson's *Milton*, vi. 475, is given a facsimile of Milton's signature. It is 'the only authentic specimen of his handwriting of later date than 1652' known to Professor Masson. *Ib.* p. 477 *n.*

[3] Johnson refers, I think, to the following passage in *An Apology for Smectymnuus*, written when he was a bachelor:—'I think with them who both in prudence and elegance of spirit would choose a virgin of mean fortunes honestly bred before the wealthiest widow.' *Works*, i. 254.

Johnson, who married a widow, said of a friend:—'He has done a very foolish thing, Sir ; he has married a widow, when he might have

had a maid.' Boswell's *Johnson*, ii. 77. There was royal precedent for this. Henry II, the Black Prince, Henry IV, Edward IV, Richard III, and Henry VIII all married widows. See also *post*, SHEFFIELD, 20.

[4] The words seem cold when we remember how Milton described her in *Sonnets*, No. xxiii.

[5] It was not Phillips, but Dr. Birch, who related this. He was told by Elizabeth Foster, Milton's grand-daughter, who had it from her mother, that 'Milton's widow, though she owned that he died worth £1,500, yet allowed his three daughters but £100 each.' Milton's *Works*, 1753, Preface, p. 76. See *post*, MILTON, 174.

Aubrey describes her 'a gent. person, a peacefull and agreable humour.' *Brief Lives*, ii. 65.

The writer of Milton's Life in *Biog. Brit.* (p. 3116) says that 'he saw her at Namptwich, where she lived about the year 1724. She seemed to have no notion of her husband's great fame, and said he left no great matter at his death.' For her excellence as a wife see Masson's *Milton*, vi. 476.

[6] 'Thou art in the right (says he); you, as other women, would ride in your coach; for me, my aim is to live and die an honest man.' Richard-

If he considered the Latin secretary as exercising any of the powers of government, he that had shared authority either with the Parliament or Cromwell might have forborne to talk very loudly of his honesty[1]; and if he thought the office purely ministerial, he certainly might have honestly retained it under the king. But this tale has too little evidence to deserve a disquisition; large offers and sturdy rejections are among the most common topicks of falsehood.

106   He had so much either of prudence or gratitude that he forbore to disturb the new settlement with any of his political or ecclesiastical opinions, and from this time devoted himself to poetry and literature[2]. Of his zeal for learning in all its parts he gave a proof by publishing the next year (1661) *Accidence commenced Grammar*[3]; a little book which has nothing remarkable, but that its author, who had been lately defending the supreme powers of his country and was then writing *Paradise Lost*, could descend from his elevation to rescue children from the perplexity of grammatical confusion, and the trouble of lessons unnecessarily repeated[4].

107   About this time Elwood the quaker, being recommended to him as one who would read Latin to him, for the advantage of his conversation[5], attended him every afternoon, except on

son, who tells this story (*Explanatory Notes*, &c., Pref. p. 100), says he had it from Henry Bendish, a descendant of Oliver Cromwell. Milton's widow said that 'her husband was applied to by message from the King, and was invited to write for the Court.' Newton's *Milton*, Pref, p. 80. Professor Masson (vi. 639) thinks the story incredible.

[1] Johnson judged Dryden much less harshly when he wrote:—'It is natural to hope that a comprehensive is likewise an elevated soul, and that whoever is wise is also honest. . . . But enquiries into the heart are not for man; we must now leave him to his Judge.' *Post*, DRYDEN, 120.

[2] 'At his Majesty's happy return,' wrote Marvell, 'J. M. did partake . . . of his regal clemency, and has ever since expiated himself in a retired silence.' *The Rehearsal Transprosed*, Second Part, 1673, p. 379.

[3] *Works*, iii. 441. Professor Masson believes that it was mainly written

in 'the days of Milton's pedagogy.' It was published, not in 1661, but in 1669. Masson's *Milton*, vi. 640.

[4] *Post*, MILTON, 147; WATTS, 22. 'Mrs. Barbauld had his [Johnson's] best praise, and deserved it; no man was more struck than Mr. Johnson with voluntary descent from possible splendour to painful duty.' *John. Misc.* i. 157.
'Thy soul was like a Star, and dwelt apart:
Thou hadst a voice whose sound was like the sea:
Pure as the naked heaven, majestic, free,
So didst thou travel on life's common way,
In cheerful godliness; and yet thy heart   [lay.'
The lowliest duties on herself did WORDSWORTH, *Poet. Works*, 1870–4, iii. 68.

[5] *Life of Ellwood*, p. 89; *post*, MILTON, 140, 145.

Sundays. Milton, who, in his letter to Hartlib[1], had declared that 'to read [smatter] Latin with an English mouth is as ill a hearing as Law French[2],' required that Elwood should learn and practise the Italian pronunciation, which, he said, was necessary, if he would talk with foreigners[3]. This seems to have been a task troublesome without use. There is little reason for preferring the Italian pronunciation to our own, except that it is more general; and to teach it to an Englishman is only to make him a foreigner at home. He who travels, if he speaks Latin, may so soon learn the sounds which every native gives it, that he need make no provision before his journey; and if strangers visit us, it is their business to practise such conformity to our modes as they expect from us in their own countries[4]. Elwood complied with the directions, and improved himself by his attendance; for he relates that Milton, having a curious ear, knew by his voice when he read what he did not understand, and would stop him and ' open the most difficult passages[5].'

In a short time he took a house in the Artillery Walk, leading to Bunhill fields[6]; the mention of which concludes the register of Milton's removals and habitations. He lived longer in this place than in any other. **108**

He was now busied by *Paradise Lost*[7]. Whence he drew the original design has been variously conjectured by men who cannot bear to think themselves ignorant of that which, at last, neither diligence nor sagacity can discover. Some find the hint in an Italian tragedy[8]. Voltaire tells a wild and unauthorised story of a farce seen by Milton in Italy, which opened thus : ' Let the Rainbow be the Fiddlestick of the Fiddle of Heaven[9].' It **109**

---

[1] *Ante*, MILTON, 14.

[2] *Works*, i. 278. In his Grammar he says :—' Few will be persuaded to pronounce Latin otherwise than their own English.' *Ib.* iii. 441.

Law French is called by Blackstone that ' barbarous dialect, an evident and shameful badge of tyranny and foreign servitude.' *Comm.* iii. 317.

[3] *Life of Ellwood*, p. 89. Sorbière (*post*, SPRAT, 6) in his *Voyage en Angleterre* (1664), p. 68, says : ' Les Anglais s'expliquent en latin d'un certain accent, et avec une prononciation qui ne le rend pas moins difficile que leur langue.'

Evelyn, hearing the exercises at West-minster School, condemned 'their odd pronouncing of Latin, so that out of England none were able to understand it, or endure it.' *Diary*, i. 372.

[4] See Boswell's *Johnson*, ii. 404.

[5] *Life of Ellwood*, p. 90.

[6] For this house see Masson's *Milton*, vi. 482. The present Milton Street close by is not the street where he lived, but the old Grub Street. *Ib.* p. 485.

[7] *Post*, MILTON, 207.

[8] Newton, in a note on *Paradise Lost*, i. 16, gives the name of this tragedy as *Il Paradiso perso*, but he adds :—' It is all a pretence.'

[9] Voltaire describes it as ' une

has been already shewn that the first conception was a tragedy or mystery [1], not of a narrative but a dramatick work, which he is supposed to have begun to reduce to its present form about the time (1655) when he finished his dispute with the defenders of the King [2].

110   He long before had promised to adorn his native country by some great performance, while he had yet perhaps no settled design, and was stimulated only by such expectations as naturally arose from the survey of his attainments and the consciousness of his powers [3].   What he should undertake it was difficult to determine.   He was ' long chusing, and began late [4].'

111   While he was obliged to divide his time between his private studies and affairs of state, his poetical labour must have been often interrupted ; and perhaps he did little more in that busy time than construct the narrative, adjust the episodes, proportion the parts, accumulate images and sentiments, and treasure in his memory or preserve in writing such hints as books or meditation would supply.   Nothing particular is known of his intellectual operations while he was a statesman, for, having every help and accommodation at hand, he had no need of uncommon expedients.

112   Being driven from all publick stations he is yet too great not to be traced by curiosity to his retirement, where he has been found by Mr. Richardson, the fondest of his admirers, sitting ' before his door in a grey coat of coarse cloth [in a grey coarse cloth coat], in warm sultry [sunny] weather, to enjoy the fresh air ; and so, as well as in his own room, receiving the visits of people of distinguished parts as well as quality [5].   His visitors of

comédie intitulée *Adam, ou le Péché originel*, écrite par un certain Andreino [Andreini]...La scène s'ouvre par un chœur d'anges, et Michel parle ainsi au nom de ses confrères :—" Que l'arc-en-ciel soit l'archet du violon du firmament ; que les sept planètes soient les sept notes de notre musique ; que le temps batte exactement la mesure,&c."' *Œuvres*, viii. 414.

' This relation of Voltaire's was perfectly true, as far as relates to the existence of the play, the *Adamo* of Andreini.' JAMES BOSWELL, JUN., Johnson's *Works*, vii. 100 n.

[1] *Ante*, MILTON, 87.

[2] Aubrey records, on the authority of E. Phillips, that ' Milton began *Paradise Lost* about two yeares before the King came in, and finished about three yeares after the King's restauracion.' *Brief Lives*, ii. 69.

[3] *Ante*, MILTON, 47.

[4] *Par. L.* ix. 26 ; *ante*, MILTON, 86.

[5] Richardson does not say that he had seen him, but writes :—' I have heard many years since,' &c.   *Explanatory Notes*, &c., Pref. p. 4.

' At the time of his abode in Petty France [1652-60, *ante*, MILTON, 96 n.] he was frequently visited by persons of high quality must now be imagined to be few [1]; but men of parts might reasonably court the conversation of a man so generally illustrious, that foreigners are reported by Wood to have visited the house in Bread-street where he was born [2].

According to another account he was seen in a small house, 113 'neatly enough dressed in black cloaths, sitting in a room hung with rusty green ; pale but not cadaverous, with chalkstones in his hands. He said, that if it were not for the gout, his blindness would be tolerable [3].'

In the intervals of his pain, being made unable to use the 114 common exercises, he used to swing in a chair, and sometimes played upon an organ [4].

He was now confessedly and visibly employed upon his poem, 115 of which the progress might be noted by those with whom he was familiar; for he was obliged, when he had composed as many lines as his memory would conveniently retain, to employ some friend in writing them, having, at least for part of the time, no regular attendant. This gave opportunity to observations and reports.

Mr. Philips observes that there was a very remarkable circum- 116 stance in the composure of *Paradise Lost*,

quality, and by all learned foreigners of note.' Phillips' *Milton*, p. 36.

[1] Phillips mentions members of the nobility 'and many persons of eminent quality' visiting him here ; 'nor were the visits of foreigners ever more frequent than in this place almost to his dying day.' *Ib.* p. 39. See also Toland's *Milton*, p. 139.

[2] 'The only inducement of severall foreigners that came over into England was chiefly to see Oliver Protector and Mr. John Milton; and would see the house and chamber wher *he* was borne. He was much more admired abrode then at home.' AUBREY, *Brief Lives*, ii. 72. See also Wood's *Fasti Oxon.* i. 486, and Masson's *Milton*, iv. 350.
The house was destroyed in the Great Fire of 1666.

[3] This account Richardson (*Explanatory Notes*, &c., Pref. p. 4) had 'from an ancient clergyman in Dorsetshire, Dr. Wright, who found him in a small house, he thinks but one room on a floor; in that, up one pair of

stairs, which was hung with a rusty green, he found John Milton, sitting in an elbow-chair, black cloaths and neat enough, pale but not cadaverous, his hands and fingers gouty, and with chalk stones.'
In the evidence given about his nuncupative will (*post*, MILTON, 162) he is one time described as dining in the kitchen, and another time in 'his lodging chamber.' *Milton's Poems*, ed. T. Warton, Preface, pp. 35, 37.

[4] 'When blindness and age confined him he played much upon an organ he kept in the house, and had a pully to swing and keep him in motion.' Toland's *Milton*, p. 150.
In his academy the students are to spend some time 'in recreating and composing their travailed spirits with the solemn and divine harmonies of music heard or learned.' *Works*, i. 283.
'Where Milton introduces music in his poems he talks the language of a master.' HAWKINS, *Hist. of Music*, i, Preface, p. 9. See *post*, MILTON, 159.

' which I have a particular reason,' says he, ' to remember ; for whereas I had the perusal of it from the very beginning for some years, as I went from time to time to visit him, in parcels of ten, twenty, or thirty verses at a time (which, being written by whatever hand came next, might possibly want correction as to the orthography and pointing), having, as the summer came on, not been shewed any for a considerable while, and desiring the reason thereof, was answered that his vein never happily flowed but from the Autumnal Equinox to the Vernal ; and that whatever he attempted at other times was never to his satisfaction, though he courted his fancy never so much : so that, in all the years he was about this poem, he may be said to have spent half his time therein [1].'

117   Upon this relation Toland[2] remarks, that in his opinion Philips has mistaken the time of the year ; for Milton, in his Elegies, declares that with the advance of the Spring he feels the increase of his poetical force, ' redeunt in carmina vires[3].' To this it is answered, that Philips could hardly mistake time so well marked ; and it may be added that Milton might find different times of the year favourable to different parts of life. Mr. Richardson conceives it impossible that ' such a work should be suspended for six months, or for one. It may go on faster or slower, but it must go on[4].' By what necessity it must continually go on, or why it might not be laid aside and resumed, it is not easy to discover.

118   This dependance of the soul upon the seasons, those temporary

---

[1] Phillips' *Milton*, p. 36. ' From Mr. E. Phillips :—All the time of writing his *Paradise Lost* his veine began at the autumnall aequinoctiall and ceased at the vernall (or thereabouts ; I believe about May).' AUBREY, *Brief Lives*, ii. 68.

His widow said that ' he used to compose his poetry chiefly in winter.' Newton's *Milton*, Pref. p. 80.

Crabbe fancied that he composed best in autumn ; ' but there was something in a sudden fall of snow that appeared to stimulate him in a very extraordinary manner.' Crabbe's *Works*, 1834, i. 262.

' My father observed that his best working days were " in the early spring, when Nature begins to waken from her winter sleep." ' *Life of Tennyson*, i. 374.

[2] ' Toland and Tindal, prompt at priests to jeer.'
     POPE, *The Dunciad*, ii. 399.
For *Toland's Invitation to Dismal to dine with the Calf's Head Club* see Swift's *Works*, xii. 293. See also *post*, SWIFT, 31.

[3] ' Fallor? an et nobis redeunt in carmina vires,
    Ingeniumque mihi munere veris adest ? ' *Eleg*. v. 5.
Milton was only twenty when he wrote this.

[4] ' I cannot comprehend that a man with such a work in his head can suspend it for six months together, or but one ; though it may go on more slowly, but it must go on.' Richardson's *Explanatory Notes*, &c., Pref. p. 113.

and periodical ebbs and flows of intellect, may, I suppose, justly
be derided as the fumes of vain imagination. ' Sapiens dominabitur astris[1].' The author that thinks himself weather-bound
will find, with a little help from hellebore[2], that he is only idle or
exhausted[3]; but while this notion has possession of the head, it
produces the inability which it supposes. Our powers owe much
of their energy to our hopes ; 'possunt quia posse videntur[4].'
When success seems attainable, diligence is enforced; but when it
is admitted that the faculties are suppressed by a cross wind or
a cloudy sky the day is given up without resistance ; for who can
contend with the course of Nature ?

From such prepossessions Milton seems not to have been free. 119
There prevailed in his time an opinion that the world was in its
decay, and that we have had the misfortune to be produced in the
decrepitude of Nature. It was suspected that the whole creation
languished, that neither trees nor animals had the height or bulk
of their predecessors, and that every thing was daily sinking by
gradual diminution[5]. Milton appears to suspect that souls partake
of the general degeneracy, and is not without some fear that his
book is to be written in ' an age too late' for heroick poesy[6].

Another opinion wanders about the world, and sometimes finds 120
reception among wise men—an opinion that restrains the operations of the mind to particular regions, and supposes that a

[1] 'They [the stars] so gently incline that a wise man may resist
them ; *sapiens dominabitur astris:*
they rule us, but God rules them.'
BURTON, *Anatomy of Melancholy,*
1660, p. 57.
[2] 'Expulit elleboro morbum bilemque
meraco.' HORACE, *Epis.* ii. 2. 137.
[3] For Gray's ' fantastick foppery '
as regards 'happy moments' for writing see *post*, GRAY, 26.
Johnson in 1758 wrote in *The
Idler*, No. xi :—' This distinction of
seasons is produced only by imagination operating on luxury. . . . He that
shall resolutely excite his faculties,
or exert his virtues, will soon make
himself superior to the seasons.'
Reynolds agreed with him in this.
Boswell's *Johnson*, i. 332 *n.*
'A man,' said Dr. Johnson, ' may
write at any time, if he will set himself doggedly to it.' *Ib.* v. 40. Nevertheless in 1773 he recorded that he

'had always considered the time
between Easter and Whitsuntide as
propitious to study.' *John. Misc.* i.
67. Two years after he published
the *Life of Milton* he regretfully
wrote :—' I thought myself above
assistance or obstruction from the
seasons.' *John. Letters*, ii. 233.
[4] *Aeneid*, v. 231.
[5] This view was put forth by
Bishop Godfrey Goodman in *The
Fall of Man, or the Corruption of
Nature proved by the Light of
Natural Reason*, 1616, and refuted
in *An Apology or Declaration of the
Power and Providence of God in
the Government of the World*, by
Dr. George Hakewill, 1635 [1627].
Johnson's *Works*, vii. 103 *n.*
[6] 'unless an age too late, or cold
Climate, or years, damp my intended
wing
Depress'd.' *Paradise Lost*, ix. 44.

luckless mortal may be born in a degree of latitude too high or
too low for wisdom or for wit. From this fancy, wild as it is, he
had not wholly cleared his head, when he feared lest the 'climate'
of his country might be 'too cold' for flights of imagination.

121   Into a mind already occupied by such fancies, another not
more reasonable might easily find its way. He that could fear lest
his genius had fallen upon too old a world or too chill a climate,
might consistently magnify to himself the influence of the seasons,
and believe his faculties to be vigorous only half the year.

122   His submission to the seasons was at least more reasonable
than his dread of decaying Nature or a frigid zone, for general
causes must operate uniformly in a general abatement of mental
power; if less could be performed by the writer, less likewise
would content the judges of his work. Among this lagging race
of frosty grovellers he might still have risen into eminence by
producing something which 'they should not willingly let die[1].'
However inferior to the heroes who were born in better ages, he
might still be great among his contemporaries, with the hope of
growing every day greater in the dwindle of posterity: he might
still be the giant of the pygmies, the one-eyed monarch of the
blind[2].

123   Of his artifices of study or particular hours of composition we
have little account, and there was perhaps little to be told.
Richardson, who seems to have been very diligent in his enquiries,
but discovers always a wish to find Milton discriminated from
other men, relates, that

'he would sometimes lie awake whole nights, but not a verse
could he make; and on a sudden his poetical faculty would rush
upon him with an *impetus* or *œstrum*, and his daughter was
immediately called to secure what came. At other times he
would dictate perhaps forty lines in a breath, and then reduce
them to half the number[3].'

[1] *Ante*, MILTON, 25.
[2] 'Being asked if Barnes knew a
good deal of Greek, Johnson answered, "I doubt, Sir, he was *uno-
culus inter caecos*."' Boswell's *Johnson*, iv. 19.
[3] 'Other stories I have heard concerning the posture he was usually
in when he dictated; that he sat
leaning backward obliquely in an
easy chair, with his leg flung over
the elbow of it; that he frequently

compos'd lying in bed in a morning.
I have been well inform'd that when
he could not sleep, but lay awake
whole nights, he try'd; not one verse
could he make; at other times flow'd
easy his unpremeditated verse [*Paradise Lost*, ix. 24], with a certain *impetus* and *Æstro* [*sic*], as himself
seem'd to believe. Then, at what
hour soever, he rung for his daughter
to secure what came. I have been
also told he would dictate many,

These bursts of lights and involutions of darkness, these 124 transient and involuntary excursions and retrocessions of invention, having some appearance of deviation from the common train of Nature, are eagerly caught by the lovers of a wonder. Yet something of this inequality happens to every man in every mode of exertion, manual or mental. The mechanick cannot handle his hammer and his file at all times with equal dexterity; there are hours, he knows not why, when 'his hand is out.' By Mr. Richardson's relation casually conveyed much regard cannot be claimed. That in his intellectual hour Milton called for his daughter 'to secure what came,' may be questioned, for unluckily it happens to be known that his daughters were never taught to write[1]; nor would he have been obliged, as is universally confessed, to have employed any casual visiter in disburthening his memory, if his daughter could have performed the office.

The story of reducing his exuberance has been told of other 125 authors, and, though doubtless true of every fertile and copious mind, seems to have been gratuitously transferred to Milton[2].

What he has told us, and we cannot now know more, is that 126 he composed much of his poem in the night and morning, I suppose before his mind was disturbed with common business; and that he poured out with great fluency his ' unpremeditated verse[3].' Versification, free, like his, from the distresses of rhyme, must by a work so long be made prompt and habitual; and, when his thoughts were once adjusted, the words would come at his command.

At what particular times of his life the parts of his work were 127 written cannot often be known. The beginning of the third book shews that he had lost his sight; and the Introduction to

perhaps 40 lines, as it were in a breath, and then reduce them to half the number.' Richardson's *Explanatory Notes*,&c., Pref. p.114. See *post*, MILTON, 161.

[1] *Post*, MILTON, 140, 174. Elizabeth Foster, his granddaughter, told Newton that ' he kept his daughters at a great distance, and would not allow them to learn to write, which he thought unnecessary for a woman.' Newton's *Milton*, Pref. p. 83.

'He hath two daughters living [Mary and Deborah]; Deborah was his amanuensis.' AUBREY, *Brief Lives*, ii. 64. For their signatures to a document see *post*, MILTON, 174 *n*.

[2] *Post*, POPE, 299; GRAY, 26.

[3] 'If answerable style I can obtain
Of my celestial patroness, who deigns
Her nightly visitation unimplor'd,
And dictates to me slumb'ring, or inspires
Easy my unpremeditated verse.'
Paradise Lost, ix. 20.
See also *ib*. iii. 32; vii. 28.

His widow reported that ' on his waking in a morning he would make her write down sometimes twenty or thirty verses.' Newton's *Milton*, Pref. p. 80.

the seventh that the return of the King had clouded him with
discountenance, and that he was offended by the licentious festivity of the Restoration. There are no other internal notes of
time. Milton, being now cleared from all effects of his disloyalty,
had nothing required from him but the common duty of living in
quiet, to be rewarded with the common right of protection; but
this, which, when he sculked from the approach of his King, was
perhaps more than he hoped, seems not to have satisfied him, for
no sooner is he safe than he finds himself in danger, 'fallen on
evil days and evil tongues, and with darkness and with danger
compass'd round¹.' This darkness, had his eyes been better
employed, had undoubtedly deserved compassion; but to add the
mention of danger was ungrateful and unjust². He was fallen
indeed on 'evil days'; the time was come in which regicides
could no longer boast their wickedness. But of 'evil tongues' for
Milton to complain required impudence at least equal to his other
powers—Milton, whose warmest advocates must allow that he
never spared any asperity of reproach or brutality of insolence.

128   But the charge itself seems to be false, for it would be hard to
recollect any reproach cast upon him, either serious or ludicrous,
through the whole remaining part of his life. He pursued his
studies or his amusements without persecution, molestation, or
insult. Such is the reverence paid to great abilities, however
misused: they who contemplated in Milton the scholar and the
wit were contented to forget the reviler of his King.

129   When the plague (1665) raged in London, Milton took refuge
at Chalfont in Bucks³, where Elwood, who had taken the house
for him, first saw a complete copy of *Paradise Lost*, and, having
perused it, said to him, 'Thou hast said a great deal upon
Paradise Lost, what hast thou to say upon *Paradise Found*⁴?'

¹   'though fall'n on evil days,
On evil days though fall'n, and evil
   tongues;   [compass'd round,
In darkness, and with dangers
And solitude.' *Par. Lost*, vii. 25.
² 'He was in perpetual terror of
being assassinated; though he had
escaped the talons of the law, he
knew he had made himself enemies
in abundance. He was so dejected
he would lie awake whole nights.
He then kept himself as private as
he could. This Dr. Tancred Robin-

son had from a relation of Milton's,
Mr. Walker of the Temple.' Richardson's *Explanatory Notes*, &c., Pref.
p. 94.
³ In the first edition, 'in Essex.'
'The great pit in Finsbury,' into
which the dead were thrown, described by Defoe (*Works*, ed. 1877,
v. 45), was close to Bunhill Row.
⁴ 'I took a pretty box for him in
Giles Chalfont. . . . After some common discourses had passed between
us, he called for a manuscript of his;

Next year, when the danger of infection had ceased, he 130 returned to Bunhill-fields, and designed the publication of his poem. A license was necessary, and he could expect no great kindness from a chaplain of the archbishop of Canterbury[1]. He seems, however, to have been treated with tenderness; for though objections were made to particular passages, and among them to the simile of the sun eclipsed in the first book[2], yet the license was granted; and he sold his copy, April 27, 1667, to Samuel Simmons, for an immediate payment of five pounds[3], with a stipulation to receive five pounds more when thirteen hundred should be sold of the first edition, and again, five pounds after the sale of the same number of the second edition, and another five pounds after the same sale of the third. None of the three editions were to be extended beyond fifteen hundred copies[4].

The first edition was ten books, in a small quarto[5]. The titles 131

which being brought he delivered to me, bidding me take it home with me, and read it at my leisure; and when I had so done return it to him with my judgment thereupon.... He asked me how I liked it.... I pleasantly said to him, "thou hast said much here of *Paradise Lost*, but what hast thou to say of *Paradise Found*?" He made me no answer, but sat some time in a muse; then brake off that discourse, and fell upon another subject.' *Life of Ellwood*, p. 144.

[1] By the licensing Act of 1662 poetry, which in 1643 had been placed under the masters of St. Paul's School (*ante*, MILTON, 58 *n*.), was now under the Archbishop. [For the scrivener's copy of Book i, which appears to have been the actual MS. placed in the hands of the compositors, see Additional Appendix A, at end of Volume i.]

For the licenser's chaplain, the Rev. Thomas Tomkyns, author of *The Inconveniencies of Toleration*, see Masson's *Milton*, vi. 506.

[2] 'as when the sun new-ris'n
Looks through the horizontal misty
air,
Shorn of his beams; or from behind the moon, [sheds
In dim eclipse, disastrous twilight
On half the nations, and with fear
of change

Perplexes monarchs.'
Paradise Lost, i. 594.
'We had like to be eternally deprived of this treasure by the Licenser, who would needs suppress the whole poem for imaginary treason in these lines.' Toland's *Milton*, p. 219.

[3] 'When the bookseller offered Milton five pounds for his *Paradise Lost* he did not reject it, and commit his poem to the flames, nor did he accept the miserable pittance as the reward of his labour; he knew that the real price of his work was immortality, and that posterity would pay it.' LORD CAMDEN, *Parl. Hist.* xvii. 1000. The copyright lasted till 1774, when perpetual copyrights were brought to an end by a decision of the House of Lords. *Ib.* pp. 953–1003; *Letters of Hume to Strahan*, p. 275.

[4] Professor Masson points out (*Milton*, vi. 508) that *Paradise Lost* was published at 'a bad time commercially.' The booksellers had suffered terribly by the Fire. Pepys recorded on Oct. 5, 1666, that he hears 'there is above £150,000 of books burned; all the great booksellers almost undone.' *Diary*, iii. 300.

[5] 'It was printed with wonderful accuracy.' Masson's *Milton*, vi. 517. 'It was sold,' says Malone, 'for three shillings, as appears from a note on

were varied from year to year[1]; and an advertisement and the arguments of the book were omitted in some copies, and inserted in others[2].

132 The sale gave him in two years a right to his second payment, for which the receipt was signed April 26, 1669[3]. The second edition was not given till 1674; it was printed in small octavo, and the number of books was increased to twelve, by a division of the seventh and twelfth[4], and some other small improvements were made[5]. The third edition was published in 1678[6], and the widow, to whom the copy was then to devolve, sold all her claims to Simmons for eight pounds, according to her receipt given Dec. 21, 1680[7]. Simmons had already agreed to transfer the whole right to Brabazon Aylmer for twenty-five pounds; and Aylmer sold to Jacob Tonson half, August 17, 1683, and half, March 24, 1690, at a price considerably enlarged[8]. In the history of *Paradise Lost* a deduction thus minute will rather gratify than fatigue[9].

133 The slow sale and tardy reputation of this poem have been always mentioned as evidences of neglected merit and of the uncertainty of literary fame, and enquiries have been made and conjectures offered about the causes of its long obscurity and late reception. But has the case been truly stated? Have not lamentation and wonder been lavished on an evil that was never felt?

134 That in the reigns of Charles and James the *Paradise Lost* received no publick acclamations is readily confessed. Wit and literature were on the side of the Court; and who that solicited favour or fashion would venture to praise the defender of the regicides[10]? All that he himself could think his due, from 'evil

the title page of my copy.' Malone's *Dryden*, i. 114.

[1] There were 'at least nine different forms of title page.' Masson's *Milton*, vi. 622.

[2] Much of this information and of what follows is given in Richardson's *Explanatory Notes*, &c., Pref. p. 116. See also Masson's *Milton*, vi. 624.

[3] For this receipt see *ib*. vi. 628.

[4] Tenth.

[5] Masson's *Milton*, vi. 713.

[6] *Ib.* vi. 779.

[7] £5 was due for the second edition; and another £5 would be due when the third edition was sold. She accepted for this £3 down. The total payment was £18—equal to about £63 at the present day. *Ib.* vi. 780.

[8] For Tonson's rudeness to Dryden see *post*, DRYDEN, 187. Tonson being asked 'what poem he ever got the most by, immediately named *Paradise Lost*.' Spence's *Anec.* p. 344. 'The best portrait of Tonson (that by Kneller) represents him with *Paradise Lost* in his hand.' Cunningham's *Lives of the Poets*, i. 123. See also *post*, MILTON, 175.

[9] This sentence is not in the first edition.

[10] Between the Restoration and the publication of *Paradise Lost* 'the public mentions of Milton had all been in the vein of continued exe-

tongues' in 'evil days,' was that reverential silence which was generously preserved. But it cannot be inferred that his poem was not read or not, however unwillingly, admired.

The sale, if it be considered, will justify the publick [1]. Those 135 who have no power to judge of past times but by their own, should always doubt their conclusions. The call for books was not in Milton's age what it is in the present. To read was not then a general amusement; neither traders nor often gentlemen thought themselves disgraced by ignorance [2]. The women had not then aspired to literature [3], nor was every house supplied with a closet of knowledge. Those, indeed, who professed learning were not less learned than at any other time; but of that middle race of students who read for pleasure or accomplishment and who buy the numerous products of modern typography, the number was then comparatively small. To prove the paucity of readers [4], it may be sufficient to remark that the nation had been satisfied, from 1623 to 1664, that is, forty-one years, with only two editions of the works of Shakespeare, which probably did not together make one thousand copies [5].

cration and regret that he had not been hanged.' For instances of these see Masson's *Milton*, vi. 636.

[1] 'The sale would be proof in itself that the poem had at once made a very strong impression.' *Ib.* vi. 628.

[2] 'Feb. 15, 1684. Dr. [afterwards Archbishop] Tenison told me there were thirty or forty young men in his parish, either governors to young gentlemen or chaplains to noblemen, who being reproved by him on occasion for frequenting taverns or coffee-houses told him they would study if they had books.' EVELYN, *Diary*, ii. 204.

[3] *Post*, ADDISON, 160; BLACK-MORE, 9; POPE, 41. Lady M. W. Montagu wrote on July 20, 1710:— 'We are permitted no books but such as tend to the weakening and effeminating of the mind.' *Letters*, 1837, i. 157. See also *ib.* iii. 31, 45.

John Clarke, Master of Hull Grammar School, in his *Essay upon Study*, 1731, p. 251, says:—'It is a great absurdity in the education of ladies to tease them with learning the French tongue, which they have no more real occasion for than Welsh or wild Irish.' Those who do not intend to marry he advises to study Latin. For Clarke see *post*, MILTON, 233.

'It is a little hard that not one gentleman's daughter in a thousand should be brought to read or understand her own natural tongue, or to be judge of the easiest books that are written in it. . . . They are not so much as taught to spell in their childhood, nor can ever attain to it in their whole lives.' SWIFT, *Works*, ix. 210.

'Our wives read Milton, and our daughters plays.'

POPE, *Imit. Hor.*, *Epis.* ii. 1. 172.

[4] 'No poem ever appeared in an age less fitted or less inclined to read, like, or understand it than did *Paradise Lost*.' CAMPBELL, *Brit. Poets*, p. 705.

'Late, very late, correctness grew our care, [from civil war.' When the tir'd Nation breath'd

POPE, *Imit. Hor.*, *Epis.* ii. 1. 272.

[5] The first edition of Dryden's *Fables* (*post*, DRYDEN, 184) probably consisted of 1,000 copies. A second edition was not called for till fourteen years later. Malone's *Dryden*, i. 328.

136   The sale of thirteen hundred copies in two years, in opposition to so much recent enmity and to a style of versification new to all and disgusting to many, was an uncommon example of the prevalence of genius. The demand did not immediately increase ; for many more readers than were supplied at first the nation did not afford. Only three thousand were sold in eleven years; for it forced its way without assistance : its admirers did not dare to publish their opinion, and the opportunities now given of attracting notice by advertisements were then very few. The means of proclaiming the publication of new books have been produced by that general literature which now pervades the nation through all its ranks.

137   But the reputation and price of the copy still advanced, till the Revolution put an end to the secrecy of love, and *Paradise Lost* broke into open view with sufficient security of kind reception [1].

138   Fancy can hardly forbear to conjecture with what temper Milton surveyed the silent progress of his work, and marked his reputation stealing its way in a kind of subterraneous current through fear and silence. I cannot but conceive him calm and confident, little disappointed, not at all dejected, relying on his own merit with steady consciousness, and waiting without impatience the vicissitudes of opinion and the impartiality of a future generation [2].

139   In the mean time he continued his studies, and supplied the want of sight by a very odd expedient, of which Philips gives the following account [3] :

140   Mr. Philips tells us,

'that though our author had daily about him one or other to read, some persons of man's estate, who, of their own accord, greedily catched at the opportunity of being his readers, that they might as well reap the benefit of what they read to him as oblige him by the benefit of their reading [4], and others of younger years were sent by their parents to the same end ; yet excusing only the eldest daughter, by reason of her bodily infirmity and difficult utterance of speech (which, to say truth, I doubt was the principal cause of excusing her), the other

---

[1] See Appendix N.
[2] *Ante*, MILTON, 26. For the general low estimation of his character during his lifetime see *Milton's Poems*, ed. T. Warton, p. 571.
　In *The Lives, &c., of the Eng. Dram. Poets* by Langbaine and

Gildon, published in 1698 (p. 100), it is stated of Milton :—'The time or place of his birth, education, or death I am ignorant of.'
[3] Phillips' *Milton*, p. 41.
[4] *Ante*, MILTON, 107.

two were condemned to the performance of reading and exactly pronouncing of all the languages of whatever book he should at one time or other think fit to peruse, viz. the Hebrew (and I think the Syriac), the Greek, the Latin, the Italian, Spanish, and French [1]. All which sorts of books to be confined to read, without understanding one word, must needs be a trial of patience almost beyond endurance. Yet it was endured by both for a long time, though the irksomeness of this employment could not be always concealed, but broke out more and more into expressions of uneasiness ; so that at length they were all, even the eldest also, sent out to learn some curious and ingenious sorts of manufacture, that are proper for women to learn ; particularly embroideries in gold or silver [2].'

In the scene of misery which this mode of intellectual labour 141 sets before our eyes, it is hard to determine whether the daughters or the father are most to be lamented. A language not understood can never be so read as to give pleasure, and very seldom so as to convey meaning. If few men would have had resolution to write books with such embarrassments, few likewise would have wanted ability to find some better expedient.

Three years after his *Paradise Lost* (1667 [3]), he published his 142 *History of England*, comprising the whole fable of Geoffry of Monmouth, and continued to the Norman invasion [4]. Why he should have given the first part, which he seems not to believe,

---

[1] 'He had a man read to him. The first thing he read was the Hebrew Bible, and that was at 4 h. mané, ½ h. + [i.e. at 4 a.m., for more than half an hour]. Then he contemplated. At 7 his man came to him again, and then read to him again, and wrote till dinner. . . . His daughter, Deborah, could read to him Latin, Italian and French, and Greeke.' AUBREY, *Brief Lives*, ii. 68.

Prescott wrote in 1827 :—' My excellent reader reads to me Spanish with a true Castilian accent, two hours a day, without understanding a word of it.' Ticknor's *Prescott*, 1864, p. 77.

[2] *Ante*, MILTON, 124 ; *post*, 170, 173.

'"Where," asked Mr. Wordsworth, " could Milton have picked up such notions in a country which had seen so many women of learning and talent ? But his opinion of what women ought to be, it may be pre-

sumed, is given in the unfallen Eve, as contrasted with the right condition of Man before his Maker : —

'He for God only, she for God in
    him.' [*Paradise Lost*, iv. 299.]

" Now that," said Mr. Wordsworth earnestly, "*is* a low, a very low, and a very false estimate of woman's condition." ' Wordsworth's *Memoirs*, ii. 465.

[3] In the first edition, 1670, the date of the publication of the *History*. *Paradise Lost* was published in 1667.

[4] *The History of Britain, That part especially now call'd England. From the first Traditional Beginning, continu'd to the Norman Conquest. Collected out of the ancientest and best Authors thereof.* By John Milton. 1670. Four of the six books he wrote before March 1648-9. When he finished is not known. *Ante*, MILTON, 83, 85 ; *Works*, iv. 1 ; Masson's *Milton*, vi. 642.

and which is universally rejected, it is difficult to conjecture[1]. The style is harsh; but it has something of rough vigour, which perhaps may often strike though it cannot please.

143   On this history the licenser again fixed his claws, and before he would transmit it to the press tore out several parts. Some censures of the Saxon monks were taken away, lest they should be applied to the modern clergy[2]; and a character of the Long Parliament and Assembly of Divines was excluded[3], of which the author gave a copy to the Earl of Anglesea[4], and which, being afterwards published, has been since inserted in its proper place.

144   The same year were printed *Paradise Regained* and *Sampson Agonistes*[5], a tragedy written in imitation of the Ancients and never designed by the author for the stage. As these poems were published by another bookseller it has been asked, whether Simmons was discouraged from receiving them by the slow sale of the former? Why a writer changed his bookseller a hundred years ago I am far from hoping to discover. Certainly he who in two years sells thirteen hundred copies of a volume in quarto,

[1] 'I have determined to bestow the telling over even of these reputed tales, be it for nothing else but in favour of our English poets and rhetoricians, who by their art will know how to use them judiciously.' *Works*, iv. 2.

Hume says of the history of the Heptarchy:—'Even the great learning and vigorous imagination of Milton sunk under the weight.' *Hist. of Eng.* i. 28.

[2] Phillips' *Milton*, p. 39. He says of the monkish historians:—'This we must expect, in civil matters to find them dubious relaters, and still to the best advantage of what they term Holy Church, meaning indeed themselves: in most other matters of religion, blind, astonished, and struck with superstition as with a planet; in one word Monks.' *Works*, iv. 79. This passage was not struck out by the censors, for it is in the first edition, p. 97. For Gibbon's scorn of monks see his *Memoirs*, p. 57.

[3] *Works*, iv. 81. It was published in 1681 under the title of *Character of the Long Parliament*. Professor Masson (vi. 808) doubts it being a fragment of the *History*.

[4] Phillips' *Milton*, p. 39; Toland's *Life of Milton*, p. 139.

The Earl, when Arthur Annesley, 'had been the chief manager of the Restoration along with Monk.' He was probably one of those who got Milton included in the Act of Oblivion (*ante*, MILTON, 102). Masson's *Milton*, vi. 187.

'Antony Wood represents this lord as an artful time-server; by principle a Calvinist, by policy a favourer of the Papists. Burnet paints him as a tedious and ungraceful orator, as a grave, abandoned, and corrupt man, whom no party would trust. The benign author of the *Biographia Britannica* (a work which I cannot help calling *Vindicatio Britannica*, or a defence of everybody) humanely applies his softening pencil.' HORACE WALPOLE, *Works*, i. 412. See Burnet's *Hist.* i. 104.

[5] The title-page bears the date of 1671. These poems were licensed on July 2, 1670, and 'may have appeared late in that year.' Masson's *Milton*, vi. 651. See *post*, MILTON, 265, 266.

bought for two payments of five pounds each, has no reason to repent his purchase.

When Milton shewed *Paradise Regained* to Elwood, 'This,' 145 said he [1], 'is owing to you; for you put it in [into] my head by the question you put to me at Chalfont, which otherwise [before] I had not thought of.'

His last poetical offspring was his favourite. He could not, as 146 Elwood relates, endure to hear *Paradise Lost* preferred to *Paradise Regained* [2]. Many causes may vitiate a writer's judgement of his own works. On that which has cost him much labour he sets a high value, because he is unwilling to think that he has been diligent in vain: what has been produced without toilsome efforts is considered with delight as a proof of vigorous faculties and fertile invention; and the last work, whatever it be, has necessarily most of the grace of novelty [3]. Milton, however it happened, had this prejudice, and had it to himself [4].

To that multiplicity of attainments and extent of comprehension 147 that entitle this great author to our veneration may be added a kind of humble dignity, which did not disdain the meanest services to literature [5]. The epick poet, the controvertist, the politician, having already descended to accommodate children with a book of rudiments, now in the last years of his life composed a book of Logick [6], for the initiation of students in philosophy, and published (1672) *Artis Logicæ plenior Institutio ad Petri Rami methodum concinnata* [7], that is, 'A new Scheme of Logick, according to the Method of Ramus.' I know not whether even in this book he did not intend an act of hostility against the Universities; for

---

[1] 'In a pleasant tone he said to me,' &c. *Life of Ellwood*, p. 145.

[2] The passage to which Johnson refers is not in *Ellwood's Life*, but in Phillips' *Milton*, p. 39. Neither is it there stated that *Paradise Regained* was Milton's favourite. '*Paradise Regained*,' Phillips wrote, 'is generally censured to be much inferior to the other; though he could not hear with patience any such thing when related to him.' See *ante*, COWLEY, 114.

[3] 'Pope knew that the mind is always enamoured of its own productions, and did not trust his first fondness.' *Post*, POPE, 302.

[4] 'An author and his reader are not always of a mind.' *Post*, THOMSON, 24.

'*Paradise Regained* Wordsworth thought the most perfect in execution of anything written by Milton; that and *The Merchant of Venice* in language he thought almost faultless.' Wordsworth's *Memoirs*, ii. 311. 'However inferior its kind is to *Paradise Lost* its execution is superior.' COLERIDGE, H. C. Robinson's *Diary*, 1869, i. 311.

[5] *Ante*, MILTON, 106.

[6] 'It was probably an old manuscript which he found among his papers.' Masson's *Milton*, vi. 685.

[7] *Works*, vi. 195.

Ramus was one of the first oppugners of the old philosophy, who disturbed with innovations the quiet of the schools [1].

148 His polemical disposition, again revived. He had now been safe so long that he forgot his fears, and published a treatise *Of true Religion, Heresy, Schism, Toleration, and the best Means to prevent the Growth of Popery* [2].

149 But this little tract is modestly written, with respectful mention of the Church of England and an appeal to the thirty-nine articles [3]. His principle of toleration is agreement in the sufficiency of the Scriptures, and he extends it to all who, whatever their opinions are, profess to derive them from the sacred books [4]. The papists appeal to other testimonies, and are therefore in his opinion not to be permitted the liberty of either publick or private worship; for though they plead conscience, 'we have no warrant,' he says, 'to regard conscience which is not grounded in [on] Scripture [5].'

150 Those who are not convinced by his reasons may be perhaps delighted with his wit: the term 'Roman catholick' is, he says, 'one of the Pope's bulls; it is particular universal, or catholick schismatick [6].'

151 He has, however, something better. As the best preservative against Popery he recommends the diligent perusal of the Scrip-

---

[1] In Milton's abridgement of Freigius's *Petri Rami Vita* we read how in Paris, 'P. Ramus repente ad praetorii tribunalis capitalem contentionem . . . rapitur, novique criminis accusatur, quod scilicet, Aristotelem oppugnando, artes enervaret.' *Works*, vi. 355. Ramus fell in the massacre of St. Bartholomew. 'Ses ennemis traînèrent son corps sanglant à la porte de tous les colléges, pour faire amende honorable à la philosophie d'Aristote.' VOLTAIRE, *Œuvres*, xxvi. 299.

For Europe divided by Ramism and Aristotelianism see Masson's *Milton*, i. 264.

[2] *Of True Religion, Haeresie, Schism, Toleration, And what best Means may be us'd against the Growth of Popery*. The Author J. M. London, 1673, *Works*, iv. 259; Masson's *Milton*, vi. 687, 690.

The king's declaration in 1672, 'suspending the execution of all penal laws against Papists and Nonconformists,' had, in 1673, set the House of Commons 'in a flame; they saw Popery and slavery lay at the bottom.' They passed the Test Act, by which all Papists, the Duke of York among them, were excluded from office. The Nonconformists, though they were hit by the Act, in their dread of Popery made no opposition. Burnet's *Hist.* i. 343, 384–92.

Milton maintains that 'of all known sects, or pretended religions at this day in Christendom—Popery is the only, or the greatest, heresy.' *Works*, iv. 260; *post*, MILTON, 165.

[3] *Works*, iv. 260. The Church of England he speaks of as 'our church.' *Ib.* p. 266. 'He adjusted himself to the necessity' of the times. Masson's *Milton*, vi. 693. See also *ante*, MILTON, 18.

[4] *Works*, iv. 263; *post*, MILTON, 166.

[5] *Ib.* iv. 265.

[6] 'It is a mere contradiction, one of the Pope's bulls, as if he should say, universal particular, a Catholic schismatic.' *Ib.* p. 261.

tures; a duty, from which he warns the busy part of mankind not to think themselves excused [1].

He now reprinted his juvenile poems with some additions [2].   152

In the last year of his life he sent to the press, seeming to take 153 delight in publication, a collection of Familiar Epistles in Latin; to which, being too few to make a volume, he added some academical exercises [3], which perhaps he perused with pleasure, as they recalled to his memory the days of youth; but for which nothing but veneration for his name could now procure a reader.

When he had attained his sixty-sixth year the gout, with which 154 he had been long tormented, prevailed over the enfeebled powers of nature. He died by a quiet and silent expiration, about the tenth of November 1674, at his house in Bunhill-fields [4], and was buried next his father in the chancel of St. Giles at Cripplegate [5]. His funeral was very splendidly and numerously attended [6].

Upon his grave there is supposed to have been no memorial[7]; but 155

---

[1] 'Neither let the countryman, the tradesman, the lawyer, the physician, the statesman, excuse himself by his much business from the studious reading thereof.' *Works*, iv. p. 267.

[2] For the title see *ante*, MILTON, 14*n*. To the ten sonnets of the edition of 1645 (*ante*, MILTON, 59) nine were added. Masson's *Milton*, vi. 688. Phillips printed four in 1694 at the end of his *Life of Milton* prefixed to *Letters of State*—those to Fairfax, Cromwell, and Cyriack Skinner for the first time. The fourth, the sonnet to Vane, sent to him on July 3, 1652, had been printed in 1662 in George Sikes's *Life and Death of Sir Henry Vane*, p. 93; where it is described as 'composed by a learned gentleman.' Aubrey wanted to get copies of the first two. 'Were they made in commendation of the devill,' he wrote, ''twere all one to me; 'tis the ὕψος [sublimity] that I look after.' *Brief Lives*, ii. 70.

[3] *Ioannis Miltoni Angli Epistolarum Familiarium Liber Unus: Quibus accesserunt Eiusdem, iam olim in Collegio Adolescentis, Prolusiones Quaedam Oratoriae*, 1674, *Works*, vi. 109. The printer was not suffered by the Government to include Milton's *Letters of State*. Masson's *Milton*, vi. 724. For their

publication in 1676 see *ib.* p. 791, and for the discovery of the MS. copy in 1823 see *ib.* pp. 805, 816. See also *ante*, MILTON, 8.

For Milton's publication in 1674 of a translation of a Latin tract about John Sobieski see *Works*, iv. 314; Masson's *Milton*, vi. 725. In 1682 was published his *Brief History of Moscovia*. *Works*, iv. 271; Masson's *Milton*, vi. 812.

[4] 'He died of the gowt struck in, the 9th or 10th of November, 1674.' AUBREY, *Brief Lives*, ii. 66. He died on Nov. 8. Masson's *Milton*, vi. 731.

[5] In the same church, on Aug. 22, 1620, Oliver Cromwell had been married to Elizabeth Bourchier. Carlyle's *Cromwell*, 1857, i. 37.

[6] 'He was attended from his house to the Church by several gentlemen then in town, his principal wellwishers and admirers.' Phillips' *Milton*, p. 40.

'All his learned and great friends in London, not without a friendly concourse of the vulgar, accompanied his body.' Toland's *Life of Milton*, p. 149.

[7] 'He lies buried in St. Giles's Cripplegate, upper end of chancell at the right hand, vide his gravestone. —Memorandum, his stone is now removed; for about two yeares since (now, 1681) the two steppes to the

in our time a monument has been erected in Westminster-Abbey *To the Author of Paradise Lost*, by Mr. Benson, who has in the inscription bestowed more words upon himself than upon Milton[1].

156   When the inscription for the monument of Philips, in which he was said to be *soli Miltono secundus*[2], was exhibited to Dr. Sprat, then dean of Westminster, he refused to admit it; the name of Milton was, in his opinion, too detestable to be read on the wall of a building dedicated to devotion[3]. Atterbury, who succeeded him, being author of the inscription, permitted its reception. 'And such has been the change of publick opinion,' said Dr. Gregory[4], from whom I heard this account, 'that I have seen erected in the church a statue[5] of that man, whose name I once knew considered as a pollution of its walls.'

157   Milton has the reputation of having been in his youth eminently

communion table were raysed.' AU-BREY, *Brief Lives*, ii. 66.

For the reported violation of his grave in 1790 see *N. & Q.* 7 S. ix. 361, and for Cowper's stanzas on 'The wretches who have dared profane

His dread sepulchral rest,'
see Cowper's *Works*, x. 26.

'A neat marble monument was set up in 1793.' *Ann. Reg.* 1793, ii. 36.

'When the proposition was agitated that monuments should be erected in St. Paul's as well as in Westminster Abbey' Johnson thought Milton's should be the first. Boswell's *Johnson*, ii. 239.

[1] Johnson, in his letter on the benefit given to Milton's granddaughter (*post*, MILTON, 175), wrote:—'To ensure a participation of fame with a celebrated poet, many, who would perhaps have contributed to starve him when alive, have heaped expensive pageants upon his grave.' Boswell's *Johnson*, i. 227.

Carlyle wrote on Coleridge's death: 'Carriages in long files, as I hear, were rushing all round Highgate when the old man lay near to die. Foolish carriages! Not one of them would roll near him (except to splash him with their mud) while he lived. ... To complete the Farce-Tragedy, they have only to bury him in Westminster Abbey.' *Early Letters of J. W. Carlyle*, 1889, p. 258.

'On Poets' Tombs see Benson's titles writ.' POPE, *The Dunciad*, iii. 325. 'On two unequal crutches propt he came,
Milton's on this, on that one Johnston's name.' *Ib.* iv. 111.
For Johnston see Boswell's *Johnson*, v. 95. See also *post*, POPE, 195; THOMSON, 6 *n*.

[2] 'Uni in hoc laudis genere Miltono secundus, primoque paene par.' *Post*, JOHN PHILIPS, 8.

[3] For Sprat's praise of Cromwell see *post*, SPRAT, 22.

[4] Perhaps David Gregory, D.D., Dean of Christ Church, Oxford, from 1756 to 1767. For some Latin hexameters by Dr. George, Provost of King's College, Cambridge, 'on the reception of Milton's monument into the venerable repository of kings and prelates,' see *Milton's Poems*, ed. T. Warton, p. 574.

Vincent Bourne, Usher of Westminster School, ends his lines *In Miltonum* (*Poetical Works*, 1826, p. 41):—
'Salve, sancta mihi sedes, tuque, unice vates,
Extructumque decus tumuli, et simulacra verendi
Ipsa senis, laurique comae, et tu muneris author
Egregii.—Tanto signatum nomine marmor   [annos.'
Securum decus et seros sibi vindicet
[5] A bust.

beautiful, so as to have been called the Lady of his college. His
hair, which was of a light brown, parted at the foretop, and hung
down upon his shoulders, according to the picture which he has
given of Adam [1]. He was, however, not of the heroick stature,
but rather below the middle size, according to Mr. Richardson,
who mentions him as having narrowly escaped from being 'short
and thick [2].' He was vigorous and active, and delighted in the
exercise of the sword, in which he is related to have been eminently skilful. His weapon was, I believe, not the rapier, but the
backsword, of which he recommends the use in his book on
Education [3].

His eyes are said never to have been bright [4]; but, if he was 158
a dexterous fencer, they must have been once quick.

His domestick habits, so far as they are known, were those of 159
a severe student [5]. He drank little strong drink of any kind, and
fed without excess in quantity [6], and in his earlier years without

[1]   'hyacinthin locks
Round from his parted forelock
manly hung
Clust'ring, but not beneath his
shoulders broad.'
            Paradise Lost, iv. 301.
[2] In one of his *Prolusiones Oratoriae* he said :—'A quibusdam audivi
nuper domina. At cur videor illis
parum masculus?' *Works*, vi. 181.
    In his *Defensio Secunda* he writes :
—'Statura fateor non sum procera ;
sed quae mediocri tamen quam
parvae propior sit.' *Ib*. v. 213.
    'He was of a moderate stature, and
well proportion'd, and of a ruddy
complexion, light brown hair, and
had handsome features, yet his eyes
were none of the quickest. When
he was a student in Cambridge he
was so fair and clear that many call'd
him *the lady of Christ's Coll.*
His deportment was affable, and his
gait erect and manly, bespeaking
courage and undauntedness. On
which account he wore a sword while
he had his sight, and was skill'd in
using it. He had a delicate tuneable
voice, an excellent ear, could play on
the organ, and bear a part in vocal
and instrumental music.' WOOD,
Fasti Oxon. i. 486.
    See also Aubrey's *Brief Lives*, ii. 67,
where it is added :—'His harmonicall
and ingeniose soul did lodge in a

beautifull and well-proportioned body,'
and Toland's *Life of Milton*, p. 149.
    'He was rather a middle siz'd than
a little man, and well proportion'd.
Latterly he was—No ; Not short and
thick, but he would have been so,
had he been something shorter and
thicker than he was. . . . His hair was
a light brown, which he wore parted
atop, and somewhat flat, long and
waving, a little curl'd.' Richardson's
Explanatory Notes, &c., Pref. p. 2.
    George Vertue said that Milton's
daughter told him that her father
'was of a fair complexion, a little red
in the cheeks, and light-brown lank
hair.' Bentham's *Works*, x. 53.
[3] 'The exercise which I commend
first is the exact use of their weapon,
to guard or to strike safely with edge
or point.' *Works*, i. 283. See also
ib. v. 213.
[4] He described his eyes, when he
was blind, as 'sine nube, clari ac
lucidi, ut eorum qui acutissimum
cernunt.' *Ib*. v. 213.
'His eie was a darke gray.' AUBREY,
Brief Lives, ii. 67. 'The colour of
his eyes was inclined to blue, not
deep.' Richardson's *Explanatory
Notes*, &c., Pref. p. 3.
[5] For this account of his habits see
Newton's *Milton*, Preface, p. 68.
[6] 'Temperate man, rarely dranke
between meales.' Aubrey's *Brief*

delicacy of choice[1]. In his youth he studied late at night[2]; but afterwards changed his hours, and rested in bed from nine to four in the summer, and five in winter[3]. The course of his day was best known after he was blind. When he first rose he heard a chapter in the Hebrew Bible, and then studied till twelve ; then took some exercise for an hour ; then dined ; then played on the organ[4], and sung, or heard another sing ; then studied to six ; then entertained his visiters till eight ; then supped, and, after a pipe of tobacco and a glass of water, went to bed.

160   So is his life described ; but this even tenour appears attainable only in Colleges. He that lives in the world will sometimes have the succession of his practice broken and confused. Visiters, of whom Milton is represented to have had great numbers[5], will come and stay unseasonably ; business, of which every man has some, must be done when others will do it.

161   When he did not care to rise early he had something read to him by his bedside[6]; perhaps at this time his daughters were employed. He composed much in the morning and dictated in the day, sitting obliquely in an elbow-chair with his leg thrown over the arm[7].

162   Fortune appears not to have had much of his care. In the civil wars he lent his personal estate to the parliament, but when, after the contest was decided, he solicited repayment, he met not only with neglect, but 'sharp rebuke[8]'; and, having tired both

Lives, ii. 68. ' He was extraordinary temperate in his diet, and was no friend to sharp or strong liquors.' Toland's *Life of Milton*, p. 150.

[1] *Ante*, MILTON, 44 ; *post*, 174.

[2] ' Pater me puerulum humaniorum literarum studiis destinavit; quas ita avide arripui, ut ab anno aetatis duodecimo vix unquam ante mediam noctem a lucubrationibus cubitum discederem ; quae prima oculorum pernicies fuit.' *Works*, v. 230.

' From his brother, Christopher Milton :—when he went to schoole, when he was very young, he studied very hard, and sate-up very late, commonly till 12 or one o'clock at night, and his father ordered the mayde to sitt-up for him.' Aubrey's *Brief Lives*, ii. 63.

In 1642 he described himself as ' up and stirring, in winter often ere the sound of any bell awake men to labour or to devotion ; in summer, as oft with the bird that first rouses, or not much tardier, to read good authors, or cause them to be read, till the attention be weary, or memory have its full fraught.' *Works*, i. 220.

[3] Toland's *Life of Milton*, p. 150. See also Aubrey's *Brief Lives*, ii. 68.

[4] *Ante*, MILTON, 114.

[5] *Ante*, MILTON, 112.

[6] Toland's *Life of Milton*, p. 150.

[7] *Ante*, MILTON, 123 *n*.

[8] ' Rebuke them sharply.' *Epistle to Titus*, i. 13.
' Sharply thou hast insisted on rebuke.'
    Paradise Regained, i. 468.

Johnson, I think, refers to the loss mentioned a few lines further down, described by Phillips (p. 43) :—' He lost no less than £2,000 which he had put for security and improvement into the Excise Office ; but, neglecting to recall it in time, could never after get

himself and his friends, was given up to poverty and hopeless indignation, till he shewed how able he was to do greater service. He was then made Latin secretary, with two hundred pounds a year [1], and had a thousand pounds for his *Defence of the People* [2]. His widow, who after his death retired to Namptwich in Cheshire, and died about 1729 [3], is said to have reported that he lost two thousand pounds by entrusting it to a scrivener; and that, in the general depredation upon the Church, he had grasped an estate of about sixty pounds a year belonging to Westminster-Abbey, which, like other sharers of the plunder of rebellion, he was afterwards obliged to return [4]. Two thousand pounds, which he had placed in the Excise-office, were also lost [5]. There is yet no reason to believe that he was ever reduced to indigence [6]: his wants being few were competently supplied. He sold his library before his death [7], and left his family fifteen hundred pounds; on which his widow laid hold, and only gave one hundred to each of his daughters [8].

it out, with all the power and interest he had in the great ones of those times.'

[1] *Ante*, MILTON, 64. Professor Masson (iv. 82, 578) thinks his salary was '15*s*. 10½*d*. a day, or £288 a year,—equivalent to about £1,000 a year now.' In 1655, his work being lighter, his salary was reduced to £150, but it was settled on him for life. Masson's *Milton*, v. 177, 180. The Restoration, of course, put an end to the settlement.

[2] *Ante*, MILTON, 68.

[3] In 1727. Masson's *Milton*, vi. 747.

[4] Birch and Newton both record these losses on the authority of Elizabeth Foster (*post*, MILTON, 174), 'who had heard of them from her mother.' Birch's *Milton's Works, to which is prefixed an account of his Life*, &c., 1753, Preface, p. 77; Newton's *Milton*, p. 82.

[5] Phillips' *Milton*, p. 43; Wood's *Fasti Oxon*. i. 486.

[6] *Ante*, MILTON, 73 *n*. After all his losses by the Restoration, Professor Masson thinks he had about £200 a year left. In the Great Fire his house in Bread Street was burnt down, '"which was all the real estate he had then left," as Wood tells us.' Masson's *Milton*, vi. 445, 504.

[7] 'He thought he might sell it more

to the advantage of his heirs than they could. His enemies reported that poverty constrained him to part with his books.' Toland's *Life of Milton*, p. 148.

[8] His widow 'applied for probate of the nuncupative or word-of-mouth will,' which his brother testified he had made to him. 'Brother,' he said, 'the portion due to me from my former wife's father I leave to the unkind children I had by her; but I have received no part of it.... All the residue of my estate I leave to the disposal of my loving wife.' The Court rejected the will, but granted her letters of administration. 'Administration gave her two-thirds of the property, one-third as widow, another as administratrix; the remaining third to be distributed equally among the daughters.' Johnson did not know of this will; 'the documents relating to it were first printed by Warton in his second edition of Milton's *Minor Poems*, in 1791.' Masson's *Milton*, vi. 727, 739, 740. Warton had the assistance of Sir William Scott (Lord Stowell) in explaining the judgement. For the invalidating of the will see *Milton's Poems*, ed. T. Warton, Preface, p. 42.

Milton's daughters, his brother

163   His literature was unquestionably great [1]. He read all the languages which are considered either as learned or polite [2]: Hebrew, with its two dialects [3], Greek, Latin, Italian, French, and Spanish. In Latin his skill was such as places him in the first rank of writers and criticks; and he appears to have cultivated Italian with uncommon diligence. The books in which his daughter, who used to read to him, represented him as most delighting, after Homer, which he could almost repeat, were Ovid's *Metamorphoses* and Euripides [4]. His Euripides is, by Mr. Cradock's kindness, now in my hands: the margin is sometimes noted, but I have found nothing remarkable [5].

164   Of the English poets he set most value upon Spenser, Shakespeare, and Cowley [6]. Spenser was apparently his favourite [7]; Shakespeare he may easily be supposed to like, with every other skilful reader [8], but I should not have expected that Cowley, whose ideas of excellence were different [9] from his own, would have had much of his approbation. His character of Dryden, who sometimes visited him, was that he was a good rhymist, but no poet [10].

165   His theological opinions are said to have been first Calvinistical, and afterwards, perhaps when he began to hate the Presbyterians, to have tended towards Arminianism. In the mixed questions of theology and government [11] he never thinks that he

deposed, 'had lived apart from their father four or five years.' *Milton's Poems*, ed. T. Warton, Preface, p. 33. His servant had only once seen one of them in the twelve months before his death. *Ib.* p. 36. See also *ante*, MILTON, 104, 140.

[1] For Pattison's criticism of this statement see his *Milton*, p. 130. He makes Johnson say that 'his literature was immense'—a term Johnson would have used of no man's literature.

[2] Among these German is not included by Johnson.

[3] He studied Hebrew, Chaldee, and Syriac. Phillips' *Milton*, p. 18.

[4] Newton's *Milton*, Pref. pp. 71, 81. From Euripides he took his motto for *Areopagitica* and *Tetrachordon*. 'Fondness for Euripides makes Milton too didactic when action was required.' LANDOR, *Imag. Conv.* iv. 262.

[5] 'It has Milton's name, with the price of the book, *viz.* 12s. 6d.; also the date 1634, all in his own hand.'

Milton's Poems, ed. T. Warton, p. 569. It is now in the British Museum. See also *John. Misc.* ii. 70.

[6] This comes from Milton's widow. Newton's *Milton*, Pref. p. 80; *ante*, COWLEY, 174.

[7] 'Milton has acknowledged to me that Spenser was his original.' DRYDEN, *Works*, xi. 210.

In the *Areopagitica* (*Works*, i. 300) he mentions 'our sage and serious poet Spenser.'

[8] See his *Epitaph on Shakespeare*, and *L'Allegro*, l. 133.

[9] In first edition, 'so different.'

[10] Newton's *Milton*, Pref. p. 80; *post*, MILTON, 177 *n.*; DRYDEN, 71. T. Warton, in a note on *Lycidas*, l. 11, points out that there and in *Paradise Lost*, i. 16, Milton uses *rhyme* for *verse*. Warton quotes Hurd as saying that 'Milton was a very bad rhymist.' *Milton's Poems*, pp. 3, 361.

[11] In 1641-2 Milton in his *Reason of Church Government* (*ante*, MILTON, 47) supported 'a Church govern-

can recede far enough from popery or prelacy ; but what Baudius says of Erasmus seems applicable to him : ' magis habuit quod fugeret, quam quod sequeretur[1].' He had determined rather what to condemn than what to approve. He has not associated himself with any denomination of Protestants : we know rather what he was not, than what he was. He was not of the church of Rome[2] ; he was not of the church of England.

To be of no church is dangerous[3]. Religion, of which the **166** rewards are distant and which is animated only by Faith and Hope, will glide by degrees out of the mind unless it be invigorated and reimpressed by external ordinances, by stated calls to worship, and the salutary influence of example[4]. Milton, who appears to have had full conviction of the truth of Christianity, and to have regarded the Holy Scriptures with the profoundest veneration, to have been untainted by any heretical peculiarity of opinion[5], and to have lived in a confirmed belief of the immediate

ment somewhat after the model of the Presbyterian Kirk of Scotland.' Masson's *Milton*, ii. 376.

' Milton's visions of Church and State were precisely intended for Paradise. . . . The very genius of human sagacity could never have legislated for the Garden of Eden with half the effect.' *Quarterly Review*, No. 71, p. 50.

[1] Johnson recorded in his Diary at Lleweney : ' Baudius on Erasmus.' Boswell's *Johnson*, v. 444.

[2] The final paragraph of his last tract (*ante*, MILTON, 148) begins :— ' The last means to avoid Popery is to amend our lives.' It ends :—' Let us therefore . . . amend our lives with all speed, lest through impenitency we run into that stupidity which we now seek all means so warily to avoid, the worst of superstitions, and the heaviest of all God's judgments, Popery.' *Works*, iv. 269.

For the absurd assertion, attributed to his brother, that he died a Papist see Hearne's *Remains*, i. 115 ; *Hist. MSS. Com.* Report vii. App. p. 244 ; *N. & Q.* 7 S. xi. 306 ; and Pattison's *Milton*, p. 154. See also *post*, GARTH, 96.

[3] ' God sends his Spirit of Truth
    henceforth to dwell
In pious hearts, an inward oracle

To all truth requisite for men to know.'
    Paradise Regained, i. 462.

[4] Milton, in *Areopagitica*, describes how a wealthy man ' finds out some divine of note and estimation. To him he adheres, resigns the whole warehouse of his religion, with all the locks and keys, into his custody. . . . He entertains him, gives him gifts, feasts him, lodges him ; his religion comes home at night, prays, is liberally supped, and sumptuously laid to sleep ; rises, is saluted, and after the malmsey, or some well-spiced bruage, and better breakfasted than he whose morning appetite would have gladly fed on green figs between Bethany and Jerusalem, his religion walks abroad at eight, and leaves his kind entertainer in the shop trading all day without his religion.' *Works*, i. 316.

[5] Milton in his last tract maintains that ' the hottest disputes among Protestants ' will be found to be on things not ' absolutely necessary to salvation.' Among Protestants he reckons Arians and Socinians. *Ib.* iv. 262.

In 1823 was discovered in the Old State Paper Office a Latin MS. entitled *Ioannis Miltoni Angli De Doctrina Christiana*, &c. It was edited and translated by Dr. Charles R. Sumner, afterwards Bishop of Win-

and occasional agency of Providence, yet grew old without any visible worship. In the distribution of his hours, there was no hour of prayer, either solitary or with his household[1]; omitting publick prayers, he omitted all.

167   Of this omission the reason has been sought, upon a supposition which ought never to be made, that men live with their own approbation, and justify their conduct to themselves. Prayer certainly was not thought superfluous by him, who represents our first parents as praying acceptably in the state of innocence, and efficaciously after their fall[2]. That he lived without prayer can hardly be affirmed; his studies and meditations were an habitual prayer. The neglect of it in his family was probably a fault for which he condemned himself, and which he intended to correct, but that death, as too often happens, intercepted his reformation[3].

168   His political notions were those of an acrimonious and surly republican, for which it is not known that he gave any better reason than that 'a popular government was the most frugal; for the trappings of a monarchy would set up an ordinary commonwealth[4].' It is surely very shallow policy, that supposes money

chester, and published in 1825. The translation was reprinted by Bohn in 1861. 'The opinions of Milton,' writes Sumner, 'were in reality nearly Arian, ascribing to the Son as high a share of divinity as was compatible with the denial of his self-existence and eternal generation, but not admitting his co-equality and co-essentiality with the Father.' *A Treatise of Christian doctrine*, &c., ed. 1861, Preface, p. 31. On the other hand 'the doctrine of the satisfaction of Christ is so scripturally enforced as to leave on that point nothing to be desired.' *Ib.* p. 33. In these two points Dr. Samuel Clarke was like Milton. Boswell's *Johnson*, iii. 248; iv. 416.

'Milton was undoubtedly a high Arian in his mature life.' COLERIDGE, *Table Talk*, 1884, p. 24. See also Masson's *Milton*, vi. 816–38; *ante*, MILTON, 18, 83 *n.*

'It is said that the discovery of his Arianism in this rigid generation has already impaired the sale of *Paradise Lost*.' HALLAM, *Introd. to the Lit. of Europe*, 1837–9, iv. 418.

[1] 'In the latter part of his life he was not a profest member of any particular sect among Christians; he frequented none of their assemblies, nor made use of their peculiar rites in his family.' Toland's *Life of Milton*, p. 151.

'He frequented no public worship, nor used any religious rite in his family.' Newton's *Milton*, Pref. p. 76.

The reviewer of the *Lives* in *Ann. Reg.* 1779, ii. 184 *n.*, writes of the statement in the text: 'As to family prayer it appears to be a calumny drawn from an expression of Toland's. . . . Bishop Newton has altered this into *his not using any religious rites in his family*. From the Bishop Dr. Johnson roundly concludes that he *never used prayer in his family.*'

[2] *Paradise Lost*, v. 209; x. 1097.

[3] Johnson is here thinking of himself. On his seventy-first birthday he recorded:—'I have forgotten or neglected my resolutions, or purposes which I now humbly and timorously renew. Surely I shall not spend my whole life with my own total disapprobation.' *John. Misc.* i. 94.

[4] 'Sir Robert Howard [*post*, DRYDEN, 17] having demanded of him what made him side with the

to be the chief good ; and even this without considering that the support and expence of a Court is for the most part only a particular kind of traffick, by which money is circulated without any national impoverishment [1].

Milton's republicanism was, I am afraid, founded in an envious 169 hatred of greatness, and a sullen desire of independence ; in petulance impatient of controul, and pride disdainful of superiority. He hated monarchs in the state and prelates in the church ; for he hated all whom he was required to obey [2]. It is to be suspected that his predominant desire was to destroy rather than establish, and that he felt not so much the love of liberty as repugnance to authority [3].

It has been observed that they who most loudly clamour for 170 liberty do not most liberally grant it [4]. What we know of Milton's character in domestick relations is, that he was severe and arbitrary. His family consisted of women ; and there appears in his books something like a Turkish contempt of females, as subordinate and inferior beings. That his own daughters might not break the ranks, he suffered them to be depressed by a mean and penurious education [5]. He thought woman made only for obedience, and man only for rebellion.

republicàns, Milton answered, among other reasons, "because theirs was the most frugal government ; for that the trappings of a monarchy might set up an ordinary commonwealth."' Toland's *Life of Milton*, p. 139.

[1] Considering the vicious use of money in the Court of Charles II, Johnson is here upholding Mandeville's doctrine, that private vices are public benefits. Boswell's *Johnson*, iii. 291. For 'money circulating' see *ib*. ii. 429 ; iii. 177, 249.

[2] Give me the liberty to know, to utter, and to argue freely according to conscience, above all liberties.' MILTON, *Works*, i. 325.

'I never knew that time in England when men of truest religion were not counted sectaries.' *Ib*. ii. 399.

'Milton's mind could not be narrowed by anything.' COWPER, Southey's *Cowper*, vii. 63.

[3] 'Milton is falsely represented by some as a democrat. He was an aristocrat in the truest sense of the word.' WORDSWORTH, *Memoirs*, ii. 472.

'He was a most determined aristocrat, an enemy to popular elections. ... He was of opinion that the government belonged to the wise, and he thought the people fools.' COLERIDGE, H. C. Robinson's *Diary*, i. 311.

In *The Ready and Easy Way to establish a Free Commonwealth* (*ante*, MILTON, 94) there are such passages as the following :—'Most voices ought not always to prevail where main matters are in question.' *Works*, iii. 404. 'Safest therefore to me it seems, ... that none of the Grand Council be moved, unless by death or just conviction of some crime ; for what can be expected firm or steadfast from a floating foundation ?' *Ib*. p. 414.

[4] For 'clamours for liberty' see *post*, THOMSON, 22.

[5] *Ante*, MILTON, 124, 140.

'Of all that men have said of woman nothing is more loftily conceived than the well-known passage at the end of Book viii of *Paradise Lost* [ll. 546-559]. ... But in directing the bringing up of his daughters, Milton

171 Of his family some account may be expected [1]. His sister, first married to Mr. Philips, afterwards married Mr. Agar, a friend of her first husband, who succeeded him in the Crown-office [2]. She had by her first husband Edward and John, the two nephews whom Milton educated [3]; and by her second two daughters [4].

172 His brother, Sir Christopher, had two daughters, Mary and Catherine [5], and a son Thomas, who succeeded Agar in the Crown-office, and left a daughter living in 1749 in Grosvenor-street [6].

173 Milton had children only by his first wife: Anne, Mary, and Deborah. Anne, though deformed, married a master-builder, and died of her first child. Mary died single. Deborah married Abraham Clark, a weaver in Spitalfields, and lived seventy-six years, to August 1727 [7]. This is the daughter of whom publick mention has been made. She could repeat the first lines of Homer, the *Metamorphoses*, and some of Euripides, by having often read

puts his own typical woman entirely on one side. His practice is framed on the principle that

"nothing lovelier can be found In woman, than to study household good." ' [*Paradise Lost*, ix. 233.] Pattison's *Milton*, p. 146.
One of Evelyn's daughters knew Italian and French. Another, he wrote, 'has read most of the Greek and Latin authors, using her talents with great modesty.' *Diary*, ii. 223, 336.
'Learning and knowledge are perfections in us, not as we are men, but as we are reasonable creatures, in which order of beings the female world is upon the same level with the male.' ADDISON, *The Guardian*, No. 155.

[1] Cunningham (*Lives of the Poets*, i. 138) quotes from *Add. MSS. in the British Museum*, 4244, p. 53, an account by Dr. Birch of Milton's family, partly copied by him from the poet's entries on a blank leaf of a Bible.

[2] Phillips' *Milton*, p. 7; *ante*, MILTON, 5. Agar, in his will, 'disposed of such "goods and chattels" as "with much industry" he had "scrambled for amongst others in this wicked world."' Masson's *Milton*, vi. 771.

[3] *Ante*, MILTON, 5, 35, 42. Of any descendants of theirs nothing is known. Masson's *Milton*, vi. 767,

770. This sister, Anne Milton, had also by her first husband that 'fair infant' whose death Milton lamented in an elegy.

[4] One of these died early; the other 'was the wife of a David Moore.' Of their son, afterwards Sir Thomas Moore, there are many descendants 'of high respectability.' *Ib.* vi. 771, 775.

[5] 'They were living at Holloway about 1734. Their names were corrupted into Melton.' Johnson's *Works*, 1787, ii. 44. 'A third daughter was married to Mr. Pendlebury, a clergyman.' *Birch MS.* 'Nothing more is known of her.' Masson's *Milton*, vi. 763.

[6] Newton wrote in 1748 :—' There is a Mrs. Milton living in Grosvenor Street, the granddaughter of Sir Christopher.' Newton's *Milton*, Pref. p. 83.

[7] Deborah was born on May 2, 1652. Masson's *Milton*, iv. 468. When she married, Clarke was a 'weaver' in Dublin. 'He came over to London "during the troubles in Ireland under King James II."' *Ib.* vi. 751. 'She married in Dublin to one Mr. Clarke (sells silk &c.); very like her father.' AUBREY, *Brief Lives*, ii. 68. Aubrey had at first described Clarke as a mercer.

them. Yet here incredulity is ready to make a stand. Many repetitions are necessary to fix in the memory lines not understood; and why should Milton wish or want to hear them so often! These lines were at the beginning of the poems. Of a book written in a language not understood the beginning raises no more attention than the end, and as those that understand it know commonly the beginning best, its rehearsal will seldom be necessary. It is not likely that Milton required any passage to be so much repeated as that his daughter could learn it, nor likely that he desired the initial lines to be read at all; nor that the daughter, weary of the drudgery of pronouncing unideal sounds, would voluntarily commit them to memory.

To this gentlewoman Addison made a present, and promised **174** some establishment; but died soon after[1]. Queen Caroline sent her fifty guineas[2]. She had seven sons and three daughters; but none of them had any children, except her son Caleb and her daughter Elizabeth. Caleb went to Fort St. George[3] in the East Indies, and had two sons, of whom nothing is now known[4]. Elizabeth married Thomas Foster, a weaver in Spitalfields, and had seven children, who all died. She kept a petty grocer's or chandler's shop, first at Holloway, and afterwards in Cock-lane near Shoreditch Church[5]. She knew little of her grandfather, and that little was not good. She told of his harshness to his daughters, and his refusal to have them taught to write[6]; and, in

---

[1] See Appendix O.

[2] Pounds. Dr. Birch, who records this, had it from Elizabeth Foster, whom he visited in the spring of 1738. Birch's *Milton*, 1753, Pref., p. 77.

[3] Now known as Madras.

[4] Caleb Clarke was there certainly as early as 1703. In 1717 he was parish-clerk. He died in 1719. There is an entry on April 2, 1727, of the baptism of his elder son's daughter. 'With this registration all trace of Milton's posterity in India ceases.' Masson's *Milton*, vi. 755. Milton's grandson probably arrived at Fort St. George when its governor was Elihu Yale, who gave his name to the American University. He was certainly under Thomas Pitt, grandfather of the Earl of Chatham, and Gulston Addison, brother of Joseph Addison. See Addison's *Works*, v. 374.

[5] 'She has now [1748] for some years, with her husband, kept a little chandler's or grocer's shop, lately at the lower Halloway [*sic*] in the road between Highgate and London, and at present in Cock Lane not far from Shoreditch Church.' Newton's *Milton*, p. 84. (This is not the Cock Lane famous for its ghost, which was near Smithfield. Boswell's *Johnson*, i. 406.) She died on May 9, 1754, 'at her house, the sign of the Sugar Loafe, opposite to the Thatched House in Islington.' She was born in Nov. 1688. *N. & Q.* 2 S. iii. 265.

[6] 'That he kept his daughters at a great distance, and would not allow them to write, which he thought unnecessary for a woman.' Birch's *Milton*, Preface, p. 77. In the *Chetham Soc. Misc.* vol. i. p. 1, there is a facsimile of the signatures of Milton's

opposition to other accounts, represented him as delicate, though temperate in his diet [1].

175   In 1750, April 5, *Comus* was played for her benefit.   She had so little acquaintance with diversion or gaiety, that she did not know what was intended when a benefit was offered her.   The profits of the night were only one hundred and thirty pounds [2], though Dr. Newton [3] brought a large contribution ; and twenty pounds were given by Tonson, a man who is to be praised as often as he is named [4].   Of this sum one hundred pounds was placed in the stocks, after some debate between her and her husband in whose name it should be entered ; and the rest augmented their little stock, with which they removed to Islington. This was the greatest benefaction that *Paradise Lost* ever procured the author's descendents [5]; and to this he who has now attempted to relate his Life, had the honour of contributing a Prologue [6].

daughters to three receipts. Anne, not being able to write, made her mark. Mary spelt her name 'Millton' and began it with a small letter ; Deborah wrote her Christian name 'Deboroh.' See *ante*, MILTON, 124, 140.

[1] 'He was very temperate in his eating and drinking, but what he had he always loved to have of the best.' Newton's *Milton*, Pref. p. 82. *Ante*, MILTON, 44, 159.

[2] The benefit produced her above £130.' *Gent. Mag.* 1750, p. 183.

[3] Dr. Thomas Newton, afterwards Bishop of Bristol, who for his edition of *Paradise Lost* with a *Life of Milton* prefixed (1749) received £630, and for *Paradise Regained* (1752) £105. *Gent. Mag.* 1787, p. 76.

[4] 'The elder Tonson from about 1720 seems to have transferred his business to his nephew Jacob Tonson,' who died in 1736, four months before his uncle, and was succeeded by his son, also named Jacob, who, 'after having carried on the business of a bookseller with great liberality, died without issue in 1767.' He is the man praised in the text. From about 1712, their shop was opposite Catherine Street in the Strand, now No. 141 (since rebuilt). Their successor was Andrew Millar, and his was Thomas

Cadell. Malone's *Dryden*, i. 523–39; Hume's *Letters to Strahan*, p. 33.

For Johnson's character of Richard Tonson, 'the last commercial name of a family which will be long remembered,' see *post*, DRYDEN, 184 *n*.

'The Tonsons had a virtual [? a real] monopoly of Milton's poetry for forty years. . . . When they were rolling in wealth, a goodly portion of it derived from traffic in Milton's poetry, Milton's widow was alive in very straitened gentility at Nantwich, and Milton's youngest daughter and her children were in penury in Spitalfields.' Masson's *Milton*, vi. 788. For copyright see *ante*, MILTON, 130 *n*.

[5] In 1725 Parliament, on the recommendation of the king, showed its gratitude to John Hampden, 'by empowering the Commissioners of the Treasury to compound with his great-grandson, late Treasurer of the Navy, for a debt of £48,000 he owed to the Crown. This deficiency was occasioned by his embarking in the South Sea scheme.' SMOLLETT, *Hist. of Eng.* ii. 445.

[6] 'What though she shine with no Miltonian fire,
    No fav'ring muse her morning dreams inspire ;
    Yet softer claims the melting heart engage,

IN the examination of Milton's poetical works I shall pay so 176
much regard to time as to begin with his juvenile productions.
For his earlier pieces he seems to have had a degree of fondness
not very laudable: what he has once written he resolves to
preserve, and gives to the publick an unfinished poem, which he
broke off because he was 'nothing satisfied with what he had
done [1],' supposing his readers less nice than himself. These pre-
ludes to his future labours are in Italian, Latin, and English [2].
Of the Italian I cannot pretend to speak as a critick, but I have
heard them commended by a man well qualified to decide their
merit [3]. The Latin pieces are lusciously elegant ; but the delight
which they afford is rather by the exquisite imitation of the
ancient writers, by the purity of the diction, and the harmony of
the numbers, than by any power of invention or vigour of sentiment [4]. They are not all of equal value ; the elegies excell [5] the

Her youth laborious, and her blameless age ;
Her's the mild merits of domestic life,
The patient sufferer and the faithful
wife.' JOHNSON, *Works*, i. 116.

The prologue was spoken by
Garrick. See also Boswell's *Johnson*,
i. 227, for Johnson's letter in *The
General Advertiser* in support of the
benefit.

[1] ' This subject [*The Passion*] the
author finding to be above the years
he had when he wrote it, and nothing
satisf'd with what was begun, left it
unfinisht.'

Johnson (*Letters*, ii. 7) writing about
the publication of Hawkesworth's
papers, says :—' I am for letting none
stand that are only relatively good,
as they were written in youth. The
Buyer has no better bargain when he
pays for mean performances, by being
told that the authour wrote them
young.' See also *ante*, MILTON, 11.

[2] For Cowper's translation of the
Italian and Latin poems see Southey's
Cowper, x. 130–92.

[3] ' Unhappily Italian poetry in the
age of Milton was almost at its worst,
and he imitated what he heard repeated or praised.' LANDOR, *Imag.
Conver.* iv. 284.

For the contempt felt by Italians
for the *Seicentisti*—the Italian writers
of the seventeenth century—see
Masson's *Milton*, i. 762. See also

ib. i. 826 *n.* for Saffi's criticism of these
sonnets. While 'the metaphors,'
he says, 'remind one of the false
literary taste then prevalent in Italy,
. . . the measure of the verse is generally correct, nay, more than this,
musical ; and one feels, in perusing
these poems, that the mind of the
young aspiring poet had, from Petrarch to Tasso, listened attentively
to the gentlest notes of the Italian
Muse, though unable to reproduce
them fully in a form of his own.'

Baretti speaks of ' Milton's imper-
fect attempts to write Italian poetry.'
*An Account of the Manners, &c., of
Italy*, 1768, i. 108.

[4] ' You may find a few minute
faults in Milton's Latin verses ; but
you will not persuade me that, if
these poems had come to us *as* written
in the age of Tiberius, we should not
have considered them to be very
beautiful.' COLERIDGE, *Table Talk*,
1884, p. 242.

' Milton's Latin verses are distinguished from most Neo-latin verse
by being a vehicle of real emotion.'
PATTISON, *Milton*, p. 41.

[5] Milton speaks of ' the smooth
elegiac poets whom both for the
pleasing sound of their numerous
writing, which in imitation I found
most easy, and most agreeable to
nature's part in me,' &c. *Works*, i.
223.

odes, and some of the exercises on Gunpowder Treason might have been spared [1].

177 The English poems [2], though they make no promises of *Paradise Lost* [3], have this evidence of genius, that they have a cast original and unborrowed. But their peculiarity is not excellence : if they differ from verses of others, they differ for the worse; for they are too often distinguished by repulsive harshness ; the combinations of words are new, but they are not pleasing ; the rhymes and epithets seem to be laboriously sought and violently applied [4].

178 That in the early parts of his life he wrote with much care appears from his manuscripts, happily preserved at Cambridge, in which many of his smaller works are found as they were first written, with the subsequent corrections [5]. Such reliques shew how excellence is acquired : what we hope ever to do with ease we may learn first to do with diligence [6].

[1] He wrote four epigrams *In Proditionem Bombardicam*, and a poem of 226 lines, in heroic verse, *In Quintum Novembris*. 'This poem,' wrote Landor, 'which ends poorly, is a wonderful work for a boy of seventeen.' *Imag. Conver.* iv. 296.

A century later, when Johnson entered Pembroke College, 'the fifth of November was kept with great solemnity, and exercises upon the subject of the day were required.' Boswell's *Johnson*, i. 60.

[2] *Ante*, MILTON, 59, 152.

[3] 'In *Comus* may very plainly be discovered the dawn or twilight of *Paradise Lost*.' *Post*, MILTON, 194.

[4] 'Milton had neither the ease of doing it [rhyming], nor the graces of it ; which is manifest in his *Juvenilia*, or verses written in his youth, where his rhyme is always constrained and forced, and comes hardly from him, at an age when the soul is most pliant, and the passion of love makes almost every man a rhymer, though not a poet.' DRYDEN, *Works*, xiii. 20. See *ante*, MILTON, 164.

[5] 'Of the 22 English pieces in the volume of 1645 [*ante*, MILTON, 59] the original drafts of 10 still exist in the volume of Milton MSS. in Trinity College, Cambridge,' among them *Lycidas* and *Comus*. Masson's *Milton*, iii. 451, 452 *n.* 'Passages are frequently erased and rewritten;

sometimes rewritten twice ; invariably the alteration is for the better.' *Ib.* i. 658 *n.* See also Dr. Aldis Wright's preface to the *Facsimile of the MS. of Milton's Minor Poems . . . in Trinity College, Cambridge*, 1899.

[6] 'Johnson used to say that he made it a constant rule to talk as well as he could both as to sentiment and expression, by which means what had been originally effort became familiar and easy.' Boswell's *Johnson*, iv. 183. See also *ib.* i. 204.

'The habits of correct writing may produce, without labour or design, the appearance of art and study.' GIBBON, *Memoirs*, p. 1.

'Do not let anybody persuade you that . . . an immortal style can be the growth of mere genius. " Multa tulit fecitque " [HORACE, *Ars Poet.* l. 413] must be the motto of all those who are to last.' WORDSWORTH, R. P. Gillies's *Memoirs*, ii. 165.

'Milton talks of " pouring easy his unpremeditated verse " ['inspires easy my,' &c. *Paradise Lost*, ix. 23]. It would be harsh, untrue and odious to say there is anything like cant in this ; but it is not true to the letter, and tends to mislead.' WORDSWORTH, *Memoirs*, ii. 256.

Ruskin wrote to Dante Rossetti in 1854 : 'All beautiful work—singing, painting, dancing, speaking—is the *easy* result of long and painful

Those who admire the beauties of this great poet sometimes 179
force their own judgement into false approbation of his little pieces,
and prevail upon themselves to think that admirable which is
only singular. All that short compositions can commonly attain
is neatness and elegance. Milton never learned the art of
doing little things with grace; he overlooked the milder excellence
of suavity and softness : he was a 'Lion' that had no skill 'in
dandling the Kid[1].'

One of the poems on which much praise has been bestowed is 180
Lycidas[2]; of which the diction is harsh, the rhymes uncertain,
and the numbers unpleasing. What beauty there is we must
therefore seek in the sentiments and images. It is not to be considered as the effusion of real passion; for passion runs not after
remote allusions and obscure opinions. Passion plucks no berries
from the myrtle and ivy, nor calls upon Arethuse and Mincius,
nor tells of 'rough satyrs and fauns with cloven heel[3].' 'Where
there is leisure for fiction there is little grief[4].'

In this poem there is no nature, for there is no truth; there is no 181
art, for there is nothing new. Its form is that of a pastoral, easy,
vulgar, and therefore disgusting : whatever images it can supply are
long ago exhausted; and its inherent improbability always forces
dissatisfaction on the mind. When Cowley tells of Hervey that they
studied together, it is easy to suppose how much he must miss
the companion of his labours and the partner of his discoveries[5];
but what image of tenderness can be excited by these lines!

practice.' *Ruskin: Rossetti: Pre-*
raphaelitism, p. 29.
'The easier an actor makes his art
appear, the greater must have been
the pains it cost him.' MACREADY,
Reminiscences, ii. 442.
[1] 'Sporting the lion ramp'd, and in
his paw
Dandl'd the kid.' *Par. Lost*, iv. 343.
Hannah More 'expressed a won-
der that the poet who had written
Paradise Lost should write such
poor sonnets. JOHNSON.—Milton,
Madam, was a genius that could
cut a Colossus from a rock, but
could not carve heads upon cherry-
stones.' Boswell's *Johnson*, iv. 305.
[2] *Ante*, MILTON, 22.
[3] 'Rough Satyrs danc'd, and Fauns
with clov'n heel
From the glad sound would not
be absent long.' *Lycidas*, l. 34.

[4] A writer in *The Quarterly Review*, No. 71, p. 46, quoting this line
says :—' In general this may be true;
in the case of Milton its truth may
be doubted. . . . His mind was perfect
fairy-land; and every thought which
entered it, whether grave or gay,
magnificent or mean, quickly partook
of a fairy form. . . . There is no universal language of grief. It takes
its complexion from the country, the
age, the individual. In its paroxysms
no man thinks of writing verses
of any kind. We exclaim, as King
David does, "My son! My son!"
When the paroxysm is past, every
man will write such verses (if he
write them at all) as the ordinary
turn of his mind dictates.' See *post*,
LYTTELTON, 9 *n*.
[5] 'Say, for you saw us, ye immortal
lights,

'We drove a field, and both together heard
What time the grey fly winds her sultry horn,
Battening our flocks with the fresh dews of night [1].'

We know that they never drove a field, and that they had no flocks to batten; and though it be allowed that the representation may be allegorical, the true meaning is so uncertain and remote that it is never sought because it cannot be known when it is found.

182 Among the flocks and copses and flowers appear the heathen deities, Jove and Phœbus, Neptune and Æolus, with a long train of mythological imagery, such as a College easily supplies. Nothing can less display knowledge or less exercise invention than to tell how a shepherd has lost his companion and must now feed his flocks alone, without any judge of his skill in piping ; and how one god asks another god what is become of Lycidas, and how neither god can tell. He who thus grieves will excite no sympathy; he who thus praises will confer no honour [2].

How oft unweary'd have we spent
  the nights,   [for love
Till the Ledaean stars so fam'd
Wonder'd at us from above!
We spent them not in toys, in
  lusts, or wine ;
  But search of deep philosophy,
  Wit, eloquence and poetry ;
Arts which I lov'd, for they, my
  friend, were thine.'
Eng. Poets, vii. 130; *ante*, COWLEY, 108.
  [1] *Lycidas*, l. 27. These ideas, writes T. Warton (*Milton's Poems*, p. 36), are not more unnatural 'than when Cowley says that the twin-stars of Leda, so famed for love, looked down upon the twin students with wonder from above.'
  [2] For Johnson's condemnation of pastoral poetry see *ante*, COWLEY, 7 ; MILTON, 34 ; *post*, CONGREVE, 13 ; FENTON, 22 ; GAY, 32; HAMMOND, 6 ; POPE, 313; A. PHILIPS, 11 ; SHENSTONE, 25, and *The Rambler*, Nos. 36, 37. In the *Life of Savage*, written in 1744, he first shows his scorn of it for its want of nature and truth. *Post*, SAVAGE, 262.
  ' Johnson has passed sentence of condemnation upon *Lycidas*, and has taken occasion from that charming poem to expose to ridicule (what is indeed ridiculous enough) the

childish prattlement of pastoral compositions, as if *Lycidas* was the prototype and pattern of them all. The liveliness of the description, the sweetness of the numbers, the classical spirit of antiquity that prevails in it, go for nothing.' COWPER, Southey's *Cowper*, iii. 314.
  ' I have been reading *Comus* and *Lycidas* with wonder and a sort of awe. Tennyson once said that *Lycidas* was a touchstone of poetic taste.' E. FITZGERALD, *Letters to F. Kemble*, p. 178.
  For Cervantes's ridicule of pastoral poetry see *Don Quixote*, Part ii. Bk. iv. chs. 15, 21. Swift writes in *Apollo's Edict*:—
' Your tragic heroes shall not rant,
Nor shepherds use poetic cant.'
            Works, xiv. 128.
  [Dr. Birkbeck Hill left an unfinished note in which he points out that *Lycidas* can be read without emotion, and that there is only one tender line in it—'Young Lycidas,' &c.; whereas he could not read Wordsworth's *Brothers* aloud or his *Michael*. Johnson had no contempt for Virgil's *Eclogues*. He learnt or relearnt them by heart in his old age (Boswell's *Johnson*, ii. 288, iv. 218); and yet they are quite as artificial as *Lycidas* —and beautiful as they are, the

This poem has yet a grosser fault. With these trifling fictions 183 are mingled the most awful and sacred truths, such as ought never to be polluted with such irreverent combinations. The shepherd likewise is now a feeder of sheep, and afterwards an ecclesiastical pastor, a superintendent of a Christian flock. Such equivocations are always unskilful; but here they are indecent, and at least approach to impiety, of which, however, I believe the writer not to have been conscious [1].

Such is the power of reputation justly acquired that its blaze 184 drives away the eye from nice examination. Surely no man could have fancied that he read *Lycidas* with pleasure had he not known its author.

Of the two pieces, *L'Allegro* and *Il Penseroso*[2], I believe opinion 185 is uniform; every man that reads them, reads them with pleasure[3]. The author's design is not, what Theobald has remarked, merely to shew how objects derived their colours from the mind, by representing the operation of the same things upon the gay and

---

finest of them does not rise to its height.]

[1] Johnson points out that in *The Hind and the Panther* 'the name Pan is given to the Supreme Being.' *Post*, DRYDEN, 295. He might have objected to 'all-judging Jove' in *Lycidas*, l. 82.

'*Lycidas* opens up a patriot passion so vehement and dangerous, that, like that which stirred the Hebrew prophet, it is compelled to veil itself from power, or from sympathy, in utterance made purposely enigmatical.' PATTISON, *Milton*, p. 29.

[2] Pattison (*ib.* p. 23) says that the Italian word is not *Penseroso* but *Pensieroso*, and that it does not signify 'thoughtful, or contemplative, but anxious, full of cares.' Mr. W. H. David quotes in *N. & Q.* 7 S. viii. 326 from a *French-Italian Dictionary*, Geneva, 1644:—' *Pensif*, penseroso, che pensa.' Dr. Skeat writes:—' It is clear that Mark Pattison forgot the difference between modern Italian and that of an earlier period,' and refers to Florio's *Italian Dictionary*, 1598. *N. & Q.* 7 S. viii. 394. See LANDOR, *Imag. Conver.* iv. 273.

[3] *Ante*, MILTON, 59. Goldsmith says of the two poems:—' The intro-

duction to both in irregular measure is borrowed from the Italians, and hurts an English ear.' *Works*, iii. 436.

Dr. Warton wrote in 1756:—' *L'Allegro* and *Il Penseroso* are now universally known, but by a strange fatality they lay in a sort of obscurity, the private enjoyment of a few curious readers, till they were set to admirable music by Mr. Handel.' *Essay on Pope*, i. 40.

Mrs. Delany heard them performed in 1755. In a note to her *Auto. &c.* iii. 334, it is stated that the Oratorio —*Allegro, Penseroso, and Moderato* —was composed by Handel in fifteen days, and was performed once in 1755. Hawkins calls *Il Moderato* 'a senseless adjunct.' *Hist. of Music*, v. 416 n.

' I remember being so charmed with Milton's *Allegro* and *Penseroso* when I was a boy that I was never weary of them.' COWPER, Southey's *Cowper*, iv. 177.

Horace Walpole wrote in 1791:— ' I would not give this last week's fine weather for all the four *Seasons* in blank verse. There is more nature in six lines of *L'Allegro* and *Il Penseroso* than in all the laboured imitations of Milton. What is there in Thomson of original?' *Letters*, ix. 347.

the melancholy temper, or upon the same man as he is differently disposed ; but rather how, among the successive variety of appearances, every disposition of mind takes hold on those by which it may be gratified.

186   The *chearful* man hears the lark in the morning; the *pensive* man hears the nightingale in the evening. The *chearful* man sees the cock strut, and hears the horn and hounds echo in the wood; then walks 'not unseen[1]' to observe the glory of the rising sun or listen to the singing milk-maid, and view the labours of the plowman and the mower; then casts his eyes about him over scenes of smiling plenty, and looks up to the distant tower, the residence of some fair inhabitant: thus he pursues rural gaiety through a day of labour or of play, and delights himself at night with the fanciful narratives of superstitious ignorance.

187   The *pensive* man at one time walks 'unseen[2]' to muse at midnight, and at another hears the sullen curfew. If the weather drives him home he sits in a room lighted only by 'glowing embers[3]'; or by a lonely lamp outwatches the North Star to discover the habitation of separate souls, and varies the shades of meditation by contemplating the magnificent or pathetick scenes of tragick and epick poetry. When the morning comes, a morning gloomy with rain and wind, he walks into the dark trackless woods[4], falls asleep by some murmuring water, and with melancholy enthusiasm expects some dream of prognostication or some musick played by aerial performers.

188   Both Mirth and Melancholy are solitary, silent inhabitants of the breast that neither receive nor transmit communication ; no mention is therefore made of a philosophical friend or a pleasant companion. The seriousness does not arise from any participation of calamity, nor the gaiety[5] from the pleasures of the bottle.

189   The man of *chearfulness* having exhausted the country tries what 'towered cities[6]' will afford, and mingles with scenes of

---

[1] *L'Allegro*, l. 57.
[2] *Il Penseroso*, l. 65.
[3] *Ib.* l. 79.
[4] Though the morn may be 'usher'd with a shower,' he only goes out
   'when the sun begins to fling His flaring beams.'   *Ib.* l. 131.
[5] In the first edition :—'Seriousness does not, &c. . . . nor gaiety,' &c.

T. Warton (*Milton's Poems*, p. 97) remarks on this observation :—'The truth is that Milton means to describe the cheerfulness of the philosopher or the student, the amusements of a contemplative mind. . . . The critic does not appear to have entered into the spirit of our author's *Allegro*.'
[6] *L'Allegro*, l. 117.

splendor, gay assemblies, and nuptial festivities; but he mingles a mere spectator as, when the learned comedies of Jonson or the wild dramas of Shakespeare are exhibited, he attends the theatre [1].

The *pensive* man never loses himself in crowds, but walks the 190 cloister or frequents the cathedral. Milton probably had not yet forsaken the Church.

Both his characters delight in musick; but he seems to think 191 that chearful notes would have obtained from Pluto a compleat dismission of Eurydice, of whom solemn sounds only procured a conditional release [2].

For the old age of Chearfulness he makes no provision; but 192 Melancholy he conducts with great dignity to the close of life. His Chearfulness is without levity, and his Pensiveness without asperity [3].

Through these two poems the images are properly selected 193 and nicely distinguished, but the colours of the diction seem not sufficiently discriminated. I know not whether the characters are kept sufficiently apart. No mirth can, indeed, be found in his melancholy; but I am afraid that I always meet some melancholy in his mirth. They are two noble efforts of imagination.

The greatest of his juvenile performances is the *Mask of Comus* [4], 194 in which may very plainly be discovered the dawn or twilight of *Paradise Lost* [5]. Milton appears to have formed very early that system of diction and mode of verse which his maturer judgement approved, and from which he never endeavoured nor desired to deviate.

Nor does *Comus* afford only a specimen of his language: it 195 exhibits likewise his power of description and his vigour of sentiment, employed in the praise and defence of virtue [6]. A

---

[1] *L'Allegro*, l. 131.

[2] 'Such strains as would have won the ear
Of Pluto, to have quite set free
His half regain'd Eurydice.'
                    Ib. l. 148.
'Such notes as warbled to the string
Drew iron tears down Pluto's cheek,
And made Hell grant what love did seek.' *Il Penseroso*, l. 106.

[3] In the first edition this sentence follows the first sentence of the next paragraph.

[4] *Ante*, MILTON, 21, 175. How slow it was in becoming known is

shown in *The Tatler*, for Nov. 24, 1709 (No. 98), where a quotation from it is introduced as 'a passage in a Mask writ by Milton, where two brothers are introduced seeking after their sister,' &c.

[5] *Ante*, MILTON, 177.

[6] 'In January, 1815, Shelley's grandfather died. Shelley went down into Sussex; his father would not suffer him to enter the house, but he sat outside the door and read *Comus*, while the reading of his grandfather's will went on inside.' MATTHEW ARNOLD, *Essays in Criticism*, 1888, p. 232.

work more truly poetical is rarely found; allusions, images, and descriptive epithets embellish almost every period with lavish decoration. As a series of lines, therefore, it may be considered as worthy of all the admiration with which the votaries have received it.

196 As a drama it is deficient. The action is not probable. A Masque, in those parts where supernatural intervention is admitted, must indeed be given up to all the freaks of imagination; but so far as the action is merely human it ought to be reasonable, which can hardly be said of the conduct of the two brothers, who, when their sister sinks with fatigue in a pathless wilderness, wander both away in search of berries too far to find their way back, and leave a helpless Lady to all the sadness and danger of solitude. This however is a defect over-balanced by its convenience.

197 What deserves more reprehension is that the prologue spoken in the wild wood by the attendant Spirit is addressed to the audience; a mode of communication so contrary to the nature of dramatick representation that no precedents can support it [1].

198 The discourse of the Spirit is too long, an objection that may be made to almost all the following speeches; they have not the spriteliness of a dialogue animated by reciprocal contention, but seem rather declamations deliberately composed and formally repeated on a moral question. The auditor therefore listens as to a lecture, without passion, without anxiety [2].

199 The song of Comus has airiness and jolity [3]; but, what may recommend Milton's morals as well as his poetry, the invitations to pleasure are so general that they excite no distinct images of corrupt enjoyment, and take no dangerous hold on the fancy.

200 The following soliloquies of Comus and the Lady are elegant, but tedious. The song [4] must owe much to the voice, if it ever can delight. At last the Brothers enter, with too much tranquillity; and when they have feared lest their sister should be in danger, and hoped that she is not in danger, the Elder makes a speech in praise of chastity [5], and the Younger finds how fine it is to be a philosopher [6].

[1] 'Johnson makes an unanswerable objection to the prologue.' LANDOR, *Imag. Conver.* iv. 284.
[2] 'Yet he listens with elevation and delight.' T. WARTON, *Milton's Poems*, p. 262.
[3] l. 93.
[4] l. 230.
[5] l. 418.
[6] l. 476.

Then descends the Spirit in form of a shepherd[1]; and the 201 Brother, instead of being in haste to ask his help, praises his singing, and enquires his business in that place. It is remarkable that at this interview the Brother is taken with a short fit of rhyming[2]. The Spirit relates that the Lady is in the power of Comus, the Brother moralises again, and the Spirit makes a long narration, of no use because it is false, and therefore unsuitable to a good Being.

In all these parts the language is poetical and the sentiments 202 are generous, but there is something wanting to allure attention.

The dispute between the Lady and Comus[3] is the most ani- 203 mated and affecting scene of the drama, and wants nothing but a brisker reciprocation of objections and replies, to invite attention and detain it.

The songs are vigorous and full of imagery; but they are 204 harsh in their diction, and not very musical in their numbers.

Throughout the whole the figures are too bold and the language 205 too luxuriant for dialogue: it is a drama in the epick style, inelegantly splendid, and tediously instructive[4].

The *Sonnets* were written in different parts of Milton's life upon 206 different occasions. They deserve not any particular criticism; for of the best it can only be said that they are not bad, and perhaps only the eighth and the twenty-first are truly entitled to this slender commendation[5]. The fabrick of a sonnet, however adapted to the Italian language, has never succeeded in ours,

---

[1] l. 490. [2] ll. 495–512.
[3] ll. 659–813.
[4] According to Dr. Warton there were at the end of the eighteenth century many who thought *The Fairy Queen, Palamon and Arcite, The Tempest,* and *Comus* 'childish and romantic.' Warton's *Pope's Works,* Preface, p. 55.
'Johnson must have lost all the senses that are affected by poetry when he calls the whole drama *tediously instructive.* There is, indeed, here and there prolixity; yet refreshing springs burst out profusely in every part of the wordy wilderness.' LANDOR, *Imag. Conver.* iv. 284.
Johnson admits that in all its parts it is 'truly poetical.' *Ante,* MILTON, 195.
[5] *Ante,* MILTON, 55, 152.

'Milton's sonnets are in several places incorrect, and sometimes uncouth in language, and, perhaps, in some, inharmonious; yet, upon the whole, I think the music exceedingly well suited to its end; that is, it has an energetic and varied flow of sound crowding into narrow room more of the combined effect of rhyme and blank verse than can be done by any other kind of verse I know of.' WORDSWORTH, *Memoirs,* i. 287.
'and when a damp
Fell round the path of Milton, in his hand   [he blew
The Thing became a trumpet, whence
Soul-animating strains—alas too few!'
WORDSWORTH, *Poet. Works,* ii. 309.
'A few of Milton's sonnets are extremely bad; the rest are excellent.' LANDOR, *Imag. Conver.* iv. 285.

which, having greater variety of termination, requires the rhymes to be often changed.

207   Those little pieces may be dispatched without much anxiety; a greater work calls for greater care. I am now to examine *Paradise Lost*, a poem which, considered with respect to design, may claim the first place, and with respect to performance the second, among the productions of the human mind [1].

208   By the general consent of criticks the first praise of genius is due to the writer of an epick poem, as it requires an assemblage of all the powers which are singly sufficient for other compositions [2]. Poetry is the art of uniting pleasure with truth, by calling imagination to the help of reason. Epick poetry undertakes to teach the most important truths by the most pleasing precepts, and therefore relates some great event in the most affecting manner. History must supply the writer with the rudiments of narration, which he must improve and exalt by a nobler art, must animate by dramatick energy, and diversify by retrospection and anticipation; morality must teach him the exact bounds and different shades of vice and virtue; from policy and the practice of life he has to learn the discriminations of character and the tendency of the passions, either single or combined; and physiology [3] must supply him with illustrations and images. To put these materials to poetical use is required an imagination capable of painting nature and realizing fiction. Nor is he yet a poet till he has

---

[1] *Ante*, MILTON, 109. 'The first place among our English poets is due to Milton.' ADDISON, *The Spectator*, No. 262. 'If Milton's *Paradise Lost* falls short of the *Aeneid* or *Iliad* in this respect [the arts of working on the imagination], it proceeds rather from the fault of the language in which it is written than from any defect of genius in the author.' *Ib.* No. 417.

'I recur to the *Paradise Lost* incessantly as the noblest specimen in the world of eloquence, harmony and genius.' LANDOR, *Imag. Conver.* iv. 245.

Macaulay thought that 'Milton's fame would have stood higher if only the first four books had been preserved. He would then have been placed above Homer.' Trevelyan's *Macaulay*, ii. 200.

[2] 'The most perfect work of poetry, says our master Aristotle, is tragedy [*Poetics*, xxvii. 15]. . . . But . . . an heroick poem is certainly the greatest work of human nature.' DRYDEN, *Works*, xiii. 36. See also *ib.* xiv. 129.

Horace Walpole, perhaps in answer to Johnson, describes an epic poem as 'that most senseless of all the species of poetic compositions, and which pedants call the *chef-d'œuvre* of the human mind. . . . When nothing has been impossible to genius in every other walk, why has everybody failed in this but the inventor, Homer? . . . Milton, all imagination, and a thousand times more sublime and spirited [than Virgil], has produced a monster.' *Letters*, viii. 235.

[3] *Ante*, MILTON, 39 *n.*

attained the whole extension of his language, distinguished all the delicacies of phrase, and all the colours of words, and learned to adjust their different sounds to all the varieties of metrical modulation [1].

Bossu is of opinion that the poet's first work is to find a *moral*, 209 which his fable is afterwards to illustrate and establish [2]. This seems to have been the process only of Milton: the moral of other poems is incidental and consequent; in Milton's only it is essential and intrinsick. His purpose was the most useful and the most arduous: 'to vindicate the ways of God to man [3]'; to shew the reasonableness of religion, and the necessity of obedience to the Divine Law [4].

To convey this moral there must be a *fable*, a narration 210 artfully constructed so as to excite curiosity and surprise expectation [5]. In this part of his work Milton must be confessed to have equalled every other poet. He has involved in his account of the Fall of Man the events which preceded, and those that were to follow it: he has interwoven the whole system of theology with such propriety that every part appears to be necessary, and scarcely any recital is wished shorter for the sake of quickening the progress of the main action.

The subject of an epick poem is naturally an event of great 211 importance. That of Milton is not the destruction of a city,

[1] In *Rasselas*, ch. x, Imlac enumerates the qualities needed in a poet. Rasselas exclaims:—'Enough! thou hast convinced me that no human being can ever be a poet.'

[2] 'La première chose par où l'on doit commencer pour faire une Fable, est de choisir l'instruction et le point de Morale qui lui doit servir de fond, selon le dessein et la fin que l'on se propose.' LE BOSSU, *Traité du Poëme Épique*, l. 1. ch. 7.
Dryden adopts Le Bossu's rule. *Works*, xvii. 303. Addison rejects it. *The Spectator*, No. 369. Voltaire attacks 'cette règle bizarre que le père Lebossu a prétendu établir, c'est de choisir son sujet avant les personnages, et de disposer toutes les actions qui se passent dans le poème avant de savoir à qui on les attribuera.' *Œuvres*, viii. 371. 'Son *Traité sur le Poëme épique* a beaucoup de réputation, mais il ne fera jamais de

poètes.' *Ib.* xvii. 117. See *post*, SMITH, 10.

[3] 'I may assert Eternal Providence,
And justify the ways of God to men.' *Paradise Lost*, i. 25.
Johnson, in his *Dictionary*, misquoting these lines, gives them under *Vindicate*. He was misled by Pope's line—
'But vindicate the ways of God to man.' *Essay on Man*, i. 16.

[4] 'In the *Paradise Lost*—indeed in every one of his poems—it is Milton himself whom you see; his Satan, his Adam, his Raphael, almost his Eve, are all John Milton; and it is a sense of this intense egotism that gives me the greatest pleasure in reading Milton's works. The egotism of such a man is a revelation of spirit.' COLERIDGE, *Table Talk*, 1884, p. 231.

[5] Johnson here borrows something from Addison's *Spectator*, No. 267.

the conduct of a colony, or the foundation of an empire. His subject is the fate of worlds, the revolutions of heaven and of earth ; rebellion against the Supreme King raised by the highest order of created beings ; the overthrow of their host and the punishment of their crime ; the creation of a new race of reasonable creatures ; their original happiness and innocence, their forfeiture of immortality, and their restoration to hope and peace [1].

212   Great events can be hastened or retarded only by persons of elevated dignity. Before the greatness displayed in Milton's poem all other greatness shrinks away. The weakest of his agents are the highest and noblest of human beings, the original parents of mankind ; with whose actions the elements consented ; on whose rectitude or deviation of will depended the state of terrestrial nature and the condition of all the future inhabitants of the globe [2].

213   Of the other agents in the poem the chief are such as it is irreverence to name on slight occasions [3]. The rest were lower powers ;

> ' of which the least could wield
> Those elements, and arm him with the force
> Of all their regions [4] ' ;

powers which only the controul of Omnipotence restrains from laying creation waste, and filling the vast expanse of space with ruin and confusion. To display the motives and actions of beings thus superiour, so far as human reason can examine them or human imagination represent them, is the task which this mighty poet has undertaken and performed.

214   In the examination of epick poems much speculation is commonly employed upon the *characters*. The characters in the

---

[1] ' When Milton conceived the glorious plan of an English epic, he soon saw the most striking subjects had been taken from him ; that Homer had taken all morality for his province, and Virgil exhausted the subject of politics.' GIBBON, *Misc. Works*, iv. 150.

[2] ' The moral which reigns in Milton is the most universal and most useful that can be imagined ; it is in short this, that obedience to the will of God makes men happy, and that disobedience makes them miserable.' ADDISON, *The Spectator*, No. 369.

[3] ' The principal actors are man in his greatest perfection, and woman in her highest beauty. Their enemies are the fallen angels ; the Messiah their friend, and the Almighty their protector.' ADDISON, *ib.* No. 267.

[4]   ' the least of whom could wield These elements,' &c.
Paradise Lost, vi. 221.

Paradise Lost which admit of examination are those of angels and of man ; of angels good and evil, of man in his innocent and sinful state.

Among the angels the virtue of Raphael is mild and placid, of 215 easy condescension and free communication [1] ; that of Michael is regal and lofty, and, as may seem, attentive to the dignity of his own nature. Abdiel and Gabriel appear occasionally, and act as every incident requires ; the solitary fidelity of Abdiel is very amiably painted [2].

Of the evil angels the characters are more diversified. To 216 Satan, as Addison observes, such sentiments are given as suit 'the most exalted and most depraved being [3].' Milton has been censured by Clarke [4] for the impiety which sometimes breaks from Satan's mouth. For there are thoughts, as he justly remarks, which no observation of character can justify, because no good man would willingly permit them to pass, however transiently, through his own mind. To make Satan speak as a rebel, without any such expressions as might taint the reader's imagination, was indeed one of the great difficulties in Milton's undertaking, and I cannot but think that he has extricated himself with great happiness [5]. There is in Satan's speeches little that can give pain to a pious ear. The language of rebellion cannot be the same with that of obedience. The malignity of Satan foams in haughtiness and obstinacy ; but his expressions are commonly general, and no otherwise offensive than as they are wicked [6].

The other chiefs of the celestial rebellion are very judiciously 217 discriminated in the first and second books ; and the ferocious character of Moloch appears, both in the battle and the council, with exact consistency [7].

---

[1] 'Nor must we omit the person of Raphael, who, amidst his tenderness and friendship for man, shows such a dignity and condescension in all his speech and behaviour as are suitable to a superior nature.' ADDISON, *The Spectator*, No. 273.

[2] *Paradise Lost*, v. 803–end.

[3] 'His sentiments . . . are suitable to a created being of the most exalted and depraved nature.' *The Spectator*, No. 303.

[4] Author of the *Essay on* [*upon*] *Study*. [By John Clarke, Master of the Grammar School in Hull, 1731, p.

204.] JOHNSON. *Ante*, MILTON, 135 *n*.

[5] 'It was easier for Homer and Virgil to dash the truth with fiction, as they were in no danger of offending the religion of their country by it. But as for Milton, . . . he was obliged to proceed with the greatest caution. . . . His story is capable of pleasing the most delicate reader, without giving offence to the most scrupulous.' ADDISON, *The Spectator*, No. 267.

[6] Johnson would not have said this of Dante's *Inferno*, had he read it.

[7] *Paradise Lost*, ii. 43 ; vi. 357.

218 To Adam and to Eve are given during their innocence such sentiments as innocence can generate and utter. Their love is pure benevolence and mutual veneration ; their repasts are without luxury and their diligence without toil. Their addresses to their Maker have little more than the voice of admiration and gratitude. Fruition left them nothing to ask, and Innocence left them nothing to fear [1].

219 But with guilt enter distrust and discord, mutual accusation, and stubborn self-defence ; they regard each other with alienated minds, and dread their Creator as the avenger of their transgression. At last they seek shelter in his mercy, soften to repentance, and melt in supplication. Both before and after the Fall the superiority of Adam is diligently sustained.

220 Of the *probable* and the *marvellous*, two parts of a vulgar epick poem which immerge the critick in deep consideration [2], the *Paradise Lost* requires little to be said. It contains the history of a miracle, of Creation and Redemption ; it displays the power and the mercy of the Supreme Being : the probable therefore is marvellous, and the marvellous is probable. The substance of the narrative is truth ; and as truth allows no choice, it is, like necessity, superior to rule. To the accidental or adventitious parts, as to every thing human, some slight exceptions may be made. But the main fabrick is immovably supported.

221 It is justly remarked by Addison that this poem has, by the nature of its subject, the advantage above all others, that it is universally and perpetually interesting [3]. All mankind will,

---

[1] ' En effet, il est à remarquer que dans tous les autres poëmes l'amour est regardé comme une faiblesse ; dans Milton seul il est une vertu. Le poète a su lever d'une main chaste le voile qui couvre ailleurs les plaisirs de cette passion ; il transporte le lecteur dans le jardin de délices ; il semble lui faire goûter les voluptés pures dont Adam et Ève sont remplis ; il ne s'élève pas au-dessus de la nature humaine, mais au-dessus de la nature corrompue.' VOLTAIRE, *Œuvres*, viii. 421.

[2] ' Aristotle observes that the fable in an epic poem should abound in circumstances that are both credible and astonishing ; or, as the French critics choose to phrase it, the fable should be filled with the probable and the marvellous.' ADDISON, *The Spectator*, No. 315.

' Le Poëme Héroïque doit avoir des Fictions pour être une Poésie ; et les Fictions, pour être reçues et agréées par le jugement, doivent être *vraisemblables.*' DESMARÊTS, *Défense du Poëme Héroïque*, p. 87, quoted in *Œuvres de Boileau*, ii. 98 *n.*

[3] *The Spectator*, No. 273.

' *Paradise Lost* is losing its hold over our imagination. . . . It would have been a thing incredible to Milton that the hold of the Jewish Scriptures over the imagination of English men and women could ever be weakened. This process, however, has already commenced.' Pattison's *Milton*, p. 199.

through all ages, bear the same relation to Adam and to Eve, and must partake of that good and evil which extend to themselves.

Of the *machinery* [1], so called from Θεὸς ἀπὸ μηχανῆς [2], by which **222** is meant the occasional interposition of supernatural power, another fertile topic of critical remarks, here is no room to speak, because every thing is done under the immediate and visible direction of Heaven ; but the rule is so far observed that no part of the action could have been accomplished by any other means.

Of *episodes* I think there are only two, contained in Raphael's **223** relation of the war in heaven [3] and Michael's prophetick account of the changes to happen in this world [4]. Both are closely connected with the great action ; one was necessary to Adam as a warning, the other as a consolation.

To the compleatness or *integrity* of the design nothing can be **224** objected ; it has distinctly and clearly what Aristotle requires, a beginning, a middle, and an end [5]. There is perhaps no poem of the same length from which so little can be taken without apparent mutilation. Here are no funeral games [6], nor is there any long description of a shield [7]. The short digressions at the beginning of the third, seventh, and ninth books might doubtless be spared ; but superfluities so beautiful who would take away ? or who does not wish that the author of the *Iliad* had gratified succeeding ages with a little knowledge of himself? Perhaps no passages are more frequently or more attentively read than those extrinsick paragraphs ; and, since the end of poetry is pleasure, that cannot be unpoetical with which all are pleased.

The questions, whether the action of the poem be strictly *one*, **225** whether the poem can be properly termed *heroick* [8], and who is

---

[1] Pope, in his Dedication of *The Rape of the Lock*, says:—'The machinery is a term invented by the critics to signify that part which the deities, angels, or demons are made to act in a poem.' In a note on *Iliad*, xxiv. 141, he writes :—' It may be thought that so many interpositions of the Gods, such messages from heaven to earth, and down to the seas, are needless machines.' See also *post*, DRYDEN, 207 *n*. ; POPE, 55, 59 ; and Boswell's *Johnson*, iv. 17.

[2] See Aristotle's *Poetics*, xv. 10.

[3] *Paradise Lost*, v. 577–vi. end.

[4] *Ib.* xi. 334–xii. end.
Addison reckons the creation of the world as part of the first episode. *The Spectator*, No. 267.

[5] Aristotle's *Poetics*, vii. 3 ; *The Spectator*, No. 267 ; *post*, DRYDEN, 363.

[6] *Iliad*, xxiii. 257 ; *Aeneid*, v. 104.

[7] *Iliad*, xviii. 478.

[8] 'There is nothing in nature more irksome than general discourses, especially when they turn chiefly upon words. For this reason I shall waive the discussion of that point which was started some years since,

the hero, are raised by such readers as draw their principles of judgement rather from books than from reason. Milton, though he intituled *Paradise Lost* only a 'poem¹,' yet calls it himself 'heroick song².' Dryden, petulantly and indecently, denies the heroism of Adam because he was overcome; but there is no reason why the hero should not be unfortunate except established practice, since success and virtue do not go necessarily together³. Cato is the hero of Lucan, but Lucan's authority will not be suffered by Quintilian to decide⁴. However, if success be necessary, Adam's deceiver was at last crushed; Adam was restored to his Maker's favour, and therefore may securely resume his human rank.

226   After the scheme and fabrick of the poem must be considered its component parts, the sentiments, and the diction.

227   The *sentiments*, as expressive of manners or appropriated to characters, are for the greater part unexceptionably just.

228   Splendid passages containing lessons of morality or precepts of prudence occur seldom. Such is the original formation of this poem that as it admits no human manners till the Fall, it can

whether Milton's *Paradise Lost* may be called an heroick poem.' ADDISON, *The Spectator*, No. 267.

¹ In the title to the second edition he describes it as 'a Poem in twelve books.'

² ' Since first this subject for Heroick Song
Pleas'd me, long choosing, and beginning late.'
Paradise Lost, ix. 25.

³ Dryden, after maintaining that Homer, Virgil, and Tasso completed 'the file of heroic poets,' and after mentioning 'a crowd of little poets who press for admission,' continues: —'Spenser has a better plea for his *Fairy Queen*, had his action been finished, or had been one. And Milton, if the devil had not been his hero instead of Adam, if the giant had not foiled the knight, and driven him out of his stronghold, to wander through the world with his lady-errant.' *Works*, xiv. 144. See *post*, ADDISON, 141.

'He that looks for an hero in *Paradise Lost* searches for that which Milton never intended; but if

he will needs fix the name of an hero upon any person in it, it is certainly the Messiah who is the hero, both in the principal action and in the chief episodes.' ADDISON, *Spectator*, No. 297.

'I assert, with Mr. Dryden, that the Devil is in truth the Hero; his plan, which he lays, pursues, and at last executes, being the subject of the poem.' CHESTERFIELD, *Letters to his Son*, ii. 138.

Burns wrote on June 11, 1787:— 'Give me a spirit like my favourite Hero, Milton's *Satan*.' He quotes *Paradise Lost*, i. 250–3. H. Sotheran's *Catalogue*, 1899, No. 12, lot 21.

'There is neither truth nor wit in saying that Satan is hero of the piece, unless, as is usually the case in human life, he is the greatest hero who gives the widest sway to the worst passions. It is Adam who acts and suffers most, and on whom the consequences have most influence. This constitutes him the main character.' LANDOR, *Imag. Conver.* iv. 201.

⁴ *Post*, ROWE, 35.

give little assistance to human conduct. Its end is to raise the thoughts above sublunary cares or pleasures. Yet the praise of that fortitude, with which Abdiel maintained his singularity of virtue against the scorn of multitudes [1], may be accommodated to all times ; and Raphael's reproof of Adam's curiosity after the planetary motions, with the answer returned by Adam [2], may be confidently opposed to any rule of life which any poet has delivered.

The thoughts which are occasionally called forth in the pro- 229 gress are such as could only be produced by an imagination in the highest degree fervid and active, to which materials were supplied by incessant study and unlimited curiosity. The heat of Milton's mind might be said to sublimate his learning, to throw off into his work the spirit of science, unmingled with its grosser parts.

He had considered creation in its whole extent, and his de- 230 scriptions are therefore learned. He had accustomed his imagination to unrestrained indulgence, and his conceptions therefore were extensive. The characteristick quality of his poem is sublimity [3]. He sometimes descends to the elegant, but his element is the great. He can occasionally invest himself with grace ; but his natural port is gigantick loftiness [4]. He can please when pleasure is required ; but it is his peculiar power to astonish.

He seems to have been well acquainted with his own genius, 231 and to know what it was that Nature had bestowed upon him more bountifully than upon others [5] ; the power of displaying the vast, illuminating the splendid, enforcing the awful, darkening the gloomy, and aggravating the dreadful : he therefore chose a subject on which too much could not be said, on which he might tire his fancy without the censure of extravagance.

The appearances of nature and the occurrences of life did not 232 satiate his appetite of greatness. To paint things as they are requires a minute attention, and employs the memory rather than the fancy. Milton's delight was to sport in the wide regions of

---

[1] *Paradise Lost*, v. 872.

[2] *Ib.* viii. 66–197.

[3] 'Milton's chief talent, and indeed his distinguishing excellence, lies in the sublimity of his thoughts.' ADDISON, *The Spectator*, No. 279.

[4] Algarotti terms it *gigantesca sublimità Miltoniana*. JOHNSON.
Baretti describes the King of Prussia as 'deigning to take the

trouble of gilding all Algarotti's copper.' *An Account of the Manners, &c., of Italy*, i. 202.
On Algarotti's death in 1764 Voltaire wrote of him to *La Gazette Littéraire* :—'Il était comme votre journal, il appartenait à l'Europe.' *Œuvres*, xliii. 369. See *post*, GRAY, 40.

[5] *Ante*, MILTON, 26, 138.

possibility; reality was a scene too narrow for his mind. He sent his faculties out upon discovery, into worlds where only imagination can travel, and delighted to form new modes of existence, and furnish sentiment and action to superior beings, to trace the counsels of hell, or accompany the choirs of heaven.

233 But he could not be always in other worlds : he must sometimes revisit earth, and tell of things visible and known. When he cannot raise wonder by the sublimity of his mind he gives delight by its fertility.

234 Whatever be his subject he never fails to fill the imagination. But his images and descriptions of the scenes or operations of Nature do not seem to be always copied from original form, nor to have the freshness, raciness, and energy of immediate observation. He saw Nature, as Dryden expresses it, 'through the spectacles of books [1]'; and on most occasions calls learning to his assistance [2]. The garden of Eden brings to his mind the vale of Enna, where Proserpine was gathering flowers [3]. Satan makes his way through fighting elements, like Argo between the Cyanean rocks, or Ulysses between the two *Sicilian* whirlpools, when he shunned Charybdis 'on the larboard [4].' The mythological allusions have been justly censured, as not being always used with notice of their vanity [5]; but they contribute variety to the narra-

---

[1] 'He [Shakespeare] was naturally learned ; he needed not the spectacles of books to read nature ; he looked inwards, and found her there.' DRYDEN, *Works*, xv. 344. Johnson quotes these words in his Preface to *Shakespeare, Works*, v. 153.
'Unhappily both Johnson and Dryden saw Nature from between the houses of Fleet Street. If ever there was a poet who knew her well, and described her in all her loveliness, it was Milton.' LANDOR, *Imag. Conver.* iv. 244.
[2] *Post*, MILTON, 268. 'For the enumeration of the Syrian and Arabian deities, it may be observed that Milton has comprised, in one hundred and thirty very beautiful lines, the two large and learned syntagmas which Selden had composed on that abstruse subject.' GIBBON, *The Decline and Fall*, ii. 4 *n.*
[3] *Paradise Lost*, iv. 268.
[4] *Ib.* ii. 1010–1020.

'The last fault which I shall take notice of in Milton's style is the frequent use of what the learned call technical words, or terms of art. . . . I have often wondered how Mr. Dryden could translate a passage out of Virgil after the following manner :—
" Tack to the larboard, and stand off to sea,
Veer starboard sea and land."
[Dryden's *Aeneid*, iii. 526 ; Virgil's *Aeneid*, iii. 412.]
'Milton makes use of larboard in the same manner.' ADDISON, *The Spectator*, No. 297. See *post*, MILTON, 263 ; DRYDEN, 255, 336.
[5] 'I do not find fault with these allusions where the poet himself represents them as fabulous, as he does in some places, but where he mentions them as truths and matters of fact.' ADDISON, *The Spectator*, No. 297.
'What has been adverse to Milton's art of illusion is, that the belief that the gods of the heathen world were

tion, and produce an alternate exercise of the memory and the fancy.

His similes are less numerous and more various than those of **235** his predecessors [1]. But he does not confine himself within the limits of rigorous comparison : his great excellence is amplitude, and he expands the adventitious image beyond the dimensions which the occasion required. Thus, comparing the shield of Satan to the orb of the Moon, he crowds the imagination with the discovery of the telescope and all the wonders which the telescope discovers [2].

Of his moral sentiments it is hardly praise to affirm that they **236** excel those of all other poets ; for this superiority he was indebted to his acquaintance with the sacred writings. The ancient epick poets, wanting the light of Revelation, were very unskilful teachers of virtue : their principal characters may be great, but they are not amiable. The reader may rise from their works with a greater degree of active or passive fortitude, and sometimes of prudence ; but he will be able to carry away few precepts of justice, and none of mercy.

From the Italian writers it appears that the advantages of even **237** Christian knowledge may be possessed in vain. Ariosto's pravity [3] is generally known ; and, though the *Deliverance of Jerusalem* may be considered as a sacred subject, the poet has been very sparing of moral instruction.

In Milton every line breathes sanctity of thought [4] and purity **238** of manners, except when the train of the narration requires the introduction of the rebellious spirits ; and even they are compelled

the rebellious angels has ceased to be part of the common creed of Christendom. Milton was nearly the last of our great writers who was fully possessed of the doctrine.' PATTISON, *Milton*, p. 198.

See De Quincey's *Works*, vi. Preface, p. 14, for a criticism on the passage in the text, beginning :—'The word *vanity* is here used in an old-world Puritanical sense for falsehood or visionariness.'

[1] E. FitzGerald writes that Tennyson in his youth 'used to say that the two grandest of all similes were those of the ships hanging in the air [ii. 636], and " the gunpowder one " [iv. 814], which he used slowly and grimly to enact in the days that are no more. He certainly then thought Milton the sublimest of all the gang ; his diction modelled on Virgil, as perhaps Dante's.' FitzGerald's *Letters*, ii. 193. Of the simile of the ships ' Tennyson said, " What simile was ever so vast as this ? " ' Tennyson's *Life*, ii. 519.

[2] *Paradise Lost*, i. 286 ; v. 261.

[3] Johnson gives *depravity* in his *Dictionary*, but without any instance of its use. In the *New Eng. Dict.* only one instance, in its sense of corruption, is given earlier than the *Lives of the Poets*.

[4]   ' indu'd
With sanctity of reason.'
Paradise Lost, vii. 507.

to acknowledge their subjection to God in such a manner as excites reverence and confirms piety.

239 Of human beings there are but two; but those two are the parents of mankind, venerable before their fall for dignity and innocence, and amiable after it for repentance and submission [1]. In their first state their affection is tender without weakness, and their piety sublime without presumption. When they have sinned they shew how discord begins in mutual frailty [2], and how it ought to cease in mutual forbearance; how confidence of the divine favour is forfeited by sin, and how hope of pardon may be obtained by penitence and prayer. A state of innocence we can only conceive, if indeed in our present misery it be possible to conceive it; but the sentiments and worship proper to a fallen and offending being we have all to learn, as we have all to practise.

240 The poet whatever be done is always great [3]. Our progenitors in their first state conversed with angels; even when folly and sin had degraded them they had not in their humiliation 'the port of mean suitors [4];' and they rise again to reverential regard when we find that their prayers were heard.

241 As human passions did not enter the world before the Fall, there is in the *Paradise Lost* little opportunity for the pathetick; but what little there is has not been lost. That passion which is peculiar to rational nature, the anguish arising from the consciousness of transgression and the horrours attending the sense of the Divine Displeasure, are very justly described and forcibly impressed [5]. But the passions are moved only on one occasion; sublimity is the general and prevailing quality in this poem—sublimity variously modified, sometimes descriptive, sometimes argumentative.

242 The defects and faults of *Paradise Lost*, for faults and defects every work of man must have, it is the business of impartial criticism to discover. As in displaying the excellence of Milton I have not made long quotations, because of selecting beauties there had been no end, I shall in the same general manner

---

[1] 'The whole species of mankind was in two persons. . . . We have, however, four distinct characters in these two persons. We see man and woman in the highest innocence and perfection, and in the most abject state of guilt and infirmity.' ADDISON, *The Spectator*, No. 273.

[2] In the first edition, 'natural frailty.'

[3] 'Shakespeare is always great, when some great occasion is presented to him.' DRYDEN, *Works*, xv. 344.

[4] 'Yet their port Not of mean suitors.' *Par. L.* xi. 8.

[5] *Ib.* x. 714.

mention that which seems to deserve censure; for what Englishman can take delight in transcribing passages, which, if they lessen the reputation of Milton, diminish in some degree the honour of our country[1]?

The generality of my scheme does not admit the frequent notice 243 of verbal inaccuracies which Bentley, perhaps better skilled in grammar than in poetry[2], has often found, though he sometimes made them, and which he imputed to the obtrusions of a reviser whom the author's blindness obliged him to employ[3].   A supposition rash and groundless, if he thought it true; and vile and pernicious, if, as is said, he in private allowed it to be false[4].

The plan of *Paradise Lost* has this inconvenience, that it com- 244 prises neither human actions nor human manners.   The man and woman who act and suffer are in a state which no other man or woman can ever know.   The reader finds no transaction in which he can be engaged, beholds no condition in which he can by any effort of imagination place himself; he has, therefore, little natural curiosity or sympathy.

We all, indeed, feel the effects of Adam's disobedience; we all 245 sin like Adam, and like him must all bewail our offences; we have restless and insidious enemies in the fallen angels, and in the blessed spirits we have guardians and friends; in the Redemption of mankind we hope to be included: in the description of heaven and hell we are surely interested, as we are all to reside hereafter either in the regions of horrour or of bliss[5].

[1] Landor on this remarks:—'There is no pleasure [delight] in transcribing such passages; but there is great utility. . . . Johnson has himself done great good by exposing great faults in great authors.   His criticism on Milton's highest work is the most valuable of all his writings.   He seldom is erroneous in his censures; but he never is sufficiently excited to admiration of what is purest and highest in poetry.' *Imag. Conver.* iv. 244.

[2] 'Bentley not only was destitute of poetical talent, but had contracted an aversion to the rapturous flights of genius and glowing language which distinguish the divine poem.' MONK, *Life of Bentley*, ii. 310.

[3] 'The friend or acquaintance, whoever he was, to whom Milton committed his copy and the overseeing of the press, did so vilely execute that trust that Paradise, under his ignorance and audaciousness, may be said to be twice lost.' Preface to Bentley's *Paradise Lost*.

[4] 'The ideal agency of the reviser of *Paradise Lost* was only a device to take off the odium of perpetually condemning and altering the words of the great poet: Bentley seems to have thought that the readers of his notes could better endure the censure of a nameless editor than of Milton, the glory of our country.' MONK, *Life of Bentley*, ii. 313.

[5] *Ante*, COWLEY, 147.   Dryden examines the position of those who, maintaining that the moderns cannot succeed in epic poems so well as the

246 But these truths are too important to be new: they have been taught to our infancy; they have mingled with our solitary thoughts and familiar conversation, and are habitually interwoven with the whole texture of life. Being therefore not new they raise no unaccustomed emotion in the mind: what we knew before we cannot learn; what is not unexpected, cannot surprise.

247 Of the ideas suggested by these awful scenes, from some we recede with reverence, except when stated hours require their association; and from others we shrink with horrour, or admit them only as salutary inflictions, as counterpoises to our interests and passions. Such images rather obstruct the career of fancy than incite it [1].

248 Pleasure and terrour are indeed the genuine sources of poetry; but poetical pleasure must be such as human imagination can at least conceive, and poetical terrour such as human strength and fortitude may combat. The good and evil of Eternity are too ponderous for the wings of wit [2]; the mind sinks under them in passive helplessness, content with calm belief [3] and humble adoration.

249 Known truths however may take a different appearance, and be conveyed to the mind by a new train of intermediate images. This Milton has undertaken, and performed with pregnancy and

ancients, 'lay the fault on our religion.' *Works*, xiii. 21.

'The principal actors in this poem are not only our progenitors, but our representatives. We have an actual interest in everything they do, and no less than our utmost happiness is concerned, and lies at stake in their behaviour.... We are embarked with them on the same bottom, and must be partakers of their happiness and misery.' ADDISON, *The Spectator*, No. 273.

'The first book of the *Paradise Lost* is in truth so terrible, and so nearly akin to my own miserable speculations in the subject of it, that I am a little apprehensive, unless my spirits were better, that the study of it might do me material harm.' COWPER, S. J. Davey's *Auto. Cata.* 1889, p. 40.

Bentham, speaking of his childhood, said:—'I read the *Paradise Lost*, and it frightened me. There was the

pandemonium with all its flames. The book looked like something between true and false, and I did not know how much might be true.' *Works*, x. 21. See also Chesterfield's *Letters to his Son*, iii. 370.

[1] 'De la foi d'un Chrétien les mystères terribles
D'ornements égayés ne sont point susceptibles.
L'Évangile à l'esprit n'offre de tous côtés
Que pénitence à faire et tourments mérités.'
BOILEAU, *L'Art poétique*, iii. 199. See *ante*, COWLEY, 146; *post*, DRYDEN, 141.

[2] *Post*, YOUNG, 155. 'Dr. Johnson had forgotten the *Night Thoughts* when he said that "the good and evil of Eternity are too ponderous for the wings of wit."' SOUTHEY, Cowper's *Works*, ii. 144.

[3] There was little calmness in Johnson's belief.

vigour of mind peculiar to himself. Whoever considers the few
radical positions which the Scriptures afforded him will wonder by
what energetick operations he expanded them to such extent and
ramified them to so much variety, restrained as he was by religious
reverence from licentiousness of fiction.

Here is a full display of the united force of study and genius ; 250
of a great accumulation of materials, with judgement to digest
and fancy to combine them : Milton was able to select from
nature or from story, from ancient fable or from modern science,
whatever could illustrate or adorn his thoughts. An accumulation
of knowledge impregnated his mind, fermented by study and
exalted by imagination[1].

It has been therefore said without an indecent hyperbole by 251
one of his encomiasts, that in reading *Paradise Lost* we read
a book of universal knowledge [2].

But original deficience cannot be supplied. The want of human 252
interest is always felt. *Paradise Lost* is one of the books which
the reader admires and lays down, and forgets to take up again.
None ever wished it longer than it is[3]. Its perusal is a duty
rather than a pleasure [4]. We read Milton for instruction, retire

---

[1] In the first edition, 'sublimed by
imagination.'

'Whereas, in reading Milton, you
never lose the sense of laborious
and condensed fulness, in reading
Homer you never lose the sense of flowing and abounding ease.' MATTHEW
ARNOLD, *On Translating Homer*,
1896, p. 73.

[2] Perhaps Johnson refers to the
Latin verses of Dr. Samuel Barrow,
which begin :—
'Qui legis Amissum Paradisum,
    grandia magni
Carmina Miltoni, quid nisi cuncta
    legis ? '
Newton's *Milton*, Preface, p. 87.

Landor, criticizing *Paradise Lost*,
xi. 129–135, writes :—' At the restoration of learning it was very pardonable to seize on every remnant of
antiquity, and to throw together into
one great storeroom whatever could
be collected from all countries, and
from all authors, sacred and profane.
Dante has done it, sometimes rather
ludicrously. Milton here copies his
Argus.' *Imag. Conver.* iv. 240.

'I don't think I've read Milton

these forty years ; the whole scheme
of the poem, and certain parts of
it, looming as grand as anything
in my memory ; but I never could
read ten lines together without stum-
bling at some pedantry that tipped
me at once out of Paradise, or even
Hell, into the Schoolroom, worse
than either.' E. FITZGERALD, *Letters*, ii. 193.

[3] This line is not in the first edition.
' "Nobody ever wished it longer,"
says Dr. Johnson, nor the moon
rounder, he might have added. Why,
'tis the perfectness and completeness
of it which makes us imagine that not
a line could be added to it, or diminished from it, with advantage. Would
we have a cubit added to the stature
of the Medicean Venus ? Do we wish
her taller ? LAMB, *Mrs. Leicester's
School and Other Writings*, ed. 1885,
p. 350.

[4] 'Addison has made Milton an
universal favourite, with whom readers
of every class think it necessary to be
pleased.' *Post*, ADDISON, 162.

'Si on lit Homère par une espèce
de devoir, on lit et on relit l'Arioste

harassed and overburdened, and look elsewhere for recreation; we desert our master, and seek for companions [1].

253 Another inconvenience of Milton's design is that it requires the description of what cannot be described, the agency of spirits. He saw that immateriality supplied no images, and that he could not show angels acting but by instruments of action; he therefore invested them with form and matter. This being necessary was therefore defensible; and he should have secured the consistency of his system by keeping immateriality out of sight, and enticing his reader to drop it from his thoughts. But he has unhappily perplexed his poetry with his philosophy. His infernal and celestial powers are sometimes pure spirit and sometimes animated body. When Satan walks with his lance upon the 'burning marle [2]' he has a body; when in his passage between hell and the new world he is in danger of sinking in the vacuity and is supported by a gust of rising vapours [3] he has a body; when he animates the toad [4] he seems to be mere spirit that can penetrate matter at pleasure; when he 'starts up in his own shape [5],' he has at least a determined form; and when he is brought before Gabriel he has ' a spear and a shield [6],' which he had the power of hiding in the toad, though the arms of the contending angels are evidently material.

pour son plaisir.' VOLTAIRE, Œuvres, viii. 392.

' The perusal of Spenser's work becomes so tedious that one never finishes it from the mere pleasure which it affords. It soon becomes a kind of task-reading.' HUME, Hist. of Engl. v. 492.

' There was a period of his life when Fox used to say that he could not forgive Milton for having occasioned him the trouble of reading through a poem (Paradise Lost), three parts of which were not worth reading.' Rogers's Table-Talk, p. 92.

' Paradise Lost has been more admired than read. The poet's wish and expectation that he should find " fit audience, though few " has been fulfilled. . . . An appreciation of Milton is the last reward of consummated scholarship.' PATTISON, Milton, p. 215.

' Still govern thou my song,
Urania, and fit audience find, though
few.' Paradise Lost, vii. 30.

[1] Post, DRYDEN, 312. 'Was there,' asked Johnson, 'ever yet anything written by mere man that was wished longer by its readers, excepting Don Quixote, Robinson Crusoe, and The Pilgrim's Progress?' John. Misc. i. 332.

In a note on Henry V. v. 2 he writes:—' The comick scenes of the history of Henry the fourth and fifth are now at an end, and all the comick personages are now dismissed. Falstaff and Mrs. Quickly are dead; Nym and Bardolph are hanged; Gadshill was lost immediately after the robbery; Poins and Peto have vanished since, one knows not how; and Pistol is now beaten into obscurity. I believe every reader regrets their departure.'

[2] Paradise Lost, i. 296.
[3] Ib. ii. 931–8.
[4] Ib. iv. 800.   [5] Ib. iv. 819.
[6]   'nor wanted in his grasp
What seem'd both spear and shield.' Ib. iv. 989.

The vulgar inhabitants of Pandæmonium, being 'incorporeal 254
spirits,' are 'at large though without number[1]' in a limited space,
yet in the battle when they were overwhelmed by mountains
their armour hurt them, 'crushed in upon their substance, now
grown gross by sinning[2].' This likewise happened to the un-
corrupted angels, who were overthrown 'the sooner for their arms,
for unarmed they might easily as spirits have evaded by contraction or remove[3].' Even as spirits they are hardly spiritual,
for 'contraction' and 'remove' are images of matter; but if they
could have escaped without their armour, they might have
escaped from it and left only the empty cover to be battered.
Uriel, when he rides on a sun-beam, is material[4]; Satan is material
when he is afraid of the prowess of Adam[5].

The confusion of spirit and matter which pervades the whole 255
narration of the war of heaven fills it with incongruity; and the
book in which it is related is, I believe, the favourite of children,
and gradually neglected as knowledge is increased.

After the operation of immaterial agents which cannot be ex- 256
plained may be considered that of allegorical persons, which have
no real existence. To exalt causes into agents, to invest abstract
ideas with form, and animate them with activity has always been
the right of poetry. But such airy beings are for the most part
suffered only to do their natural office, and retire. Thus Fame
tells a tale[6] and Victory hovers over a general or perches on
a standard[7]; but Fame and Victory can do no more. To give
them any real employment or ascribe to them any material
agency is to make them allegorical no longer, but to shock the
mind by ascribing effects to non-entity. In the *Prometheus* of
Æschylus we see Violence and Strength, and in the *Alcestis* of
Euripides we see Death, brought upon the stage, all as active
persons of the drama; but no precedents can justify absurdity.

Milton's allegory of Sin and Death[8] is undoubtedly faulty. Sin 257

[1] *Paradise Lost*, i. 789.
[2] 'Their armour help'd their harm,
  crush'd in and bruis'd
  Into their substance pent, ...
  ... though Spirits of purest light,
  Purest at first, now gross by
  sinning grown.' *Ib.* vi. 656.
[3] 'The sooner for their arms; un-
  arm'd they might
  Have easily, as Spirits, evaded
  swift

By quick contraction or remove.'
        Ib. vi. 595.
[4] *Ib.* iv. 555.
[5] *Ib.* ix. 484.
[6] As Rumour does in the opening
  of 2 *Henry IV.*
[7] '. . . Victory sits on our helms.'
        Richard III. v. 3.
[8] *Paradise Lost*, ii. 648. Atterbury
wrote to Pope in 1717 :—'I challenge
you, with all your partiality, to show

is indeed the mother of Death, and may be allowed to be the portress of hell ; but when they stop the journey of Satan, a journey described as real, and when Death offers him battle, the allegory is broken. That Sin and Death should have shewn the way to hell might have been allowed ; but they cannot facilitate the passage by building a bridge, because the difficulty of Satan's passage is described as real and sensible, and the bridge ought to be only figurative[1]. The hell assigned to the rebellious spirits is described as not less local than the residence of man. It is placed in some distant part of space, separated from the regions of harmony and order by a chaotick waste and an unoccupied vacuity[2] ; but Sin and Death worked up a 'mole of aggregated soil[3],' cemented with asphaltus[4] ; a work too bulky for ideal architects.

258   This unskilful allegory appears to me one of the greatest faults of the poem ; and to this there was no temptation, but the author's opinion of its beauty[5].

259   To the conduct of the narrative some objections may be made. Satan is with great expectation brought before Gabriel in Paradise, and is suffered to go away unmolested[6]. The creation of man is represented as the consequence of the vacuity left in heaven by the expulsion of the rebels[7] ; yet Satan mentions it as a report 'rife in heaven' before his departure[8].

260   To find sentiments for the state of innocence was very difficult ; and something of anticipation perhaps is now and then discovered. Adam's discourse of dreams[9] seems not to be the speculation of a new-created being. I know not whether his answer to the

---

me in Homer anything equal to the Allegory of Sin and Death, either as to the greatness and justness of the invention, or the height and beauty of the colouring.' Pope's *Works* (Elwin and Courthope), ix. 9.

[1] *Paradise Lost*, ii. 1024. 'Johnson's remarks on the allegory of Milton are just and wise ; so are those on the non-materiality or non-immateriality of Satan.' LANDOR, *Imag. Conver.* iv. 243.

[2] *Paradise Lost*, ii. 890. Tennyson said :—' I think that Milton's vague hell is much more awful than Dante's hell marked off into divisions.' Tennyson's *Life*, ii. 518.

[3] 'Aggravated' in the third edition must be a misprint. In the first edition Johnson has 'aggregated,' as

in *Paradise Lost*, x. 293. In his *Dictionary* he quotes the verse under *aggregate*.

[4] 'Asphaltic slime.' *Ib.* x. 298.

[5] Addison, allowing that it is 'a very beautiful and well-invented allegory,' adds :—' I cannot think that persons of such a chimerical existence are proper actors in an epic poem ; because there is not that measure of probability annexed to them which is requisite in writings of this kind.' *The Spectator*, No. 273. See also *ib.* No. 297.

[6] *Paradise Lost*, iv. 866–end.

[7] *Ib.* vii. 150.

[8]   'whereof so rife There went a fame in heav'n.' *Ib.* i. 650.

[9] *Ib.* v. 100.

angel's reproof for curiosity does not want something of propriety: it is the speech of a man acquainted with many other men [1]. Some philosophical notions, especially when the philosophy is false [2], might have been better omitted. The angel in a comparison speaks of 'timorous deer [3],' before deer were yet timorous, and before Adam could understand the comparison.

Dryden remarks that Milton has some flats among his elevations [4]. This is only to say that all the parts are not equal. In every work one part must be for the sake of others; a palace must have passages, a poem must have transitions. It is no more to be required that wit should always be blazing than that the sun should always stand at noon. In a great work there is a vicissitude of luminous and opaque parts, as there is in the world a succession of day and night. Milton, when he has expatiated in the sky, may be allowed sometimes to revisit earth; for what other author ever soared so high or sustained his flight so long? 261

Milton, being well versed in the Italian poets, appears to have borrowed often from them [5]; and, as every man catches something from his companions, his desire of imitating Ariosto's levity has disgraced his work with the 'Paradise of Fools'; a fiction not in itself ill-imagined, but too ludicrous for its place [6]. 262

---

[1] *Paradise Lost*, viii. 179.
[2] As where Raphael brings in the Ptolemaic system. *Ib.* viii. 15–178. See also *ib.* iii. 481–3, and Masson's *Milton*, vi. 523–51.
[3]   'as a herd
Of goats or timorous flock.'
        Paradise Lost, vi. 856.
[4] 'Milton's *Paradise Lost* is admirable; but am I therefore bound to maintain that there are no flats amongst his elevations, when it is evident he creeps along sometimes for above an hundred lines together?' DRYDEN, *Works*, xii. 300.
'It is true Milton runs into a flat of thought, sometimes for an hundred lines together; but it is when he is got into a track of Scripture.' *Ib.* xiii. 19. 'A track of theology' would be nearer the truth.
'Milton's strong pinion now not heav'n can bound,
    Now serpent-like in prose he sweeps the ground,
In quibbles angel and archangel join,

And God the Father turns a school-divine.'
POPE, *Imit. of Hor.*, *Epis.* ii. 1. 99.
Gray, speaking of a long poem, said:—'To produce effect it was absolutely necessary to have weak parts. He instanced in Homer, and particularly in Milton, who, in parts of his poem, rolls on in sounding words that have but little meaning.' Mitford's *Gray*, v. 36.
[5] 'I am sure that I myself, and many others, find a peculiar charm in those passages of such great masters as Virgil or Milton where they adopt the creation of a bygone poet, or reclothe it, more or less, according to their own fancy.' TENNYSON, *Life*, i. 258.
[6] *Paradise Lost*, iii. 440–497.
'Such allegories rather savour of the spirit of Spenser and Ariosto than of Homer and Virgil.' ADDISON, *The Spectator*, No. 297.
'Even the least portions [of heroick poems] must be of the epick kind; all

263   His play on words, in which he delights too often [1]; his equivocations, which Bentley endeavours to defend by the example
of the ancients [2]; his unnecessary and ungraceful use of terms
of art [3], it is not necessary to mention, because they are easily
remarked and generally censured, and at last bear so little proportion to the whole that they scarcely deserve the attention of
a critick.

264   Such are the faults of that wonderful performance *Paradise
Lost*; which he who can put in balance with its beauties must be
considered not as nice but as dull, as less to be censured for
want of candour than pitied for want of sensibility.

265   Of *Paradise Regained* [4] the general judgement seems now to
be right, that it is in many parts elegant, and every-where
instructive. It was not to be supposed that the writer of
Paradise Lost could ever write without great effusions of fancy
and exalted precepts of wisdom. The basis of *Paradise
Regained* is narrow; a dialogue without action can never please
like an union of the narrative and dramatick powers [5]. Had this
poem been written, not by Milton but by some imitator, it would
have claimed and received universal praise [6].

266   If *Paradise Regained* has been too much depreciated [7], *Sampson
Agonistes* has in requital been too much admired [8]. It could only

things must be grave, majestical and
sublime, nothing of a foreign nature,
like the trifling *novels* which Ariosto
and others have inserted in their
poems.' DRYDEN, *Works*, xiv. 130.

[1] 'The only piece of pleasantry in
Paradise Lost is where the evil
spirits are described as rallying the
angels upon the success of their newly
invented artillery [Book vi. 607–
629]. This passage I look upon to
be the most exceptionable in the
whole poem, as being nothing else
but a string of puns, and those too
very indifferent.' ADDISON, *The Spectator*, No. 279.

[2] 'These passages of Satan and
Belial's insulting and jesting mockery
have been often censur'd; especially
by an ingenious gentleman who had
a settled aversion to all *puns*, as they
are call'd; which niceness, if carried
to extremity, will depreciate half of
the good sayings of the old Greek
and Latin wits.' BENTLEY, *Para-

dise Lost*, vi. 615 *n.*
'The wit, which Milton calls the
pleasant vein, is worthy of newly-
made devils who never had heard
any before.' LANDOR, *Imag. Conver.*
iv. 224.

[3] *Ante*, MILTON, 234.

[4] *Ante*, MILTON, 146.

[5] 'The speakers are no more than
the abstract principles of good and
evil, two voices who hold a rhetori-
cal disquisition through four books
and two thousand lines.' PATTISON,
Milton, p. 192. The rhetoric, however, glows at times with the hidden
fire of indignation at the 'evil days'
on which the poet has fallen.

[6] 'Coleridge says of it:—" In its
kind it is the most perfect poem
extant."' *Ib.* p. 195.

[7] Wesley describes it as :
'The last faint effort of an expiring Muse.' *Journal*, 1827, iii. 368.

[8] '*Samson Agonistes* equals, if not
exceeds, any of the most perfect

be by long prejudice and the bigotry of learning that Milton could prefer the ancient tragedies with their encumbrance of a chorus to the exhibitions of the French and English stages [1] ; and it is only by a blind confidence in the reputation of Milton that a drama can be praised in which the intermediate parts have neither cause nor consequence, neither hasten nor retard the catastrophe.

In this tragedy are however many particular beauties, many just sentiments and striking lines ; but it wants that power of attracting attention which a well-connected plan produces [2]. 267

Milton would not have excelled in dramatick writing [3] ; he knew human nature only in the gross, and had never studied the shades of character, nor the combinations of concurring or the perplexity of contending passions. He had read much and knew what books could teach ; but had mingled little in the world, and was deficient in the knowledge which experience must confer [4]. 268

Through all his greater works there prevails an uniform peculiarity of *Diction*, a mode and cast of expression which bears little resemblance to that of any former writer, and which is so 269

tragedies which were ever exhibited on the Athenian stage.' Newton's *Milton*, Preface, p. 63.

'It has been opposed, with all the confidence of triumph, to the dramatic performances of other nations. . . . The whole drama, if its superfluities were cut off, would scarcely fill a single act ; yet this is the tragedy which ignorance has admired and bigotry applauded.' JOHNSON, *The Rambler*, Nos. 139, 140.

Atterbury wrote to Pope in 1722:— 'I wish you would review and polish *Samson Agonistes*. It is written in the very spirit of the ancients, it deserves your care, and is capable of being improved, with little trouble, into a perfect model and standard of tragic poetry.' Pope's *Works* (Elwin and Courthope), ix. 49.

'*Comus* is rich in beautiful and sweet flowers, and in exuberant leaves of genius ; but the ripe and mellow fruit is in *Samson Agonistes*. When he wrote that his mind was Hebraized. Indeed, his genius fed on the writings of the Hebrew prophets.' WORDS-WORTH, *Memoirs*, ii. 472.

'Wordsworth concurred, he said, with Johnson in this, that it had *no middle*, but the beginning and end

are equally sublime.' H. C. Robinson's *Diary*, iii. 84.

'*Samson* has more of the antique spirit than any production of any other modern poet. Milton is very great.' GOETHE, Eckermann's *Conversations*, 1850, ii. 220. See also H. C. Robinson's *Diary*, ii. 437, 440 *n*.

[1] In the Preface Milton speaks of Aeschylus, Sophocles, and Euripides as 'the three tragic poets unequalled yet by any, and the best rule to all who endeavour to write tragedy.'

[2] For 'the vehement exhibition of Milton's personality' both in *Samson Agonistes* and *Paradise Regained* see Masson's *Milton*, vi. 658, 670.

[3] 'I wonder that he who ventured (contrary to the practice of all other epic poets) to imitate Homer's lownesses in the narrative should not also have copied his plainness and perspicuity in the dramatic parts ; since in his speeches (where clearness above all is necessary) there is frequently such transposition and forced construction, that the very sense is not to be discovered without a second or third reading.' POPE, Postscript to *The Odyssey*, 1760, iv. 281.

[4] *Ante*, MILTON, 234.

far removed from common use that an unlearned reader when he first opens his book finds himself surprised by a new language [1].

270   This novelty has been, by those who can find nothing wrong in Milton, imputed to his laborious endeavours after words suitable to the grandeur of his ideas [2]. 'Our language,' says Addison, 'sunk under him [3].' But the truth is, that both in prose and verse, he had formed his style by a perverse and pedantick principle. He was desirous to use English words with a foreign idiom [4]. This in all his prose is discovered and condemned, for there judgement operates freely, neither softened by the beauty nor awed by the dignity of his thoughts; but such is the power of his poetry that his call is obeyed without resistance, the reader feels himself in captivity to a higher and a nobler mind, and criticism sinks in admiration.

271   Milton's style was not modified by his subject: what is shown with greater extent in *Paradise Lost* may be found in *Comus*. One source of his peculiarity was his familiarity with the Tuscan poets: the disposition of his words is, I think, frequently Italian [5]; perhaps sometimes combined with other tongues. Of him, at last, may be said what Jonson says of Spenser, that 'he wrote no

---

[1] 'I found in Milton a true sublimity, lofty thoughts, which were clothed with admirable Grecisms, and ancient words which he had been digging from the mines of Chaucer and Spenser, and which, with all their rusticity, had somewhat of venerable in them.' DRYDEN, *Works*, xiii. 117. 'Instead of sprinkling old words [in *Paradise Lost*] he has dealt them with too free a hand, even sometimes to the obscuring of his sense.' *Ib.* vii. 309.

Addison describes 'those several ways of speech with which Milton has so very much enriched, and in some places darkened, the language of his poem.' *The Spectator*, No. 285.

'George II asked, when somebody was highly praising Milton, "Why did he not write his *Paradise Lost* in prose?"' Warton's *Pope's Works*, iv. 199.

Stephen Duck, the peasant poet (*post*, SAVAGE, 236), 'read *Paradise Lost* over twice or thrice with a dictionary, before he could under-

stand the language. He studied it as others study the classics.' *Gent. Mag.* 1736, p. 317.

[2] *Post*, DRYDEN, 339 *n.*

[3] 'Our language sunk under him, and was unequal to that greatness of soul which furnished him with such glorious conceptions.' *The Spectator*, No. 297.

[4] 'The great pest of language is frequency of translation. No book was ever turned from one language into another without imparting something of its native idiom; this is the most mischievous and comprehensive innovation.' JOHNSON, *Works*, v. 48.

[5] *Ante*, MILTON, 22.

Landor, criticizing *Il Penseroso*, l. 156—

'To walk the studious cloisters pale,' writes:—'Milton was very Italian in his custom of adding a second epithet after the substantive, where one had preceded it.' *Imag. Conver.* iv. 276.

[As the reading of the line thus quoted by Landor is disputed, Warton and most later editors giving 'studious cloister's pale,' another example

language[1],' but has formed what Butler calls 'a Babylonish Dialect[2],' in itself harsh and barbarous, but made by exalted genius and extensive learning the vehicle of so much instruction and so much pleasure that, like other lovers, we find grace in its deformity[3].

Whatever be the faults of his diction he cannot want the praise 272 of copiousness and variety; he was master of his language in its full extent, and has selected the melodious words with such diligence that from his book alone the Art of English Poetry might be learned.

After his diction something must be said of his versification[4]. 273 'The measure,' he says, 'is the English heroick verse without rhyme[5].' Of this mode he had many examples among the

may be found in 'Warble his native wood-notes wild.' *L'Allegro*, l. 134.]

' Many, if not most of Milton's odd constructions, are to be sought in the *Divina Commedia*, I think, rather than in the ancients.' LOWELL, *Letters*, ii. 433.

[1] 'Spenser, in affecting the ancients, writ no language.' JONSON, *Works*, 1756, vii. 128. See also *The Rambler*, No. 121.

[2] *Hudibras*, i. 1. 93.

[3] ' Milton's style in his *Paradise Lost* is not natural; 'tis an exotic style. As his subject lies a good deal out of the world it has a particular propriety in those parts of the poem; and when he is on earth, wherever he is describing our parents in Paradise, you see he uses a more easy and natural way of writing.' POPE, Spence's *Anec.* p. 174.

' Milton is never quaint, never twangs through the nose, but is everywhere grand and elegant, without resorting to musty antiquity for his beauties. On the contrary, he took a long stride forward, left the language of his own day far behind him, and anticipated the expressions of a century yet to come.' COWPER, *Works*, vi. 294.

[4] Johnson examines Milton's versification in *The Rambler*, Nos. 86, 88, 90, 94.

' Milton,' wrote Cowper, ' of all English poets that ever lived had certainly the finest ear.' In another letter he speaks of 'the unacquainted-ness of modern ears with the divine harmony of Milton's numbers and the principles upon which he constructed them.' *Works*, v. 269; vi. 12.

'The poet's peculiar excellence, above all others, was in his exquisite perception of rhythm, and in the boundless variety he has given it both in verse and prose. Virgil comes nearest to him in his assiduous study of it, and in his complete success.' LANDOR, *Longer Prose Works*, ii. 206.

' More than once,' writes F. T. Palgrave, 'did Tennyson impress upon me that Milton must have framed his metre upon that "ocean-roll of rhythm," which underlies the hexameters of Virgil; quoting, as a perfect example, the four lines, "Continuo ventis surgentibus . . . " (*Geor.* i. 356), in which the rising of a storm is painted.' Tennyson's *Life*, ii. 500.

'Milton certainly modelled his English verse on Virgil, as Tennyson observed to me some forty years ago.' E. FITZGERALD, *More Letters*, p. 218.

'Dobson's Latin translation of *Paradise Lost* [*post*, POPE, 195] is about the greatest feat ever performed in modern Latin verse, and it shows by a crucial experiment how little Milton really has in common with Virgil.' GOLDWIN SMITH, *Lectures and Essays*, 1881, p. 324. See also Courthope's *Hist. of Eng. Poetry*, 1903, iii. 444.

[5] 'The measure is English,' &c. Preface to *Paradise Lost*.

Italians[1], and some in his own country. The Earl of Surrey is said to have translated one of Virgil's books without rhyme[2], and besides our tragedies a few short poems had appeared in blank verse[3]; particularly one tending to reconcile the nation to Raleigh's wild attempt upon Guiana, and probably written by Raleigh himself[4]. These petty performances cannot be supposed to have much influenced Milton, who more probably took his hint from Trisino's *Italia Liberata*[5]; and, finding blank verse easier than rhyme, was desirous of persuading himself that it is better[6].

274 'Rhyme,' he says, and says truly, 'is no necessary adjunct of true poetry[7].' But perhaps of poetry as a mental operation metre or musick is no necessary adjunct; it is however by the musick of metre that poetry has been discriminated in all languages, and in languages melodiously constructed with a due proportion of long and short syllables metre is sufficient. But one language cannot communicate its rules to another; where metre is scanty and imperfect some help is necessary. The musick of the English heroick line strikes the ear so faintly that it is easily lost, unless all the syllables of every line co-operate together; this co-operation can be only obtained by the preservation of every verse unmingled with another as a distinct system of sounds, and this distinctness is obtained and preserved by the artifice of rhyme[8]. The variety

---

[1] *Post*, MILTON, 275.

[2] 'He translated the second and fourth books of Virgil [*Aeneid*] into blank verse. This is the first composition in blank verse extant in the English language. The diction is often poetical, and the versification varied with proper pauses.' WARTON, *Hist. of Eng. Poetry*, ed. 1871, iv. 35.

[3] Warton mentions Abraham Fleming's 'blank-verse translation of the *Bucolics* and *Georgics*, in alexandrines, in 1589.' *Ib*. iv. 39.

[4] [This poem, *De Guiana Carmen Epicum*, signed G. C., is prefixed to *A Relation of the Second Voyage to Guiana performed and written in the year* 1596 *by Laurence Keymis Gent*. Contained in Hakluyt's *Voyages* (1598-1600), vol. iii. p. 668. It consists of about 200 lines in blank verse. Raleigh is certainly not the author. Cunningham (*Lives of the Poets*, vol. i. p. 163 *n*.) states that

Oldys attributes it to George Chapman. Mr. A. H. Bullen (*Dict. Nat. Biog*. x. 48) also gives Chapman as author.]

[5] 'In [1548] Trissino published his *Italia Liberata da' Goti*, professedly written in imitation of the *Iliad*, without rhyme. His design was to destroy the terza rima of Dante.' WARTON, *Hist. of Engl. Poetry*, iv. 39.

[6] See Appendix P.

[7] 'Rhyme being no necessary adjunct or true ornament of poem or good verse,' &c. Preface to *Paradise Lost*.

Marvell thus ends his lines *On Milton's Paradise Lost* (*Poet. Works*, 1870, p. 76) :—
'Thy verse created like thy theme sublime　　[needs not rhyme.'
In number, weight, and measure,

[8] 'I am ready to depose on oath that I find every syllable as distinguishably and clearly either long

of pauses, so much boasted by the lovers of blank verse, changes the measures of an English poet to the periods of a declaimer[1]; and there are only a few skilful and happy readers of Milton who enable their audience to perceive where the lines end or begin. 'Blank verse,' said an ingenious critick[2], 'seems to be verse only to the eye[3].'

Poetry may subsist without rhyme, but English poetry will 275 not often please; nor can rhyme ever be safely spared but where the subject is able to support itself[4]. Blank verse makes some approach to that which is called the 'lapidary style[5]'; has neither the easiness of prose nor the melody of numbers, and therefore tires by long continuance. Of the Italian writers without rhyme, whom Milton alleges as precedents[6], not one is popular; what reason could urge in its defence has been confuted by the ear[7].

or short in our language as in any other.' COWPER, Southey's *Cowper*, vi. 346.

'Je crois la rime nécessaire à tous les peuples qui n'ont pas dans leur langue une mélodie sensible, marquée par les longues et par les brèves, et qui ne peuvent employer ces dactyles et ces spondées qui font un effet si merveilleux dans le latin.' VOLTAIRE, *Œuvres*, xxxv. 435.

[1] 'This I had the honour to tell Dr. Johnson; and I said:—" Quin, the actor, taught it me; and called it The Pause of Suspension."' MRS. PIOZZI, *Auto.* 1861, ii. 138.

[2] Mr. Locke of Norbury Place. Boswell's *Johnson*, iv. 43.

[3] Coleridge, in *Biog. Lit.* 1847, ii. 86, giving an extract from Wordsworth's *Brothers*, as first published, and referring to one line, continues:— 'If any ear could suspect that these sentences were ever printed as metre, on those very words alone could the suspicion have been founded.'

[4] *Post*, ROSCOMMON, 30; DRYDEN, 20, 265; SOMERVILE, 8; THOMSON, 47; DYER, 11; SHENSTONE, 31; YOUNG, 160; AKENSIDE, 17.

[5] *Ante*, MILTON, 27.

[6] 'Some both Italian and Spanish poets of prime note have rejected rhyme.' Preface to *Paradise Lost*. 'Trissino is commonly regarded as the inventor of blank verse in Italy, in his *Sofonisba* printed in 1524. It

was, I think, first introduced into Spanish by Boscan and Garcilasso in 1543. Boscan's *Leandro*, a tale nearly 3,000 lines long, may still be read with pleasure for the gentle and sweet passages it contains.' TICKNOR, *History of Spanish Literature*, 1872, i. 516. See also Warton's *History of Eng. Poetry*, iv. 39. For Caro's *Aeneid* in blank verse see *post*, DRYDEN, 203 *n*.

'Till barbarous ages, and more barbarous times,
Debased the majesty of verse to rhymes;
. . . . . .
But Italy, reviving from the trance
Of Vandal, Goth, and monkish ignorance,
With pauses, cadence, and well-vowelled words,
And all the graces a good ear affords,
Made rhyme an art, and Dante's polished page
Restored a silver, not a golden age.'
DRYDEN, *To the Earl of Roscommon*, l. 11.

For Roscommon's attack on rhyme see *English Poets*, xv. 91.

[7] 'Those two divine excellencies of music and poetry are grown in a manner to be little more but the one fiddling and the other rhyming, and are indeed very worthy the ignorance of the friar and the barbarousness of the Goths that introduced them among us.' TEMPLE, *Works*, 1757, iii. 454.

276 But whatever be the advantage of rhyme I cannot prevail on myself to wish that Milton had been a rhymer [1], for I cannot wish his work to be other than it is; yet like other heroes he is to be admired rather than imitated. He that thinks himself capable of astonishing may write blank verse, but those that hope only to please must condescend to rhyme.

277 The highest praise of genius is original invention. Milton cannot be said to have contrived the structure of an epick poem, and therefore owes reverence to that vigour and amplitude of mind to which all generations must be indebted for the art of poetical narration, for the texture of the fable, the variation of incidents, the interposition of dialogue, and all the stratagems that surprise and enchain attention. But of all the borrowers from Homer Milton is perhaps the least indebted [2]. He was naturally a thinker for himself, confident of his own abilities [3] and disdainful of help or hindrance; he did not refuse admission to the thoughts or images of his predecessors [4], but he did not seek them. From his contemporaries he neither courted nor received support; there is in his writings nothing by which the pride of other authors might be gratified or favour gained, no exchange of praise nor solicitation of support. His great works were performed under discountenance and in blindness, but difficulties vanished at his touch; he was born for whatever is arduous; and his work is not the greatest of heroick poems, only because it is not the first.

---

[1] 'I am not persuaded the *Paradise Lost* would not have been more nobly conveyed to posterity, not perhaps in heroic couplets, although even *they* could sustain the subject if well balanced, but in the stanza of Spenser or of Tasso, or in the terza rima of Dante, which the powers of Milton could easily have grafted on our language.' BYRON, *Works*, 1854, ix. 91.

'To this metre, as used in the *Paradise Lost*, our country owes the glory of having produced one of the only two poetical works in the grand style which are to be found in the modern languages; the Divine Comedy of Dante is the other.' MATTHEW ARNOLD, *On Translating Homer*, 1896, p. 72.

[2] His widow 'being asked whether he did not often read Homer and Virgil, she understood it as an imputation upon him for stealing from those authors, and answered with eagerness that he stole from nobody but the Muse who inspired him; and being asked by a lady present who the Muse was, replied it was God's grace, and the Holy Spirit that visited him nightly.' Newton's *Milton*, Pref. p. 80.

'There is scarce any author who has written so much, and upon such various subjects, and yet quotes so little from his contemporary authors.' *Ib.* p. 72. Swift went beyond him in scarcely ever 'taking a single thought from any writer, ancient or modern.' *Post*, SWIFT, 141.

[3] *Ante*, MILTON, 26, 138, 231.

[4] 'Milton has acknowledged to me that Spenser was his original.' DRYDEN, *Works*, xi. 210.

APPENDIX I (Page 85)

'The writing of deeds and charters was one of the employments of the regular clergy. After the dissolution of religious houses the business of a scrivener became a lay profession; and 14 Jac. [1617] a company of scriveners was incorporated, about which time they took themselves to the writing of wills, leases, &c. Francis Kirkman, in *The Unlucky Citizen*, 1673, relates that almost all the business of the city in making leases, mortgages, &c., and procuring money on securities of ground and houses, was transacted by these men, who hence assumed the name of money scriveners. The furniture of a scrivener's shop was a sort of pew for the master, desks for the apprentices, and a bench for the clients to sit on till their turn came.' HAWKINS, *Hist. of Music*, 1776, iii. 367. See also Masson's *Milton*, i. 24. Johnson in his *Dictionary* defines *money-scrivener* as 'one who raises money for others.' For 'the griping scrivener' see Dryden's *Works*, xii. 369.

'Among the psalm-tunes composed into four parts by sundry authors, and published by Thomas Ravenscroft in 1633, there are many, particularly that common one called York Tune, with the name John Milton; the tenor of this tune is so well known that within memory half the nurses in England were used to sing it by way of lullaby; and the chimes of many country churches have played it six or eight times in four and twenty hours from time immemorial.' HAWKINS, *Hist. of Music*, iii. 368. See also Aubrey's *Brief Lives*, ii. 62; Phillips' *Milton*, p. 4; T. Warton's *Milton's Poems*, p. 523; Masson's *Milton*, i. 50; and *N. & Q.* 8 S. v. 346.

APPENDIX J (Page 86)

It was from the elder brother, Edward, that this account is derived. In 1694 he published *Letters of State written by Mr. John Milton . . . To which is added An Account of his Life. Together with several of his Poems.* John Phillips lived by his pen, often sinking into obscenity. For many years he was 'in the closest intimacy with Titus Oates.' Masson's *Milton*, v. 259, 382; vi. 462, 767. Aubrey describes him as 'very happy at jiggish poetry.' *Brief Lives*, ii. 152. Edward, though he wrote a licentious book (Masson's *Milton*, v. 383), was generally decent in his writings. He was a tutor in the families of Evelyn and of the Earls of Pembroke and Arlington. *Ib.* vi. 763. Evelyn recorded under Oct. 24, 1663 :—'Mr Edward Philips came to be my son's preceptor; this gentleman was nephew to Milton who wrote against Salmasius's *Defensio*, but was not at all infected with his principles.' *Diary*, i. 399. For his *History of Poetry* see MILTON, 42. 'His chief performance is the fourth edition of Baker's *Chronicle*.' Masson's *Milton*, vi. 481.

APPENDIX K (Page 90)

For Samuel Hartlib, 'the son of a Polish merchant of German extraction' by an English wife, 'who made London his head-quarters,' see Masson's *Milton*, iii. 193. Evelyn describes him as 'honest and learned Mr. Hartlib, a public-spirited and ingenious person, who had propagated many useful things and arts.' *Diary*, i. 326. Pepys attended the wedding of his daughter 'Nan Hartlib, which was kept at Goring House, with very great state, cost, and noble company.' *Diary*, i. 115.

In *A Shelf of Old Books* by Mrs. James T. Fields, New York, 1895, p. 147, is given a facsimile of the following title-page :—*Poems, &c., upon Several Occasions. By Mr. John Milton. Both English and Latin, &c. Composed at several times. With a small Tractate of Education. To Mr. Hartlib.* London, Printed for Tho. Dring at the Blew Anchor next Mitre Court over against Fetter Lane in Fleet-street, 1673. 'It belonged to Thomas Gray when a schoolboy, his name being written nine times by himself upon the title-page.'

The original tract had no title-page, but the following heading on the first page :—' OF EDUCATION : TO MASTER SAMUEL HARTLIB.' Masson's *Milton*, iii. 233. See MILTON, 152.

APPENDIX L (Page 106)

For Milton's *Doctrine of Divorce* see *Works*, i. 332–end; ii. 1–63. The first edition appeared in 1643, probably as early as Aug. 1. Masson's *Milton*, iii. 44. Its title was *The Doctrine and Discipline of Divorce, Restor'd, to the good of both Sexes, from the Bondage of Canon Law and other mistakes, to Christian Freedom, guided by the Rule of Charity*, &c. The second edition, published in Feb. 1643-4, has a different title, and is 'a great enlargement.' *Ib.* p. 64. Among the causes of divorce 'there is no word of desertion.' *Ib.* p. 72.

The second tract was *The Judgement of Martin Bucer concerning Divorce. Writt'n to Edward the Sixt, in his Second Book of the Kingdom of Christ. And now English. Wherein a late Book restoring the Doctrine and Discipline of Divorce is heer confirm'd and justify'd by the authoritie of Martin Bucer. To the Parlament of England.* It was published on July 15, 1644. Bucer had been appointed by Edward VI Professor of Divinity at Cambridge. Masson's *Milton*, iii. 255 ; *Works*, ii. 64.

'The four chief Places of Scripture' were Gen. i. 27, 28, compared and explained by Gen. ii. 18, 23, 24 ; Deut. xxiv. 1, 2 ; Matt. v. 31, 32, with Matt. xix from ver. 3 to 11 ; 1 Cor. vii. from ver. 10 to 16. *Ib.* ii. 111. *The Tetrachordon* appeared on March 4, 1644-5. Masson's *Milton*, iii. 301. Johnson passes over Milton's fourth tract on divorce —*Colasterion*, published on the same day as *Tetrachordon. Ib.* p. 313 ; *Works*, ii. 240. In his *Treatise on Christian Doctrine* (Bk. i. ch. 10), published after his death (MILTON, 166 *n.*), he argued for the lawfulness of polygamy. See Masson's *Milton*, vi. 830.

APPENDIX M (Page 110)

The *Eikon Basilike* was published on or before Feb. 9, 1648-9. There were, it is said, fifty editions in various languages within a year. Masson's *Milton*, iv. 36 *n.*, 129 *n.*

Lord Chancellor Hyde, in answer to Dr. Gauden, who pressed him for a better reward than the poor bishopric of Exeter (he expected Winchester, and obtained Worcester), wrote about the authorship of this book on March 13, 1660-1:—'Truly when it ceases to be a secret, I know nobody will be glad of it but Mr. Milton.' Todd on *Eikon*, p. 20.

'It was,' writes Burnet, 'universally believed to be the King's own. . . . It had the greatest run, in many impressions, that any book has had in our age. There was in it a nobleness and justness of thought, with a greatness of style, that made it to be looked on as the best writ book in the English language. . . . I was bred up with a high veneration of it.' Burnet adds that in 1673 the Duke of York (James II) told him that 'Dr. Gawden writ it.' Burnet's *History of my own Time*, 1724, i. 50-1.

Toland also prints (*Life of Milton*, p. 84) a memorandum in the hand of the Earl of Anglesea (MILTON, 143) within a copy of *Eikon Basilike*, discovered on the sale of his library in 1686, stating that 'King Charles II and the Duke of York did both . . . assure me that this . . . was made by Dr. Gauden.'

'Its real author, Dr. John Gauden, caught with great felicity the higher motives which were never absent from Charles' mind. . . . The greedily devoured volumes served to create an ideal image of Charles which went far to make the permanent overthrow of the monarchy impossible.' GARDINER, *Civil War*, iv. 325.

Macaulay, after telling how the licenser of the press, in 1693, authorized the publication of a book by Dr. Anthony Walker, an intimate friend of Gauden, asserting from personal knowledge that Gauden was the author of the *Eikon Basilike*, continues :—'If he had authorized the publication of a work in which the *Gospel of St. John* or the *Epistle to the Romans* had been represented as spurious, the indignation of the High Church party could hardly have been greater. The question was not literary, but religious. Doubt was impiety. The Blessed Martyr was an inspired penman, his *Icon* a supplementary revelation. . . . [James] Fraser [the licenser] found it necessary to resign his place.' *Hist. of England*, vi. 361.

Southey believed it to be genuine (*Life and Corres.*, 1850, v. 81).

[See also E. Almack, *Bibliography of the . . . Eikon Basilike* (1896), important from the bibliographical point of view ; and W. H. Hutton, *Influence of Christianity upon National Character, illustrated by the Lives and Legends of the English Saints* (Bampton Lectures for 1903, published by Messrs. Wells, Gardner & Co.), pp. 337-52. Mr. Hutton expresses his views as to the authorship at p. 348 *n.* 2.]

APPENDIX N (PAGE 144)

Milton is not mentioned by Baxter (Warton's *Milton's Poems*, p. 573) or, I think, by Clarendon in his *History* or *Life*. Dryden, in 1674, described *Paradise Lost* as 'undoubtedly one of the greatest, most noble, and most sublime poems which either this age or nation has produced.' *Works*, v. 112.

In 1678 Rymer wrote of 'that *Paradise Lost* of Milton's, which some are pleased to call a poem.' *The Tragedies of the Last Age*, p. 143.

In 1680 Roscommon praised it. *Eng. Poets*, xv. 91, 92.

In 1685 Temple, in his essay *Of Poetry*, wrote :—' After these three [Ariosto, Tasso, and Spenser] I know none of the moderns that have made any achievements in heroic poetry worth recording.' *Works*, iii. 420.

Before 1688 Somers (afterwards Lord Chancellor) encouraged Tonson to print 'a new and elegant edition of *Paradise Lost* [the fourth].' There were above 500 subscribers. Atterbury, in 1687, sent Tonson thirty-one names from Oxford. Dryden wrote for it his lines on Milton. Malone's *Dryden*, i. 202.

Tonson, in the duodecimo edition of 1711, says of this 'elegant edition,' that 'notwithstanding the price of it was four times greater than before, the sale increased double the number every year. The work is now generally known and esteemed.' See also Richardson's *Explanatory Notes*, &c., Pref. p. 118; Masson's *Milton*, vi. 784.

Jonathan Richardson, born about 1665, had in his youth honoured Shakespeare, Cowley, Dryden, and other poets, but had never heard of Milton. 'I happened,' he writes, 'to find *Paradise Lost* in Mr. Riley's painting-room [Riley died in 1691]. From that hour all the rest (Shakespeare excepted) faded in my estimation or vanished.' Richardson's *Explanatory Notes*, &c., Pref. p. 118.

Burnet wrote of *Paradise Lost* before 1705 :—' Tho' Milton affected to write in blank verse without rhyme, and made many new and rough words, yet it was esteemed the beautifullest and perfectest poem that ever was writ, at least in our language.' *History*, ed. 1724, i. 163.

Shaftesbury, in 1710, described *Paradise Lost* as 'our most approved heroick poem.' *Characteristics*, 1714, i. 276.

Milton is not mentioned in Pope's *Essay on Criticism*, published in 1711.

In 1711–12 Addison's series of papers on *Paradise Lost* appeared in *The Spectator*. *Post*, ADDISON, 162.

Dennis wrote (*Original Letters*, 1721, p. 174) :—' *Paradise Lost* had been printed forty years before it was known to the greatest part of England that there barely was such a book.'

Swift wrote of it in 1732 :—' Few either read, liked, or understood it ; and it gained ground merely by its merit.' *Works*, xvii. 396.

The same year Bentley, in the Preface to his edition of *Paradise Lost*, says that 'for above sixty years it has passed upon the whole nation for a perfect, absolute, faultless composition.' Bentley, however, wished to prove the need of emendations.

In *The Table of Modern Fame* in *Dodsley's Museum*, Sept. 13, 1746, i. 489, supposed to be by Akenside, after Pope has been seated Milton is granted the last seat but one. 'He is now admitted for the first time, and was not but with difficulty admitted at all. But have patience . . . he may perhaps at last obtain the highest, or at least the second place.' See also Warton's *Essay on Pope*, ii. 54.

Newton's edition of *Paradise Lost*, published in 1749, reached its eighth edition by 1775. Newton's *Works*, ed. 1782, i. 50.

Johnson, in 1750, in his Prologue for Milton's granddaughter, says :—

> 'At length our mighty bard's victorious lays
> Fill the loud voice of universal praise.' *Works*, i. 115.

Warburton wrote in 1757 :—'The present fashion for Milton makes us as ready to learn our religion from the *Paradise Lost*; though it be certain he was as poor and fanciful a divine as Shakespeare was a licentious historian.' Warburton's *Pope*, iv. 154.

'In 1763 I calculate,' writes Professor Masson, '*Paradise Lost* was in its forty-sixth edition. . . .There had been four translations into German, two into Dutch, three into French, and two into Italian, and at least one into Latin.' Masson's *Milton*, vi. 789. The *British Museum Catalogue* shows that it has been translated also into Armenian, Bohemian, Danish, Greek, Hebrew, Hungarian, Icelandic, Manx, Polish, Portuguese, Russian, Spanish, Swedish, and Welsh. For Milton's reputation as a poet in his lifetime see Masson's *Milton*, vi. 776. It is rash to differ from Professor Masson; I think, however, that he exaggerates this reputation. See on this subject an interesting note in Cunningham's *Lives of the Poets*, i. 124.

APPENDIX O (Page 159)

'Deborah Clarke,' writes Dr. Birch, 'gave Dr. Ward, Professor of Rhetoric at Gresham College, who saw her not long before her death, the following account, which he communicated to me, Feb. 10, 1737–8. "She informed me that she and her sisters used to read to their father in eight languages, which by practice they were capable of doing with great readiness and accuracy, though they understood what they read in no other language but English ; and their father used often to say in their hearing :—'One tongue was enough for a woman.' None of them were ever sent to school, but all taught at home by a mistress kept for that purpose. *Isaiah, Homer*, and Ovid's *Metamorphoses* were books which they were often called to read to their father ; and at my desire she repeated a considerable number of verses from the beginning of both these poets with great readiness. I knew who she was upon the first sight of her, by the similitude of her countenance with her father's picture. And upon my telling her so, she informed me that Mr. Addison told her the same thing, upon her going to wait on him. For he, upon hearing she was living, sent for her, and desired, if she had any papers of her father's, she would bring them with her, as an evidence of her being Mr. Milton's daughter. But immediately upon her being introduced to him, he said, 'Madam, you need no other voucher ; your face is a sufficient testimonial whose daughter you are.' And he then made her a handsome present of a purse of guineas, with a promise of procuring her an annual provision for her life; but he dying soon after, she lost the benefit of his generous design. She appeared to be a woman of good sense and a genteel behaviour, and to bear the inconvenience of a low fortune with decency and prudence."' T. BIRCH, *Milton's Works*, 1753, Preface, p. 76. See also *Gent. Mag.* 1776, p. 200; Newton's *Milton*, Preface, p. 81; Bentham's *Works*, x. 52.

APPENDIX P (PAGE 192)

Milton, in the Preface to *Paradise Lost*, speaks of 'the troublesome and modern bondage of rhyming.'

Two or three years earlier than Milton's Preface, Boileau had written:—

' Maudit soit le premier, dont la verve insensée
  Dans les bornes d'un vers renferma sa pensée,
  Et donnant à ses mots une étroite prison,
  Voulut avec la rime enchaîner la raison.'   *Satires*, ii. 53.

'Shakespeare, to shun the pains of continual rhyming, invented that kind of writing which we call blank verse, into which the English tongue so naturally slides that in writing prose it is hardly to be avoided.' DRYDEN, *Works*, ii. 136. 'Whatever cause Milton alleges for the abolishing of rhyme, his own particular reason is plainly this, that rhyme was not his talent.' *Ib.* xiii. 20. 'He who can write well in rhyme may write better in blank verse.' *Ib.* xiv. 211.

'Je me souviendrai toujours que je demandai au célèbre Pope, pourquoi Milton n'avait pas rimé son *Paradis perdu*, et qu'il me répondit:—"Because he could not, parce qu'il ne le pouvait pas."' VOLTAIRE, *Œuvres*, xxxv. 435. 'Un poète anglais est un homme libre qui asservit sa langue à son génie; le Français est un esclave de la rime. . . . L'Anglais dit tout ce qu'il veut, le Français ne dit que ce qu'il peut.' *Ib.* i. 310.

Cowper wrote, after finishing *The Task*:—'I do not mean to write blank verse again. Not having the music of rhyme, it requires so close an attention to the pause and the cadence, and such a peculiar mode of expression, as render it, to me at least, the most difficult species of poetry that I have ever meddled with.' Southey's *Cowper*, v. 105. See also *ib.* p. 89.

Tennyson said to Allingham on Sept. 2, 1880:—'It is much easier to write rhyme than good blank verse.' *Allingham MSS.*

Addison describes how Milton

'Unfettered in majestic numbers walks.'
Addison's *Works*, i. 24.

'He that writes in rhymes dances in fetters.'
PRIOR, *Eng. Poets*, xxxiii. 207.

'For rhyme with reason may dispense,
And sound has right to govern sense.'   *Ib.* p. 155.

BUTLER[1]

OF the great author of *Hudibras* there is a life prefixed to the 1 later editions of his poem by an unknown writer[2], and therefore of disputable authority; and some account is incidentally given by Wood[3], who confesses the uncertainty of his own narrative: more, however, than they knew cannot now be learned, and nothing remains but to compare and copy them.

SAMUEL BUTLER was born in the parish of Strensham[4] 2 in Worcestershire, according to his biographer, in 1612[5]. This account Dr. Nash finds confirmed by the register. He was christened Feb. 14[6].

His father's condition is variously represented. Wood mentions 3 him as competently wealthy[7], but Mr. Longueville[8], the son of Butler's principal friend, says he was an honest farmer with some small estate, who made a shift to educate his son at the grammar school of Worcester, under Mr. Henry Bright[9], from whose care he removed for a short time to Cambridge; but for a want of money was never made a member of any college. Wood leaves us rather doubtful whether he went to Cambridge or Oxford; but at last makes him pass six or seven years at Cambridge, without knowing in what hall or college[10]: yet it can hardly be imagined that

[1] 'In the last [seventeenth] century the strange fashion of calling Butler by the name of Hudibras was very general; even so late as 1738 Dr. Birch placed the Life of the poet in the *General Dictionary* under the title of Hudibras.' Malone's *Dryden*, iii. 206.

[2] First published in 1732.

[3] Wood gives this account in the *Life of William Prynne*, on whom Butler had fathered two letters written by himself. *Ath. Oxon.* iii. 874. See also Aubrey's *Brief Lives*, i. 135.

[4] Strensham was held by a Royalist garrison at the time of the Civil War. It surrendered in 1646. Nash's *Worcestershire*, ii. 390.

[5] 1613 N. S.

[6] Nash's *Worcestershire*, ii. 391. Feb. 13 according to Wood, and the author of his *Life*. Grey's *Hudibras*, 1806, Preface, p. 5. All Johnson's quotations from Nash's *History of Worcestershire* are given first in the edition of the *Lives of the Poets* published in 1783.

[7] 'His father was a person of competent estate near 300*l*. per an.' *Ath. Oxon.* iii. 874.

[8] *Post*, BUTLER, 20 *n*.

[9] Aubrey calls him 'the famous school master of those times.' *Brief Lives*, ii. 162.

[10] Aubrey, who knew Butler well, writes:—'His father was a man but of slender fortune, and to breed

he lived so long in either university, but as belonging to one house or another, and it is still less likely that he could have so long inhabited a place of learning with so little distinction as to leave his residence uncertain. Dr. Nash has discovered that his father was owner of a house and a little land, worth about eight pounds a year, still called ' Butler's tenement [1].'

4   Wood has his information from his brother, whose narrative placed him at Cambridge, in opposition to that of his neighbours which sent him to Oxford. The brother's seems the best authority, till, by confessing his inability to tell his hall or college, he gives reason to suspect that he was resolved to bestow on him an academical education ; but durst not name a college for fear of detection [2].

5   He was for some time, according to the author of his Life, clerk to Mr. Jefferys of Earl's-Croomb in Worcestershire, an eminent justice of the peace [3]. In his service he had not only leisure for study, but for recreation ; his amusements were musick and painting, and the reward of his pencil was the friendship of the celebrated Cooper [4]. Some pictures, said to be his, were shewn to Dr. Nash, at Earl's Croomb, but when he enquired for them some years afterwards he found them destroyed, to stop windows, and owns that they hardly deserved a better fate [5].

him at schoole was as much education as he was able to reach to. . . . He never was at the university.' *Brief Lives*, i. 135. The author of the *Life* says that ' being become an excellent school-scholar, he went for some little time to Cambridge, but was never matriculated.' Grey's *Hudibras*, Preface, p. 5.

[1] Nash's *Worcestershire*, ii. 391.

[2] 'He went, as his brother now living affirms, to the University of Cambridge ; yet others of the neighbourhood say to Oxon, but whether true I cannot tell. . . . After he had continued in Cambridge about six or seven years, but in what college or hall his brother knows not,' &c. *Ath. Oxon.* iii. 875.

[3] Grey's *Hudibras*, Preface, p. 5.

[4] 'Butler's love to and skill in painting made a great friendship between him and Mr. Samuel Cowper (prince of limners of this age). . . . He [Butler] painted well, and made it

(sometime) his profession.' AUBREY, *Brief Lives*, i. 135, 138. Evelyn, in 1662, 'had the honour to hold the candle whilst this rare limner [Cooper] was crayoning of the King's face and head to make the stamps for the new milled money now contriving.' *Diary*, i. 381. Cooper painted Mrs. Pepys. 'He is a most admirable workman, and good company.' PEPYS, *Diary*, iv. 484. His wife was sister of Pope's mother. Walpole's *Anec. of Painting*, 1782, iii. 115 ; Pope's *Works* (Elwin and Courthope), v. 5.

[5] This sentence is not in the first edition. Nash saw them in 1738. ' In 1774 I found they had served to stop up windows and save the tax ; and indeed they were not fit for much else.' NASH, *Worcestershire*, ii. 391.

The tax (1775) rose gradually from twopence on every window, the lowest rate, upon houses with not more than seven windows, to two

He was afterwards admitted into the family of the Countess of 6
Kent, where he had the use of a library; and so much recommended
himself to Selden that he was often employed by him in literary
business. Selden, as is well known, was steward to the Countess,
and is supposed to have gained much of his wealth by managing
her estate [1].

In what character Butler was admitted into that Lady's 7
service, how long he continued in it, and why he left it, is, like
the other incidents of his life, utterly unknown [2].

The vicissitudes of his condition placed him afterwards in the 8
family of Sir Samuel Luke, one of Cromwell's officers [3]. Here he
observed so much of the character of the sectaries that he is said
to have written or begun his poem at this time; and it is likely
that such a design would be formed in a place where he saw the
principles and practices of the rebels, audacious and undisguised
in the confidence of success.

At length the King returned, and the time came in which 9
loyalty hoped for its reward [4]. Butler, however, was only made
secretary to the Earl of Carbery, president of the principality of
Wales, who conferred on him the stewardship of Ludlow Castle
when the Court of the Marches was revived [5].

---

shillings, the highest rate, upon
houses with twenty-five windows and
upwards. Adam Smith's *Wealth of
Nations*, 1811, iii. 292.

[1] According to Aubrey, 'after the
Earle's death he married her. . . . He
never owned the marriage till after
her death, upon some lawe account.'
Brief Lives, ii. 220-1. The editor
adds that she 'bequeathed her estate
to him.' *Ib.* p. 225. 'The story is probably false.' *Dict. Nat. Biog.* li. 220.
The author of Butler's *Life* describes
the Countess as 'that great encou-
rager of learning,' and Selden as 'that
living library of learning.' Grey's
Hudibras, Preface, p. 6.

[2] 'He wayted some yeares on her;
she gave her gentlemen 20 *li.* per
annum a-piece.' *Brief Lives*, i. 138.

[3] He was member for Bedford, and
a victim of Pride's Purge on Dec. 6,
1648. Carlyle's *Cromwell*, 1857, i.
346; ii. 387; Rushworth's *Hist. Coll.*
vii. 1355. He had been 'a Colonel in
the parliament army, and Scoutmaster
General in the counties of Bedford,

Surrey,' &c. Grey's *Hudibras*, i. 59.
In the couplet (canto 1. 1. 903) that
stands:—
'Tis sung, there is a valiant Mama-
  luke
In foreign land, yclep'd ——.'
It is suggested 'that the chasm is to
be filled up with Sir Samuel Luke,
because the line before it is of ten
syllables, and the general measure of
the verse is of eight.' *Ib.* i. 147. As
he died before the publication of
Hudibras there seems no reason for
the suppression.

[4] Waller writes in his lines, *To the
King upon His Majesty's Happy
Return:*—
'But above all the Muse-inspired
  train
Triumph, and raise their drooping
  heads again;
Kind heav'n at once has in your
  person sent
Their sacred judge, their guard and
  argument.' *Eng. Poets*, xvi. 152.

[5] *Ante*, MILTON, 21. For the
Court of the Council of the Marches

10   In this part of his life he married Mrs. Herbert, a gentlewoman of a good family, and lived, says Wood, upon her fortune, having studied the common law but never practised it [1]. A fortune she had, says his biographer, but it was lost by bad securities.

11   In 1663 [2] was published the first part, containing three cantos, of the poem of *Hudibras*, which, as Prior relates, was made known at Court by the taste and influence of the Earl of Dorset [3]. When it was known it was necessarily admired; the king quoted, the courtiers studied, and the whole party of the royalists applauded it [4]. Every eye watched for the golden shower which was to fall upon the author, who certainly was not without his part in the general expectation.

12   In 1664 the second part appeared; the curiosity of the nation was rekindled, and the writer was again praised and elated [5]. But praise was his whole reward. Clarendon, says Wood, gave him

of Wales see Owen Edwards's *Wales*, 1902, p. 321. 'It was abolished by the Long Parliament in 1642, restored in 1660, and finally abolished in 1689.' *Ib.* p. 328.

'Tradition at Ludlow still points out a room in the entrance-gateway where Butler kept his pen, ink, and paper for anything he had on hand.' Masson's *Milton*, vi. 300. See also *ib.* i. 604.

[1] *Ath. Oxon.* iii. 875. 'He married a good jointeresse, the relict of — Morgan, by which meanes he lives comfortably.' Aubrey's *Brief Lives*, i. 36.

In the *Life* she is called 'Mrs. Herbert, but no widow, as our Oxford antiquary has reported.' Grey's *Hudibras*, Preface, p. 7.

[2] At the end of 1662.

[3] *Post*, DORSET, 13. 'Butler owed it to him that the Court tasted his *Hudibras*.' PRIOR, *Eng. Poets*, xxxii. 127.

For the titles of the three parts see Cunningham's *Lives of the Poets*, i. 174, and for the earliest editions see *N. & Q.* 7 S. iii. 446; iv. 244, 418.

[4] 'Dec. 26, 1662. We falling into discourse of a new book of drollery in use, called *Hudebras* [*sic*], I would needs go find it out, and met with it at the Temple: cost me 2*s*. 6*d*. But when I come to read it, it is so silly an abuse of the Presbyter Knight going to the wars that I am ashamed of it; and by and by meeting at Mr. Townsend's at dinner, I sold it to him for 18*d*.' PEPYS, *Diary*, ii. 85. 'Feb. 6, 1662-3. And so to a bookseller's in the Strand, and there bought *Hudibras* again, it being certainly some ill humour to be so against that which all the world cries up to be the example of wit, for which I am resolved once more to read him, and see whether I can find it or no.' *Ib.* p. 105.

According to an advertisement quoted in Masson's *Milton*, vi. 339, from *The Kingdom's Intelligencer*, Jan. 5, 1661-2, the book was published by that date; but there must, I think, be a mistake in this.

[5] Towards the end of 1663. 'Nov. 28, 1663. To Paul's Church Yard, and there looked upon the second part of *Hudibras*, which I buy not, but borrow to read, to see if it be as good as the first, which the world cried so mightily up, though it hath not a good liking in me, though I had tried but twice or three times reading to bring myself to think it witty.' Pepys's *Diary*, ii. 250. On Dec. 10 he bought both parts, 'the book now in greatest fashion for drollery, though I cannot, I confess, see enough where the wit lies.' *Ib.* p. 255.

reason to hope for 'places and employments of value and credit[1]';
but no such advantages did he ever obtain. It is reported that
the King once gave him three hundred guineas[2]; but of this
temporary bounty I find no proof[3].

Wood relates that he was secretary to Villiers, Duke of Buck- 13
ingham, when he was Chancellor of Cambridge[4]; this is doubted
by the other writer, who yet allows the Duke to have been his
frequent benefactor[5]. That both these accounts are false there is
reason to suspect, from a story told by Packe in his account of
the Life of Wycherley[6], and from some verses which Mr. Thyer
has published in the author's remains[7].

'Mr. Wycherley,' says Packe, 'had always laid hold of an 14
[any] opportunity which offered of representing to the Duke
of Buckingham how well Mr. Butler had deserved of the royal
family by writing his inimitable *Hudibras*, and that it was a
reproach to the Court that a person of his loyalty and wit should
suffer in obscurity, and under the wants he did. The Duke
always seemed to hearken to him with attention enough, and after
some time undertook to recommend his pretensions to his
Majesty. Mr. Wycherley, in hopes to keep him steady to his

[1] *Ath. Oxon.* iii. 875. 'The King
and Lord Chancellor Hyde both promised him great matters, but to this
day he haz got *no* employment, only
the King gave him — *li*.' Aubrey's
Brief Lives, i. 136. Aubrey adds that
the Chancellor 'haz his picture in his
library over the chimney.' Evelyn
says that 'he placed it in the room
where he used to eat and dine in
public.' *Diary*, iii. 301.

[2] £300, according to *Gen. Hist.
Dict.* vi. 299, quoted in Grey's *Hudibras*, Preface, p. 44.

[3] See *post*, OTWAY, 15, for 'the
common reward of loyalty in those
times,'—neglect. Dryden, in his *Threnodia Augustalis*, l. 377 (*Works*, x.
80), says of the Muses and Charles
II :—
'Though little was their hire, and
light their gain,
Yet somewhat to their share he
threw.'
In his *Essay on Satire* he writes :—
'Being encouraged only with fair
words by King Charles II, my little
salary ill paid,' &c. *Ib.* xiii. 31. See
post, DRYDEN, 277.
'Charles II knew his people, and

rewarded merit.' JOHNSON, Boswell's
Johnson, ii. 341.

[4] *Ath. Oxon.* iii. 875; Aubrey's *Brief
Lives*, i. 137. He was Chancellor from
1670 to 1674. *Graduati Cant.* 1823,
App. p. 4. He was Zimri in *Absalom
and Achitophel*, ll. 544-68. Pope, in
Moral Essays, iii. 299, describes him
dying where he had
'No wit to flatter left of all his
store,' &c.
See also *post*, DRYDEN, 93.
In the *Catalogue of the Record
Office Museum*, p. 78, the Memoran-
dum of the Duke's approval of a pe-
tition about a Fellowship at Trinity
College is signed 'Sa. Butler.'

[5] Grey's *Hudibras*, Preface, p. 8.

[6] Jacob's *Poet. Reg.* i. 276; Packe's
Misc. 1719, p. 183.

[7] Johnson refers, I think, to a character not in verse but in prose, which
begins :—'A Duke of Bucks is one
that has studied the whole body of
vice,' and ends :—'He endures
pleasures with less patience than
other men do their pains.' *Remains*,
ii. 72. For Thyer see *post*, BUTLER,
20.

word, obtained of his Grace to name a day, when he might introduce that modest and unfortunate poet to his new patron. At last an appointment was made, and the place of meeting was agreed to be the Roebuck. Mr. Butler and his friend attended accordingly: the Duke joined them ; but, as the d—l would have it, the door of the room where they sat was open, and his Grace, who had seated himself near it, observing a pimp of his acquaintance (the creature too was a knight) trip by with a brace of Ladies, immediately quitted his engagement, to follow another kind of business, at which he was more ready than in doing good offices to men of desert [1], though no one was better qualified than he, both in regard to his fortune and understanding [2], to protect them ; and, from that time to the day of his death, poor Butler never found the least effect of his promise [3] ! '

15   Such is the story. The verses are written with a degree of acrimony such as neglect and disappointment might naturally excite, and such as it would be hard to imagine Butler capable of expressing against a man who had any claim to his gratitude.

16   Notwithstanding this discouragement and neglect he still prosecuted his design, and in 1678 published the third part, which still leaves the poem imperfect and abrupt [4]. How much more he originally intended or with what events the action was to be concluded, it is vain to conjecture. Nor can it be thought strange that he should stop here, however unexpectedly. To write without reward is sufficiently unpleasing [5]. He had now arrived at an age when he might think it proper to be in jest no longer, and perhaps his health might now begin to fail [6].

17   He died in 1680 ; and Mr. Longueville, having unsuccessfully solicited a subscription for his interment in Westminster Abbey,

---

[1] Dryden writes of the Duke :—
'In squand'ring wealth was his peculiar art ;
Nothing went unrewarded but desert.'
        Absalom and Achitophel, l. 559.
[2] 'He had no sort of literature, only he was drawn into chemistry ; and for some years he thought he was very near finding the philosopher's stone.' BURNET, *Hist. of my own Time*, i. 107.
[3] Johnson had this story in mind when he wrote *The Rambler*, No. 27.
[4] For the publication of the third part see *N. & Q.* 6 S. vi. 150, 311.

[5] 'No man but a blockhead,' said Johnson, 'ever wrote except for money.' Boswell's *Johnson*, iii. 19.
Aubrey, at the end of his *Life of Butler*, writes : — 'Memorandum — satyricall witts disoblige whom they converse with, &c. ; and consequently make to themselves many enemies and few friends ; and this was his manner and case.' *Brief Lives*, i. 138.
[6] 'He haz been much troubled with the gowt, and particularly 1679 he stirred not out of his chamber from October till Easter. He dyed of a consumption, September 25, 1680.' *Ib.* i. 136.

buried him at his own cost in the church-yard of Covent Garden [1]. Dr. Simon Patrick [2] read the service.

Granger was informed by Dr. Pearce, who named for his authority Mr. Lowndes of the treasury, that Butler had an yearly pension of an hundred pounds [3]. This is contradicted by all tradition, by the complaints of Oldham [4], and by the reproaches of Dryden [5]; and I am afraid will never be confirmed. 18

About sixty years afterwards Mr. Barber, a printer, Mayor of London [6], and a friend to Butler's principles, bestowed on him 19

[1] *Biog. Brit.* 1748, p. 1075.
'About 25 of his old acquaintance at his funerall. I myself being one of the eldest helped to carry his pall, with Tom Shadwell at the foot. . . . His coffin covered with black bayes.' AUBREY'S *Brief Lives*, i. 136.

It was owing to the cost that Goldsmith was not buried in the Abbey. Goldsmith's *Works*, 1801, Preface, i. 115.

[2] Afterwards Bishop, first of Chichester, next of Ely. He was at this time Rector of St. Paul's, Convent Garden, where, six years later, Evelyn heard him in a sermon ' perstringing the profane way of mirth and intemperance of this ungodly age.' *Diary*, ii. 269.

[3] The story came to Granger through Zachary Pearce, Bishop of Rochester, who had it from 'a gentleman of unquestionable veracity,' who heard it from Lowndes. Granger's *Biog. Hist.* 1775, iv. 40. For Granger see Boswell's *Johnson*, iii. 91, and for Pearce see *ib.* i. 292; iii. 112. [This paragraph is not in the first edition.]

Swift wrote on May 21, 1711:—
'My uncle and Lowndes married two sisters, and Lowndes is a great man at the Treasury.' Swift's *Works*, ii. 261. See also *ib.* xvi. 191, and *Eng. Poets*, xxxvi. 211, for Gay's lines:—
'To my Ingenious and Worthy Friend William Lowndes, Esq., Author of that Celebrated Treatise in Folio called the Land-Tax Bill.

[4] 'On Butler who can think without just rage,
The glory and the scandal of his age ? . . .
Of all his gains by verse he could not save

Enough to purchase flannel and a grave;
Reduced to want, he in due time fell sick,
Was fain to die, and be interred on tick.'
OLDHAM, *Works*, 1703, p. 420.

[5] Dryden makes the Hind say to the Church of England:—
'Unpitied Hudibras, your champion friend,
Has shown how far your charities extend.
This lasting verse shall on his tomb be read,
"He shamed you living, and upbraids you dead." '
The Hind and the Panther, iii. 247.

In a letter to Lord Treasurer Rochester, pressing for payment of 'half a yeare of my salary,' Dryden wrote:—''Tis enough for one age to have neglected Mr. Cowley and sterv'd Mr. Butler.' *Works*, xviii. 104.

Otway, in his *Prologue to Lee's Constantine*, says of youthful poets:—
'Prevent the malice of their stars in time,
And warn them early from the sin of rhyme:
Tell them how Spenser starv'd, how Cowley mourn'd,
How Butler's faith and service was return'd.'
Eng. Poets, xv. 226; *post*, OTWAY.

See also quotations from Dennis and Cibber in Cunningham's *Lives of the Poets*, i. 177.

[6] He was Lord Mayor in 1732-3. Swift's *Letters to Chetwode*, p. 180. There is no life of him in the *D. N. B.*; but see *An Impartial History of Life, Character, . . . and Travels of Mr. John Barber, City-Printer*, &c., published by Curll, 1741.]

a monument in Westminster Abbey, thus inscribed:

M. S.
SAMUELIS BUTLERI,
Qui *Strenshamiæ* in agro *Vigorn.* nat. 1612,
obiit *Lond.* 1680.
Vir doctus imprimis, acer, integer;
Operibus Ingenii, non item præmiis, fœlix:
Satyrici apud nos Carminis Artifex egregius;
Quo simulatæ Religionis Larvam detraxit,
Et Perduellium scelera liberrime exagitavit:
Scriptorum in suo genere Primus et Postremus.
Ne, cui vivo deerant ferè omnia,
Deesset etiam mortuo Tumulus,
Hoc tandem posito marmore curavit
JOHANNES BARBER, Civis *Londinensis*, 1721 [1].

20   After his death were published three small volumes of his
posthumous works [2]; I know not by whom collected or by what
authority ascertained [3]; and, lately, two volumes more have been
printed by Mr. Thyer of Manchester, indubitably genuine [4]. From
none of these pieces can his life be traced or his character discovered. Some verses, in the last collection, shew him to have
been among those who ridiculed the institution of the Royal
Society [5], of which the enemies were for some time very numerous
and very acrimonious; for what reason it is hard to conceive,
since the philosophers professed not to advance doctrines but to

[1] Samuel Wesley's epigram on this monument ends:—
'The poet's fate is here in emblem shewn,
He asked for bread, and he received a stone.'
        Southey's *Specimens*, i. 369.
[2] They were published in 1715-19 in 3 vols. 12mo. 'Except the *Ode on Duval the Highwayman* and two prose tracts they were all spurious.' Cunningham's *Lives of the Poets*, i. 177; *N. & Q.* 3 S. viii. 354.
[3] 'Mr. Longueville, a bencher of the Inner Temple, was the last patron and friend that poor old Butler had, and in his old age he supported him. Otherwise he might have been liter-ally starved. All that Butler could do to recompense him was to make him his heir, that is to give him his remains, but in loose papers and in-digested. But Mr. Longueville hath

reduced them into method and order, and some of them have been since printed.' *Lives of the Norths*, 1826, ii. 188, 190. See also *ib.* iii. 305. For LONGUEVILLE, see *ante*, BUTLER, 3, 17.
[4] R. Thyer, Keeper of the Public Library at Manchester, published in 1759 *The Genuine Remains in Verse and Prose of Samuel Butler*. From Mr. Longueville the MSS. passed to his son Charles, and from him to John Clarke, of Walgherton, in Cheshire, who let Thyer publish them, and subscribed for twenty sets. See List of Subscribers and Preface to vol. i; *post*, BUTLER, 40; POPE, 75 *n*.
[5] He ridiculed it in verse in *The Elephant in the Moon* and in prose in *An Occasional Reflection on Dr. Charlton's feeling a Dog's Pulse at Gresham College. By R. B. Esq.* [Robert Boyle]. *Remains*, i. 1, 404.

produce facts[1]; and the most zealous enemy of innovation must admit the gradual progress of experience, however he may oppose hypothetical temerity.

In this mist of obscurity passed the life of Butler, a man whose [21] name can only perish with his language. The mode and place of his education are unknown; the events of his life are variously related; and all that can be told with certainty is, that he was poor[2].

THE poem of *Hudibras* is one of those compositions of which [22] a nation may justly boast, as the images which it exhibits are domestick, the sentiments unborrowed and unexpected, and the strain of diction original and peculiar[3]. We must not however suffer the pride, which we assume as the countrymen of Butler, to make any encroachment upon justice, nor appropriate those honours which others have a right to share. The poem of *Hudibras* is not wholly English; the original idea is to be found in the *History of Don Quixote*, a book to which a mind of the greatest powers may be indebted without disgrace[4].

Cervantes shews a man who, having by the incessant perusal of [23] incredible tales subjected his understanding to his imagination, and familiarised his mind by pertinacious meditation to trains of[5] incredible events and scenes of impossible existence, goes out in

[1] *Ante*, COWLEY, 31; *post*, DRYDEN, 257; SPRAT, 5 *n*.; ADDISON, 43.

[2] 'There is a strong similitude between the lives of almost all our English poets. The Ordinary of Newgate, we are told, has but one story, which serves for the life of every hero that comes within the circle of his pastoral care; however unworthy the resemblance appears, it may be asserted that the history of one poet might serve with as little variation for that of any other. Born of creditable parents, who gave him a pious education; however in spite of all their endeavours, in spite of all the exhortations of the minister of the parish on Sundays, he turned his mind from following good things, and fell to—writing verses. Spenser, in short, lived poor, was reviled by the critics of his time, and died at last in the utmost distress.' GOLDSMITH, *Works*, iv. 204.

[3] 'There is more thinking,' said Johnson, 'in Milton and in Butler than in any of our poets.' Boswell's *Johnson*, ii. 239.

[4] 'Le poëme d'*Hudibras* semble être un composé de la *Satyre Ménippée* et de *Don Quichotte*; il a sur eux l'avantage des vers. Il a celui de l'esprit: la *Satyre Ménippée* n'en approche pas; elle n'est qu'un ouvrage très médiocre; mais à force d'esprit l'auteur d'*Hudibras* a trouvé le secret d'être fort au-dessus de *Don Quichotte*. Le goût, la naïveté, l'art de narrer, celui de bien entremêler les aventures, celui de ne rien prodiguer, valent bien mieux que de l'esprit: aussi *Don Quichotte* est lu de toutes les nations et *Hudibras* n'est lu que des Anglais.' VOLTAIRE, *Œuvres*, xxiv. 128.

See *post*, POPE, 225, for the resemblance of *The Memoirs of Scriblerus* to *Don Quixote*.

[5] In the first edition, 'to think on.'

the pride of knighthood to redress wrongs and defend virgins, to rescue captive princesses, and tumble usurpers from their thrones, attended by a squire whose cunning, too low for the suspicion of a generous mind, enables him often to cheat his master.

24 The hero of Butler is a Presbyterian Justice who, in the confidence of legal authority and the rage of zealous ignorance, ranges the country to repress superstition and correct abuses, accompanied by an Independent Clerk, disputatious and obstinate, with whom he often debates, but never conquers him.

25 Cervantes had so much kindness for Don Quixote that, however he embarrasses him with absurd distresses, he gives him so much sense and virtue as may preserve our esteem: wherever he is or whatever he does he is made by matchless dexterity commonly ridiculous, but never contemptible.

26 But for poor Hudibras, his poet had no tenderness; he chuses not that any pity should be shewn or respect paid him: he gives him up at once to laughter and contempt, without any quality that can dignify or protect him.

27 In forming the character of Hudibras and describing his person and habiliments the author seems to labour with a tumultuous confusion of dissimilar ideas. He had read the history of the mock knights-errant; he knew the notions and manners of a presbyterian magistrate, and tried to unite the absurdities of both, however distant, in one personage. Thus he gives him that pedantick ostentation of knowledge which has no relation to chivalry, and loads him with martial encumbrances that can add nothing to his civil dignity. He sends him out *a colonelling* [1], and yet never brings him within sight of war.

28 If Hudibras be considered as the representative of the presbyterians it is not easy to say why his weapons should be represented as ridiculous or useless, for, whatever judgement might be passed upon their knowledge or their arguments, experience had sufficiently shewn that their swords were not to be despised.

29 The hero, thus compounded of swaggerer and pedant, of knight and justice, is led forth to action, with his squire Ralpho, an Independent enthusiast.

30 Of the contexture of events planned by the author, which is called the action of the poem, since it is left imperfect no judge-

---

[1] 'Then did Sir Knight abandon dwelling,
And out he rode a colonelling.' *Hudibras*, i. 1. 13.

ment can be made. It is probable that the hero was to be led through many luckless adventures, which would give occasion, like his attack upon the 'bear and fiddle [1],' to expose the ridiculous rigour of the sectaries; like his encounter with Sidrophel and Whacum [2], to make superstition and credulity contemptible; or, like his recourse to the low retailer of the law [3], discover the fraudulent practices of different professions.

What series of events he would have formed, or in what manner 31 he would have rewarded or punished his hero, it is now vain to conjecture. His work must have had, as it seems, the defect which Dryden imputes to Spenser [4]: the action could not have been one; there could only have been a succession of incidents, each of which might have happened without the rest, and which could not all co-operate to any single conclusion.

The discontinuity of the action might however have been easily 32 forgiven if there had been action enough; but I believe every reader regrets the paucity of events, and complains that in the poem of *Hudibras*, as in the history of Thucydides, there is more said than done. The scenes are too seldom changed, and the attention is tired with long conversation.

It is indeed much more easy to form dialogues than to contrive 33 adventures. Every position makes way for an argument, and every objection dictates an answer. When two disputants are engaged upon a complicated and extensive question, the difficulty is not to continue, but to end the controversy. But whether it be that we comprehend but few of the possibilities of life, or that life itself affords little variety, every man who has tried knows how much labour it will cost to form such a combination of circumstances, as shall have at once the grace of novelty and credibility, and delight fancy without violence to reason.

Perhaps the dialogue of this poem is not perfect. Some power 34 of engaging the attention might have been added to it, by quicker

---

[1] The argument of the first canto of Part i ends:—
'Th' adventure of the bear and fiddle Is sung, but breaks off in the middle.'
[2] In Part ii. canto 3.
[3] Part iii. canto 3, line 577.
[4] 'There is no uniformity in the design of Spenser: he aims at the accomplishment of no one action; he raises up a hero for every one of his adventures, and endows each of them with some particular moral virtue, which renders them all equal, without subordination or preference. ... Had he lived to finish his poem in the six remaining legends, it had certainly been more of a piece, but could not have been perfect, because the model was not true.' DRYDEN, *Works*, xiii. 17.

reciprocation, by seasonable interruptions, by sudden questions, and by a nearer approach to dramatick spriteliness; without which fictitious speeches will always tire, however sparkling with sentences and however variegated with allusions [1].

35 The great source of pleasure is variety. Uniformity must tire at last, though it be uniformity of excellence. We love to expect; and, when expectation is disappointed or gratified, we want to be again expecting. For this impatience of the present, whoever would please must make provision. The skilful writer *irritat, mulcet* [2]; makes a due distribution of the still and animated parts. It is for want of this artful intertexture and those necessary changes that the whole of a book may be tedious, though all the parts are praised [3].

36 If inexhaustible wit could give perpetual pleasure no eye would ever leave half-read the work of Butler; for what poet has ever brought so many remote images so happily together? It is scarcely possible to peruse a page without finding some association of images that was never found before. By the first paragraph the reader is amused, by the next he is delighted, and by a few more strained to astonishment; but astonishment is a toilsome pleasure; he is soon weary of wondering, and longs to be diverted.

'Omnia vult [vis] belle, Matho, dicere: dic aliquando
Et bene, dic neutrum, dic aliquando male [4].'

37 Imagination is useless without knowledge: nature gives in vain the power of combination, unless study and observation supply materials to be combined. Butler's treasures of knowledge appear proportioned to his expence; whatever topick employs his mind he shews himself qualified to expand and illustrate it with all the accessories that books can furnish: he is found not only to have travelled the beaten road, but the bye-paths of literature; not only to have taken general surveys, but to have examined particulars with minute inspection.

38 If the French boast the learning of Rabelais [5], we need not be afraid of confronting them with Butler [6].

---

[1] 'Though scarcely any author was ever able to express his thoughts in so few words, he often employs too many thoughts on one subject, and thereby becomes prolix after an unusual manner.' Hume's *Hist. of England*, viii. 337.

[2] HORACE, *Epis.* ii. 1. 212.

'Enrage, compose.' POPE, *Imit. Hor., Epis.* ii. 1. 344.

[3] *Post*, DRYDEN, 270.

[4] MARTIAL, *Epig.* x. 46.

[5] 'Rabelais était profondément savant, et tournait la science en ridicule.' VOLTAIRE, *Œuvres*, xii. 178.

[6] '*Hudibras* is perhaps one of the

But the most valuable parts of his performance are those which 39
retired study and native wit cannot supply.   He that merely
makes a book from books may be useful, but can scarcely be
great.   Butler had not suffered life to glide beside him unseen or
unobserved.   He had watched with great diligence the operations
of human nature and traced the effects of opinion, humour,
interest, and passion.   From such remarks proceeded that great
number of sententious distichs which have passed into conversation, and are added as proverbial axioms to the general stock
of practical knowledge.

When any work has been viewed and admired the first 40
question of intelligent curiosity is, how was it performed ?   *Hudibras* was not a hasty effusion ; it was not produced by a sudden
tumult of imagination, or a short paroxysm of violent labour.
To accumulate such a mass of sentiments at the call of accidental
desire or of sudden necessity is beyond the reach and power of
the most active and comprehensive mind.   I am informed by
Mr. Thyer of Manchester, the excellent editor of this author's
reliques[1], that he could shew something like *Hudibras* in prose.
He has in his possession the common-place book, in which Butler
reposited, not such events or precepts as are gathered by reading ;
but such remarks, similitudes, allusions, assemblages, or inferences
as occasion prompted or meditation produced; those thoughts
that were generated in his own mind, and might be usefully
applied to some future purpose.   Such is the labour of those who
write for immortality.

But human works are not easily found without a perishable part. 41
Of the ancient poets every reader feels the mythology tedious and
oppressive[2].   Of *Hudibras* the manners, being founded on opinions,
are temporary and local, and therefore become every day less

---

most learned compositions that is to
be found in any language.'   HUME,
Hist. of England, viii. 337.

  ' No work in our language contains more learning than *Hudibras*.'
J. WARTON, *Essay on Pope,* ii. 473.

  [1] *Ante,* BUTLER, 20.

  [2] *Post,* WALLER, 152 ; DRYDEN,
238 ; SMITH, 49 ; ROWE, 10 ; GAY,
28 ; GRANVILLE, 26 ; TICKELL, 17 ;
POPE, 325 ; THOMSON, 29 ; GRAY,
45 ; Boswell's *Johnson,* iv. 16, 17.

  ' When the torch of ancient learning was rekindled, so cheering were
its beams, that our eldest poets, cut
off by Christianity from all accredited
machinery, and deprived of all acknowledged guardians and symbols
of the great objects of nature, were
naturally induced to adopt, as a poetic
language, those fabulous personages,
those forms of the supernatural in nature, which had given them such dear
delight in the poems of their great
masters.'   COLERIDGE, *Biog. Lit.* ii.
80.

intelligible and less striking. What Cicero says of philosophy is true likewise of wit and humour, that 'time effaces the fictions of opinion, and confirms the determinations of Nature[1].' Such manners as depend upon standing relations and general passions are co-extended with the race of man; but those modifications of life and peculiarities of practice which are the progeny of error and perverseness, or at best of some accidental influence or transient persuasion, must perish with their parents.

42 Much therefore of that humour which transported the last century with merriment is lost to us, who do not know the sour solemnity, the sullen superstition, the gloomy moroseness, and the stubborn scruples of the ancient Puritans; or, if we know them, derive our information only from books or from tradition, have never had them before our eyes, and cannot but by recollection and study understand the lines in which they are satirised. Our grandfathers knew the picture from the life; we judge of the life by contemplating the picture[2].

43 It is scarcely possible, in the regularity and composure of the present time, to image the tumult of absurdity and clamour of contradiction which perplexed doctrine, disordered practice[3], and disturbed both publick and private quiet in that age, when subordination was broken and awe was hissed away; when any

---

[1] 'Opinionum enim commenta delet dies, naturae iudicia confirmat.' *De Natura Deorum*, ii. 2, 5.

[2] In 1744 Dr. Grey wrote of him :— 'He is still the unrivalled darling of his own country.' *Hudibras*, Preface, p. 40. Grey had the common fault of editors—whatever he saw the world saw. Ten years earlier Voltaire had written:—'On ne lit plus le Dante dans l'Europe, parce que tout y est allusion à des faits ignorés; il en est de même d'*Hudibras*. La plupart des railleries de ce livre tombent sur la théologie et les théologiens du temps. Il faudrait à tout moment un commentaire. La plaisanterie expliquée cesse d'être plaisanterie, et un commentateur de bons mots n'est guère capable d'en dire.' *Œuvres*, xxiv. 131.

In 1754 Dr. Delany wrote that he had lived to see 'Cowley and even Butler almost as much neglected as Durfey.' *Observations on Orrery's Swift*, p. 126.

Johnson wrote four years later:— 'Those who had felt the mischief of discord and the tyranny of usurpation read *Hudibras* with rapture; for every line brought back to memory something known, and gratified resentment by the just censure of something hated. But the book which was once quoted by princes, and which supplied conversation to all the assemblies of the gay and witty, is now seldom mentioned, and even by those that affect to mention it is seldom read.' *The Idler*, No. 59.

In 1775 Johnson said:—' There is in *Hudibras* a great deal of bullion which will always last. But to be sure the brightest strokes of his wit owed their force to the impression of the characters which was upon men's minds at the time.' Boswell's *Johnson*, ii. 369.

[3] These two words are not in the first edition.

unsettled innovator who could hatch a half-formed notion produced it to the publick ; when every man might become a preacher, and almost every preacher could collect a congregation.

The wisdom of the nation is very reasonably supposed to reside 44 in the parliament.   What can be concluded of the lower classes of the people when in one of the parliaments summoned by Cromwell it was seriously proposed that all the records in the Tower should be burnt, that all memory of things past should be effaced, and that the whole system of life should commence anew [1] ?

We have never been witnesses of animosities excited by the use 45 of minced pies and plumb porridge [2], nor seen with what abhorrence those who could eat them at all other times of the year would shrink from them in December [3].   An old Puritan, who was alive in my childhood, being at one of the feasts of the church invited by a neighbour to partake his cheer, told him that if he would treat him at an alehouse with beer, brewed for all times and seasons, he should accept his kindness, but would have none of his superstitious meats or drinks [4].

One of the puritanical tenets was the illegality of all games of 46 chance, and he that reads Gataker upon *Lots* [5] may see how

---

[1] Mr. C. H. Firth informs me that 'the Parliament supposed to have proposed the burning of the Records was the Barebones Parliament, 1653. The charge is no doubt a calumny, so far as the Parliament was concerned. (Cf. Godwin's *Commonwealth of England*, iii. 573, for its real aims.) But the proposal was really made by Hugh Peters, in 1651. See his *Good Work for a Good Magistrate*, p. 33.'

[2] ' Rather than fail, they will defy
That which they love most tenderly ;
Quarrel with minc'd pies, and disparage
Their best and dearest friend plum-porridge.'
Hudibras, i. 1. 225.

[3] In a note on the above lines Grey quotes the following verses :—
' All plums the prophets' sons despise,
And spice broths are too hot ;
Treason 's in a December pie
And death within the pot ;
Christmas farewell, thy days (I fear)

And merry days are done ;
So they may keep feasts all the year,
Our Saviour shall have none.'

[4] ' I have heard of a Clergyman ejected from his living by the Parliament Visitors for being a scandalous eater of custard.   Not that it was a superstitious meat, but because it was a delicacy.' HAWKINS, Johnson's *Works*, 1787, i. 191.

[5] When Johnson was detained by storms on the Isle of Col he one day ' amused himself by reading Gataker *On Lots* . . . ; a very learned book of the last age, which had been found in the garret of Col's house, and which he said was a treasure here.' Boswell's *Johnson*, v. 302. The book is entitled, *Of the Nature and Use of Lots : A Treatise historicall and theologicall.* By Thomas Gataker, 1619. Pattison calls Gataker, Selden, and Usher ' the three most eminent men for learning in England at that day.' *Life of Milton*, p. 130.

much learning and reason one of the first scholars of his age thought necessary, to prove that it was no crime to throw a die, or play at cards, or to hide a shilling for the reckoning [1].

47   Astrology however, against which so much of the satire is directed, was not more the folly of the Puritans than of others. It had in that time a very extensive dominion. Its predictions raised hopes and fears in minds which ought to have rejected it with contempt [2]. In hazardous undertakings care was taken to begin under the influence of a propitious planet; and when the king was prisoner in Carisbrook Castle, an astrologer was consulted what hour would be found most favourable to an escape [3].

48   What effect this poem had upon the publick, whether it shamed imposture or reclaimed credulity, is not easily determined. Cheats can seldom stand long against laughter [4]. It is certain that the credit of planetary intelligence wore fast away; though some men of knowledge, and Dryden among them, continued to believe that conjunctions and oppositions had a great part in the distribution of good or evil, and in the government of sublunary things [5].

49   Poetical action ought to be probable upon certain suppositions, and such probability as burlesque requires is here violated only by one incident. Nothing can shew more plainly the necessity of doing something, and the difficulty of finding something to do, than that Butler was reduced to transfer to his hero the flagellation of Sancho, not the most agreeable fiction of Cervantes; very suitable indeed to the manners of that age and nation, which

---

[1] South, preaching on *Prov.* xvi. 33, 'The lot is cast into the lap, but the whole disposing of it is of the Lord,' says:—'I cannot think myself engaged from these words to discourse of lots, as to their nature, use, and allowableness; and that, not only in matters of moment and business, but also of recreation; which latter is indeed impugned by some, though better defended by others.' *Sermons,* i, 201.

[2] In 1643 Parliament appointed a Licenser of the Press 'for the Mathematicks, Almanacks, and Prognostications.' Rushworth's *Hist. Coll.* v. 336. In Feb. 1651-2, certain leading Independent divines petitioned Parliament 'to take some speedy course for the utter suppressing of that abominable cheat of Judicial Astrology.' Masson's *Milton,* iv. 392.

[3] Lilly, the astrologer, says that, 'with his Majesty's consent,' he was asked to ascertain by his art, 'in what quarter of this nation he might be most safe,' if he escaped. At a second consultation he 'elected a day and hour when to receive the Commissioners' sent by Parliament; and, agreeing to what they proposed, 'with all speed to come up with them to London.' He does not say that he was consulted about the hour of escape. Lilly's *Life and Times,* 1826, pp. 61, 63.

[4] See *post,* AKENSIDE, 6, for Johnson's attack on 'Shaftesbury's foolish assertion of the efficacy of ridicule for the discovery of truth.'

[5] *Post,* DRYDEN, 191.

ascribed wonderful efficacy to voluntary penances, but so remote from the practice and opinions of the Hudibrastick time that judgement and imagination are alike offended.

The diction of this poem is grossly familiar, and the numbers 50 purposely neglected, except in a few places where the thoughts by their native excellence secure themselves from violation, being such as mean language cannot express [1]. The mode of versification has been blamed by Dryden, who regrets that the heroick measure was not rather chosen [2]. To the critical sentence of Dryden the highest reverence would be due, were not his decisions often precipitate and his opinions immature [3]. When he wished to change the measure, he probably would have been willing to change more. If he intended that when the numbers were heroick the diction should still remain vulgar, he planned a very heterogeneous and unnatural composition. If he preferred a general stateliness both of sound and words, he can be only understood to wish that Butler had undertaken a different work.

The measure is quick, spritely, and colloquial, suitable to the 51 vulgarity of the words and the levity of the sentiments [4]. But

---

[1] The following passages are instances of this :—
' The moon pull'd off her veil of light,
That hides her face by day from sight
(Mysterious veil of brightness made,
That's both her lustre and her shade),
And in the lanthorn of the night
With shining horns hung out her light,' &c. *Hudibras*, ii. 1. 905.
'For though outnumber'd, overthrown,
And by the fate of war run down,
Their duty never was defeated,
Nor from their oaths and faith retreated ;
For loyalty is still the same,
Whether it win or lose the game ;
True as the dial to the sun,
Although it be not shin'd upon.'
Ib. iii. 2. 169.

[2] 'The choice of his numbers is suitable enough to his design, as he has managed it ; but in any other hand the shortness of his verse, and the quick returns of rhyme, had debased the dignity of style. And besides, the double rhyme (a necessary companion of burlesque writing) is not so proper for manly satire, for it

turns earnest too much to jest, and gives us a boyish kind of pleasure. ... It is indeed below so great a master to make use of such a little instrument. . . . After all, he has chosen this kind of verse, and has written the best in it ; and had he taken another he would always have excelled.' DRYDEN, *Works*, xiii. 112.

' It is a dispute among the critics whether burlesque poetry runs best in heroic verse, like that of *The Dispensary* [*post*, GARTH, 17], or in doggerel, like that of *Hudibras*. I think where the low character is to be raised the heroic is the proper measure ; but when an hero is to be pulled down and degraded, it is done best in doggerel.' ADDISON, *The Spectator*, No. 249.

[3] *Post*, DRYDEN, 202.

[4] ' I am afraid that great numbers of those who admire the incomparable *Hudibras*, do it more on account of these doggerel rhymes than of the parts that really deserve admiration. I am sure I have heard the
  "pulpit, drum ecclesiastic,
Was beat with fist instead of a stick ; " [i. 1. 11]

such numbers and such diction can gain regard only when they are used by a writer whose vigour of fancy and copiousness of knowledge entitle him to contempt of ornaments, and who, in confidence of the novelty and justness of his conceptions, can afford to throw metaphors and epithets away [1]. To another that conveys common thoughts in careless versification, it will only be said, 'Pauper videri Cinna vult, et est pauper [2].' The meaning and diction will be worthy of each other, and criticism may justly doom them to perish together.

52   Nor even though another Butler should arise, would another *Hudibras* obtain the same regard. Burlesque consists in a disproportion between the style and the sentiments, or between the adventitious sentiments and the fundamental subject. It therefore, like all bodies compounded of heterogeneous parts, contains in it a principle of corruption. All disproportion is unnatural; and from what is unnatural we can derive only the pleasure which novelty produces. We admire it awhile as a strange thing; but, when it is no longer strange, we perceive its deformity. It is a kind of artifice, which by frequent repetition detects itself; and the reader, learning in time what he is to expect, lays down his book, as the spectator turns away from a second exhibition of those tricks, of which the only use is to shew that they can be played [3].

and
" There was an ancient sage philosopher,
    Who [That] had read Alexander Ross over," [i. 2. 1]
more frequently quoted than the finest pieces of wit in the whole poem.' ADDISON, *The Spectator*, No. 60.

[1] Prior wrote of Butler :—
'Yet he, consummate master, knew When to recede, and where pursue: His noble negligences teach What other toils despair to reach.'
English Poets, xxxiii. 158.   See *post*, PRIOR, 64.

[2] MARTIAL, *Epig.* viii. 19. Dryden says of a poet :—' He doubly starves all his verses, first for want of thought, and then of expression. His poetry neither has wit in it, nor seems to have it; like him in Martial, " Pauper videri Cinna vult, et est pauper." ' *Works*, xv. 288.

[3] *Post*, JOHN PHILIPS, 11.

Fielding, in the Preface to *Joseph Andrews*, writing of burlesque, says : ' But though we have sometimes admitted this in our diction, we have carefully excluded it from our sentiments and characters; for there it is never properly introduced, unless in writings of the burlesque kind, which this is not intended to be. Indeed, no two species of writing can differ more widely than the comic and the burlesque; for as the latter is ever the exhibition of what is monstrous and unnatural, and where our delight, if we examine it, arises from the surprising absurdity, as in appropriating the manners of the highest to the lowest, or *e converso*, so in the former we should ever confine ourselves strictly to nature, from the just imitation of which will flow all the pleasure we can this way convey to a sensible reader.'

ROCHESTER

JOHN WILMOT, afterwards Earl of Rochester, the son of 1
Henry, Earl of Rochester, better known by the title of Lord
Wilmot, so often mentioned in Clarendon's *History*[1], was born
April 10, 1647 [2], at Ditchley, in Oxfordshire. After a grammatical
education at the school of Burford, he entered a nobleman into
Wadham College in 1659, only twelve years old; and in 1661, at
fourteen, was, with some other persons of high rank, made master
of arts by Lord Clarendon in person[3].

He travelled afterwards into France and Italy; and, at his 2
return, devoted himself to the Court. In 1665 he went to sea
with Sandwich, and distinguished himself at Bergen by uncommon
intrepidity[4]; and the next summer served again on board [the
ship commanded by[5]] Sir Edward Spragge, who, in the heat of
the engagement, having a message of reproof to send to one of his
captains, could find no man ready to carry it but Wilmot, who,
in an open boat, went and returned amidst the storm of shot[6].

But his reputation for bravery was not lasting: he was 3
reproached with slinking away in street quarrels and leaving his
companions to shift as they could without him; and Sheffield,
Duke of Buckingham, has left a story of his refusal to fight him[7].

[1] 'Wilmot loved debauchery, but
shut it out from his business; never
neglected that, and seldom miscarried
in it. Goring had a much better
understanding, and a sharper wit,
except in the very exercise of debauchery, and then the other was
inspired.' CLARENDON, *Hist.* v. 2.
See also *ib.* iv. 472.

[2] 'He was born anno 1647, on
April the 1st day, 11 h. 7 m. a.m., and
endued with a noble and fertile muse.
The sun governed the horoscope, and
the moon ruled the birth hour. The
conjunction of Venus and Mercury
in M. Coeli, in sextile of Luna, aptly
denotes his inclination to poetry.
The great reception of Sol with Mars
and Jupiter posited so near the latter,
bestowed a large stock of generous

and active spirits, which constantly
attended on this excellent native's
mind, insomuch that no subject came
amiss to him.' Gadbury's *Ephemeris*,
1698, quoted in *Ath. Oxon.* iii. 1230 *n*.
Burnet places his birth in 1648. *Some
passages of the Life and Death of
John, Earl of Rochester*, 1680, p. 1.

[3] 'He was admitted very affection-
ately into the fraternity by a kiss on
the left cheek from the Chancellor of
the University.' *Ath. Oxon.* iii. 1229.

[4] *Life*, by Burnet, p. 9.

[5] These four words, omitted also in
the first edition, are supplied from
Burnet's *Life*, p. 10.

[6] *Ib.* p. 11.

[7] *Post*, SHEFFIELD, 3. If Rochester
was cowardly, Sheffield was a ruffian.
They were, he says, to fight on horse-

4   He had very early an inclination to intemperance, which he totally subdued in his travels[1]; but when he became a courtier he unhappily addicted himself to dissolute and vitious company, by which his principles were corrupted and his manners depraved. He lost all sense of religious restraint; and, finding it not convenient to admit the authority of laws which he was resolved not to obey, sheltered his wickedness behind infidelity.

5   As he excelled in that noisy and licentious merriment which wine incites, his companions eagerly encouraged him in excess, and he willingly indulged it, till, as he confessed to Dr. Burnet, he was for five years together continually drunk, or so much inflamed by frequent ebriety as in no interval to be master of himself[2].

6   In this state he played many frolicks, which it is not for his honour that we should remember, and which are not now distinctly known. He often pursued low amours in mean disguises, and always acted with great exactness and dexterity the characters which he assumed.

7   He once erected a stage on Tower-hill, and harangued the populace as a mountebank; and, having made physick part of his study, is said to have practised it successfully[3].

8   He was so much in favour with King Charles that he was made one of the gentlemen of the bedchamber, and comptroller of Woodstock Park[4].

back, because 'Lord Rochester told me he was so weak with a distemper that he found himself unfit to fight at all any way, much less a-foot. . . . My anger against him being quite over, because I was satisfied that he never spoke those words I resented, I took the liberty of representing what a ridiculous story it would make if we returned without fighting. . . . I must be obliged in my own defence to lay the fault on him, by telling the truth of the matter.' His second spread it abroad. *Works*, 1729, ii. 8.

Scott, quoting the passage, twice speaks of Rochester's infamy, but passes over in silence the other's brutality. Scott's *Dryden*, xv. 215.

For Rochester's cowardly brutality to Dryden see *post*, DRYDEN, 105.

His father was charged with 'want of mettle' early in the Civil War. Clarendon's *Hist.* iii. 188 *n*.

[1] *Life*, p. 11.
[2] 'Not all the while under the visible effects of it, but his blood was so inflamed that he was not, in all that time, cool enough to be perfectly master of himself.' *Life*, p. 12. See also Hearne's *Collections*, ed. C. E. Doble, 1889, iii. 263.
[3] 'He set up in Tower Street for an Italian mountebank, where he practised physic for some weeks not without success. He took pleasure to disguise himself as a porter, or as a beggar; sometimes to follow some mean amours. He would go about in odd shapes, in which he acted his part so naturally that even those who were in the secret could perceive nothing by which he might be discovered.' *Life*, p. 27. See also Burnet's *History*, i. 294.
[4] 'He was raunger of Woodstock-parke, and lived often at the lodge at

Having an active and inquisitive mind he never, except in his 9
paroxysms of intemperance, was wholly negligent of study ; he
read what is considered as polite learning so much that he is
mentioned by Wood as the greatest scholar of all the nobility [1].
Sometimes he retired into the country and amused himself with
writing libels, in which he did not pretend to confine himself to
truth [2].

His favourite author in French was Boileau, and in English 10
Cowley [3].

Thus in a course of drunken gaiety and gross sensuality, with 11
intervals of study perhaps yet more criminal [4], with an avowed
contempt of all decency and order, a total disregard to every
moral, and a resolute denial of every religious obligation, he
lived worthless and useless, and blazed out his youth and his
health in lavish voluptuousness, till, at the age of one and
thirty, he had exhausted the fund of life, and reduced himself to
a state of weakness and decay.

At this time he was led to an acquaintance with Dr. Burnet, to 12
whom he laid open with great freedom the tenour of his opinions
and the course of his life, and from whom he received such con-

the west end, a very delightfull place,
and noble prospects westwards. Here
his lordship had severall lascivious
pictures drawen.' AUBREY, *Brief
Lives*, ii. 304.

[1] 'He was a person of most rare
parts, and his natural talent was excellent, much improved by learning and industry, being thoroughly
acquainted with the classic authors,
both Greek and Latin ; a thing very
rare (if not peculiar to him) among
those of his quality.' *Ath. Oxon.* iii.
1229.

'He had made himself master of
the ancient and modern wit, and of the
modern French and Italian, as well as
the English.' *Life*, p. 7.

His tutor told Hearne that 'he
understood very little or no Greek,
and that he had but little Latin.'
Hearne's *Coll.* iii. 263.

The standard of learning among
the nobility was not high : Evelyn
wrote of the Earl of Essex in 1680 :—
'He is a sober, wise, judicious, and
pondering person, not illiterate beyond the rate of most noblemen in

this age.' *Diary*, ii. 149.

[2] 'He said the lies in these libels
came often in as ornaments, that
could not be spared without spoiling
the beauty of the poem.' *Life*, p. 26.

'He found out a footman that
knew all the Court, and he furnished
him with a red coat and a musket as
a sentinel, and kept him all the winter
long every night at the doors of such
ladies as he believed might be in
intrigues.... When he was furnished
with materials he used to retire into
the country for a month or two, to
write libels.' BURNET, *Hist. of my
own Time*, i. 295.

[3] *Life*, p. 8. 'Lord Rochester said
[of Cowley], though somewhat profanely :—"Not being of God, he
could not stand."' DRYDEN, *Works*,
xi. 224.

[4] Johnson held them as perhaps
more criminal, as he directed his
studies 'to fortify his mind by dis-
possessing it all he could of the
belief and apprehensions of religion,'
and also 'to strengthen these ill
principles in others.' *Life*, pp. 15, 16.

viction of the reasonableness of moral duty and the truth of Christianity as produced a total change both of his manners and opinions[1]. The account of those salutary conferences is given by Burnet, in a book intituled *Some Passages of the Life and Death of John Earl of Rochester*, which the critick ought to read for its elegance, the philosopher for its arguments, and the saint for its piety. It were an injury to the reader to offer him an abridgement[2].

13 He died July 26, 1680, before he had completed his thirty-fourth year; and was so worn away by a long illness that life went out without a struggle[3].

14 Lord Rochester was eminent for the vigour of his colloquial wit[4], and remarkable for many wild pranks and sallies of extravagance. The glare of his general character diffused itself upon his writings; the compositions of a man whose name was heard so often were certain of attention, and from many readers certain of applause[5]. This blaze of reputation is not yet quite extinguished; and his poetry still retains some splendour beyond that which genius has bestowed[6].

15 Wood and Burnet give us reason to believe that much was imputed

---

[1] *Life*, p. 30. He wrote to Burnet shortly before his death:—'If God be yet pleased to spare me longer in this world I hope in your conversation to be exalted to that degree of piety, that the world may see how much I abhor what I so long loved, and how much I glory in repentance in God's service.' *Hist. of my own Time*, Preface, p. 17.

'Nor was the King pleased with my being sent for by the Earl when he died; he fancied that he had told me many things of which I might make an ill use; yet he had read the book that I writ concerning him and spoke well of it.' *Ib.* ii. 122.

[2] 'I asked if Burnet had not given a good Life of Rochester. JOHNSON. We have a good *Death*; there is not much *Life*.' Boswell's *Johnson*, iii. 191.

[3] 'He lay much silent; once they heard him praying very devoutly. And on Monday, about two of the clock in the morning, he died without any convulsion, or so much as a groan.' *Life*, p. 157.

'At length, after a short but pleasant life, this noble and beautiful count paid his last debt to nature.' *Ath. Oxon.* iii. 1232. 'The writings of this *noble and beautiful count*, as Anthony Wood calls him (for his Lordship's vices were among the fruits of the Restoration, and consequently not unlovely in that biographer's eyes),' &c. HORACE WALPOLE, *Works*, i. 399.

The dissolute Earl of Sandwich (the fourth earl) was Rochester's grandson. *Post*, SHEFFIELD, 3 *n.*

[4] 'His wit had in it a peculiar brightness, to which none could ever arrive.' BURNET, *History*, i. 294.

[5] 'Mr. Andrew Marvell, who was a good judge of witt, was wont to say that he was the best English satyrist, and had the right veine.' AUBREY, *Brief Lives*, ii. 304.

[6] 'Lord Rochester's poems have much more obscenity than wit, more wit than poetry, more poetry than politeness.' WALPOLE, *Works*, i. 399.

to him which he did not write[1]. I know not by whom the original collection was made or by what authority its genuineness was ascertained. The first edition was published in the year of his death, with an air of concealment, professing in the title page to be printed at Antwerp[2].

Of some of the pieces, however, there is no doubt. The 16 Imitation of Horace's Satire[3], the Verses to Lord Mulgrave[4], the Satire against Man[5], the Verses upon *Nothing*[6], and perhaps some others, are, I believe, genuine, and perhaps most of those which the late collection exhibits[7].

As he cannot be supposed to have found leisure for any course 17 of continued study, his pieces are commonly short, such as one fit of resolution would produce.

[1] *Ath. Oxon.* iii. 1230. 'When anything extraordinary that way [libels and satires] came out, as a child is fathered sometimes by its resemblance, so was it laid at his door as its parent and author.' BURNET, *Life*, p. 14. 'The three most eminent wits of that time, on whom all the lively libels were fastened, were the Earls of Dorset and Rochester, and Sir Charles Sedley.' BURNET, *History*, i. 294.

[2] '*Poems on Several Occasions*, Antwerp [London] 1680, octavo.' Walpole's *Works*, i. 400. This edition is not in the British Museum. In the 'Advertisement' of his *Funeral Sermon* by Robert Parsons it is stated that 'all the lewd and profane poems and libels of the late Lord Rochester have been (contrary to his dying request) published to the world.' *N. & Q.* 6 S. v. 424. For a reward offered in the *London Gazette*, No. 1567, Nov. 22-25, 1680, for the discovery of the printer of this 'Libel of lewd scandalous Poems' see Cunningham's *Lives of the Poets*, i. 192. For Curll's impudence about an edition of his poems see Pope's *Works* (Elwin and Courthope), vi. 421 *n*., and for Stevens's 'castration' of them for the *English Poets*, at Johnson's request, see Boswell's *Johnson*, iii. 191.

[3] *Eng. Poets*, xv. 63.

[4] *Ib.* p. 38. For Lord Mulgrave (Sheffield, Duke of Buckingham) see *ante*, ROCHESTER, 3; *post*, SHEF-FIELD, 3.

[5] *Eng. Poets*, xv. 45. Mr. Lecky records of Tennyson:—'I can still remember the almost terrific force he threw into the noble lines of Rochester on the *Vanity of Human Reason*.
'Reason, an *ignis fatuus* of the mind,
Which leaves the light of Nature, sense, behind;
Pathless and dangerous wandering ways it takes
Through Error's fenny bogs and thorny brakes;
Whilst the misguided follower climbs with pain
Mountains of whimsies heaped in his own brain.
.   .   .   .   .
Till [Then] Old Age and Experience, hand in hand,
Lead him to Death, and *make* him understand,
After a search so painful and so long,
That *all* his life he has been in the wrong.' [*Eng. Poets*, xv. 45.]
Tennyson's *Life*, ii. 201.
The italics are Mr. Lecky's; marking, no doubt, Tennyson's emphasis. The Master of Balliol often repeated these verses. *Life of Jowett*, ii. 38.

[6] *Eng. Poets*, xv. 55; *post*, POPE, 18.

[7] In 1685 was published Fletcher's '*Valentinian, A Tragedy. As 'tis altered by the late Earl of Rochester.*' The Preface contains a defence of Rochester.

18 His songs have no particular character: they tell, like other songs, in smooth and easy language of scorn and kindness, dismission and desertion, absence and inconstancy, with the common places of artificial courtship. They are commonly smooth and easy; but have little nature, and little sentiment.

19 His imitation of Horace on Lucilius is not inelegant or unhappy. In the reign of Charles the Second began that adaptation, which has since been very frequent, of ancient poetry to present times[1]; and perhaps few will be found where the parallelism is better preserved than in this. The versification is indeed sometimes careless, but it is sometimes vigorous and weighty[2].

20 The strongest effort of his Muse is his poem upon *Nothing*[3]. He is not the first who has chosen this barren topick for the boast of his fertility. There is a poem called *Nihil* in Latin by Passerat, a poet and critick of the sixteenth century in France[4]; who, in his own epitaph, expresses his zeal for good poetry thus:

'Molliter ossa quiescent
Sint modo carminibus non onerata malis[5].'

21 His works are not common, and therefore I shall subjoin his verses.

[1] *Ante*, COWLEY, 125. Sprat, speaking of Cowley's adaptations, says: 'This way of leaving verbal translations, and chiefly regarding the sense and genius of the author, was scarce heard of in England before this present age. I will not presume to say that Mr. Cowley was the absolute inventor of it. Nay, I know that others had the good luck to recommend it first in print. Yet I appeal to you, Sir [Mr. Clifford], whether he did not conceive it, and discourse of it, and practise it as soon as any man.' Hurd's *Cowley*, i. 28.
In the first years of the reign of Charles II Boileau was bringing out his adaptations. He was the model to Pope and Johnson.

[2] Lord Dorset and Lord Rochester should be considered as holiday-writers; as gentlemen that diverted themselves now and then with poetry rather than as poets.' POPE, Spence's *Anec.* p. 281.

[3] It was 'printed on one side of a sheet of paper in two columns.' WALPOLE, *Works*, i. 399.

'French truth and British policy make a conspicuous figure *in nothing*, as the Earl of Rochester has very well observed in his admirable poem upon that barren subject.' ADDISON, *The Spectator*, No. 305.
'French truth, Dutch prowess, British policy,
Hibernian learning, Scotch civility,
Spaniards' dispatch, Danes' wit, are mainly seen in thee.'
Eng. Poets, xv. 57.

[4] In a note on Voltaire's 'Observations' on the French translation of *Tristram Shandy*, where he speaks of '*la satire Ménippée*,' it is said that Passerat was one 'des sept joyeux auteurs de ce malin chef-d'œuvre de plaisanterie.' *Œuvres de Voltaire*, xlii. 432.

[5] 'Je dis comme Passerat :—
"Mea molliter ossa quiescent,"' &c.
Ménagiana, vi. 255.
In a note it is added :—'Ce sont les deux derniers vers des six que fit Passerat pour son épitaphe, qu'on peut voir dans l'église des Jacobins de la rue S.-Jacques.'

In examining this performance *Nothing* must be considered as 22 having not only a negative but a kind of positive signification; as I need not fear thieves, I have *nothing*; and *nothing* is a very powerful protector[1]. In the first part of the sentence it is taken negatively; in the second it is taken positively, as an agent. In one of Boileau's lines it was a question, whether he should use *à rien faire* or *à ne rien faire*; and the first was preferred, because it gave *rien* a sense in some sort positive[2]. *Nothing* can be a subject only in its positive sense, and such a sense is given it in the first line:

'*Nothing*, thou elder brother ev'n to shade.'

In this line I know not whether he does not allude to a curious book *De Umbra*, by Wowerus, which, having told the qualities of *Shade*, concludes with a poem in which are these lines:

'Jam primum terram validis circumspice claustris
Suspensam totam, decus admirabile mundi
Terrasque tractusque maris, camposque liquentes
Aeris et vasti laqueata palatia cœli—
Omnibus UMBRA prior[3].'

The positive sense is generally preserved with great skill 23 through the whole poem, though sometimes in a subordinate sense the negative *nothing* is injudiciously mingled[4]. Passerat confounds the two senses.

Another of his most vigorous pieces is his Lampoon on Sir 24

---

[1] 'Felix cui nihil est (fuerant haec vota Tibullo);
Non timet insidias: fures, incendia temnit.
Sollicitas sequitur nullo sub iudice lites.' *Post*, ROCHESTER, 28.

[2] 'Sans ce métier, fatal au repos de ma vie,
Mes jours pleins de loisir couleraient sans envie,
Je n'aurais qu'à chanter, rire, boire d'autant;
Et comme un gras chanoine, à mon aise, et content,
Passer tranquillement, sans souci, sans affaire,
La nuit à bien dormir, et le jour à rien faire.' *Satires*, ii. 57.
The editor quotes La Fontaine's *Épitaphe*, which ends:—
'Quant à son tems, bien le sçût dispenser;

Deux parts en fit, dont il soûloit passer
L'une à dormir, et l'autre à ne rien faire.'
He adds: 'M. Despréaux [Boileau] demanda à l'Académie, laquelle de ces deux manières, la sienne, ou celle de La Fontaine, valoit mieux. Il passa tout d'une voix, que la sienne étoit la meilleure, parce qu'en ôtant la négative, *Rien faire* devenoit une espèce d'occupation.' *Œuvres de Boileau*, i. 46. See also *ib.* v. 188.
[3] Joan. Wouweri, *Dies Aestiva sive De Umbra Paegnion*, 1610, p. 130. See *post*, YALDEN, 17.
[4] 'Yet this of thee the wise may freely say,
Thou from the virtuous nothing tak'st away,
And to be part with thee the wicked wisely pray.' *Eng. Poets*, xv. 56.

Car Scroop[1], who, in a poem called *The Praise of Satire*[2], had some lines like these :

> 'He who can push into a midnight fray
> His brave companion, and then run away,
> Leaving him to be murder'd in the street,
> Then put it off with some buffoon conceit ;
> Him, thus dishonour'd, for a wit you own,
> And court him as top fidler of the town[3].'

25   This was meant of Rochester, whose 'buffoon conceit' was, I suppose, a saying often mentioned, that 'every Man would be a Coward if he durst[4],' and drew from him those furious verses[5] ; to which Scroop made in reply an epigram, ending with these lines :

> 'Thou canst hurt no man's fame with thy ill word ;
> Thy pen is full as harmless as thy sword[6].'

26   Of the *Satire against Man* Rochester can only claim what remains when all Boileau's part is taken away[7].

27   In all his works there is sprightliness and vigour, and every where may be found tokens of a mind which study might have carried to excellence.   What more can be expected from a life spent in ostentatious contempt of regularity, and ended before the abilities of many other men began to be displayed[8]?

---

[1] *Eng. Poets*, xv. p. 67.

[2] *A Defence of Satyr.*

[3] I quote from memory. JOHNSON.
'To fatal midnight quarrels can betray
His brave companion, and then run away,
Leaving him to be murder'd in the street,
Then put it off with some buffoon conceit ;
This, this is he, you should beware of all,
Yet him a pleasant witty man you call :
To whet your dull debauches up and down,
You seek him as top fidler of the town.'
Roxburghe Ballads, iv. 570.

[4] 'The good he acts, the ill he does endure,
'Tis all from fear, to make himself secure.
Merely for safety after fame they thirst ;

For all men would be cowards if they durst.'
ROCHESTER, *Eng. Poets*, xv. 50.

[5] The following is a specimen of the poet's fury :—
'Who needs wilt be an ugly Beau-Garçon,
Spit at and shunn'd by every girl in town ;
Where dreadfully Love's scare-crow thou art plac'd,
To fright the tender flock that long to taste ;
While every coming maid, when you appear,
Starts back for shame, and straight turns chaste for fear.'   *Ib.* p. 68.

[6] *Roxburghe Ballads*, iv. 571.

[7] *Ante*, ROCHESTER, 16. Boileau's eighth satire is entitled *La Satire sur l'Homme.*

[8] 'George Steevens made the selection of Rochester's poems which appear in Dr. Johnson's edition.' Jacob Tonson early in the century

'Poema Cl. V. JOANNIS PASSERATII,   28
Regii in Academia Parisiensi Professoris.
Ad ornatissimum virum ERRICUM MEMMIUM[1]

Janus adest, festæ poscunt sua dona Kalendæ,
Munus abest festis quod possim offerre Kalendis.
Siccine Castalius nobis exaruit humor?
Usque adeò ingenii nostri est exhausta facultas,
Immunem ut videat redeuntis janitor anni?
Quod nusquam est, potius nova per vestigia quæram.

Ecce autem partes dum sese versat in omnes
Invenit mea Musa NIHIL, ne despice munus.
Nam NIHIL est gemmis, NIHIL est pretiosius auro.
Huc animum, huc igitur vultus adverte benignos :
Res nova narratur quæ nulli audita priorum,
Ausonii et Graii dixerunt cætera vates,
Ausoniæ indictum NIHIL est Græcæque Camœnæ.

E cœlo quacunque Ceres sua prospicit arva,
Aut genitor liquidis orbem complectitur ulnis
Oceanus, NIHIL interitus et originis expers.
Immortale NIHIL, NIHIL omni parte beatum.
Quòd si hinc majestas et vis divina probatur,
Num quid honore deûm, num quid dignabimur aris?
Conspectu lucis NIHIL est jucundius almæ,
Vere NIHIL, NIHIL irriguo formosius horto,
Floridius pratis, Zephyri clementius aura ;
In bello sanctum NIHIL est, Martisque tumultu :
Justum in pace NIHIL, NIHIL est in fœdere tutum.
Felix cui NIHIL est, fuerant hæc [quæ] vota Tibullo :
Non timet insidias : fures, incendia temnit :
Sollicitas sequitur nullo sub judice lites.
Ille ipse invictis qui subjicit omnia fatis [plantis]
Zenonis sapiens[2], NIHIL admiratur et optat.
Socraticique gregis fuit ista scientia quondam,

had made a selection. Johnson's *Works*, vii. 162 *n*.

'The very name of Rochester is offensive to modest ears; yet does his poetry discover such energy of style and such poignancy of satire as give ground to imagine what so fine a genius, had he fallen in a more happy age, and had followed better models, was capable of producing. The ancient satirists often used great liberty in their expressions ; but their freedom no more resembles the licentiousness of Rochester than the nakedness of an Indian does that of a common prostitute.' HUME, *History*, viii. 336.

[1] *Nihil.* Henrico Memmio, pro xeniis. Per Ioannem Passeratium. P.R. Paris. 1587.

[2] In the first edition and a later one that I examined it is 'Junonis sapiens.' Whether 'Zenonis sapiens' is Johnson's emendation, I do not know. It must be the right reading.

Scire NIHIL, studio cui nunc incumbitur uni.
Nec quicquam in ludo mavult didicisse juventus,
Ad magnas quia ducit opes, et culmen honorum.
Nosce NIHIL, nosces fertur quod Pythagoreæ
Grano hærere fabæ, cui vox adjuncta negantis.
Multi Mercurio freti duce viscera terræ
Pura liquefaciunt simul, et patrimonia miscent,
Arcano instantes operi, et carbonibus atris,
Qui tandem exhausti damnis, fractique labore,
Inveniunt atque inventum NIHIL usque requirunt.
Hoc dimetiri non ulla decempeda possit :
Nec numeret Libycæ numerum qui callet arenæ :
Et Phœbo ignotum NIHIL est, NIHIL altius astris.
Tùque, tibi licet eximium sit mentis acumen,
Omnem in naturam penetrans, et in abdita rerum,
Pace tua, Memmi, NIHIL ignorare vidêris.
Sole tamen NIHIL est, et puro clarius igne.
Tange NIHIL, dicesque NIHIL sine corpore tangi.
Cerne NIHIL, cerni dices NIHIL absque colore.
Surdum audit loquitúrque NIHIL sine voce, volátque
Absque ope pennarum, et graditur sine cruribus ullis.
Absque loco motuque NIHIL per inane vagatur.
Humano generi utilius NIHIL arte medendi.
Ne rhombos igitur, neu Thessala murmura tentet
Idalia vacuum trajectus arundine pectus,
Neu legat Idæo Dictæum in vertice gramen.
Vulneribus sævi NIHIL auxiliatur amoris.
Vexerit et quemvis trans mœstas portitor undas,
Ad superos hunc imo NIHIL revocabit ab orco.
Inferni NIHIL inflectit præcordia regis,
Parcarúmque colos, et inexorabile pensum.
Obruta Phlegræis campis Titania pubes
Fulmineo sensit NIHIL esse potentius ictu :
Porrigitur magni NIHIL extra mœnia mundi :
Diíque NIHIL metuunt. Quid longo carmine plura
Commemorem ? virtute NIHIL præstantius ipsa,
Splendidius NIHIL est ; NIHIL est Jove denique majus.
Sed tempus finem argutis imponere nugis :
Ne tibi si multa laudem mea carmina charta,
De NIHILO, NIHILI pariant [pariant Nihili] fastidia versus [1].'

[1] According to Hawkins (*Life of Johnson*, p. 17) 'for the insertion of this poem Johnson had, as it is said, no other aid than his own recollection.'

ROSCOMMON

WENTWORTH DILLON, Earl of Roscommon, was the [1]
son of James Dillon and Elizabeth Wentworth, sister to
the earl of Strafford.   He was born in Ireland [2] during the
lieutenancy of Strafford, who, being both his uncle and his
godfather, gave him his own surname.   His father, the third
earl of Roscommon, had been converted by Usher to the
protestant religion [3], and when the popish rebellion broke out
Strafford, thinking the family in great danger from the fury of
the Irish, sent for his godson, and placed him at his own seat in
Yorkshire, where he was instructed in Latin ; which he learned so
as to write it with purity and elegance, though he was never able
to retain the rules of grammar.

Such is the account given by Mr. Fenton, from whose notes on [2]
Waller [4] most of this account must be borrowed, though I know
not whether all that he relates is certain.   The instructer whom
he assigns to Roscommon is one Dr. Hall, by whom he cannot
mean the famous Hall, then an old man and a bishop [5].

When the storm broke out upon Strafford, his house was a [3]
shelter no longer ; and Dillon, by the advice of Usher, was sent
to Caen, where the Protestants had then an university, and continued his studies under Bochart [6].

[1] 'In the *Gentleman's Magazine* for
May, 1748 [p. 214], Johnson wrote
a *Life of Roscommon*, with notes,
which he afterwards much improved,
indented the notes into text, and
inserted it amongst his *Lives of the
English Poets.*'   Boswell's *Johnson*,
i. 191.

[2] About 1633. *Dict. Nat. Biog.*
Strafford entered Dublin as Lord
Deputy in July, 1633.   Gardiner's
Hist. of Engl. viii. 34.

[3] Wood's *Fasti Oxon.* ii. 390.
'It was his grandfather, Sir Robert
Dillon, second Earl, who was converted from popery ; and his conversion is recited in the patent of Sir

James, the first Earl, as one of the
grounds of his creation.'   MALONE,
Johnson's *Works*, vii. 164 *n.*

[4] Fenton's *Waller*, 1744 : *Observations*, &c., p. 138.   See *post*, FEN-
TON, 15.

[5] It seems impossible to identify
this 'Dr. Hall.'   The 'famous Hall'
is of course Joseph Hall, who was
born in 1574 and made Bishop of
Exeter in 1627, and of Norwich in
1641.   He died in 1656.

[6] 'Samuel Bochart was minister
of a Calvinist congregation at Caen,
and, being professor in the Calvinist
College there, was a teacher of such
repute as to attract pupils from

4 Young Dillon, who was sent to study under Bochart, and who is represented as having already made great proficiency in literature, could not be more than nine years old. Strafford went to govern Ireland in 1633, and was put to death eight years afterwards. That he was sent to Caen is certain; that he was a great scholar may be doubted.

5 At Caen he is said to have had some preternatural intelligence of his father's death.

6 'The lord Roscommon, being a boy of ten years of age, at Caen in Normandy, one day was, as it were, madly extravagant in playing, leaping, getting over the tables, boards [table-boards], &c. He was wont to be sober enough; they said, God grant this bodes no ill-luck to him! In the heat of this extravagant fit he cries out, *My father is dead*. A fortnight after news came from Ireland that his father was dead. This account I had from Mr. Knolles, who was his governor, and then with him,—since secretary to the earl of Strafford; and I have heard his lordship's relations confirm the same.' *Aubrey's Miscellany* [1].

7 The present age is very little inclined to favour any accounts of this kind, nor will the name of Aubrey much recommend it to credit; it ought not however to be omitted because better evidence of a fact cannot easily be found than is here offered, and it must be by preserving such relations that we may at last judge how much they are to be regarded. If we stay to examine this account, we shall see difficulties on both sides: here is a relation of a fact given by a man who had no interest to deceive and who could not be deceived himself, and here is, on the other hand, a miracle which produces no effect: the order of nature is interrupted to discover not a future but only a distant event, the knowledge of which is of no use to him to whom it is revealed [2]. Between these difficulties, what way shall be found? Is reason or testimony to be rejected? I believe what Osborne says of an appearance of sanctity may be applied to such impulses or anticipations as this: 'Do not wholly slight them, because

---

England. . . . We may perhaps trace the "unspotted lays" of the poet [*post*, ROSCOMMON, 24] to his Calvinist master.' PATTISON, *Essays*, i. 247.

[1] *Miscellanies upon various Subjects*, by John Aubrey, 1784, p. 162.

[2] Johnson, after giving the evidences for second sight, continues:—'Strong reasons for incredulity will readily occur. This faculty of seeing things out of sight is local and commonly useless. It is a breach of the common order of things, without any visible reason or perceptible benefit.' *Works*, ix. 106.

they may be true ; but do not easily trust them, because they may be false[1].'

The state both of England and Ireland was at this time such, [8] that he who was absent from either country had very little temptation to return ; and therefore Roscommon when he left Caen travelled into Italy, and amused himself with its antiquities, and particularly with medals, in which he acquired uncommon skill.

At the Restoration, with the other friends of monarchy, he [9] came to England, was made captain of the band of pensioners, and learned so much of the dissoluteness of the court that he addicted himself immoderately to gaming, by which he was engaged in frequent quarrels, and which undoubtedly brought upon him its usual concomitants, extravagance and distress[2].

After some time a dispute about part of his estate forced him [10] into Ireland, where he was made by the duke of Ormond captain of the guards, and met with an adventure thus related by Fenton :—

'He was at Dublin as much as ever distempered with the same [11] fatal affection for play, which engaged him in one adventure that well deserves to be related. As he returned to his lodgings from a gaming-table, he was attacked in the dark by three ruffians, who were employed to assassinate him. The earl defended himself with so much resolution that he dispatched one of the aggressors ; whilst a gentleman, accidentally passing that way, interposed, and disarmed another ; the third secured himself by flight. This generous assistant was a disbanded officer, of a good family and fair reputation ; who, by what we call the partiality of fortune, to avoid censuring the iniquities of the times, wanted even a plain suit of cloaths to make a decent appearance at the castle. But

[1] 'Despise not a profession of holiness, because it may be true ; but have a care how you trust it, for fear it should be false.' Francis Osborne's *Works*, 1673, p. 103.

'I expressed a liking for Mr. Francis Osborne's works, and asked Johnson what he thought of that writer. He answered :—"A conceited fellow. Were a man to write so now, the boys would throw stones at him."' Boswell's *Johnson*, ii. 193.

'Mr. Osborne says that "a woman is the most cowardly of all the creatures God ever made"—a sentiment more remarkable for its bluntness than for its truth.' *Tom Jones*, Bk. iv.

ch. 13. See also Boswell's *Johnson*, i. 405.

[2] 'Jan. 6, 1661–2. This evening, according to custom, his Majesty opened the revels of that night by throwing the dice himself in the privy-chamber, where was a table set on purpose, and lost his £100. (The year before he won £1,500.) The ladies also played very deep. I came away when the Duke of Ormond had won about £1,000.' EVELYN, *Diary*, i. 381. 'Jan. 8, 1667–8. I saw deep and prodigious gaming at the Groom-Porter's, vast heaps of gold squandered away in a vain and profuse manner.' *Ib.* ii. 35.

his lordship, on this occasion, presenting him to the Duke of Ormond, with great importunity prevailed with his grace that he might resign his post of captain of the guards to his friend ; which for about three years the gentleman enjoyed, and, upon his death, the duke returned the commission to his generous benefactor.'

12 When he had finished his business he returned to London ; was made Master of the Horse to the Dutchess of York ; and married the Lady Frances, daughter of the Earl of Burlington [1], and widow of Colonel Courteney.

13 He now busied his mind with literary projects, and formed the plan of a society for refining our language [2], and fixing its standard ; 'in imitation,' says Fenton, 'of those learned and polite societies with which he had been acquainted abroad [3].' In this design his friend Dryden is said to have assisted him [4].

14 The same design, it is well known, was revived by Dr. Swift in the ministry of Oxford [5]; but it has never since been publickly mentioned, though at that time great expectations were formed, by some, of its establishment and its effects. Such a society might perhaps without much difficulty be collected ; but that it would produce what is expected from it may be doubted [6].

---

[1] Pepys, on April 29, 1667, records ' a match for my Lord Hinchingbroke to a daughter of my Lord Burlington's, where there is great alliance, £10,000 portion ; a civil family, and relation to my Lord Chancellor, whose son hath married one of the daughters.' *Diary*, iv. 29.

[2] 'After the praise of refining the taste of a nation the highest eulogy, perhaps, which can be bestowed upon any author is to say that he corrupted it.' ADAM SMITH, *Moral Sentiments*, 1812, p. 342.

[3] Fenton's *Waller*, 1744: *Observations*, &c., p. 140. *Ante*, MILTON, 25 *n*. Sprat speaks of 'a proposal for erecting an English Academy.' *Hist. of the Royal Soc.* 1667, p. 40. Pattison says of this period :—'In France Academies were still in all the freshness of youth, and had not yet become mere empty titles of honour, or clubs for the publication of Transactions.' *Essays*, i. 257.

'The project of forming a high court of letters for France was no dream. Richelieu in great measure fulfilled it.' M. ARNOLD, *Essays in Criticism*, 1884, p. 46. See also Sainte-Beuve's *Causeries*, xiv. 195.

[4] Dryden, in the Dedication of his *Rival Ladies* (*Works*, ii. 134 ; *post*, DRYDEN, 16), says :—' I am sorry that (speaking so noble a language as we do) we have not a more certain measure of it, as they have in France, where they have an Academy erected for that purpose, and endowed with large privileges by the present King.'

[5] *Post*, SWIFT, 40. See also *post*, PRIOR, 14.

[6] ' It [our language] never wanted this care more than at that period ; nor could two men have been found more proper to execute most parts of that plan than Dryden, the greatest master of the powers of language, and Roscommon, whose judgment was sufficient to correct the exuberances of his associate. Since them chaster writers have by degrees refined our tongue. . . . Such authors fix a standard by their writings. . . . Academies and dictionaries are impotent authorities : who that thinks Machiavel an incompetent guide would

The Italian academy seems to have obtained its end. The 15
language was refined, and so fixed that it has changed but little.
The French academy thought that they refined their language,
and doubtless thought rightly: but the event has not shewn that
they fixed it ; for the French of the present time is very different
from that of the last century [1].

In this country an academy could be expected to do but little. 16
If an academician's place were profitable it would be given by
interest ; if attendance were gratuitous it would be rarely paid,
and no man would endure the least disgust. Unanimity is
impossible, and debate would separate the assembly.

But suppose the philological decree made and promulgated, 17
what would be its authority ? In absolute governments there is
sometimes a general reverence paid to all that has the sanction of
power and the countenance of greatness. How little this is the
state of our country needs not to be told. We live in an age in
which it is a kind of publick sport to refuse all respect that cannot
be enforced [2]. The edicts of an English academy would probably
be read by many, only that they might be sure to disobey them.

That our language is in perpetual danger of corruption cannot 18
be denied ; but what prevention can be found? The present
manners of the nation would deride authority, and therefore
nothing is left but that every writer should criticise himself [3].

All hopes of new literary institutions were quickly suppressed 19

obey the Crusca.' HORACE WAL-
POLE, *Works*, i. 518. The Accademia
della Crusca is the Italian Academy.
Boswell's *Johnson*, i. 298, 443.
  [1] Grimm wrote in 1755 :—'Ils [les
philosophes] s'imaginent que la langue dépend absolument de la litté-
rature, et de l'état des arts et des
lettres dans un pays. C'est le peuple
qui la parle qui est le maître de la
langue, et non pas les gens de lettres
qui l'écrivent.' *Mémoires histori-
ques*, &c., 1814, i. 152.
' Poets that lasting marble seek
  Must carve in Latin or in Greek ;
  We write in sand; our language
    grows,
  And, like the tide, our work o'erflows.'
        WALLER, *Eng. Poets*, xvi. 173.
  [2] 'Johnson burst forth, "Subordination is sadly broken down in this age.
No man, now, has the same authority

which his father had,—except a gaoler.
No master has it over his servants :
it is diminished in our colleges ; nay,
in our grammar schools."' Boswell's
Johnson, iii. 262.
  [3] 'If an Academy should be established for the cultivation of our style,
which I, who can never wish to see
dependence multiplied, hope the
spirit of English liberty will hinder
or destroy,' &c. JOHNSON, *Works*,
v. 48. See also *John. Misc.* i. 436.
  ' The deterrent effect of the Académie [des Sciences] on the spread
of Evolution in France has been most
striking. Even at the present day
[1887] a member of the Institute does
not feel quite happy in owning to
a belief in Darwinism. We may
indeed be thankful that we are " devoid of such a blessing."' *Life of
Charles Darwin*, 1892, p. 261.

by the contentious turbulence of King James's reign; and Roscommon, foreseeing that some violent concussion of the State was at hand, purposed to retire to Rome, alleging that *it was [would be] best to sit near [next] the chimney when the chamber smoaked*[1], a sentence of which the application seems not very clear.

20 His departure was delayed by the gout, and he was so impatient either of hinderance or of pain that he submitted himself to a French empirick, who is said to have repelled the disease into his bowels.

21 At the moment in which he expired he uttered, with an energy of voice that expressed the most fervent devotion, two lines of his own version of *Dies Iræ*:

'My God, my Father, and my Friend,
Do not forsake me in my end[2].'

He died in 1684[3]; and was buried with great pomp in Westminster-Abbey.

22 His poetical character is given by Mr. Fenton:[4]

'In his writings,' says Fenton, 'we view the image of a mind which [that] was naturally serious and solid; richly furnished and adorned with all the ornaments of learning [art and science, and those ornaments] unaffectedly disposed in the most regular and elegant order. His imagination might have probably been more fruitful and sprightly if his judgement had been less severe. But that severity (delivered in a masculine, clear, succinct style) contributed to make him so eminent in the didactical manner, that no man with justice can affirm he was ever equalled by any of our [own] nation, without confessing at the same time that he is inferior to none. In some other kinds of writing his genius seems to have wanted fire to attain the point of perfection; but who can attain it?'

23 From this account of the riches of his mind, who would not imagine that they had been displayed in large volumes and

---

[1] Fenton's *Waller : Observations,* &c., p. 141.
'"Where is my uncle?" asked Morton. "In Edinburgh," replied Alison; "the honest man thought it was best to gang and sit by the chimley when reek rase."' *Old Mortality, Tales of my Landlord,* (1818), vol. iii. 292. See also *Woodstock* (1871), p. 270.
[2] The first line of the triplet is:—
'Prostrate my contrite heart I rend.'
Eng. Poets, xv. 123.

Roscommon's is certainly a free version of

'Oro supplex et acclinis,
Cor contritum quasi cinis,
Gere curam mei finis.'

[3] 'His will was made January 4, 1684-5, and proved the latter end of that month.' Prior's *Malone,* p. 404.
[4] Fenton's *Waller : Observations,* &c., p. 141.

numerous performances? Who would not, after the perusal of
this character, be surprised to find that all the proofs of this genius,
and knowledge, and judgement are not sufficient to form a single
book, or to appear otherwise than in conjunction with the works
of some other writer of the same petty size[1]? But thus it is that
characters are written: we know somewhat, and we imagine the
rest. The observation, that his imagination would probably have
been more fruitful and spritely if his judgement had been less
severe, may be answered, by a remarker somewhat inclined to
cavil, by a contrary supposition, that his judgement would probably have been less severe if his imagination had been more fruitful.
It is ridiculous to oppose judgement to imagination; for it does
not appear that men have necessarily less of one as they have more
of the other.

We must allow of Roscommon, what Fenton has not mentioned 24
so distinctly as he ought, and what is yet very much to his honour,
that he is perhaps the only correct writer in verse before Addison[2];
and that if there are not so many or so great beauties in his
compositions as in those of some contemporaries, there are at
least fewer faults. Nor is this his highest praise; for Mr. Pope
has celebrated him as the only moral writer of King Charles's
reign:

> 'Unhappy Dryden! in all Charles's days,
> Roscommon only boasts unspotted lays[3].'

His great work is his *Essay on Translated Verse*[4]; of 25

---

[1] 'They were published together
with those of Duke in an octavo
volume in 1717.' Johnson's *Works*,
ed. 1787, ii. 211.

[2] *Post*, ADDISON, 157; PRIOR, 71;
POPE, 30. 'Roscommon is one of
the most renowned writers in the
reign of Charles II, but one of the
most careless too.' HORACE WAL-
POLE, *Works*, i. 518.

[3] *Imit. Hor., Epis.* ii. 1. 213.
Pope praises him also in the *Essay
on Criticism*, l. 725, as
> 'not more learn'd than good,
With manners gen'rous as his noble
blood;
To him the wit of Greece and Rome
was known,
And ev'ry author's merit but his
own.'
'Of all the considerable writers

of this age Sir William Temple is
almost the only one that kept himself
altogether unpolluted by that inunda-
tion of vice and licentiousness which
overwhelmed the nation.' HUME,
Hist. of Eng. viii. 337. Milton
Hume places in the age of the Commonwealth; Bunyan he passes over,
together with the great divines and
philosophers.

[4] *Eng. Poets*, xv. 79.
'Yet modestly he does his work
survey,
And calls a finished poem an Essay.'
DRYDEN, *Works*, xi. 28.
Johnson, in his *Dictionary*, quoting
this couplet, defines *Essay* as 'a loose
sally of the mind; an irregular indi-
gested piece; not a regular and
orderly composition.' Dryden says of
his own *Essay of Dramatic Poetry* :—

which Dryden writes thus in the preface to his *Miscellanies*[1]:

'It was my Lord Roscommon's *Essay on Translated Verse*,' says Dryden, 'which made me uneasy, till I tried whether or no I was capable of following his rules, and of reducing the speculation into practice. For many a fair precept in poetry is like a seeming demonstration in [the] mathematicks, very specious in the diagram, but failing in the mechanick operation. I think I have generally observed his instructions: I am sure my reason is sufficiently convinced both of their truth and usefulness; which, in other words, is to confess no less a vanity than to pretend that I have, at least in some places, made examples to his rules.'

26   This declaration of Dryden will, I am afraid, be found little more than one of those cursory civilities which one author pays to another[2]; for when the sum of Lord Roscommon's precepts is collected it will not be easy to discover how they can qualify their reader for a better performance of translation than might have been attained by his own reflections.

27   He that can abstract his mind from the elegance of the poetry, and confine it to the sense of the precepts, will find no other direction than that the author should be suitable to the translator's genius; that he should be such as may deserve a translation; that he who intends to translate him should endeavour to understand him; that perspicuity should be studied, and unusual and uncouth names sparingly inserted; and that the style of the original should be copied in its elevation and depression. These are the rules that are celebrated as so definite and important; and for the delivery of which to mankind so much honour has been paid. Roscommon

---

'It only can be excused ... by the modesty of the title—*An Essay*.' *Works*, xiii. 3. For Denham's use of the word *ante*, DENHAM, 7 *n*. Addison says that some of the *Spectators* 'run out into the wildness of those compositions which go by the name of Essays.' *The Spectator*, No. 476.

[1] *The Second Miscellany*, 1685; Dryden's *Works*, xii. 282. The *Essay* appeared in 1684. That same year Dryden wrote to Tonson:—'I am of your opinion that you should reprint it, and that you may safely venture on a thousand more.' *Ib*. xviii. 105.

[2] One of Dryden's 'civilities' is outrageously ridiculous. He wrote of Roscommon:—
'How will sweet Ovid's ghost be pleased to hear
His fame augmented by a British peer.'   *Works*, xi. 29.
Addison in his *Account of the Greatest English Poets* (*post*, ADDISON, 128; *Works*, i. 25) wrote:—
'Nor must Roscommon pass neglected by,
That makes ev'n rules a noble poetry:
Rules whose deep sense and heavenly numbers show
The best of critics and of poets too.'
Addison in *The Spectator*, No. 253, calls the *Essay* 'a masterpiece in its kind.'

has indeed deserved his praises had they been given with discernment, and bestowed not on the rules themselves, but the art with which they are introduced, and the decorations with which they are adorned.

The *Essay*, though generally excellent, is not without its faults. 28 The story of the Quack, borrowed from Boileau[1], was not worth the importation; he has confounded the British and Saxon mythology:

> 'I grant that from some mossy idol oak,
>   In double rhymes, our *Thor* and *Woden* spoke[2].'

The oak, as I think Gildon has observed[3], belonged to the British druids, and Thor and Woden were Saxon deities. Of the 'double rhymes,' which he[4] so liberally supposes, he certainly had no knowledge.

His interposition of a long paragraph of blank verses is unwar- 29 rantably licentious[5]. Latin poets might as well have introduced a series of iambicks among their heroicks[6].

His next work is the translation of the *Art of Poetry*[7], which 30 has received in my opinion not less praise than it deserves[8]. Blank verse left merely to its numbers has little operation either on the ear or mind: it can hardly support itself without bold figures and striking images. A poem frigidly didactick without rhyme is so near to prose that the reader only scorns it for pretending to be verse[9].

Having disentangled himself from the difficulties of rhyme, he 31

[1] *Eng. Poets*, xv. 87; BOILEAU, *L'Art poétique*, iv. 1.

[2] *Eng. Poets*, xv. 91.

[3] In *The Laws of Poetry*, 1721, p. 343.

[4] 'Know Eusden thirsts no more for sack or praise;
He sleeps among the dull of ancient days;
Safe where no critics damn, no duns molest,
Where wretched Withers, Ward, and Gildon rest.'
POPE, *The Dunciad*, i. 293.

[5] 'He' should refer to Gildon; it means, of course, Roscommon.

[6] He calls it '*An Essay on Blank Verse out of Paradise Lost. Bk. vi.*' *Eng. Poets*, xv. 92 n.

[6] Of this poem one couplet survives:

'Immodest words admit of no defence,
For want of decency is want of sense.' *Ib.* p. 83.
The two following lines are not quite forgotten:—
'And choose an author as you choose a friend.' *Ib.* p. 82.
'The multitude is always in the wrong.' *Ib.* p. 85.

[7] *Ib.* p. 129. It appeared in 1679-80. Cunningham's *Lives of the Poets*, i. 207.

[8] Waller says of this translation:—
'Poets lose half the praise they should have got,
Could it be known what they discreetly blot.'
Eng. Poets, xvi. 175.

[9] *Ante*, MILTON, 274.

may justly be expected to give the sense of Horace with great exactness, and to suppress no subtilty of sentiment for the difficulty of expressing it. This demand, however, his translation will not satisfy; what he found obscure, I do not know that he has ever cleared.

32   Among his smaller works the Eclogue of Virgil [1] and the *Dies Iræ* are well translated, though the best line in the *Dies Iræ* is borrowed from Dryden [2]. In return, succeeding poets have borrowed from Roscommon.

33   In the verses on the Lap-dog the pronouns *thou* and *you* are offensively confounded, and the turn at the end is from Waller [3].

34   His versions of the two odes of Horace [4] are made with great liberty, which is not recompensed by much elegance or vigour.

35   His political verses [5] are spritely, and when they were written must have been very popular.

36   Of the scene of Guarini [6], and the prologue to *Pompey* [7], Mrs. Phillips, in her letters to Sir Charles Cotterel, has given the history [8].

---

[1] *Eng. Poets*, xv. 104. 'The *Silenus* [Ecl. vi] of my Lord Roscommon cannot be too much commended.' DRYDEN, *Works*, xiv. 213.

[2] The best line is :—
'In storms of guilty terror tost.'
I do not recall a corresponding line in Dryden. That poet borrowed from Roscommon in the last stanza of his *Ode on Mrs. Anne Killigrew*, which begins :—
'When in mid-air the golden trump shall sound,
To raise the nations under ground.'
Works, xi. 112.
Roscommon has :—
'And wake the nations under ground.'
Eng. Poets, xv. 121.

[3] 'How fondly human passions turn! What we then envied, now we mourn.'
ROSCOMMON, *Ib.* xv. 118.
'Under how hard a law are mortals born !
Whom now we envy, we anon must mourn.'
WALLER, *Ib.* xvi. 103.

[4] *Ib.* xv. 111, 126.

[5] I have restored the reading of the first edition. In the 1783 edition, it is 'poetical verses.' The title is :—*The*

Ghost of the Old House of Commons to the New One, appointed to meet at Oxford [in 1681]. *Ib.* p. 116.

[6] *Pastor Fido*, v. 2. *Ib.* p. 113.

[7] *Prologue to Pompey, a Tragedy, Translated by Mrs. Cath. Philips from the French of Monsieur Corneille. Ib.* 123.

[8] *Letters from Orinda to Poliarchus*, 1705, p. 79. Cotterel was Master of the Ceremonies. Evelyn's *Diary*, ii. 38. Katherine Philips was born in Jan. 1631-2, and died in 1664. 'She tooke sermons *verbatim* when she was but 10 yeares old.' AUBREY, *Brief Lives*, ii. 153. 'She was esteemed the most applauded poetess of our nation.' Her works were published in 1667 under the title of *Poems by the most deservedly admired Mrs. Katherine Philipps, the matchless Orinda. Ath. Oxon.* iii. 787.
Cowley celebrated her in an ode entitled *On Orinda's Poems* and in another on her death. *Eng. Poets*, vii. 206, 255.
'Eliza's glory lives in Spenser's song ;   [Orinda young.'
And Cowley's verse keeps fair
PRIOR, *Eng. Poets*, xxxii. 154.
Jeremy Taylor dedicated to her

'Lord Roscommon,' says she, 'is certainly one of the most promising young noblemen [the most hopeful young nobleman] in Ireland. He has paraphrased a Psalm¹ admirably [well] and a scene of *Pastor Fido* very finely, in some [many] places much better than Sir Richard Fanshaw². This was undertaken merely in [This last he undertook purely out of] compliment to me, who happened to [having heard me] say that it was the best scene in [the] Italian, and the worst in [the] English. He was only [but] two hours about it. It begins thus:

> "Dear happy groves, and you the dark retreat
> Of silent horrour, Rest's eternal seat."'

From these lines, which are since somewhat mended³, it **37** appears that he did not think a work of two hours fit to endure the eye of criticism without revisal.

When Mrs Phillips was in Ireland, some ladies that had seen **38** her translation of *Pompey* resolved to bring it on the stage at Dublin, and, to promote their design, Lord Roscommon gave them a prologue, and Sir Edward Dering⁴ an Epilogue ; 'which,' says she, 'are the best performances of those kinds I ever saw.' If this is not criticism, it is at least gratitude. The thought of bringing Cæsar and Pompey into Ireland, the only Country over which Cæsar never had any power, is lucky⁵.

Of Roscommon's works the judgement of the publick seems **39** to be right. He is elegant, but not great ; he never labours after exquisite beauties, and he seldom falls into gross faults. His versification is smooth, but rarely vigorous, and his rhymes are remarkably exact. He improved taste if he did not enlarge

---

his *Discourse of Friendship*—'To the most ingenious and excellent M. K. P. [Mrs. Katherine Phillips].' Taylor's *Works*, 1864, i. 69. See also *post*, WALLER, 147 ; POPE, 171. Campbell gives two specimens of her poetry. *British Poets*, p. 212. For her family see *N. & Q.* 2 S. v. 202.

¹ *Psalm* 148 ; *Eng. Poets*, xv. 98.
² *Ante*, DENHAM, 25.
³ 'Ah, happy grove ! dark and secure retreat
    Of sacred silence, rest's eternal seat.' *Eng. Poets*, xv. 113.
⁴ Of Surrendon, Kent. Evelyn's

Diary, ii. 149. 'April 11, 1665. At noon dined at the Sun, behind the 'Change, with Sir Edward Deering ..., we having made a contract with Sir Edward this day about timber.' PEPYS, *Diary*, iii. 3.
⁵ 'When he the Thames, the Danube, and the Nile
    Had stain'd with blood, peace flourish'd in this isle ;
    And you alone may boast you never saw
    Caesar till now, and now can give him law.'
Prologue to Pompey, 1663 ; *Eng. Poets*, xv. 124.

knowledge, and may be numbered among the benefactors to English literature [1].

[1] 'His *Essay on Translated Verse* and his translation of Horace's *Art of Poetry* have great merit; in the rest of his poems there are scarce above four lines that are striking, as these:—

"The law appear'd with Maynard at their head,
In legal murder none so deeply read."

And these in the apparition of Tom Ross to his pupil the Duke of Monmouth:—

"Like Samuel, at thy necromantic call,
I rise to tell thee, God has left thee, Saul."' WALPOLE, *Works*, i. 518.

The first couplet is from *The Ghost of the Old House of Commons*. The first line runs:—

'The robe was summon'd, Maynard in the head,
In legal murder none so deeply read.' *Eng. Poets*, xv. 117.

The second couplet is from *Ross's Ghost*. *Ib.* p. 125.

OTWAY

1

O F THOMAS OTWAY, one of the first names in the
English drama [1], little is known [2]; nor is there any part
of that little which his biographer can take pleasure in relating.

He was born at Trottin [3] in Sussex, March 3, 1651, the son
of Mr. Humphry Otway, rector of Woolbedding. From Win-
chester-school, where he was educated, he was entered in 1669
a commoner of Christ-church [4], but left the university without
a degree; whether for want of money, or from impatience of
academical restraint, or mere eagerness to mingle with the world
is not known.

It seems likely that he was in hope of being busy and conspicuous; for he went to London and commenced player [5],

[1] 'Johnson always appeared not to be sufficiently sensible of the merit of Otway.' Boswell's *Johnson*, iv. 21.

[2] Johnson has apparently drawn on *Biog. Brit.* Supplement, p. 137, for Otway's *Life*. The poet, in the Dedication of *Venice Preserved*, says: —'A steady faith and loyalty to my Prince was all the inheritance my father left me.' He describes himself in his *Poet's Complaint* (*Eng. Poets*, xv. 178):—

'I am a wretch of honest race;
My parents not obscure, nor high in
     titles were,
     They left me heir to no disgrace.
My father was (a thing now rare)
Loyal and brave, my mother chaste
     and fair.
The pledge of marriage-vows was
     only I;
Alone I liv'd, their much lov'd fonded
     boy: [high
They gave me generous education;
They strove to raise my mind, and
     with it grew their joy.
The sages that instructed me in arts
     And knowledge oft would praise
          my parts,   [hearts.'
     And cheer my parents' loving

A writer in *Gent. Mag.* 1745, p. 99, says:—'His person was of the middle size, inclinable to fatness. He had a thoughtful, speaking eye, and that was all.'

[3] Trotton. The river Arun runs by it.
'Wild Arun too has heard thy strains,
     And Echo, 'midst my native plains,
          Been sooth'd by Pity's lute.
There first the wren thy myrtles
          shed
On gentlest Otway's infant head,
     To him thy cell was shown.'
COLLINS, *Ode to Pity, Eng. Poets*, lviii. 15.

[4] *Ath. Oxon.* iv. 168. He matriculated on May 27, 1669, aged 17, but left Oxford in 1672, without a degree. *Dict. Nat. Biog.*

[5] 'The world was wide, but whither
          should I go?
     I whose blooming hopes all wither'd
          were,
     Who'd little fortune, and a deal
          of care?
     To Britain's great metropolis I
          stray'd,
     Where Fortune's general game is
          play'd.' *Eng. Poets*, xv. 179.

but found himself unable to gain any reputation on the stage[1].

4   This kind of inability he shared with Shakespeare and Jonson, as he shared likewise some of their excellencies. It seems reasonable to expect that a great dramatick poet should without difficulty become a great actor; that he who can feel could express; that he who can excite passion should exhibit with great readiness its external modes: but since experience has fully proved that of those powers, whatever be their affinity, one may be possessed in a great degree by him who has very little of the other, it must be allowed that they depend upon different faculties or on different use of the same faculty; that the actor must have a pliancy of mien, a flexibility of countenance, and a variety of tones, which the poet may be easily supposed to want; or that the attention of the poet and the player have been differently employed—the one has been considering thought, and the other action; one has watched the heart, and the other contemplated the face.

5   Though he could not gain much notice as a player, he felt in himself such powers as might qualify for a dramatick author; and in 1675, his twenty-fifth year, produced *Alcibiades*, a tragedy; whether from the *Alcibiade* of Palaprat[2] I have not means to enquire. Langbain, the great detector of plagiarism, is silent[3].

6   In 1677 he published *Titus and Berenice*, translated from Racine[4], with *The Cheats of Scapin* from Molière[5], and in 1678 *Friendship in Fashion*, a comedy, which, whatever might be its

---

[1] 'In *The Jealous Bridegroom* by Mrs. Bhen [Behn], Mr. Otway having an inclination to turn actor, Mrs. Bhen gave him the King in the play for a probation part; but he being not used to the stage, the full house put him to such a sweat and tremendous agony, being dasht, spoilt him for an actor.' DOWNES, *Roscius Anglicanus*, 1789, p. 43.

[2] In *Les Œuvres de Palaprat*, 1697, *Alcibiade* is not included. Neither is it mentioned in his life in *Nouv. Biog. gén.*
Voltaire says of Brueys: 'La petite comédie du *Grondeur*, supérieure à toutes les farces de Molière, et celle de *L'Avocat Patelin*, . . . le feront connaître tant qu'il y aura en France un théâtre. Palaprat l'aida dans ces deux jolies pièces.' *Œuvres*, xvii. 58.

[3] In his *Account of the English Dramatic Poets*. See *post*, DRYDEN, 25, 29, 92.

[4] 'Rapin,' which is found in the first and third editions of the *Lives*, must be a slip of Johnson's pen for Racine. Otway's play is taken from that poet's *Bérénice*, which was brought out in 1670—the same year as Corneille's *Tite et Bérénice*.

[5] 'This play, with the farce, being perfectly well acted had good success.' *Roscius Anglicanus*, p. 48.

first reception [1], was, upon its revival at Drury-lane in 1749, hissed off the stage for immorality and obscenity [2].

Want of morals or of decency did not in those days exclude 7 any man from the company of the wealthy and the gay if he brought with him any powers of entertainment; and Otway is said to have been at this time a favourite companion of the dissolute wits [3]. But, as he who desires no virtue in his companion has no virtue in himself, those whom Otway frequented had no purpose of doing more for him than to pay his reckoning. They desired only to drink and laugh; their fondness was without benevolence, and their familiarity without friendship. Men of wit, says one of Otway's biographers, received at that time no favour from the Great but to share their riots; 'from which they were dismissed again to their own narrow circumstances. Thus they languished in poverty without the support of innocence [4].'

[1] 'It was acted with general applause.' LANGBAINE, *Dram. Poets*, p. 398.

[2] It was revived on Jan. 22, 1749-50. Cunningham's *Lives of the Poets*, i. 212.

Garrick had been manager of the theatre for more than two years. In the Prologue at the opening in 1747, written for him by Johnson, he had said of 'the wits of Charles':—

'Themselves they studied; as they felt, they writ;
Intrigue was plot, obscenity was wit.

.   .   .   .   .

Yet bards like these aspir'd to lasting praise,
And proudly hop'd to pimp in future days.
Their cause was gen'ral, their supports were strong;
Their slaves were willing, and their reign was long;
Till shame regain'd the post that sense betray'd,
And virtue call'd oblivion to her aid.'
Johnson's *Works*, i. 23.

Of Garrick's shameful revival of this play no mention is made by his biographers Davies and Murphy. In 1749 he wrote to Foote, who had heard that he was to be taken off in the play:—'The character of Melagene, exclusive of some little immoralities, which can never be applied to you, is that of a very smart, pleasant, conceited fellow, and a good mimic.' *Garrick Corres.* i. 55.

[3] 'I miss'd the brave and wise, and in their stead
On every sort of vanity I fed.
Gay coxcombs, cowards, knaves, and prating fools,
Bullies of o'er-grown bulks and little souls,
Gamesters, half wits and spend-thrifts (such as think
Mischievous midnight frolics, bred by drink,
    Are gallantry and wit,
Because to their lewd understandings fit)
Were those wherewith two years at least I spent.'
OTWAY, *The Poet's Complaint, Eng. Poets*, xv. 179.

[4] 'From whence they were to return to their own narrow circumstances with the loss of their modesty and virtue. Thus they languished in poverty without the support of innocence.' Otway's *Works*, 1712, Pref.

In Johnson's *Works*, vii. 174, 'imminence,' which, though it gives no sense, is the reading of both the first and third editions [1783], is changed into 'eminence.' Both are clearly misprints for 'innocence.'

Savage suffered from the same treatment as Otway. *Post*, SAVAGE, 97.

8   Some exception however must be made. The Earl of Ply-
mouth[1], one of King Charles's natural sons, procured for him
a cornet's commission in some troops then sent into Flanders.
But Otway did not prosper in his military character; for he soon
left his commission behind him, whatever was the reason, and
came back to London in extreme indigence[2], which Rochester
mentions with merciless insolence in the *Session of the Poets*[3]:

> 'Tom Otway came next, Tom Shadwell's dear zany,
> And swears for heroicks he writes best of any;
> *Don Carlos* his pockets so amply had fill'd,
> That his mange was quite cured, and his lice were all kill'd.
>
> . . . .
>
> But Apollo had seen his face on the stage,   ⎞
> And prudently did not think fit to engage   ⎬
> The scum of a play-house, for the prop of an age.' ⎠

9   *Don Carlos*, from which he is represented as having received so
much benefit, was played in 1675. It appears, by the Lampoon,
to have had great success, and is said to have been played thirty
nights together. This however it is reasonable to doubt, as so long
a continuance of one play upon the stage is a very wide deviation
from the practice of that time; when the ardour for theatrical
entertainments was not yet diffused through the whole people,
and the audience, consisting nearly of the same persons, could be
drawn together only by variety[4].

---

[1] 'He was carousing one day with Lord Pl—th, and then starving a month in low company at an ale-house on Tower Hill.' *Gent. Mag.* 1745, p. 99. The earl died, without heir, in 1680. Courthope's *Hist. Peerage*, 1857, p. 385.

[2] He mentions his being 'cashiered' in the Epilogue to *Caius Marius*, and continues:—

> 'Therefore, when he received that fatal doom,
> This play came forth, in hopes his friends would come
> To help a poor disbanded soldier home.'
>   Davies's *Dram. Misc.* iii. 193.

[3] The title of his poem is *A Trial of the Poets for the Bays, Eng. Poets*, xv. 41. Otway, in his *Poet's Complaint*, attacks
>   ' that blundering sot
> Who a late *Session of the Poets* wrote.'

He describes the writer as one who
> '. . . for old shoes and scraps repeats old plays.' *Ib.* p. 184.

Rochester is probably described in the next lines:—
> 'Then next there follow'd, to make up the throng,
> Lord Lampoon and Monsieur Song.'

He had been Otway's patron. See the Preface to *Don Carlos* and the Dedication of *Titus and Berenice*, quoted in Malone's *Dryden*, i. 122. Rochester turned on Dryden as he turned on Otway. *Post*, DRYDEN, 62. For an earlier *Session of the Poets*, see *ante*, COWLEY, 41.

[4] 'All the parts being admirably acted it lasted successively ten days; it got more money than any preceding modern tragedy.' *Roscius Anglicanus*, p. 46.

The Orphan was exhibited in 1680. This is one of the few 10 plays that keep possession of the stage[1], and has pleased for almost a century through all the vicissitudes of dramatick fashion. Of this play nothing new can easily be said. It is a domestick tragedy drawn from middle life. Its whole power is upon the affections, for it is not written with much comprehension of thought or elegance of expression. But if the heart is interested, many other beauties may be wanting, yet not be missed[2].

The same year produced *The History and Fall of Caius* 11 *Marius*; much of which is borrowed from the *Romeo and Juliet* of Shakespeare[3].

In 1683 was published the first, and next year the second, parts 12 of *The Soldier's Fortune*[4], two comedies now forgotten; and in 1685[5] his last and greatest dramatick work, *Venice preserved*, a tragedy, which still continues to be one of the favourites of the publick[6], notwithstanding the want of morality in the original design[7], and the despicable scenes of vile comedy with which he

[1] Macready acted in it in 1811. Macready's *Reminiscences*, i. 53.

[2] 'Mrs. Barry told me that she never pronounced those three words in *The Orphan*, "Ah! poor Castalio," without teares.' GILDON, *Complete Art of Poetry*, 1718, i. 290. Voltaire, after condemning the play as revolting, continues:—'L'auteur dédie sa pièce à la duchesse de Cleveland; avec la même naïveté qu'il a écrit sa tragédie, il félicite cette dame d'avoir eu deux enfans de Charles II.' *Œuvres*, xlii. 149.

[3] Langbaine instances 'the characters of Marius Junior, and Lavinia the Nurse, and Sulpitius; which last is carried on to the end of the play, though Mr. Dryden says in his *Postscript to Granada* [*post*, DRYDEN, 49; *Works*, iv. 239] "that Shakespeare said himself that he was forced to kill Mercutio in the third act to prevent being killed by him."' *Dram. Poets*, p. 397.

'March 1, 1661-2. *Romeo and Juliet* is a play of itself the worst that ever I heard.' PEPYS, *Diary*, i. 330. For nearly eighty years it lay neglected by the actors, till Garrick brought it out in 1748, with the catastrophe rendered more affecting. *Writers and Readers*, by G. B. Hill, p. 62.

Langbaine however said that 'it is accounted among the best of Shakespeare's plays.' *Dram. Poets*, p. 462.

[4] In 1676 *The Soldier's Fortune*, and Durfey's *Fond Husband*, 'took extraordinary well, and being perfectly acted got the company great reputation and profit.' *Roscius Anglicanus*, p. 46. The former was printed in 1681. The second part was entitled *The Atheist, or The Second Part of the Soldier's Fortune*. Jacob's *Poet. Reg.* i. 196.

[5] It was printed in 1682.

[6] It, *The Orphan*, and Southerne's *Fatal Marriage* 'took above all the modern plays that succeeded [till 1706].' *Roscius Anglicanus*, p. 48. In *Brit. Mus. Cata.* there are twenty-three editions of *Venice Preserved* in English, four in French, two in Dutch, and one in German, Italian, and Russian: Tonson paid £15 for the copyright. Davies's *Dram. Misc.* iii. 268.

[7] 'It has been observed that Otway has founded his tragedy on so wrong a plot that the greatest characters in it are those of rebels and traitors.' ADDISON, *The Spectator*, No. 39. Addison adds that 'the sounding of the clock in *Venice Preserved* makes the hearts of the whole audience

has diversified his tragick action [1]. By comparing this with his *Orphan* it will appear that his images were by time become stronger, and his language more energetick. The striking passages are in every mouth [2]; and the publick seems to judge rightly of the faults and excellencies of this play, that it is the work of a man not attentive to decency nor zealous for virtue; but of one who conceived forcibly and drew originally by consulting nature in his own breast.

13 Together with those plays he wrote the poems which are in the late collection, and translated from the French the *History of the Triumvirate* [3].

14 All this was performed before he was thirty-four years old; for

quake.' *The Spectator*, No. 44. I remember how my heart quaked more than fifty years ago, when I saw the play at Sadler's Wells Theatre.

[1] 'In performance it is purged of these despicable scenes.' *Biog. Dram.* iii. 377.

'Il est désagréable qu'on ne nous ait pas traduit fidèlement cette *Venise*; on nous a privé d'un sénateur qui mord les jambes de sa maîtresse, qui fait le chien, qui aboie, et qu'on chasse à coups de fouet.' VOLTAIRE, *Œuvres*, xlii. 149.

'Johnson,' writes Northcote, 'in his peremptory manner pronounced that there was not forty good lines to be found in *Venice Preserved*. Goldsmith asserted that, notwithstanding, it was of all tragedies the one nearest equal to Shakespeare. "Poh!" said Johnson. "What stuff in these lines!—

'What feminine tales hast thou been list'ning to [ache got
Of unair'd shirts, catarrhs and tooth-
By thin-soled shoes? [Act iii. sc. 2]."'
"True," said Goldsmith; "to be sure, that is very like to Shakespeare."' S. Gwynne's *Memorials of an Eighteenth Century Painter*, p. 97.

Goldsmith, in *The Bee*, No. 8, calls 'Otway, next to Shakespeare, the greatest genius England ever produced in tragedy.' *Works*, iii. 127.

'Who sees not that the Grave-digger in *Hamlet*, the Fool in *Lear*, have a kind of correspondency to, and fall in with, the subjects which they seem to interrupt, while the comic stuff in *Venice Preserved*, and the doggerel nonsense of the Cook

and his poisoning associates in the *Rollo* of Beaumont and Fletcher, are pure irrelevant, impertinent discords.' LAMB, *Poems*, &c. 1888, p. 281.

'The comic scenes are particularly good. It is they alone which account for, and go near to justify the conspiracy; for we see in them how utterly unfit for government the Senate had become.' GOETHE, quoted in H. C. Robinson's *Diary*, 1869, i. 187.

[2] They are, I think, all forgotten. [Yet here and there a line like, 'Angels are painted fair to look like you' (*Venice Preserved*, i. 1), may be said still to live.]

'When, in 1794, the Rev. Wm. Jackson fell in the dock from poison, previous to being sentenced to death for high treason, he pressed the hand of his counsel, muttering, "We have deceived the Senate." This, quoted from *Venice Preserved*, shows the deep impression that powerful play had produced. This incident is described in *Secret Service under Pitt*, p. 192.' *N. & Q.* 8 S. vi. 38. They are Pierre's dying words in the last act.

'Ours is a trophy which will not
    decay   [Moor,
With the Rialto; Shylock, and the
And Pierre, cannot be swept or
    worn away—
The keystones of the arch! though
    all were o'er,   [shore.'
For us repeopled were the solitary
        BYRON, *Childe Harold*, iv. 4.

[3] *Histoire des deux Triumvirats*, by S. de Broé. Otway's translation appeared the year after his death.

he died April 14, 1685[1], in a manner which I am unwilling to mention. Having been compelled by his necessities to contract debts, and hunted, as is supposed, by the terriers of the law, he retired to a publick house on Tower-hill, where he is said to have died of want[2]; or, as it is related by one of his biographers[3], by swallowing, after a long fast, a piece of bread which charity had supplied. He went out, as is reported, almost naked, in the rage of hunger, and, finding a gentleman in a neighbouring coffee-house, asked him for a shilling. The gentleman gave him a guinea, and Otway going away bought a roll, and was choaked with the first mouthful. All this, I hope, is not true; and there is this ground of better hope, that Pope, who lived near enough to be well informed, relates in Spence's memorials that he died of a fever caught by violent pursuit of a thief that had robbed one of his friends[4]. But that indigence and its concomitants, sorrow and despondency, pressed hard upon him has never been denied, whatever immediate cause might bring him to the grave.

Of the poems which the late collection admits, the longest is 15 *The Poet's Complaint of his Muse*[5], part of which I do not understand[6]; and in that which is less obscure I find little to commend. The language is often gross, and the numbers are harsh. Otway had not much cultivated versification[7], nor much replenished his

---

[1] *Ath. Oxon.* iv. 170.

[2] In a note at the end of *The Tatler*, May 9, 1710 (ed. 1789, iii. 169), is the following:—'At Drury Lane Theatre on Thursday, May 11, *Caius Marius*, a Trag. by T. Otway, acted at the Duke's Theatre. 4 to. 1680. Its ingenious author, after suffering severely for his want of oeconomy, died in a spunging-house on Tower Hill, known by the sign of a Bull, about five years after the publication of this play at the age of 35.'

Wood wrote of George Peele:— 'When or where he died I cannot tell; for so it is, and always hath been, that most poets die poor and consequently obscurely, and a hard matter it is to trace them to their graves.' *Ath. Oxon.* i. 688.

[3] *Cibber's Lives*, ii. 334.

[4] This anecdote is not in the first edition. Spence had it, not from Pope, but Dennis, who was twenty-eight when Otway died. 'Otway had an intimate friend (one Blackstone) who was shot; the murderer fled towards Dover, and Otway pursued him. In his return he drank water when violently heated, and so got a fever, which was the death of him.' Spence's *Anec.* p. 44.

'When he died he had about him the copy of a tragedy, which, it seems, he had sold for a trifle to Bentley the bookseller. I have seen an advertisement at the end of one of L'Estrange's political papers offering a reward to any one who should bring it to his shop.' GOLDSMITH, *Works*, iii. 128. He had written four acts only. See *ib. n.* for a copy of the advertisement in *The Observator* of Nov. 27, 1686.

[5] *Eng. Poets*, xv. 175. Printed in 1680.

[6] Rochester calls him 'puzzling Otway.' *Ib.* xv. 63.

[7] 'Not but the tragic spirit was our own,
    And full in Shakespeare, fair in Otway shone;

mind with general knowledge. His principal power was in moving the passions, to which Dryden in his latter years left an illustrious testimony [1]. He appears, by some of his verses, to have been a zealous royalist, and had what was in those times the common reward of loyalty ; he lived and died neglected [2].

But Otway fail'd to polish or refine,
And fluent Shakespeare scarce effac'd a line.'
POPE, *Imit. Hor., Epis.* ii. 1. 276.
[1] In his preface to Fresnoy's *Art of Painting*. JOHNSON. It was published in 1695. Dryden writes of the power of expressing the passions :—'We call it the gift of our Apollo—not to be obtained by pains or study, if we are not born to it ; for the motions which are studied are never so natural as those which break out in the height of a real passion. Mr. Otway possessed this part as thoroughly as any of the ancients or moderns.' *Works*, xvii. 325 ; *post*, DRYDEN, 325. For Fresnoy see *ib.* 146.
'Otway in the Preface to *Don Carlos* (1676) alludes to Dryden :— "*Don Carlos* never failed to draw tears from the eyes of the auditors ; I mean those whose souls were capable of so noble a pleasure . . . though a *certain writer*, that shall be nameless (but you may guess at him by what follows), being asked his opinion of the play, very gravely *cock'd*, and cried :—'I'gad, he knew not a line in it he would be author of.' "' Malone's *Dryden*, i. 501.
'Otway has admirably succeeded in the tender and melting part of his tragedies.' ADDISON, *The Spectator*, No. 39. 'Tender' is the epithet often applied to Otway. In Gay's *Three Hours after Marriage*, 1717, pp. 19, 22, the writer of a tragedy and a player talk of 'the tender Otway'; 'the tenderness of Otway.'
Thomson, in the *Prologue to Tancred and Sigismunda*, mentions 'soft Otway's tender woe.' Voltaire twice speaks of him as known in England as 'le tendre Otway.' *Œuvres*, xlii. 129, 144. 'I once asked Dr. Johnson if he did not think Otway a good painter of tender scenes, and he replied, "Sir, he is all tenderness."'

DR. BURNEY, *Hist. of Music*, 1789, iii. 598 *n.*
'Otway has written but two tragedies, out of six, that are pathetic. I believe he did it without much design ; as Lillo has done in his *Barnwell*. 'Tis a talent of nature rather than an effect of judgment to write so movingly.' POPE, Spence's *Anec.* p. 215.
'Otway's excellencies lay in painting directly from nature, in catching every emotion just as it rises from the soul, and in all the powers of the moving and pathetic.' GOLDSMITH, iii. 127.
Borrow, joining Otway with Milton and Butler, says :—'They have left a fame behind them which shall never die.' *Lavengro*, 1888, p. 133.
[2] Otway, dedicating *Venice Preserved* to the king's mistress, the Duchess of Portsmouth, wrote :— 'When I had enemies, that with malicious power kept back and shaded me from those royal beams whose warmth is all I have or hope to live by, your noble pity and compassion found me where I was far cast backward from my blessing ; down in the rear of fortune ; called me up, and placed me in the shine, and I have felt its comfort.'
Hume ends his *Hist. of England* with the following sentence:—'Otway, though a professed royalist, could not even procure bread by his writings ; and he had the singular fate of dying literally of hunger. These incidents throw a great stain on the memory of Charles, who had discernment, loved genius, was liberal of money, but attained not the praise of true generosity.'
For the neglect of Butler see *ante*, BUTLER, 18, and of 'Dr. Hodges who, in the height of the Great Plague, continued in London,' see Boswell's *Johnson*, ii. 341 *n.*

WALLER[1]

EDMUND WALLER was born on the third of March, 1605, at Colshill in Hertfordshire[2]. His father was Robert Waller, Esquire, of Agmondesham in Buckinghamshire, whose family was originally a branch of the Kentish Wallers[3], and his mother was the daughter of John Hampden, of Hampden in the same county, and sister to Hampden, the zealot of rebellion[4].

His father died while he was yet an infant, but left him an 2 yearly income of three thousand five hundred pounds[5], which, rating together the value of money and the customs of life, we may reckon more than equivalent to ten thousand at the present time.

He was educated by the care of his mother at Eaton[6], and 3

[1] 'Waller,' wrote Johnson, 'never had any critical examination before.' *John. Letters*, ii. 68 ; *ante*, COWLEY, 1 *n*. Among Johnson's authorities for this *Life* are the *Life of Waller* prefixed to his *Poems upon Several Occasions*, 1711, and *Observations on some of Mr. Waller's Poems* in Fenton's *Works of Waller*, 1729 (my references are to the edition of 1744).

'In the Life of Waller, Johnson gives a distinct and animated narrative of publick affairs in that variegated period, with strong yet nice touches of character ; and having a fair opportunity to display his political principles, does it with an unqualified manly confidence, and satisfies his readers how nobly he might have executed a *Tory History* of his country.' Boswell's *Johnson*, iv. 39.

[2] 'He was born at Winchmore-hill in the parish of Agmundesham, commonly called Amersam [now Amersham], in Bucks, on March 13, 1605-6.' *Ath. Oxon.* iii. 46. 'Though Coleshill be in Agmundesham 'tis in the county of Hertford.' *Life*, p. 3. Winchmoor Hill is close to Coleshill. 'He was baptized on March 9.' Cunningham's *Lives of the Poets*, i. 219.

[3] For his grandfather's will see *N. & Q.* 1 S. v. 619. The Kentish Wallers were 'of Groombridge and Speldhurst, near Tunbridge Wells.' Cunningham's *Lives of the Poets*, i. 219.

[4] Hampden's father, William by name, not John, and Waller's mother were children of Griffith Hampden. Hampden's mother was a daughter of Sir Henry Cromwell, the Protector's grandfather. Hampden therefore was first cousin to Oliver Cromwell and to Edmund Waller. *Ath. Oxon.* iii. 47 *n*.

'Waller derived his poetick witt from the Hamdens ; several of them have been poets.' AUBREY, *Brief Lives*, ii. 279. Johnson in his *Dictionary* defines *zealot* as 'one passionately ardent in any cause. Generally used in dispraise.'

[5] *Life*, p. 3. 'His paternall estate and by his first wife was 3,000 *li.* per annum.' *Brief Lives*, ii. 274.

[6] 'He sayes that he was bred under severall ill, dull, ignorant school-masters, till he went to Mr. Dobson at [High] Wickham, who was a good schoolmaster, and had been an Eaton scholar.' *Ib.* ii. 278. In the *Life of Waller*, p. 7, it is said he went to Eton. It is accepted at Eton that he was educated there ; but, on inquiry, I cannot learn that there is any proof.

removed afterwards to King's College in Cambridge[1]. He was sent to parliament in his eighteenth, if not in his sixteenth year[2], and frequented the court of James the First, where he heard a very remarkable conversation, which the writer of the Life prefixed to his Works, who seems to have been well informed of facts, though he may sometimes err in chronology, has delivered as indubitably certain[3].

4 'He found Dr. Andrews, bishop of Winchester, and Dr. Neale, bishop of Durham, standing behind his Majesty's chair; and there happened something [very] extraordinary,' continues this writer, 'in the conversation those prelates had with the king, on which Mr. Waller did often reflect. His Majesty asked the bishops, "My Lords, cannot I take my subjects money, when I want it, without all this formality of [in] parliament?" The bishop of Durham readily answered, "God forbid, Sir, but you should: you are the breath of our nostrils." Whereupon the King turned and said to the bishop of Winchester, "Well, my Lord, what say you?" "Sir," replied the bishop, "I have no skill to judge of parliamentary cases." The King answered, "No put-offs, my Lord; answer me presently." "Then, Sir," said he, "I think it is lawful for you to take my brother Neale's money; for he offers it." Mr. Waller said the company was pleased with this answer, and the wit of it seemed to affect the King; for, a certain lord coming in soon after, his Majesty cried out, "Oh, my lord, they say you lig with my Lady." "No, Sir," says his Lordship in confusion, "but I like her company, because she has so much wit." "Why then," says the King, "do you not lig with my Lord of Winchester there?"'

5 Waller's political and poetical life began nearly together. In his eighteenth year he wrote the poem that appears first in his works, on the Prince's Escape at St. Andero[4], a piece which justifies the observation made by one of his editors, that he attained, by a felicity like instinct, a style which perhaps will

---

[1] He entered on March 22, 1620; there is no record of his taking his degree. *Dict. Nat. Biog.* [He was admitted at Lincoln's Inn on July 3, 1622. *Linc. Inn Admission Reg.* i. 190. There seems to be no record of his being called to the bar, but in 1628 the letting of his chambers was before the Benchers. *Black Books of Linc. Inn,* ii. 277.]

[2] *Life,* p. 5. Pleading for his life before the House of Commons (*post,* WALLER, 60) he said:—'If you look on my education, it hath been almost from my childhood in this House.' Fenton's *Waller,* p. 278. See also *post,* WALLER, 92. He is reported as having said on Jan. 28, 1677–8:—'I have sat here fifty years.' *Parl. Hist.* iv. 904. There is no proof that he entered before Feb. 1623–4. *Dict. Nat. Biog.*

[3] *Life,* p. 8. Hume quotes this anecdote in his *History,* vi. 75.

[4] *Post,* WALLER, 123. *Eng. Poets,* xvi. 17. It was on Sept. 12, 1623, that the prince escaped drowning at Santander. Gardiner's *Hist. of Eng.* v. 120.

never be obsolete; and that 'were we to judge only [barely] by the wording, we could not know what was wrote at twenty, and what at fourscore¹.' His versification was in his first essay such as it appears in his last performance². By the perusal of Fairfax's translation of Tasso, to which, as Dryden relates³, he confessed himself indebted for the smoothness of his numbers, and by his own nicety of observation, he had already formed such a system of metrical harmony as he never afterwards much needed or much endeavoured to improve⁴. Denham corrected his numbers by experience, and gained ground gradually upon the ruggedness of his age; but what was acquired by Denham was inherited by Waller.

The next poem, of which the subject seems to fix the time, is 6 supposed by Mr. Fenton to be the Address to the Queen, which he considers as congratulating her arrival, in Waller's twentieth year⁵. He is apparently mistaken; for the mention of the nation's obligations to her frequent pregnancy proves that it was written when she had brought many children⁶. We have therefore no date of any other poetical production before that which the murder of the Duke of Buckingham occasioned⁷: the steadiness with which the King received the news in the chapel deserved indeed to be rescued from oblivion.

Neither of these pieces that seem to carry their own dates 7

---

¹ From the preface to the second part of Waller's *Poems*, 1690, reprinted in Fenton's *Waller*, p. 289.

² If we have this poem as he wrote it (of which there is no proof, *post*, WALLER, 7), Milton was but fourteen, Denham eight, and Cowley five when he was writing such verses as the following: —

'He rent the crown from vanquish'd
   Henry's head;
Rais'd the White Rose, and trampled on the Red.
  .   .   .   .   .   .
With the sweet sound of this harmonious lay,
About the keel delighted dolphins
   play.' *Eng. Poets*, xvi. 17-18.
The first collection of his poems appeared in 1645.

³ Preface to his *Fables*. JOHNSON. 'Many besides myself have heard our famous Waller own that he derived the harmony of his numbers from *Godfrey of Bulloigne*, which was turned into English by Mr. Fairfax.' DRYDEN, *Works*, xi. 210. See also *Life*, p. 65.

⁴ 'When he was a brisque young sparke, and first studyed poetry, "Methought," said he, "I never saw a good copie of English verses; they want smoothnes; then I began to essay."' AUBREY, *Brief Lives*, ii. 275. *Post*, WALLER, 142.

⁵ The queen arrived on June 12, 1625.

⁶ The mistake is Johnson's, who has confused two poems — one *To the Queen*, the other *Of the Queen*. The first was written to congratulate her arrival; in the second 'the nation's obligations' are thus expressed: —

'Joy of our age and safety of the next,
For which so oft thy fertile womb is
   vext.' *Eng. Poets*, xvi. 30, 34.

⁷ On Aug. 23, 1628. *Eng. Poets*, xvi. 23; *post*, WALLER, 124.

could have been the sudden effusion of fancy. In the verses on the Prince's escape, the prediction of his marriage with the princess of France must have been written after the event[1]; in the other, the promises of the King's kindness to the descendants of Buckingham[2], which could not be properly praised till it had appeared by its effects, shew that time was taken for revision and improvement. It is not known that they were published till they appeared long afterwards with other poems[3].

8   Waller was not one of those idolaters of praise who cultivate their minds at the expence of their fortunes. Rich as he was by inheritance, he took care early to grow richer by marrying Mrs. Banks, a great heiress in the city[4], whom the interest of the court was employed to obtain for Mr. Crofts[5]. Having brought him a son, who died young, and a daughter, who was afterwards married to Mr. Dormer of Oxfordshire[6], she died in childbed, and left him a widower of about five and twenty, gay and wealthy, to please himself with another marriage.

9   Being too young to resist beauty, and probably too vain to think himself resistible, he fixed his heart, perhaps half fondly and half ambitiously, upon the Lady Dorothea Sidney, eldest daughter of the Earl of Leicester, whom he courted by all the poetry in which Sacharissa is celebrated: the name is derived from the Latin appellation of *sugar*, and implies, if it means any thing, a spiritless mildness and dull good-nature, such as excites rather tenderness than esteem, and such as, though always treated with kindness, is never honoured or admired[7].

10   Yet he describes Sacharissa as a sublime predominating beauty, of lofty charms and imperious influence, on whom he looks with

[1] The poet describes how Charles,
'His loins yet full of ungot princes, all
His glory in the bud, lets nothing fall
That argues fear; if any thought annoys
The Gallant Youth, 'tis love's untasted joys;
And dear remembrance of that fatal glance
For which he lately pawn'd his heart in France.' *Eng. Poets*, xvi. 20.
[2] *Ib.* p. 24.
[3] The first volume of his *Poems* appeared in 1645, when he was abroad. In an edition published in 1664 he complained of 'the many and gross faults' of this first publication, which had been made without his consent. Fenton's *Waller*, p. 285; *N. & Q.* 5 S. ix. 333.
[4] On July 15, 1631. Cunningham's *Lives of the Poets*, i. 265.
[5] *Ante*, DENHAM, 15; *post*, WALLER, 91.
[6] *Life*, p. 18.
[7] 'Sacharissa is a name which recalls to mind what is related of the Turks, who in their gallantries think *Sucar Birpara*, i. e. bit of sugar, to be the most polite and endearing compliment they can use to the ladies.' FENTON, *Observations*, p. 66.

amazement rather than fondness, whose chains he wishes, though in vain, to break, and whose presence is 'wine that inflames to madness[1].'

His acquaintance with this high-born dame gave wit no oppor- 11 tunity of boasting its influence; she was not to be subdued by the powers of verse, but rejected his addresses, it is said, with disdain, and drove him away to solace his disappointment with Amoret or Phillis. She married in 1639 the Earl of Sunderland, who died at Newberry in the king's cause[2]; and, in her old age, meeting somewhere with Waller, asked him when he would again write such verses upon her; 'When you are as young, Madam,' said he, 'and as handsome, as you were then[3].'

In this part of his life it was that he was known to Clarendon, 12 among the rest of the men who were eminent in that age for genius and literature; but known so little to his advantage, that they who read his character[4] will not much condemn Sacharissa that she did not descend from her rank to his embraces, nor think every excellence comprised in wit.

The Lady was, indeed, inexorable; but his uncommon qualifi- 13 cations, though they had no power upon her, recommended him to the scholars and statesmen, and undoubtedly many beauties of that time, however they might receive his love, were proud of his praises. Who they were, whom he dignifies with poetical names, cannot now be known. Amoret, according to Mr. Fenton, was the Lady Sophia Murray[5]. Perhaps by traditions preserved in families more may be discovered.

[1] 'Sacharissa's beauty's wine,
Which to madness doth incline;
Such a liquor as no brain
That is mortal can sustain.'
Eng. Poets, xvi. 64.
For a reference to these lines see Boswell's *Johnson*, ii. 360.

[2] 'Here fell the Earl of Sunderland; a lord of great fortune, tender years (being not above three and twenty years of age), and an early judg- ment; who, having no command in the army, attended upon the King's person under the obligation of hon- our; and putting himself that day in the King's troop a volunteer, before they came to charge, was taken away by a common bullet.' Clarendon's *Hist.* iv. 239.
His only son was the shameless

minister of Charles II and James II, through whom the Dukes of Marl- borough and Earls Spencer are de- scended from Waller's Sacharissa.

[3] 'She asked him in raillery, "When, Mr. Waller, will you write such fine verses upon me again?" "Oh, Ma- dame," said he, "when your Lady- ship is as young again."' *Life*, p. 117.
For a copy of verses to her 'among the State Papers in the Record Office' see *N. & Q.* 4 S. iii. 1.

[4] *Post*, WALLER, 90.

[5] Fenton's *Waller: Observations*, p. 73. She, with Lady Daubigny (*post*, WALLER, 57), was charged with complicity in Waller's plot. "'I do not mean,' she said boldly to the Committee of Safety, "to give an

14   From the verses written at Penshurst it has been collected that he diverted his disappointment by a voyage, and his biographers, from his poem on the Whales, think it not improbable that he visited the Bermudas; but it seems much more likely that he should amuse himself with forming an imaginary scene than that so important an incident, as a visit to America, should have been left floating in conjectural probability [1].

15   From his twenty-eighth to his thirty-fifth year he wrote his pieces on the Reduction of Sallee [2]; on the Reparation of St. Paul's [3]; to the King on his Navy [4]; the panegyrick on the Queen Mother [5]; the two poems to the Earl of Northumberland [6]; and perhaps others, of which the time cannot be discovered.

16   When he had lost all hopes of Sacharissa he looked round him for an easier conquest, and gained a Lady of the family of Bresse, or Breaux [7]. The time of his marriage is not exactly known. It has not been discovered that this wife was won by his poetry; nor is any thing told of her, but that she brought him many children. He doubtless praised some whom he would have been afraid to marry, and perhaps married one whom he would have been ashamed to praise. Many qualities contribute to domestick happiness upon which poetry has no colours to bestow, and many airs and sallies may delight imagination which he who

account to such fellows as you are." A few voices were raised in the House for sending the two ladies before a court-martial; but in the end respect for their sex prevailed.' GARDINER, *Great Civil War*, 1897, i. 158. Likely enough, she was one of 'the ladies of great honour' whom, according to Clarendon, Waller betrayed. *Post*, WALLER, 47.

[1] The poem is entitled *The Battel of the Summer Islands*—a name given to the Bermudas by Sir George Summers, who was wrecked there about 1609. Fenton points out that Waller in his last poem to Sacharissa says:—
'Ah! cruel nymph! from whom her
    humble swain
Flies for relief unto the raging main.'
                [*Eng. Poets*, xvi. 61.]
    Fenton adds:—'If he was a proprietor of the Summer Islands, as it is reported he was, he might perhaps at that time accompany his friend the

Earl of Warwick, who had a large share in that plantation.' Fenton's *Waller*, pp. 43, 52, and *Observations*, p. 85.
    Aubrey recorded in 1680:—'He wrote verses of the Bermudas 50 yeares since, upon the information of one that had been there; walking in his fine woods, the poetique spirit came upon him.' *Brief Lives*, ii. 276. See *post*, WALLER, 127, and *Eng. Poets*, xvi. 70.
    [2] *Ib.* p. 26; *post*, WALLER, 125.
    [3] *Ib.* p. 27; *post*, WALLER, 125.
    [4] *Ib.* p. 24; *post*, WALLER, 124.
    [5] *Ib.* p. 37.
    [6] *Ib.* pp. 44, 46.
    [7] In his epitaph she is described as 'ex Bressyorum familiá.' *Life*, p. 81. Aubrey spells the name Brace. She was, he says, 'beautifull and very prudent.' *Brief Lives*, ii. 274. The passage that follows is quoted in Boswell's *Johnson*, ii. 57.

flatters them never can approve. There are charms made only for distant admiration. No spectacle is nobler than a blaze.

Of this wife his biographers have recorded that she gave him 17 five sons and eight daughters.

During the long interval of parliament he is represented as 18 living among those with whom it was most honourable to converse, and enjoying an exuberant fortune with that independence and liberty of speech and conduct which wealth ought always to produce. He was however considered as the kinsman of Hampden, and was therefore supposed by the courtiers not to favour them.

When the parliament was called in 1640 it appeared that 19 Waller's political character had not been mistaken. The King's demand of a supply produced one of those noisy speeches which disaffection and discontent regularly dictate ; a speech filled with hyperbolical complaints of imaginary grievances. ' They,' says he, ' who think themselves already undone can never apprehend themselves in danger, and they who [that] have nothing left can never give freely [1].' Political truth is equally in danger from the praises of courtiers and the exclamations of patriots.

He then proceeds to rail at the clergy, being sure at that time 20 of a favourable audience. His topick is such as will always serve its purpose ; an accusation of acting and preaching only for preferment : and he exhorts the Commons ' carefully to provide for their protection against Pulpit Law [2].'

It always gratifies curiosity to trace a sentiment. Waller has in 21 this speech quoted Hooker in one passage [3], and in another has copied him, without quoting [4].

' Religion,' says Waller, ' ought to be the first thing in our purpose and desires ; but that which is first in dignity is not always to precede in order of time, for well-being supposes a being ; and the first impediment which men naturally endeavour to remove, is the want of those things without which they cannot subsist. God first assigned unto Adam maintenance of life, and gave him a title to the rest of the creatures before he appointed a law to observe.'

' God first assigned Adam,' says Hooker, ' maintenance of life, 22 and then appointed him a law to observe.—True it is that the

[1] Fenton's *Waller*, p. 258 ; *Parl. Hist.* ii. 556.

[2] ' Since they are so ready to let loose the consciences of their Kings, we are the more carefully to provide for our protection against this pulpit-law by declaring and reinforcing the municipal laws of this Kingdom.' Fenton's *Waller*, p. 262.

[3] *Ib.* p. 262.   [4] *Ib.* p. 263.

kingdom of God must be the first thing in our purpose and desires; but inasmuch as a righteous life presupposeth life, inasmuch as to live virtuously it is impossible, except we live; therefore the first impediment which naturally we endeavour to remove is penury, and want of things without which we cannot live [1].'

23 The speech is vehement; but the great position, that grievances ought to be redressed before supplies are granted, is agreeable enough to law and reason [2]; nor was Waller, if his biographer may be credited [3], such an enemy to the King as not to wish his distresses lightened, for he relates

'That the King sent particularly to Waller, to second his demand of some subsidies to pay off the army; and Sir Henry Vane objecting against first voting a supply, because the King would not accept unless it came up to his proportion, Mr. Waller spoke earnestly to Sir Thomas Jermyn, comptroller of the household, to save his master from the effects of so bold a falsity; "for," he said, "I am but a country gentleman, and cannot pretend to know the King's mind": but Sir Thomas durst not contradict the secretary [4]; and his son, the Earl of St. Albans, afterwards told Mr. Waller that his father's cowardice ruined the King.'

24 In the Long Parliament which, unhappily for the nation, met Nov. 3, 1640 [5], Waller represented Agmondesham the third time [6]; and was considered by the discontented party as a man sufficiently trusty and acrimonious to be employed in managing the prosecution of Judge Crawley, for his opinion in favour of ship money; and his speech shews that he did not disappoint their expectations. He was probably the more ardent, as his uncle Hampden had been particularly engaged in the dispute, and by a sentence which seems generally to be thought unconstitutional particularly injured [7].

---

[1] *Eccl. Polity*, Book i. sect. 10.
[2] Fenton's *Waller*, p. 263.
[3] *Life*, p. 20.
[4] Sir Henry Vane was Secretary of State. Clarendon accuses him of having acted that part maliciously, 'to bring all into confusion.' *Hist. of the Rebell.* i. 245. 'It is incredible,' writes Dr. Gardiner, 'that Vane should have acted thus without express authority from Charles.' *Hist. of Eng.* ix. 115.
[5] *Post*, WALLER, 65. 'For the authority of law, for the security of property, for the peace of our streets,

for the happiness of our homes, our gratitude is due, under Him who raises and pulls down nations at His pleasure, to the Long Parliament, to the Convention, and to William of Orange.' MACAULAY, *History*, iii. 413.
[6] He sat for St. Ives, Cornwall. *Parl. Hist.* ii. 604.
[7] Waller charged Crawley with 'a crime peculiar to himself and of great malignity.' 'Adding despair to our misery he tells us from the Bench that ship-money was a right so inherent in the Crown that it

He was not however a bigot to his party, nor adopted all their 25 opinions. When the great question, whether Episcopacy ought to be abolished, was debated [1], he spoke against the innovation so coolly, so reasonably, and so firmly that it is not without great injury to his name that his speech, which was as follows, has been hitherto omitted in his works [2]:

'There is no doubt but the sense of what this nation hath suf- 26 fered from the present Bishops hath produced these complaints, and the apprehensions men have of suffering the like in time to come make so many desire the taking away of Episcopacy; but I conceive it is possible that we may not now take a right measure of the minds of the people by their petitions, for when they subscribed them the Bishops were armed with a dangerous commission of making new canons, imposing new oaths, and the like; but now we have disarmed them of that power. These petitioners lately did look upon Episcopacy as a beast armed with horns and claws, but now that we have cut and pared them (and may, if we see cause, yet reduce it into narrower bounds) it may, perhaps, be more agreeable. Howsoever, if they be still in passion, it becomes us soberly to consider the right use and antiquity thereof, and not to comply further with a general desire than may stand with a general good.

'We have already shewed that episcopacy and the evils thereof 27 are mingled like water and oil, we have also in part severed them; but I believe you will find that our laws and the present government of the church are mingled like wine and water, so inseparable that the abrogation of at least a hundred of our laws is desired in these petitions. I have often heard a noble answer of the Lords commended in this house to a proposition of like nature, but of less consequence; they gave no other reason of their refusal but this, *Nolumus mutare Leges Angliæ*: it was the bishops who so answered then [3]; and it would become the dignity

would not be in the power of an Act of Parliament to take it away.' Fenton's *Waller*, pp. 268, 273, and *Observations*, p. 165.

This speech was made on July 6, 1641. *Parl. Hist.* ii. 869. '20,000 copies of it were sold in one day.' *Life*, p. 21. 'Crawley was restrained from going circuit, Aug. 5. Probably he joined the king.' *Dict. Nat. Biog.*

[1] The debate began on Feb. 8, 1641. 'Slight as the difference might be between those who took opposite sides on that day, their parting gave the colour to English political life which has distinguished it ever since, and which has distinguished every

free government which has followed in the steps of our forefathers.' GARDINER, *Hist. of Eng.* ix. 281.

[2] This speech has been retrieved from a paper printed at that time by the writers of the *Parliamentary History*. JOHNSON.

Johnson had found this *History* [*The Parliamentary or Constitutional History of England, . . . to 1660*, 24 vols. 1751-62] in the library at Streatham. Boswell's *Johnson*, iv. 36 *n.* [The speech is in vol. ix. p. 347, but its delivery is assigned to June 11, 1641.]

[3] This sentence should, I think, run:—' It was the bishops who were so answered then.' Blackstone

and wisdom of this house to answer the people now with a *Nolumus mutare.*

28 'I see some are moved with a number of hands against the Bishops, which, I confess, rather inclines me to their defence ; for I look upon episcopacy as a counterscarp or out-work, which, if it be taken by this assault of the people, and, withall, this mystery once revealed, *That we must deny them nothing when they ask it thus in troops*, we may in the next place have as hard a task to defend our property as we have lately had to recover it from the Prerogative. If, by multiplying hands and petitions, they prevail for an equality in things ecclesiastical, the next demand perhaps may be *Lex Agraria*, the like equality in things temporal.

29 'The Roman story tells us, That when the people began to flock about the senate, and were more curious to direct and know what was done than to obey, that Common-wealth soon came to ruin ; their *Legem rogare* grew quickly to be a *Legem ferre* ; and after, when their legions had found that they could make a Dictator, they never suffered the senate to have a voice any more in such election.

30 'If these great innovations proceed I shall expect a flat and level in learning too, as well as in church-preferments : *Honos alit Artes*[1]. And though it be true that grave and pious men do study for learning-sake and embrace virtue for itself, yet it is as true that youth, which is the season when learning is gotten, is not without ambition, nor will ever take pains to excel in any thing when there is not some hope of excelling others in reward and dignity.

31 'There are two reasons chiefly alleged against our church-government.

32 'First, Scripture, which, as some men think, points out another form.

33 'Second, the abuses of the present superiors.

34 'For Scripture, I will not dispute it in this place ; but I am confident that whenever an equal division of lands and goods shall be desired, there will be as many places in Scripture found out which seem to favour that, as there are now alleged against the prelacy or preferment in the church. And, as for abuses,

quotes the reply of the earls and barons to the bishops at the Parliament of Merton, 1236 :—'Et omnes comites et barones una voce responderunt, quod nolunt leges Angliae mutare, quae hucusque usitatae sunt et approbatae.' *Com.* i. 19.

[1] CICERO, *Tusc.* i. 2. 4.

'A few shining dignities, prebends, deaneries, bishopricks are the pious fraud that induces and decoys the parents to risk their children's fortune in the Church. . . . Do but once level all your preferments, and you'll soon be as level in your learning. For, instead of the flower of the English youth, you'll have only the refuse sent to your academies, and those, too, cramped and crippled in their studies for want of aim and emulation.' BENTLEY, *Works*, 1836, iii. 389.

'Pious fraud' is from *Hudibras*, i. 3. 1145.

where you are now, in the Remonstrance, told what this and that poor man hath suffered by the bishops, you may be presented with a thousand instances of poor men that have received hard measure from their landlords, and of worldly goods abused, to the injury of others and disadvantage of the owners.

'And therefore, Mr. Speaker, my humble motion is, That we 35 may settle men's minds herein, and, by a question, declare our resolution to reform, that is not to abolish, Episcopacy.'

It cannot but be wished that he, who could speak in this manner, 36 had been able to act with spirit and uniformity.

When the Commons began to set the royal authority at open 37 defiance, Waller is said to have withdrawn from the house, and to have returned with the king's permission ; and, when the king set up his standard, he sent him a thousand broad-pieces [1]. He continued, however, to sit in the rebellious conventicle, but 'spoke,' says Clarendon [2], 'with great sharpness and freedom, which, now there [were so few there that used it, and there] was no danger of being outvoted, was not restrained ; and therefore used as an argument against those who were gone upon pretence that they were not suffered to deliver their opinion freely in the house, which could not be believed, when all men knew what liberty Mr. Waller took, and spoke every day with impunity against the sense and proceedings of the house.'

Waller, as he continued to sit, was one of the commissioners 38 nominated by the parliament to treat with the king at Oxford [3], and when they were presented the King said to him, 'Though you are the last, you are not the lowest nor the least in my favour [4].' Whitlock, who, being another of the commissioners, was witness of this kindness, imputes it to the king's knowledge of the plot in which Waller appeared afterwards to have been engaged against the parliament. Fenton, with equal probability, believes that his attempt to promote the royal cause arose from his sensibility of the king's tenderness [5]. Whitlock

---

[1] 'This statement,' says the author of his *Life* (p. 23), is taken from 'a manuscript written by one of his nearest relations.' Broad-piece is 'a name applied after the introduction of the guinea in 1663 to the "Unite," or 20 shilling-piece ("Jacobus" and "Carolus") of the preceding reigns, which were much broader and thinner than the new milled coinage.' *New Eng. Dict.*

[2] *History*, iv. 58. Clarendon introduces him as 'one Mr. Waller.'
[3] They were received by the king on Feb. 1, 1642-3. Clarendon's *Hist.* iii. 402 ; Gardiner's *Civil War*, i. 89.
[4] 'Though you are the last, yet you are not the worst nor the least in our favour.' Whitelocke's *Memorials*, p. 70.
[5] Fenton's *Waller : Observations*, p. 167. Dr. Gardiner, who calls

says nothing of his behaviour at Oxford : he was sent with several others to add pomp to the commission, but was not one of those to whom the trust of treating was imparted.

39 The engagement, known by the name of Waller's plot, was soon afterwards discovered [1]. Waller had a brother-in-law, Tomkyns, who was clerk of the Queen's council, and at the same time had a very numerous acquaintance and great influence in the city. Waller and he, conversing with great confidence, told both their own secrets and those of their friends, and, surveying the wide extent of their conversation, imagined that they found in the majority of all ranks great disapprobation of the violence of the Commons, and unwillingness to continue the war. They knew that many favoured the king whose fear concealed their loyalty, and many desired peace though they durst not oppose the clamour for war ; and they imagined that if those who had these good intentions could be informed of their own strength, and enabled by intelligence to act together, they might overpower the fury of sedition by refusing to comply with the ordinance for the twentieth part and the other taxes levied for the support of the rebel army, and by uniting great numbers in a petition for peace. They proceeded with great caution. Three only met in one place, and no man was allowed to impart the plot to more than two others, so that if any should be suspected or seized more than three could not be endangered [2].

40 Lord Conway joined in the design, and, as Clarendon imagines [3], incidentally mingled, as he was a soldier, some martial hopes or projects, which however were only mentioned, the main design being to bring the loyal inhabitants to the knowledge of each other ; for which purpose there was to be appointed one in every district, to distinguish the friends of the king, the adherents to the parliament, and the neutrals. How far they proceeded does not appear ; the result of their enquiry, as Pym declared [4], was, that within the walls for one that was for the Royalists, there were three against them ; but that without the walls for one that was

Charles's speech indiscreet, says that 'Waller had long been secretly working for the King.'
[1] Johnson's authority for much that follows is the *Life*, p. 25. The conspirators were arrested on May, 31, 1643. Gardiner's *Civil War*, i. 146.

[2] In the first edition the paragraph ends at ' peace.'
[3] *History*, iv. 60.
[4] *Parliamentary History*, vol. xii. [p. 287]. JOHNSON. See Cobbett's *Parl. Hist.* iii. 125.

against them, there were five for them. Whether this was said from knowledge or guess was perhaps never enquired.

It is the opinion of Clarendon [1] that in Waller's plan no 41 violence or sanguinary resistance was comprised; that he intended only to abate the confidence of the rebels by publick declarations, and to weaken their powers by an opposition to new supplies. This, in calmer times, and more than this, is done without fear; but such was the acrimony of the Commons that no method of obstructing them was safe.

About this time another design was formed by Sir Nicholas 42 Crispe, a man of loyalty that deserves perpetual remembrance; when he was a merchant in the city he gave and procured the king in his exigencies an hundred thousand pounds [2], and, when he was driven from the Exchange, raised a regiment and commanded it.

Sir Nicholas flattered himself with an opinion that some 43 provocation would so much exasperate, or some opportunity so much encourage, the King's friends in the city, that they would break out in open resistance, and then would want only a lawful standard and an authorised commander, and extorted from the King, whose judgement too frequently yielded to importunity, a commission of array, directed to such as he thought proper to nominate, which was sent to London by the Lady Aubigney [3]. She knew not what she carried, but was to deliver it on the communication of a certain token which Sir Nicholas imparted.

This commission could be only intended to lie ready till the 44 time should require it. To have attempted to raise any forces would have been certain destruction; it could be of use only when

---

[1] *History*, iv. 62. Dr. Gardiner describes the plot as dangerous. *Civil War*, i. 144.

[2] 'He projected such a trade to Holland, France, and other countries, in the wars, as was worth to the King (though wandering up and down his kingdom and forced away from his great mart) £100,000 yearly, Sir Nicholas keeping most ports open for his Majesty's occasions.' David Lloyd's *Memoirs*, &c. 1668, p. 617.

'May 6, 1645. The Commons ordered an allowance of £8,000 *per annum* for the Prince Elector, £2,000

of it out of the King's revenue, and the rest out of the estates of the Lord Cottington and Sir N. Crispe.' Whitelocke's *Memorials of the English Affairs*, 1732, p. 145. See also Clarendon's *Hist.* iv. 63; Gardiner's *Civil War*, i. 84.

[3] Dr. Gardiner writes the name Daubigny. *Civil War*, i. 148. Her husband fell at Edgehill. 'It was believed that he fell by his own men, not without the suspicion of an officer of his own.' Clarendon's *Hist.* iii. 286 *n*. See *ante*, WALLER, 13 *n*.

the forces should appear.   This was, however, an act preparatory
to martial hostility.   Crispe would undoubtedly have put an end
to the session of parliament had his strength been equal to his
zeal : and out of the design of Crispe, which involved very little
danger, and that of Waller, which was an act purely civil, they
compounded a horrid and dreadful plot.

45   The discovery of Waller's design is variously related.   In
Clarendon's *History*[1] it is told that a servant of Tomkyns, lurk-
ing behind the hangings when his master was in conference with
Waller, heard enough to qualify him for an informer, and carried
his intelligence to Pym.   A manuscript, quoted in the Life of
Waller[2], relates that 'he was betrayed by his sister Price, and
her presbyterian chaplain Mr. Goode, who stole some of his
papers ; and if he had not strangely dreamed the night before
that his sister had betrayed him, and thereupon burnt the rest of
his papers by the fire that was [left] in his chimney, he had
certainly lost his life by [for] it.'   The question cannot be decided.   It is not unreasonable to believe that the men in power
receiving intelligence from the sister would employ the servant
of Tomkyns to listen at the conference, that they might avoid an
act so offensive as that of destroying the brother by the sister's
testimony.

46   The plot was published in the most terrifick manner.   On the
31st of May [1643], at a solemn fast, when they were listening
to the sermon, a messenger entered the church[3], and communicated
his errand to Pym, who whispered it to others that were placed
near him, and then went with them out of the church, leaving
the rest in solicitude and amazement.   They immediately sent
guards to proper places, and that night apprehended Tomkyns
and Waller : having yet traced nothing but that letters had been
intercepted, from which it appeared that the parliament and the
city were soon to be delivered into the hands of the cavaliers.

47   They perhaps yet knew little themselves, beyond some general
and indistinct notices.

'But Waller,' says Clarendon[4], 'was so confounded with fear
[and apprehension] that he confessed whatever he had heard,
said [said, heard], thought, or seen ; all that he knew of himself,

---

[1] Vol. iv. p. 66.   [2] P. 28.
[3] St. Margaret's, Westminster.   Gardiner's *Civil War*, iii. 146.
[4] *History*, iv. 67.

and all that he suspected of others, without concealing any person, of what degree or quality soever, or any discourse which [that] he had ever upon any occasion entertained with them ; what such and such ladies of great honour, to whom, upon the credit of his [great] wit and great [very good] reputation, he had been admitted, had spoke to him in their chambers upon [of] the proceedings in the Houses and how they had encouraged him to oppose them ; what correspondence and intercourse they had with some Ministers of State at Oxford, and how they conveyed [derived] all intelligence thither.'

He accused the Earl of Portland and Lord Conway as co-operating in the transaction ; and testified that the Earl of Northumberland had declared himself disposed in favour of any attempt that might check the violence of the Parliament, and reconcile them to the King.

He undoubtedly confessed much which they could never have 48 discovered, and perhaps somewhat which they would wish to have been suppressed ; for it is inconvenient, in the conflict of factions, to have that disaffection known which cannot safely be punished.

Tomkyns was seized on the same night with Waller, and 49 appears likewise to have partaken of his cowardice ; for he gave notice of Crispe's commission of array, of which Clarendon never knew how it was discovered [1]. Tomkyns had been sent with the token appointed, to demand it from Lady Aubigney, and had buried it in his garden, where, by his direction, it was dug up ; and thus the rebels obtained, what Clarendon confesses them to have had, the original copy.

It can raise no wonder that they formed one plot out of these 50 two designs, however remote from each other, when they saw the same agent employed in both, and found the commission of array in the hands of him who was employed in collecting the opinions and affections of the people.

Of the plot, thus combined, they took care to make the most. 51 They sent Pym among the citizens, to tell them of their imminent danger and happy escape ; and inform them, that the design was to seize the ' Lord Mayor and all the Committee of Militia, and would not spare one of them [2].' They drew up a vow and cove-

---

[1] *Hist.* iv. p. 66 ; Gardiner's *Civil War*, i. 111, 148.
[2] These words are not in the report of Pym's speech, 'corrected by his own hand for the press.'

Parl. Hist. iii. 121. The design is mentioned in a paper issued by the House of Commons. Rushworth's *Hist. Coll.* v. 322.

nant, to be taken by every member of either house, by which he declared his detestation of all conspiracies against the parliament, and his resolution to detect and oppose them. They then appointed a day of thanksgiving for this wonderful delivery; which shut out, says Clarendon, all doubts whether there had been such a deliverance, and whether the plot was real or fictitious.

52   On June 11, the Earl of Portland and Lord Conway were committed, one to the custody of the mayor, and the other of the sheriff; but their lands and goods were not seized.

53   Waller was still to immerse himself deeper in ignominy. The Earl of Portland and Lord Conway denied the charge, and there was no evidence against them but the confession of Waller, of which undoubtedly many would be inclined to question the veracity. With these doubts he was so much terrified, that he endeavoured to persuade Portland to a declaration like his own, by a letter extant in Fenton's edition[1]:

'But for me,' says he, 'you had never known any thing of this business, which was prepared for another, and therefore I cannot imagine why you should hide [wed] it so far as to contract your own ruin by concealing it, and persisting unreasonably to hide that truth, which without you already is and will every day be made more manifest. Can you imagine yourself bound [obliged] in honour to keep that secret, which is already revealed by another; or possible it should still be a secret, which is known to one of the other sex?... If you [still] persist to be cruel to yourself for their [others'] sakes who [that] deserve it not, it will nevertheless be made appear, ere long I fear, to your ruin. Surely [Sure], if I had the happiness to wait on you, I could move you to compassionate both yourself and me, who, [as] desperate as my case is, am desirous to die with the honour of being known to have declared the truth [. . .]. You have no reason [vainly] to contend to hide what is already revealed—inconsiderately to throw away yourself [yourself away] for the interest of others, [and such] to whom you are less obliged than you are aware of.'

54   This persuasion seems to have had little effect. Portland sent (June 29) a letter to the Lords to tell them that he

'is in custody, as he conceives, without any charge; and that, by what Mr. Waller hath threatened him with since he was imprisoned, he doth apprehend a very cruel, long, and ruinous restraint: he therefore prays, that he may not find the effects of Mr. Waller's threats, by a long and close imprisonment; but may be speedily

[1] P. 280.

brought to a legal trial, and then he is confident the vanity and falsehood of those informations which have been given against him will appear [1].'

In consequence of this letter the Lords ordered Portland and Waller to be confronted ; when the one repeated his charge, and the other his denial. The examination of the plot being continued (July 1), Thinn, usher of the house of Lords, deposed that Mr. Waller having had a conference with the Lord Portland in an upper room, Lord Portland said, when he came down, ' Do me the favour to tell my Lord Northumberland [1] that Mr. Waller has extremely pressed me to save my own life and his, by throwing the blame upon the Lord Conway and the Earl of Northumberland.' **55**

Waller, in his letter to Portland, tells him of the reasons which he could urge with resistless efficacy in a personal conference ; but he over-rated his own oratory : his vehemence, whether of persuasion or intreaty, was returned with contempt [2]. **56**

One of his arguments with Portland is, that the plot is already known to a woman. This woman was doubtless Lady Aubigney, who, upon this occasion, was committed to custody ; but who, in reality, when she delivered the commission, knew not what it was. **57**

The parliament then proceeded against the conspirators, and committed their trial to a council of war. Tomkyns and Chaloner were hanged near their own doors [3]. Tomkyns, when he came to die, said it was a *foolish business* [4]; and indeed there seems to have been no hope that it should escape discovery, for though never more than three met at a time, yet a design so extensive must, by necessity, be communicated to many, who could not be expected to be all faithful and all prudent. Chaloner was attended at his execution by Hugh Peters [5]. His crime was that **58**

---

[1] *Parl. Hist. of England*, 1751-62, xii. 317.

[2] Dr. Gardiner says of Waller's letter :—' It leaves in my mind very little doubt that Portland was the liar.' *Civil War*, i. 156 n. He adds:— ' But Waller was so abject in his terror that when Conway and Portland bluntly denied the truth of the accusation public feeling was strong in their favour.'

[3] One in Holborn and the other in Cornhill. Clarendon's *Hist.* iv. 75.

Forty-two years later Cornish, a victim of James II and Jeffreys, was in like manner hanged on ' a gibbet set up where King Street meets Cheapside, in sight of the house where he had long lived in general respect.' Macaulay's *England*, ii. 247.

[4] Rushworth's *Hist. Coll.* v. 326.

[5] *Ib.* p. 327.

he had commission to raise money for the King; but it appears not that the money was to be expended upon the advancement of either Crispe or Waller's plot[1].

59 The Earl of Northumberland, being too great for prosecution, was only once examined before the Lords[2]. The Earl of Portland and lord Conway persisting to deny the charge, and no testimony but Waller's yet appearing against them, were, after a long imprisonment, admitted to bail. Hassel, the King's messenger, who carried the letters to Oxford, died the night before his trial. Hampden escaped death, perhaps by the interest of his family; but was kept in prison to the end of his life[3]. They whose names were inserted in the commission of array were not capitally punished, as it could not be proved that they had consented to their own nomination, but they were considered as malignants, and their estates were seized.

60 'Waller, though confessedly,' says Clarendon, 'the most guilty, with incredible dissimulation affected such a remorse of conscience that his trial was put off, out of Christian compassion, till he might recover his understanding.' What use he made of this interval, with what liberality and success he distributed flattery and money, and how, when he was brought (July 4) before the House, he confessed and lamented, and submitted and implored, may be read in the *History of the Rebellion* (B. vii.)[4]. The speech, to which Clarendon ascribes the preservation of his 'dear-bought life,' is inserted in his works[5]. The great historian, however,

[1] This sentence is not in the first edition. In his dying speech he said:—'As Mr. Waller was the mouth from the Lords, as he did declare, so I was the unhappy instrument from Mr. Waller to the rest.' Rushworth's *Hist. Coll.* v. 327.

[2] 'For the accusation of the Earl of Northumberland, it was proceeded tenderly in; for though the violent party was heartily incensed against him, as a man weary of them, yet his reputation was still very great.' CLARENDON, *History*, iv. 77.

[3] Alexander Hampden. Rushworth's *Hist. Coll.* v. 323. In the first edition the sentence ran:—'Hampden was kept,' &c. Dr. Gardiner says that 'he fell ill, and ultimately died in confinement.' *Civil War*, i. 157. Between the arrest of the conspirators

and their trial John Hampden, Waller's first cousin, received his death wound at Chalgrove.

[4] 'By drawing visitants to himself of the most powerful ministers of all factions he had, by his liberality and penitence, his receiving vulgar and vile sayings from them with humility and reverence, as clearer convictions and informations than in his life he had ever had; and distributing great sums to them for their prayers and ghostly counsel, so satisfied them that they satisfied others.' Clarendon's *Hist.* iv. 78.

[5] Fenton's *Waller*, p. 275; also in Rushworth's *Hist. Coll.* v. 328; *Parl. Hist.* iii. 140. He would not suffer this speech to be inserted in his poems after the Restoration. Aubrey's *Brief Lives*, ii. 276.

seems to have been mistaken in relating that 'he prevailed' in the principal part of his supplication, 'not to be tried by a Council of War [1]'; for, according to Whitlock, he was by expulsion from the House abandoned to the tribunal which he so much dreaded, and, being tried and condemned, was reprieved by Essex [2]; but after a year's imprisonment, in which time resentment grew less acrimonious, paying a fine of ten thousand pounds, he was permitted 'to recollect himself in another country [3].'

Of his behaviour in this part of his life it is not necessary to 61 direct the reader's opinion. 'Let us not,' says his last ingenious biographer [4], 'condemn him with untempered severity, because he was not a prodigy which the world hath seldom seen, because his character included not the poet, the orator, and the hero [5].'

For the place of his exile he chose France, and staid some time 62 at Roan, where his daughter Margaret was born, who was afterwards his favourite and his amanuensis [6]. He then removed to

---

[1] 'He prevailed not to be tried by a Council of War, and thereby preserved his dear-bought life.' Clarendon's *Hist.* iv. 78.

[2] Whitelocke's *Memorials*, 1732, p. 70. This is also Rushworth's account, vol. v. p. 330.
According to Dr. Gardiner:— 'He could not appear before a court-martial without leave given by the House. ... He was expelled the House [on July 4], but he remained in prison for many months, untried and unsentenced, till the throng of events had almost blotted out the memory of his crime.' *Civil War*, i. 158.

[3] 'He had leave to recollect himself in another country (for his liberty was to be in banishment) how miserable he had made himself in obtaining that leave to live out of his own.' Clarendon's *Hist.* iv. 79.
'The Houses [in Sept. 1644] hardly knew where to turn for money. In their distress they . . . offered to pardon him on his engagement to leave the country and to pay £10,000. Waller caught at the bargain.' Gardiner's *Civil War*, ii. 37.
'He had much adoe to save his life ; and in order to it, sold his estate in Bedfordshire, about 1,300 *li.* per annum, to Dr. Wright, M.D., for

10,000 *li.* (much under value) which was procured in 24 hours' time, or els he had been hanged. ... With which money he bribed the whole House, which was the first time a House of Commons was ever bribed.' AUBREY, *Brief Lives*, ii. 276.

[4] *The Life of Edmund Waller*, by Percival Stockdale (prefixed to an edition of Waller's *Works*), 1772, p. 63. For Stockdale see Boswell's *Johnson*, ii. 113 ; *John. Misc.* ii. 330.
Sir Walter Scott, telling a story of the Ettrick Shepherd's locking up 'twae folk come frae Glasgow (he said) to provoke mey to fecht a duel,' continues :—'I am afraid we must apply to Hogg the apology which is made for Waller by his biographer.' Scott quotes the passage in the text. *Journal*, 1891, p. 454.

[5] Waller, addressing Charles II on the Restoration, says :—
'Like your Great Master you the storm withstood,
And pitied those who love with frailty shew'd.'
Eng. Poets, xvi. 151.
'In this allusion Mr. Waller seems to touch tenderly upon his own want of resolution.' FENTON, *Observations*, p. 124.

[6] *Life*, p. 40.

Paris, where he lived with great splendour and hospitality[1]; and from time to time amused himself with poetry, in which he sometimes speaks of the rebels and their usurpation in the natural language of an honest man[2].

63   At last it became necessary for his support to sell his wife's jewels, and being reduced, as he said, at last 'to the rump jewel[3],' he solicited from Cromwell permission to return, and obtained it by the interest of colonel Scroop, to whom his sister was married[4]. Upon the remains of a fortune, which the danger of his life had very much diminished, he lived at Hall-barn[5], a house built by himself, very near to Beaconsfield[6], where his mother resided. His mother, though related to Cromwell and Hampden[7], was zealous for the royal cause, and, when Cromwell visited her, used to reproach him; he in return would throw a napkin at her, and say he would not dispute with his aunt[8]; but finding in time that she acted for the king as well as talked, he made her a prisoner

---

[1] *Life*, p. 40. Evelyn thus describes his passage down the Loire from Roanne in July 1646:—'The next day we arrived at Orleans, taking our turns to row. Sometimes we footed it through pleasant fields and meadows; sometimes we shot at fowls and other birds; nothing came amiss; sometimes we played at cards, whilst others sung, or were composing verses; for we had the great poet, Mr. Waller, in our company.' *Diary*, i. 252. See also *ib.* p. 225.

[2] Johnson refers to the lines *To my Lady Morton*, *Eng. Poets*, xvi. 125. Fenton says in a note on this poem that 'Mazarin seems to have reverenced Cromwell more than his Maker.' *Observations*, p. 108.

[3] 'Except my Lord St. Alban's [*ante*, COWLEY, 12, 44; *post*, WALLER, 104], there was no English table but Mr. Waller's; which was so costly to him that he used to say he was at last come to the rump jewel.' *Life*, p. 40.

[4] *Ib.* p. 42. 'Adrian Scroop of Buckinghamshire, Esq., descended from the ancient lords of that name.' *Ath. Oxon.* iii. 47 *n*. On Oct. 17, 1660 Evelyn 'met the quarters, mangled, cut and reeking,' of Scroop and three other regicides, 'as they were brought from the gallows in baskets on the hurdle.' *Diary*, i. 360.

On Jan. 13, 1651-2 he had recorded:—'I took leave of Mr. Waller, who had obtained of the rebels permission to return.' *Ib.* p. 286.

[5] In the first edition 'Hillburn.' Malone, visiting Burke in 1789, recorded:—'We dined this day at Hall-barn, as it is now called, though Dr. Johnson, in his *Life of Waller*, calls it Hill-barn [*sic*].' Prior's *Malone*, p. 155. He adds:—'The house was built by Waller himself, but there have been considerable additions. Mr. Waller, the present owner, is a young man, the sixth I believe from the poet. The estate is now not more than about £1,500 *per annum*.' *Ib.* p. 162.

[6] 'He residing mostly at Hall Barn, near Beaconsfield, he was on all occasions called Mr. Waller of Beaconsfield; the greatest honour that poor but pleasant town has to boast of.' *Life*, p. 42.

[7] *Ante*, WALLER, 1. Her brother, William, married Cromwell's aunt, Elizabeth Cromwell.

[8] The *Life*, p. 6, whence this anecdote is taken, continues:—'for so he used to call her, though not quite so nearly related.'

to her own daughter, in her own house. If he would do any thing, he could not do less.

Cromwell, now protector, received Waller as his kinsman to 64 familiar conversation. Waller, as he used to relate, found him sufficiently versed in ancient history[1]; and when any of his enthusiastick friends came to advise or consult him, could sometimes overhear him discoursing in the cant of the times, but when he returned he would say, 'Cousin Waller, I must talk to these men in [after] their own way,' and resumed the common style of conversation[2].

He repaid the Protector for his favours (1654) by the famous 65 *Panegyrick*, which has been always considered as the first of his poetical productions[3]. His choice of encomiastick topicks is very judicious, for he considers Cromwell in his exaltation, without enquiring how he attained it; there is consequently no mention of the rebel or the regicide[4]. All the former part of his hero's life is veiled with shades, and nothing is brought to view but the chief, the governor, the defender of England's honour, and the enlarger of her dominion. The act of violence by which he obtained the supreme power is lightly treated, and decently justified. It was certainly to be desired that the detestable band[5] should be dissolved which had destroyed the church, murdered the King, and filled the nation with tumult and oppression; yet Cromwell had not the right of dissolving them, for all that he had before done could be justified only by supposing them invested with lawful authority. But combinations of wickedness would overwhelm the world by the advantage which licentious principles afford, did not those who have long practised perfidy grow faithless to each other[6].

In the poem on the war with Spain are some passages at 66

---

[1] 'Very well read in the Greek and Roman story.' *Life*, p. 43.

[2] 'And would then go on where they left off.' *Ib.* p. 43.

[3] *A Panegyric to my Lord Protector, Eng. Poets*, xvi. 136; *post*, WALLER, 128; ADDISON, 128. There is no copy of the first edition in the British Museum, but in the *Catalogue* the conjectural date of *The Anti-Panegyrick* is 1654.

[4] Scott says of Dryden's *Elegy on Cromwell* (*post*, DRYDEN, 7):— 'Although a panegyric on an usurper, the topics of praise are selected with attention to truth, and are, generally speaking, such as Cromwell's worst enemies could not have denied to him.' Scott's *Dryden*, 1821, i. 41.

[5] The Long Parliament. *Ante*, WALLER, 24.

[6] 'I remember (said Johnson) this remark of Sir Thomas Browne's, "Do the devils lie? No; for then Hell could not subsist."' Boswell's *Johnson*, iii. 293.
'O shame to men! devil with devil
    damn'd
Firm concord holds.'
            Paradise Lost, ii. 496.

least equal to the best parts of the *Panegyrick*, and in the conclusion the poet ventures yet a higher flight of flattery, by recommending royalty to Cromwell and the nation [1]. Cromwell was very desirous, as appears from his conversation, related by Whitlock [2], of adding the title to the power of monarchy, and is supposed to have been with-held from it, partly by fear of the army and partly by fear of the laws, which, when he should govern by the name of King, would have restrained his authority. When therefore a deputation was solemnly sent to invite him to the Crown he, after a long conference, refused it ; but is said to have fainted in his coach when he parted from them [3].

67   The poem on the death of the Protector [4] seems to have been dictated by real veneration for his memory.   Dryden and Sprat [5] wrote on the same occasion ; but they were young men, struggling into notice, and hoping for some favour from the ruling party. Waller had little to expect; he had received nothing but his pardon from Cromwell, and was not likely to ask any thing from those who should succeed him.

68   Soon afterwards the Restauration supplied him with another subject ; and he exerted his imagination, his elegance, and his melody with equal alacrity for Charles the Second [6].   It is not

---

[1] The poet, after recounting the capture of
'Their huge capacious galleons stuffed with plate,'
speaking of 'our great Protector,' continues :—
'His conqu'ring head has no more room for bays.
Then let it be as the glad nation prays :
Let the rich ore forthwith be melted down,
And the state fix'd by making him a crown ;
With ermine clad and purple, let him hold
A royal sceptre made of Spanish gold.' *Eng. Poets*, xvi. 144.

[2] 'Nov. 7, 1652. It was about this time, in a fair evening, I began walking in St. James's Park to refresh myself after business of toil, and for a little exercise, that the Lord General Cromwell, meeting with me, saluted me with more than ordinary courtesy.' WHITELOCKE, *Memorials of the English Affairs*, 1732, 548.

[3] Mr. C. H. Firth informs me that he knows of no authority for this story. 'In itself it is improbable, for Cromwell refused the Crown at Whitehall, where he was living.'

[4] *Eng. Poets*, xvi. 147. It contains the famous instance of the bathos, quoted in *The Art of Sinking*, ch. xi :—
'Under the tropic is our language spoke,
And part of Flanders hath receiv'd our yoke.'
'He would not suffer this poem to be inserted in the edition of his Poems since the restauration of King Charles II.' AUBREY, *Brief Lives*, ii. 276.

[5] *Post*, DRYDEN, 7 ; SPRAT, 2. The three poems were printed in 1659 under the title of *Poems upon the Death of his late Highnesse Oliver Lord Protector of England, Scotland and Ireland*. Written by Mr. Edm. Waller, Mr. Jo. Dryden, Mr. Sprat of Oxford.

[6] *Eng. Poets*, xvi. 148. 'It was registered on May 30, 1660, the day after His Majesty's entry into Whitehall.' Masson's *Milton*, vi. 12.

possible to read, without some contempt and indignation, poems of the same author, ascribing the highest degree of 'power and piety' to Charles the First [1], then transferring the same 'power and piety' to Oliver Cromwell [2]; now inviting Oliver to take the Crown, and then congratulating Charles the Second on his recovered right. Neither Cromwell nor Charles could value his testimony as the effect of conviction, or receive his praises as effusions of reverence; they could consider them but as the labour of invention and the tribute of dependence.

Poets, indeed, profess fiction, but the legitimate end of fiction 69 is the conveyance of truth; and he that has flattery ready for all whom the vicissitudes of the world happen to exalt must be scorned as a prostituted mind that may retain the glitter of wit, but has lost the dignity of virtue.

The *Congratulation* was considered as inferior in poetical merit 70 to the *Panegyrick*, and it is reported that when the king told Waller of the disparity he answered, ' Poets, Sir, succeed better in fiction than in truth [3].'

The *Congratulation* is indeed not inferior to the *Panegyrick* 71 either by decay of genius or for want of diligence, but because Cromwell had done much, and Charles had done little. Cromwell

---

[1] 'The world's restorer once could not endure
That finish'd Babel should those men secure
Whose pride design'd that fabric to have stood
Above the reach of any second flood:
To thee, His chosen, more indulgent, He
Dares trust such pow'r with so much piety.'
To the King on his Navy. Eng. Poets, xvi. 24.

[2] 'When fate or error had our age misled,
And o'er this nation such confusion spread;
The only care which could from heav'n come down
Was so much power and piety in one.'
A Panegyric to my Lord Protector. Ib. p. 140.

[3] Fenton gives *Ménagiana* as his authority for this anecdote, where we read (iii. 332) :—'Le roi les ayant lus, lui reprocha qu'il en avait fait de meilleurs pour Cromwel [*sic*]. Walher [*sic*] lui dit :—" Sire, nous autres poètes, nous réussissons mieux en fictions qu'en vérités."' *Observations*, p. 122.

'Cette réponse n'était pas si sincère que celle de l'ambassadeur hollandais, qui, lorsque le même roi se plaignait que l'on avait moins d'égards pour lui que pour Cromwell, répondit :—" Ah! sire, ce Cromwell était tout autre chose."' VOLTAIRE, *Œuvres*, xxiv. 123.

There was fiction enough in the *Congratulation*; ex. gr. :—
'Faith, law and piety (that banish'd train),
Justice and truth with you return again;
The city's trade and country's easy life
Once more shall flourish without fraud or strife.'
Eng. Poets, xvi. 152.

wanted nothing to raise him to heroick excellence but virtue ; and virtue his poet thought himself at liberty to supply. Charles had yet only the merit of struggling without success, and suffering without despair. A life of escapes and indigence could supply poetry with no splendid images.

72   In the first parliament summoned by Charles the Second (March 8 [1], 1661), Waller sat for Hastings in Sussex, and served for different places in all the parliaments of that reign. In a time when fancy and gaiety were the most powerful recommendations to regard it is not likely that Waller was forgotten. He passed his time in the company that was highest, both in rank and wit, from which even his obstinate sobriety did not exclude him. Though he drank water he was enabled by his fertility of mind to heighten the mirth of Bacchanalian assemblies ; and Mr. Saville said, that 'no man in England should keep him company without drinking but Ned Waller [2].'

73   The praise given him by St. Evremond is a proof of his reputation [3]; for it was only by his reputation that he could be known as a writer to a man who, though he lived a great part of a long life upon an English pension, never condescended to understand the language of the nation that maintained him [4].

74   In parliament ' he was,' says Burnet, ' the delight of the house,

---

[1] May 8. *Parl. Hist.* iv. 178.

[2] ' King Charles, in his diversions at the Duke of Buckingham's and other places, always made Mr. Waller a party, excusing his drinking with the company ; upon which Mr. Saville used to say,' &c. *Life of Waller*, p. 47.

' It is observed in Waller's *Life*, in the *Biographia Britannica* [vi. 4110], that he drank only water; and that while he sat in a company who were drinking wine, "he had the dexterity to accommodate his discourse to the pitch of theirs as it *sunk*."' Boswell's *Johnson*, iii. 327 *n*.

See also Aubrey's *Brief Lives*, ii. 277.

The Earl of Rochester wrote to Saville :—' Preserve me from the imminent peril of sobriety ; which, for want of good wine more than company, is very like to befal me. Remember what pains I have formerly taken to wean you from your per-

nicious resolutions of discretion and wisdom.' Rochester's *Familiar Letters*, 1697, p. 1.

Henry Saville was Groom of the Bedchamber to the Duke of York ; afterwards Vice-Chamberlain to Charles II. Pepys's *Diary*, iii. 123 ; v. 126.

[3] St. Evremond described Waller to Corneille as ' one of the finest wits of the age.' He added :—' You are the only writer of our nation whose sentiments have the advantage to touch his.' *Life*, p. 49. See also *ib.* pp. 61, 63, 71. For St. Evremond's praise of Waller see his *Œuvres Meslées*, 1709, ii. 128 ; iii. 145, 240; for La Fontaine's praise see *ib.* iii. 133, 151. I do not find in these volumes St. Evremond's description to Corneille.

[4] He was born in 1613. He fled from France in 1661, was pensioned by Charles II, and befriended by William III. He died in 1703.

and though old [even at eighty] said the liveliest things of any among them [1].' This however is said in his account of the year seventy-five, when Waller was only seventy. His name as a speaker occurs often in Grey's *Collections* [2]; but I have found no extracts that can be more quoted as exhibiting sallies of gaiety than cogency of argument [3].

He was of such consideration that his remarks were circulated **75** and recorded. When the duke of York's influence was high both in Scotland and England, it drew, says Burnet, a lively reflection from Waller, the celebrated wit. ' He said the house of commons had resolved that the duke should not reign after the king's death; but the king, in opposition to them, had [was] resolved that he should reign even in [during] his life [4].' If there appear no extraordinary *liveliness* in this *remark*, yet its reception proves the speaker to have been a *celebrated wit*, to have had a name which the men of wit were proud of mentioning.

He did not suffer his reputation to die gradually away, which **76** may easily happen in a long life, but renewed his claim to poetical distinction from time to time as occasions were offered, either by publick events or private incidents; and, contenting himself with the influence of his muse, or loving quiet better than influence, he never accepted any office of magistracy.

He was not however without some attention to his fortune, **77** for he asked from the King (in 1665) the provostship of Eaton College, and obtained it [5]; but Clarendon refused to put the seal to the grant, alleging that it could be held only by a clergyman.

---

[1] Burnet, *Hist.* i. 436; *post*, WALLER, 97.

[2] *Debates in the House of Commons*, 1667-94. Collected by the Hon. Anchitel Grey. 1763. 8vo. 10 vols. Lowndes's *Bibl. Man.* p. 1781.

[3] In the first edition, 'that can be quoted as exhibiting any representation of abilities displayed rather in sallies,' &c.

[4] 'The King walked about with a small train of the necessary attendants, when the Duke had a vast following; which drew a lively reflection from Waller, the celebrated wit.' Burnet's *Hist.* ii. 201. Johnson injures the reflection by changing 'was' into 'had.' 'The House had resolved,' but the king 'was resolved.'

[5] 'The King gave him nothing but a grant of the Provostship of Eton.' *Life*, p. 48. Richard Allestree was appointed. In the Preface to his *Sermons* (1684) it is said that 'a great interest was made by a layman, who probably might succeed upon the advantage of his [Allestree's] refusal, notwithstanding that the Provost be actually the Parson of Eton Parish.' For Prior's seeking the office see *post*, PRIOR, 49 *n*. In 1623 Bacon had in vain sought it 'for a cell to retire into.' *Cata. of MSS. in the Museum of the Record Office*, p. 72.

It is known that Sir Henry Wotton qualified himself for it by Deacon's orders [1].

78   To this opposition the *Biographia* imputes the violence and acrimony with which Waller joined Buckingham's faction in the prosecution of Clarendon [2].   The motive was illiberal and dishonest, and shewed that more than sixty years had not been able to teach him morality.   His accusation is such as conscience can hardly be supposed to dictate without the help of malice.   'We were to be governed by janizaries instead of parliaments, and are in danger from a worse plot than that of the fifth of November; then, if the Lords and Commons had been destroyed, there had been a succession; but here both had been destroyed for ever [3].' This is the language of a man who is glad of an opportunity to rail, and ready to sacrifice truth to interest at one time, and to anger at another.

79   A year after the Chancellor's banishment another vacancy gave him encouragement for another petition, which the King referred to the council, who, after hearing the question argued by lawyers for three days, determined that the office could be held only by a clergyman, according to the act of uniformity, since the provosts had always received institution, as for a parsonage, from the bishops of Lincoln.   The King then said, he could not break the law which he had made; and Dr. Zachary Cradock, famous for a single sermon, at most for two sermons, was chosen by the Fellows [4].

80   That he asked any thing else is not known; it is certain that he obtained nothing, though he continued obsequious to the court through the rest of Charles's reign.

81   At the accession of King James (in 1685) he was chosen for

[1] Wotton was appointed in 1623. 'He was made Deacon with all convenient speed.' Walton's *Lives*, 1838, p. 134.

[2] *Biog. Brit.* p. 4111.

[3] This is apparently a paraphrase of the following passage in Anchitel Grey's *Debates*, i. 29 :—'Government by Bashaws—Our late rebellion had Commons, but in this government not so much as a Rump left—It outgoes the 5th of November. Both Houses blown up, and slavery by this upon posterity.'

In 1667 he was one of the managers in a Conference with the House of Lords about committing Clarendon to prison. *Parl. Hist.* iv. 388.

[4] *A Sermon preached before the King, Feb.* 10, 1677-8 [on *Eccles.* ix. 2]. It was published in 1678, a fifth edition in 1695, and another edition in 1740. [This sermon and one on *Timothy* i. 5 make up a book of fifty-four pages published in 1742.] *Brit. Mus. Cata.*

'I have heard of an eminent preacher, who could never be prevailed upon to print but one sermon (the best, perhaps, that ever passed

parliament, being then fourscore, at Saltash in Cornwall; and wrote
a *Presage of the Downfall [Ruin] of the Turkish Empire*, which
he presented to the King on his birthday [1]. It is remarked, by his
commentator Fenton, that in reading Tasso [2] he had early imbibed
a veneration for the heroes of the Holy War, and a zealous enmity
to the Turks, which never left him. James however, having soon
after begun what he thought a holy war at home, made haste to
put all molestation of the Turks out of his power.

James treated him with kindness and familiarity, of which 82
instances are given by the writer of his Life [3]. One day, taking
him into the closet, the King asked him how he liked one of the
pictures: 'My eyes,' said Waller, 'are dim, and I do not know
it [I know not who it is].' The King said it was the princess of
Orange. 'She is,' said Waller, 'like the greatest woman in the world.'
The King asked who was that? and was answered, Queen
Elizabeth. 'I wonder,' said the King, 'you should think so; but
I must confess she had a wise council.' 'And, Sir,' said Waller,
'did you [your Majesty] ever know a fool chuse a wise one?' Such
is the story, which I once heard of some other man. Pointed axioms
and acute replies fly loose about the world, and are assigned successively to those whom it may be the fashion to celebrate [4].

When the King knew that he was about to marry his daughter 83
to Dr. Birch, a clergyman [5], he ordered a French gentleman to tell
him that 'the King wondered he could think of marrying his
daughter to a falling church.' 'The King,' says Waller, 'does me
great honour in taking notice of my domestick affairs; but I have
lived long enough to observe that this falling church has got
a trick of rising again.'

He took notice to his friends of the King's conduct, and said 84
that "he would be left like a whale upon the strand [6].' Whether
he was privy to any of the transactions which ended in the
Revolution is not known. His heir joined the prince of Orange [7].

the press), to which the public gave
the title of DR. CRADOCK'S WORKS.'
Sewell's *Life of J. Philips*, p. 14.

  [1] The grossness of his flattery is
seen in the following couplet:—
'A Prince more fit for such a glorious
    task
Than England's King from heav'n
    we cannot ask.'
        Eng. Poets, xvi. 199.
  [2] In Fairfax's translation. *Obser-*

vations, p. 30.

  [4] *Post*, SHEFFIELD, 14.
  [5] Dr. Peter Birch, Minister of St.
James's. Aubrey's *Brief Lives*, ii.
280.
  'Nov. 5, 1686. I went to St.
Martin's, where Dr. Birch preached
very boldly against the Papists.'
EVELYN, *Diary*, ii. 270.
  [6] *Life*, p. 52.
  [7] *Ib.*

[3] P. 51.

85   Having now attained an age beyond which the laws of nature
seldom suffer life to be extended otherwise than by a future
state, he seems to have turned his mind upon preparation for the
decisive hour, and therefore consecrated his poetry to devotion.
It is pleasing to discover that his piety was without weakness ;
that his intellectual powers continued vigorous ; and that the lines
which he composed when 'he, for age, could neither read nor
write,' are not inferior to the effusions of his youth [1].

86   Towards the decline of life he bought a small house with a little
land at Colshill [2], and said 'he should be glad to die like the
stag, where he was roused [3].'   This however did not happen.
When he was at Beaconsfield he found his legs grow tumid [4] ; he
went to Windsor, where Sir Charles Scarborough [5] then attended
the King, and requested him, as both a friend and physician, to
tell him *what that swelling meant.* 'Sir,' answered Scarborough,
'your blood will run no longer. '   Waller repeated some lines of
Virgil [6], and went home to die.

87   As the disease increased upon him he composed himself for his
departure, and calling upon Dr. Birch to give him the holy sacra-

[1] 'When we for age could neither
read nor write,
The subject made us able to indite :
The soul with nobler resolutions
deckt,
The body stooping, does herself
erect.
.   .   .   .   .   .
The soul's dark cottage, batter'd
and decay'd,
Lets in new light, thro' chinks
that time has made ;
Stronger by weakness, wiser men
become,
As they draw near to their eternal
home.
Leaving the old, both worlds at
once they view
That stand upon the threshold of
the new.' *Eng. Poets,* xvi. 235.
See *post,* WALLER, 133.
[2] Thomas Ellwood (*ante,* MILTON,
107), 'whose love of letters and humanity made his conversation much
desired by Mr. Waller, lived at that
pleasant village.' *Life,* p. 55. Ellwood, in his *Autobiography,* does
not mention Waller.
[3] 'Said he to his cousin Hampden,
A stagge, when he is hunted, and

neer spent, alwayes returnes home.'
Aubrey's *Brief Lives,* ii. 278.
'And as a hare, whom hounds and
horns pursue,
Pants to the place from whence at
first he flew,
I still had hopes, my long vexations
past,
Here to return—and die at home at
last.'
GOLDSMITH, *The Deserted Village,*
l. 39.
[4] 'His legs began to swell.' *Life,*
p. 56.
'So easy is Johnson's style in these
Lives that I do not recollect more
than three uncommon or learned
words ; one, when giving an account
of the approach of Waller's mortal
disease, he says, "he found his legs
grow tumid."' Boswell's *Johnson,* iv.
39.
[5] *Ante,* COWLEY, 22.
[6] Perhaps *Georgics,* iii. 66.
'Optima quaeque dies miseris morta-
libus aevi
Prima fugit : subeunt morbi, tristis-
que senectus,
Et labor, et durae rapit inclementia
mortis.'

ment, he desired his children to take it with him, and made an earnest declaration of his faith in Christianity. It now appeared what part of his conversation with the great could be remembered with delight. He related that, being present when the duke of Buckingham talked profanely before King Charles, he said to him, 'My Lord, I am a great deal older than your grace, and have, I believe, heard more arguments for atheism than ever your grace did ; but I have lived long enough to see there is nothing in them ; and so I hope your grace will[1].'

He died October 21, 1687, and was buried at Beaconsfield, with 88 a monument erected by his son's executors, for which Rymer wrote the inscription, and which I hope is now rescued from dilapidation[2].

He left several children by his second wife ; of whom, his 89 daughter was married to Dr. Birch. Benjamin, the eldest son, was disinherited and sent to New Jersey, as wanting common understanding[3]. Edmund, the second son, inherited the estate, and represented Agmondesham in parliament[4], but at last turned Quaker[5]. William, the third son, was a merchant in London. Stephen, the fourth, was an eminent Doctor of Laws, and one of the Commissioners for the Union[6]. There is said to have been a fifth, of whom no account has descended[7].

The character of Waller, both moral and intellectual, has been 90 drawn by Clarendon[8], to whom he was familiarly known, with

---

[1] *Life*, p. 57.

[2] For the burial-place see Aubrey's *Brief Lives*, ii. 278, and for Rymer's inscription see *Life*, p. 80.

[3] ' His eldest, Benjamin, was so far from inheriting his father's wit that he had not a common portion ; so he was sent to Jersey, a colony in the West Indies, where he is still living in obscurity and oblivion.' *Ib.* p. 58.

Many Americans, I am informed, trace their descent to him, asserting that it was in Virginia he settled. A letter in *N. & Q.* 7 S. vii. 487 from Mr. F. Waller of Washington makes this very doubtful. He says that ' one or more of the sons of Dr. John Waller of Newport Pagnell, a prominent citizen there between 1670 and 1688, emigrated to Virginia,' and he asks for information connecting this doctor with the family of the poet.

[4] From 1688-9 to 1698. *Parl. Hist.* v. 26, 541, 958. An Edmund

Waller was in parliament in Walpole's ministry. ' He was a very dull man and spoke obscurely, and in the meanest language, but was supposed to understand the revenue.' HORACE WALPOLE, *Philobiblon Soc. Misc.* x. 37.

[5] *Life*, p. 60. Perhaps Ellwood converted him. *Ante*, WALLER, 86 *n*.

[6] The names of the Commissioners are given in Smollett's *History*, ii. 75.

[7] Johnson and Boswell found a great-grandson of the poet a student at Aberdeen in 1773. ' We were told,' writes Boswell, ' the present Mr. Waller was a plain country gentleman ; and his son would be such another.' Boswell's *Johnson*, v. 85. ' A Portion of the Library of Major-General Waller, collected by the Poet and his Descendants,' was sold by Messrs. Sotheby & Co. on Dec. 12, 1900.

[8] *Life of Clarendon*, i. 53. See also *History of the Rebellion*, iv. 58.

nicety, which certainly none to whom he was not known can presume to emulate. It is therefore inserted here, with such remarks as others have supplied; after which, nothing remains but a critical examination of his poetry.

91   'Edmund Waller,' says Clarendon, 'was born to a very fair estate, by the parsimony or frugality of a wise father and mother: and he thought it so commendable an advantage that he resolved to improve it with his utmost care, upon which in his nature he was too much intent; and, in order to that, he was so much reserved and retired that he was scarce ever heard of, till by his address and dexterity he had gotten a very rich wife in the city [1], against all the recommendation and countenance and authority of the Court, which was thoroughly engaged on the behalf of Mr. Crofts [2]; and which used to be successful in that age against any opposition. He had the good fortune to have an alliance and friendship with Dr. Morley [3], who had assisted and instructed him in the reading many good books, to which his natural parts and promptitude inclined him, especially the poets; and at the age when other men used to give over writing verses (for he was near thirty years when he first engaged himself in that exercise; at least that he was known to do so), he surprised the town with two or three pieces of that kind; as if a tenth Muse had been newly born, to cherish drooping poetry. The Doctor at that time brought him into that company which was most celebrated for good conversation; where he was received and esteemed, with great applause and respect. He was a very pleasant discourser, in earnest and in jest, and therefore very grateful to all kind of company, where he was not the less esteemed for being very rich.

92   'He had been even nursed in parliaments, where he sat when he was very young [4]; and so, when they were resumed again (after a long intermission), he appeared in those assemblies with great advantage; having a graceful way of speaking, and by thinking much on [upon] several arguments (which his temper and complexion, that had much of melancholic, inclined him to), he seemed often to speak upon the sudden, when the occasion had only administered the opportunity of saying what he had thoroughly considered, which gave a great lustre to all he

---

[1] *Ante*, WALLER, 8.

[2] *Ib.* Clarendon, describing how in 1655 the Earl of Bristol and Crofts were wooing the same lady, adds that 'Crofts wanted not art and address to encourage him in those attempts, and could bear repulses with more tranquillity of mind and acquiescence than the other could.' *History*, vii. 97. See *ante*, WALLER, 8. [For William Crofts, created Baron Crofts

of Saxham at Brussels in 1658, see *ante*, DENHAM, 15. Crofts lent his surname to the luckless Duke of Monmouth, who was when a boy entrusted to his care.]

[3] George Morley, afterwards Bishop of Winchester. Isaac Walton dedicated to him his *Lives*. Clarendon drew his character. *Life of Clarendon*, i. 55.

[4] *Ante*, WALLER, 3. Clarendon

said ; which yet was rather of delight than weight [1]. There needs no more be said to extol the excellence and power of his wit, and pleasantness of his conversation, than that it was of magnitude enough to cover a world of very great faults ; that is, so to cover them, that they were not taken notice of to his reproach ; viz. a narrowness in his nature to the lowest degree ; an abjectness and want of courage to support him in any virtuous undertaking ; an insinuation and servile flattery to the height the vainest and most imperious nature could be contented with ; that it preserved and won his life from those who were most resolved to take it, and in an occasion in which he ought to have been ambitious to have lost it ; and then preserved him again from the reproach and contempt that was due to him for so preserving it, and for vindicating it at such a price ; that it had power to reconcile him to those whom he had most offended and provoked ; and continued to his age with that rare felicity, that his company was acceptable where his spirit was odious ; and he was at least pitied, where he was most detested.'

Such is the account of Clarendon, on which it may not be 93 improper to make some remarks [2].

'He was very little known till he had obtained a rich wife in 94 the city [3].'

He obtained a rich wife about the age of three-and-twenty [4], an age before which few men are conspicuous much to their advantage. He was known however in parliament and at court ; and, if he spent part of his time in privacy, it is not unreasonable to suppose that he endeavoured the improvement of his mind as well as of his fortune.

That Clarendon might misjudge the motive of his retirement is 95 the more probable, because he has evidently mistaken the commencement of his poetry, which he supposes him not to have attempted before thirty. As his first pieces were perhaps not printed the succession of his compositions was not known ; and Clarendon, who cannot be imagined to have been very studious of poetry, did not rectify his first opinion by consulting Waller's book.

had written, 'in his infancy.' *Life of Clarendon*, i. 54.

[1] 'He is something magisteriall, and haz a great mastership of the English language. He is of admirable and gracefull elocution, and exceeding ready.' AUBREY, *Brief Lives*, ii. 276.

[2] For an instance of Waller's affectation about his memory, which

Johnson said 'he would record if he lived to revise his *Life*,' see *John. Misc*. ii. 153. For his memory see Aubrey's *Brief Lives*, ii. 279.

[3] This is an instance of Johnson's habit of enclosing a paraphrase in quotation marks.

[4] 'She left him a widower of about five-and-twenty.' *Ante*, WALLER, 8.

96 Clarendon observes that he was introduced to the wits of the age by Dr. Morley; but the writer of his *Life* relates that he was already among them, when, hearing a noise in the street, and enquiring the cause, they found 'a son of Ben Jonson' under an arrest [1]. This was Morley, whom Waller set free at the expence of one hundred pounds, took him into the country as director of his studies, and then procured him admission into the company of the friends of literature. Of this fact, Clarendon had a nearer knowledge than the biographer, and is therefore more to be credited.

97 The account of Waller's parliamentary eloquence is seconded by Burnet, who, though he calls him 'the delight of the house,' adds that 'he was only concerned to say that which should make him be applauded; he never laid the business of the House to heart, being a vain and empty though a witty man [2].'

98 Of his insinuation and flattery it is not unreasonable to believe that the truth is told. Ascham, in his elegant description of those whom in modern language we term Wits, says that they are *open flatterers and privy mockers* [3]. Waller shewed a little of both, when, upon sight of the Dutchess of Newcastle's verses on the death of a Stag [4], he declared that he would give all his own compositions to have written them; and, being charged with the exorbitance of his adulation, answered that 'nothing was too much to be given, that a Lady might be saved from the disgrace

---

[1] 'At one of their meetings they heard a noise in the street, and were told "a son of Ben Jonson's" was arrested. They sent for him, and he proved Mr. Morley, afterwards Bishop of Winchester.' *Life*, p. 11. 'Morley was the son of Francis Morley, Esq., by his wife, who was Denham's sister.' *Dict. Nat. Biog.* Aubrey (*Brief Lives*, ii. 15) states that 'my Lord of Winton [Morley] knew Ben Jonson very well.'

[2] Burnet's *Hist.* i. 436; *ante*, WALLER, 74. Fenton quotes Dryden as saying that 'Burnet was venomously nice in his commendations.' *Observations*, p. 135.

[3] Ascham, in *The Schoolmaster*, ed. Arber, p. 33, describes 'quick wits' as 'privy mockers.' A few lines earlier he speaks of them as 'flattering their betters.'

[4] *The Hunting of a Stag.* The following is a specimen:—

'Single he was; his horns were all his helps
To guard him from a multitude of whelps;
Besides a company of men were there,
If dogs should fail, to strike him everywhere.'
Poems and Phancies, written by the Thrice Noble, Illustrious and Excellent Princess, the Lady Marchioness of Newcastle, 1664, p. 142.

Lamb mentions her in *The Essays of Elia*, 1889, p. 157:—'The poets and romancical writers (as dear Margaret Newcastle would call them).' See also *ib*. p. 36, and *Letters of Lamb*, ii. 138. 'She seems,' wrote Southey, 'rather a creature of romance than of real life.' *Corres. of Southey and C. Bowles*, p. 341. See also *post*, DRYDEN, 43.

Her husband was made a Duke in 1664.

of such a vile performance [1].' This however was no very mischievous or very unusual deviation from truth : had his hypocrisy been confined to such transactions he might have been forgiven though not praised; for who forbears to flatter an author or a lady ?

Of the laxity of his political principles and the weakness of his 99 resolution he experienced the natural effect by losing the esteem of every party. From Cromwell he had only his recall, and from Charles the Second, who delighted in his company, he obtained only the pardon of his relation Hampden and the safety of Hampden's son [2].

As far as conjecture can be made from the whole of his writing 100 and his conduct he was habitually and deliberately a friend to monarchy. His deviation towards democracy proceeded from his connection with Hampden, for whose sake he prosecuted Crawley with great bitterness [3]; and the invective which he pronounced on that occasion was so popular, that twenty thousand copies are said by his biographer to have been sold in one day [4].

It is confessed that his faults still left [5] him many friends, at 101 least many companions. His convivial power of pleasing is universally acknowledged; but those who conversed with him intimately found him not only passionate, especially in his old age, but resentful, so that the interposition of friends was sometimes necessary [6].

[1] 'Being taxed for his insincerity he answered that he could do no less in gallantry than be willing to devote all his own papers to keep a lady from the disgrace of having written anything so ill.' KATHERINE PHILIPS, *Letters from Orinda*, 1705, p. 206.

[2] 'When, about 1683, his cousin John Hampden, Esq., grandson of Colonel Hampden [Shipmoney Hampden], was prosecuted for high treason, he had the favour of obtaining his pardon, and protecting his son from the need of one.' *Life*, p. 48.

Sprat, in his *Account of the Horrid Conspiracy* (*post*, SPRAT, 9), pp. 21, 140, tells how Hampden, 'who has renewed and continued the hereditary malignity of his house against the Royal Family, was fined £40,000, and ordered to give sureties for his good behaviour during life,' as an accomplice in the Rye House Plot. 'This sentence,' says Burnet, 'amounted to an imprisonment for life.' *Hist.* ii. 194. The pardon obtained for him by Waller was escape from a capital sentence. His son needed no protection. Perhaps Richard Hampden, son of 'Colonel Hampden,' and father of the man pardoned, is meant. He had been one of Cromwell's Lords.

[3] *Ante*, WALLER, 24.

[4] *Life*, p. 16.

[5] In the first edition, by a misprint, 'lost.'

Johnson, in writing, always used the long *s* in the middle of a word.

[6] 'He is of somewhat above a middle stature, thin body, not at all robust: fine thin skin, his face somewhat of an olivaster; his hayre frizzd, of a brownish colour ; full

102   His wit and his poetry naturally connected him with the polite writers of his time: he was joined with Lord Buckhurst in the translation of Corneille's *Pompey*[1]; and is said to have added his help to that of Cowley in the original draught of *The Rehearsal*[2].

103   The care of his fortune, which Clarendon imputes to him in a degree little less than criminal, was either not constant or not successful; for, having inherited a patrimony of three thousand five hundred a year in the time of James the First, and augmented it at least by one wealthy marriage, he left, about the time of the Revolution, an income of not more than twelve or thirteen hundred, which, when the different value of money is reckoned, will be found perhaps not more than a fourth part of what he once possessed.

104   Of this diminution, part was the consequence of the gifts which he was forced to scatter, and the fine which he was condemned to pay at the detection of his plot; and if his estate, as is related in his *Life*, was sequestered, he had probably contracted debts when he lived in exile; for we are told that at Paris he lived in splendor, and was the only Englishman, except the Lord St. Albans[3], that kept a table.

105   His unlucky plot compelled him to sell a thousand a year[4]; of the waste of the rest there is no account, except that he is confessed by his biographer to have been a bad œconomist. He seems to have deviated from the common practice: to have been a hoarder in his first years, and a squanderer in his last.

---

eye, popping out, and working; ovall faced, his forehead high and full of wrinkles. His head but small, braine very hott, and apt to be cholerique— *Quanto doctior, eo iracundior.*— Cicero.' *Brief Lives*, ii. 276.

[1] For Waller's translation of Act I see Fenton's *Waller*, p. 241. Johnson does not mention Buckhurst's aid in his *Life of Dorset*. Dryden, dedicating to him his *Dramatic Poesy*, defending his own rhymed plays, says:—' I am sure my adversaries can bring no such arguments against me as those with which the fourth act of *Pompey* will furnish me in its defence.' *Works*, xv. 278.

' June 23, 1666. Read *Pompey the Great*, a play translated from the French by several noble persons; among others, my Lord Buckhurst, that to me is but a mean play, and the words and sense not very extraordinary.' Pepys, *Diary*, iii. 217.

According to Pope, Godolphin was one of the translators. Warton's *Pope*, iv. 185. For Mrs. Philips's rival translation see *ante*, Roscommon, 36; *post*, Waller, 147.

[2] *Post*, Dryden, 94 *n.*

[3] *Ante*, Cowley, 7, 44; Waller, 23, 63 *n.* ' He was the Queen's chief officer, and governed all her receipts, and he loved plenty so well that he would not be without it, whatever others suffered.' Clarendon's *Hist.* v. 555. See also *ib.* vi. 352.

[4] *Ante*, Waller, 60; *Life*, p. 36.

Of his course of studies or choice of books nothing is known, 106
more than that he professed himself unable to read Chapman's
translation of Homer without rapture[1]. His opinion concerning
the duty of a poet is contained in his declaration, that 'he would
blot from his works any line that did not contain some motive to
virtue[2].'

THE characters, by which Waller intended to distinguish 107
his writings, are spriteliness and dignity: in his smaller pieces
he endeavours to be gay[3]; in the larger, to be great. Of his airy
and light productions the chief source is gallantry; that attentive
reverence of female excellence which has descended to us from
the Gothick ages[4]. As his poems are commonly occasional and
his addresses personal, he was not so liberally supplied with
grand as with soft images; for beauty is more easily found than
magnanimity.

The delicacy which he cultivated restrains him to a certain 108
nicety and caution, even when he writes upon the slightest matter.
He has therefore in his whole volume nothing burlesque[5], and
seldom any thing ludicrous or familiar. He seems always to do
his best[6], though his subjects are often unworthy of his care.
It is not easy to think without some contempt on an author who
is growing illustrious in his own opinion by verses, at one time,
To a Lady, who can do anything, but sleep, when she pleases[7]. At
another, *To a Lady, who can sleep, when she pleases*[8]. Now, *To
a Lady, on her passing through a crowd of people*[9]. Then, *On*

---

[1] 'Mr. Dryden tells us, Mr. Waller
used to say he could never read
Chapman's *Homer* without transport.'
Life, p. 66. Dryden wrote, 'without
incredible pleasure and extreme
transport.' *Works*, xii. 67.

[2] The authority for this is Knightly
Chetwood in his *Life of Virgil. Ib.*
xiii. 315.
'No writing is good that does not
tend to better mankind some way or
other. Mr. Waller has said, "that
he wished everything of his burnt
that did not drive some moral."
Even in love-verses it may be flung
in by the way.' POPE, Spence's *Anec.*
p. 203.

[3] 'Waller often attempted easy
writing, but seldom attained it; for

he is too frequently driven into
transpositions.' JOHNSON, *The Idler*,
No. 77.

[4] The Middle Ages. The *Gothick*
of Johnson and his contemporaries
is the *mediaeval* of our time. The
earliest use of 'Middle Ages' given
in *New Eng. Dict.* is Hallam's in
1818.

[5] For an instance of unintentional
burlesque see *ante*, WALLER, 67 *n.*

[6] 'Poets lose half the praise they
    should have got,
Could it be known what they dis-
    creetly blot.'
WALLER, *Eng. Poets*, xvi. 175.

[7] *Ib.* p. 34.

[8] *Ib.* p. 53.

[9] *Ib.* p. 55.

a braid of divers colours woven by four fair Ladies[1]; On a tree cut in paper[2]; or, To a Lady, from whom he received the copy of verses on the paper-tree, which for many years had been missing[3].

109　Genius now and then produces a lucky trifle. We still read the *Dove* of Anacreon[4] and *Sparrow* of Catullus[5], and a writer naturally pleases himself with a performance which owes nothing to the subject. But compositions merely pretty have the fate of other pretty things, and are quitted in time for something useful: they are flowers fragrant and fair, but of short duration; or they are blossoms to be valued only as they foretell fruits.

110　Among Waller's little poems are some, which their excellency ought to secure from oblivion; as, *To Amoret*, comparing the different modes of regard with which he looks on her and *Sacharissa*[6], and the verses *On Love*, that begin 'Anger in hasty words or blows[7].'

111　In others he is not equally successful; sometimes his thoughts are deficient, and sometimes his expression.

112　The numbers are not always musical, as

> 'Fair Venus, in thy soft arms
> 　　The god of rage confine;
> For thy whispers are the charms
> 　　Which only can divert his fierce design.
> What though he frown, and to tumult do incline;
> 　　Thou the flame
> 　　Kindled in his breast canst tame,
> With that snow which unmelted lies on thine[8].'

113　He seldom indeed fetches an amorous sentiment from the depths of science[9]; his thoughts are for the most part easily understood, and his images such as the superficies of nature readily supplies; he has a just claim to popularity because he writes to common degrees of knowledge, and is free at least from philosophical

---

[1] *Eng. Poets*, xvi. 135.

[2] *Ib.* p. 167.　[3] *Ib.* p. 168.

[4] According to Mrs. Piozzi Johnson said of Anacreon's *Dove*:—'As I never was struck with anything in the Greek language till I read that, so I never read anything in the same language that pleased me as much.' *John. Misc.* i. 176. See *ib.* for his translation of it. 'Though I began these verses,' he said, 'when I was sixteen years old, I never could find time to make an end of them before I was sixty-eight.'

[5] Catullus's *Ad Passerem Lesbiae* and *Luctus in Morte Passeris* 'seem to have been admired, both by the ancients and the moderns, above all the rest. Beautiful indeed they are.' LANDOR, *Longer Prose Works*, ii. 212.

[6] *Ante*, WALLER, 9; *Eng. Poets*, xvi. 62.

[7] *Ib.* p. 79.

[8] *Ib.* p. 36.

[9] As did the metaphysical poets. *Ante*, COWLEY, 65.

pedantry, unless perhaps the end of a song *To the Sun* may be excepted, in which he is too much a Copernican[1]. To which may be added the simile of the Palm in the verses *On her passing through a crowd*[2], and a line in a more serious poem on *The Restoration*, about vipers and treacle[3], which can only be understood by those who happen to know the composition of the Theriaca[4].

His thoughts are sometimes hyperbolical, and his images 114 unnatural:

> 'The plants admire,
> No less than those of old did Orpheus' lyre;
> If she sit down, with tops all tow'rds her bow'd,
> They round about her into arbours crowd:
> Or if she walks [walk], in even ranks they stand,
> Like some well-marshal'd and obsequious band[5].'

In another place:

> 'While in the park I sing, the listening deer
> Attend my passion, and forget to fear:
> When to the beeches I report my flame,
> They bow their heads, as if they felt the same:
> To gods appealing, when I reach their bowers,
> With loud complaints they answer me in showers.
> To thee a wild and cruel soul is given,
> More deaf than trees, and prouder than the heaven[6]!'

On the head of a Stag:

> 'O fertile head! which every year
> Could such a crop of wonder bear!
> The teeming earth did never bring
> So soon, so hard, so huge a thing:

---

[1] 'Well does this prove
The error of those antique books
Which made you move
About the world: her charming looks
Would fix your beams, and make it ever day,
Did not the rolling earth snatch her away.'
Eng. Poets, xvi. 48.
'This stanza alludes to the Copernican system. . . . Dr. Donne and Mr. Cowley industriously affected to entertain the fair sex with such philosophical allusions; which, in his riper age, Mr. Waller as industriously avoided.' FENTON, *Observations*, p. 61.

[2] *Ib.* p. 69; *Eng. Poets*, xvi. 55.

[3] 'All winds blow fair that did the world embroil;
Your vipers treacle yield, and scorpions oil.' *Ib.* p. 150.

[4] *Treacle* is derived, through the old *triacle*, from the Latin *theriaca*, an antidote against poisons, especially venomous bites. Bailey (*Eng. Dict.* ed. 1773) defines it as 'a physical composition made of vipers and other ingredients; also a sort of syrup drawn from sugar.' See *post*, GARTH, 11.

[5] *Eng. Poets*, xvi. 51. The conceit in the fourth line is found also in Pope's *Pastorals*, ii. 74:—
'Trees, where you sit, shall crowd into a shade.'

[6] *Eng. Poets*, xvi. p. 60.

Which might it never have been cast,
Each year's growth added to the last,
These lofty branches had supply'd
The Earth's bold sons' prodigious pride :
Heaven with these engines had been scal'd,
When mountains heap'd on mountains fail'd[1].'

115   Sometimes having succeeded in the first part he makes a feeble conclusion. In the song of *Sacharissa's and Amoret's Friendship*, the two last stanzas ought to have been omitted[2].

116   His images of gallantry are not always in the highest degree delicate :

'Then shall my love this doubt displace,
    And gain such trust, that I may come
And banquet sometimes on thy face,
    But make my constant meals at home[3].'

117   Some applications may be thought too remote and unconsequential, as in the verses on the *Lady dancing* :

'The sun, in figures such as these,
Joys with the moon to play :
    To the sweet strains they advance,
Which do result from their own spheres ;
        As this nymph's dance
Moves with the numbers which she hears[4].'

118   Sometimes a thought which might perhaps fill a distich is expanded and attenuated till it grows weak and almost evanescent :

'Chloris ! since first our calm of peace
    Was frighted hence, this good we find,
Your favours with your fears increase,
    And growing mischiefs make you kind.
So the fair tree, which still preserves
    Her fruit and state, while no wind blows,
In storms from that uprightness swerves ;
    And the glad earth about her strows
With treasure from her yielding boughs[5].'

119   His images are not always distinct, as in the following passage he confounds *Love* as a person with *love* as a passion :

[1] *Eng. Poets*, xvi. 104.
[2] *Ib.* p. 65.
[3] *Ib.* p. 85. Prior imitated this verse in *A Better Answer. Eng. Poets*, xxxii. 260.
' So when I am wearied with wandering all day

To thee, my delight, in the evening I come :
No matter what beauties I saw in my way ;
They were but my visits, but thou art my home.'
[4] *Ib.* xvi. p. 95.   [5] *Ib.* p. 98.

'Some other nymphs, with colours faint,
And pencil slow, may Cupid paint,
And a weak heart in time destroy;
She has a stamp, and prints the Boy:
Can, with a single look, inflame
The coldest breast, the rudest tame [1].'

His sallies of casual flattery are sometimes elegant and happy, 120
as that *In return for the Silver Pen* [2], and sometimes empty and
trifling, as that *Upon the Card torn by the Queen* [3]. There are
a few lines *Written in the Dutchess's Tasso*, which he is said by
Fenton to have kept a summer under correction [4]. It happened
to Waller, as to others, that his success was not always in proportion to his labour [5].

Of these petty compositions, neither the beauties nor the 121
faults deserve much attention. The amorous verses have this
to recommend them, that they are less hyperbolical than those
of some other poets. Waller is not always at the last gasp; he
does not die of a frown, nor live upon a smile. There is however
too much love, and too many trifles. Little things are made too
important; and the Empire of Beauty is represented as exerting
its influence further than can be allowed by the multiplicity of
human passions and the variety of human wants. Such books
therefore may be considered as shewing the world under a false
appearance, and, so far as they obtain credit from the young
and unexperienced, as misleading expectation and misguiding
practice [6].

Of his nobler and more weighty performances the greater 122
part is panegyrical; for of praise he was very lavish, as is observed
by his imitator, Lord Lansdown:

[1] *Eng. Poets*, xvi. p. 99.
[2] *Ib.* p. 97. [3] *Ib.* p. 239.
[4] *Ib.* p. 202. The lines are but
ten in number. 'I very well remember to have heard the Duke
of Buckinghamshire say, that the
author employed the greatest part of
a summer in composing and correcting them.' FENTON, *Observations*,
p. 153.
[5] 'That admirable writer has the
best and worst verses of any among
our great English poets.' ADDISON,
The Tatler, No. 163.
[6] Johnson, in his *Preface to Shakespeare*, speaking of lovers, says:—

'... to distress them as nothing
human ever was distressed, to deliver
them as nothing human ever was
delivered, is the business of a modern
dramatist. For this, probability is
violated, life is misrepresented, and
language is depraved. But love is
only one of many passions; and as
it has no great influence upon the
sum of life, it has little operation in
the dramas of a poet [Shakespeare]
who caught his ideas from the living
world, and exhibited only what he
saw before him.' Johnson's *Works*,
v. 107. See also Boswell's *Johnson*,
ii. 122.

'No satyr stalks [lurks] within the [this] hallow'd ground, ⎞
But queens [nymphs] and heroines, kings and gods ⎟
   abound ;   ⎬
Glory and arms and love are all the sound [1].' ⎠

123   In the first poem, on the danger of the Prince on the coast of Spain, there is a puerile and ridiculous mention of Arion at the beginning [2]; and the last paragraph, on the Cable, is in part ridiculously mean, and in part ridiculously tumid [3]. The poem however is such as may be justly praised, without much allowance for the state of our poetry and language at that time.

124   The two next poems are upon the King's behaviour at the death of Buckingham [4], and upon his Navy [5].

He has, in the first, used the pagan deities with great propriety:

''Twas want of such a precedent as this
   Made the old heathen frame their gods amiss [6].'

In the poem on the Navy those lines are very noble which suppose the King's power secure against a second Deluge, so noble that it were almost criminal to remark the mistake of *centre* for *surface*, or to say that the empire of the sea would be worth little if it were not that the waters terminate in land [7].

125   The poem upon Sallee has forcible sentiments, but the conclusion is feeble [8]. That on the Repairs of St. Paul's has some-

[1] *Eng. Poets*, xxxviii. 14 ; *post*, GRANVILLE, 3.

[2] *Eng. Poets*, xvi. 17.

[3] *Ante*, WALLER, 5. A rope was thrown from a ship to the boat in which the prince and several grandees were tossing about.
'Twice was the cable hurl'd in vain ; the fates [states.
Would not be moved for our sister For England is the third successful throw,
And then the Genius of that land they know.' *Eng. Poets*, xvi. 22.

[4] *Of His Majesty's receiving the News of the Duke of Buckingham's Death*. *Ante*, WALLER, 6 ; *Eng. Poets*, xvi. 23.
[The king, who was at prayers when the news was 'whispered in his ears, . . . continued unmoved and without the least change in his countenance till prayers were ended ; when he suddenly departed to his chamber and threw himself upon his bed, lamenting with much passion and with abundance of tears the loss.' Clarendon's *Hist.* i. 54.]

[5] *Ante*, WALLER, 15 ; *Eng. Poets*, xvi. 24.   [6] *Ib.* p. 24.
[7] 'Should Nature's self invade the world again, [liquid main,
And o'er the centre spread the Thy pow'r were safe ; and her destructive hand
Would but enlarge the bounds of thy command ; [lord of all,
Thy dreadful fleet would style thee And ride in triumph o'er the drowned ball.' *Ib.* p. 25.
Mr. C. L. Ford in *N. & Q.* 9 S. iv. 11 suggests that 'by the "centre" Waller means the earth itself,' as the word is used in *Troilus and Cressida*, i. 3. 85 ; *Paradise Lost*, i. 74.
[8] 'Hither he sends the chief among his peers, [presents bears,
Who in his bark proportion'd To the renown'd for piety and force,
Poor captives manumis'd and matchless horse.'
Eng. Poets, xvi. 27.

thing vulgar and obvious, such as the mention of Amphion[1];
and something violent and harsh, as,

> 'So all our minds with his conspire to grace
> The Gentiles' great apostle, and deface
> Those state-obscuring sheds, that like a chain
> Seem'd to confine, and fetter him again[2];
> Which the glad saint shakes off at his command,
> As once the viper from his sacred hand.
> So joys the aged oak, when we divide
> The creeping ivy from his injur'd side.'

Of the two last couplets the first is extravagant, and the second mean.

His praise of the Queen is too much exaggerated, and the 126 thought, that she 'saves lovers, by cutting off hope, as gangrenes are cured by lopping the limb[3],' presents nothing to the mind but disgust and horror.

Of *The Battle of the Summer Islands*[4] it seems not easy to 127 say whether it is intended to raise terror or merriment: the beginning is too splendid for jest, and the conclusion too light for seriousness. The versification is studied, the scenes are diligently displayed, and the images artfully amplified; but as it ends neither in joy nor sorrow it will scarcely be read a second time.

The *Panegyrick* upon Cromwell[5] has obtained from the publick 128 a very liberal dividend of praise, which however cannot be said to have been unjustly lavished; for such a series of verses had rarely appeared before in the English language. Of the lines some are grand, some are graceful, and all are musical. There is now and then a feeble verse or a trifling thought; but its great fault is the choice of its hero[6].

The poem of *The War with Spain* begins with lines more 129

---

[1] *Eng. Poets*, xvi. 27.

[2] The 'sheds' were the houses built up against the walls. They were pulled down. 'Before the end of 1632 the long nave stood exposed to view in its unrivalled proportions.' GARDINER, *Hist. of Eng.* vii. 246.

[3] 'She saves the lover, as we gangrenes stay,
> By cutting hope, like a lopt limb, away.' *Eng. Poets*, xvi. 33.

[4] *Ib.* p. 70; *ante*, WALLER, 14.

[5] *Eng. Poets*, xvi. 136; *ante*, WALLER, 65.

[6] 'When black ambition stains a public cause,
> A monarch's sword when mad vainglory draws,
> Not Waller's wreath can hide the nation's scar,
> Nor Boileau turn the feather to a star.' Pope, *Epil. Sat.* ii. 228.
> For Boileau see his *Ode sur la Prise de Namur*, l. 113.

vigorous and striking than Waller is accustomed to produce[1]. The succeeding parts are variegated with better passages and worse. There is something too far-fetched in the comparison of the Spaniards drawing the English on, by saluting St. Lucar with cannon, *to lambs awakening the lion by bleating*[2]. The fate of the Marquis and his Lady, who were burnt in their ship, would have moved more had the poet not made him die like the Phœnix, because he had spices about him, nor expressed their affection and their end by a conceit at once false and vulgar:

> 'Alive, in equal flames of love they burn'd,
> And now together are to ashes turn'd[3].'

130   The verses to Charles on his Return were doubtless intended to counterbalance the panegyric on Cromwell. If it has been thought inferior to that with which it is naturally compared, the cause of its deficience has been already remarked[4].

131   The remaining pieces it is not necessary to examine singly. They must be supposed to have faults and beauties of the same kind with the rest. The Sacred Poems[5] however deserve particular regard; they were the work of Waller's declining life, of those hours in which he looked upon the fame and the folly of the time past with the sentiments which his great predecessor Petrarch bequeathed to posterity, upon his review of that love and poetry which have given him immortality[6].

132   That natural jealousy which makes every man unwilling to allow much excellence in another, always produces a disposition to believe that the mind grows old with the body, and that he whom we are now forced to confess superior is hastening daily to a level with ourselves. By delighting to think this of the living, we learn to think it of the dead; and Fenton, with all his kindness for Waller, has the luck to mark the exact time when his genius passed the zenith, which he places at his fifty-fifth year[7].

---

[1] *Eng. Poets*, xvi. 143; *post*, DRYDEN, 250.

[2] 'So heedless lambs which for their mothers bleat
Wake hungry lions, and become their meat.' *Eng. Poets*, xvi. 144.

[3] *Ib.* p. 146.

[4] *Ante*, WALLER, 70.

[5] *Eng. Poets*, xvi. 205-36; *ante*, WALLER, 85.

[6] 'Petrarca, like Boccaccio, regretted at the close of life, not only the pleasure he had enjoyed, but also the pleasure he had imparted to the world. Both of them, as their mental faculties were diminishing, and their animal spirits were leaving them apace, became unconscious how incomparably greater was the benefit than the injury done by their writings.' LANDOR, *Longer Prose Works*, ii. 265.

[7] Fenton says of Waller's poem *To the King upon his Return*:—'Its date coincides with the fifty-fifth year

This is to allot the mind but a small portion. Intellectual decay is doubtless not uncommon; but it seems not to be universal[1]. Newton was in his eighty-fifth year improving his *Chronology*[2], a few days before his death; and Waller appears not, in my opinion, to have lost at eighty-two any part of his poetical power.

His Sacred Poems do not please like some of his other works; 133 but before the fatal fifty-five, had he written on the same subjects, his success would hardly have been better.

It has been the frequent lamentation of good men that verse 134 has been too little applied to the purposes of worship, and many attempts have been made to animate devotion by pious poetry; that they have very seldom attained their end is sufficiently known, and it may not be improper to enquire why they have miscarried[3].

Let no pious ear be offended if I advance, in opposition to many 135 authorities, that poetical devotion cannot often please. The doctrines of religion may indeed be defended in a didactick poem, and he who has the happy power of arguing in verse will not lose it because his subject is sacred. A poet may describe the beauty and the grandeur of Nature, the flowers of the Spring, and the harvests of Autumn, the vicissitudes of the Tide, and the revolutions of the Sky, and praise the Maker for his works in lines which no reader shall lay aside. The subject of the disputation is not piety, but the motives to piety; that of the description is not God, but the works of God.

Contemplative piety, or the intercourse between God and the 136 human soul, cannot be poetical. Man admitted to implore the mercy of his Creator and plead the merits of his Redeemer is already in a higher state than poetry can confer.

The essence of poetry is invention; such invention as, by 137 producing something unexpected, surprises and delights. The topicks of devotion are few, and being few are universally known; but, few as they are, they can be made no more; they can receive

---

of Mr. Waller's age; from which time his genius began to decline apace from its meridian.' *Observations*, p. 121.

[1] 'JOHNSON. I value myself upon this that there is nothing of the old man in my conversation. I am now sixty-eight; and I have no more of it than at twenty-eight.' Boswell's *Johnson*, iii. 336. See also *ib.* iv. 181.

[2] *General Dict. Hist. and Crit.* vii. 297. For Gibbon's study of Newton's *Chronology* see his *Memoirs*, pp. 45, 63, 129.

[3] *Ante*, COWLEY, 146.

no grace from novelty of sentiment, and very little from novelty of expression.

138 Poetry pleases by exhibiting an idea more grateful to the mind than things themselves afford. This effect proceeds from the display of those parts of nature which attract, and the conceal-ment of those which repel, the imagination : but religion must be shewn as it is ; suppression and addition equally corrupt it, and such as it is, it is known already.

139 From poetry the reader justly expects, and from good poetry always obtains, the enlargement of his comprehension and eleva-tion of his fancy; but this is rarely to be hoped by Christians from metrical devotion. Whatever is great, desirable, or tremendous, is comprised in the name of the Supreme Being. Omnipotence cannot be exalted ; Infinity cannot be amplified ; Perfection cannot be improved.

140 The employments of pious meditation are Faith, Thanksgiving, Repentance, and Supplication. Faith, invariably uniform, cannot be invested by fancy with decorations. Thanksgiving, the most joyful of all holy effusions, yet addressed to a Being without passions, is confined to a few modes, and is to be felt rather than expressed. Repentance, trembling in the presence of the judge, is not at leisure for cadences and epithets [1]. Supplication of man to man may diffuse itself through many topicks of persuasion, but supplication to God can only cry for mercy.

141 Of sentiments purely religious, it will be found that the most simple expression is the most sublime. Poetry loses its lustre and its power, because it is applied to the decoration of something more excellent than itself. All that pious verse can do is to help the memory and delight the ear, and for these purposes it may be very useful ; but it supplies nothing to the mind. The ideas of Christian Theology are too simple for eloquence, too sacred for fiction, and too majestick for ornament ; to recommend them by

[1] 'Dr. Johnson would try to repeat the ... *Dies iræ, Dies illa*, he could never pass the stanza ending thus, *Tantus labor non sit cassus*, without bursting into a flood of tears ; which sensibility I used to quote against him when he would inveigh against devotional poetry, and protest that all religious verses were cold and feeble, and unworthy the subject, which ought to be treated with higher reverence, he said, than either poets or painters could presume to excite or bestow.' MRS. PIOZZI, *John. Misc.* i. 284.

The stanza runs :—

'Quaerens me sedisti lassus.
Redemisti crucem passus :
Tantus labor non sit cassus.'

In the Latin hymns is to be found the best answer to Johnson's criti-cism.

tropes and figures is to magnify by a concave mirror the sidereal hemisphere.

As much of Waller's reputation was owing to the softness and 142 smoothness of his numbers [1], it is proper to consider those minute particulars to which a versifier must attend.

He certainly very much excelled in smoothness most of the 143 writers who were living when his poetry commenced. The Poets of Elizabeth had attained an art of modulation, which was afterwards neglected or forgotten. Fairfax was acknowledged by him as his model [2]; and he might have studied with advantage the poem of Davis [3], which, though merely philosophical, yet seldom leaves the ear ungratified.

But he was rather smooth than strong [4]; of 'the full resounding 144 line,' which Pope attributes to Dryden [5], he has given very few examples. The critical decision has given the praise of strength to Denham, and of sweetness to Waller [6].

His excellence of versification has some abatements. He uses 145 the expletive *do* very frequently [7]; and though he lived [8] to see it

[1] 'But now, my Muse, a softer strain rehearse,
  Turn every line with art, and smooth thy verse;
  The courtly Waller next commands thy lays;
  Muse, tune thy verse with art to Waller's praise.'
    ADDISON, *Works*, i. 25.
The editor of Waller's *Poems*, 1690, wrote:—'He was indeed the parent of English verse, and the first that showed us our tongue had beauty and numbers in it.' Fenton's *Waller*, p. 287.
'Waller was the first refiner of English poetry, at least of English rhyme; but his performances still abound with many faults, and, what is more material, they contain but feeble and superficial beauties.' HUME, *History*, vii. 345. See *ante*, COWLEY, 63; DENHAM, 21, 35; WALLER, 5; *post*, DRYDEN, 342; PRIOR, 74 *n*.
[2] *Ante*, WALLER, 5.
[3] *Nosce Teipsum* by Sir John Davies, 1599. 'Davies carried abstract reasoning into verse with an acuteness and felicity which have seldom been equalled.' CAMPBELL, *Brit. Poets*, Pref. p. 70. See p. 100

for specimens of his poetry.
[4] 'Cowley has indeed many noble lines such as the feeble care of Waller never could produce.' *Ante*, COWLEY, 185.
[5] *Imit. Hor., Epis.* ii. 1. 267; *post*, DRYDEN, 342; POPE, 333.
[6] *Ante*, DENHAM, 34. 'Well-placing of words for the sweetness of pronunciation was not known till Mr. Waller introduced it.' DRYDEN, *Works*, iv. 233. 'They [the older writers] can produce nothing so even, sweet and flowing as Mr. Waller; nothing so majestic, so correct as Sir John Denham.' *Ib.* xv. 291. 'If I should instruct some of my fellow-poets to make well-running verses, they want genius to give them strength as well as sweetness.' *Ib.* xiv. 208.
'And praise the easy vigour of a line
  Where Denham's strength and Waller's sweetness join.'
  POPE, *Essay on Criticism*, l. 360.
[7] *Ante*, COWLEY, 189.
[8] *Used*, which is found in both the first and third editions, must be a misprint for *lived*.

almost universally ejected, was not more careful to avoid it in his last compositions than in his first. Praise had given him confidence, and, finding the world satisfied, he satisfied himself.

146   His rhymes are sometimes weak words : *so* is found to make the rhyme twice in ten lines[1], and occurs often as a rhyme through his book.

147   His double rhymes in heroick verse have been censured by Mrs. Phillips, who was his rival in the translation of Corneille's *Pompey*[2]; and more faults might be found, were not the enquiry below attention.

148   He sometimes uses the obsolete termination of verbs, as *waxeth*, *affecteth*[3]; and sometimes retains the final syllable of the preterite, as *amazed*[4], *supposed*[5], of which I know not whether it is not to the detriment of our language that we have totally rejected them.

149   Of triplets he is sparing[6], but he did not wholly forbear them ; of an Alexandrine[7] he has given no example.

150   The general character of his poetry is elegance and gaiety. He is never pathetick, and very rarely sublime[8]. He seems neither to have had a mind much elevated by nature, nor amplified by learning. His thoughts are such as a liberal conversation and large acquaintance with life would easily supply. They had however then, perhaps, that grace of novelty, which they are now often supposed to want by those who, having already found them in later books, do not know or enquire who produced them first.

[1] *Eng. Poets*, xvi. 120. In both cases it rhymes with *know*. In the same short poem it had been made also to rhyme with *allow*.

[2] Fenton's *Waller: Observations*, p. 163. She adds :—'The rule that I understood of translation, till these gentlemen informed me better, was to write so Corneille's sense as it is to be supposed Corneille would have done if he had been an Englishman ; not confined to his lines, nor his numbers (unless we can do it happily), but always to his meaning.' For Butler's double rhymes see *ante*, BUTLER, 50 *n.*, and for Pope's *post*, POPE, 377. For Mrs. Philips see *ante*, ROSCOMMON, 38, and WALLER, 102 *n.*

[3] 'So little care of what is done below

Hath the bright dame whom Heav'n affecteth so.'
               Eng. Poets, xvi. 54.

[4] 'The water consecrate for sacrifice Appears all black to her amazed eyes.' *Ib.* p. 131.

[5] 'Yet, that his piece might not exceed belief,

He cast a veil upon supposed grief.'
               Ib. p. 24.

[6] He has, I think, but four—*ib.* pp. 71, 74, 179, 183.

[7] *Ante*, COWLEY, 196 ; *post*, DRYDEN, 344 ; POPE, 376.

[8] Hume says of Waller's poems :—'They aspire not to the sublime ; still less to the pathetic. They treat of love, without making us feel any tenderness, and abound in panegyric, without exciting admiration.' *History*, vii. 345.

This treatment is unjust. Let not the original author lose by his imitators [1].

Praise however should be due before it is given. The author 151 of Waller's Life ascribes to him the first practice, of what Erythræus [2] and some late critics call *Alliteration*, of using in the same verse many words beginning with the same letter [3]. But this knack, whatever be its value, was so frequent among early writers, that Gascoign, a writer of the sixteenth century, warns the young poet against affecting it [4]; Shakespeare, in the *Midsummer Night's Dream*, is supposed to ridicule it [5]; and in another play the sonnet of Holofernes fully displays it [6].

He borrows too many of his sentiments and illustrations from 152 the old mythology [7], for which it is vain to plead the example of ancient poets : the deities which they introduced so frequently were considered as realities, so far as to be received by the imagination, whatever sober reason might even then determine. But of these images time has tarnished the splendor. A fiction, not only detected but despised, can never afford a solid basis to any position, though sometimes it may furnish a transient allusion, or slight illustration. No modern monarch can be much exalted by hearing that, as Hercules had had his *club*, he has his *navy* [8].

[1] *Post*, DRYDEN, 196.

[2] 'Latiniste vénitien, né à Venise, vivait en 1559.' *Nouv. Biog. gén.* xvi. 327.

[3] 'That way of using the same initial letters in a line, which throws the verse off more easily, was first introduced by him, as in this verse :—
"Oh ! how I long my careless limbs to lay." [*Eng. Poets*, xvi. 72.] Mr. Dryden imitated it to affectation, as many others since him have also done.' *Life*, p. 79.
Atterbury, writing to Pope about his couplet :—
'Virtue unmoved can hear the call, And face the flash that melts the ball'
[*Epitaph on John Hughes and Sarah Drew*, end], says :—'Waller, for the sake of the F and the B (of which he was remarkably fond), would have chosen to say :—
"And face the flash that *burns* the ball."' *Atterbury Corres.* ii. 75.
Alliteration is not in Johnson's *Dictionary*. Eight years after its

publication Churchill wrote :—
'Apt alliteration's artful aid.'
Poems, 1766, i. 101.
The word was in print as early as 1656. *New Eng. Dict.*

[4] 'That figure which is expressed in repetition of sundry words beginning all with one letter, being modestly used, lendeth good grace to a verse ; but they do so hunt a letter to death that they make it *crambé*, and *Crambe bis posita mors est.*' *Certayne Notes of Introduction in English Verse*, 1575, *Arber's Reprints*, 1868, p. 36.

[5] Act i. sc. 2.

[6] *Love's Labour's Lost*, iv. 2. The last eleven words are not in the first edition of the *Lives*.

[7] *Ante*, BUTLER, 41 ; WALLER, 123, 125.

[8] 'His club Alcides, Phoebus has his bow,
Jove has his thunder, and your navy You.'
To the King, Eng. Poets, xvi. 198.

153 But of the praise of Waller, though much may be taken away, much will remain, for it cannot be denied that he added something to our elegance of diction, and something to our propriety of thought ; and to him may be applied what Tasso said, with equal spirit and justice, of himself and Guarini, when, having perused the *Pastor Fido*, he cried out, ' If he had not read *Aminta*, he had not excelled it [1].'

154 AS Waller professed himself to have learned the art of versification from Fairfax [2] it has been thought proper to subjoin a specimen of his work, which, after Mr. Hoole's translation, will perhaps not be soon reprinted [3]. By knowing the state in which Waller found our poetry, the reader may judge how much he improved it [4].

I [5].

> ' Erminiaes steed (this while) his mistresse bore
> Through forrests thicke among the shadie treene,
> Her feeble hand the bridle raines forlore,
> Halfe in a swoune she was for feare I weene ;
> But her flit courser spared nere the more,
> To beare her through the desart woods vnseene
>   Of her strong foes, that chas'd her through the plaine,
>   And still pursu'd, but still pursu'd in vaine.

[1] ' It is said that Tasso, on seeing the *Pastor Fido* represented, looked vexed and said :—" If Guarini had not seen my *Amintas* he had not excelled it." ' BARETTI, *The Italian Library*, 1757, p. 120.
' Tasso's *Aminta* infinitely transcends Guarini's *Pastor Fido*, as having more of nature in it, and being almost wholly clear from the wretched affectation of learning.' DRYDEN, *Works*, xiii. 324.
Chesterfield (*Letters*, ii. 341) thus described the *Pastor Fido* :—' A parcel of shepherds and shepherdesses, with the *true pastoral simplicity*, talk metaphysics, epigrams, *concetti* and quibbles by the hour to each other.' See also *post*, GAY, 32 ; A. PHILIPS, 16.
' I am desirous of laying hold on Mr. Waller's memory on all occasions and thereby acknowledging to the world that, unless he had written, none of us could write.' DRYDEN, *Works*, xviii. 6.

[2] *Ante*, WALLER, 5, 143.
[3] Boswell's *Johnson*, i. 383. Charles Lamb wrote on Jan. 5, 1797 :—' Fairfax I have been in quest of a long time. Johnson, in his *Life of Waller*, gives a most delicious specimen of him, and adds, in the true manner of that delicate critic, as well as amiable man, " It may be presumed that this old version will not be much read after the elegant translation of my friend, Mr. Hoole." I endeavoured—I wished to gain some idea of Tasso from this Mr. Hoole, the great boast and ornament of the India House, but soon desisted. I found him more vapid than smallest small beer "sun-vinegared." ' *Letters of Lamb*, i. 59.
[4] For somewhat similar praise of Cowley and Denham see *ante*, COWLEY, 202 ; DENHAM, 42.
[5] [Book vii of *Godfrey of Bulloigne or the Recouerie of Ierusalem, done into English heroicall Verse by Edw. Fairfax, Gent.* 1600.]

2.

'Like as the wearie hounds at last retire,
Windlesse, displeased, from the fruitlesse chace,
When the slie beast Tapisht in bush and brire,
No art nor paines can rowse out of his place:
The Christian knights so full of shame and ire
Returned backe, with faint and wearie pace:
   Yet still the fearefull Dame fled, swift as winde,
   Nor euer staid, nor euer lookt behinde.

3.

'Through thicke and thinne, all night, all day, she driued,
Withouten comfort, companie or guide,
Her plaints and teares with euery thought reuiued,
She heard and saw her greefes, but nought beside.
But when the sunne his burning chariot diued
In Thetis waue, and wearie teame vntide,
   On Iordans sandie banks her course she staid
   At last, there downe she light, and downe she laid.

4.

'Her teares, her drinke; her food, her sorrowings,
This was her diet that vnhappie night:
But sleepe (that sweet repose and quiet brings)
To ease the greefes of discontented wight,
Spred foorth his tender, soft, and nimble wings,
In his dull armes foulding the virgin bright;
   And loue, his mother, and the graces kept
   Strong watch and warde, while this faire Ladie slept.

5.

'The birds awakte her with their morning song,
Their warbling musicke pearst her tender eare,
The murmuring brookes and whistling windes among
The ratling boughes, and leaues, their parts did beare;
Her eies vnclos'd beheld the groues along
Of swaines and shepherd groomes, that dwellings weare;
   And that sweet noise, birds, winds, and waters sent,
   Prouokte againe the virgin to lament.

6.

'Her plaints were interrupted with a sound,
That seem'd from thickest bushes to proceed,
Some iolly shepherd sung a lustie round,
And to his voice had tun'd his oaten reed;
Thither she went, an old man there she found
(At whose right hand his little flock did feed),

Set making baskets, his three sonnes among,
That learn'd their fathers art, and learn'd his song.

7.

'Beholding one in shining armes appeare
The seelie man and his were sore dismaid;
But sweet Erminia comforted their feare,
Her ventall vp, her visage open laid,
You happie folke, of heau'n beloued deare,
Work on (quoth she) vpon your harmlesse traid,
　　These dreadfull armes I beare no warfare bring
　　To your sweet toile, nor those sweet tunes you sing.

8.

'But father, since this land, these townes and towres,
Destroied are with sword, with fire and spoile,
How may it be vnhurt, that you and yours
In safetie thus, applie your harmlesse toile?
My sonne (quoth he) this poore estate of ours
Is euer safe from storme of warlike broile;
　　This wildernesse doth vs in safetie keepe,
　　No thundring drum, no trumpet breakes our sleepe.

9.

'Haply iust heau'ns defence and shield of right,
Doth loue the innocence of simple swaines,
The thunderbolts on highest mountaines light,
And seld or neuer strike the lower plaines:
So kings haue cause to feare *Bellonaes* might,
Not they whose sweat and toile their dinner gaines,
　　Nor euer greedie soldier was entised
　　By pouertie, neglected and despised.

10.

'O pouertie, chefe of the heau'nly brood,
Dearer to me than wealth or kingly crowne!
No wish for honour, thirst of others good,
Can moue my hart, contented with mine owne:
We quench our thirst with water of this flood,
Nor fear we poison should therein be throwne:
　　These little flocks of sheepe and tender goates
　　Giue milke for food, and wooll to make us coates.

11.

'We little wish, we need but little wealth,
From cold and hunger vs to cloath and feed;

These are my sonnes, their care preserues from stealth
Their fathers flocks, nor servants moe I need :
Amid these groues I walke oft for my health,
And to the fishes, birds and beastes giue heed,
　How they are fed, in forrest, spring and lake,
　And their contentment for ensample take.

12.

'Time was (for each one hath his doting time,
These siluer locks were golden tresses than)
That countrie life I hated as a crime,
And from the forrests sweet contentment ran,
To Memphis stately pallace would I clime,
And there became the mightie Caliphes man,
　And though I but a simple gardner weare,
　Yet could I marke abuses, see and heare.

13.

'Entised on with hope of future gaine,
I suffred long what did my soule displease ;
But when my youth was spent, my hope was vaine,
I felt my natiue strength at last decrease ;
I gan my losse of lustie yeeres complaine,
And wisht I had enioy'd the countries peace ;
　I bod the court farewell, and with content
　My later age here haue I quiet spent.

14.

'While thus he spake, Erminia husht and still
His wise discourses heard, with great attention,
His speeches graue those idle fancies kill,
Which in her troubled soule bred such dissention ;
After much thought reformed was her will,
Within those woods to dwell was her intention,
　Till fortune should occasion new afford,
　To turne her home to her desired Lord.

15.

'She said therefore, O shepherd fortunate !
That troubles some didst whilom feele and proue,
Yet liuest now in this contented state,
Let my mishap thy thoughts to pitie moue,
To entertaine me as a willing mate
In shepherds life, which I admire and loue ;
　Within these pleasant groues perchance my hart,
　Of her discomforts, may vnload some part.

16.

'If gold or wealth of most esteemed deare,
If iewels rich, thou diddest hold in prise,
Such store thereof, such plentie haue I here,
As to a greedie minde might well suffice:
With that downe trickled many a siluer teare,
Two christall streames fell from her watrie eies;
   Part of her sad misfortunes than she told,
   And wept, and with her wept that shepherd old.

17.

'With speeches kinde, he gan the virgin deare
Towards his cottage gently home to guide;
His aged wife there made her homely cheare,
Yet welcomde her, and plast her by her side.
The Princesse dond a poore pastoraes geare,
A kerchiefe course vpon her head she tide;
   But yet her gestures and her lookes (I gesse)
   Were such, as ill beseem'd a shepherdesse.

18.

'Not those rude garments could obscure, and hide,
The heau'nly beautie of her angels face,
Nor was her princely ofspring damnifide,
Or ought disparag'de, by those labours bace;
Her little flocks to pasture would she guide,
And milke her goates, and in their folds them place,
   Both cheese and butter could she make, and frame
   Her selfe to please the shepherd and his dame.'

POMFRET[1]

OF Mr. JOHN POMFRET nothing is known but from [1] a slight and confused account prefixed to his poems by a nameless friend[2], who relates that he was the son of the Rev. Mr. Pomfret, rector of Luton in Bedfordshire, that he was bred at Cambridge, entered into orders, and was rector of Malden in Bedfordshire, and might have risen in the Church, but that when he applied to Dr. Compton, bishop of London[3], for institution to a living of considerable value, to which he had been presented[4], he found a troublesome obstruction raised by a malicious interpretation of some passage in his *Choice*, from which it was inferred that he considered happiness as more likely to be found in the company of a mistress than of a wife[5].

This reproach was easily obliterated; for it had happened to [2]

---

[1] Pomfret was one of the four poets inserted in the collection on Johnson's recommendation. *Post*, WATTS, 1. Among the poets passed over who belong to the period included in the *Lives* are Crashaw, Lovelace, Herrick, Marvell, Churchill, and Chatterton. The omission of Goldsmith was due to a bookseller, who, owning the copyright of one of his works, refused to come into the project. Boswell's *Johnson*, iii. 100 *n*.

[2] In the edition of 1736 it is at the end of the volume. Mr. Seccombe in the *Dict. of Nat. Biog.* states that Pomfret was born in 1667; took his B.A. degree in 1684; on Dec. 12, 1695, was made rector of Maulden, and on June 2, 1702, rector of Milbrook, both in Bedfordshire. His father was vicar of Luton. See also *N. & Q.* 8 S. ii. 27.

[3] Burnet describes Compton as 'a generous and good-natured man, but easy and weak and much in the power of others.' *History*, iv. 333.

[4] He had already two livings.

[5] 'Would bounteous Heaven once more indulge, I'd choose
(For who would so much satis-
faction lose
As witty nymphs in conversation
give)
Near some obliging modest fair
to live.
. . . . . .
To this fair creature I'd sometimes
retire,
Her conversation would new joys
inspire,
Give life an edge so keen, no
surly care
Would venture to assault my soul,
or dare,
Near my retreat, to hide one
secret snare.
But so divine, so noble a re-
past
I'd seldom, and with moderation
taste;
For highest cordials all their virtue
lose
By a too frequent and too bold a
use;

Pomfret as to almost all other men who plan schemes of life : he had departed from his purpose, and was then married [1].

3 The malice of his enemies had however a very fatal consequence; the delay constrained his attendance in London, where he caught the small-pox, and died in 1703, in the thirty-sixth year of his age [2].

4 He published his poems in 1699 ; and has been always the favourite of that class of readers, who without vanity or criticism seek only their own amusement.

5 His *Choice* exhibits a system of life adapted to common notions and equal to common expectations ; such a state as affords plenty and tranquillity, without exclusion of intellectual pleasures. Perhaps no composition in our language has been oftener perused than Pomfret's *Choice* [3].

6 In his other poems there is an easy volubility ; the pleasure of smooth metre is afforded to the ear, and the mind is not oppressed with ponderous or entangled with intricate sentiment. He pleases many, and he who pleases many must have some species of merit.

And what would cheer the spirits in distress
Ruins our health, when taken to excess.
. . . . . .
If Heaven a date of many years would give,
Thus I'd in pleasure, ease and plenty live.
And as I near approach'd the verge of life,
Some kind relation (for I'd have no wife)
Should take upon him all my worldly care,
Whilst I did for a better state prepare.'
Eng. Poets, xvii. 8, 9, 10.
'The parenthesis was so maliciously represented to the Bishop, that his Lordship was given to understand it could bear no other construction than that Mr. Pomfret preferred a mistress before a wife.' *Life*, p. 5.
[1] He married in 1692. *N. & Q.* 8 S. ii. 27.

[2] He was buried on Dec. 1, 1702. *Ib.*
[3] *Eng. Poets*, xvii. 5. Swift wrote in 1726 :—'At a bookseller's shop some time ago I saw a book with this title—*Poems by the Author of the Choice*. Not enduring to read a dozen lines, I asked the company whether they had ever seen the book, or heard of the poem. They were all as ignorant as I.' *Works*, ix. 231.
Southey wrote in 1807 :—' Why is Pomfret the most popular of the English Poets ? The fact is certain, and the solution would be useful.' Southey's *Specimens*, i. 91. In 1819 Campbell thus criticized this statement :—' It might have been demanded with equal propriety, why London Bridge is built of Parian marble.' *British Poets*, p. 314.
In 1736 Pomfret's *Poems* reached their tenth edition. The *Choice*, no doubt, was reprinted in many collections as well as separately. ' Four quarto editions of it appeared during 1701.' *Dict. Nat. Biog.*

DORSET

OF the Earl of Dorset[1] the character has been drawn so 1 largely and so elegantly by Prior[2], to whom he was familiarly known, that nothing can be added by a casual hand; and, as its authour is so generally read, it would be useless officiousness to transcribe it.

Charles Sackville was born January 24, 1637[3]. Having been 2 educated under a private tutor he travelled into Italy, and returned a little before the Restoration. He was chosen into the first parliament that was called, for East Grinstead in Sussex[4], and soon became a favourite of Charles the Second[5]; but undertook no publick employment, being too eager of the riotous and licentious pleasures which young men of high rank, who aspired to be thought wits, at that time imagined themselves intitled to indulge[6].

One of these frolicks has, by the industry of Wood[7], come 3 down to posterity. Sackville, who was then Lord Buckhurst, with Sir Charles Sedley[8] and Sir Thomas Ogle, got drunk at

[1] The sixth Earl of Dorset.
[2] In the Dedication of his Poems to the Earl's son. *Eng. Poets*, xxxii. 125; *post*, PRIOR, 18; POPE, 387. Johnson follows also *Biog. Brit.* p. 3357.
[3] 1637-8.
[4] It met on May 8, 1661, and was not dissolved till Jan. 24, 1678-9. *Parl. Hist.* iv. 192, 1074.
[5] 'Till he was a little heated with wine he scarce ever spoke; but he was upon that exaltation a very lively man.' BURNET, *History*, i. 294. Swift, finding him described as 'one of the pleasantest companions in the world, when he likes his company,' wrote in the margin:—'Not of late years, but a very dull one.' *Works*, xii. 226.
[6] 'The wits of Charles found easier ways to fame,
Nor wished for Jonson's art or Shakespeare's flame:

Themselves they studied; as they felt they writ;
Intrigue was plot, obscenity was wit.' JOHNSON, *Works*, i. 23.
[7] *Ath. Oxon.* iv. 732.
[8] 'Sedley began to be the oracle of the poets. The King told him that nature had given him a patent to be Apollo's viceroy.' Cibber's *Lives*, iii. 95.
Rochester, after speaking of 'the poor-fed poets of the town,' continues:—
'I loathe the rabble; 'tis enough for me
If Sedley, Shadwell, Shephard, Wycherley,
Godolphin, Butler, Buckhurst, Buckingham,
And some few more whom I omit to name,
Approve my sense: I count their censure fame.' *Eng. Poets*, xv. 67.
Sedley was Lisideius, one of the

the Cock in Bow-street by Covent-garden, and, going into the balcony, exposed themselves to the populace in very indecent postures.   At last, as they grew warmer, Sedley stood forth naked[1], and harangued the populace in such profane language, that the publick indignation was awakened ; the crowd attempted to force the door, and, being repulsed, drove in the performers with stones, and broke the windows of the house[2].

4   For this misdemeanour they were indicted[3], and Sedley was fined five hundred pounds[4] : what was the sentence of the others is not known.   Sedley employed Killigrew and another to procure a remission from the king; but (mark the friendship of the dissolute!) they begged the fine for themselves, and exacted it to the last groat[5].

5   In 1665, Lord Buckhurst attended the Duke of York as a volunteer in the Dutch war ; and was in the battle of June 3, when eighteen great Dutch ships were taken, fourteen others were destroyed, and Opdam, the admiral who engaged the Duke, was blown up beside him, with all his crew[6].

four speakers in the dialogue in Dryden's *Essay of Dramatic Poesy.* Dryden's *Works*, xv. 273. Burnet reckons him one of ' the most eminent wits of that time,' the other two being Dorset and Rochester. *History*, i. 294.

[1] Rochester told Burnet that he and his friends ' in their frolics would have chosen sometimes to have gone naked, if they had not feared the people.' Burnet's *Rochester*, 1829, p. 203.

[2] ' The fire of his [Dorset's] youth carried him to some excesses, but they were accompanied with a most lively invention and true humour. . . . His faults brought their excuse with them, and his very failings had their beauties.' PRIOR, *Eng. Poets*, xxxii. 133.

[3] From Pepys's record on July 1, 1663, Buckhurst does not seem to have been indicted. ' It being told that my Lord Buckhurst was there, my Lord [Chief Justice Foster] asked whether it was that Buckhurst that was lately tried for robbery ; and when answered "Yes," he asked whether he had so soon forgot his deliverance at that time, and that it

would have more become him to have been at his prayers, begging God's forgiveness, than now running into such courses again.' *Diary*, ii. 184.   For this trial for robbery see *ib.* i. 328, and for Buckhurst and Sedley, five years later, ' running up and down all the night, almost naked, through the streets,' see *ib.* v. 29.

[4] The Chief Justice told Sedley ' that it was for him, and such wicked wretches as he was, that God's anger and judgment hung over us, calling him sirrah many times.' *Ib.* ii. 184. Dryden, in 1673, dedicating to him *Assignation*, wrote :—' This Dedication is only an occasion I have taken to do myself the greatest honour imaginable with posterity.' *Works*, iv. 371. ' Sir Charles Sedley was everything that an English gentleman could be.' JACOB, *Poetical Register*, i. 242. For his daughter see *post*, SHEFFIELD, 20.

[5] *Ath. Oxon.* iv. 732. ' Old courtiers will tell you twenty stories of Harry Killigrew, Fleetwood, Sheppard and others, who would often sell places that were never in being.' SWIFT, *Works*, v. 407.

[6] ' June 3, 1665. All this day by

On the day before the battle he is said to have composed the 6
celebrated song, *To all you Ladies now at land*[1], with equal
tranquillity of mind and promptitude of wit. Seldom any
splendid story is wholly true. I have heard from the late Earl
of Orrery, who was likely to have good hereditary intelligence[2],
that Lord Buckhurst had been a week employed upon it, and
only retouched or finished it on the memorable evening. But
even this, whatever it may substract from his facility, leaves him
his courage.

He was soon after made a gentleman of the bedchamber, and 7
sent on short embassies to France[3].

In 1674 the estate of his uncle James Cranfield, Earl of 8
Middlesex, came to him by its owner's death, and the title was
conferred on him the year after[4]. In 1677 he became, by the
death of his father, Earl of Dorset, and inherited the estate of his
family.

In 1684, having buried his first wife, of the family of Bagot[5], 9
who left him no child, he married a daughter of the Earl of
Northampton, celebrated both for beauty and understanding[6].

He received some favourable notice from King James[7]; but 10
soon found it necessary to oppose the violence of his innovations,
and with some other Lords appeared in Westminster-hall, to
countenance the Bishops at their trial[8].

all people upon the River, and almost
everywhere else hereabout, were
heard the guns, our two fleets being
engaged.' PEPYS, *Diary*, iii. 21.
'June 8. We have taken and sunk,
as is believed, about twenty-four of
their best ships.' *Ib.* p. 25. Hume
puts the number at nineteen. *History*,
vii. 403.

[1] *Eng. Poets*, xvii. 155. Prior said
he composed it the night before the
battle. *Ib.* xxxii. 130.

[2] The family name of the Earls of
Orrery was Boyle. Richard Boyle,
second son of the Earl of Burlington,
was killed in the battle. Pepys's
Diary, iii. 24. 'The late Earl' was
the fifth Earl. *Post*, SWIFT, 1 *n.*;
Boswell's *Johnson*, v. 238.

[3] *Eng. Poets*, xxxii. 130. In July,
1667, Nell Gwynne became his mistress. Pepys's *Diary*, iv.116. 'About
Michaelmas, 1668, she became the
King's mistress. He was sent to

France on a complimentary mission
to get him out of the way.' *Dict.
Nat. Biog.* l. 87.

'Dorset hated the Court, and despised the King, when he saw that he
was neither generous nor tender-
hearted.' BURNET, *History*, i. 294.

[4] [This uncle was Lionel, the third
Earl, on whose death the title became
extinct; not James, the second Earl,
also an uncle, who died in 1651.
Hist. Peerage (Courthope).]

[5] Daughter of Hervey Bagot, of
Pipe Hall in Warwickshire, and
widow of the Earl of Falmouth.
Collins's *Peerage*, i. 775.

[6] 'Famed for her beauty and admirable endowments of mind.' *Ib.*

[7] He was made Custos Rotulorum
of Sussex and Lord Lieutenant.
Ib. i. 775.

[8] *Ib.* p. 776. 'On this great day
the unjust Judge was overawed. He
often cast a side glance towards the

11 As enormities grew every day less supportable he found it necessary to concur in the Revolution. He was one of those Lords who sat every day in council to preserve the publick peace, after the king's departure [1]; and, what is not the most illustrious action of his life, was employed to conduct the Princess Anne to Nottingham with a guard [2], such as might alarm the populace as they passed with false apprehensions of her danger. Whatever end may be designed, there is always something despicable in a trick.

12 He became, as may be easily supposed, a favourite of King William, who, the day after his accession, made him lord chamberlain of the household [3], and gave him afterwards the garter [4]. He happened to be among those that were tossed with the King in an open boat sixteen hours, in very rough and cold weather, on the coast of Holland [5]. His health afterwards declined [6]; and on Jan. 19, 1705-6, he died at Bath.

13 He was a man whose elegance and judgement were universally confessed [7], and whose bounty to the learned and witty was generally known [8]. To the indulgent affection of the publick Lord Rochester bore ample testimony in this remark: 'I know

thick rows of Earls and Barons by whom he was watched, and before whom, in the next Parliament, he might stand at the bar.' MACAULAY, *History*, iii. 115.

[1] *Ib.* iii. 295; Collins's *Peerage*, i. 776.

[2] *Eng. Poets*, xxxii. 131.

'They could not safely attempt to reach William's quarters; for the road thither lay through a country occupied by the royal forces. It was therefore determined that Anne should take refuge with the northern insurgents.' MACAULAY, *History*, iii. 260.

[3] Collins's *Peerage*, i. 776. Smollett describes him as a man of 'invincible indolence.' *History*, i. 316.

[4] On Feb. 3, 1690-1. Collins's *Peerage*, i. 777.

[5] *Ib.* p. 777. It was in January 1690-1. 'When the King got within the Maese, so that it was thought two hours' rowing would bring him to land, being weary of the sea he went into an open boat with some of his Lords; but by mists and storms he was tossed up and down above

sixteen hours before he got safe to land. Yet neither he, nor any of those who were with him, were the worse for all this cold and wet weather.' BURNET, *Hist.* iii. 78.

[6] 'Let my friends wish me,' wrote Pope, 'as long a life as they please, I should not wish it to myself with the allay of great or much pain. My old Lord Dorset said very well in that case the tenure is not worth the fine.' Pope's *Works* (Elwin and Courthope), ix. 103. Pope perhaps had this in mind when he wrote:—
'Ease, health and life for this they must resign;
Unsure the tenure, but how vast the fine!'
POPE, *The Temple of Fame*, l. 507.

[7] 'He had the greatest wit tempered with the greatest candour, and was one of the finest critics as well as the best poets of his age.' ADDISON, *The Spectator*, No. 85. See also Horace Walpole's *Works*, i. 425.

[8] 'He was the support of all the poets of his time.' Jacob's *Poetical Register*, ii. 174. For his kindness to Prior see *post*, PRIOR, 2.

not how it is, but Lord Buckhurst may do what he will, yet is never in the wrong [1].'

If such a man attempted poetry we cannot wonder that his 14 works were praised. Dryden, whom, if Prior tells truth, he distinguished by his beneficence [2], and who lavished his blandishments on those who are not known to have so well deserved them [3], undertaking to produce authors of our own country superior to those of antiquity, says, ' I would instance your Lordship in satire, and Shakespeare in tragedy [4].' Would it be imagined that, of this rival to antiquity, all the satires were little personal invectives [5], and that his longest composition was a song of eleven stanzas [6] ?

The blame however of this exaggerated praise falls on the 15

[1] ' It was in fact true, what the Earl of Rochester said in jest to King Charles—that he did not know how it was, but my Lord Dorset might do anything, yet was never to blame.' PRIOR, *Eng. Poets*, xxxii. 133.

Rochester wrote of him :—
' For pointed satire I would Buckhurst choose,
The best good man, with the worst-natured Muse.'
Eng. Poets, xv. 65.

' Never was so much ill-nature in a pen as in his, joined with so much good-nature as was in himself even to excess ; for he was against all punishing, even of malefactors.' BURNET, *Hist*. i. 294.

' Yet soft in nature, though severe his lay,
His anger moral, and his wisdom gay.' *Post*, POPE, 387.

[2] *Post*, DRYDEN, 137. For his giving Dryden a banknote for £100 at a Christmas Day dinner see Jacob's *Poetical Register*, ii. 16, quoted in Malone's *Dryden*, i. 452.

[3] For Dryden's ' abject adulation' see *post*, DRYDEN, 170.

[4] Dryden's *Works*, xiii. 14 ; *post*, DRYDEN, 27.

' Dryden determines by him [Dorset], under the character of Eugenius, as to the laws of dramatic poetry [in the *Essay of Dramatic Poesy*, *Works*, xv. 301].' PRIOR, *Eng. Poets*, xxxii. 127. Malone points out that Crites' character better suits him, who is described as ' a person of a sharp judgment, and somewhat too delicate a taste in wit, which the world have mistaken in him for ill-nature [*Works*, xv. 285].' Malone's *Dryden*, vol. i. pt. 2 ; *Essay on Dram. Poesy*, p. 35 *n*. Whichever he is, there is this inconsistency, that while he was one of the boating party on the Thames who ' perceived the air to break about them like the noise of distant thunder, or of swallows in a chimney, on that memorable day when our navy engaged the Dutch' (Dryden's *Works*, xv. 283), he was himself fighting in the battle. *Ante*, DORSET, 5.

[5] ' The gentleman had always so much the better of the satirist that the persons touched were forced to appear rather ashamed than angry.' PRIOR, *Eng. Poets*, xxxii. 129.

The following lines addressed to the Hon. Edward Howard do not show much of ' the gentleman' :—
' Sure hasty pudding is thy chiefest dish,
With bullock's liver, or some stinking fish ;
Garbage, ox-cheeks, and tripes do feast thy brain,
Which nobly pays this tribute back again.' *Ib*. xvii. 148.

[6] His poems are contained in twenty-four pages of *Eng. Poets*, pp. 147–71. Malone thinks ' all his satires have not come down to us, at least with his name.' Malone's *Dryden*, iii. 80.

For his pieces in *State Poems*, vol. iii, see Spence's *Anec*. p. 157.

encomiast, not upon the author; whose performances are, what they pretend to be, the effusions of a man of wit, gay, vigorous, and airy[1]. His verses to Howard[2] shew great fertility of mind, and his *Dorinda* has been imitated by Pope[3].

[1] 'Your Lyric Poems are the delight and wonder of this age, and will be the envy of the next.' DRYDEN, *Works*, xiii. 5.

'Lord Dorset's things are all excellent in their way; for one should consider his pieces as a sort of epigrams; wit was his talent.' POPE, Spence's *Anec.* p. 281.

[2] *Eng. Poets*, xvii. 147, 148. Waller also ridiculed Howard. *Ib.* xvi. 181. Both satirists ridicule '*His Incomparable, Incomprehensible Poem, intitled the British Princes.*' See also Boswell's *Johnson*, ii. 108.

[3] [*On the Countess of Dorchester, Mistress to King James the Second, Eng. Poets*, xvii. 158. Pope's imitation is entitled *Artemisia*.]

STEPNEY[1]

GEORGE STEPNEY, descended from the Stepneys of 1 Pendegrast [Prendergast] in Pembrokeshire, was born at Westminster in 1663. Of his father's condition or fortune I have no account[2]. Having received the first part of his education at Westminster, where he passed six years in the College, he went at nineteen to Cambridge[3], where he continued a friendship begun at school with Mr. Montague, afterwards Earl of Halifax[4]. They came to London together, and are said to have been invited into publick life by the Duke of Dorset[5].

His qualifications recommended him to many foreign employ- 2 ments, so that his time seems to have been spent in negotiations. In 1692 he was sent envoy to the Elector of Brandenburgh; in 1693 to the Imperial Court; in 1694 to the Elector of Saxony; in 1696 to the Electors of Mentz and Cologne, and the Congress at Francfort; in 1698 a second time to Brandenburgh; in 1699 to the King of Poland; in 1701 again to the Emperor; and in 1706 to the States General[6]. In 1697 he was made one of the commissioners of trade. His life was busy, and not long.

[1] Johnson's authority in this *Life* is Jacob's *Poetical Register*, ii. 205.

[2] He was Groom of the Chamber to Charles II. *Dict. Nat. Biog.* Horace Walpole is wrong in stating that his mother was Vandyke's daughter. *Anec. of Painting*, ed. 1888, i. 336 *n.* Sir John Stepney, the fourth baronet, was her husband. Cokayne's *Complete Baronetage*, i. 178. The poet's mother was Mary, daughter of Sir Bernard Whetstone, Knt. *Dict. Nat. Biog.*

[3] He was elected Scholar of Trinity College in 1682, and Fellow in 1687. *Dict. Nat. Biog.*

[4] *Post*, HALIFAX, 2. Stepney bequeathed to him 'a golden cup and a hundred tomes of his library.' Addison's *Works*, v. 363.

[5] The sixth Earl of Dorset. It was his son to whom the dukedom was granted in 1720. *Ante*, DORSET, 8. ''Twas he that recommended the late Lord Halifax to King William, promoted Mr. Prior, preferred Mr. Mainwaring, Mr. Stepney and many others.' JACOB, *Poetical Register*, ii. 175. According to the *Life of Halifax*, 1715, p. 7, Stepney 'desired to be excused out of his love to a retired life.'

[6] Addison, sending him the beginning of his *Dialogues on Medals*, wrote :—'I cannot hope that one who is so well acquainted with the persons of our present modern princes should find any pleasure in a discourse on the faces of such as made a figure in the world above a thousand years ago.' Addison's *Works*, v. 338.

He died in 1707, and is buried in Westminster-Abbey, with this epitaph, which Jacob transcribed [1].

H. S. E.
GEORGIUS STEPNEIUS, Armiger,
Vir
Ob Ingenii acumen,
Literarum Scientiam,
Morum Suavitatem,
Rerum Usum,
Virorum Amplissimorum Consuetudinem,
Linguæ, Styli, ac Vitæ Elegantiam,
Præclara Officia cum Britanniæ tum Europæ præstita,
Sua ætate multum celebratus;
Apud posteros semper celebrandus;
Plurimas Legationes obiit
Ea Fide, Diligentia, ac Felicitate,
Ut Augustissimorum Principum
Gulielmi et Annæ
Spem in illo repositam
Numquam fefellerit,
Haud raro superaverit.
Post longum honorum Cursum
Brevi Temporis Spatio confectum,
Cum Naturæ parum, Famæ satis vixerat,
Animam ad altiora aspirantem placide efflavit.

On the Left Hand:

G. S.
Ex Equestri Familia Stepneiorum,
De Pendegrast, in Comitatu
Pembrochiensi oriundus,
Westmonasterii natus est, A.D. 1663.
Electus in Collegium
Sancti Petri Westmonast. A. 1676.
Sanctæ Trinitatis Cantab. 1682.
Consiliariorum quibus Commercii
Cura commissa est 1697.
Chelseiæ mortuus, et, comitante
Magna procerum
Frequentia, huc elatus, 1707 [2].

3   It is reported that the juvenile compositions of Stepney made grey authors blush [3]. I know not whether his poems will appear

---

[1] *Poetical Register*, ii. 205.
[2] Luttrell (vi. 215) recorded that on Sept. 22, 1707, 'the corpse of Mr. Stepney was interred in great state;

the pall was carried up by two dukes, two earls, and two barons.' He died on Sept. 15. *N. & Q.* 2 S. xi. 225.
[3] *Post*, SMITH, 6. Addison,

such wonders to the present age. One cannot always easily find the reason for which the world has sometimes conspired to squander praise [1]. It is not very unlikely that he wrote very early as well as he ever wrote ; and the performances of youth have many favourers, because the authors yet lay no claim to publick honours, and are therefore not considered as rivals by the distributors of fame.

He apparently professed himself a poet, and added his name to 4 those of the other wits in the version of *Juvenal* [2], but he is a very licentious translator, and does not recompense his neglect of the author by beauties of his own. In his original poems, now and then a happy line may perhaps be found, and now and then a short composition may give pleasure. But there is in the whole little either of the grace of wit, or the vigour of nature.

writing to him, spoke of 'the great respect I shall always have for so extraordinary a character.' Addison's *Works*, v. 349.

In *Characters of the Court of Queen Anne* he is described as 'a gentleman of admirable natural parts, very learned, one of the best poets now in England, and perhaps equal to any that ever was.' As a marginal note on 'poets' Swift wrote :—'Scarce of a third rate.' Swift's *Works*, xii. 236.

[1] 'The learned often bewail the loss of ancient writers whose characters have survived their works ; but, perhaps, if we could now retrieve them, we should find them only the Granvilles [*post*, GRANVILLE], Montagues [*post*, HALIFAX], Stepneys, and Sheffields [*post*, SHEFFIELD], of their time, and wonder by what infatuation or caprice they could be raised to notice.' *The Rambler*, No. 106.

[2] *Post*, DRYDEN, 140, 299. Stepney translated Satire viii. *Eng. Poets*, xvii. 200.

J. PHILIPS

1 JOHN PHILIPS was born on the 30th of December, 1676, at
   Bampton in Oxfordshire ; of which place his father Dr. Stephen
Philips, archdeacon of Salop, was minister. The first part of his
education was domestick, after which he was sent to Winchester,
where, as we are told by Dr. Sewel, his biographer[1], he was soon
distinguished by the superiority of his exercises ; and, what is less
easily to be credited, so much endeared himself to his schoolfellows
by his civility and good-nature, that they without murmur or ill-
will saw him indulged by the master with particular immunities.
It is related that when he was at school he seldom mingled
in play with the other boys, but retired to his chamber, where his
sovereign pleasure was to sit hour after hour while his hair was
combed by somebody, whose service he found means to procure[2].

2 At school he became acquainted with the poets ancient and
modern, and fixed his attention particularly on Milton[3].

3 In 1694 he entered himself at Christ-church, a college at that
time in the highest reputation, by the transmission of Busby's
scholars to the care, first of Fell[4], and afterwards of Aldrich[5].

[1] *The Life and Character of Mr. John Philips,* written by Mr. [George] Sewell. 2nd ed. London, 1715.

[2] 'I have been informed by one who was at school with him, that he would sit almost absolutely without motion for several hours together, enjoying the pleasure it gave him with the highest degree of sensibility. It was in these intervals chiefly, that he read Milton.' *Biog. Brit.* p. 3353.
'Many people take delight in the combing of their hair. . . . More than once I have fallen into the hands of men who could imitate any measure of songs in combing the hair, so as sometimes to express very intelligibly Iambics, Trochees and Dactyls, &c., whence there arose to me no small delight.' Isaac Vossius's *De Poematum Cantu,* &c., 1673, p. 62, quoted in Hawkins's *Hist. of Music,* iv. 275.

[3] *Biog. Brit.* p. 3353; *Life,* p. 5.

[4] For Dr. Busby, Head Master of Westminster School, see *post,* DRYDEN, 4, and for the link between the School and Christ Church see *post,* SMITH, 4.
John Fell, Bishop of Oxford and Dean of Christ Church, 'kept up the exercise of his house severely. . . . He would constantly take his rounds in his coll. go to the chambers of noblemen and gent. commoners, and examine what progress they made in their studies.' *Ath. Oxon.* iv. 196.
'Feb. 24, 1665. Dr. Fell preached before the King, a very formal discourse, and in blank verse, according to his manner.' EVELYN, *Diary,* i. 413.
He was the servile Dean, who, in compliance with the demand of the Court, deprived Locke of his studentship. King's *Life of Locke,* 1858, pp. 147, 149, 175.

[5] Between Fell, who died in 1686,

Here he was distinguished as a genius eminent among the eminent, and for friendship particularly intimate with Mr. Smith, the author of *Phædra and Hippolytus* [1]. The profession which he intended to follow was that of physick ; and he took much delight in natural history, of which botany was his favourite part [2].

His reputation was confined to his friends and to the university ; 4 till about 1703 he extended it to a wider circle by *The Splendid Shilling*, which struck the publick attention with a mode of writing new and unexpected [3].

This performance raised him so high, that when Europe 5 resounded with the victory of Blenheim he was, probably with an occult opposition to Addison, employed to deliver the acclamation of the Tories [4]. It is said that he would willingly have declined the task [5], but that his friends urged it upon him. It appears that he wrote this poem at the house of Mr. St. John [6].

Blenheim was published in 1705. The next year produced his 6 greatest work, the poem upon *Cider* [7], in two books ; which was received with loud praises, and continued long to be read, as an imitation of Virgil's *Georgick*, which needed not shun the presence of the original [8].

and Aldrich, who was made Dean in 1689, came John Massey, ' one of the new converts to Romanism.' Burnet's *Hist.* ii. 321 ; Hearne's *Remains*, i. 82. ' Aldrich visited the chambers of young gentlemen, on purpose to see that they employed their time in useful and commendable studies.' *Ib.* i. 211. Philips praises him in *Cyder*. *Eng. Poets*, xvii. 290.

[1] *Post*, SMITH, 15, 51.

[2] Smith wrote of him :—
' Judicious physic's noble art to gain,
All drugs and plants explored, alas
    in vain ! ' *Eng. Poets*, xxv. 115.

[3] ' I find it in *A Collection of Poems* printed in 1701 for David Brown and Ben. Tooke.' Cunningham's *Lives of the Poets*, ii. 22. It was published separately in 1705.
Eng. Poets, xvii. 239. Addison, in *The Tatler*, No. 249, makes a shilling ' in a soft-silver sound give an account of his life and adventures. . . . The first adventure was my being in a poet's pocket, who was so taken with the brightness and novelty of my appearance, that it gave occasion to the finest burlesque poem in the

British language, entitled from me *The Splendid Shilling.*'
Cowper thus mentions the poem in *The Task*, Bk. iii. l. 455 :—
' And in thy numbers, Philips, shines
    for aye
The solitary Shilling.'

[4] *Eng. Poets*, xvii. 245. *Post*, ADDISON, 25, 130 ; PRIOR, 17.

[5] *Life*, p. 16.

[6] Afterwards Viscount Bolingbroke. Philips, at the end of *Blenheim*, writes :—
' Thus, from the noisy world exempt,
    with ease   [groves
And plenty blest, amid the mazy
(Sweet solitude !), where warbling
    birds provoke
The silent Muse, delicious rural seat
Of St. John, English Memmius, I
    presumed
To sing Britannic trophies, inexpert
Of war.' *Eng. Poets*, xvii. 261.

[7] It was published in 1707-8. Tonson gave forty guineas for it. Cunningham's *Lives of the Poets*, ii. 22.

[8] ' It comes the nearest of any poem to the *Georgicks.*' *Life*, p. 18. *Post*, PHILIPS, 15.

7   He then grew probably more confident of his own abilities, and
began to meditate a poem on *The Last Day*[1], a subject on which
no mind can hope to equal expectation[2].

8   This work he did not live to finish; his diseases, a slow consumption and an asthma, put a stop to his studies[3], and on Feb. 15,
1708[4], at the beginning of his thirty-third year, put an end to his
life. He was buried in the cathedral of Hereford; and Sir Simon
Harcourt[5], afterwards Lord Chancellor, gave him a monument in
Westminster Abbey[6]. The inscription at Westminster was written,
as I have heard, by Dr. Atterbury, though commonly given
to Dr. Freind[7].

His Epitaph at Hereford:

JOHANNES PHILIPS

Obiit 15 die Feb. Anno $\begin{cases} \text{Dom. 1708.} \\ \text{Ætat. suæ 32.} \end{cases}$

Cujus
Ossa si requiras, hanc Urnam inspice;
Si Ingenium nescias, ipsius Opera consule;
Si Tumulum desideras,
Templum adi *Westmonasteriense:*

[1] Smith wrote of him :—
'Oh! had relenting Heav'n prolonged
    his days,
The towering bard had sung in
    nobler lays
How the last trumpet wakes the lazy
    dead;
How saints aloft the cross triumphant
    spread;
How opening heavens their happy
    regions shew;
And yawning gulphs with flaming
    vengeance glow;
And saints rejoice above, and sinners
    howl below.'
        Eng. Poets, xxv. 113.

[2] *Post*, YOUNG, 155.
[3] A passage in Smith's poem
shows a great difference in domestic
arrangements. Addressing a friend
he says :—
'Your care had long his fleeting life
    restrained,
One table fed you, *and one bed
    contained*;
For his dear sake long restless nights
    you bore,

While rattling coughs his heaving
    vessels tore.' *Eng. Poets*, xxv. 108.
[4] 1709 N.S. [Underhill's *Poetical
Works of John Gay*, 1893, i. 275].
[5] Philips, in *Cyder*, addressing
Harcourt's son, who was in Italy,
continues :—
    'At length, dear youth, return,
            .   .   .   .   .   .
Return, and let thy father's worth
    excite
Thirst of pre-eminence.'
            Eng. Poets, xvii. 297.
    For Pope's epitaph on the 'dear
youth' see *post*, POPE, 401.
[6] Hearne describes it as 'a burlesque upon monuments.' *Remains*,
iii. 141.
'I am against stuffing Westminster
Abbey with any one's statue till a
hundred years or so have proved
whether posterity is as warm about
a man's merits as we are. What
a vast monument is erected to Cider
Philips!' E. FitzGerald, *More
Letters*, &c., p. 26.
[7] *Post*, PRIOR, 44 *n.*; *John. Misc.*
ii. 378 *n.*

Qualis quantusque Vir fuerit,
Dicat elegans illa et preclara,
Quæ cenotaphium ibi decorat,
Inscriptio.
Quàm interim erga Cognatos pius et officiosus,
Testetur hoc saxum
A MARIA PHILIPS Matre ipsius pientissimâ
Dilecti Filii Memoriæ non sine Lacrymis dicatum.

His Epitaph at Westminster:

Herefordiæ conduntur Ossa,
Hoc in Delubro statuitur Imago,
Britanniam omnem pervagatur Fama
JOHANNIS PHILIPS:
Qui Viris bonis doctisque juxta charus,
Immortale suum Ingenium,
Eruditione multiplici excultum,
Miro animi candore,
Eximiâ morum simplicitate,
Honestavit.
Litterarum Amœniorum sitim,
Quam Wintoniæ Puer sentire cœperat,
Inter Ædis Christi Alumnos jugiter explevit.
In illo Musarum Domicilio
Præclaris Æmulorum studiis excitatus,
Optimis scribendi Magistris semper intentus,
Carmina sermone Patrio composuit
A Græcis Latinisque fontibus feliciter deducta,
Atticis Romanisque auribus omnino digna,
Versuum quippe Harmoniam
Rythmo didicerat,
Antiquo illo, libero, multiformi
Ad res ipsas apto prorsus, et attemperato,
Non Numeris in eundem ferè orbem redeuntibus,
Non Clausularum similiter cadentium sono
Metiri:
Uni in hoc laudis genere Miltono secundus [1],
Primoque pœne Par.
Res seu Tenues, seu Grandes, seu Mediocres
Ornandas sumserat,
Nusquam non quod decuit,
Et vidit, et assecutus est,
Egregius, quocunque Stylum verteret,
Fandi author, et Modorum artifex.
Fas sit Huic,

---

[1] *Ante*, MILTON, 136.

Auso licèt à tuâ Metrorum Lege discedere
O Poesis Anglicanæ Pater, atque Conditor, Chaucere,
Alterum tibi latus claudere,
Vatum certe Cineres, tuos undique stipantium
Non dedecebit Chorum.
SIMON HARCOURT Miles,
Viri benè de se, de Litteris meriti
Quoad viveret Fautor,
Post Obitum piè memor,
Hoc illi Saxum poni voluit.
J. PHILIPS, STEPHANI, S. T. P. Archidiaconi
Salop. Filius, natus est Bamptoniæ
in agro Oxon. Dec. 30, 1676.
Obiit Herefordiæ, Feb. 15, 1708.

9   Philips has been always praised without contradiction as a man
modest, blameless, and pious ; who bore narrowness of fortune
without discontent, and tedious and painful maladies without
impatience ; beloved by those that knew him, but not ambitious
to be known. He was probably not formed for a wide circle.
His conversation is commended for its innocent gaiety, which
seems to have flowed only among his intimates[1] ; for I have been
told that he was in company silent and barren, and employed
only upon the pleasures of his pipe. His addiction to tobacco is
mentioned by one of his biographers, who remarks that in all his
writings, except *Blenheim*, he has found an opportunity of celebrating the fragrant fume[2]. In common life he was probably one
of those who please by not offending, and whose person was loved
because his writings were admired. He died honoured and
lamented, before any part of his reputation had withered, and
before his patron St. John had disgraced him[3].

10   His works are few. *The Splendid Shilling*[4] has the uncommon

---

[1] 'Must he no more divert the tedious
        day ?
    Nor sparkling thoughts in antique
        words convey ?
    No more to harmless irony descend,
    To noisy fools a grave attention lend,
    Nor merry tales with learn'd quota-
        tions blend ? '
        SMITH, *Eng. Poets*, xxv. 114.
[2] 'As the custom of smoking tobacco was highly in vogue when he
first came to college from the example of the Dean (Aldrich), so he
fell in with the general taste.' *Biog.*

Brit. p. 3355.
        His Latin Ode *Ad Henricum St.
John* begins :—
    ' O qui recisae finibus Indicis
    Benignus herbae das mihi divitem
    Haurire succum, et suaveolentes
    Saepe tubis iterare fumos.'
            Eng. Poets, xvii. 262.
    See also *ib.* pp. 236, 240.
[3] For Johnson's scorn of Pope's
' all-accomplished St. John ' (*Epil.
Sat.* ii. 139) see Boswell's *Johnson*, i.
268.
[4] In Smith's poem *In Memory of*

merit of an original design, unless it may be thought precluded by the ancient *Centos*. To degrade the sounding words and stately construction of Milton, by an application to the lowest and most trivial things, gratifies the mind with a momentary triumph over that grandeur which hitherto held its captives in admiration; the words and things are presented with a new appearance, and novelty is always grateful where it gives no pain.

But the merit of such performances begins and ends with the 11 first author. He that should again adapt Milton's phrase to the gross incidents of common life, and even adapt it with more art, which would not be difficult, must yet expect but a small part of the praise which Philips has obtained; he can only hope to be considered as the repeater of a jest[1].

'The parody on Milton,' says Gildon, 'is the only tolerable 12 production of its author[2].' This is a censure too dogmatical and violent. The poem of *Blenheim* was never denied to be tolerable, even by those who do not allow its supreme excellence. It is indeed the poem of a scholar, 'all inexpert of war[3]'; of a man who writes books from books, and studies the world in a college. He seems to have formed his ideas of the field of *Blenheim* from the battles of the heroick ages or the tales of chivalry with very little comprehension of the qualities necessary to the composition of a modern hero, which Addison has displayed with so much propriety[4]. He makes Marlborough behold at distance the slaughter

---

Philips the following lines seem to show that the two poets shared 'the garret vile' described in *The Splendid Shilling* :—
'What sounding lines his abject theme express !
What shining words the pompous Shilling dress !
There, there my cell, immortal made, outvies
The frailer piles which o'er its ruins rise.' *Eng. Poets*, xxv. 110.
By 'the frailer piles' is meant, I think, Peckwater Quadrangle, Christ Church, which, as Hearne tells us, was 'about half done.' Hearne's *Remains*, i. 211.
[1] *Ante*, BUTLER, 52, and *post*, SOMERVILE, 8.
' *The Splendid Shilling* has been

an hundred times imitated without success. The truth is, the first thing in this way must preclude all future attempts, for nothing is so easy as to burlesque any man's manner when we are once showed the way.' GOLDSMITH, *Works*, iii. 437.
[2] [Gildon, speaking of writers 'who because they could write with justness upon a comic or ludicrous subject persuaded themselves that they could write as well upon all those that were serious,' cites as an instance ' the author of *The Splendid Shilling*, . . . for the author of the Parodie never did anything else worth looking on.' *The Laws of Poetry*, p. 321.]
[3] 'Inexpert of war.' *Ante*, PHILIPS, 5 *n*.
[4] *Post*, ADDISON, 130.

made by Tallard, then haste to encounter and restrain him, and
mow his way through ranks made headless by his sword[1].

13   He imitates Milton's numbers indeed, but imitates them very
injudiciously. Deformity is easily copied ; and whatever there is
in Milton which the reader wishes away, all that is obsolete,
peculiar, or licentious is accumulated with great care by Philips[2].
Milton's verse was harmonious, in proportion to the general state
of our metre in Milton's age, and, if he had written after the
improvements made by Dryden, it is reasonable to believe that
he would have admitted a more pleasing modulation of numbers
into his work[3] ; but Philips sits down with a resolution to make
no more musick than he found : to want all that his master wanted,
though he is very far from having what his master had. Those
asperities therefore that are venerable in the *Paradise Lost* are
contemptible in the *Blenheim*[4].

14   There is a Latin ode written to his patron St. John, in return for
a present of wine and tobacco, which cannot be passed without
notice. It is gay and elegant, and exhibits several artful accom-
modations of classick expressions to new purposes. It seems
better turned than the odes of Hannes[5].

[1]   ' till Churchill, viewing where
The violence of Tallard most pre-
vailed,
Came to oppose his slaughtering arm.

        .   .   .   .   .   .

            In Gallic blood again
He dews his reeking sword, and
strews the ground
With headless ranks.'
            Eng. Poets, xvii. 251.

[2] ' Imitation is of two sorts ; the
first is, when we force to our own
purposes the thoughts of others ; the
second consists in copying the imperfections or blemishes of celebrated
authors. . . . I have seen sundry
poems in imitation of Milton, where,
with the utmost exactness, and not so
much as one exception, *nevertheless*
was *nathless*, *embroidered* was
broidered, *hermits* were *eremites*. . . .
And in very deed there is no other
way by which the true modern
poet could read to any purpose
the works of such men as Milton
and Shakespeare.' SWIFT, *Works*,
xiii. 53. In a note it is said :—' Swift
alluded to Philips's *Cyder*, of which
he often expressed a strong disappro-

bation, and particularly on account
of these antiquated words.'
    Steele, in *The Spectator*, No. 140,
also censures Philips :—' Thus the
imitators of Milton seem to place
all the excellency of that sort of
writing either in the uncouth or antique words, or something else which
was highly vicious, though pardonable in that great man.'
    [3] *Post*, DRYDEN, 343.
    [4] ' Philips, by Phoebus and his Aldrich
taught,
Sings with that heat wherewith
his Churchill fought ;
Unfettered, in great Milton's strain
he writes,
Like Milton's angels whilst his
hero fights.'
    TICKELL, *Eng. Poets*, xxxix. 296.
' Philips's *Splendid Shilling* is the
earliest and one of the best of our
parodies : but *Blenheim* is as complete a burlesque upon Milton as
The Splendid Shilling, though it
was written and read with gravity.'
CAMPBELL, *Brit. Poets*, p. 318.
    [5] [This ode I am willing to mention,
because there seems to be an error

To the poem on *Cider*, written in imitation of the *Georgicks*, 15 may be given this peculiar praise, that it is grounded in truth; that the precepts which it contains are exact and just, and that it is therefore at once a book of entertainment and of science. This I was told by Miller, the great gardener and botanist, whose expression was, that 'there were many books written on the same subject in prose, which do not contain so much truth as that poem ¹.'

In the disposition of his matter so as to intersperse precepts 16 relating to the culture of trees with sentiments more generally alluring, and in easy and graceful transitions from one subject to another, he has very diligently imitated his master; but he unhappily pleased himself with blank verse, and supposed that the numbers of Milton, which impress the mind with veneration, combined as they are with subjects of inconceivable grandeur, could be sustained by images which at most can rise only to elegance ². Contending angels may shake the regions of heaven in blank verse; but the flow of equal measures and the embellishment of rhyme must recommend to our attention the art

in all the printed copies, which is, I find, retained in the last. They all read:—
'Quam Gratiarum cura decentium
O ! O ! labellis cui Venus insidet.'
[*Eng. Poets*, xvii. 263.]
The author probably wrote:
'Quam Gratiarum cura decentium
Ornat; labellis cui Venus insidet.'
JOHNSON.]
The error is retained in the edition (*Eng. Poets*) of 1790, to which my references are given.
'Dr. Hannes was a practising physician at Oxford. He was a contributor to the *Musae Anglicanae*, 2 vols. 8vo, Oxon., 1692–99.' Addison's *Works*, v. 319. See also *ib.* i. 248 for Addison's ode *Ad D. D. Hannes, Insignissimum Medicum et Poetam.*'
For the trick by which Dr. Hannes pushed himself up into practice see the *Life of Dr. Radcliffe*, p. 42. See also *post*, SMITH, 14.
¹ 'It does not always follow,' said Johnson, 'that a man who has written a good poem on an art, has practised it. Philip Miller told me, that in Philips's *Cyder*, a poem, all the pre-

cepts were just, and indeed better than in books written for the purpose of instructing; yet Philips had never made cyder.' Boswell's *Johnson*, v. 78.
'The motto,' writes Dr. Warton (Pope's *Works*, i. 334), 'prefixed to Philips's *Cyder* was elegant.
"Honos erit huic quoque pomo?"
[VIRGIL, *Ecl.* ii. 53.]
Atterbury suggested the interrogation point.' The same motto, with the interrogation point, is inscribed in a scroll over Philips's bust in Westminster Abbey. Crull's *Antiquities of St. Peter's*, ii. 35.
An Italian translation was published at Florence in 1749; a second edition in 1752. *Brit. Mus. Cata.*
² Thomson addresses him as:—
'Philips, Pomona's bard, the second thou
Who nobly durst in rhyme-unfetter'd verse,
With British freedom sing the British song.'
The Seasons: Autumn, l. 644.
In the first edition of *Autumn* the first line runs (l. 639):—'Philips, facetious bard.'

of engrafting, and decide the merit of the 'redstreak' and 'pearmain¹.'

17   What study could confer Philips had obtained ; but natural deficience cannot be supplied. He seems not born to greatness and elevation. He is never lofty, nor does he often surprise with unexpected excellence ; but perhaps to his last poem may be applied what Tully said of the work of Lucretius, that ' it is written with much art, though with few blazes of genius ².'

18   The following fragment, written by Edmund Smith, upon the works of Philips, has been transcribed from the Bodleian manuscripts.

'A prefatory Discourse to the Poem on Mr. Philips, with a character of his writings.

' IT is altogether as equitable some account should be given of those who have distinguished themselves by their writings, as of those who are renowned for great actions. It is but reasonable they, who contribute so much to the immortality of others, should have some share in it themselves ; and since their genius only is discovered by their works, it is just that their virtues should be recorded by their friends. For no modest men (as the person I write of was in perfection) will write their own panegyricks ; and it is very hard that they should go without reputation, only because they the more deserve it. The end of writing Lives is for the imitation of the readers. It will be in the power of very few to imitate the duke of Marlborough ; we must be content with admiring his great qualities and actions, without hopes of following them. The private and social virtues are more easily transcribed. The Life of Cowley³ is more instructive, as well as more fine, than any we have in our language. And it is to be wished, since Mr. Philips had so many of the good qualities of that poet, that I had some of the abilities of his historian.

19   'The Grecian philosophers have had their Lives written, their morals commended, and their sayings recorded. Mr. Philips had all the virtues to which most of them only pretended, and all their integrity without any of their affectation.

¹ 'The Pippin burnisht o'er with gold, the Moyle
Of sweetest honeyed taste, the fair Permain
Tempered, like comeliest nymph, with red and white.
   .   .   .   .   .
Yet let her to the Red-streak yield, that once   [lized,
Was of the sylvan kind, uncivi-
Of no regard, till Scudamore's skilful hand

Improved her, and by courtly discipline
Taught her the savage nature to forget.' *Eng. Poets*, xvii. 285–6.
² [*Epp. Ad Q. Fratrem*, Oxon. 1902, ii. 9. 25. The text is corrupt : see notes to above. Johnson probably used a copy of Lambinus's *Cicero*, 1594, bought by C. Burney at the sale of his library in 1785 and now in the possession of Mr. C. E. Doble.]
³ By Sprat. *Ante*, COWLEY, 1.

'The French are very just to eminent men in this point ; not 20 a learned man nor a poet can die, but all Europe must be acquainted with his accomplishments[1]. They give praise and expect it in their turns[2]: they commend their Patrus[3] and Molières as well as their Condes and Turennes ; their Pellisons[4] and Racines have their elogies as well as the prince whom they celebrate ; and their poems, their mercuries, and orations, nay their very gazettes, are filled with the praises of the learned.

'I am satisfied, had they a Philips among them and known how 21 to value him ; had they one of his learning, his temper, but above all of that particular turn of humour, that altogether new genius, he had been an example to their poets and a subject of their panegyricks, and perhaps set in competition with the ancients, to whom only he ought to submit.

'I shall therefore endeavour to do justice to his memory, since 22 nobody else undertakes it. And indeed I can assign no cause why so many of his acquaintance (that are as willing and more able than myself to give an account of him) should forbear to celebrate the memory of one so dear to them, but only that they look upon it as a work entirely belonging to me.

'I shall content myself with giving only a character of the 23

[1] He refers to the *Éloges* of the Academy. Voltaire, in his *Lettres sur les Anglais*, says :—'Un jour un bel esprit de ce pays-là me demanda les Mémoires de l'Académie Française ; elle n'écrit point de mémoires, lui répondis-je ; mais elle a fait imprimer soixante ou quatre-vingts volumes de complimens. Il en parcourut un ou deux ; il ne put jamais entendre ce style, quoiqu'il entendît fort bien tous nos bons auteurs. Tout ce que j'entrevois, me dit-il, dans ces beaux discours, c'est que le récipiendaire ayant assuré que son prédécesseur était un grand homme, que le Cardinal de Richelieu était un très grand homme, le chancelier Séguier un assez grand homme, le directeur lui répond la même chose, et ajoute que le récipiendaire pourrait bien aussi être une espèce de grand homme, et que pour lui directeur, il n'en quitte pas sa part. . . . On s'est imposé une espèce de loi d'ennuyer le public.' VOLTAIRE, *Œuvres*, xxiv. 145.

[2] 'Call Tibbald Shakespeare, and he'll swear the Nine,
Dear Cibber ! never matched one ode of thine.'
POPE, *Imit. Hor. Epis.* ii. 2. 137.

[3] 'Patru (Olivier), né à Paris, en 1604, le premier qui ait introduit la pureté de la langue dans le barreau. Mort en 1681.' VOLTAIRE, *Œuvres*, xvii. 139.
'Mais pour moi, que l'éclat ne saurait décevoir,
Qui mets au rang des biens l'esprit et le savoir,
J'estime autant Patru, même dans l'indigence,
Qu'un commis engraissé des malheurs de la France.'
BOILEAU, *Épîtres*, v. 95.
[4] 'Pellisson-Fontanier (Paul), né en 1624 ; poète médiocre, à la vérité, mais homme très savant et très éloquent. . . . Mort en 1693.' VOLTAIRE, *Œuvres*, xvii. 139.
Boileau in the couplet (*Satires*, viii. 209) which runs :—
'L'or même à la laideur donne un teint de beauté :
Mais tout devient affreux avec la pauvreté,'
had at first written :—
'L'or même à Pélisson,' &c.
In a note it is stated that ' Pélisson était d'une laideur si étonnante, qu'une dame lui dit un jour, qu'il abusait de la permission que les hommes ont d'être laids.' *Œuvres*, i. 130.

person and his writings, without meddling with the transactions of his life, which was altogether private : I shall only make this known observation of his family, that there were scarce so many extraordinary men in any one. I have been acquainted with five of his brothers (of which three are still living), all men of fine parts, yet all of a very unlike temper and genius. So that their fruitful mother, like the mother of the gods, seems to have produced a numerous offspring, all of different though uncommon faculties. Of the living, neither their modesty nor the humour of the present age permits me to speak : of the dead, I may say something.

24   'One of them had made the greatest progress in the study of the law of nature and nations of any one I know. He had perfectly mastered, and even improved, the notions of Grotius, and the more refined ones of Puffendorf. He could refute Hobbes with as much solidity as some of greater name, and expose him with as much wit as Echard[1]. That noble study, which requires the greatest reach of reason and nicety of distinction, was not at all difficult to him. 'Twas a national loss to be deprived of one who understood a science so necessary, and yet so unknown in England. I shall add only, he had the same honesty and sincerity as the person I write of, but more heat. The former was more inclined to argue, the latter to divert : one employed his reason more ; the other his imagination : the former had been well qualified for those posts, which the modesty of the latter made him refuse. His other dead brother would have been an ornament to the college of which he was a member. He had a genius either for poetry or oratory ; and, though very young, composed several very agreeable pieces. In all probability he would have wrote as finely, as his brother did nobly. He might have been the Waller, as the other was the Milton of his time. The one might celebrate Marlborough, the other his beautiful offspring. This had not been so fit to describe the actions of heroes as the virtues of private men. In a word, he had been fitter for my place ; and while his brother was writing upon the greatest men that any age ever produced, in a style equal to them, he might have served as a panegyrist on him.

25   'This is all I think necessary to say of his family. I shall proceed to himself and his writings ; which I shall first treat of, because I know they are censured by some out of envy, and more out of ignorance.

26   '*The Splendid Shilling*, which is far the least considerable, has the more general reputation, and perhaps hinders the character of the rest. The style agreed so well with the burlesque that

[1] John Eachard, D.D., published two Dialogues on Hobbes. ' I have known men, happy enough at ridicule, who upon grave subjects were perfectly stupid ; of which Dr. Eachard of Cambridge, who writ *The Contempt of the Clergy*, was a great instance.' SWIFT, *Works*, ix. 234.

the ignorant thought it could become nothing else. Every body is pleased with that work. But to judge rightly of the other requires a perfect mastery of poetry and criticism, a just contempt of the little turns and witticisms now in vogue, and, above all, a perfect understanding of poetical diction and description.

'All that have any taste of poetry will agree, that the great 27 burlesque is much to be preferred to the low. It is much easier to make a great thing appear little, than a little one great: Cotton and others of a very low genius have done the former[1]; but Philips, Garth[2], and Boileau[3] only the latter.

'A picture in miniature is every painter's talent; but a piece 28 for a cupola, where all the figures are enlarged, yet proportioned to the eye, requires a master's hand.

'It must still be more acceptable than the low burlesque, 29 because the images of the latter are mean and filthy, and the language itself entirely unknown to all men of good breeding. The style of Billingsgate would not make a very agreeable figure at St. James's. A gentleman would take but little pleasure in language, which he would think it hard to be accosted in, or in reading words which he could not pronounce without blushing. The lofty burlesque is the more to be admired, because, to write it, the author must be master of two of the most different talents in nature. A talent to find out and expose what is ridiculous, is very different from that which is to raise and elevate. We must read Virgil and Milton for the one, and Horace and *Hudibras* for the other. We know that the authors of excellent comedies have often failed in the grave style, and the tragedian as often in comedy. Admiration and laughter are of such opposite natures that they are seldom created by the same person. The man of mirth is always observing the follies and weaknesses, the serious writer the virtues or crimes of mankind; one is pleased with contemplating a beau, the other a hero. Even from the same object they would draw different ideas: Achilles would appear in very different lights to Thersites and Alexander. The one would admire the courage and greatness of his soul; the other would ridicule the vanity and rashness of his temper. As the satyrist says to Hannibal:

> "I curre per Alpes,
> Ut pueris placeas, et declamatio fias[4]."

---

[1] Charles Cotton published in 1664 and 1672 *Scarronides, or Virgile Travestie.* Lowndes's *Bibl. Man.*

[2] In *The Dispensary. Post,* GARTH, 17.

[3] In *Le Lutrin.*

[4] 'I, demens, et saevas curre per Alpes,' &c. JUV. *Sat.* x. 166.
'He left the name at which the world grew pale
To point a moral, or adorn a tale.'
JOHNSON, *Vanity of Human Wishes,* l. 221.

30   'The contrariety of style to the subject pleases the more
strongly, because it is more surprising; the expectation of the
reader is pleasantly deceived, who expects an humble style from
the subject, or a great subject from the style. It pleases the
more universally, because it is agreeable to the taste both of the
grave and the merry : but more particularly so to those who have
a relish of the best writers, and the noblest sort of poetry. I
shall produce only one passage out of this poet, which is the
misfortune of his Galligaskins :

> " My Galligaskins, which [that] have long withstood
> The winter's fury and encroaching frosts,
> By time subdued (what will not time subdue ! [1])."

This is admirably pathetical. and shews very well the vicissitudes of sublunary things. The rest goes on to a prodigious
height ; and a man in Greenland could hardly have made a more
pathetick and terrible complaint. Is it not surprising that the
subject should be so mean, and the verse so pompous ? that the
least things in his poetry, as in a microscope, should grow great
and formidable to the eye ? especially considering that, not
understanding French, he had no model for his style ? that he
should have no writer to imitate, and himself be inimitable ?
that he should do all this before he was twenty ? at an age,
which is usually pleased with a glare of false thoughts, little
turns, and unnatural fustian ? at an age, at which Cowley, Dryden,
and I had almost said Virgil, were inconsiderable ? So soon was
his imagination at its full strength, his judgement ripe, and his
humour complete.

31   'This poem was written for his own diversion, without any
design of publication. It was communicated but to *me* ; but
soon spread, and fell into the hands of pirates. It was put out,
vilely mangled, by Ben Bragge [2]; and impudently said to be
corrected by the author. This grievance is now grown more
epidemical ; and no man now has a right to his own thoughts, or
a title to his own writings [3]. Xenophon answered the Persian,

---

[1] *Eng. Poets*, xvii. 243. Galligaskins were 'a kind of wide hose or
breeches worn in the 16th and 17th
centuries ; later, a more or less
ludicrous term for loose breeches in
general.' *New Eng. Dict.*
  [2] '"Whereas a false copy is published by B. Bragg of an imitation of
Milton, under the title of *The
Splendid Shilling*, &c. This is to
give notice that it will be printed
next week from a true copy." *The
Daily Courant*, Thursday, Feb. 1,
1705.' Cunningham's *Lives of the
Poets*, ii. 31.

[3] It was the statute of the 8th of
Queen Anne that 'for the first time
conferred directly upon authors a
qualified and time-limited property
in their compilations and productions.'
Till that time ' the author's copy was
the manuscript, and the only way
open to him for dealing with that
was to sell it out and out as John
Milton did *Paradise Lost*, or to
persuade the Crown to give him a
grant of letters patent for a term of
years.' A. BIRRELL, *Copyright in
Books*, 1899, pp. 74, 92. For 'letters
patent' see *post*, POPE, 130 *n.*

who demanded his arms, " We have nothing now left but our arms
and our valour ; if we surrender the one, how shall we make use
of the other ¹ ? " Poets have nothing but their wits and their
writings ; and if they are plundered of the latter, I don't see what
good the former can do them. To pirate, and publickly own it,
to prefix their names to the works they steal, to own and avow
the theft, I believe, was never yet heard of but in England. It
will sound oddly to posterity, that, in a polite nation, in an enlightened age, under the direction of the most wise, most learned, and
most generous encouragers of knowledge in the world, the property
of a mechanick should be better secured than that of a scholar ;
that the poorest manual operations should be more valued than
the noblest products of the brain ; that it should be felony to rob
a cobler of a pair of shoes, and no crime to deprive the best author
of his whole subsistence ; that nothing should make a man a sure
title to his own writings but the stupidity of them ; that the
works of Dryden should meet with less encouragement than
those of his own Flecknoe ², or Blackmore ; that Tillotson and
St. George, Tom Thumb ³ and Temple, should be set on an equal
foot. This is the reason why this very paper has been so long
delayed ; and while the most impudent and scandalous libels are
publickly vended by the pirates, this innocent work is forced to
steal abroad as if it were a libel.

'Our present writers are by these wretches reduced to the same 32
condition Virgil was, when the centurion seized on his estate ⁴.
But I don't doubt that I can fix upon the Mæcenas of the present
age, that will retrieve them from it. But, whatever effect this
piracy may have upon us, it contributed very much to the
advantage of Mr. Philips ; it helped him to a reputation, which
he neither desired nor expected, and to the honour of being put
upon a work of which he did not think himself capable ; but the
event shewed his modesty. And it was reasonable to hope, that
he, who could raise mean subjects so high, should still be more
elevated on greater themes ; that he, that could draw such noble
ideas from a shilling, could not fail upon such a subject as the
duke of Marlborough, " which is capable of heightening even the
most low and trifling genius." And, indeed, most of the great
works which have been produced in the world have been owing
less to the poet than the patron. Men of the greatest genius are
sometimes lazy, and want a spur ; often modest, and dare not

---

¹ It was Theopompus, an Athenian,
who gave this answer. *Anabasis*, ii.
I. 12.

² *Post*, DRYDEN, 136.

³ The earliest mention in the *Brit.
Mus. Cata.* of Tom Thumb is *A
Comment upon the History of Tom
Thumb*, 1711, a parody of Addison's
papers on *Chevy Chase*. [It is included in the *Misc. Works* of ' William Wagstaffe,' 1726. Dilke (*Papers
of a Critic*, 1875, i. 369, reprinted
from *N. & Q.* 3 S. i. 381) holds that
Swift wrote it.]

⁴ *Eclogues*, i. and ix.

venture in publick; they certainly know their faults in the worst things; and even their best things they are not fond of, because the idea of what they ought to be is far above what they are. This induced me to believe that Virgil desired his work might be burnt, had not the same Augustus that desired him to write them, preserved them from destruction [1]. A scribling beau may imagine a Poet *may* be induced to write, by the very pleasure he finds in writing; but that is seldom, when people are necessitated to it [2]. I have known men row, and use very hard labour, for diversion, which, if they had been tied to, they would have thought themselves very unhappy.

33   'But to return to *Blenheim*, that work so much admired by some, and censured by others. I have often wished he had wrote it in Latin, that he might be out of the reach of the empty criticks, who would have as little understood his meaning in that language as they do his beauties in his own.

34   'False criticks have been the plague of all ages; Milton himself, in a very polite court, has been compared to the rumbling of a wheelbarrow: he had been on the wrong side, and therefore could not be a good poet. *And this, perhaps, may be Mr. Philips's case* [3].

35   'But I take generally the ignorance of his readers to be the occasion of their dislike. People that have formed their taste upon the French writers, can have no relish for Philips: they admire points and turns, and consequently have no judgement of what is great and majestick; he must look little in their eyes, when he soars so high as to be almost out of their view. I cannot therefore allow any admirer of the French to be a judge of Blenheim, nor any who takes Bouhours for a compleat critick [4]. He generally judges of the ancients by the moderns, and not the moderns by the ancients; he takes those passages of their own authors to be really sublime which come the nearest to it; he often calls that a noble and a great thought which is only a pretty and fine one, and has more instances of the sublime out of Ovid *de Tristibus*, than he has out of all Virgil.

---

[1] 'Qui, quum gravari morbo sese sentiret, scrinia saepe et magna instantia petivit, crematurus Aeneida; quibus negatis, testamento comburi iussit, ut rem inemendatam imperfectamque. Verum Tucca et Varius monuerunt id Augustum non permissurum.' *Life of Virgil attributed to Donatus.* Delphin Virgil, Preface, p. 8.

[2] 'JOHNSON. No man but a blockhead ever wrote except for money.' Boswell's *Johnson*, iii. 19. 'No, Sir, nothing excites a man to write but necessity.' *Ib. n.* 3. See also *ib.* iv.

219; *post*, POPE, 298.

[3] Philips died before the Tories, with his patron St. John, came into power.

[4] 'Bouhours, whom I look upon to be the most penetrating of all the French critics, has taken pains to show that it is impossible for any thought to be beautiful which is not just, and has not its foundation in the nature of things; that the basis of all wit is truth; and that no thought can be valuable of which good sense is not the ground-work.' ADDISON, *The Spectator*, No. 62.

'I shall allow, therefore, only those to be judges of Philips, who 36 make the ancients, and particularly Virgil, their standard.

'But, before I enter on this subject, I shall consider what is 37 particular in the style of Philips, and examine what ought to be the style of heroick poetry, and next inquire how far he is come up to that style.

'His style is particular, because he lays aside rhyme, and writes 38 in blank verse, and uses old words, and frequently postpones the adjective to the substantive, and the substantive to the verb ; and leaves out little particles, *a* and *the* ; *her* and *his* ; and uses frequent appositions. Now let us examine, whether these alterations of style be conformable to the true sublime. . . .'

WALSH

1　WILLIAM WALSH, the son of Joseph Walsh, Esq., of Abberley in Worcestershire, was born in 1663, as appears from the account of Wood [1], who relates that at the age of fifteen he became, in 1678, a gentleman commoner [2] of Wadham College.

2　He left the university without a degree, and pursued his studies in London and at home; that he studied, in whatever place, is apparent from the effect, for he became, in Mr. Dryden's opinion, 'the best critick in the nation [3].'

3　He was not, however, merely a critick or a scholar, but a man of fashion, and, as Dennis remarks, ostentatiously splendid in his dress [4]. He was likewise a member of parliament and a courtier, knight of the shire for his native county in several parliaments; in another the representative of Richmond in Yorkshire [5]; and gentleman of the horse to Queen Anne under the duke of Somerset [6].

4　Some of his verses shew him to have been a zealous friend to the Revolution [7]; but his political ardour did not abate his rever-

---

[1] *Ath. Oxon.* iv. 741.

[2] *Post*, HALIFAX, 4 *n.*

[3] 'Who, without flattery, is the best critic of our nation.' DRYDEN, *Works*, xv. 192. For Dryden's 'mint of flattery,' which was never impoverished, see *post*, DRYDEN, 172. See also his *Works*, xviii. 181, for his letter to Walsh criticizing his faulty English.

[4] 'He loved to be well dressed.' *Post*, POPE, 40.
'Warburton told Mr. Hamilton that Pope and others had undoubted proof that Walsh at one time was reduced to such distress by prodigality as to become the hostler of an inn.' MALONE, Prior's *Malone*, p. 388.

[5] He was elected for Worcestershire in the general elections of 1698, 1700–1, and 1702, and for Richmond in those of 1705 and 1707. *Parl. Hist.* v. 1189, 1231; vi. 45, 447, 593.

[6] The Duke was Master of the Horse.

[7] 'I would as soon murder a man for his estate as prosecute him for his religious and speculative errors; and since I am in a way of quoting verses, I will give you three out of Walsh's famous Ode to King William:—
"Nor think it a sufficient cause
　To punish men [man] by penal laws,
　For not believing right."
[*Eng. Poets*, xvii. 392.]'
CHESTERFIELD, *Works*, 1779, iv. 273.
Pope, writing to Swift about the number of masses required to save the souls of his friends, says:—'Walsh was not only a Socinian, but (what you will own is harder to be saved) a Whig. He cannot modestly be rated at less than a hundred.' Pope's *Works* (Elwin and Courthope), vii. 5.

ence or kindness for Dryden, to whom he gave a *Dissertation on Virgil's Pastorals*, in which, however studied, he discovers some ignorance of the laws of French versification [1].

In 1705 he began to correspond with Mr. Pope, in whom he [5] discovered very early the power of poetry. Their letters are written upon the pastoral comedy of the Italians, and those pastorals which Pope was then preparing to publish [2].

The kindnesses which are first experienced are seldom forgotten. [6] Pope always retained a grateful memory of Walsh's notice, and mentioned him in one of his latter pieces among those that had encouraged his juvenile studies :

'Granville the polite,
And knowing Walsh, would tell me I could write [3].'

In his *Essay on Criticism* he had given him more splendid [7] praise [4], and, in the opinion of his learned commentator [5], sacrificed a little of his judgement to his gratitude.

The time of his death I have not learned. It must have [8] happened between 1707, when he wrote to Pope, and 1711 [6], when Pope praised him in his Essay. The epitaph makes him forty-six years old : if Wood's account be right, he died in 1709 [7].

---

[1] This Dissertation, according to Malone (Malone's *Dryden*, iii. 563), was written by Knightly Chetwood, as is shown by Dryden's letter of Dec. 1697, in Dryden's *Works*, xviii. 139. See *post*, DRYDEN, 305 *n*. For the criticism on French versification see his *Works*, xiii. 341.

[2] 'Another of my earliest acquaintance,' said Pope, 'was Walsh. I was with him at his seat in Worcestershire for a good part of the summer of 1705, and showed him my *Essay on Criticism* in 1706. Walsh died the year after.' Spence, *Anec.* p. 194. Walsh wrote to him four letters. *Post*, POPE, 30; Pope's *Works* (Elwin and Courthope), vi. 49-60.

[3] *Prol. Sat.* l. 135.

[4] 'Such late was Walsh—the Muse's judge and friend,
Who justly knew to blame or to commend ;
To failings mild, but zealous for desert ;
The clearest head, and the sincerest heart.

This humble praise, lamented shade ! receive,
This praise at least a grateful Muse may give :
The Muse whose early voice you taught to sing,
Prescrib'd her heights, and prun'd her tender wing
(Her guide now lost), no more attempts to rise,
But in low numbers short excursions tries.' *Essay on Criticism*, l. 729.

[5] Dr. Warton. Warton's *Essay on Pope*, i. 198. Warburton had said much the same. Warburton's *Pope's Works*, i. 159.

[6] In the third edition 1721—no doubt a misprint for 1711, the date correctly given in the first edition.

[7] His epitaph in Abberley Church says that he died at Marlborough on March 16, 1707, aged 46: Nash's *Worcestershire*, i. 4, where his portrait and a picture of his house are given. Luttrell (vi. 280), writing on March 18, 1707–8, mentions his death, so that he died on March 16, 1708 N. S.

9   He is known more by his familiarity with greater men, than by anything done or written by himself.

10   His works are not numerous. In prose he wrote *Eugenia, a Defence of Women* [1], which Dryden honoured with a Preface.

Æsculapius, or the Hospital of Fools, published after his death [2].

A collection of Letters and Poems, amorous and gallant, was published in the volumes called Dryden's *Miscellany*, and some other occasional pieces [3].

11   To his Poems and Letters is prefixed a very judicious preface upon Epistolary Composition and Amorous Poetry [4].

12   In his *Golden Age Restored* [5], there was something of humour, while the facts were recent ; but it now strikes no longer. In his imitation of Horace, the first stanzas are happily turned [6] ; and in all his writings there are pleasing passages. He has however more elegance than vigour, and seldom rises higher than to be pretty [7].

[1] *A Dialogue concerning Women, Being a Defence of the Sex. Written to Eugenia.* 1691. For Dryden's Preface see his *Works*, xviii. 5.

[2] In *Poems and Translations by Several Hands*, 1714.

[3] [The edition of *Miscellany Poems* in six volumes published by Tonson in 1716, wherein *Letters and Poems Amorous and Gallant by William Walsh* are included (vol. iv. pp. 335–395), has no just title to the name by which it goes of Dryden's *Miscellany Poems.* See Mr. W. D. Christie's bibliographical notice of the *Miscellany Poems* edited by Dryden, in Dryden's *Select Poems*, Introd. p. 60.]

Dryden wrote to Walsh (n. d.) :—
'Your apostrophe's to your Mistresse, where you break off the thrid of your discourse and address yourself to her, are, in my opinion, as fine turnes of gallantry as I have mett with anywhere.' *Works*, xviii. 183.

'Walsh's letters seem written as exercises, and were never sent to any living mistress or friend.' *Post*, POPE, 171.

See Boswell's *Johnson*, ii. 133, for some lines from Walsh's *Retirement*, which Johnson 'quoted with great pathos.' The last line but one,

'In her blest arms contented could I live,'
he changed into
    'With such a one,' &c.
            Eng. Poets, xvii. 364.

[4] Johnson, in *The Rambler*, No. 152, writing of 'criticisms upon the epistolary style,' says of the Preface to this collection as published in *Dryden's Misc.* :—'The observations with which Walsh has introduced his pages of inanity are such as give him little claim to the rank assigned him by Dryden among the critics [*ante*, WALSH, 2].' In the reprint of the Preface in *Eng. Poets*, xvii. 333, these 'pages of inanity' have disappeared.

[5] *Eng. Poets*, xvii. 393.

[6] HORACE, *Odes*, iii. 3.
It begins :—
'The man that's resolute and just,
    Firm to his principles and trust,
        Nor hopes nor fears can blind;
No passions his designs control,
Not Love, that tyrant of the soul,
    Can shake his steady mind.'
            Eng. Poets, xvii. 390.

[7] His prettiest lines are, perhaps, the following :—
'I can endure my own despair,
    But not another's hope.'
                Ib. p. 366.

DRYDEN[1]

O F the great poet whose life I am about to delineate, the 1 curiosity which his reputation must excite will require a display more ample than can now be given. His contemporaries, however they reverenced his genius, left his life unwritten ; and nothing therefore can be known beyond what casual mention and uncertain tradition have supplied.

JOHN DRYDEN was born August 9, 1631[2], at Aldwincle 2 near Oundle, the son of Erasmus Dryden of Tichmersh, who was the third son of Sir Erasmus Dryden, Baronet, of Canons Ashby[3]. All these places are in Northamptonshire, but the original stock of the family was in the county of Huntingdon[4].

He is reported by his last biographer, Derrick[5], to have 3 inherited from his father an estate of two hundred a year, and to have been bred, as was said, an Anabaptist. For either of these particulars no authority is given[6]. Such a fortune ought to have

[1] 'When I was a young fellow (said Johnson) I wanted to write the *Life of Dryden.*' Boswell's *Johnson*, iii. 71. 'He told us he had sent Derrick to Dryden's relations to gather materials for his *Life* ; and he believed Derrick had got all that he himself should have got ; but it was nothing.' *Ib.* v. 240. See also *ib.* i. 456 ; iv. 44 ; *John. Letters*, ii. 68. For Derrick see Boswell's *Johnson*, i. 394, 456, and for his attempt 'to gather materials' see *post*, DRYDEN, 188 ; Dryden's *Misc. Works*, 1760, Preface, p. 9.

'Johnson had a mind precisely formed to relish the excellences of Dryden—more vigorous than refined ; more reasoning than impassioned.' HALLAM, *Edin. Review*, No. xxv. 117.

[2] According to Malone there is 'no satisfactory evidence' of the date of his birth. Malone's *Dryden's Prose Works*, i. 3. On his tombstone 1632 is the date of his birth. *Post*, DRYDEN, 156 *n.*

[3] Wood's *Ath. Oxon.* iii. 809. Wood adds that Fuller had the same birthplace. Dryden says of the Earl of Exeter :—' In a village belonging to his family I was born.' *Works*, xv. 191. Sir Erasmus was the 'generous grandsire' of the poet's *Epistle to John Driden*, l. 188, who, 'for refusing to pay loan-money to Charles I, was

"In a loathsome dungeon doomed to lie."'

Christie's *Select Poems of Dryden*, Introd. p. 11.

[4] Dryden's great-great-grandfather came from Staffhill, Cumberland. Malone's *Dryden*, i. 10 ; *Works*, i. 18.

[5] Dryden's *Misc. Works*, 1760, Preface, p. 14.

[6] For his income see *post*, DRYDEN, 182. 'His father,' writes Malone, 'acted as a Justice of the Peace during the usurpation, and was probably a zealous Presbyterian, as his elder brother, Sir John Driden, certainly was. ... Derrick's authority was probably

secured him from that poverty which seems always to have oppressed him ; or if he had wasted it, to have made him ashamed of publishing his necessities. But though he had many enemies, who undoubtedly examined his life with a scrutiny sufficiently malicious, I do not remember that he is ever charged with waste of his patrimony [1]. He was indeed sometimes reproached for his first religion [2]. I am therefore inclined to believe that Derrick's intelligence was partly true, and partly erroneous [3].

4 From Westminster School, where he was instructed as one of the king's scholars by Dr. Busby [4], whom he long after continued to reverence, he was in 1650 elected to one of the Westminster scholarships at Cambridge [5].

5 Of his school performances has appeared only a poem on the death of Lord Hastings [6], composed with great ambition of such

the lampoons of the last age.' Malone's *Dryden*, i. 23, 37 *n.* For extracts from these lampoons see *ib.* pp. 9 *n.*, 38–40. His father died in June 1654. *Works*, i. 26. From the Rev. F. M. Stopford, Rector of Tichmarsh, I have the following extract from the register of his church :— 'Sepulti. 1670—Maria Driden. 72 an. Vidua. Jany. 14.' She died on Jan. 14, 1670-1.

[1] 'His little estate at Blakesley is at this day [1800] occupied by a grandson of the tenant who held it in Dryden's time. He relates that his grandfather was used to take great pleasure in talking of the poet. He was, he said, the easiest and the kindest landlord in the world.' Malone's *Dryden*, i. 471.

[2] This sentence is not in the first edition, the previous paragraph continuing :—'or considered as a deserter from another religion.'

[3] In the first edition :—'Derrick was misinformed.'

[4] See *ante*, STEPNEY, 1 ; JOHN PHILIPS, 3 ; *post*, DRYDEN, 208 ; SMITH, 29 ; DUKE, 1 ; KING, 2 ; HALIFAX, 2 ; ROWE, 2 ; PRIOR, 2, for the poets educated by Busby. He was head master from 1638 to 1695. Sargeaunt's *Westminster School*, p. 268. Locke and South were Dryden's schoolfellows. Malone's *Dryden*, i. 13. 'Busby educated more youths that were afterwards eminent in the Church and State than any master of his time.' WOOD, *Ath. Oxon.* iv. 418.

'Every one of the confederated band' of Christ Church men who defended Boyle's *Phalaris* against Bentley were his pupils. Monk's *Bentley*, i. 90.

'He strictly forbad the use of notes, and for our Greek and Latin authors we had nothing but the plain text.' H. FELTON, *Dissertation on the Classics*, p. 41.

Two of Dryden's sons were under him in 1682. *Works*, xviii. 99. In 1693 the poet dedicated to him the *Fifth Satire of Persius*. *Ib.* xiii. 249. In 1699 he wrote about the correction of some of his own verses :—'I am now in feare that I purged them out of their spirit ; as our Master Busby us'd to whip a boy so long till he made him a confirm'd blockhead.' *Ib.* xviii. 158. See also *John. Misc.* ii. 304.

[5] Dr. Aldis Wright informs me that Dryden was admitted at Trinity College on May 18, 1650, and matriculated on July 6.

[6] The eldest son of the Earl of Huntingdon. He died in 1649. 'No less than 98 elegies were made on him by the wits of the age, and published in 1650 under the title of *Lachrymae Musarum.*' Collins's *Peerage*, ii. 101. The number, says Christie, was only thirty-three. *Select Poems*, Introd. p. 13.

conceits as, notwithstanding the reformation begun by Waller and Denham, the example of Cowley still kept in reputation [1]. Lord Hastings died of the small-pox, and his poet has made of the pustules, first rosebuds, and then gems ; at last exalts them into stars, and says,

> 'No comet need foretell his change drew on,
> Whose corps might seem a constellation [2].'

At the university he does not appear to have been eager of 6 poetical distinction, or to have lavished his early wit either on fictitious subjects or publick occasions. He probably considered that he who purposed to be an author ought first to be a student [3]. He obtained, whatever was the reason, no fellowship in the College [4]. Why he was excluded cannot now be known, and it is vain to guess ; had he thought himself injured, he knew how to complain. In the *Life of Plutarch* he mentions his education in the College with gratitude [5] ; but in a prologue at Oxford, he has these lines :

> 'Oxford to him a dearer name shall be
> Than his own mother-university ;

[1] In 1672 Dryden wrote :—'Mr. Cowley's authority is almost sacred to me.' *Works*, iv. 24. In 1693 he wrote :—'That noble wit of Scotland, Sir George Mackenzie, asked me why I did not imitate in my verses the turns of Mr. Waller and Sir John Denham. . . . This hint first made me sensible of my own wants. . . . I looked over the darling of my youth, the famous Cowley ; there I found the points of wit and quirks of epigram.' *Ib.* xiii. 116 ; *post*, DRYDEN, 217, 222, 236.

[2] *Works*, xi. 96. For another early poem see *ib.* xi. 1 ; Malone's *Dryden*, i. 14.

[3] At the universities Cowley (*ante*, COWLEY, 9), Milton (*ante*, MILTON, 11), Prior (*Eng. Poets*, xxxii. 143), and Johnson (Boswell's *Johnson*, i. 61) each 'lavished his early wit.'

[4] Malone quotes the following order from 'the *Conclusion Book* in the Archives of the College, p. 221 ' :—'July 19, 1652. Agreed then, that Dryden be put out of Commons for a fortnight at least, and that he goe not out of the colledg during the time aforesaid, excepting to sermons, without express

leave, and that at the end of the fortnight he read a confession of his crime in the hall at the three Fellowes tables. His crime was his disobedience to the Vice-Master, and his contumacy in taking his punishment inflicted by him.' Malone's *Dryden*, i. 16. 'The tables were the tables of the Fellows formerly in use.' *Ib.* i. Part 2, p. 134.

An entry on April 23, 1655, shows that Dryden, who was a Bachelor of Arts, was to forfeit his scholarship unless he returned to reside. This he did not do. 'Having ceased to be a scholar he was ineligible for a fellowship.' *Select Poems*, Introd. p. 15. For Milton's not getting a fellowship see *ante*, MILTON, 11. The degree of M.A. was conferred on Dryden in 1668 by Archbishop Sheldon. Malone's *Dryden*, i. 553.

[5] 'I read Plutarch in the library of Trinity College, to which foundation I gratefully acknowledge a great part of my education.' *Works*, xvii. 55. See *ib.* xiv. 216, where he says that many tutors at the university 'are the most positive blockheads in the world.'

Thebes did his rude [green] unknowing youth engage ;
He chooses Athens in his riper age [1].'

7 It was not till the death of Cromwell, in 1658, that he became a publick candidate for fame [2], by publishing *Heroic Stanzas on the late Lord Protector* [3], which, compared with the verses of Sprat and Waller on the same occasion [4], were sufficient to raise great expectations of the rising poet.

8 When the king was restored Dryden, like the other panegyrists of usurpation, changed his opinion, or his profession, and published *Astrea Redux, a poem on the happy restoration and return of his most sacred Majesty King Charles the Second* [5].

9 The reproach of inconstancy was, on this occasion, shared with such numbers that it produced neither hatred nor disgrace ; if he changed, he changed with the nation. It was, however, not totally forgotten when his reputation raised him enemies [6].

10 The same year he praised the new king in a second poem on his restoration [7]. In the *Astrea* was the line,

'An horrid *stillness* first *invades* the *ear,*
And in that silence we a [the] tempest fear [8],'

for which he was persecuted with perpetual ridicule [9], perhaps with more than was deserved. *Silence* is indeed mere privation ; and, so considered, cannot *invade* [10] ; but privation likewise cer-

---

[1] *Works*, x. 386. Dryden, in 1673, sending the Earl of Rochester 'a prologue and epilogue, which I made for our players when they went down to Oxford,' continues:—'By the event your Lordship will judge how easy 'tis to pass anything upon an university, and how gross flattery the learned will endure.' *Ib.* xviii. 95. The letter perhaps gives the date of the prologue quoted in the text ; in that case the epilogue must be the one given in x. 325.
For the good taste of an Oxford audience see *post,* TICKELL, 4 *n.*

[2] His elegy on Hastings was published in 1650.

[3] *Works*, ix. 10. For Dryden's receipt on Oct. 19, 1657, for £50 from Secretary Thurloe see Masson's *Milton*, v. 375. [Christie thinks it not improbable that Dryden had been employed as secretary by his relative Sir Gilbert Pickering, one of Cromwell's Privy Council and Chamberlain of his household. *Select Poems,* Introd. p. 17.]

[4] *Three Poems upon the Death of his Late Highness Oliver Lord Protector,* &c. Written by Mr. Edmund Waller, Mr. John Dryden, Mr. Sprat of Oxford. London, 1659. 4to. See *ante,* WALLER, 67 ; *post,* DRYDEN, 234 ; SPRAT, 2. 'Dryden's poem was doubtless published before the end of 1658.' *Select Poems,* Introd. p. 57.

[5] *Post,* DRYDEN, 236 ; *Works,* ix. 32. 'Most' is not in the title.

[6] He never republished his lines on Cromwell. 'They were reprinted by his adversaries in a broadsheet in 1681.' Malone's *Dryden,* i. 44.

[7] *A Panegyric on his Coronation,* 1661. *Works,* ix. 54 ; *post,* DRYDEN, 240.

[8] *Works,* ix. 32.

[9] See Scott's note, *ib.*

[10] Pope made the zephyrs to 'lament in silence.' *Post,* POPE, 313.

tainly is *darkness*, and probably *cold*, yet poetry has never been refused the right of ascribing effects or agency to them as to positive powers. No man scruples to say that *darkness* hinders him from his work, or that *cold* has killed the plants. Death is also privation, yet who has made any difficulty of assigning to Death a dart and the power of striking?

In settling the order of his works there is some difficulty, for, 11 even when they are important enough to be formally offered to a patron, he does not commonly date his dedication; the time of writing and publishing is not always the same; nor can the first editions be easily found, if even from them could be obtained the necessary information.

The time at which his first play was exhibited is not certainly 12 known, because it was not printed till it was some years afterwards altered and revived [1], but since the plays are said to be printed in the order in which they were written, from the dates of some those of others may be inferred [2]; and thus it may be collected that in 1663, in the thirty-second year of his life, he commenced a writer for the stage [3], compelled undoubtedly by necessity, for he appears never to have loved that exercise of his genius, or to have much pleased himself with his own dramas.

Of the stage, when he had once invaded it, he kept possession 13 for many years; not indeed without the competition of rivals, who sometimes prevailed, or the censure of criticks, which was often poignant and often just; but with such a degree of reputation as made him at least secure of being heard, whatever might be the final determination of the publick [4].

---

[1] He wrote *The Duke of Guise*, 'in the year of the Restoration; but 'it was damned in private.' *Works*, vii. 146; *post*, DRYDEN, 68.

[2] Johnson, in dealing with the plays, apparently aims at following the chronological order as he got it from Langbaine. *Post*, DRYDEN, 64 *n*. Nevertheless the six plays assigned to 1678 (*post*, DRYDEN, 92) he distributes over paragraphs 29, 48, 63, 71, 78. Dryden, in an 'Advertisement' prefixed to *King Arthur*, 'put,' he writes, 'the plays in the order I wrote them.' Malone's *Dryden*, i. 56. See also *ib*. p. 218 for this list, supplemented by the dates of entry at Stationers' Hall.

[3] 'Feb. 3, 1663-4. In Covent Garden to-night I stopped at the great Coffee-house there; where Dryden, the poet, I knew at Cambridge, and all the wits of the town.' PEPYS, *Diary*, ii. 280.

[4] Hume, fifty-five years after Dryden's death, speaks of 'the total oblivion to which are now condemned' all the plays of the Restoration. 'Dryden's plays, excepting a few scenes, are utterly disfigured by vice or folly.' *Hist. of Eng.* viii. 335. Horace Walpole wrote a few years later:—' Dryden's tragedies are a compound of bombast and heroic obscenity, inclosed in the most beautiful numbers.' *Anec. of Painting*, iii. 4.

14   His first piece was a comedy called *The Wild Gallant*[1]. He began with no happy auguries; for his performance was so much disapproved that he was compelled to recall it, and change it from its imperfect state to the form in which it now appears, and which is yet sufficiently defective to vindicate the criticks[2].

15   I wish that there were no necessity of following the progress of his theatrical fame, or tracing the meanders of his mind through the whole series of his dramatick performances; it will be fit however to enumerate them, and to take especial notice of those that are distinguished by any peculiarity intrinsick or concomitant; for the composition and fate of eight and twenty dramas include too much of a poetical life to be omitted.

16   In 1664 he published *The Rival Ladies*[3], which he dedicated to the Earl of Orrery, a man of high reputation both as a writer and a statesman[4]. In this play he made his essay of dramatick rhyme[5], which he defends in his dedication[6], with sufficient certainty of a favourable hearing; for Orrery was himself a writer of rhyming tragedies[7].

17   He then joined with Sir Robert Howard in *The Indian Queen*, a tragedy in rhyme. The parts which either of them wrote are not distinguished[8].

18   *The Indian Emperor* was published in 1667[9]. It is a tragedy

[1] *Works*, ii. 21. [Produced at the King's Theatre, in Feb. 1663. *Select Poems*, Introd. p. 20, but not published till 1669. Malone's *Dryden*, i. 218.]

[2] In the Preface he writes:—I made the town my judges, and the greater part condemned it. . . . Yet it was received at Court.' *Works*, ii. 27. It seems to have had some run, for Evelyn saw it on Feb. 5, 1662-3 (*Diary*, i. 396), and Pepys on Feb. 23, who described it as 'so poor a thing as I never saw in my life almost.' *Diary*, ii. 119. It was ridiculed in *The Rehearsal*, ed. Arber, p. 66.

[3] *Works*, ii. 125. Pepys, who saw it on Aug. 4, 1664, calls it 'a very innocent and most pretty witty play.' *Diary*, ii. 362. See also *ib.* iii. 239.

[4] Dryden says in the Dedication:—'The Muses have seldom employed your thoughts but when some violent fit of the gout has snatched you from affairs of state.' *Works*, ii. 131. *Ante*, DENHAM, 23; Bos-

well's *Johnson*, v. 237.

[5] The play is mostly in blank verse.

[6] *Works*, ii. 137. See also *ib.* xv. 364.

[7] Horace Walpole (*Works*, i. 514) quotes from Orrery's *Black Prince*, Act v:—
'When to the wars of Aquitaine I went
I made a friendship with the Earl of Kent.'

[8] Dryden's wife (*post*, DRYDEN, 157) was Howard's sister. Pepys recorded on Jan. 27, 1663-4:—'Observed the street full of coaches at the new play, at *The Indian Queen*.' *Diary*, ii. 276. 'The play is good, but spoiled with the rhyme, which breaks the sense.' *Ib.* p. 278. See also Evelyn's *Diary*, i. 400. For *The Indian Queen* see *Works*, ii. 223. 'The versification is much superior to that of Howard's other plays.' Malone's *Dryden*, i. 57.

[9] *Works*, ii. 288. 'It was probably acted in the winter of 1664-5.' Malone's *Dryden*, i. 57.

in rhyme, intended for a sequel to Howard's *Indian Queen*. Of this connection notice was given to the audience by printed bills, distributed at the door ; an expedient supposed to be ridiculed in *The Rehearsal*, when Bayes tells how many reams he has printed, to instil into the audience some conception of his plot [1].

In this play is the description of Night [2], which Rymer has made [19] famous by preferring it to those of all other poets [3].

The practice of making tragedies in rhyme was introduced [20] soon after the Restoration, as it seems, by the earl of Orrery, in compliance with the opinion of Charles the Second, who had formed his taste by the French theatre [4] ; and Dryden, who wrote, and made no difficulty of declaring that he wrote, only to please, and who perhaps knew that by his dexterity of versification he was more likely to excel others in rhyme than without it, very rapidly adopted his master's preference [5]. He therefore made

---

[1] 'Besides, Sir, I have printed above a hundred sheets of paper to insinuate the plot into the boxes.' *The Rehearsal*, ed. Arber, p. 39. *Post*, DRYDEN, 94.

[2] *Works*, ii. 360.

[3] For Rymer see *post*, DRYDEN, 200. In the Preface to his translation of Rapin's *Reflections on Aristotle's Treatise of Poesie* he quotes descriptions by Apollonius, Virgil [*Aen.* iv. 522–8] (one of whose lines [l. 524] he mends, to make it more poetical), Tasso, Marino, Chapelain, and Le Moyne, to all of which he prefers Dryden's.

Johnson, comparing the description of night in *Macbeth*, ii. 2, says :—'He that reads Dryden finds himself lulled with serenity, and disposed to solitude and contemplation. He that peruses Shakespeare looks round alarmed, and starts to find himself alone.' Johnson's *Shakespeare*, vi. 404.

'Dryden's lines are vague, bombastic and senseless.' WORDSWORTH, *Works*, 1857, vi. 370. See also *post*, YOUNG, 168 *n.*; *John. Misc.* i. 186.

[4] Dryden writes in his Dedication :—'The most eminent persons for wit and honour in the Royal Circle have judged no way so fit as verse to entertain a noble audience, or to express a noble passion. *Works*, ii. 285.

'Nov. 26, 1661. I saw *Hamlet* played, but now the old plays began to disgust this refined age, since his Majesty's being so long abroad.' EVELYN, *Diary*, i. 380.

'In nature the most violent passions are silent; in tragedy they must speak, and speak with dignity too. Hence the necessity of their being written in verse, and, unfortunately for the French from the weakness of their language, in rhymes. And for the same reason Cato the Stoic, expiring at Utica, rhymes masculine and feminine at Paris ; and fetches his last breath at London in most harmonious and correct blank verse.' CHESTERFIELD, *Letters to his Son*, iii. 256. See also Southey's *Cowper*, ii. 351, and Cunningham's *Lives of the Poets*, i. 275, for a quotation from Orrery's *Letters*, p. 65.

[5] 'The practice first, and then the continuation of rhyme, shows that it attained the end, which was to please; and if that cannot be compassed here, I will be the first who shall lay it down ; for I confess my chief endeavours are to delight the age in which I live.' *Works*, ii. 297.

'Poeta quom primum animum ad scribendum adpulit,
Id sibi negoti credidit solum dari,
Populo ut placerent quas fecisset fabulas.' TER. *Prol. to And.* l. 1.

rhyming tragedies till, by the prevalence of manifest propriety, he seems to have grown ashamed of making them any longer [1].

21 To this play is prefixed a very vehement defence of dramatick rhyme [2], in confutation of the preface to *The Duke of Lerma* [3], in which Sir Robert Howard had censured it.

22 In 1667 he published *Annus Mirabilis, The Year of Wonders*, which may be esteemed one of his most elaborate works [4].

23 It is addressed to Sir Robert Howard by a letter, which is not properly a dedication [5]; and, writing to a poet, he has interspersed many critical observations, of which some are common, and some perhaps ventured without much consideration. He began even now to exercise the domination of conscious genius, by recommending his own performance: 'I am [well] satisfied that as the Prince and General [Rupert and Monk] are incomparably the best subjects [subject] I ever had [excepting only the royal family], so what [also that this] I have written on them is much better than what I have performed on any other [. . .], as I have endeavoured to adorn my poem with noble thoughts, so much more to express those thoughts with elocution [6].'

24 It is written in quatrains or heroick stanzas of four lines; a measure which he had learned from the *Gondibert* of Davenant, and which he then thought the most majestick that the English language affords [7]. Of this stanza he mentions the encumbrances, increased as they were by the exactness which the age required [8]. It was throughout his life very much his custom to recommend

'The reign of rhyming tragedies lasted about fifteen years, from 1662 to 1676. A few heroic plays afterward appeared, but they were not long-lived.' Malone's *Dryden*, i. 2.431.

'Dryden's heroic plays are bad, not because they are in rhyme, but because they are absurd; the rhyme is their chief merit.' CHRISTOPHER NORTH, *Blackwood*, 1845, p. 143.

[2] A play in rhyme is as absurd in English as a tragedy of hexameters would have been in Greek or Latin.' ADDISON, *The Spectator*, No. 39.

'In Dryden's time they did not understand, or anyhow had forgotten, how to write blank verse.' TENNYSON, *Life*, ii. 385. Milton lived to within two years of the end of 'the reign of rhyming tragedies,' but he belonged to the past. For blank verse and rhyme see *ante*, MILTON,

273; *post*, DRYDEN, 203, 264.
[2] *A Defence of an Essay of Dramatic Poesy. Works*, ii. 291.
[3] *The Great Favourite, or the Duke of Lerma*, 1668.
[4] *Works*, ix. 79; *post*, DRYDEN, 247. Pepys read it on Feb. 2, 1666-7, and found it 'a very good poem.' *Diary*, iii. 390.
[5] *Works*, ix. 90.
[6] *Ib.* ix. 94, 95.
[7] *Ib.* ix. 92; *post*, DRYDEN, 247; HAMMOND, 8. For *Gondibert*, see *post*, DRYDEN, 235.
[8] 'In quatrains the poet is to bear along in his head the troublesome sense of four lines together. For those who write correctly in this kind must needs acknowledge that the last line of the stanza is to be considered in the composition of the first.' *Works*, ix. 92.

his works by representation of the difficulties that he had encountered, without appearing to have sufficiently considered that where there is no difficulty there is no praise.

There seems to be in the conduct of Sir Robert Howard and 25 Dryden towards each other something that is not now easily to be explained. Dryden, in his dedication to the earl of Orrery, had defended dramatick rhyme [1]; and Howard, in the preface to a collection of plays, had censured his opinion [2]. Dryden vindicated himself in his *Dialogue on Dramatick Poetry* [3]; Howard, in his Preface to *The Duke of Lerma* [4], animadverted on the Vindication; and Dryden, in a Preface to *The Indian Emperor* [5], replied to the Animadversions with great asperity, and almost with contumely [6]. The dedication to this play is dated the year [7] in which the *Annus Mirabilis* was published. Here appears a strange inconsistency; but Langbaine affords some help, by relating that the answer to Howard was not published in the first edition of the play, but was added when it was afterwards reprinted [8]; and as *The Duke of Lerma* did not appear till 1668 [9], the same year in which the *Dialogue* was published, there was time enough for enmity to grow up between authors who, writing both for the theatre, were naturally rivals [10].

[1] *Ante*, DRYDEN, 16; *Works*, ii. 134 (1664).

[2] In the Preface to *Four New Plays* (1665).

[3] *Essay of Dramatic Poesy* (1667-8), *Works*, xv. 273; *post*, DRYDEN, 27.

[4] *The Great Favourite, or the Duke of Lerma* (summer of 1668). Malone's *Dryden*, i. 91.

[5] Second edition (1668), *Works*, ii. 291; *ante*, DRYDEN, 18. 'As a peace-offering the preface was cancelled with such care, that (writes Malone) I have never met with an ancient copy of the play in which it was found.' Malone's *Dryden*, i. 92; *ib*. i. 2. 156. In 1697 Dryden described Howard as 'that excellent person.' *Works*, xiv. 171.

[6] *Ib*. ii. 299. Professor Masson points out that 'the paragraph entitled "The Verse," prefixed to the fifth issue of copies of *Paradise Lost* in 1668, is Milton's contribution to the controversy' about blank verse and rhyme. Masson's *Milton*, vi. 634.

In Dryden's Preface is a passage which Johnson probably had in mind when he wrote :—'Mr. Davies has got great success as an author, generated by the corruption of a bookseller.' Boswell's *Johnson*, iii. 434. Dryden said of Howard :—'The Muses have lost him, but the commonwealth gains by it; the corruption of a poet is the generation of a statesman.' *Works*, ii. 301.

[7] Oct. 12, 1667. *Ib*. ii. 288.

[8] Langbaine's *Dram. Poets*, p. 165. Gerard Langbaine, son of the Provost of Queen's College, Oxford, 'by his mother's fondness became idle, a great jockey, married, and run out of a good part of his estate. But being a man of parts, he took up, lived a retired life, and improved much his natural and gay geny [genius] that he had to dramatic poetry.' *Ath. Oxon*. iv. 364. See *ante*, OTWAY, 5; *post*, DRYDEN, 29, 92.

[9] Pepys saw it acted the first time on Feb. 20, 1667-8. *Diary*, iv. 363.

[10] Dryden defended rhyme in his

26   He was now so much distinguished that in 1668 he succeeded
Sir William Davenant as poet-laureat. The salary of the laureat [1]
had been raised in favour of Jonson, by Charles the First, from
an hundred marks to one hundred pounds a year and a tierce
of wine [2]; a revenue in those days not inadequate to the conveniencies of life.

27   The same year he published his *Essay on* [*of*] *Dramatick
Poetry* [3], an elegant and instructive dialogue, in which we are
told by Prior that the principal character is meant to represent
the duke of Dorset [4]. This work seems to have given Addison
a model for his *Dialogues upon Medals* [5].

28   *Secret Love, or the Maiden Queen*, is a tragi-comedy [6]. In the
preface he discusses a curious question, whether a poet can judge
well of his own productions [7] : and determines very justly that of
the plan and disposition [8], and all that can be reduced to principles of science, the author may depend upon his own opinion ;
but that in those parts where fancy predominates self-love may
easily deceive [9]. He might have observed, that what is good only
because it pleases cannot be pronounced good till it has been
found to please [10].

29   *Sir Martin Marall* is a comedy, published without preface or
dedication, and at first without the name of the author [11]. Lang-

Dedication (1664). Howard censured
it in his Preface to *Four New Plays*
(1665). Dryden vindicated it in his
Dialogue (1667). Howard animadverted on the vindication in the Preface to *The Duke of Lerma* (1668).
Dryden rejoined in the Preface to
The Indian Emperor, second edition
(1668).

[1] Johnson, in his *Dictionary*, gives
laureate (not *laureat*) only as an
adjective.

[2] See Appendix Q.

[3] In 1667-8. *Ante*, DRYDEN, 25.

[4] The Earl of Dorset. *Ante*,
DORSET, 14 *n*. For Johnson's mistake about his title see *post*, PRIOR,
18 ; A. PHILIPS, 3.

[5] *Post*, ADDISON, 20. Addison
said that he imitated Fontenelle's
Dialogues on the Plurality of Worlds.
Addison's *Works*, v. 338.

[6] *Works*, ii. 413. On March 2,
1666-7, Pepys recorded of this play :—
'There is a comical part done by
Nell [Gwynne], which is Florimell,

that I never can hope ever to see the
like done again by man or woman.
The King and Duke of York were
at the play.' *Diary*, iii. 417. It
was printed in 1668. Malone's *Dryden*, i. 218.

[7] 'The author himself is the best
judge of his own performance.' GIB-
BON, *Memoirs*, p. 191.

[8] 'The plan and disposition' of
Johnson is, in Dryden, either 'the
fabric and contrivance' or 'the frame
and contexture.' *Works*, ii. 418.

[9] *Ib.* ii. 418. Pepys, on Jan. 18,
1667-8, bought the play, 'which Mr.
Dryden himself in his Preface seems
to brag of, and indeed is a good play.'
Diary, iv. 327.

[10] *Ante*, COWLEY, 38; *post*, SMITH,
49 ; ADDISON, 136; POPE, 280;
Boswell's *Johnson*, i. 200.

[11] *Works*, iii. 1. It was printed in
1668. Malone's *Dryden*, i. 218. Pepys,
who saw it acted on Aug. 16, 1667, describes it as 'made by my Lord Duke
of Newcastle, but, as everybody says,

baine charges it, like most of the rest, with plagiarism, and observes that the song is translated from Voiture, allowing however that both the sense and measure are exactly observed [1].

The Tempest is an alteration of Shakespeare's play, made by Dryden in conjunction with Davenant, 'whom,' says he, 'I found of so quick a fancy that nothing was proposed to him in [on] which he could not suddenly produce a thought extremely pleasant and surprising; and those first thoughts of his, contrary to the Latin proverb, were not always the least happy; and as his fancy was quick, so likewise were the products of it remote and new. He borrowed not of any other, and his imaginations were such as could not easily enter into any other man [2].' **30**

The effect produced by the conjunction of these two powerful minds was that to Shakespeare's monster Caliban is added a sister-monster Sicorax; and a woman, who, in the original play, had never seen a man, is in this brought acquainted with a man that had never seen a woman [3]. **31**

corrected by Dryden. . . . I never laughed so in all my life, and at very good wit therein, not fooling.' *Diary*, iv. 157.

'The Duke giving Mr. Dryden a bare translation of it out of a comedy of Molière [*L'Étourdi*], he adapted the part purposely for the mouth of Mr. Nokes, and curiously polished the whole. This and *Love in a Tub* [by Etherege] got the company more money than any preceding comedy.' DOWNES, *Roscius Anglicanus*, p. 38.

[1] The following is the opening stanza of each poem:—

' L'Amour sous sa loy
N'a jamais eu d'amant plus heureux
    que moy.
Bénit soit son flambeau,
Son carquois, son bandeau !
Je suis amoureux :
Et le ciel ne voit point d'amant plus
    heureux.'
            Œuvres de Voiture, 1665, ii. 42.
' Blind Love, to this hour,
Had never, like me, a slave under
    his power ;
    Then blest be the dart
    That he threw at my heart ;
    For nothing can prove
A joy so great as to be wounded with
    love.'   Dryden's *Works*, iii. 75.
[2] *Works*, iii. 107.   'Davenant,'

writes Dryden, 'first taught me to admire Shakespeare.' *Ib.* p. 106. He died on April 7, 1668. The Preface is dated Dec. 1, 1669. *Ib.* p. 108. Pepys saw it acted on Nov. 7, 1667. *Diary*, iv. 257. For Davenant's influence on Dryden see *post*, DRYDEN, 235.

[3] ' Davenant designed the counterpart to Shakespeare's plot, that those two characters of innocence and love might the more illustrate and commend each other.' Dryden's *Works*, iii. 106.

' How much this comedy is now esteemed, though the foundation were Shakespeare's, all people know.' LANGBAINE, *Dram. Poets*, p. 463.

Macready acted Prospero in this ' mélange' in 1821. In 1839 he produced Shakespeare's *Tempest*, 'a play which had never been seen before.' It ran fifty-five nights. Macready's *Reminiscences*, i. 226 ; ii. 144.

' It was a singular felicity that Dryden's operas were set to music by Purcell. In *The Tempest* are some of the finest airs and sweetest harmonies that ever delighted the ear. Dryden had no skill in music. His wife had been a scholar of Purcell.' HAWKINS, Johnson's *Works*, 1787, ii. 447.

32 About this time, in 1673 [1], Dryden seems to have had his quiet much disturbed by the success of *The Empress of Morocco*, a tragedy written in rhyme by Elkanah Settle; which was so much applauded as to make him think his supremacy of reputation in some danger. Settle had not only been prosperous on the stage, but, in the confidence of success, had published his play, with sculptures [2] and a preface of defiance [3]. Here was one offence added to another; and, for the last blast of inflammation, it was acted at Whitehall by the court-ladies [4].

33 Dryden could not now repress these emotions, which he called indignation, and others jealousy; but wrote upon the play and the dedication such criticism as malignant impatience could pour out in haste [5].

34 Of Settle he gives this character [6].

'He's an animal of a most deplored understanding, without [reading and] conversation. His being is in a twilight of sense and some glimmering of thought, which he can never fashion into wit or English. His style is boisterous and rough-hewn, his rhyme incorrigibly lewd, and his numbers perpetually harsh and ill-sounding. The little talent which he has is fancy. He sometimes labours with a thought, but, with the pudder he makes to bring it into the world, 'tis commonly still-born; so

[1] As the last play mentioned, *The Tempest*, was published in the winter of 1669-70, and the *Notes and Observations* which Johnson goes on to criticize were not published till 1674, paragraphs 32-42 should have come later.

[2] 'It was the first play that ever was sold in England for two shillings, and the first that ever was printed with cuts.' DENNIS, Preface to *Remarks upon Pope's Homer*. Three quarters of a century later Dodsley was selling *Irene* and seven other tragedies for eighteenpence each. See advertisement at the end of *Theatrical Records*, 1756. Goldsmith did not like 'sculptures.' 'The vulgar,' he writes, 'buy every book rather from the excellence of the sculptor than the writer.' Goldsmith's *Works*, iii. 87.

[3] 'There is no preface; the defiance occurs in the Dedication.' Cunningham's *Lives of the Poets*, i. 281.

[4] Dennis's *Remarks*, &c., Preface; *post*, DRYDEN, 101. For Rochester's

Prologue to the play see *Eng. Poets*, xv. 71.

[5] *Notes and Observations on the Empress of Morocco; or some few Erratas to be printed instead of the Sculptures with the second Edition of that Play*, 1674. Langbaine's *Dram. Poets*, p. 440; Dryden's *Works*, xv. 393.

'Mr. Dryden, Mr. Shadwell and Mr. Crown began to grow jealous, and they three wrote Remarks on *The Empress of Morocco*.' DENNIS, *Remarks*, &c., Preface.

Of these *Notes*, &c., Malone writes: —'The Preface, I think, from internal evidence is Dryden's; and one passage in the body of the piece, and the Postscript, though I have some doubts concerning the latter.' Malone's *Dryden*, ii. 271. Paragraphs 34 and 35 in the text belong to the Preface (*Works*, xv. 399, 400), and 41 to the passage (*ib.* pp. 402-4). The rest therefore is not Dryden's.

[6] See *post*, DRYDEN, 116, for a second character of Settle.

that, for want of learning and elocution, he will never be able to express any thing either naturally or justly ! '

This is not very decent ; yet this is one of the pages in which **35** criticism prevails most over brutal fury. He proceeds :

' He has a heavy hand at fools, and a great felicity in writing nonsense for them. Fools they will be in spite of him. His King, his two Empresses, his villain, and his sub-villain, nay his hero, have all a certain natural cast of the father. . . . Their folly was born and bred in them, and something of the Elkanah will be visible.'

This is Dryden's general declamation ; I will not withhold from **36** the reader a particular remark. Having gone through the first act, he says :

' To conclude this act with the most rumbling piece of nonsense spoken yet,

> "To flattering lightning our feign'd smiles conform,
> Which back'd with thunder do but gild a storm."

Conform a smile to lightning, make a *smile* imitate *lightning*, and *flattering lightning* ; lightning sure is a threatening thing. And this lightning must *gild a storm*.   Now if I must conform my smiles to lightning, then my smiles must gild a storm too ; to *gild* with *smiles* is a new invention of gilding. And gild a storm by being *backed with thunder*. Thunder is part of the storm ; so one part of the storm must help to *gild* another part, and help by *backing* ; as if a man would gild a thing the better for being backed, or having a load upon his back.   So that here is *gilding* by *conforming, smiling, lightning, backing*, and *thundering*. The whole is as if I should say thus, I will make my counterfeit smiles look like a flattering stone-horse, which, being backed with a trooper, does but gild the battle. I am mistaken if nonsense is not here pretty thick sown. Sure the poet writ these two lines aboard some smack in a storm, and, being sea-sick, spewed up a good lump of clotted nonsense at once.'

Here is perhaps a sufficient specimen ; but as the pamphlet, **37** though Dryden's, has never been thought worthy of republication and is not easily to be found, it may gratify curiosity to quote it more largely.

> ' " Whene'er she bleeds,
> He no severer a damnation needs,
> That dares pronounce the sentence of her death,
> Than the infection that attends that breath."

That attends that breath.—The poet is at *breath* again ; *breath* can never 'scape him ; and here he brings in a *breath* that must be *infectious* with *pronouncing* a sentence ; and this sentence is not to be pronounced till the condemned party *bleeds*, that is, she must be executed first, and sentenced after ; and the *pronouncing* of this *sentence* will be infectious, that is, others will catch the disease of that sentence, and this infecting of others will torment a man's self.   The whole is thus : *when she bleeds, thou needest no greater hell or torment to thyself than infecting of others by pronouncing a sentence upon her.*   What hodge-podge does he make here !   Never was Dutch grout such clogging, thick, indigestible stuff.   But this is but a taste to stay the stomach ; we share a more plentiful mess presently.

38   'Now to dish up the poet's broth that I promised :

> " For when we're dead and our freed souls enlarg'd,
> Of nature's grosser burden we're discharg'd,
> Then gently, as a happy lover's sigh,
> Like wandering meteors through the air we'll fly,
> And in our airy walk, as subtle guests,
> We'll steal into our cruel fathers' breasts,
> There read their souls, and track each passion's sphere :
> See how Revenge moves there, Ambition here.
> And in their orbs view the dark characters
> Of sieges, ruins, murders, blood and wars.
> We'll blot out all those hideous draughts, and write
> Pure and white forms ; then with a radiant light
> Their breasts encircle, till their passions be
> Gentle as nature in its infancy :
> Till soften'd by our charms their furies cease,
> And their revenge resolves into a peace.
> Thus by our death their quarrel ends,
> Whom living we made foes, dead we'll make friends."

If this be not a very liberal mess, I will refer myself to the stomach of any moderate guest.   And a rare mess it is, far excelling any Westminster white-broth.   It is a kind of giblet porridge, made of the giblets of a couple of young geese, stodged full of *meteors, orbs, spheres, track, hideous draughts, dark characters, white forms,* and *radiant lights,* designed not only to please appetite and indulge luxury, but it is also physical, being an approved medicine to purge choler, for it is propounded by Morena as a receipt to cure their fathers of their choleric humours : and were it written in characters as barbarous as the words, might very well pass for a doctor's bill.   To conclude, it is porridge, 'tis a receipt, 'tis a pig with a pudding in the belly, 'tis I know not what ; for, certainly, never any one that pretended to write sense had the impudence before to put such stuff as this into the mouths of those that were to speak it before an audience, whom he did not take to be all fools ; and after that to print it too, and expose it to the examination of the world. But let us see what we can make of this stuff:

"For when we're dead and our freed souls enlarg'd "—

Here he tells us what it is to be *dead*; it is to have *our freed souls set free*. Now if to have a soul set free is to be dead, then to have a *freed soul* set free is to have a dead man die.

"Then gently, as a happy lover's sigh "—

They two like one *sigh*, and that one *sigh* like two wandering meteors,

"—shall fly through the air "—

That is, they shall mount above like falling stars, or else they shall skip like two Jacks with lanthorns, or Will with a wisp, and Madge with a candle.

'*And in their airy walk steal into their cruel fathers' breasts,* **39** *like subtle guests.* So that their *fathers' breasts* must be in an airy *walk*, an airy *walk* of a *flier*. *And there they will read their souls, and track the spheres of their passions.* That is, these walking fliers, Jack with a lanthorn, &c. will put on his spectacles, and fall a *reading souls*, and put on his pumps and fall a *tracking of spheres*; so that he will read and run, walk and fly at the same time! Oh! Nimble Jack. *Then he will see, how revenge here, how ambition there*—The birds will hop about. *And then view the dark characters of sieges, ruins, murders, blood, and wars, in their orbs: Track the characters* to their forms! Oh! rare sport for Jack. Never was place so full of game as these breasts! You cannot stir but flush a sphere, start a character, or unkennel an orb!'

Settle's is said to have been the first play embellished with **40** sculptures[1]; those ornaments seem to have given poor Dryden great disturbance[2]. He tries however to ease his pain by venting his malice in a parody[3].

'The poet has not only been so impudent to expose all this **41** stuff, but so arrogant to defend it with an epistle; like a saucy booth-keeper that, when he had put a cheat upon the people, would wrangle and fight with any that would not like it or would offer to discover it: for which arrogance our poet receives this correction; and to jerk him a little the sharper, I will not transpose [trans-prose] his verse, but by the help of his own words trans-nonsense sense, that, by my stuff, people may judge the better what his is:

[1] *Ante*, DRYDEN, 32.
[2] See *post*, LYTTELTON, 17, for 'poor Lyttelton.'
[3] For the lines parodied see *Works*, xv. 404 *n.*

'Great Boy, thy tragedy and sculptures done
From press, and plates in fleets do homeward come:
And in ridiculous and humble pride,
Their course in ballad-singers' baskets guide,
Whose greasy twigs do all new beauties take,
From the gay shews thy dainty sculptures make.
Thy lines a mess of rhyming nonsense yield,
A senseless tale, with flattering [fluttering] fustian fill'd.
No grain of sense does in one line appear,
Thy words big bulks of boisterous bombast bear.
With noise they move, and from players' mouths rebound,
When their tongues dance to thy words' empty sound.
By thee inspir'd the [thy] rumbling verses roll,
As if that rhyme and bombast lent a soul:
And with that soul they seem taught duty too,
To huffing words does humble nonsense bow,
As if it would thy worthless worth enhance,
To th' lowest rank of fops thy praise advance;
To whom, by instinct, all thy stuff is dear;
Their loud claps echo to the theatre.
From breaths of fools thy commendation spreads,
Fame sings thy praise with mouths of loggerheads.
With noise and laughing each thy fustian greets,
'Tis clapt by quires of empty-headed cits,
Who have their tribute sent, and homage given,
As men in whispers send loud noise to heaven.

'Thus I have daubed him with his own puddle: and now we are come from aboard his dancing, masking, rebounding, breathing fleet; and as if we had landed at Gotham, we meet nothing but fools and nonsense.'

42 Such was the criticism to which the genius of Dryden could be reduced, between rage and terrour; rage with little provocation and terrour with little danger. To see the highest minds thus levelled with the meanest may produce some solace to the consciousness of weakness, and some mortification to the pride of wisdom. But let it be remembered, that minds are not levelled in their powers but when they are first levelled in their desires. Dryden and Settle had both placed their happiness in the claps of multitudes[1].

43 *The Mock Astrologer*[2], a comedy, is dedicated to the illustrious

[1] 'When a poet is thoroughly provoked he will do himself justice, however dear it cost him. . . . The vengeance we defer is not forgotten.' DRYDEN, *Works*, xiv. 157. See also *ib.* xiii. 82; *post*, DRYDEN, 173.

[2] Its first title is *An Evening's Love. Works*, iii. 227. It was printed in 1671. Malone's *Dryden*, i. 218. 'June 20, 1668. I saw this new

duke of Newcastle, whom he courts by adding to his praises those of his lady, not only as a lover but a partner of his studies. It is unpleasing to think how many names once celebrated are since forgotten. Of Newcastle's works nothing is now known but his treatise on horsemanship [1].

The Preface seems very elaborately written, and contains many 44 just remarks on the Fathers of the English drama. Shakespeare's plots, he says, are in the hundred novels of Cinthio ; those of Beaumont and Fletcher in Spanish stories ; Jonson only made them for himself [2]. His criticisms upon tragedy, comedy, and farce are judicious and profound [3]. He endeavours to defend the immorality of some of his comedies by the example of former writers [4]; which is only to say, that he was not the first nor perhaps the greatest offender. Against those that accused him of plagiarism he alleges a favourable expression of the king : ' He only desired that they, who accuse me of thefts, would steal him

play, and do not like it, it being very smutty.

'June 22. Calling this day at Herringman's [Dryden's publisher], he tells me Dryden do himself call it but a fifth-rate play.' PEPYS, *Diary*, iv. 478.

'June 19, 1668. To a new play, *The Evening Lover* [*sic*], a foolish plot, and very profane ; it afflicted me to see how the stage was degenerated, and polluted by the licentious times.' EVELYN, *Diary*, ii. 37.

[1] *A New Method, &c., to dress Horses, and work them according to Nature by the Subtlety of Art*, London, 1667, fol. There was an earlier version in French. Antwerp, 1658. 'The Duke, though "amorous in poetry and music" as my Lord Clarendon says, was fitter to break Pegasus for a manage [riding-school] than to mount him on the steeps of Parnassus. Of all the riders of that steed perhaps there have not been a more fantastic couple than his Grace and his faithful Duchess, who was never off her pillion. . . . She says "that it pleased God to command his servant Nature to *indue* her with a poetical and philosophical genius even from her birth."' HORACE WALPOLE, *Works*, i. 383.

For Clarendon's character of New-

castle see *Hist. of the Rebel.* 1826, iv. 516.

According to Langbaine she published twenty-six plays. *Dram. Poets*, p. 390.

She has a place in *The Dunciad*, i. 141 :—

' Here swells the shelf with Ogilby the great ;
There, stamp'd with arms, Newcastle shines complete.'

See also *ante*, WALLER, 98 ; *post*, POPE, 260 *n.*; Pepys's *Diary*, iv. 15, 27 ; Evelyn's *Diary*, ii. 26 ; Malone's *Dryden*, i. 2. 338.

[2] ' Ben Jonson, indeed, has designed his plots himself, but no man has borrowed so much from the ancients.' *Works*, iii. 252.

[3] Writing of humour Dryden says :— 'Jonson was the only man of all ages and nations who has performed it well.' *Ib.* iii. 242. Dr. Johnson would not have allowed this, who, writing of comedies, says :—'The stream of time, which is continually washing away the dissoluble fabricks of other poets, passes without injury by the adamant of Shakespeare.' Johnson's *Works*, v. 113.

[4] He instances Plautus, Terence, Jonson, and Beaumont and Fletcher. *Works*, iii. 247 ; *post*, DRYDEN, 204.

plays like mine [1]'; and then relates how much labour he spends in fitting for the English stage what he borrows from others [2].

45 *Tyrannick Love, or the Virgin Martyr* [3], was another tragedy in rhyme, conspicuous for many passages of strength and elegance and many of empty noise and ridiculous turbulence. The rants of Maximin have been always the sport of criticism, and were at length, if his own confession may be trusted, the shame of the writer [4].

46 Of this play he takes care to let the reader know that it was contrived and written in seven weeks [5]. Want of time was often his excuse, or perhaps shortness of time was his private boast in the form of an apology.

47 It was written before *The Conquest of Granada*, but published after it [6]. The design is to recommend piety: ' I considered that pleasure was not the only end of poesy, and that even the instructions of morality were not so wholly the business of a poet, as that [the] precepts and examples of piety were to be omitted; for to leave that employment altogether to the clergy were to forget that religion was first taught in verse, which the laziness or dulness of succeeding priesthood turned afterwards into prose [7].' Thus foolishly could Dryden write, rather than not shew his malice to the parsons [8].

48 The two parts of *The Conquest of Granada* [9] are written with a seeming determination to glut the publick with dramatick

[1] *Works*, iii. 250.

[2] Even Langbaine, in the Appendix to *Dram. Poets*, owns that 'he so polishes other men's thoughts, that, though they are mean in themselves, yet by a new turn which he gives them they appear beautiful and sparkling.'

[3] *The Royal Martyr, Works*, iii. 369. First acted in the winter of 1668-9, and printed in 1670. Malone's *Dryden*, i. 94, 218.

[4] 'A famous modern poet used to sacrifice every year a Statius to Virgil's manes. . . . I remember some verses of my own Maximin and Almanzor, which cry vengeance upon me for their extravagance, and which I wish heartily in the same fire with Statius and Chapman.' *Works*, vi. 404. *Post*, DRYDEN, 334.

[5] *Ib.* iii. 379; *post*, DRYDEN, 64, 264.

[6] In the Preface *The Conquest* is mentioned. *Works*, iii. 379. That play was not however registered till Feb. 20, 1670-1, nor published till 1672. Malone's *Dryden*, i. 94.

[7] *Works*, iii. 376.

[8] *Post*, DRYDEN, 179.

[9] *Works*, iv. 1. 119. [*Almanzor and Almahide, or the Conquest of Granada*, in two parts, each being a separate play. *Select Poems*, Introd. p. 26.] 'They were probably produced in the autumn of 1669 and the spring of 1670.' Malone's *Dryden*, i. 94. Evelyn records that in Feb. 1670-1 there 'was acted at Whitehall Theatre the famous play called *The Siege of Granada*, two days successively. There were indeed very glorious scenes and perspectives.' *Diary*, ii. 60. According to Gildon 'these plays always had the effect of comedy on the audience.' Malone's *Dryden*, i. 2. 228.

wonders; to exhibit in its highest elevation a theatrical meteor of incredible love and impossible valour, and to leave no room for a wilder flight to the extravagance of posterity[1]. All the rays of romantick heat, whether amorous or warlike, glow in Almanzor by a kind of concentration. He is above all laws; he is exempt from all restraints; he ranges the world at will, and governs wherever he appears. He fights without enquiring the cause, and loves in spite of the obligations of justice, of rejection by his mistress, and of prohibition from the dead. Yet the scenes are, for the most part, delightful; they exhibit a kind of illustrious depravity and majestick madness: such as, if it is sometimes despised, is often reverenced, and in which the ridiculous is mingled with the astonishing[2].

In the Epilogue to the second part of *The Conquest of Gra-* 49 *nada*, Dryden indulges his favourite pleasure of discrediting his predecessors[3]; and this Epilogue he has defended by a long postscript[4]. He had promised a second dialogue, in which he should more fully treat of the virtues and faults of the English poets, who have written in the dramatick, epick, or lyrick way. This promise was never formally performed; but, with respect to the dramatick writers, he has given us in his prefaces and in this postscript something equivalent: but his purpose being to exalt himself by the comparison, he shows faults distinctly, and only praises excellence in general terms.

A play thus written, in professed defiance of probability[5], 50 naturally drew down upon itself the vultures of the theatre[6].

---

[1] 'In the *Grand Cyrus* Artamenes exterminates with his own hand at least a hundred thousand fighting men. These monstrous fictions constituted the amusement of the young and gay in the age of Charles II.' SCOTT, Dryden's *Works*, iv. 2.

[2] 'At an early age there are few poems which make a more deep impression upon the imagination than *The Conquest of Granada.*' SCOTT, *Ib.* iv. 6.

[3] ' Fame then was cheap, and the first comer sped;
And they have kept it since by being dead.
. . . .
Wit 's now arrived to a more high degree;

Our native language more refined and free.
Our ladies and our men now speak more wit
In conversation than those poets writ.' *Ib.* iv. 224.
In another passage he writes:—'I am made [by my critics] a detractor from my predecessors, whom I confess to have been my masters in the art.' *Ib.* iv. 375.

[4] *Ib.* iv. 225.

[5] 'Il n'y a que le vraisemblable qui touche dans la tragédie.' RACINE, Preface to *Bérénice.*

[6] Bayes says in *The Rehearsal*, p. 91 :—'Why, I have designed a Conquest that cannot possibly, I gad, be acted in less than a whole week.'

One of the criticks that attacked it was Martin Clifford, to whom
Sprat addressed the *Life of Cowley*, with such veneration of his
critical powers as might naturally excite great expectations of
instruction from his remarks[1]. But let honest credulity beware
of receiving characters from contemporary writers. Clifford's
remarks, by the favour of Dr. Percy[2], were at last obtained ; and,
that no man may ever want them more, I will extract enough to
satisfy all reasonable desire.

51   In the first Letter his observation is only general:

'You do live,' says he, 'in as much ignorance and darkness as
you did in the womb : your writings are like a jack-of-all-trades
shop ; they have a variety, but nothing of value ; and if thou
art not the dullest plant-animal that ever the earth produced, all
that I have conversed with are strangely mistaken in thee.'

52   In the second, he tells him that Almanzor is not more copied
from Achilles[3] than from Ancient Pistol.

'But I am,' says he, 'strangely mistaken if I have not seen this
very Almanzor of yours in some disguise about this town and
passing under another name. Pr'ythee tell me true, was not this
Huffcap once the Indian Emperor, and at another time did he
not call himself Maximin ? Was not Lyndaraxa once called
Almeria ? I mean under Montezuma the Indian Emperor. I
protest and vow they are either the same, or so alike that I cannot,
for my heart, distinguish one from the other. You are therefore
a strange unconscionable thief ; thou art not content to steal from
others, but dost rob thy poor wretched self too.'

53   Now was Settle's time to take his revenge. He wrote a vindication of his own lines ; and, if he is forced to yield any thing,
makes reprisals upon his enemy. To say that his answer is
equal to the censure is no high commendation. To expose
Dryden's method of analysing his expressions, he tries the same
experiment upon the description of the ships in *The Indian
Emperor*[4], of which however he does not deny the excellence ;

See also Langbaine's *Dram. Poets*,
p. 157.
    [1] Cowley's *Select Works*, 1777.
Preface, p. 3. Clifford was made
Master of the Charterhouse in 1671.
'Little is known of him.' Malone's
Dryden, i. 95. See *post*, DRYDEN, 94.
    [2] The author of the *Reliques*.
Clifford's *Four Letters* were not
published till 1687. Malone's *Dryden*,

i. 199.
    [3] 'The first image I had of Alman-
zor was from the Achilles of Homer.'
DRYDEN, *Works*, iv. 26.
    [4] 'At last, as far as I could cast my
        eyes
    Upon the sea, somewhat, me-
        thought, did rise,
    Like bluish mists, which, still
        appearing more,

but intends to shew that by studied misconstruction every thing
may be equally represented as ridiculous. After so much of
Dryden's elegant animadversions, justice requires that something
of Settle's should be exhibited. The following observations are
therefore extracted from a quarto pamphlet of ninety five pages[1]:

> ' " Fate after him below with pain did move,   54
> And victory could scarce keep pace above[2]."

These two lines, if he can show me any sense or thought in, or any
thing but bombast and noise, he shall make me believe every
word in his observations on *Morocco* sense[3].

' In *The Empress of Morocco* were these lines :   55

> " I'll travel then to some remoter sphere,
> Till I find out new worlds, and crown you there."

On which Dryden made this remark :

" I believe our learned author takes a sphere for a country :
the sphere of Morocco, as if Morocco were the globe of earth and
water ; but a globe is no sphere neither, by his leave," &c. So
sphere must not be sense, unless it relate to a circular motion
about a globe, in which sense the astronomers use it. I would
desire him to expound these lines in *Granada* :

> " I'll to the turrets of the palace go,
> And add new fire to those that fight below.
> Thence, hero-like [Hero-like], with torches by my side
> (Far be the omen tho'), my Love I'll [will] guide.
> No, like his better fortune I'll appear,   ⎞
> With open arms, loose vail and flowing hair,   ⎬
> Just flying forward from my rowling sphere[4]."   ⎠

I wonder, if he be so strict, how he dares make so bold with
sphere himself, and be so critical in other men's writings. Fortune is fancied standing on a globe, not on a *sphere*, as he told us
in the first Act[5].

Took dreadful shapes, and moved
  towards the shore.
   .   .   .   .   .   .
The object I could first distinctly
  view
Was tall straight trees, which on
  the waters flew ;
Wings on their sides instead of
  leaves did grow,
Which gathered all the breath the
  winds could blow ;   [palaces,
And at their roots grew floating
Whose outblowed bellies cut the
  yielding seas.'   *Works*, ii. 331.

[1] Entitled *Notes and Observations on the Empress of Morocco Revised*, &c., 1674.
[2] *Works*, iv. 50. The extravagance is paralleled by Johnson's couplet on Shakespeare :—
'Existence saw him spurn her bounded reign,
And panting time toiled after him in vain.' Johnson's *Works*, i. 23.
[3] *Notes*, &c., p. 53.
[4] *Works*, iv. 68.
[5] *Notes*, &c., p. 70.

56 ' Because " Elkanah's similes are the most unlike things to what they are compared in the world," I'll venture to start a simile in his *Annus Mirabilis*: he gives this poetical description of the ship called the *London* :

" The goodly *London* in her gallant trim,
    The Phenix-daughter of the vanquisht [vanished] old,
Like a rich bride does to the ocean swim,
    And on her shadow rides in floating gold.

" Her flag aloft spread ruffling in [to] the wind,
    And sanguine streamers seem'd [seem] the flood to fire :
The weaver, charm'd with what his loom design'd,
    Goes on to sea, and knows not to retire.

" With roomy decks, her guns of mighty strength,
    Whose low-laid mouths each mounting billow laves,
Deep in her draught, and warlike in her length,
    She seems a sea-wasp flying on the waves [1]."

What a wonderful pother is here, to make all these poetical beautifications of a ship ! that is, a *phenix* in the first stanza, and but a *wasp* in the last ; nay, to make his humble comparison of a *wasp* more ridiculous, he does not say it flies [flew] upon the waves as nimbly as a wasp, or the like, but it seemed a *wasp*. But our author at the writing of this was not in his altitudes, to compare ships to floating palaces [2] ; a comparison to the purpose was a perfection he did not arrive to till his *Indian Emperor's* days. But perhaps his similitude has more in it than we imagine ; this ship had a great many guns in her, and they, put all together, made the sting in the wasp's tail : for this is all the reason I can guess why it seemed a *wasp*. But, because we will allow him all we can to help out, let it be a *phenix sea-wasp*, and the rarity of such an animal may do much towards the heightening the fancy [3].

57 ' It had been much more to his purpose, if he had designed to render the senseless [Authour's] play little, to have searched for some such pedantry as this:

" Two ifs scarce make one possibility [4]."

" If justice will take all and nothing give,
    Justice, methinks, is not distributive [5]."

" To die or kill you, is the alternative,
    Rather than take your life, I will not live [6]."

Observe, how prettily our author chops logick in heroick

---

[1] Stanzas 151–3.
[2] *Ante*, DRYDEN, 53 *n*.
[3] *Notes*, &c., p. 74.
[4] *Works*, iv. 54.
[5] *Ib*. iv. 57.
[6] *Ib*. iv. 91.

verse. Three such fustian canting words as *distributive, alternative,*
and *two ifs,* no man but himself would have come within the
noise of. But he's a man of general learning, and all comes into
his play.

'Twould have done well too if he could have met with a rant 58
or two worth the observation; such as

> " Move swiftly, Sun, and fly a lover's pace,
>   Leave months and weeks behind thee in thy race[1]."

But surely the Sun, whether he flies a lover's or not a lover's
pace, leaves weeks and months, nay years too, behind him in his
race.

'Poor Robin, or any other of the Philomathematicks, would
have given him satisfaction in the point[2].

> " If I could [would] kill thee now, thy fate's so low,   59
>   That I must stoop ere I can give the blow.
>   But mine is fixt so far above thy crown,
>   That all thy men,
>   Piled on thy back, can never pull it down[3]."

'Now where that is, Almanzor's fate is fixt, I cannot guess;
but wherever it is, I believe Almanzor, and think that all Abdalla's
subjects, piled upon one another, might not pull down his fate so
well as without piling: besides, I think Abdalla so wise a man,
that if Almanzor had told him piling his men upon his back
might do the feat, he would scarce bear such a weight for the
pleasure of the exploit; but it is a huff, and let Abdalla do it if
he dare[4].

> " The people like a headlong torrent go,   60
>   And every dam they break or overflow.
>   But, unoppos'd, they either lose their force,
>   Or wind in volumes to their former course[5]."

A very pretty allusion, contrary to all sense or reason. Torrents,
I take it, let them wind never so much, can never return to their
former course, unless he can suppose that fountains can go upwards, which is impossible; nay more, in the foregoing page he
tells us so too. A trick of a very unfaithful memory,

> " But can no more than fountains upward flow[6]."

---

[1] *Works,* iv. 222; *post,* DRYDEN,
330. 'I have really hope from spring;
and am ready, like Almanzor, to bid
the sun *fly swiftly,* and *leave weeks
and months behind him.* The sun has
looked for six thousand years upon
the world to little purpose, if he does
not know that a sick man is almost
as impatient as a lover.' *Letters of*
Johnson, ii. 373.

[2] *Poor Robin's Almanack* began
in 1664 and ended in 1776. It was continued as *Old Poor Robin's Almanack*
till 1828. *Brit. Mus. Cata.*

[3] *Works,* iv. 77.

[4] *Notes,* &c., p. 77.

[5] *Works,* iv. 78.

[6] *Ib.*

Which of a *torrent*, which signifies a rapid stream, is much more impossible. Besides, if he goes to quibble, and say that it is possible by art water may be made return and the same water run twice in one and the same channel, then he quite confutes what he says; for it is by being opposed that it runs into its former course : for all engines that make water so return, do it by compulsion and opposition. Or, if he means a headlong torrent for a tide, which would be ridiculous, yet they do not wind in volumes, but come fore-right back (if their upright lies straight to their former course), and that by opposition of the sea-water, that drives them back again [1].

61   'And for fancy, when he lights of any thing like it, 'tis a wonder if it be not borrowed. As here, for example of, I find this fanciful thought in his *Ann. Mirab.*[2]

> " Old father Thames raised up his reverend head,
>   But feared the fate of Simoeis would return ;
> Deep in his ooze he sought his sedgy bed,
>   And shrunk his waters back into his urn."

This is stolen from Cowley's *Davideis*, p. 9.

> "Swift Jordan started, and strait backward fled,
> Hiding amongst [among] thick reeds his aged head [3]."

> "And when the Spaniards their assault begin,
> At once beat those without and these within [4]."

This Almanzor speaks of himself; and sure for one man to conquer an army within the city and another without the city at once, is something difficult; but this flight is pardonable to some we meet with in *Granada*. Osmin [Ozmyn], speaking of Almanzor :

> "Who, like a tempest that outrides the wind,
> Made a just battle, ere the bodies join'd [5]."

Pray what does this honourable person mean by a "*tempest that outrides the wind*"! A tempest that outrides itself. To suppose a tempest without wind, is as bad as supposing a man to walk without feet; for if he supposes the tempest to be something distinct from the wind, yet as being the effect of wind only, to come before the cause is a little preposterous; so that, if he takes it one way, or if he takes it the other, those two *ifs* will scarce make one *possibility*[6].' Enough of Settle.

62   *Marriage Alamode*[7] is a comedy dedicated to the Earl of Rochester, whom he acknowledges not only as the defender of

[1] *Notes, &c.,* p. 80.
[2] Stanza 232.
[3] *Notes,* &c., p. 82. Cowley's *Davideis,* 1674, p. 9; *Eng. Poets,* viii. 187.
[4] *Works,* iv. 60.
[5] *Ib.* iv. 50.
[6] *Notes,* &c., p. 82.
[7] *Works,* iv. 247.

his poetry, but the promoter of his fortune [1]. Langbaine places this play in 1673 [2]. The earl of Rochester therefore was the famous Wilmot [3], whom yet tradition always represents as an enemy to Dryden, and who is mentioned by him with some disrespect in the preface to *Juvenal* [4].

The Assignation, or Love in a Nunnery, a comedy, was driven 63 off the stage, 'against the opinion,' as the author says, 'of the best judges [5].' It is dedicated in a very elegant address to Sir Charles Sedley [6]; in which he finds an opportunity for his usual complaint of hard treatment and unreasonable censure [7].

Amboyna [8] is a tissue of mingled dialogue in verse and prose, 64 and was perhaps written in less time than *The Virgin Martyr* [9];

[1] 'There is,' he wrote, 'no such persecution as that of fools. . . . They make it their business to chase wit from the knowledge of princes, lest it should disgrace their ignorance. . . . If our general good fortune had not raised up your Lordship to defend us, I know not whether anything had been more ridiculous in Court than writers. . . . What I never can forget, you have not only been careful'of my reputation, but of my fortune.' *Works*, iv. 254-6.

[2] *Dram. Poets*, p. 166. 'It appears to have been acted in May, 1672; it was printed in 1673.' Malone's *Dryden*, i. 106.

[3] John Wilmot, Earl of Rochester (*ante*, ROCHESTER, 13), died in 1680. Laurence Hyde received the same title in Nov. 1682.

[4] In this Preface, written in 1693, Dryden says of the lines on Dorset (*ante*, DORSET, 13 *n.*) that Rochester 'has given all the commendation which his self-sufficiency could afford to any man. In that character, methinks, I am reading Jonson's verses to the memory of Shakespeare; an insolent, sparing and invidious panegyric.' *Works*, xiii. 5. (For these verses see Johnson's *Shakespeare*, Preface, p. 153.) In 1673 Dryden had gone so far in flattery as to write to Rochester: 'The best comic writers of our age have copied . . . the decencies of behaviour from your Lordship.' An unconscious prophet he added:—'From the patron of wit you may become its tyrant.' *Works*,

iv. 253, 257. Rochester turned on him as he turned on Otway. *Ante*, OTWAY, 8 *n.*; *post*, DRYDEN, 93, 101, 105; Malone's *Dryden*, i. 121.

[5] *Works*, iv. 365. It was acted in 1672-3, and printed in 1673. Malone's *Dryden*, i. 107. 'It succeeded ill in the representation, against the opinion of many the best judges of our age, to whom you know I read it ere it was presented publicly.' *Works*, iv. 370.

[6] *Ib.* iv. 369; *ante*, DORSET, 3.

[7] *Post*, DRYDEN, 102, 173.

[8] *Amboyna: or the Cruelties of the Dutch to the English Merchants.* First acted and printed in 1673. *Works*, v. 1; Malone's *Dryden*, i. 108.

In 1652 the English Commonwealth demanded £700,000 from the Dutch, as compensation for the loss 'of the fruits in the Molucca Islands, Banda and Amboyna, from the time (1622-3) that by the slaughter of our men we were thence expelled.' Milton's *Works*, iv. 369; Masson's *Milton*, iv. 374. For the torture and massacre of English merchants by the Dutch see Gardiner's *Hist. of Eng.* 1883, v. 241.

Horace Walpole describes the Dutch as 'a people too apt even in their depressed state to hazard barbarous and brutal infraction of treaties and humanity, when a glimpse of commercial interest invites it.' *Anec. of Painting*, ii. 98.

[9] *Royal Martyr*. *Ante*, DRYDEN, 45.

though the author thought not fit either ostentatiously or mournfully to tell how little labour it cost him, or at how short a warning he produced it [1]. It was a temporary performance, written in the time of the Dutch war, to inflame the nation against their enemies [2]; to whom he hopes, as he declares in his Epilogue, to make his poetry not less destructive than that by which Tyrtæus of old animated the Spartans [3]. This play was written in the second Dutch war in 1673 [4].

65   *Troilus and Cressida* is a play altered from Shakespeare [5], but so altered that even in Langbaine's opinion, 'the last scene in the third act is a masterpiece [6].' It is introduced by a discourse on *the grounds of criticism in tragedy*, to which I suspect that Rymer's book [7] had given occasion.

66   *The Spanish Fryar* [8] is a tragi-comedy, eminent for the happy coincidence and coalition of the two plots [9]. As it was written

[1] In the Dedication he says that 'it was contrived and written in a month.' *Works*, v. 8. *Ante*, DRYDEN, 46.

[2] 'But hope not either language, plot, or art;
'Twas writ in haste, but with an English heart.'
Prologue, Works, v. 11.

[3] *Ib.* v. 92. Chesterfield, speaking in 1737 on the Stage Licensing Bill, said (*Misc. Works*, ii. 334):—'When the Court had a mind to fall out with the Dutch, Dryden wrote his *Amboyna*, in which he represents the Dutch as a pack of avaricious, cruel ungrateful rascals; and when the Exclusion Bill was moved in Parliament, he wrote his *Duke of Guise* [*post*, DRYDEN, 68], in which those who were for preserving the religion of their country were exposed under the character of the Duke of Guise and his party, who leagued together for excluding Henry IV of France from the throne, on account of his religion.'

[4] Johnson, who had hitherto followed the year in dealing with the plays, now skips five years. He (returns), *post*, DRYDEN, 71, to those omitted, and goes through them regularly, except that he places *Limberham* (1680) before *Oedipus* (1679). See *ante*, DRYDEN, 12, and the Preface to the *Lives*, where he says:—'I am not without suspicion that some of

Dryden's works are placed in wrong years. I have followed Langbaine as the best authority for his plays.'

[5] *Works*, vi. 241. Probably first acted in the winter of 1678-9; printed in 1679. Malone's *Dryden*, i. 118.

[6] *Dram. Poets*, p. 173. Act iii has but two scenes. In the first part of the second scene Dryden adds to Pandarus's grossness. It is of the second part that Langbaine speaks; of this Dryden says:—'The occasion of raising it was hinted to me by Mr. Betterton.' *Works*, vi. 257.

[7] *Post*, DRYDEN, 200.

[8] *Works*, vi. 393. According to Malone (i. 119) 'it was probably first acted in Feb. 1681-2.' The title-page is dated 1681. A book printed in 1681-2 would have been dated 1682. A play was never printed before it was acted.

[9] Addison speaks of 'the beauty which the critics admire in it, where the two different plots look like counterparts and copies of one another.' *The Spectator*, No. 267. Hallam, after showing that in *The Merchant of Venice* there are two underplots, 'the courtship of Bassanio and Portia, which is happily connected with the main plot, and that of Lorenzo and Jessica, which is quite episodical,' continues:—'In *The Spanish Friar* there is not, even by accident, any relation between the

against the Papists [1] it would naturally at that time have friends and enemies ; and partly by the popularity which it obtained at first, and partly by the real power both of the serious and risible part, it continued long a favourite of the publick [2].

It was Dryden's opinion, at least for some time, and he main- 67 tains it in the dedication of this play, that the drama required an alternation of comick and tragick scenes, and that it is necessary to mitigate by alleviations of merriment the pressure of ponderous events and the fatigue of toilsome passions. ' Whoever,' says he, ' cannot perform both parts, *is but half a writer for the stage* [3].'

The Duke of Guise [4], a tragedy written in conjunction with 68 Lee [5], as *Oedipus* had been before, seems to deserve notice only for the offence which it gave to the remnant of the Covenanters,

adventures of Lorenzo in his intrigue, and the love and murder which goes forward in the palace.' *Edinburgh Review*, vol. 13, p. 126.

[1] In his Dedication Dryden describes himself as 'recommending a Protestant play to a Protestant patron.' *Works*, vi. 410. In his *Parallel of Poetry and Painting* (*ib.* xvii. 327 ; *post*, DRYDEN, 146) he writes :— ' Neither can I defend my *Spanish Fryar*, as fond as otherwise I am of it, from this imputation [of being ' Gothic ']．' In confessing his fondness he sank the convert in the author. He was now a Papist.

The play was forbidden by James II. When in June, 1689, it was revived by Queen Mary's command, ' some unhappy expressions forced her to hold up her fan.' One of them was Pedro's speech in Act i. sc. 1, where he says of the Queen of Arragon :—' She usurps the throne, keeps the old King in prison, and at the same time is praying for a blessing. O religion and roguery, how they go together ! ' *A Letter by the Earl of Nottingham*, quoted in Malone's *Dryden*, i. 214.

[2] ' It produced vast profit to the Company.' *Roscius Ang.* p. 47. Gibbon saw it acted in 1762. *Misc. Works*, i. 154.

[3] ' The feast is too dull and solemn without the fiddles. . . . A several genius is required to either way ; and, without both of them, a man, in my opinion, is but half a poet for the stage.' *Works*, vi. 410.

In 1707 the comic scenes of *Marriage Alamode* (*ante*, DRYDEN, 62) and of *The Maiden Queen* (*ante*, 28) were put together as one play, as being ' utterly independent of the serious scenes,' and were so acted for several years. Cibber's *Apology*, p. 192.

[4] First acted towards the end of 1682 ; printed in 1683. *Works*, vii. 1 ; Malone's *Dryden*, i. 120. See *ante*, DRYDEN, 12 *n*.

[5] *Post*, DRYDEN, 81. In 1695 Dryden described Lee as a poet ' who had a great genius for tragedy,' but ' following the fury of his natural temper made every man, and woman too, in his plays stark raging mad ; there was not a sober person to be had for love or money.' *Works*, xvii. 320. See also *ib.* xviii. 118.

For Addison's admiration of a line in his *Rival Queens* see *The Spectator*, No. 39, and *John. Letters*, i. 207. This play was acted as late as 1820. Macready's *Reminiscences*, i. 193. For his ' pathetic reading' see Cibber's *Apology*, p. 71, and for some ' harmonious lines of his' see *Joseph Andrews*, bk. iii. ch. 10. In *Tom Jones*, bk. vi. ch. 12, Fielding calls him ' the gigantic poet.' For his death see Warton's *Essay on Pope*, ii. 109.

Gray speaks of his ' Bedlam tragedy, which had twenty-five acts and some odd scenes.' *Letters*, i. 96.

and in general to the enemies of the court, who attacked him with great violence, and were answered by him [1]; though at last he seems to withdraw from the conflict, by transferring the greater part of the blame or merit to his partner [2]. It happened that a contract had been made between them, by which they were to join in writing a play ; and 'he happened,' says Dryden, 'to claim the [performance of that] promise just upon the finishing of a poem, when I would have been glad of a little respite.—Two thirds of it belonged to him ; and to me only the first scene of the play; the whole fourth act, and the first half or somewhat more of the fifth.'

69　　This was a play written professedly for the party of the duke of York, whose succession was then opposed [3]. A parallel is intended between the Leaguers of France and the Covenanters of England [4]; and this intention produced the controversy [5].

70　　*Albion and Albania* [*sic*] is a musical drama or opera, written, like *The Duke of Guise*, against the Republicans. With what success it was performed I have not found [6].

71　　*The State of Innocence and Fall of Man* [7] is termed by him an

[1] In *The Vindication of the Duke of Guise* (1683), *Works*, vii. 146.

[2] *Ib.* pp. 149, 167.

[3] The Exclusion Bill passed the Commons in Oct. 1680, but was thrown out by the Lords. Macaulay's *History*, i. 269.

[4] *Post*, DRYDEN, 122. Dryden, in 1660 in *Astraea Redux*, l. 101, described Henry of Navarre as

'Shocked by a covenanting League's vast powers,
As holy and as Catholic as ours.'

[5] The play, writes Dryden, 'was persecuted with so notorious malice by one side that it procured us the partiality of the other. . . . They [the faction] could boast that the theatres were true Protestant. . . . But let them now assure themselves that they can make the major part of no assembly, except it be a meeting house.' *Works*, vii. 13.

[6] *Albion and Albanius, ib.* vii. 221. Printed in 1685. Malone's *Dryden*, i. 219.

'Being acted on a very unlucky day, being the day the Duke of Monmouth landed in the West, the nation being in great consternation, it was

performed but six times.' *Roscius Anglicanus*, p. 55.

It was first acted on June 6, 1685. Monmouth landed on June 11 ; the news reached London on June 13. Malone's *Dryden*, i. 187. Dryden, in the Dedication of *King Arthur* (*post*, DRYDEN, 85), says that 'the Prologue to it, which was the opera of *Albion and Albanius*, was often practised before Charles II at Whitehall, though he lived not to see the performance of it on the stage.' *Works*, viii. 129. See also *ib.* vii. 240.

[7] *Ib.* v. 93. Published towards the end of 1674. [Johnson here returns to the plays he had skipped between 1674 and 1679; see *ante*, DRYDEN, 64 *n*.] Milton, who died on Nov. 8 of that year, is spoken of as 'the deceased author.' *Ib.* v. 111 ; Malone's *Dryden*, i. 109. According to Aubrey, Dryden 'went to him to have leave to putt his *Paradise Lost* into a drama in rhymne. Mr. Milton recieved him civilly, and told him he would give him leave to tagge his verses.' *Brief Lives*, ii. 72. 'He alluded to the fashion then of wearing tags of metal

opera ; it is rather a tragedy in heroick rhyme, but of which the personages are such as cannot decently be exhibited on the stage [1]. Some such production was foreseen by Marvel, who writes thus to Milton :

> 'Or if a work so infinite be [he] spann'd,
> Jealous I was lest [that] some less skilful hand,
> Such as disquiet always what is well,
> And by ill-imitating would excel,
> Might hence presume the whole creation's day
> To change in scenes, and shew it in a play [2].'

It is another of his hasty productions ; for the heat of his imagination raised it in a month [3].

This composition is addressed to the princess of Modena, then **72** dutchess of York, in a strain of flattery which disgraces genius, and which it was wonderful that any man that knew the meaning of his own words could use without self-detestation. It is an attempt to mingle earth and heaven, by praising human excellence in the language of religion [4].

The preface contains an apology for heroick verse and poetick **73** licence ; by which is meant not any liberty taken in contracting

---

at the end of their ribbons.' Newton's *Milton*, Preface, p. 57.

Marvell, in the poem quoted in the text, addressing Milton says :—
' Well might'st thou scorn thy readers to allure
With tinkling rhyme, of thy own sense secure ;
While the Town-Bayes writes all the while and spells,
And like a pack-horse tires without his bells.
Their fancies like our bushy-points appear ;
The poets tag them, we for fashion wear.'
Johnson, in his Dictionary, under *To Tag* quotes from Dryden 'tagged with rhyme.'
In Gay's *Three Hours after Marriage* (1717, p. 25) a poetess complains that Dr. Fossile has thrown into the flames ' the tag of a new comedy.'
[1] Satan and Raphael are among the personages. It was never acted. *Works*, v. 111. Dryden has a hit at the Dutch, when he makes Lucifer,

after Beelzebub had excluded 'the ignoble crowd of vulgar devils,' address the ' dark divan ' as
' Most high and mighty lords, who better fell
From heaven to rise States-General of hell.' *Ib.* p. 129.
[2] *On Milton's Paradise Lost,* Marvell's *Poems*, ed. 1870, p. 75.
Dennis, writing of Dryden's praise of Milton in the preface to *The State of Innocence*, adds :—' Yet Mr. Dryden at that time knew not half the extent of Milton's excellence, as more than twenty years afterwards he confessed to me.' Dennis's *Original Letters*, ed. 1721, p. 75.
Lee, addressing Dryden, says of Milton :—
' He was the golden ore which you refined.'
Dryden's *Works*, v. 109.
[3] *Ib.* v. 111 ; *ante*, DRYDEN, 46.
[4] ' Your person,' he wrote to the Duchess, ' is so admirable that it can scarce receive addition when it shall be glorified.' *Works*, v. 107. For his flattery see *post*, DRYDEN, 88, 170.

or extending words, but the use of bold fictions and ambitious figures [1].

74 The reason which he gives for printing what was never acted cannot be overpassed : ' I was induced to it in my own defence, many hundred copies of it being dispersed abroad without my knowledge or consent, and every one gathering new faults, it became at length a libel against me [2].' These copies as they gathered faults were apparently manuscript ; and he lived in an age very unlike ours if many hundred copies of fourteen hundred lines were likely to be transcribed. An author has a right to print his own works, and needs not seek an apology in falsehood ; but he that could bear to write the dedication felt no pain in writing the preface.

75 *Aureng Zebe* [3] is a tragedy founded on the actions of a great prince then reigning, but over nations not likely to employ their criticks upon the transactions of the English stage. If he had known and disliked his own character, our trade was not in those times secure from his resentment [4]. His country is at such a distance that the manners might be safely falsified and the incidents feigned ; for remoteness of place is remarked by Racine to afford the same conveniencies to a poet as length of time [5].

76 This play is written in rhyme ; and has the appearance of being the most elaborate of all the dramas [6]. The personages are imperial [7]; but the dialogue is often domestick, and therefore

---

[1] ' Poetic licence I take to be the liberty which poets have assumed to themselves in all ages of speaking things in verse which are beyond the severity of prose.' *Works*, v. 122.

[2] *Ib.* v. 111.

[3] *Works*, v. 179; *post*, DRYDEN, 264. It was acted as early as the spring of 1675, and printed the following winter. Malone's *Dryden*, i. 115.

[4] He is drawn by Dryden as a faultless hero.

[5] ' On peut dire que le respect que l'on a pour les héros s'augmente à mesure qu'ils s'éloignent de nous. *Major e longinquo reverentia.* L'éloignement des païs répare en quelque sorte la trop grande proximité des temps.' RACINE, Preface to *Bajazet.*

[6] ' Our author,' says Dryden in the Prologue,
' to confess a truth, though out of time, [tress, Rhyme.
Grows weary of his long-loved mis-
. . . . .
What verse can do, he has performed in this, [of his.'
Which he presumes the most correct *Works*, v. 201. See *ante*, DRYDEN, 20.

[7] ' The impropriety of thoughts in the speeches of the Great Mogul and his Empress has been generally censured. Take the sentiments out of the shining dress of words, and they would be too coarse for a scene in Billingsgate.' ADDISON, *The Guardian*, No. 110. See *The Rambler*, No. 125, for a scene in this play in which ' every circumstance concurs to turn tragedy to farce.'

susceptible of sentiments accommodated to familiar incidents. The complaint of life is celebrated[1], and there are many other passages that may be read with pleasure.

This play is addressed to the earl of Mulgrave, afterwards duke 77 of Buckingham, himself, if not a poet, yet a writer of verses, and a critick. In this address Dryden gave the first hints of his intention to write an epick poem. He mentions his design in terms so obscure that he seems afraid lest his plan should be purloined, as, he says, happened to him when he told it more plainly in his preface to Juvenal[2]. 'The design,' says he, 'you know is great, the story English, and neither too near the present times, nor too distant from them[3].'

All for Love, or the World well lost[4], a tragedy founded upon 78 the story of Antony and Cleopatra, he tells us, 'is the only play which he wrote for himself'; the rest were 'given to the people[5].' It is by universal consent accounted the work in which he has admitted the fewest improprieties of style or character; but it has one fault equal to many, though rather moral than critical, that by admitting the romantick omnipotence of Love[6], he has recommended as laudable and worthy of imitation that conduct which through all ages the good have censured as vicious, and the bad despised as foolish[7].

---

[1] *Works*, v. 258. It is quoted in Boswell's *Johnson*, iv. 303. See also *ib*. ii. 125. Macaulay, after quoting from *Clarinda's Journal* in *The Spectator*, No. 323, how 'Kitty repeated the eight best lines in *Aurengzebe*,' continues:—'There are not eight finer lines in Lucretius.' *Hist. of Eng.* vi. 135 *n*.

[2] *Post*, DRYDEN, 140, 145.

[3] 'The subject of which you know is great, the story English, and neither too far distant from the present age, nor too near approaching it.' *Works*, v. 196.

[4] *Ib*. v. 303. It was probably first acted in the early winter of 1677-8, as it was registered at Stationers' Hall on Jan. 31, 1677-8. It was printed in 1678. Malone's *Dryden*, i. 116.

[5] Dryden says of *The Spanish Friar*:—'The faults of that drama are in the kind of it, which is tragicomedy. But it was given to the people; and I never writ anything for myself but *Antony and Cleopatra*.' *Works*, xvii. 333.

[6] 'Johnson laughed at the notion that a man never can be really in love but once, and considered it as a mere romantick fancy.' Boswell's *Johnson*, ii. 460.

[7] Antony says in his dying speech to Cleopatra:
'But grieve not, while thou stayest,
   My last disastrous times:
Think we have had a clear and
   glorious day,   [storm
And Heaven did kindly to delay the
Just till our close of evening. Ten
   years' love,
And not a moment lost, but all
   improved
To the utmost joys,—what ages
   have we lived!
And now to die each other's; and,
   so dying,
While hand in hand we walk in
   groves below,

79 Of this play the prologue and the epilogue, though written upon the common topicks of malicious and ignorant criticism, and without any particular relation to the characters or incidents of the drama, are deservedly celebrated for their elegance and spriteliness.

80 *Limberham, or the kind Keeper* [1], is a comedy, which after the third night was prohibited as too indecent for the stage. What gave offence was in the printing, as the author says, altered or omitted. Dryden confesses that its indecency was objected to; but Langbaine, who yet seldom favours him, imputes its expulsion to resentment, because it 'so much exposed the keeping part of the town [2].'

81 *Oedipus* [3] is a tragedy formed by Dryden and Lee in conjunction from the works of Sophocles, Seneca, and Corneille [4]. Dryden planned the scenes, and composed the first and third acts [5].

82 *Don Sebastian* is commonly esteemed either the first or second of his dramatick performances [6]. It is too long to be all acted [7],

Whole troops of lovers' ghosts shall flock about us,
And all the train be ours.'
　　　　　Works, v. 432.

[1] Printed in 1678. Malone's *Dryden*, i. 116. On the title-page the date is 1680.

[2] *Dram. Poets*, p. 164. Dryden writes in the Dedication:—'It was intended for an honest satire against our crying sin of *keeping*; how it would have succeeded I can but guess, for it was permitted to be acted only thrice.' *Works*, vi. 9.

Malone had seen a MS. copy of the play, 'found by Bolingbroke among the sweepings of Pope's study, in which a pen had been drawn through several exceptionable passages that do not appear in the printed play.' Malone's *Dryden*, i. 118. See also Prior's *Malone*, p. 255.

Johnson in his Dictionary gives neither *keep* nor *keeper* in the sense in which they are used here.

[3] *Works*, vi. 121. Printed in 1679. Malone's *Dryden*, i. 118.

[4] *Works*, vi. 131. For Lee see *ante*, DRYDEN, 68.

[5] 'I writ the first and third acts, and drew the scenery of the whole play.' *Works*, vii. 203. Johnson defines *scenery*, as here used, as 'the

disposition and consecution of the scenes of a play.'

'It took prodigiously, being acted ten nights together.' *Roscius Anglicanus*, p. 47. The Company of the King's Playhouse, in the document quoted *post*, DRYDEN, 91 *n*., complain that Dryden, with Lee, 'has given *Oedipus* to the Duke's Company, contrary to his agreement, to the almost undoing of the Company, this being the only Poet remaining to us.'

Addison, in *The Spectator*, No. 40, referring to *Oedipus*, 'shows how a *rant* pleases beyond the most just and natural thought that is not pronounced with vehemence.'

See *John. Misc.* ii. 62 for Cradock's revision of this play; also *post*, AKENSIDE, 24 *n*.

[6] *Works*, vii. 285. It was first acted and printed in 1690. Malone's *Dryden*, i. 211, 218. 'It was, as I have heard, acted with great applause.' LANGBAINE, *Dram. Poets*, p. 161. Pope reckoned it, *All for Love*, and *The Spanish Friar* as the best of Dryden's plays. Spence's *Anec.* p. 171.

[7] Dryden says in the Preface:—'The first day's audience convinced me that the poem was insupportably too long. . . . Above 1,200 lines have been cut off from it since it was first

and has many characters and many incidents; and though it is not without sallies of frantick dignity, and more noise than meaning, yet as it makes approaches to the possibilities of real life, and has some sentiments which leave a strong impression [1], it continued long to attract attention. Amidst the distresses of princes and the vicissitudes of empire are inserted several scenes which the writer intended for comick; but which, I suppose, that age did not much commend, and this would not endure. There are, however, passages of excellence universally acknowledged; the dispute and the reconciliation of Dorax and Sebastian has always been admired [2].

This play was first acted in 1690, after Dryden had for some years discontinued dramatick poetry [3].

Amphitryon is a comedy derived from Plautus and Molière [4]. 83 The dedication is dated Oct. 1690. This play seems to have succeeded at its first appearance; and was, I think, long considered as a very diverting entertainment.

Cleomenes [5] is a tragedy, only remarkable as it occasioned an 84 incident related in *The Guardian*, and allusively mentioned by

---

delivered to the actors.' When printed the lines were restored. *Works*, vii. 306-8.

[1] Addison, criticizing this play, continues:—'Dryden, indeed, is generally wrong in his sentiments.' *The Guardian*, No. 110.

[2] Dorax or Alonzo was a Portuguese renegade. The beginning of this passage is somewhat comical:—
'SEBASTIAN (*solus*). Reserved behaviour, open nobleness,
A long mysterious track of a stern bounty;
But now the hand of fate is on the curtain,
And draws the scene to sight.
Re-enter Dorax, having taken off his turban, and put on a peruke, hat, and cravat.
DORAX. Now do you know me?
SEBASTIAN. Thou should'st be Alonzo.' *Works*, vii. 433.
See *The Rambler*, No. 125, for Dryden's 'improprieties' in this play and *Aurengzebe*.

[3] *Post*, DRYDEN, 139.

[4] *Works*, viii. 1. First acted in 1690. Malone's *Dryden*, i. 212, 219. Cibber describes 'the cold, flat, and unaffect-

ing manner' in which Dryden 'gave his first reading of this play to the actors.' *Apology*, p. 71.

[5] *Works*, viii. 203. First acted in May, 1692, and printed in that year. Southerne (*post*, DRYDEN, 90) wrote the same year that 'Mr. Dryden, falling sick last summer, bequeathed to my care the last act.' Malone's *Dryden*, i. 212, 219. Malone publishes the following receipt:—
'Oct. ye 6th, 1691.
Receiv'd the sum of Thirty Guinneys, for which I resign to Mr. Tonson all my right in the printing ye copy of *Cleomenes*, a tragedy.
Witnesse my hand,
John Dryden.
Witnesse
John Dryden, Jun.' *Ib.* i. 455.
Tonson told Atterbury that '*Cleomenes* had the fortune to please the town.' 'Therefore I read it over,' wrote Atterbury, 'and found what I expected in it—much prophaneness.' *Atterbury Corres.* ii. 16. Macready (*Reminiscences*, i. 354) describes it as 'a play that has all the marks of a decaying intellect upon it.'

Dryden in his preface [1]. As he came out from the representation, he was accosted thus by some airy stripling : 'Had I been left alone with a young beauty, I would not have spent my time like your Spartan.' 'That, Sir,' said Dryden, 'perhaps is true; but give me leave to tell you, that you are no hero.'

85 *King Arthur* is another opera. It was the last work that Dryden performed for King Charles [2], who did not live to see it exhibited; and it does not seem to have been ever brought upon the stage [3]. In the dedication to the marquis of Halifax there is a very elegant character of Charles, and a pleasing account of his latter life [4]. When this was first brought upon the stage, news that the duke of Monmouth had landed was told in the theatre,

[1] He mentions that 'foolish objection which is raised against me by the sparks, for Cleomenes not accepting the favours of Cassandra. They would not have refused a fair lady! I grant they would not ; but let them grant me that they are not heroes ; and so much for the point of honour.' *Works*, viii. 221. For the scene see *ib.* p. 324. 'In *The Guardian*, No. 45, by Steele, this remark assumes a more lively air by being converted into an *extempore* saying. . . . "I can only answer, as I remember Mr. Dryden did," &c. . . . The tale most probably was formed on the passage in the Preface.' Malone's *Dryden*, ii. 229.

[2] 'This poem was the last piece of service which I had the honour to do for my gracious master, King Charles II.' *Works*, viii. 129. For Dryden's complaint of the king's neglect see *post*, DRYDEN, 144 *n*.

[3] This is a mistake. It was first acted and printed in 1691. Malone's *Dryden*, i. 212, 219 ; *Works*, viii. 123. According to *Roscius Anglicanus*, p. 57, 'it was very gainful to the Company.' Cibber says that, 'though the success in appearance was very great,' the expenses were still greater. *Apology*, p. 110. Collier describes it as 'a strange jumble and hotch potch of matters . . . the Hell of Heathenism and the Hell of Revelation ; a fit of smut, and then a jest about original sin.' *A Short View of the English Stage*, 3rd ed. 1698, p. 188.

'Dec. 25, 1770. I went to *King Arthur*, and was tired to death, both of the nonsense of the piece and the execrable performance.' HORACE WALPOLE, *Letters*, v. 272.

'It was set to music by Purcell, and is yet [1787] a favourite entertainment.' HAWKINS, Johnson's *Works*, 1787, ii. 339. It was revived in 1842-3. Macready's *Reminiscences*, ii. 208.

E. FitzGerald wrote in 1851 :— 'I am just now looking with great delight into Purcell's *King Arthur*, real noble *English* music, much of it ; and assuredly the prototype of much of Handel.' *Letters*, i. 270.

[4] 'Let his human frailties be forgotten, and his clemency and moderation (the inherent virtues of his family) be remembered with a grateful veneration. . . . He was master of too much good sense to delight in heavy conversation, and whatever his favourites of state might be, yet those of his affection were men of wit. He was easy with these, and complied only with the former. But in the latter part of his life, which certainly required to be most cautiously managed, his secret thoughts were communicated but to few ; and those selected of that sort who were *Amici omnium horarum*, able to advise him in a serious consult, and afterwards capable of entertaining him with pleasant discourse as well as profitable.' *Works*, viii. 131-3. See also Boswell's *Johnson*, i. 442 ; ii. 341.

upon which the company departed, and *Arthur* was exhibited no more [1].

His last drama was *Love triumphant*, a tragi-comedy [2]. In his dedication to the Earl of Salisbury he mentions 'the lowness of fortune to which he has voluntarily reduced himself, and of which he has no reason to be ashamed [3].' **86**

This play appeared in 1694. It is said to have been unsuccessful [4]. The catastrophe, proceeding merely from a change of mind, is confessed by the author to be defective [5]. Thus he began and ended his dramatick labours with ill success [6].

From such a number of theatrical pieces it will be supposed by most readers that he must have improved his fortune; at least, that such diligence with such abilities must have set penury at defiance. But in Dryden's time the drama was very far from that universal approbation which it has now obtained. The playhouse was abhorred by the Puritans, and avoided by those who desired the character of seriousness or decency. A grave lawyer would have debased his dignity, and a young trader would have impaired his credit, by appearing in those mansions of dissolute licentiousness [7]. The profits of the theatre when so many classes of the people were deducted from the audience were not great, and the poet had for a long time but a single night. The first that had two nights was Southern [8], and the **87**

---

[1] This sentence was added to the second edition in forgetfulness of the statement that this opera was never brought upon the stage. The piece interrupted by Monmouth's landing was *Albion and Albanius, ante,* DRYDEN, 70.

[2] *Works*, viii. 365. First acted about Dec. 1693, and printed in 1694. Malone's *Dryden*, i. 214, 219. As a second title Dryden had thought of *Neither Side to Blame. Works*, xviii. 189.

[3] *Ib.* viii. 373. See *post*, DRYDEN, 136, for his loss of the laureateship.

[4] Malone (i. 217) quotes from a *Letter from a Gentleman in London to a Friend in the Country*, March 22, 1693-4 :—'It was damned by the universal cry of the town, *nemine contradicente*, but the conceited poet.'

[5] 'Aristotle, I acknowledge, has declared that the catastrophe which is made from the change of will is not of the first order of beauty.' *Works*, viii. 374.

[6] *Ante*, DRYDEN, 14.

[7] 'The play-houses in so dissolute a time were become nests of prostitution, and the stage was defiled beyond all example; Dryden, the great master of dramatic poesy, being a monster of immodesty and of impurity of all sorts.' BURNET, *History*, i. 300. See *post*, DRYDEN, 124, 175; CONGREVE, 18.

[8] 'In the dedication of *Sir Antony Love* in 1691 Southern speaks of his being interested in the third and sixth representation.' Malone's *Dryden*, i. 454. For Southerne see *post*, DRYDEN, 90; FENTON, 11.

In the document signed by the players (*post*, DRYDEN, 91 *n*.) it is stated that 'the Company did also at Mr. Dryden's earnest request give him a third day for his last new play called

first that had three was Rowe. There were, however, in those days arts of improving a poet's profit, which Dryden forbore to practise[1]; and a play therefore seldom produced him more than a hundred pounds, by the accumulated gain of the third night[2] the dedication, and the copy.

88 Almost every piece had a dedication, written with such elegance and luxuriance of praise as neither haughtiness nor avarice could be imagined able to resist. But he seems to have made flattery too cheap. That praise is worth nothing of which the price is known[3].

89 To increase the value of his copies he often accompanied his work with a preface of criticism, a kind of learning then almost new in the English language, and which he, who had considered with great accuracy the principles of writing, was able to distribute copiously as occasions arose. By these dissertations the publick judgement must have been much improved; and Swift, who conversed with Dryden, relates that he regretted the success of his own instructions, and found his readers made suddenly too skilful to be easily satisfied[4].

All for Love.' Rowe was only five years old at that time.

Cibber, in 1704, had his third and sixth day for *The Careless Husband*. See the Dedication. In the last act of *Love's Last Shift* he speaks of 'the duns a poet has in the morning upon the fourth day of his new play.'

Gay had four nights for *The Beggar's Opera. N. & Q.* 1 S. i. 178.

Aaron Hill (*Works*, 1754, ii. 370) wrote, in 1749, of his *Merope* :—'The balance of my three nights' benefits came but to £148.'

[1] In Cibber's *Lives*, v. 328, it is stated that, while Dryden had never made more than £100 by a play, Southerne, by one of his, cleared £700. 'Southern was not beneath the drudgery of solicitation, and often sold his tickets at a very high price by applying to persons of distinction.' He sold the copyright of *The Spartan Dame* for £150. *Biog. Dram.* i. 680.

[2] Shadwell, in James II's reign, received for a third night at Drury Lane, 'at single prices, £130, which was the greatest receipt they ever had at that house at single prices. Boxes, 4s. 0d.; Pit, 2s. 6d.; First Gal-

lery, 1s. 6d.; Upper Gallery, 1s. 0d.' *Roscius Anglicanus*, p. 56.

Before 1762 Drury Lane 'held no more than £220; the charge on the author's night was £63. In 1762 the house was enlarged to a receipt of £335.' Murphy's *Garrick*, p. 362.

Johnson, it seems, only cleared £195 17s. by his three nights of *Irene*. For the copy he received £100. Boswell's *Johnson*, i. 198 *n*.

[3] *Ante*, DRYDEN, 72 ; *post*, 170, 172.

[4] 'The word *relates* (writes Malone, i. 239) seems to refer to some passage in Swift's works ; but I have in vain sought for it.' The passage is the following from *A Tale of a Tub* :—'He [Dryden] hath often said to me in confidence that the world would have never suspected him to be so great a poet, if he had not assured them so frequently in his prefaces that it was impossible they could either doubt or forget it. Perhaps it may be so ; however, I much fear his instructions have edified out of their place, and taught men to grow wiser in certain points, where he never intended they should.' Swift's *Works*, x. 125.

Malone quotes 'somewhat similar

His prologues had such reputation that for some time a play 90
was considered as less likely to be well received if some of his
verses did not introduce it. The price of a prologue was two
guineas, till being asked to write one for Mr. Southern, he
demanded three, 'Not,' said he, 'young man, out of disrespect
to you, but the players have had my goods too cheap [1].'

Though he declares that in his own opinion his genius was not 91
dramatick [2], he had great confidence in his own fertility; for
he is said to have engaged by contract to furnish four plays
a year [3].

It is certain that in one year, 1678, he published *All for Love*, 92
Assignation, two parts of *The Conquest of Granada, Sir Martin
Marall*, and *The State of Innocence*, six complete plays [4]; with
a celerity of performance which, though all Langbaine's charges
of plagiarism [5] should be allowed, shews such facility of composition, such readiness of language, and such copiousness of

sentences in Dryden' from *Works*,
vi. 134, vii. 235.

For Swift's 'perpetual malevolence
to Dryden' see *post*, SWIFT, 18.

[1] For Dryden's Prologues and Epilogue for Southerne's plays see *Works*,
x. 374, 377, 391, and for his poetical
Epistle to him see *ib.* xi. 46. Pope
described Southerne as

'Tom, whom heaven sent down to
raise

The price of prologues and of plays.'
*To Mr. T. Southern, on his Birth-
day*, 1742.
Warburton adds in a note: 'This
alludes to a story Mr. Southern
told of Dryden about the same time
to Mr. P. and Mr. W.' The price,
Warburton says, was raised from
four to six guineas. He adds that
'he was the first who brought the
booksellers to give £100 for the copy
of a play.' Warburton's *Pope*, vi. 66.

How they found their account in
this I cannot understand, seeing that
the usual price of a play was one
shilling, or eighteenpence at most.

For Gray's account of Southerne in
1737 see his *Letters*, i. 8.

[2] *Post*, DRYDEN, 264, 329.

[3] In Messrs. Sotheran & Co.'s *Cata.
of Autos.* No. 12 (1899), Lot 64, is a
document signed by some of the
players, which states:—'Whereas

upon Mr. Dryden's binding himself
to write 3 Plays a yeare, the
said Mr. Dryden was admitted and
continued as a Sharer in the King's
Playhouse for divers yeares, and
received for his share and a quarter
3 or 4 hundred pounds *communibus
annis*, but though he received the
moneys, we received not the Plays,
not one in a yeare.' See also Malone's
Dryden, i. 72, and *The Rehearsal*, p. 40.

[4] Johnson's authority is Jacob's
Poet. Register, i. 82. Of these six
All for Love was published in 1678
(*ante*, DRYDEN, 78); *Assignation* in
1673 (*ante*, 63); *Conquest of Granada*
in 1672 (*ante*, 48); *Sir Martin Marall*
in 1668 (*ante*, 29); and *The State of
Innocence* in 1674 (*ante*, 71). In
sixteen years (1667 to the end of
1682) he produced eighteen dramas.
'From 1667 to 1670 he probably
wrote five or six plays. There is
good ground for believing that Shakespeare, for several years, composed
two plays in each year.' Malone's
Dryden, i. 78.

Ticknor quotes 'the anecdotes of
Montalvan that Lopez wrote five full-
length dramas in fifteen days.' *Span.
Lit.* ii. 203, quoted in *Century Cyclo.*
p. 1030.

[5] *Ante*, OTWAY, 5; DRYDEN, 25,
29.

sentiment, as since the time of Lopez de Vega perhaps no other author has possessed.

93 He did not enjoy his reputation, however great, nor his profits, however small, without molestation. He had criticks to endure, and rivals to oppose. The two most distinguished wits of the nobility, the duke of Buckingham[1] and earl of Rochester[2], declared themselves his enemies.

94 Buckingham characterised him in 1671 by the name of Bayes in *The Rehearsal*[3], a farce which he is said to have written with the assistance of Butler[4] the author of *Hudibras*, Martin Clifford of the Charterhouse[5], and Dr. Sprat, the friend of Cowley, then his chaplain[6]. Dryden and his friends laughed at the length of time, and the number of hands employed upon this performance[7]; in which, though by some artifice of action it yet keeps possession of the stage[8], it is not possible now to find any thing that might not have been written without so long delay, or a confederacy so numerous[9].

95 To adjust the minute events of literary history is tedious and troublesome[10]; it requires indeed no great force of understanding, but often depends upon enquiries which there is no opportunity of making, or is to be fetched from books and pamphlets not always at hand.

96 *The Rehearsal* was played in 1671[11], and yet is represented as

---

[1] *Ante*, BUTLER, 13.

[2] *Ante*, DRYDEN, 62.

[3] 'It is said Mr. Waller had a hand in it, with Mr. Clifford, Mr. Cowley, and some other wits, and that it was at first written like a comment on several plays.' Waller's *Poems*, 1712, Preface, p. 37; *ante*, WALLER, 102.

[4] Butler is not mentioned in the account in Waller's *Poems*.

[5] *Ante*, DRYDEN, 50.

[6] *Post*, SPRAT, 4.

[7] Dryden's *Works*, xi. 44; *Eng. Poets*, xxv. 142, for Duke's attack on Buckingham. Malone's *Dryden*, i. 95.

[8] For Cibber acting Bayes about 1717 see *post*, POPE, 233.
Garrick wrote on Feb. 6, 1741 :— 'I have the greatest success imaginable in the part of Bayes, and instead of clapping me they huzza.' *Catalogue of Peel Heirlooms*, June 12, 1900, Lot 72.

[9] 'The abilities of this lord [Buckingham] appear in no instance more amazing than that, being exposed by two of the greatest poets [Dryden and Pope], he has exposed one of them ten times more severely. Zimri is an admirable portrait, but Bayes is an original creation.' HORACE WALPOLE, *Works*, i. 416. For Zimri see *Absalom and Achitophel*, l. 544, and for Pope's lines see *Moral Essays*, iii. 299. Pope's birth took place the year after Buckingham died.

[10] For Johnson's inattention to minute accuracy see Boswell's *Johnson*, iii. 359 *n.*; iv. 36 *n.*, 51 *n.*

[11] First acted on Dec. 7, 1671, and printed in 1672. Malone's *Dryden*, i. 99. Evelyn recorded on Dec. 14, 1672 :—'Went to see the Duke of Buckingham's ridiculous farce and rhapsody, called *The Recital* [*sic*]; buffooning all plays, yet profane enough.' *Diary*, ii. 73. Evelyn's

ridiculing passages in *The Conquest of Granada* and *Assignation*, which were not published till 1678, in *Marriage Alamode* published in 1673, and in *Tyrannick Love* of 1677 [1]. These contradictions shew how rashly satire is applied [2].

It is said that this farce was originally intended against 97 Davenant [3], who in the first draught was characterised by the name of Bilboa. Davenant had been a soldier and an adventurer.

There is one passage in *The Rehearsal* still remaining, which 98 seems to have related originally to Davenant. Bayes hurts his nose, and comes in with brown paper applied to the bruise [4]; how this affected Dryden does not appear. Davenant's nose had suffered such diminution by mishaps among the women, that a patch upon that part evidently denoted him [5].

It is said likewise that Sir Robert Howard was once meant. The design was probably to ridicule the reigning poet, whoever he might be.

Much of the personal satire, to which it might owe its first 99 reception, is now lost or obscured [6]. Bayes probably imitated the dress and mimicked the manner of Dryden; the cant words which are so often in his mouth may be supposed to have been Dryden's habitual phrases or customary exclamations [7]. Bayes, when he is to write, is blooded and purged [8]: this, as Lamotte relates himself to have heard, was the real practice of the poet [9].

dates cannot be fully trusted. See Preface to his *Diary*, p. 7.

[1] *Tyrannick Love* was acted in 1668-9, and *The Conquest* as early as 1670. Though they were not published they could still be ridiculed. There is not a single allusion to *Marriage Alamode* in *The Rehearsal*; nor, in the original edition, to *Assignation*. Malone's *Dryden*, i. 100, 102.

[2] On the title-page of the fifth edition, published the year of Buckingham's death, it is stated that the play contains 'Amendments and large Additions by the Author.' *The Rehearsal*, p. 18.

[3] *Ante*, DRYDEN, 26.

[4] 'BAYES. Ah, gadsookers, I have broke my nose.... Pray, Sir, can you help me to a wet piece of brown paper?' *The Rehearsal*, p. 65. In the next act he enters 'with a paper on his nose.'

[5] See Aubrey's *Brief Lives*, i. 205.

The portrait of Davenant prefixed to the folio edition of his works (1673) shows a nose that had 'suffered diminution.' It contrasts oddly with his great wig, crowned by a chaplet of bay leaves.

[6] See Appendix R.

[7] 'By gad,' 'I vow to Gad,' 'I gad,' and 'gadsookers' are Bayes's common exclamations. See also Davies's *Dram. Misc.* iii. 308. In *The Rehearsal*, 1710, p. 31 *n.*, it is said that 'it is the constant style of Failer in *The Wild Gallant*.'

[8] 'If I am to write familiar things as Sonnets to Armida and the like, I make use of stewed prunes only; but when I have a grand design in hand I ever take physic and let blood.' *The Rehearsal*, 5th ed., 1687, Act ii. sc. 1. See also Southey's *Cowper*, v. 107.

[9] *An Essay upon Poetry and Painting*, by Charles Lamotte, D.D., 1730, p. 103.

100   There were other strokes in *The Rehearsal* by which malice
was gratified: the debate between Love and Honour[1], which
keeps prince Volscius in a single boot[2], is said to have alluded
to the misconduct of the duke of Ormond, who lost Dublin to
the rebels while he was toying with a mistress[3].

101   The earl of Rochester, to suppress the reputation of Dryden,
took Settle into his protection, and endeavoured to persuade the
publick that its approbation had been to that time misplaced[4].
Settle was a while in high reputation: his *Empress of Morocco*,
having first delighted the town[5], was carried in triumph to
Whitehall, and played by the ladies of the court[6]. Now was
the poetical meteor at the highest; the next moment began
its fall. Rochester withdrew his patronage; seemingly resolved,
says one of his biographers, 'to have a judgement contrary to
that of the town[7]'; perhaps being unable to endure any
reputation beyond a certain height, even when he had himself
contributed to raise it.

102   Neither criticks nor rivals did Dryden much mischief, unless
they gained from his own temper the power of vexing him, which
his frequent bursts of resentment give reason to suspect. He is
always angry at some past, or afraid of some future censure[8];
but he lessens the smart of his wounds by the balm of his own

---

[1] Davenant's *Love and Honour* is
ridiculed. *The Rehearsal*, p. 84.
   [2] *Ib.* p. 87.
   [3] Clarendon (*History*, viii. 4, 57)
tells how Ormond suffered from
'lewd discourses, which flow from
no other fountain but that of malice
and ignorance.' The chief slanderer
was 'the titular Bishop of Ferns.'
After describing the loss of Dublin
Clarendon continues :—' Malice itself
cannot fix a colourable imputation
upon him of want of fidelity or discretion.'
   Dryden, in *Absalom and Achitophel*, l. 819, writes of Ormond under
the name of Barzillai :—
'Long since, the rising rebels he
    withstood
In regions waste beyond the Jordan's
    flood.'
   See also *post*, DRYDEN, 188.
   [4] Rochester wrote the Prologue to
Settle's *Empress of Morocco*. *Eng.*

Poets, xv. 71; Dennis's *Remarks on
Homer*, Preface.
   [5] 'The town' is defined by Johnson as 'the Court end of London'
in opposition to 'the City.'
   [6] *Ante*, DRYDEN, 32.
   [7] St. Evremond, in a letter to the
Duchess of Mazarine, after telling
how Rochester 'set up Crowne in
opposition to Dryden,' continues :—
'But when Crowne's *Hierusalem* had
met with as wild success as the
Almanzors, his Lordship withdrew
his favours, as if he would still be in
contradiction to the Town.' Rochester's *Works*, 1709, Preface, p. 33.
I cannot find the original letter in
St. Evremond's *Works*.
   [8] *Ante*, DRYDEN, 63; *post*, 173;
PRIOR, 5. Macready (*Reminiscences*,
i. 353), quoting this passage, asks,
'Is not this a key to the causes of
my own disquietudes?'

approbation, and endeavours to repel the shafts of criticism by opposing a shield of adamantine confidence [1].

The perpetual accusation produced against him was that of 103 plagiarism, against which he never attempted any vigorous defence [2]; for, though he was sometimes injuriously censured, he would by denying part of the charge have confessed the rest; and as his adversaries had the proof in their own hands, he, who knew that wit had little power against facts, wisely left in that perplexity which generality produces a question which it was his interest to suppress, and which, unless provoked by vindication, few were likely to examine.

Though the life of a writer, from about thirty-five to sixty-three, 104 may be supposed to have been sufficiently busied by the composition of eight and twenty pieces for the stage [3], Dryden found room in the same space for many other undertakings.

But how much soever he wrote he was at least once suspected 105 of writing more; for in 1679 a paper of verses, called *An Essay on Satire*, was shewn about in manuscript, by which the earl of Rochester [4], the dutchess of Portsmouth [5], and others, were so much provoked that, as was supposed, for the actors were never discovered, they procured Dryden, whom they suspected as the author, to be waylaid and beaten [6]. This incident is

---

[1] *Post*, DRYDEN, 162. 'Dryden was, I am afraid, so intoxicated with his own merit that he overlooked and despised all the great satirists who constantly abused, I had almost said, libelled his works, unless they were some other way eminent, besides by their writings, such as Shadwell, who was poet laureate, and Buckingham, who was a duke.' FIELDING, *Works*, 1821, x. 122.

[2] *Ante*, DRYDEN, 29, 92; *post*, 229, 329. 'BAYES. Why, Sir, when I have anything to invent I never trouble my head about it, as other men do; but presently turn o'er this book (my *Drama Common places*) and there I have, at one view, all that *Perseus* [*sic*], *Montaigne*, *Seneca's Tragedies*, *Horace*, *Juvenal*, *Claudian*, *Pliny*, *Plutarch's Lives*, and the rest have ever thought upon this subject; and so, in a trice, by leaving out a few words, or putting in others of my own, the work is done.'

The Rehearsal, p. 33.

[3] To make up twenty-eight Johnson must reckon *The Indian Queen*. *Ante*, DRYDEN, 17.

[4] *Ante*, ROCHESTER, 3; DRYDEN, 62; *post*, SHEFFIELD, 23; Dryden's *Works*, xv. 210.

[5] Louise de Querouaille, one of Charles II's mistresses. She is coupled with another mistress, the Duchess of Cleveland, in the following triplet:—
'Yet sauntering Charles, between his beastly brace, [place, Meets with dissembling still in either Affected humour, or a painted face.'
Ib. p. 204.
Querouaille was popularly pronounced Carwell. Malone's *Dryden*, i. 135.

[6] *Ath. Oxon.* iv. 210; Malone's *Dryden*, i. 323; *Hist. MSS. Com.* xii. App. vii. p. 164; *N. & Q.* 4 S. x. 113. For the *Essay* see Dryden's *Works*, xv. 201. It is strange that any one could so have mistaken Dryden's style.

mentioned by the duke of Buckinghamshire, the true writer, in his *Art of Poetry*; where he says of Dryden,

'Though prais'd and beaten for another's rhymes,
His own deserves as great applause sometimes [1].'

106 His reputation in time was such that his name was thought necessary to the success of every poetical or literary performance, and therefore he was engaged to contribute something, whatever it might be, to many publications. He prefixed the *Life of Polybius* to the translation of Sir Henry Sheers [2]; and those of Lucian [3] and Plutarch [4] to versions of their works by different hands. Of the English *Tacitus* [5] he translated the first book, and, if Gordon be credited, translated it from the French [6]. Such a charge can hardly be mentioned without some degree of indignation; but it is not, I suppose, so much to be inferred that Dryden wanted the literature necessary to the perusal of Tacitus, as that, considering himself as hidden in a crowd, he had no awe of the publick, and writing merely for money was contented to get it by the nearest way.

107 In 1680, the *Epistles of Ovid* being translated by the poets of the time, among which one was the work of Dryden, and another of Dryden and Lord Mulgrave [7], it was necessary to introduce

---

[1] This couplet is not in the *Essay on Poetry* as printed in *Eng. Poets*, xxxii. 69. In the second edition (1691) it runs:—
'The Laureate here may justly claim
  our praise,   [mortal bays;
Crown'd by Mac-Fleckno with im-
Though prais'd and punish'd for
  another's Rhimes,
His own deserve as great Applause
  sometimes.'
In a side-note on 'Rhimes' it is added:—'A Libel, for which he was both applauded and wounded tho' intirely innocent of the whole matter.'
  In the edition of 1717, p. 307, the third line runs:—
'Though prais'd and punish'd once
  for other's rhymes.'
See *post*, SHEFFIELD, 23, 27, for Dryden's 'exalting this *Essay* so highly.'
[2] *Works*, xviii. 23. For a wonderful piece of natural history related, says Dryden, ' by my most ingenious friend, Sir Henry Shere,' see *ib*. xiv.

98, and for Dryden's character of him, see *ib*. xviii. 24. See also Pepys's *Diary*, v. 162, 185. According to Malone (i. 254) the name was Shere, not Sheres or Sheers. See also *ib*. iii. 229.
[3] *Works*, xviii. 54.
[4] *Ib*. xvii. 1.
[5] *The Annals and History of Tacitus* ... made English by several hands. 1698.
[6] 'He has done it almost literally from Mr. Amelot de la Houssaye. He follows the French author servilely and writes French English rather than trust him out of his eye.' GORDON, *Tacitus*, 1728, Preface, p. 1.
'The pompous folios of Gordon's *Tacitus* were greedily devoured' by Gibbon in his boyhood. Gibbon's *Memoirs*, p. 44.
[7] Dryden unaided translated two, *Epist. Her*. vii and xi, and one with Mulgrave [*post*, SHEFFIELD, 1], *Epist*. xvii. *Works*, xii. 25, 31, 40. *Post*, DRYDEN, 267; DUKE, 2; POPE, 17.

them by a preface; and Dryden, who on such occasions was regularly summoned, prefixed a discourse upon translation, which was then struggling for the liberty that it now enjoys[1]. Why it should find any difficulty in breaking the shackles of verbal interpretation, which must for ever debar it from elegance, it would be difficult to conjecture, were not the power of prejudice every day observed. The authority of Jonson[2], Sandys[3], and Holiday[4] had fixed the judgement of the nation; and it was not easily believed that a better way could be found than they had taken, though Fanshaw[5], Denham[6], Waller[7], and Cowley[8] had tried to give examples of a different practice[9].

In 1681 Dryden became yet more conspicuous by uniting 108 politicks with poetry, in the memorable satire called *Absalom and Achitophel*[10], written against the faction which, by lord Shaftesbury's incitement, set the duke of Monmouth at its head.

Of this poem, in which personal satire was applied to the 109 support of publick principles, and in which therefore every mind was interested, the reception was eager, and the sale so large that my father, an old bookseller[11], told me he had not known it equalled but by Sacheverell's trial[12].

The reason of this general perusal Addison has attempted to 110 derive from the delight which the mind feels in the investigation of secrets; and thinks that curiosity to decypher the names

---

[1] *Works*, xii. 7; *ante*, DENHAM, 25; *post*, DRYDEN, 223, 356.
Addison (*Works*, iv. 337) praises the French, 'when they advise a translator to find out such particular elegancies in his own tongue as bear some analogy to those he sees in the original, and to express himself by such phrases as his author would probably have made use of had he written in the language into which he is translated.'

[2] *Post*, DRYDEN, 223.

[3] *Ante*, COWLEY, 197; *post*, DRYDEN, 223; POPE, 5.

[4] *Post*, DRYDEN, 223, 299.

[5] *Ante*, DENHAM, 24; ROSCOMMON, 36.

[6] *Ante*, DENHAM, 33, 36.

[7] Waller's version of part of *Aeneid* iv (*Eng. Poets*, xvi. 130) is instanced by Dryden as paraphrase. *Post*, DRYDEN, 224 *n.*

[8] *Ante*, COWLEY, 125.

[9] 'The accuracy of Jonson found more imitators than the elegance of Fairfax; and May, Sandys and Holiday confined themselves to the task of rendering line for line, not indeed with equal felicity, for May and Sandys were poets, and Holiday only a scholar and a critic.' JOHNSON, *The Idler*, No. 69.

[10] *Works*, ix. 195. 'It was published on or before Nov. 17, 1681, in folio. Price one shilling.' Malone's *Dryden*, i. 157.

[11] *Post*, SPRAT, 19; Boswell's *Johnson*, i. 34.

[12] *Post*, KING, 13; SPRAT, 17; HALIFAX, 9; ADDISON, 14; Boswell's *Johnson*, i. 38.
'During the trial of Sacheverell our audiences were extremely weakened by the better rank of people daily attending it.' CIBBER, *Apology*, p. 241.

procured readers to the poem[1]. There is no need to enquire
why those verses were read, which to all the attractions of
wit, elegance, and harmony added the co-operation of all the
factious passions, and filled every mind with triumph or resentment.

111   It could not be supposed that all the provocation given by
Dryden would be endured without resistance or reply. Both his
person and his party were exposed in their turns to the shafts of
satire[2], which, though neither so well pointed nor perhaps so well
aimed, undoubtedly drew blood.

112   One of these poems is called *Dryden's Satire on his Muse*[3],
ascribed, though, as Pope says, falsely, to Somers, who was
afterwards Chancellor[4]. The poem, whose soever it was, has
much virulence, and some spriteliness. The writer tells all the
ill that he can collect both of Dryden and his friends.

113   The poem of *Absalom and Achitophel* had two answers, now
both forgotten : one called *Azaria and Hushai*, the other *Absalom
Senior*[5]. Of these hostile compositions Dryden apparently
imputes *Absalom Senior* to Settle, by quoting in his verses
against him the second line[6]. *Azaria and Hushai* was, as Wood
says[7], imputed to him, though it is somewhat unlikely that he
should write twice on the same occasion. This is a difficulty

[1] ' The natural pride and ambition
of the soul is very much gratified in
the reading of a fable ; for in writings
of this kind the reader comes in for
half of the performance ; everything
appears to him like a discovery of
his own ; he is busied all the while
in applying characters and circumstances, and is in this respect both a
reader and a composer.' *The Spectator*, No. 512.

[2] For the titles of these attacks see
Dryden's *Works*, ix. 204.

[3] *Satyr to his Muse*. By the Author
of *Absalom and Achitophel*. 1682.
Post, DRYDEN, 166.

[4] I do not know where Pope says
this. Jacob imputed it to Somers.
Poet. Register, ii. 193. Horace Walpole (*Works*, i. 432), including it in
Somers's writings, adds :—'This, I
think, has been disputed ; and, indeed, the gross ribaldry of it cannot
be believed to have flowed from so
humane and polished a nature.'

Nearly two years earlier Somers
had published a political poem
' without any offensive personality.'
Malone's *Dryden*, i. 166. This poem
is not in *Brit. Mus. Cata.*

Dryden, in 1699, wrote of ' having
the Chancellor my enemy.' *Works*,
xviii. 168. See also *post*, DRYDEN, 157.

[5] *Absalom Senior, or Achitophel
Transprosed. A Poem*, 1682. *Works*,
ix. 357 n.

[6] 'Who makes heaven's gate a lock
to its own key.' *Absalom and Achitophel*, ii. 446 ; *Works*, ix. 362 n. For
Settle see *ante*, DRYDEN, 32.

[7] [*Ath. Oxon.* iv. 687.] It was by
Samuel Pordage, whom Dryden
attacked—
'As lame Mephibosheth the wizard's
    son.'
    Absalom and Achitophel, ii. 405.
His father was 'a physician and
astrologer' ; he himself 'a civil
courteous person.' AUBREY, *Brief
Lives*, ii. 161.

which I cannot remove, for want of a minuter knowledge of poetical transactions.

The same year he published *The Medal* [1], of which the subject is a medal struck on lord Shaftesbury's escape from a prosecution, by the *ignoramus* of a grand jury of Londoners [2]. **114**

In both poems he maintains the same principles, and saw them both attacked by the same antagonist. Elkanah Settle, who had answered *Absalom*, appeared with equal courage in opposition to *The Medal*, and published an answer called *The Medal Reversed* [3], with so much success in both encounters that he left the palm doubtful, and divided the suffrages of the nation. Such are the revolutions of fame, or such is the prevalence of fashion, that the man whose works have not yet been thought to deserve the care of collecting them ; who died forgotten in an hospital ; and whose latter years were spent in contriving shows for fairs [4], and carrying an elegy or epithalamium, of which the beginning and end were occasionally varied, but the intermediate parts were always the same, to every house where there was a funeral or a wedding [5]— might with truth have had inscribed upon his stone **115**

' Here lies the Rival and Antagonist of Dryden [6].'

---

[1] *The Medal. A Satire against Sedition. Works*, ix. 411. Published in March 1681-2, price sixpence. Malone's *Dryden*, i. 163.

[2] See Burnet's *Hist.* ii. 122. An ignoramus is the same as ' not a true bill ' or ' not found.' Blackstone's *Comm.* 1775, iv. 305. Sprat in his *Account of the Horrid Conspiracy*, p. 23 (*post*, SPRAT, 9), says that 'the whole wicked mystery and trade of packing the *ignoramus* juries passed through the hands of the Under-Sheriffs.'

Spence heard a priest tell Pope that ' Charles II gave Dryden the hint for writing *The Medal* ... Dryden had a present of 100 broad pieces for the poem.' Spence's *Anec.* p. 171.

For a description of the medal struck see *Works*, ix. 416.

[3] Wood attributes it to Settle. *Ath. Oxon.* iv. 687. It was, says Scott, by Samuel Pordage. *Works*, ix. 419.

[4] Warburton says in a note on *The Dunciad*, iii. 283 :—' After the Revolution Settle kept a booth at Bar-

tholomew Fair, where, in the droll called *St. George for England*, he acted, in his old age, in a Dragon of Green leather of his own invention. He died in the Charterhouse.' Warburton's *Pope*, v. 158.

Young, in his *Epistle to Mr. Pope*, l. 263, tells how
' Poor Elkanah, all other changes past,
For bread in Smithfield dragons hiss'd at last.'
Langbaine says that Settle describes himself as ' one who, after all his repented follies, is resolved to honestly skulk into a corner of the stage, and there die contented.' *Dram. Poets*, App. See also *Gent. Mag.* 1745, p. 99.

[5] See *The Idler*, No. xii.

[6] ' In short Mr. Settle was then [1673] a formidable rival to Mr. Dryden ; and I remember very well that not only the Town, but the University of Cambridge was very much divided in their opinions about the preference that ought to be given to

116 Settle was for this rebellion severely chastised by Dryden under the name of Doeg, in the second part of *Absalom and Achitophel*[1], and was perhaps for his factious audacity made the city poet, whose annual office was to describe the glories of the Mayor's day[2]. Of these bards he was the last, and seems not much to have deserved even this degree of regard, if it was paid to his political opinions ; for he afterwards wrote a panegyrick on the virtues of judge Jefferies, and what more could have been done by the meanest zealot for prerogative?

117 Of translated fragments or occasional poems to enumerate the titles or settle the dates would be tedious, with little use. It may be observed that as Dryden's genius was commonly excited by some personal regard he rarely writes upon a general topick.

118 Soon after the accession of king James, when the design of reconciling the nation to the church of Rome became apparent, and the religion of the court gave the only efficacious title to its favours, Dryden declared himself a convert to popery[3]. This at

them ; and in both places the younger fry inclined to Elkanah.' DENNIS, *Remarks on Pope's Homer*, Preface.

'Elkanah Settle,' said Wilkes, 'sounds so queer ; who can expect much from that name? We should have no hesitation to give it for John Dryden in preference to Elkanah Settle, from the names only, without knowing their different merits.' Boswell's *Johnson*, iii. 76.

[1] Published about Nov. 10, 1682. *Works*, ix. 322. Most of it is by Nahum Tate (*post*, ROWE, 21), with corrections and additions by Dryden, who wrote ll. 310–509. For Doeg see l. 408. See also *post*, DRYDEN, 273.

[2] 'His office was to compose yearly panegyrics upon the Lord Mayors, and verses to be spoken in the Pageants. But that part of the Shows being at length frugally abolished, the employment of City-Poet ceased.' Warburton's *Pope*, v. 22.

His City Poems bore such titles as the following :— *Triumphs of London for the Inauguration of Sir Richard Levett, Lord Mayor of London*, Oct. 30, 1699. Lowndes's *Bibl. Man.* p. 2246, in which work more space is given to Settle than Dryden.

Pope, describing the Show, continues :—

'Now night descending, the proud scene was o'er,
But liv'd in Settle's numbers one day more.' *The Dunciad*, i. 89.

Tennyson said of these lines :— 'It is dreadful to think how satire will endure. The perfection of that couplet brings tears to one's eyes, and it pillories Settle for ever.' *Allingham MS*.

In 1683 Settle printed *A Panegyrick* on Jefferies :—

'Betimes the Long Robe's glory, and his tongue
Touched with a coal from wisdom's altar young.'

[3] Evelyn recorded under date of Jan. 19, 1685-6 :—'Dryden, the famous play-writer, and his two sons, and Mrs. Nelly (Miss to the late — [King]) were said to go to mass.' *Diary*, ii. 259. (See *ib*. i. 381, where under date of Jan. 9, 1661-2, it is said that 'at this time they began to call all lewd women *Miss*.') Evelyn's dates are not trustworthy.

The Bishop of Carlisle wrote on Jan. 27, 1686-7, that Mr. Finch, the new Warden of All Souls, 'an ingenious young gentleman, lately meeting

any other time might have passed with little censure. Sir Kenelm Digby embraced popery[1]; the two Rainolds reciprocally converted one another[2]; and Chillingworth himself was a while so entangled in the wilds of controversy as to retire for quiet to an infallible church[3]. If men of argument and study can find such difficulties or such motives, as may either unite them to the church of Rome or detain them in uncertainty, there can be no wonder that a man, who perhaps never enquired why he was a protestant, should by an artful and experienced disputant be made a papist, overborne by the sudden violence of new and unexpected arguments, or deceived by a representation which shews only the doubts on one part and only the evidence on the other.

That conversion will always be suspected that apparently concurs with interest[4]. He that never finds his error till it hinders 119

with Mr. Dryden in a coffee-house in London, publickly before all the company wished him much joy of his *new* religion. " Sir," said Dryden, " you are very much mistaken ; my religion is the *old* religion." " Nay," replyed the other, " whatever it be in itself I am sure 'tis new to you, for within these 3 days you had no religion at all." ' *Le Fleming MSS., Hist. MSS. Comm.* Report xii. App. 7, p. 202.

[1] ' Wood states that he was " trained up in the Protestant religion " [*Athen. Oxon.* iii. 688]. It is certain that he was brought up in the Roman Catholic faith which his father adopted.' S. L. LEE, *Dict. Nat. Biog.* xv. 60. [According to Aubrey, ' Anno 163 . . . tempore Caroli I^{mi} he received the sacrament in the chapell at Whitehall, and professed the Protestant religion, which gave great scandal to the Roman Catholics, but afterwards he *looked back.*' *Brief Lives,* i. 227.]

[2] ' All this while this our John Reinolds was well affected to the Romish religion, and his brother William earnest for Reformation ; which difference in judgment . . . engaged them in a strange duel . . . wherein both conquered one the other, yet neither enjoyed the victory, nor kept his prisoner ; for John Reinolds, who before was a Papist, by

these bickerings became a zealous Protestant, and William Reinolds, who before had been a zealous Protestant, became a Jesuited Papist, and wrote most pestilent books against the church and state.' Fuller's *Abel Redivivus,* ed. 1867, ii. 221. They flourished in Elizabeth's reign. [John Rainolds or Reynolds lived on to 1607, and was one of the Puritan representatives at the Hampton Court Conference in 1604.]

[3] ' I know a man that of a moderate Protestant turned a Papist, and the day that he did so . . . was convicted in conscience that his yesterday's opinion was an error. . . . The same man afterwards, upon a better consideration, became a doubting Papist, and, of a doubting Papist, a confirmed Protestant.' W. CHILLINGWORTH, *The Religion of Protestants,* &c., 1638, p. 303.

' Chillingworth had contracted such an irresolution and habit of doubting that by degrees he grew confident of nothing, and a sceptic at least in the greatest mysteries of faith.' CLARENDON, *Life,* i. 62. See also Johnson's *Works,* vi. 417 ; Gibbon's *Memoirs,* p. 74.

[4] Dryden, in *The Hind and the Panther,* iii. 221, referring, no doubt, to himself, makes the Hind say :—

' Now for my converts, who, you say, unfed,

his progress towards wealth or honour will not be thought to love Truth only for herself. Yet it may easily happen that information may come at a commodious time; and as truth and interest are not by any fatal necessity at variance, that one may by accident introduce the other. When opinions are struggling into popularity the arguments by which they are opposed or defended become more known; and he that changes his profession would perhaps have changed it before, with the like opportunities of instruction. This was then the state of popery; every artifice was used to shew it in its fairest form: and it must be owned to be a religion of external appearance sufficiently attractive [1].

120   It is natural to hope that a comprehensive is likewise an elevated soul, and that whoever is wise is also honest. I am willing to believe that Dryden, having employed his mind, active as it was, upon different studies, and filled it, capacious as it was, with other materials, came unprovided to the controversy, and wanted rather skill to discover the right than virtue to maintain it. But enquiries into the heart are not for man; we must now leave him to his Judge [2].

121   The priests, having strengthened their cause by so powerful an adherent, were not long before they brought him into action. They engaged him to defend the controversial papers found in the strong-box of Charles the Second, and, what yet was harder, to defend them against Stillingfleet [3].

122   With hopes of promoting popery he was employed to translate Maimbourg's *History of the League*, which he published with a large introduction [4]. His name is likewise prefixed to the English *Life of Francis Xavier* [5]; but I know not that he ever owned himself the translator [6]. Perhaps the use of his name was

---

Have followed me for miracles of bread.
Judge not by hearsay, but observe at least,
If since their change their loaves have been increased.'
For Macaulay's accusation that Dryden's 'conversion concurred with interest' see his *History*, ii. 455, and for Robert Bell's defence see Bell's *Dryden*, i. 55; ii. 134 *n.*, and Dryden's *Works*, i. 248 *n.* 'It is idle,' wrote Sir Leslie Stephen, 'to compare such a conversion to those of loftier minds. But, in a sense, he may well have been sincere enough.' *Dict. Nat. Biog.* xvi. 69.

[1] *Post*, GARTH, 16.
[2] *Ante*, MILTON, 105 *n.*; *post*, DRYDEN, 158, 406.
[3] See Appendix S.
[4] See Appendix S.
[5] By Father Dominic Bouhours.
[6] 'Translated into English by Mr. Dryden' is on the title-page. It was published in 1688. *Works*, xvi. 3. For Scott's remarks on it see *ib.* i. 282.

a pious fraud [1], which however seems not to have had much effect ; for neither of the books, I believe, was ever popular.

The version of *Xavier's Life* is commended by Brown, in a **123** pamphlet [2] not written to flatter ; and the occasion of it is said to have been that the Queen, when she solicited a son, made vows to him as her tutelary saint [3].

He was supposed to have undertaken to translate Varillas's **124** *History of Heresies*, and, when Burnet published Remarks upon it, to have written an *Answer* [4] upon which Burnet makes the following observation [5] :

' I have been informed from England that a gentleman, who is famous [known] both for poetry and several other things [and other things], had spent three months in translating M. Varillas's *History*, but that, as soon as my *Reflections* appeared, he discontinued his labour, finding the credit of his author was gone. Now, if he thinks it is recovered by his *Answer*, he will perhaps go on with his translation ; and this may be, for aught I know, as good an entertainment for him as the conversation that he had set on between the Hinds and Panthers, and all the rest of animals, for whom M. Varillas may serve well enough as an author : and this

---

[1] ' When pious frauds and holy shifts Are dispensations and gifts.' *Hudibras*, i. 3, 1145. See also *ib.* iii. 2, 63.
' These are called the pious frauds of friendship.' FIELDING, *Amelia*, vi. 6.

[2] *The Late Converts Exposed, or the Reasons of Mr. Bays's changing his Religion. Considered in a Dialogue, Part the Second. With Reflections on the Life of St. Xavier*, &c., 1690. One of the characters of the *Dialogue* says of the *Life* :—' The language and the style are extremely fine, both in the original and in the translation.' p. 33.

[3] *Ib.* p. 35. Dryden, in his Dedication to the Queen, after stating that Bouhours attributed the birth of Lewis XIV to Xavier's intercession, continues :—' Your Majesty, I doubt not, has the inward satisfaction of knowing that such pious prayers have not been unprofitable to you ; and the nation may one day come to understand how happy it will be for them to have a son of prayers ruling over them.' *Works*, xvi. 3. In *Britannia Rediviva, ib.* x. 288 ; *post*,

DRYDEN, 298, he addresses the babe :—
' Hail, son of prayers ! by holy violence
Drawn down from heaven.'

[4] Varillas in 1686 began the publication of his *Histoire des Révolutions arrivées dans l'Europe en matière de Religion*. Burnet the same year published *Reflections on Mr. Varillas' History*. The next year he published *A Continuation of Reflections*, &c., and *A Defence of the Reflections*, &c.
The *History* was translated by Dryden, ' at the King's command,' as is shown by an entry on April 29, 1686, in the Stationers' Register. The *Answer* was by Varillas. Malone shows that Johnson was misled ' by the imperfect citation of Burnet's words in the *General Dict.*, and by his clumsy phraseology.' The paragraph preceding the one cited in the text makes this clear. Malone's *Dryden*, i. 194. See also *post*, KING, 3.

[5] In *A Defence of the Reflections*, &c., Amsterdam, 1687, p. 138.

history and that poem are such extraordinary things of their kind, that it will be but suitable to see the author of the worst poem become likewise the translator of the worst history that the age has produced.   If his grace and his wit improve both proportionably he will hardly find that he has gained much by the change he has made, from having no religion to chuse one of the worst. It is true he had somewhat to sink from in [the] matter of wit ; but as for his morals, it is scarce possible for him to grow a worse man than he was[1].   He has lately wreaked his malice on me[2] for spoiling his three months' labour ; but in it he has done me all the honour that any man can receive from him, which is to be railed at by him.   If I had ill-nature enough to prompt me to wish a very bad wish for him, it should be that he would go on and finish his translation.   By that it will appear whether the English nation, which is the most competent judge in this matter, has, upon the seeing our debate, pronounced in M. Varillas's favour, or in mine.   It is true Mr. D. will suffer a little by it ; but at least it will serve to keep him in from other extravagancies; and if he gains little honour by this work, yet he cannot lose so much by it as he has done by his last employment.'

125   Having probably felt his own inferiority in theological controversy he was desirous of trying whether, by bringing poetry to aid his arguments, he might become a more efficacious defender of his new profession.   To reason in verse was, indeed, one of his powers[3] ; but subtilty and harmony united are still feeble, when opposed to truth.

126   Actuated therefore by zeal for Rome, or hope of fame, he published *The Hind and Panther*[4], a poem in which the church of Rome, figured by the *milk-white Hind*, defends her tenets against the church of England, represented by the *Panther*, a beast beautiful, but spotted.

127   A fable which exhibits two beasts talking Theology appears at once full of absurdity ; and it was accordingly ridiculed in *The City Mouse and Country Mouse*, a parody written by Montague, afterwards earl of Halifax, and Prior, who then gave the first specimen of his abilities[5].

---

[1] *Ante*, DRYDEN, 87 ; *post*, 170, 175.

[2] In *The Hind and the Panther*, iii. 1120–1288, where Burnet is the Buzzard.

[3] 'BAYES. Reasoning; I gad, I love reasoning in verse.' *The Rehearsal*, p. 107.

'I am of opinion that they cannot be good poets who are not accustomed to argue well.' DRYDEN, *Works*, ii. 303.   See *post*, DRYDEN, 327, 356.

[4] *Works*, x. 85 ; *post*, DRYDEN, 286.   It was published in April, 1687. Malone's *Dryden*, i. 197.

[5] *Post*, DRYDEN, 288 ; HALIFAX, 5 ; PRIOR, 5.

The conversion of such a man at such a time was not likely 128 to pass uncensured. Three dialogues were published by the facetious Thomas Brown [1], of which the two first were called *Reasons of Mr. Bayes's changing his religion*, and the third *The Reasons of Mr. Hains the player's conversion and re-conversion* [2]. The first was printed in 1688, the second not till 1690, the third in 1691. The clamour seems to have been long continued, and the subject to have strongly fixed the publick attention [3].

In the two first dialogues Bayes is brought into the company 129 of Crites and Eugenius, with whom he had formerly debated on dramatick poetry [4]. The two talkers in the third are Mr. Bayes and Mr. Hains.

Brown was a man not deficient in literature nor destitute of 130 fancy; but he seems to have thought it the pinnacle of excellence to be a *merry fellow* [5], and therefore laid out his powers upon small jests or gross buffoonery, so that his performances have little intrinsick value, and were read only while they were recommended by the novelty of the event that occasioned them.

These dialogues are like his other works: what sense or 131 knowledge they contain is disgraced by the garb in which it is exhibited. One great source of pleasure is to call Dryden 'little Bayes [6].' Ajax, who happens to be mentioned, is 'he that wore as many cowhides upon his shield as would have furnished half the king's army with shoe-leather [7].'

---

[1] An account of him is in Jacob's *Poet. Reg.* ii. 18, and Cibber's *Lives*, iii. 204. He published these *Dialogues* under the name of Dudley Tomkinson. His *Works* (not including these *Dialogues*) were published in 1715 in four vols. 12mo.

[2] 'Joe Haines declared that the Virgin Mary had appeared to him. Lord Sunderland asked him whether he had really seen the Virgin. "Yes, my Lord, I assure you it is a fact." "How was it, pray?" "Why, as I was lying in my bed the Virgin appeared to me, and said, 'Arise, Joe.'" "You lie, you rogue," said the Earl; "for if it had really been the Virgin she would have said, 'Joseph,' if it had been only out of respect to her husband."' Davies's *Dram. Misc.* iii. 284. On his recon-

version he said in a Prologue:—
'I own my crime of leaving in the lurch
My mother-playhouse—she's my mother-church.' *Ib.* p. 308.

[3] Dryden wrote in 1697:—'I hear Tom Brown is coming out upon me.' *Works*, xviii. 137. 'Brown wrote a burlesque account of Dryden's funeral in verse.' *Ib. n.* For the inscription intended for Brown's grave see Crull's *Antiquities of St. Peter's*, ii. 138.

[4] In *An Essay of Dramatic Poesy*. *Ante*, DRYDEN, 27.

[5] *Ante*, DENHAM, 22.

[6] In *The City Mouse and Country Mouse* (1687) (*post*, HALIFAX, 5) he had been thus called. Halifax's *Works*, pt. i. 47.

[7] *The Late Converts*, &c., p. 2.

132   Being asked whether he has seen *The Hind and Panther*, Crites
answers:

'Seen it, Mr. Bayes! why I can stir no where but it persues me;
it haunts me worse than a pewter-buttoned serjeant does a decayed
cit¹.   Sometimes I meet it in a band-box, when my laundress
brings home my linen; sometimes, whether I will or no, it lights
my pipe at a coffee-house; sometimes it surprises me in a trunk-
maker's shop; and sometimes it refreshes my memory for me on
the backside of a Chancery-lane parcel.   For your comfort too,
Mr. Bayes, I have not only seen it, as you may perceive, but have
read it too, and can quote it as freely upon occasion as a frugal
tradesman can quote that noble treatise the *Worth of a Penny* to
his extravagant 'prentice, that revels in [cockale], stewed apples,
and penny custards².'

133   The whole animation of these compositions arises from a pro-
fusion of ludicrous and affected comparisons.

'To secure one's chastity,' says Bayes, 'little more is necessary
than to leave off a correspondence with the other sex, which to
a wise man is no greater a punishment than it would be to
a fanatick parson to be forbid seeing *The Cheats*³ and *The
Committee*⁴, or for my Lord Mayor and Aldermen to be inter-
dicted the sight of *The London Cuckold*⁵.'—This is the general
strain, and therefore I shall be easily excused the labour of more
transcription.

134   Brown does not wholly forget past transactions:

'[As] You began,' says Crites to Bayes, 'with a very indifferent
religion, and [so] have not [much] mended the matter in your
last choice; it was but reason that your Muse, which appeared
first in a Tyrant's quarrel, should employ her last efforts to justify
the usurpations of the *Hind*⁶.'

¹ The sergeant must be of the
order described in *The Comedy of
Errors*, iv. 3. 25:—'He, Sir, that
takes pity on decayed men, and
gives them suits of durance.'
² *The Late Converts*, &c., p. 1.
³ By John Wilson, first acted in
1663. 'Lacy played Scruple, the non-
conformist minister, who in his fondness for deep potations, "too good
for the wicked; it may strengthen
them in their enormities," anticipated
the shepherd in *Pickwick*.'   *Dict.
Nat. Biog.* lxii. 105.
⁴ By Sir Robert Howard. Pepys,
who calls it 'a merry, but indifferent
play,' saw it four times. *Diary*, ii.
170; iv. 156, 250, 444.

⁵ *The Late Converts*, &c., p. 9.
This play by Edward Ravenscroft
was first acted in 1682. Till 1752 it
was commonly acted on Lord Mayor's
Day, 'in contempt, and to the disgrace of the City.'   *John. Letters*,
i. 184 *n*. Cibber says of it and of
Charles II's time that 'the most
rank play that ever succeeded was
then in the highest court-favour.'
Apology, p. 155.
'The audience in Congreve's time
were particularly fond of having a
city-cuckold dressed out for their
entertainment.'   Davies's *Dram.
Misc.* iii. 336.
⁶ *The Late Converts*, &c., p. 4.

Next year the nation was summoned to celebrate the birth of 135
the Prince. Now was the time for Dryden to rouse his imagination, and strain his voice. Happy days were at hand, and he
was willing to enjoy and diffuse the anticipated blessings. He
published a poem [1], filled with predictions of greatness and
prosperity—predictions of which it is not necessary to tell how
they have been verified.

A few months passed after these joyful notes, and every blossom 136
of popish hope was blasted for ever by the Revolution. A papist
now could be no longer Laureat [2]. The revenue, which he had
enjoyed with so much pride and praise, was transferred to Shadwell [3], an old enemy whom he had formerly stigmatised by the
name of Og [4]. Dryden could not decently complain that he was
deposed; but seemed very angry that Shadwell succeeded him,
and has therefore celebrated the intruder's inauguration in a poem
exquisitely satirical, called *Mac Flecknoe* [5], of which *The Dunciad,*

---

[1] *Britannia Rediviva.   A Poem on the Birth of the Prince, Works,* x. 281; *post*, DRYDEN, 298. The Prince was born on June 10, 1688, and the poem of 361 lines was published on June 23. Malone's *Dryden,* i. 202.

[2] See *ante,* DRYDEN, 26 and 86, where he says 'he has voluntarily reduced himself to his lowness of fortune.'   He held office till Aug. 1, 1689, on which day it became void by his not taking the oaths in accordance with the statute 1 W. and M. c. 8. Malone's *Dryden,* i. 207. In the Prologue to *Don Sebastian* he says:—
'There's no pretension
To argue loss of wit from loss of pension.'   *Works,* vii. 320.

[3] Shadwell wrote in his *Congratulatory Poem to Queen Mary on her Arrival in England*:—
'We from the Mighty States have now gained more
Than by our aid they ever got before.
Not Alva's rage would have distressed them so
As, Madam, we have done recalling you.'   Malone's *Dryden,* i. 207.
He also succeeded Dryden as Royal Historiographer.   *Ib.* For an account of him see *N. & Q.* 8 S. iv. 109.

[4] *Absalom and Achitophel,* ii. 408–

11, 457–509. See also *The Dunciad,* iii. 22.

Addison, after saying that Shadwell had a great deal of humour, continues:—'He represents an empty rake in one of his plays as very much surprised to hear one say that breaking of windows was not humour.' *The Spectator,* No. 35.

[5] *Works,* x. 428. 'It was published in quarto with the title :—*Mac-Flecknoe, or a Satyr upon the true-blew Protestant Poet, T. S.* By the Author of *Absalom and Achitophel.* The price was twopence.' It appeared on Oct. 4, 1682, more than six years before Dryden lost the laureateship. Malone's *Dryden,* i. 169.
'Richard Flecknoe [who died in 1678] was as famous as any man in his age for indifferent metre. He never could arrive with all his industry to get but one play to be acted. His acquaintance with the nobility was more than with the Muses.'   Langbaine's *Dram. Poets,* p. 199.
Dryden makes him choose Shadwell as his successor over ' the realms of Nonsense.'
'Shadwell alone of all my sons is he
Who stands confirmed in full stupidity.
The rest to some faint meaning make pretence,

as Pope himself declares, is an imitation, though more extended in its plan, and more diversified in its incidents [1].

137 It is related by Prior that Lord Dorset, when as chamberlain he was constrained to eject Dryden from his office, gave him from his own purse an allowance equal to his salary [2]. This is no romantick or incredible act of generosity; an hundred a year is often enough given to claims less cogent, by men less famed for liberality. Yet Dryden always represented himself as suffering under a publick infliction, and once particularly demands respect for the patience with which he endured the loss of his little fortune [3]. His patron might, indeed, enjoin him to suppress his bounty; but if he suffered nothing, he should not have complained.

138 During the short reign of King James he had written nothing for the stage, being, in his own opinion, more profitably employed in controversy and flattery. Of praise he might perhaps have been less lavish without inconvenience, for James was never said to have much regard for poetry [4]: he was to be flattered only by adopting his religion.

139 Times were now changed: Dryden was no longer the court-poet [5],

---

But Shadwell never deviates into sense.' *Mac Flecknoe*, ll. 6, 17-20.

[1] *Post*, POPE, 356.

[2] *Ante*, DORSET, 12; *Eng. Poets*, xxxii. 135. Malone (i. 449) shows that 'Dorset's bounty was merely temporary and occasional.'

Langbaine says Shadwell 'confesses that he owed the laureateship chiefly to the patronage of Dorset.' *Dram. Poets*, p. 443.

Nell Gwynne, in an undated letter quoted in *N. & Q.* 4 S. vii. 3, writes:—' My lord of Dorscit apiers wonse in thre munths, for he drinkes aile with Shadwell and Mr. Haris at the Dukes house all day long.'

'A Prologue by Dryden to *The Prophetess* [*Works*, x. 407] was forbid by the Lord Dorset after the first day. This happened when William was prosecuting the war in Ireland. It had some sneers at the Revolution itself, and as the poetry was good the offence was less pardonable.' CIBBER, *Apology*, p. 198.

Macaulay (*Hist.* iv. 25 *n.*) quotes some lines by Blackmore on Dryden and Dorset.

[3] 'Since this revolution, wherein I have patiently suffered the ruin of my small fortune, and the loss of that poor subsistence which I had from two kings,' &c. *Works*, xiii. 31. See also *ib.* xiv. 233; *ante*, DORSET, 14.

[4] Scott thus describes the three kings with whom Dryden had to do:—'The needy Charles, who loved literary merit without rewarding it; the saturnine James, who rewarded without loving it; and the phlegmatic William, who did neither the one nor the other.' *Works*, xiv. 210 *n.*

[5] In his *Dedication of the Georgics*, he writes of the Court:—'It is necessary for the polishing of manners to have breathed that air; but it is infectious, even to the best morals, to live always in it. . . . I commend not him who never knew a Court, but him who forsakes it because he knows it.' *Works*, xiv. 8. In the *Dedication of the Aeneis*, he says that Virgil 'proves that it is possible for a courtier not to be a knave.' *Ib.* p. 158. See *post*, DRYDEN, 183.

and was to look back for support to his former trade[1]; and having waited about two years, either considering himself as discountenanced by the publick, or perhaps expecting a second revolution, he produced *Don Sebastian* in 1690[2]; and in the next four years four dramas more[3].

In 1693 appeared a new version of Juvenal and Persius[4]. Of 140 Juvenal he translated the first, third, sixth, tenth, and sixteenth satires, and of Persius the whole work[5]. On this occasion he introduced his two sons to the publick, as nurselings of the Muses. The fourteenth of Juvenal was the work of John, and the seventh of Charles Dryden[6]. He prefixed a very ample preface in the form of a dedication to lord Dorset[7]; and there gives an account of the design which he had once formed to write an epick poem on the actions either of Arthur or the Black Prince[8]. He considered the epick as necessarily including some kind of supernatural agency, and had imagined a new kind of contest between the guardian angels of kingdoms, of whom he conceived that each might be represented zealous for his charge, without any intended opposition to the purposes of the Supreme Being, of which all created minds must in part be ignorant[9].

This is the most reasonable scheme of celestial interposition 141 that ever was formed. The surprises and terrors of enchantments, which have succeeded to the intrigues and oppositions of pagan deities, afford very striking scenes, and open a vast extent to the imagination; but, as Boileau observes, and Boileau will be seldom found mistaken[10], with this incurable defect, that in

---

[1] In the Preface to *Don Sebastian* he says that 'his misfortunes have once more brought him, against his will, upon the stage.' *Works*, vii. 306. See also *ib.* viii. 221.

Montagu, in his poem on *His Majesty's Victory in Ireland* (*post*, HALIFAX, 6), asks what poet shall celebrate it :—
'But who is equal to sustain the part ?
D—n has numbers, but he wants a heart ;
Enjoin'd a penance, which is too severe,
For playing once the fool, to persevere.' *Eng. Poets*, xxvi. 299.
[2] *Ante*, DRYDEN, 82.
[3] *Ante*, DRYDEN, 83, 84, 85, 86.

[4] *Works*, xiii. 124 ; *ante*, DRYDEN, 77 ; *post*, DRYDEN, 299 ; DUKE, 2. The title-page bears the date of 1693; but according to Malone (i. 221) it was published in Sept. 1692.
[5] *Works*, xiii. 211 ; *post*, DRYDEN, 301.
[6] *Post*, DRYDEN, 157.
[7] Entitled *An Essay on Satire.* *Works*, xiii. 1. It is in this Essay that 'he lavished his blandishments' on Dorset. *Ante*, DORSET, 14.
[8] *Works*, xiii. 24-31 ; *ante*, MILTON, 86 ; *post*, POPE, 241.
[9] *Works*, xiii. 26.
[10] 'Boileau's example alone is a sufficient authority.' DRYDEN, *Works*, xiii. 110.

a contest between heaven and hell we know at the beginning which is to prevail[1]: for this reason we follow Rinaldo to the enchanted wood with more curiosity than terror[2].

142   In the scheme of Dryden there is one great difficulty, which yet he would perhaps have had address enough to surmount. In a war justice can be but on one side, and to entitle the hero to the protection of angels he must fight in the defence of indubitable right. Yet some of the celestial beings, thus opposed to each other, must have been represented as defending guilt.

143   That this poem was never written is reasonably to be lamented. It would doubtless have improved our numbers and enlarged our language, and might perhaps have contributed by pleasing instruction to rectify our opinions and purify our manners.

144   What he required as the indispensable condition of such an undertaking, a publick stipend, was not likely in those times to be obtained. Riches were not become familiar to us, nor had the nation yet learned to be liberal[3].

145   This plan he charged Blackmore with stealing; 'only,' says he, 'the guardian angels of kingdoms were machines too ponderous for him to manage[4].'

146   In 1694 he began the most laborious and difficult of all his works, the translation of Virgil[5]; from which he borrowed two months[6], that he might turn Fresnoy's *Art of Painting* into

[1] 'Neither will Virgil's machines [*ante*, MILTON, 222] be of any service to a Christian poet. We see how ineffectually they have been tried by Tasso and by Ariosto. . . . Boileau has well observed that it is an easy matter in a Christian poem for God to bring the Devil to reason.' DRYDEN, *Works*, xviii. 116. See also *ib.* xiii. 24; Boileau's *L'Art Poétique*, iii. 193: *ante*, MILTON, 247 *n.*

[2] In Tasso's *Ger. Lib.* canto xviii.

[3] 'Being encouraged only with fair words by King Charles II, my little salary ill paid, and no prospect of a future subsistence, I was then discouraged in the beginning of my attempt; and now age has overtaken me, and want, a more insufferable evil, through the change of the times, has wholly disenabled me.' *Works*, xiii. 31.

'And Dryden, in immortal strain,
Had raised the Table Round again,

But that a ribald King and Court
Bade him toil on to make them
   sport.'
   Marmion, canto i, Introduction.
See *ante*, BUTLER, 16; OTWAY, 14; DRYDEN, 85 *n.*

[4] *Works*, xi. 241. See *post*, BLACKMORE, 7, 11.

[5] Evelyn recorded on Jan. 11, 1693-4:—'Supped at Mr. Edward Sheldon's, where was Mr. Dryden, the poet, who now intended to write no more plays, being intent on his translation of Virgil. He read his Prologue and Epilogue to his valedictory play now shortly to be acted.' *Diary*, ii. 339. For the Prologue and Epilogue to *Love Triumphant* (*ante*, DRYDEN, 86) see *Works*, viii. 378, 475. In the Prologue he says:—
'He dies, at least to us and to the
   stage.'

[6] *Works*, xvii. 291.

English prose [1]. The preface, which he boasts to have written in twelve mornings [2], exhibits a parallel of poetry and painting [3], with a miscellaneous collection of critical remarks, such as cost a mind stored like his no labour to produce them.

In 1697 he published his version of the works of Virgil [4], and, 147 that no opportunity of profit might be lost, dedicated the *Pastorals* to the lord Clifford [5], the *Georgicks* to the earl of Chesterfield [6], and the *Eneid* to the earl of Mulgrave [7]. This œconomy of flattery, at once lavish and discreet, did not pass without observation [8].

[1] Du Fresnoy died in 1665. His poem *De Arte Graphica* appeared in 1668. See Reynolds's *Works*, 1824, iii. 13, for a brief Life of him prefixed to Mason's verse translation of it, and *ib.* p. 91 for Sir Joshua's critical notes. Pope, in his *Epistle to Mr. Jervas, with Mr. Dryden's Translation of Fresnoy's Art of Painting* (*post*, POPE, 69), bids his friend
'Read these instructive leaves, in which conspire
Fresnoy's close art, and Dryden's native fire.'

[2] 'Perhaps the judges of painting and poetry, when I tell them how short a time it cost me, may make me the same answer which my Lord Rochester made to one who, to commend a tragedy, said it was written in three weeks:—"How the devil could he be so long about it?"' *Works*, xvii. 334.

[3] *Ib.* xiv. 214.

[4] *Post*, DRYDEN, 227 *n.*, 303-13. According to Pope 'he cleared every way about £1,200 by his *Virgil.*' Spence's *Anec.* p. 262. Malone (i. 237) estimates his share by the sale at £1,396. For the list of subscribers see *Works*, xiii. 277.

[5] He tells Clifford that the chronicles make 'so honourable mention' of the humanity of his ancient house in the Wars of the Roses. *Works*, xiii. 325. Shakespeare's 'fell Clifford' knew nothing of humanity.

[6] *Ib.* xiv. 1. It was the second Earl, grandfather of the famous Earl. Dryden wrote to him on Feb. 17, 1696, that he had deferred the publication 'in hopes of his return for whom for my conscience I have suffered

[James II] that I might have laid my author at his feet.' Cunningham, *Lives of the Poets*, i. 393. [For an example of Dryden's attacks on William III in his *Virgil* see T. Moore's *Memoirs*, 1854, v. 285, where Lord Holland cites the translation of 'Pulsatusve parens' [*Aen.* vi. 609], which Dryden renders (l. 825), 'expel their parents, and usurp the throne.' See also *N. & Q.* 2 S. x. 263, for other allusions to William III and the Dutch. Thus the contrast in the *Fourth Georgic* between the rivals for the royal rank among the bees as translated by Dryden evidently refers to James and William; especially where, in order to produce a likeness to William III, he renders
'ille horridus alter
Desidia latamque trahens inglorius alvum' (l. 93),
'Gaunt are his sides and sullen is his face.' l. 144.
Again, in the *Third Georgic*, Dryden translates
'Talis Hyperboreo septem subiecta trioni
Gens effrena virum Rhipaeo tunditur Euro' (ll. 381-2),
'Such are the cold Rhipaean race, and such
The savage Scythian and unwarlike Dutch. ll. 586-7.]

[7] *Works*, xiv. 129; *post*, SHEFFIELD.

[8] 'I confess to have been somewhat liberal in the business of titles. ... Our famous Dryden has ventured to proceed a point further, endeavouring to introduce also a multiplicity of god-fathers; which is an improvement of much more advantage upon a very obvious account.' SWIFT, *A*

148　This translation was censured by Milbourne, a clergyman, styled by Pope 'the fairest of criticks,' because he exhibited his own version to be compared with that which he condemned [1].

149　His last work was his *Fables*, published in 1699 [2], in consequence, as is supposed, of a contract now in the hands of Mr. Tonson, by which he obliged himself, in consideration of three hundred pounds, to finish for the press ten thousand verses [3].

150　In this volume is comprised the well-known *Ode on St. Cecilia's Day* [4], which, as appeared by a letter communicated to Dr. Birch, he spent a fortnight in composing and correcting [5]. But what is this to the patience and diligence of Boileau, whose *Equivoque*, a poem of only three hundred forty-six lines, took from his life eleven months to write it, and three years to revise it [6]!

151　Part of this book of *Fables* is the first *Iliad* in English, intended as a specimen of a version of the whole [7]. Considering into what

Tale of a Tub, Introduction, *Works*, x. 75.

[1] In a note to *The Dunciad*, ii. 349, he is described as 'the fairest of critics, who, when he wrote against Mr. Dryden's *Virgil*, did him justice in printing at the same time his own translations of him, which were intolerable.' See *post*, DRYDEN, 175, 178, 306, 357.

Luke Milbourne published his *Notes on Dryden's Virgil* in 1698.

[2] *Fables Ancient and Modern. Translated into Verse from Homer, Ovid, Boccace and Chaucer. With Original Poems.* By Mr. Dryden. 1700. *Works*, xi. 196. They were published early in March 1699-1700. *Ib.* xviii. 176; *post*, DRYDEN, 314; POPE, 17.

[3] *Post*, DRYDEN, 184-87.

[4] *Alexander's Feast*, his second ode for St. Cecilia's Day. *Works*, xi. 186; *post*, DRYDEN, 279, 318, 406; POPE, 320.

It was sung on Nov. 22 (St. Cecilia's Day), 1697, and published separately in folio in December. Malone's *Dryden*, i. 254. For a list of these odes see *ib.* p. 276, and for an account of the festival see *ib.* p. 280. See also *post*, HUGHES, 6; CONGREVE, 39.

[5] 'The letter, it is believed, does not exist.' Cunningham's *Lives of the Poets*, i. 319.

Dr. Warton tells the following

story which passed down to him from Bolingbroke through Pope and two other men: 'Mr. St. John [Bolingbroke], paying a morning visit to Dryden, found him in an unusual agitation of spirits, even to a trembling: "I have been up all night," he said; " my musical friends made me promise to write them an ode for St. Cecilia. I have been so struck with the subject which occurred to me that I could not leave it till I had completed it; here it is, finished at one sitting."' *Essay on Pope*, ii. 83.

There must be much exaggeration in this story. It might have been true of Dryden's shorter *Ode to St. Cecilia*, had not St. John been a child when it was written. For his visiting Dryden see *post*, DRYDEN, 187. ' It is possible,' writes Scott, ' that Dryden may have completed, at one sitting, the whole Ode, and yet have spent a fortnight in correction.' *Works*, i. 342. See also *post*, DRYDEN, 319.

[6] *Œuvres de Boileau*, i. 233 *n*. His diligence did not satisfy Voltaire, who says of this satire:—'Il eût pu la mieux faire; mais il y a des vers dignes de lui que l'on cite tous les jours.' *Œuvres*, xxxiii. 71.

[7] *Works*, xii. 376. He translated also the parting of Hector and Andromache. *Ib.* p. 402. 'I find him,' he wrote, 'a poet more according to

hands Homer was to fall, the reader cannot but rejoice that this project went no further [1].

The time was now at hand which was to put an end to all his 152 schemes and labours. On the first of May, 1701 [2], having been some time, as he tells us, a cripple in his limbs [3], he died in Gerard-street [4] of a mortification in his leg [5].

There is extant a wild story relating to some vexatious events 153 that happened at his funeral, which, at the end of *Congreve's Life*, by a writer of I know not what credit, are thus related, as I find the account transferred to a biographical dictionary [6] :

my genius than Virgil.' *Ib.* xviii. 160. He plays the buffoon in the last lines of book i—
    ' The thundering God,
Even he, withdrew to rest, and had his load ;
His swimming head to needful rest applied,
And Juno lay unheeded by his side.'
    [1] ' Had Mr. Dryden translated the whole work, I would no more have attempted Homer after him than Virgil.' *Preface to the Iliad*, ed. 1760, p. 51.
    [2] Dryden died on May 1, 1700. The first announcement of his illness Malone found in *The Post-Boy* of April 30—' John Dryden, Esq., the famous poet, lies a dying.' Malone adds that Johnson was misled as to the date by the *General Dict.* and the *Biog. Brit.*, which followed Pope (see his note to his epitaph on Rowe) in giving the date as 1701. Malone's *Dryden*, i. 336. For Pope's note see Warburton's *Pope*, vi. 77.
    [3] On April 11, 1700, he wrote :—' All this while I am lame at home, and have not stirred abroad this month at least.' *Works*, xviii. 178.
    [4] ' My house,' wrote Dryden, ' is in Gerard Street, the fifth door on the left hand coming from Newport Street.' *Ib.* xviii. 143. ' His best prospect,' he wrote, ' is on the garden of Leicester House.' *Ib.* vii. 303. According to Pope, ' he used most commonly to write in the ground room next the street.' Spence's *Anec.* p. 260. The house was No. 43. Wheatley's *London*, ii. 105. It has recently

been taken down. It was at the Turk's Head in this street that the Literary Club at one time met. Boswell's *Johnson*, i. 478 *n*. Burke's house, No. 37, is the present Hôtel des Étrangers.
    [5] He refused to submit to amputation. *Works*, i. 367. ' Dryden was generally an extreme sober man. For the last ten years of his life he was much acquainted with Addison, and drank with him more than he ever used to do ; probably so as to hasten his end.' DENNIS, Spence's *Anec.* p. 45. [They could not have been intimate more than six years, from 1693, when Addison was twenty-two, to 1699, when he left England, not to return until after Dryden's death in 1700.] For Addison's drinking see *post*, ADDISON, 117.
    [6] *Biog. Brit.* 1750, p. 1759. This *Life of Congreve* was published by the infamous Curll (*post*, POPE, 162) in 1730. The account is given on p. 1 of the second part. ' Charles Wilson, Esq. (the author on the title-page), is probably a fictitious person.' The Appendix (referred to *post*, DRYDEN, 191) written by Elizabeth Thomas, ' who had been honoured by Dryden with the title of Corinna, is a tissue of falsehoods. She wrote it in the Fleet Prison.' Malone's *Dryden*, i. 347. See *ib.* i. 362 *n*. for ' the audacity of this woman in publishing this false and ridiculous account of Dryden's funeral, at a time when Southerne, and probably many others who had walked at it, were yet living.' See also *post*, POPE, 29 ; *N. & Q.* 8 S. v. 322, 382, 463.

'Mr. Dryden dying on the Wednesday morning, Dr. Thomas Sprat, then bishop of Rochester and dean of Westminster, sent the next day to the lady Elizabeth Howard, Mr. Dryden's widow, that he would make a present of the ground, which was forty pounds, with all the other Abbey-fees. The lord Halifax likewise sent to the lady Elizabeth and Mr. Charles Dryden her son, that if they would give him leave to bury Mr. Dryden he would inter him with a gentleman's private funeral, and afterwards bestow five hundred pounds on a monument in the Abbey; which, as they had no reason to refuse, they accepted. On the Saturday following the company came: the corpse was put into a velvet hearse, and eighteen mourning coaches filled with company attended. When they were just ready to move the lord Jefferies, son of the lord chancellor Jefferies, with some of his rakish companions coming by, asked whose funeral it was, and being told Mr. Dryden's he said, "What, shall Dryden, the greatest honour and ornament of the nation, be buried after this private manner! No, gentlemen, let all that loved Mr. Dryden and honour his memory alight and join with me in gaining my lady's consent to let me have the honour of his interment, which shall be after another manner than this; and I will bestow a thousand pounds on a monument in the Abbey for him." The gentlemen in the coaches, not knowing of the bishop of Rochester's favour, nor of the lord Halifax's generous design (they both having, out of respect to the family, enjoined the lady Elizabeth and her son to keep their favour concealed to the world, and let it pass for their own expence), readily came out of the coaches, and attended lord Jefferies up to the lady's bedside, who was then sick; he repeated the purport of what he had before said; but she absolutely refusing, he fell on his knees, vowing never to rise till his request was granted. The rest of the company by his desire kneeled also; and the lady, being under a sudden surprise, fainted away. As soon as she recovered her speech, she cried, "No, no." "Enough, gentlemen," replied he; "my lady is very good, she says, 'Go, go.'" She repeated her former words with all her strength, but in vain; for her feeble voice was lost in their acclamations of joy: and the lord Jefferies ordered the hearsemen to carry the corpse to Mr. Russel's, an undertaker's in Cheapside[1], and leave it there till he should send orders for the embalment,

---

[1] For his bill for the funeral see *Works*, xviii. 204.

Garth, in *The Dispensary*, makes an apothecary describe himself and his brethren as we

'Who baffle nature, and dispose of
  lives,   [starves, or thrives.'
Whilst Russel, as we please, or
  Eng. Poets, xxviii. 44.

Prior, in *Alma*, iii. 290 (*ib.* xxxiii. 186), describes how Alma

'Soon ceases all the worldly bustle,
And you consign the corpse to
  Russel.'

Granville in a Prologue says:—

'Not even Russel can inter the dead.'
            Ib. xxxviii. 126.

which, he added, should be after the royal manner. His directions were obeyed, the company dispersed, and lady Elizabeth and her son remained inconsolable. The next day Mr. Charles Dryden waited on the lord Halifax and the bishop, to excuse his mother and himself by relating the real truth. But neither his lordship nor the bishop would admit of any plea; especially the latter, who had the Abbey lighted, the ground opened, the choir attending, an anthem ready set, and himself waiting for some time without any corpse to bury. The undertaker, after three days' expectance of orders for embalment without receiving any, waited on the lord Jefferies, who, pretending ignorance of the matter, turned it off with an ill-natured jest, saying, "That those who observed the orders of a drunken frolick deserved no better; that he remembered nothing at all of it; and that he might do what he pleased with the corpse." Upon this, the undertaker waited upon the lady Elizabeth and her son, and threatened to bring the corpse home, and set it before the door. They desired a day's respite, which was granted. Mr. Charles Dryden wrote a handsome letter to the lord Jefferies, who returned it with this cool answer, "That he knew nothing of the matter, and would be troubled no more about it." He then addressed the lord Halifax and the bishop of Rochester, who absolutely refused to do any thing in it. In this distress Dr. Garth sent for the corpse to the College of Physicians, and proposed a funeral by subscription, to which himself set a most noble example. At last a day, about three weeks after Mr. Dryden's decease, was appointed for the interment: Dr. Garth pronounced a fine Latin oration at the College over the corpse[1]; which was attended to the Abbey by a numerous train of coaches. When the funeral was over Mr. Charles Dryden sent a challenge to the lord Jefferies, who refusing to answer it, he sent several others, and went often himself; but could neither get a letter delivered nor admittance to speak to him: which so incensed him that he resolved, since his lordship refused to answer him like a gentleman, that he would watch an opportunity to meet and fight off-hand, though with all the rules of honour; which his lordship hearing, left the town: and Mr. Charles Dryden could never have the satisfaction of meeting

---

[1] Hearne recorded in 1726 that in this oration 'Dr. Garth did not mention one word of Jesus Christ, but made an oration as an apostrophe to the great god Apollo, to influence the minds of the audience with a wise, but, without doubt, poetical understanding, and, as a conclusion, instead of a psalm of David, repeated the 30th ode of the third book of Horace, beginning *Exegi monumen-* *tum*. He made a great many blunders in the pronunciation.' Hearne's *Remains*, ii. 267. According to Farquhar, 'the oration was great and ingenious, worthy the subject, and like the author, whose prescriptions can restore the living, and his pen embalm the dead.' Malone's *Dryden*, i. 363. For Garth's 'irreligion' see *post*, GARTH, 15.

him, though he sought it till his death with the utmost application[1].'

154   This story I once intended to omit as it appears with no great
evidence ; nor have I met with any confirmation but in a letter
of Farquhar, and he only relates that the funeral of Dryden was
tumultuary and confused[2].

155   Supposing the story true we may remark that the gradual
change of manners, though imperceptible in the process, appears
great when different times, and those not very distant, are compared.   If at this time a young drunken Lord should interrupt
the pompous regularity of a magnificent funeral what would be
the event, but that he would be justled out of the way, and
compelled to be quiet ?   If he should thrust himself into a house,
he would be sent roughly away ; and what is yet more to the
honour of the present time, I believe that those who had subscribed to the funeral of a man like Dryden would not, for such
an accident, have withdrawn their contributions.

[1] According to Malone (i. 368)
Lord Halifax was burying the body
at his own expense.   Lords Dorset,
Jeffreys, and others prevailed on the
relations to have it embalmed, and
on the President of the College of
Physicians to have it deposited there,
till a funeral in the Abbey was
arranged, for which a subscription
was raised.   The body lay in state
ten days, and on May 13 was carried
to the Abbey, after a Latin oration
by Garth, and the singing of an Ode
of Horace in the Theatre of the
College.   There is no foundation for
the story of the drunken frolic and
of the quarrel between Jeffreys and
C. Dryden.   Jeffreys, the only son of
the infamous Chancellor, was a writer
of verse. He died, without male issue,
in 1703.'   Malone's *Dryden*, i. 368.

Pope attacked Halifax for his share
in the funeral : —
' He help'd to bury whom he help'd
    to starve.'   *Prol. Sat.* l. 248.
As Chancellor of the Exchequer
'he help'd to starve' him by not
giving him a pension. See also
Luttrell's *Diary*, iv. 645.

[2] In the first edition the sentence
after 'evidence' ran as follows :—
' but having been since informed
that there is in the register of the

College of Physicians an order relating to Dryden's funeral, I can doubt
its truth no longer.'   In the Preface
to the first edition Johnson says :—
' I had been told that in the College
of Physicians there is some memorial
of Dryden's funeral, but my intelligence was not true ; the story therefore wants the credit which such
a testimony would have given it.
There is in Farquhar's *Letters* an
indistinct mention of it as irregular
and disorderly, and of the oration
which was then spoken.   More than
this I have not discovered.'

Farquhar ridiculed the mixed ceremony—'the Ode of Horace sung
instead of David's Psalms. . . . The
pomp of the ceremony was a kind of
rhapsody, and fitter, I think, for
Hudibras than him. . . . The quality
and mob, farce and heroics ; the
sublime and ridicule mixed in a
piece' [Farquhar's *Works*, 3rd ed.
pt. i. 53].   Malone's *Dryden*, i. 363 ;
Works, i. 368 *n*.

In the Register of the College is
an entry on May 3, granting 'the
request of several persons of quality'
for the reception of the body.   Malone's *Dryden*, i. 372.   For an
account of the funeral see *Gent
Mag.* 1786, i. 291.

He was buried among the poets in Westminster Abbey, where, 156
though the duke of Newcastle had, in a general dedication
prefixed by Congreve to his dramatick works, accepted thanks for
his intention of erecting him a monument [1], he lay long without
distinction, till the duke of Buckinghamshire gave him a tablet,
inscribed only with the name of DRYDEN [2].

He married the lady Elizabeth Howard, daughter of the earl 157
of Berkshire [3], with circumstances, according to the satire imputed
to lord Somers, not very honourable to either party [4]: by her he
had three sons, Charles, John, and Henry. Charles was usher
of the palace to Pope Clement the XIth [5], and visiting England
in 1704, was drowned in an attempt to swim across the Thames
at Windsor.

John was author of a comedy called *The Husband his own* 158
Cuckold [6]. He is said to have died at Rome. Henry entered

---

[1] For Congreve's Dedication see
Dryden's *Works*, ii. 13. Garth
wrote in 1717:—'Mr. Dryden, who
could make kings immortal, now
wants a poor square foot of stone.'
End of Preface to Ovid's *Metamorphoses*. Pope (*post*, POPE, 408), in
his epitaph for Rowe, says of Dryden:—
'Beneath a rude and nameless stone
    he lies.
    .   .   .   .   .
One grateful woman to thy fame
    supplies
What a whole thankless land to his
    denies.'
See also Pope's Preface to *Miscellanies in Prose* for his warning
against 'venting praise or censure
too precipitately.' Swift's *Works*,
xiii. 6.

[2] The inscription is 'J. Dryden,
Natus 1632. Mortuus May 1, 1700.
Joannes Sheffield, Dux Bucking-
hamiensis Posuit 1720.' Malone's
Dryden, i. 6; Part ii. 133. In 1720
Atterbury wrote to Pope of 'your
design of fixing Dryden's name only
below, and his bust above.' Pope's
Works (Elwin and Courthope), ix.
22. For the year of his birth see
ante, DRYDEN, 2.

[3] In St. Swithin's Church, Cannon
Street, 'the last leaf of a mouldering
register records Dec. 1, 1663,' Dry-

den's marriage. Wheatley's *London*,
iii. 343. His wife was sister of Sir
Robert Howard (*ante*, DRYDEN, 25)
and of Edward Howard (*ante*, DOR-
SET, 15). She died insane in 1714.
Works, i. 387. 'Dryden's invectives
against the marriage state are fre-
quent and bitter.' Malone's *Dryden*,
i. 393. In his last year he writes to
John Driden, who was 'uncumbered
with a wife':—
'Minds are so hardly matched that
    even the first,
Though paired by Heaven, in Para-
    dise were cursed.' *Works*, xi. 73.
[4] 'After two children and a third
    miscarriage,
By brawny brothers hector'd into
    marriage.'
Satyr to his Muse, p. 4; *ante*, DRY-
DEN, 112.
For the lampoons on Dryden see
Malone's *Dryden*, i. 161.
[5] Dryden addressed his son as
'Camariere d'Honore [*sic*], A.S.S.'
When he was ill Dryden wrote :—'If
it please God that I must die of over-
study I cannot spend my life better
than in saving his.' *Works*, xviii.
140. For verses by him see Nichols's
Select Collection of Poetry, 1780, i.
56; iv. 293.
[6] Dryden wrote the Epilogue (*ib.*
x. 425) and Congreve the Prologue,
which ends :—

into some religious order[1]. It is some proof of Dryden's sincerity in his second religion, that he taught it to his sons. A man conscious of hypocritical profession in himself is not likely to convert others; and as his sons were qualified in 1693 to appear among the translators of Juvenal[2], they must have been taught some religion before their father's change.

159		Of the person of Dryden I know not any account[3]; of his mind the portrait which has been left by Congreve[4], who knew him with great familiarity, is such as adds our love of his manners to our admiration of his genius.

'He was,' we are told, 'of a nature exceedingly humane and compassionate, ready to forgive injuries, and capable of a sincere reconciliation with those that had offended him[5]. His friendship, where he professed it, went beyond his professions. He was of a very easy, of very pleasing access; but somewhat slow, and, as it were, diffident in his advances to others: he had that in his nature which abhorred intrusion into any society whatever. He was therefore less known, and consequently his character became more liable to misapprehensions and misrepresentations: he

'There's his last refuge; if the play don't take,
	Yet spare young Dryden for his father's sake.'
			Eng. Poets, xxxiv. 216.
Dryden also wrote the Preface, when the play was printed, and bargained with the publisher. *Works*, xv. 409; xviii. 127. For his letters to Dr. Busby about his sons see *ib.* xviii. 99–102.

[1] His name was Erasmus Henry. 'He was a Captain in the Pope's Guards.' In 1710 he succeeded to the title of Baronet; he died the same year. None of the brothers married. '"All of them," says a good judge, who knew them, "were fine, ingenious and accomplished gentlemen."' Malone's *Dryden*, i. 399, 426.
Johnson's account is from *Biog. Brit.* p. 1761 *n.*

[2] *Ante*, DRYDEN, 140.

[3] 'There are,' writes Malone, 'few English poets of whose external appearance more particulars have been recorded.' From satires of the time Malone quotes such epithets as 'learned and florid'; 'cherry-cheeked dunce'; 'a fat rosy-coloured

fellow.' He had 'a sleepy eye,' and 'a large mole on his right cheek, which all his portraits exhibit.' Malone's *Dryden*, i. 430–7. 'In the *State Poems* he is "Poet-Squab, a short, thick man."' Prior's *Malone*, p. 254.
'He was not a very genteel man, he was intimate with none but poetical men. He was as plump as Mr. Pitt; of a fresh colour, and a down look, and not very conversable.' POPE, Spence's *Anec.* p. 261.

[4] For a correct version of what Congreve wrote see Appendix T.

[5] Addison, who knew Dryden well, says in *The Spectator*, No. 169:—
'The greatest wits I have conversed with are men eminent for their humanity.'
Beattie, in his *Essays*, 1779, p. 14, reproaches him for his inhumanity in a passage where he says that many of Chaucer's words no more merit reviving 'than the crowds of men who daily die, or are slain for sixpence in a battle, merit to be restored to life, if a wish could revive them.' *Works*, xv. 188. For another instance of his inhumanity see *ante*, DRYDEN, 122 *n.*

was very modest, and very easily to be discountenanced in his approaches to his equals or superiors [1]. As his reading had been very extensive, so was he very happy in a memory tenacious of every thing that he had read. He was not more possessed of knowledge than he was communicative of it; but then his communication was by no means pedantick or imposed upon the conversation, but just such, and went so far as, by the natural turn of the conversation in which he was engaged, it was necessarily promoted or required. He was extreme ready, and gentle in his correction of the errors of any writer who thought fit to consult him, and full as ready and patient to admit of the reprehensions of others in respect of his own oversights or mistakes.'

To this account of Congreve nothing can be objected but the 160 fondness of friendship; and to have excited that fondness in such a mind is no small degree of praise [2]. The disposition of Dryden, however, is shewn in this character rather as it exhibited itself in cursory conversation, than as it operated on the more important parts of life. His placability and his friendship indeed were solid virtues; but courtesy and good-humour are often found with little real worth. Since Congreve, who knew him well, has told us no more, the rest must be collected as it can from other testimonies, and particularly from those notices which Dryden has very liberally given us of himself.

The modesty which made him so slow to advance, and so easy 161 to be repulsed, was certainly no suspicion of deficient merit, or unconsciousness of his own value: he appears to have known in its whole extent the dignity of his character, and to have set a very high value on his own powers and performances [3]. He probably did not offer his conversation, because he expected it to be solicited; and he retired from a cold reception, not submissive but indignant, with such reverence of his own greatness as made him unwilling to expose it to neglect or violation.

[1] He wrote in 1679:—'For my own part I never could shake off the rustic bashfulness which hangs upon my nature.' *Works*, vi. 249.

[2] Dryden, seven years before his death, in his *Epistle to My Dear Friend Mr. Congreve* (*Works*, xi. 60), wrote:—
'But you whom every muse and grace adorn,
Whom I foresee to better fortune born,

Be kind to my remains; and O defend,
Against your judgment, your departed friend.'

[3] Johnson speaks of Milton's 'high opinion of his own powers' (*ante*, MILTON, 47), and of Addison's 'very high opinion of his own merit' (*post*, ADDISON, 109). Dryden, the year before his death, wrote to a lady:—
'I am still drudging on; always a poet, and never a good one.' *Works*, xviii. 147. See also *post*, POPE, 20.

162   His modesty was by no means inconsistent with ostentatious-
ness : he is diligent enough to remind the world of his merit, and
expresses with very little scruple his high opinion of his own
powers ; but his self-commendations[1] are read without scorn or
indignation : we allow his claims, and love his frankness[2].

163   Tradition, however, has not allowed that his confidence in
himself exempted him from jealousy of others[3].   He is accused
of envy and insidiousness ; and is particularly charged with
inciting Creech to translate Horace, that he might lose the
reputation which Lucretius had given him[4].

164   Of this charge we immediately discover that it is merely
conjectural : the purpose was such as no man would confess ;
and a crime that admits no proof, why should we believe?

165   He has been described as magisterially presiding over the
younger writers, and assuming the distribution of poetical fame ;
but he who excels has a right to teach, and he whose judgement
is incontestable may, without usurpation, examine and decide[5].

166   Congreve represents him as ready to advise and instruct ; but
there is reason to believe that his communication was rather

[1] *Ante*, DRYDEN, 102.
[2] *Post*, DRYDEN, 214.
[3] 'BAYES. I despise your Jonson
and Beaumont, that borrowed all
they writ from Nature ; I am for
fetching it purely out of my own
fancy.'
  'SMITH. But what think you of
Sir John Suckling, Sir ?
  'BAYES. By gad, I am a better
poet than he.' *The Rehearsal*, p. 51.
  'Even Dryden,' said Jacob Tonson, 'was very suspicious of rivals.
He would compliment Crowne, when
a play of his failed, but was cold to
him if he met with success.   He
used sometimes to own that Crowne
had some genius ; but then added
that his father and Crowne's mother
were very well acquainted.' Spence's
Anec. p. 45.
  For a comedy, by John Crowne,
'acted at Court by the ladies only,'
in 1674, see Evelyn's *Diary*, ii. 100.
[4] Malone (i. 506) traces this slander
to Tom Brown's *Reasons of Mr.
Bayes's changing his Religion*, Part
ii. 53 (*ante*, DRYDEN, 128 ; quoted
in the *Works*, viii. 223 n.).   To a reprint of Creech's *Lucretius* had been

prefixed some anonymous recom-
mendatory verses, assigned by Wood
(*Ath. Oxon.* iv. 739) to Dryden
among other writers.   Lines so poor
could not have been by him.   For
them see *Works*, xviii. 323 ; *N. & Q.*
6 S. iv. 24.   When Creech hanged
himself (in June, 1700) 'the act was
ascribed by some writers to the ill
success of his *Horace* (published 16
years earlier) ; and it was insinuated
that Dryden was ultimately the cause
of his end.'   His *Horace* had reached
two editions.   Creech, in the Preface,
says to Dryden :—'You are ready to
reach out a helping hand to all those
who endeavour to climb that height
where you are already seated.'   For
Dryden's praise of Creech see *Works*,
viii. 223 ; xii. 296 ; xiv. 218, and for
Creech see *post*, DRYDEN, 300.
[5] Dennis wrote to him in 1694 :—
'You with a breath can bestow or
confirm reputation ; a whole num-
berless people proclaims the praise
which you give, and the judgments
of three mighty kingdoms appear to
depend upon yours.' *Works*, xviii.
114.   See *post*, DRYDEN, 190.

useful than entertaining. He declares of himself that he was saturnine, and not one of those whose spritely sayings diverted company[1]; and one of his censurers makes him say,

> 'Nor wine nor love [Nor love nor wine] could ever see me gay;
> To writing bred, I knew not what to say[2].'

There are men whose powers operate only at leisure and in retirement, and whose intellectual vigour deserts them in conversation; whom merriment confuses, and objection disconcerts; whose bashfulness restrains their exertion, and suffers them not to speak till the time of speaking is past; or whose attention to their own character makes them unwilling to utter at hazard what has not been considered, and cannot be recalled. **167**

Of Dryden's sluggishness in conversation it is vain to search or to guess the cause. He certainly wanted neither sentiments nor language; his intellectual treasures were great, though they were locked up from his own use. 'His thoughts,' when he wrote, 'flowed in upon him so fast, that his only care was which to chuse, and which to reject[3].' Such rapidity of composition naturally promises a flow of talk, yet we must be content to believe what an enemy says of him, when he likewise says it of himself. But whatever was his character as a companion, it appears that he lived in familiarity with the highest persons of his time. It is related by Carte of the duke of Ormond that he used often to pass a night with Dryden, and those with whom Dryden consorted[4]: who they were Carte has not told; **168**

---

[1] 'My conversation is slow and dull, my humour saturnine and reserved; in short, I am none of those who endeavour to break jests in company or make repartees.' *Works*, ii. 297. 'That I admire not any comedy equally with tragedy is perhaps from the sullenness of my humour.' *Ib.* iii. 240. 'One sprightly saying of his' to his wife ['I wish I were a book and then I should have more of your company.' 'Pray my dear, if you do become a book let it be an almanac, for then I shall change you every year'] related by Horace Walpole (Prior's *Malone*, p. 436), Mr. Saintsbury has found in a French work most of which was written before his marriage. *Works*, i. 382 *n.* For Pope's want of 'vivacity

in company' see *post*, POPE, 264.

[2] In *Satyr to his Muse*, p. 4; *ante*, DRYDEN, 12.

[3] 'Thoughts, such as they are, come crowding in so fast upon me that my only difficulty is to choose or to reject.' *Works*, xi. 213.

[4] 'Once in a quarter of a year he used to have the Marquis of Halifax, the Earls of Mulgrave, Dorset, and Danby, Mr. Dryden, and others of that set of men at supper, and then they were merry, and drank hard.' Carte's *Life of Ormond*, 1851, iv. 699.

Of Carte's *Life of Ormond*, Johnson said that 'two good volumes in duodecimo might be made out of the two in folio.' Boswell's *Johnson*, v. 296. It was reprinted in Oxford

but certainly the convivial table at which Ormond sat was not surrounded with a plebeian society. He was indeed reproached with boasting of his familiarity with the great ; and Horace will support him in the opinion that to please superiors is not the lowest kind of merit [1].

169 The merit of pleasing must, however, be estimated by the means. Favour is not always gained by good actions or laudable qualities. Caresses and preferments are often bestowed on the auxiliaries of vice, the procurers of pleasure, or the flatterers of vanity. Dryden has never been charged with any personal agency unworthy of a good character: he abetted vice and vanity only with his pen. One of his enemies has accused him of lewdness in his conversation [2]; but if accusation without proof be credited, who shall be innocent [3] ?

170 His works afford too many examples of dissolute licentiousness and abject adulation ; but they were probably, like his merriment, artificial and constrained—the effects of study and meditation, and his trade rather than his pleasure [4].

171 Of the mind that can trade in corruption, and can deliberately pollute itself with ideal wickedness for the sake of spreading the contagion in society, I wish not to conceal or excuse the depravity. —Such degradation of the dignity of genius, such abuse of superlative abilities, cannot be contemplated but with grief and

in 1851 in six volumes octavo—without an index.

Dryden dedicated his *Plutarch* to the first Duke and his *Fables* to the second Duke. *Works*, xi. 197 ; xvii. 5. See also *post*, DRYDEN, 188.

[1] ' Principibus placuisse viris non ultima laus est.'
HORACE, *Epis.* i. 17. 35.

[2] ' Set up for wit and awkwardly was lewd.' *Satyr to his Muse*, p. 3.

[3] Dryden, a few years before his death, wrote to Dennis :—' I appeal to the world if I have deceived or defrauded any man ; and for my private conversation, they who see me every day can be the best witnesses whether or no it be blameless and inoffensive.' *Works*, xviii. 118. *Conversation*, as here used, is defined by Johnson as ' behaviour ; manner of acting in common life.'

' Dryden was in company the modestest man that ever conversed.'

Gent. Mag. 1745, p. 99.

[4] ' I have frequently heard it offered in his favour that his necessities obliged him to a constancy of writing for the entertainment of the town, the taste of which was very much depraved.' JACOB, *Poet. Register*, i. 86.

Burnet (*Hist. of my Own Time*, i. 300) describes him as ' a monster of immodesty and of impurity of all sorts.' Lord Lansdowne, defending him, said: 'He was so much a stranger to immodesty that modesty in too great a degree was his failing. He was a man of regular life and conversation, as all his acquaintance can vouch.' *Letter to the Author of the Reflexions Historical and Political*, &c., p. 5, quoted in *Biog. Brit.* p. 1760. For Lansdowne's indecency in one of his plays see *post*, GRANVILLE, 10.

indignation [1]. What consolation can be had Dryden has afforded, by living to repent, and to testify his repentance [2].

Of dramatick immorality he did not want examples among his predecessors, or companions among his contemporaries [3]; but in the meanness and servility of hyperbolical adulation I know not whether, since the days in which the Roman emperors were deified, he has been ever equalled, except by Afra Behn in an address to Eleanor Gwyn [4]. When once he has undertaken the task of praise he no longer retains shame in himself, nor supposes it in his patron [5]. As many odoriferous bodies are observed to diffuse perfumes from year to year without sensible diminution of bulk or weight, he appears never to have impoverished his mint of flattery by his expences, however lavish. He had all forms of excellence, intellectual and moral, combined in his mind, with endless variation ; and when he had scattered on the hero of the day the golden shower of wit and virtue, he had ready for him, whom he wished to court on the morrow, new wit and virtue with another stamp [6]. Of this kind of meanness

---

[1] 'Writers of great talents, who employ their parts in propagating immorality, and seasoning vicious sentiments with wit and humour, are to be looked upon as the pest of society and the enemies of mankind: they leave books behind them (as it is said of those who die in distempers which breed an ill will towards their own species) to scatter infection and destroy their posterity.' ADDISON, *The Spectator*, No. 166.

[2] 'O gracious God! how far have we
Profaned thy heavenly gift of poesy !
Made prostitute and profligate the Muse,
Debased to each obscene and impious use,
Whose harmony was first ordained above
For tongues of angels, and for hymns of love !'
Ode to Mrs. Killigrew, Works, xi. 107.
Dryden, after writing this, went on 'debasing his Muse.' See also *ib.* xi. 231, and *post*, DRYDEN, 175, for his penitence in the Preface to his last work.

[3] Evelyn wrote in 1666 (*Diary*, ii.

19) that he 'very seldom went to the public theatres . . . as they were abused to an atheistical liberty ; foul and undecent women now (and never till now) permitted to appear and act.'
Cibber (*Apology*, p. 155), writing of the stage half a century later, says that 'ladies rarely came upon the first days of acting a new comedy but in masks, until they had been assured they might do it without the risk of an insult to their modesty.'

[4] Prefixed to *The Feign'd Curtizans*, 1679. Malone's *Dryden*, i. 2. 323. Pope in *The Guardian*, No. 4, attacks 'this prostitution of praise,' in dedications.

[5] 'Burnet treats the Duke of Leeds severely ; the *Peerage* [Collins, 1756, i. 252] vindicates him by a dedication of Dryden's [*Works*, v. 316], which one must allow is authority to such a book ; for nothing can exceed the flattery of a genealogist but that of a dedicator.' HORACE WALPOLE, *Works*, i. 423.

[6] *Ante*, DRYDEN, 88. 'Pope never set his genius to sale.' *Post*, POPE, 270.

he never seems to decline the practice, or lament the necessity: he considers the great as entitled to encomiastick homage, and brings praise rather as a tribute than a gift, more delighted with the fertility of his invention than mortified by the prostitution of his judgement[1]. It is indeed not certain that on these occasions his judgement much rebelled against his interest. There are minds which easily sink into submission, that look on grandeur with undistinguishing reverence, and discover no defect where there is elevation of rank and affluence of riches.

173   With his praises of others and of himself is always intermingled a strain of discontent and lamentation, a sullen growl of resentment, or a querulous murmur of distress[2]. His works are undervalued, his merit is unrewarded, and 'he has few thanks to pay his stars that he was born among Englishmen[3].' To his criticks he is sometimes contemptuous, sometimes resentful, and sometimes submissive. The writer who thinks his works formed for duration mistakes his interest when he mentions his enemies[4]. He degrades his own dignity by shewing that he was affected by their censures, and gives lasting importance to names[5] which, left to themselves, would vanish from remembrance. From this principle Dryden did not oft depart; his complaints are for the greater part general; he seldom pollutes[6] his page

[1] Burke pointed out to Malone that 'these extravagant panegyrics were the vice of the time, not of the man; . . . the contest being who should go farthest in the most graceful way. . . . Butler had well illustrated the principle on which they went, where he compares their endeavours to those of the archer who draws his arrow to the head whether his object be a swan or a goose [*Hudibras*, ii. 1. 630].' Prior's *Malone*, p. 251; Malone's *Dryden*, i. 2. 322. For instances of these panegyrics see *ib.* i. 245.

[2] *Ante*, DRYDEN, 63, 102. 'To say truth, 'tis the common fortune of most scholars to be servile and poor, to complain pitifully, and lay open their wants to their respectless patrons. . . . Poverty is the Muses' patrimony.' BURTON, *Anatomy of Melancholy*, 1660, pp. 132–3.

[3] ['How I have acquitted myself of it [*Eleonora*] must be left to the opinion of the world. . . . For my comfort they are but Englishmen; and as such if they think ill of me to-day, they are inconstant enough to think well of me to-morrow. And after all I have not much to thank my fortune that I was born amongst them.' Scott's *Dryden*, 1821, xi. 125.]

[4] Boswell believed that Johnson only once 'in the whole course of his life condescended to oppose anything that was written against him.' Boswell's *Johnson*, i. 314. See also *ib.* ii. 61; v. 274; *John. Misc.* i. 270; *John. Letters*, ii. 148; *post*, ADDISON, 70.

[5] 'I have seldom answered any scurrilous lampoon, when it was in my power to have exposed my enemies; and, being naturally vindicative, have suffered in silence, and possessed my soul in quiet.' *Works*, xiii. 83.

[6] For *pollutes* see *post*, POPE,

with an adverse name. He condescended indeed to a controversy with Settle [1], in which he perhaps may be considered rather as assaulting than repelling; and since Settle is sunk into oblivion his libel remains injurious only to himself.

Among answers to criticks no poetical attacks or altercations 174 are to be included: they are, like other poems, effusions of genius, produced as much to obtain praise as to obviate censure. These Dryden practised, and in these he excelled.

Of Collier, Blackmore, and Milbourne he has made mention 175 in the preface to his *Fables* [2]. To the censure of Collier, whose remarks may be rather termed admonitions than criticisms, he makes little reply; being, at the age of sixty-eight, attentive to better things than the claps of a playhouse [3]. He complains of Collier's rudeness, and the 'horse-play of his raillery'; and asserts that 'in many places he has perverted by his glosses the meaning' of what he censures [4]; but in other things he confesses that he is justly taxed, and says, with great calmness and candour, 'I have pleaded guilty to all thoughts or [and] expressions of mine that [which] can be truly accused [argued] of obscenity, immorality, or profaneness, and retract them. If he be my enemy, let him triumph; if he be my friend, [as I have given him no personal occasion to be otherwise], he will be glad of my repentance [5].' Yet, as our best dispositions are imperfect, he left standing in the same book a reflection on Collier of great asperity, and indeed of more asperity than wit [6].

254; Boswell's *Johnson*, i. 330; iv. 404 *n.* 'The word is a wide one,' wrote Byron. Byron's *Works*, 1854, ix. 61.

[1] *Ante*, DRYDEN, 42.

[2] *Works*, xi. 240-4. See also his *Epistle to Motteux*, xi. 67. For Collier see *post*, CONGREVE, 18; for Blackmore see *ante*, DRYDEN, 145; *post*, BLACKMORE, 14; and for Milbourne see *ante*, DRYDEN, 148; *post*, 306.

[3] 'Dryden and Settle had both placed their happiness in the claps of multitudes.' *Ante*, DRYDEN, 42.

[4] 'In many places he has perverted my meaning by his glosses, and interpreted my words into blasphemy and bawdry of which they were not guilty; besides that he is too much given to horseplay in his raillery, and comes to battle like a

dictator from the plough.' *Works*, xi. 243. See *post*, ADDISON, 153.

[5] If Dryden was a sincere Roman Catholic he may well have been scared at Collier's attack on *Absalom and Achitophel*, ll. 19, 20:—

'This is downright defiance of the Living God! Here you have the very essence and spirit of blasphemy, and the Holy Ghost brought in upon the most hideous occasion. I question whether the torments and despair of the damned dare venture at such flights as these. They are beyond description; I pray God they may not be beyond pardon too.' *A Short View of the English Stage*, 3rd ed. p. 184.

[6] *Works*, xi. 243. Dryden's last Epilogue, written just before his death, begins (*ib.* viii. 502):

DRYDEN

176Blackmoreherepresentsasmadehisenemybythepoemof
Absalom and Achitophel, which 'he thinks a little hard upon [on] his fanatick patrons [in London] [1]'; and charges him with borrowing the plan of his *Arthur* from the preface to Juvenal, 'though he had,' says he, 'the baseness not to acknowledge his benefactor, but instead of it to traduce me in a libel.'

177 The libel in which Blackmore traduced him was a *Satire upon Wit* [2], in which, having lamented the exuberance of false wit and the deficiency of true, he proposes that all wit should be recoined before it is current, and appoints masters of assay who shall reject all that is light or debased.

> ' 'Tis true, that when the coarse and worthless dross
> Is purg'd away, there will be mighty loss;
> Ev'n Congreve, Southern, manly Wycherley [3],
> When thus refin'd, will grievous sufferers be;
> Into the melting-pot when Dryden comes,
> What horrid stench will rise, what noisome fumes!
> How will he shrink, when all his lewd allay
> And wicked mixture shall be purg'd away!'

Thus stands the passage in the last edition; but in the original there was an abatement of the censure, beginning thus:

> 'But what remains will be so pure, 'twill bear
> Th' examination of the most severe [4].'

Blackmore, finding the censure resented and the civility disregarded, ungenerously omitted the softer part. Such variations discover a writer who consults his passions more than his virtue; and it may be reasonably supposed that Dryden imputes his enmity to its true cause [5].

178 Of Milbourne he wrote only in general terms, such as are

'Perhaps the parson stretched a point too far,
When with our theatres he waged a war.'
[1] *Works*, xi. 241. Blackmore was a citizen and a Whig. *Post*, BLACKMORE, 5, 13.
[2] Blackmore published *A Satyr against Wit* in 1700, probably too late for Dryden to notice it in this Preface. 'The libel' was in the Preface to *King Arthur*, where Blackmore prays that any man who 'lavishes out his life and wit in propagating vice and corruption of manners may

go off the stage unpitied, complaining of neglect and poverty, the just punishment of his wit and folly.' Malone's *Dryden*, iii. 647. For Blackmore's poem see *post*, BLACKMORE, 17. Dryden replied to it in his last Prologue. Malone's *Dryden*, i. 333; *Works*, viii. 481.
[3] The poets' names are printed C—e, S—n, W—ly, D—n. *A Satyr against Wit*, 1700, p. 7.
[4] Blackmore's *Collection of Poems*, 1718, p. 89. The title of the poem is changed into *A Satyre upon Wit*.
[5] *Post*, BLACKMORE, 19.

always ready at the call of anger, whether just or not: a short extract will be sufficient:

'He pretends a [this] quarrel to me, that I have fallen foul upon [on] priesthood; if I have, I am only to ask pardon of good priests, and am afraid his share [part] of the reparation will come to little. Let him be satisfied that he shall never [not] be able to force himself upon me for an adversary; I contemn him too much to enter into competition with him [1].

. . . .

'As for the rest of those who have written against me they are such scoundrels that they deserve not the least notice to be taken of them. Blackmore and Milbourne are only distinguished from the crowd by being remembered to their infamy [2].'

Dryden indeed discovered in many of his writings an affected 179 and absurd malignity to priests and priesthood [3], which naturally raised him many enemies, and which was sometimes as unseasonably resented as it was exerted. Trapp is angry that he calls the sacrificer in the *Georgicks* the 'holy butcher [4]'; the translation is indeed ridiculous, but Trapp's anger arises from his zeal, not for the author, but the priest: as if any reproach of the follies of paganism could be extended to the preachers of truth [5].

Dryden's dislike of the priesthood is imputed by Langbaine, 180 and I think by Brown, to a repulse which he suffered when he solicited ordination [6]; but he denies, in the preface to his *Fables*,

---

[1] *Works*, xi. 240.

[2] *Ib.* xi. 244.

[3] Johnson had in mind such passages as the following:—'Religion was first taught in verse, which the laziness or dulness of succeeding priesthood turned afterwards into prose.' *Ib.* iii. 376. 'The cause of religion is but a modern motive to rebellion, invented by the Christian priesthood, refining on the heathen.' *Ib.* xiv. 148.

In the *Epistle to Motteux*, l. 17, he defends himself:—

'Nor, when accused by me, let them complain;
Their faults, and not their function,
I arraign.'   *Ib.* xi. 67.

[4] 'He calls the *priest* the *holy butcher*. If Mr. Dryden took delight in abusing priests and religion Virgil did not.' Trapp's *Aeneis*, 1718, Preface, p. 52.

'Or, by the holy butcher if he fell,

The inspected entrails could no fates foretell.' *Works*, xiv. 93.

'Aut si quam ferro mactaverat ante sacerdos.' VIRGIL, *Geor.* iii. 489.

For Trapp see *post*, DRYDEN, 202, 210.

[5] Collier, in his *Short View*, p. 103, says that Dryden, in *Don Sebastian*, 'strikes at the Bishops through the Mufti. . . . He knows the transition from one religion to another is natural, the application easy, and the audience but too well prepared.'

[6] 'Ever since a certain worthy Bishop refused orders to a certain poet Mr. Dryden has declared open defiance against the whole clergy.' LANGBAINE, *Dram. Poets*, p. 171. For Brown's attack see *Works*, i. 358 *n.*, and for Brown see *ante*, DRYDEN, 128. For other writings with the same charge see Malone's *Dryden*, i. 163.

that he ever designed to enter into the church[1]; and such a denial he would not have hazarded, if he could have been convicted of falsehood.

181 Malevolence to the clergy is seldom at a great distance from irreverence of religion, and Dryden affords no exception to this observation[2]. His writings exhibit many passages, which, with all the allowance that can be made for characters and occasions, are such as piety would not have admitted, and such as may vitiate light and unprincipled minds. But there is no reason for supposing that he disbelieved the religion which he disobeyed. He forgot his duty rather than disowned it. His tendency to profaneness is the effect of levity[3], negligence, and loose conversation, with a desire of accommodating himself to the corruption of the times, by venturing to be wicked as far as he durst. When he professed himself a convert to Popery he did not pretend to have received any new conviction of the fundamental doctrines of Christianity.

182 The persecution of criticks was not the worst of his vexations : he was much more disturbed by the importunities of want. His complaints of poverty are so frequently repeated, either with the dejection of weakness sinking in helpless misery, or the indignation of merit claiming its tribute from mankind, that it is impossible not to detest the age which could impose on such a man the necessity of such solicitations, or not to despise the man who could submit to such solicitations without necessity[4].

[1] *Works*, xi. 241.

[2] Johnson instances *Absalom and Achitophel* as containing ' too many lines irreligiously licentious.' *Post*, DRYDEN, 269.

[3] Such passages as the following, though not like many others avowedly profane, would have shocked Johnson :

' False heroes, made by flattery so,
　Heaven can strike out, like sparkles, at a blow ;
But ere a prince is to perfection brought,
He costs Omnipotence a second thought.'
　　　　　Threnodia Aug. l. 435.
' The Smith Divine, as with a careless beat,
　Struck out the mute creation at a heat ;

But when arrived at last to human race,
The Godhead took a deep considering space.'
The Hind and the Panther, i. 253.
　Dr. South, however, had said before Dryden :—' There was a consult of the whole Trinity, for the making of man.' *Sermons*, 1823, i. 379.
　Boileau also (a devout Papist) had written :—
' La terre compte peu de ces Rois bienfaisans.
　Le Ciel à les former se prépare longtemps.' *Épîtres*, i. 107.

[4] *Post*, DRYDEN, 227. In the Dedication of his *Pastorals* to Lord Clifford (*ante*, DRYDEN, 147) he writes :—' What I now offer to your Lordship is the wretched remainder of a sickly age, worn out with study

Whether by the world's neglect or his own imprudence I am **183** afraid that the greatest part of his life was passed in exigencies. Such outcries were surely never uttered but in severe pain. Of his supplies or his expences no probable estimate can now be made. Except the salary of the Laureat, to which king James added the office of Historiographer [1], perhaps with some additional emoluments, his whole revenue seems to have been casual [2]; and it is well known that he seldom lives frugally who lives by chance. Hope is always liberal, and they that trust her promises make little scruple of revelling to-day on the profits of the morrow.

Of his plays the profit was not great, and of the produce of **184** his other works very little intelligence can be had [3]. By discoursing with the late amiable Mr. Tonson [4] I could not find that any memorials of the transactions between his predecessor and Dryden had been preserved, except the following papers [5]:

'I do hereby promise to pay John Dryden, Esq., or order, on the 25th of March, 1699, the sum of two hundred and fifty guineas, in consideration of ten thousand verses, which the said

and oppressed by fortune, without other support than the constancy and patience of a Christian.' *Works*, xiii. 320.

[1] [The two appointments of Poet Laureate and Historiographer Royal were conferred on him by Charles II.] *Ante*, DRYDEN, 26 *n*.

[2] See Appendix U.

[3] In 1692 he asked 20 guineas for about 600 lines of a translation of Ovid. *Works*, xviii. 108. In 1693 Tonson wrote to him:—'All that I have for 50 guineas are but 1,446 lines [of Ovid].' *Ib*. p. 109. Two years later (during Montagu's great recoinage, Macaulay, *Hist*. vii. 259) he complained to Tonson that in some money received from him, 'besides the clipped money, there were at least 40 shillings brass.' *Ib*. p. 120. See also *ib*. p. 126. For the payment for his *Virgil*, see *ante*, DRYDEN, 147 *n*.

[4] [Cunningham(*Lives of the Poets*, i. 335) thinks this was Richard Tonson, M.P. for New Windsor. He died on Oct. 9, 1772. *Gent. Mag.* 1772, p. 496. It is more probable that Johnson refers to Jacob Tonson, his brother, who died in 1767. The two brothers were part-

ners, but Richard took little part in the business. For an agreement with Dr. Percy in 1764 to which both brothers are parties but which Jacob signs 'for self and brother,' see Nichols's *Lit. Illustr.* vi. 560. In Steevens's advertisement to his edition of Johnson's *Shakespeare* (1773) the character of Jacob Tonson is drawn —by Johnson Dr. Birkbeck Hill felt sure—in splendid terms of praise (see also *ante*, MILTON, 175). In this advertisement Jacob is described as 'the last commercial name of a family which will be long remembered.' Malone's *Shakespeare*, 1821, i. 181. Richard outlived Jacob by five years. Johnson helped Derrick in his *Life of Dryden* published in 1760 and may well have consulted Jacob Tonson at that time. Boswell's *Johnson*, i. 456. The description in the advertisement to Steevens's edition of Johnson's *Shakespeare* that Jacob Tonson's 'manners were soft and his conversation delicate' agrees with 'the amiable Mr. Tonson' of the text.]

[5] *Ante*, DRYDEN, 149. For an exact reprint see Malone's *Dryden*, i. 560.

John Dryden, Esq., is to deliver to me Jacob Tonson, when finished, whereof seven thousand five hundred verses, more or less, are already in the said Jacob Tonson's possession. And I do hereby farther promise, and engage myself, to make up the said sum of two hundred and fifty guineas three hundred pounds sterling to the said John Dryden, Esq., his executors, administrators, or assigns, at the beginning of the second impression of the said ten thousand verses.

In witness whereof I have hereunto set my hand and seal, this 20th day of March, 169⅚.

'Jacob Tonson.

'Sealed and delivered, being first duly stampt, pursuant to the acts of parliament for that purpose, in the presence of
    'Ben. Portlock.
    'Will. Congreve [1].'

'March 24th, 1698.

'Received then of Mr. Jacob Tonson the sum of two hundred sixty-eight pounds fifteen shillings, in pursuance of an agreement for ten thousand verses, to be delivered by me to the said Jacob Tonson, whereof I have already delivered to him about seven thousand five hundred, more or less ; he the said Jacob Tonson being obliged to make up the foresaid sum of two hundred sixty-eight pounds fifteen shillings three hundred pounds at the beginning of the second impression of the foresaid ten thousand verses ;

'I say, received by me
'John Dryden.

'Witness Charles Dryden.'

Two hundred and fifty guineas at 1*l*. 1*s*. 6*d*. is 268*l*. 15*s*.[2]

185   It is manifest from the dates of this contract that it relates to the volume of *Fables*, which contains about twelve thousand verses [3], and for which therefore the payment must have been afterwards enlarged.

---

[1] No doubt the poet.

[2] This sum Dryden received in the following currency :

	£	s.	d.
'In a bag in silver	100	0	0
In silver besides	21	15	6
66 Lewis d'ores at 17*s*. 6*d*.	57	15	0
83 Guyneas at £1 1*s*. 6*d*.	89	4	6
	268	15	0

250 Guyneas at £1 1*s*. 6*d*. are £268 15*s*. 0*d*.'

On June 11, 1713, the balance of £31 5*s*. making up the £300, the sum agreed on, was paid to Dryden's administratrix. Malone's *Dryden*, i. 561–2. 'This shows,' says Malone (*ib.* i. 320), 'that not more than £300 in the whole was paid.' The additional verses he gave '*ex abundanti*.' Malone reckons that 'he usually received 50 guineas for about 1,500 lines.' *Ib.* p. 456. See *ante*, MILTON, 135 *n*. The second edition was apparently published in 1713. See *Brit. Mus. Cata.*

[3] I make the number 11,924. See *post*, DRYDEN, 317.

I have been told of another letter yet remaining, in which he 186
desires Tonson to bring him money, to pay for a watch which he
had ordered for his son, and which the maker would not leave
without the price [1].

The inevitable consequence of poverty is dependence [2]. Dryden 187
had probably no recourse in his exigencies but to his bookseller.
The particular character of Tonson I do not know; but the
general conduct of traders was much less liberal in those
times than in our own; their views were narrower, and their
manners grosser [3]. To the mercantile ruggedness of that race
the delicacy of the poet was sometimes exposed. Lord Bolingbroke, who in his youth had cultivated poetry [4], related to Dr.
King of Oxford [5], that one day, when he visited Dryden, they
heard, as they were conversing, another person entering the house.
'This,' said Dryden, 'is Tonson. You will take care not to depart
before he goes away; for I have not completed the sheet which I
promised him; and if you leave me unprotected, I must suffer all
the rudeness to which his resentment can prompt his tongue [6].'

[1] Dryden was ready with the money for two watches for his sons; the difficulty seems to have arisen from the debased or clipped currency. *Works*, xviii. 128.

[2] Macaulay wrote on accepting his Indian appointment:—'The thought of becoming a bookseller's hack; of writing to relieve, not the fulness of the mind, but the emptiness of the pocket; of bearing from publishers what Dryden bore from Tonson, is horrible to me.' Trevelyan's *Macaulay*, i. 347.

[3] For 'the avarice' of booksellers see *post*, SAVAGE, 128. Fifteen years after Johnson wrote the *Life of Savage*, he wrote 'of the ruggedness of the commercial race.' *Rasselas*, ch. xv. In later life 'he uniformly expressed much regard for the book-sellers of London.' 'The booksellers are generous, liberal-minded men.' Boswell's *Johnson*, i. 304, 438.

[4] 'A few little pieces of his poetry are extant, for which he had a natural and easy turn.' HORACE WALPOLE, *Works*, i. 449, where a list of them is given.

[5] William King, Principal of St. Mary Hall, author of *Anecdotes of his own Time*, where, however, this story is not given. He knew Johnson. Boswell's *Johnson*, i. 279 *n.* See *post*, SWIFT, 65.

[6] In 1693 Tonson wrote to Dryden:—'Upon my word, I had rather have your good will than any man's alive.' *Works*, xviii. 110. The same year Dryden wrote to him:—'I am much ashamed of myself that I am so much behind-hand with you in kindness.' *Ib.* In 1696 he wrote:—'Upon trial I find all of your trade are sharpers, and you not more than others; therefore I have not wholly left you. ... I am not your enemy, and I may be your friend.' *Ib.* p. 126. For Dryden's coarse lines on him see *ib.* i. 327.

Pope wrote in 1731:—'Old Jacob Tonson is the perfect image and likeness of Bayle's *Dictionary*, so full of matter, secret history, and wit, and spirit, at almost fourscore.' *Pope* (Elwin and Courthope), viii. 279.

He is 'Genial Jacob' of *The Dunciad*, i. 57; and 'left-legg'd Jacob' of *ib.* ii. 68. See also *Pope* (Elwin and Courthope), iv. 326, and *N. & Q.* 5 S. x. 104.

188 What rewards he obtained for his poems, besides the payment of the bookseller, cannot be known : Mr. Derrick, who consulted some of his relations[1], was informed that his *Fables* obtained five hundred pounds from the dutchess of Ormond, a present not unsuitable to the magnificence of that splendid family[2] ; and he quotes Moyle as relating that forty pounds were paid by a musical society for the use of *Alexander's Feast*[3].

189 In those days the œconomy of government was yet unsettled, and the payments of the Exchequer were dilatory and uncertain : of this disorder there is reason to believe that the Laureat sometimes felt the effects ; for in one of his prefaces he complains of those who, being intrusted with the distribution of the Prince's bounty, suffer those that depend upon it to languish in penury[4].

190 Of his petty habits or slight amusements tradition has retained little[5]. Of the only two men whom I have found to whom he was personally known, one told me that at the house which he frequented, called Will's Coffee-house[6], the appeal upon any

---

[1] *Ante*, DRYDEN, 1 *n.*

[2] Dryden, in his Dedication of the *Fables* to the Duke, speaks of 'perpetual gentleness and inherent goodness' as 'running in the blood of the Ormond family.' He praises the Duke for his 'long train of generosity; profuseness of doing good.' *Works*, xi. 200, 204. The Duchess he flatters in a dedication in verse. *Ib.* p. 248, and *post*, DRYDEN, 314. See *ante*, DRYDEN, 100, for the Duke's grandfather.

Malone (i. 328) is 'inclined to read *one* instead of *five* hundred pounds.'

[3] Dryden describes Walter Moyle as 'a most ingenious young gentleman, conversant in all the studies of humanity much above his years.' *Works*, xvii. 315. See also *ib.* xviii. 57, and Malone's *Dryden*, iii. 382. His works in 3 vols. 8vo were published in 1726-7. Malone points out that Derrick, who was born after Moyle's death, writes :—'He used to say.' (See Dryden's *Misc. Works*, ed. 1760, i. Preface, p. 28.) Malone adds:—'In Moyle's works I find nothing on this subject.' *Ib.* i. 287.

On Sept. 3, 1697, Dryden wrote :— 'I am writing a song for St. Cecilia's Feast. This is troublesome, and

no way beneficial.' *Works*, xviii. 134.

[4] *Ante*, DRYDEN, 144 *n.*, 183 *n.*

[5] 'He was a great taker of snuff.' *The Rehearsal*, 1710, p. 31 *n.* 'He carried a copious supply loose in his waistcoat pocket, and generally prepared it himself.' Malone's *Dryden*, i. 518. Malone adds that 'Prince Eugene is said to have carried his snuff in the same manner; but his pocket was lined with tin.' Dryden was also fond of fishing. *Ib.* p. 520. Like Congreve (*post*, CONGREVE, 7) he read badly. 'Some of his friends have often reported of him that there was no man who read poetry with a worse grace.' THEOBALD, *The Censor*, No. 9.

[6] It took its name from its landlord, William Urwin, and stood 'on the north side of Russell Street, at the end of Bow Street. It is now (1800) No. 23, Great Russell Street. The company assembled on the first, or dining-room floor, as it was called in the last [the seventeenth] century ; and hence it is that we hear of a balcony.' Malone's *Dryden*, i. 483. The house is now No 1, Bow Street. Wheatley's *London*, iii. 517. See *ib.* for many interesting quotations about Will's.

The Tatler, in his first number,

literary dispute was made to him[1], and the other related that his armed chair, which in the winter had a settled and prescriptive place by the fire, was in the summer placed in the balcony ; and that he called the two places his winter and his summer seat[2]. This is all the intelligence which his two survivors afforded me.

One of his opinions will do him no honour in the present age, **191** though in his own time, at least in the beginning of it, he was far from having it confined to himself. He put great confidence in the prognostications of judicial astrology[3]. In the Appendix to the *Life of Congreve* is a narrative of some of his predictions wonderfully fulfilled ; but I know not the writer's means of information, or character of veracity[4]. That he had the configurations of the horoscope in his mind, and considered them as influencing the affairs of men, he does not forbear to hint :

says that when he treats of poetry ' it shall be under the article of Will's Coffee-house.' *The Spectator*, in his first, says :—' Sometimes I am seen thrusting my head into a round of politicians at Will's.'

' The worst conversation I ever remember to have heard in my life was that at Will's Coffee-house, where the wits (as they were called) used formerly to assemble ; that is to say, five or six men who had writ plays, or at least prologues, or had share in a Miscellany came thither,' &c. SWIFT, *Works*, ix. 170.

' Put on the critic's brow, and sit
  At Will's, the puny judge of wit.'
        Ib. xiv. 308.

The ' Great' Duke of Argyle often went to Will's. *Wentworth Papers*, pp. 181, 184–5. See also *post*, POPE, 13, 31 ; for Button's see *post*, ADDISON, 116.

[1] ' Cibber could tell no more but "that he remembered him a decent old man, arbiter of critical disputes at Will's."' Boswell's *Johnson*, iii. 71.

[2] 'His winter-chair and his summer-chair.' *Ib.* The second survivor was ' old Swinney '—' Owen MacSwinny, formerly director of the play-house.' HORACE WALPOLE, *Letters*, i. 118.

' Dryden employed his mornings in writing, dined *en famille*, and then went to Will's ; only he came home earlier a' nights than Addison.' POPE, Spence's *Anec.* p. 286.

[3] *Ante*, BUTLER, 47. ' The term *astrology*, at least when coupled with *judicial*, has always signified the discovery of future events by means of the position of the heavenly bodies.' *Penny Cyclo.* ii. 526.

' The science of judicial astrology, in almost every age except the present, has maintained its dominion over the mind of man.' GIBBON, *Decline and Fall*, i. 126.

Bentley, in a sermon preached in Dryden's lifetime, says of it :—' At this time of day, when all the general powers and capacities of matter are so clearly understood, he must be very ridiculous himself that doth not deride and explode the antiquated folly.' *Boyle Sermons*, ed. 1724, p. 120.

Darwin records that Earl Stanhope, father of the historian, one day said to him :—' Why don't you give up your fiddle-faddle of geology and zoology, and turn to the occult sciences ?' *Life of Charles Darwin*, 1892, p. 36.

[4] The writer was Mrs. Thomas. *Ante*, DRYDEN, 153 *n*. The narrative is quoted in *Works*, xviii. 217. She had the great advantage of writing long after the ' predictions' were fulfilled. Malone's *Dryden*, i. 405.

'The utmost malice of the [their] stars is past [1].'

'Now frequent *trines* the happier lights among,
And *high-rais'd Jove*, from his dark prison freed,
Those weights took off that on his planet hung,
Will gloriously the new-laid works succeed [2].'

He has elsewhere shewn his attention to the planetary powers [3]; and in the preface to his *Fables* has endeavoured obliquely to justify his superstition, by attributing the same to some of the Ancients [4]. The letter, added to this narrative [5], leaves no doubt of his notions or practice.

192   So slight and so scanty is the knowledge which I have been able to collect concerning the private life and domestick manners of a man, whom every English generation must mention with reverence as a critick and a poet.

193   DRYDEN may be properly considered as the father of English criticism, as the writer who first taught us to determine upon principles the merit of composition. Of our former poets the greatest dramatist wrote without rules, conducted through life and nature by a genius that rarely misled, and rarely deserted him [6]. Of the rest, those who knew the laws of propriety had neglected to teach them.

194   Two *Arts of English Poetry* were written in the days of Elizabeth by Webb and Puttenham [7], from which something

---

[1] *Annus Mirabilis*, stanza 291.

[2] *Ib.* stanza 292.

[3] 'Auspicious prince, at whose nativity
   Some royal planet ruled the southern sky.'
   Absalom and Achitophel, l. 230.
'For sure the milder planets did combine
On thy auspicious horoscope to shine,
And e'en the most malicious were in trine.'
   Ode to Mrs. Killigrew, l. 41.

[4] In his Dedication of the *Aeneis* to Lord Normanby, speaking of astrology, he says:—'But I insist not on this, because I know you believe not there is such an art; though not only Horace and Persius, but Augustus himself, thought otherwise.' *Works*, xiv. 167.

[5] *Post*, DRYDEN, 406. This sentence is not in the first edition.

[6] 'Shakespeare's adherence to general nature has exposed him to the censure of critics who form their judgments upon narrower principles. ... He engaged in dramatic poetry with the world open before him; the rules of the ancients were yet known to few; the public judgment was unformed.' JOHNSON, *Works*, v. 109, 112.
'Critics did not originally beget authors, but authors made critics.' COWPER, *Works*, v. 29.

[7] *A Discourse of English Poetrie*. By William Webbe, 1586. *The Arte of English Poesie*. [By George Puttenham.] 1859. Both these works are in Mr. Arber's *English Reprints*. In 1838 young Lowell was studying versification in Puttenham. H. E. Scudder's *Life of Lowell*, 1901, i. 67.

might be learned, and a few hints had been given by Jonson[1] and Cowley[2]; but Dryden's *Essay on Dramatick Poetry* was the first regular and valuable treatise on the art of writing.

He who, having formed his opinions in the present age of English literature, turns back to peruse this dialogue, will not perhaps find much increase of knowledge or much novelty of instruction; but he is to remember that critical principles were then in the hands of a few, who had gathered them partly from the Ancients, and partly from the Italians and French[3]. The structure of dramatick poems was not then generally understood. Audiences applauded by instinct, and poets perhaps often pleased by chance. 195

A writer who obtains his full purpose loses himself in his own lustre[4]. Of an opinion which is no longer doubted, the evidence ceases to be examined. Of an art universally practised, the first teacher is forgotten. Learning once made popular is no longer learning: it has the appearance of something which we have bestowed upon ourselves, as the dew appears to rise from the field which it refreshes. 196

To judge rightly of an author we must transport ourselves to his time, and examine what were the wants of his contemporaries, and what were his means of supplying them. That which is easy at one time was difficult at another. Dryden at least imported his science, and gave his country what it wanted before; or rather, he imported only the materials, and manufactured them by his own skill[5]. 197

[1] In his *Timber; or Discoveries made upon Men and Matter.* Jonson's *Works*, 1756, vii. 69. 'Jonson, who by studying Horace had been acquainted with the rules [of the stage], yet seemed to envy to posterity that knowledge, and, like an inventor of some useful art, to make a monopoly of his learning.' DRYDEN, *Works*, xiii. 3.

[2] In his Prefaces. *Eng. Poets*, vii. 7; viii. 109.

[3] Dryden throughout his *Essay of Dramatic Poesy* criticizes Corneille (referring no doubt to his *Discours*) and the rules of the French drama. In his *Dedication of the Aeneis* he says:—'The French are as much better critics than the English as they are worse poets.' *Works*, xiv.

162. 'Dryden has assured me that he got more from the Spanish critics alone than from the Italian and French, and all other critics put together.' BOLINGBROKE, Spence's *Anec.* 14.

[4] 'Let not the original author lose by his imitators.' *Ante*, WALLER, 150; *post*, ADDISON, 160.

[5] In his *Essay on Satire* (1693) he writes:—

'I made my early addresses to your Lordship [Earl of Dorset] in my *Essay of Dramatic Poesy*; and therein bespoke you to the world wherein I have the right of a first discoverer. . . . I was drawing the outlines of an art without any living master to instruct me in it. . . . Before the use of the loadstone, or knowledge of the

198   The dialogue on the Drama[1] was one of his first essays of
criticism, written when he was yet a timorous candidate for
reputation, and therefore laboured with that diligence which he
might allow himself somewhat to remit when his name gave
sanction to his positions, and his awe of the public was abated,
partly by custom, and partly by success. It will not be easy
to find in all the opulence of our language a treatise so artfully
variegated with successive representations of opposite probabilities,
so enlivened with imagery, so brightened with illustrations. His
portraits of the English dramatists[2] are wrought with great
spirit and diligence. The account of Shakespeare[3] may stand
as a perpetual model of encomiastick criticism ; exact without
minuteness, and lofty without exaggeration. The praise lavished
by Longinus, on the attestation of the heroes of Marathon by
Demosthenes[4], fades away before it. In a few lines is exhibited
a character, so extensive in its comprehension and so curious in
its limitations, that nothing can be added, diminished, or reformed ;
nor can the editors and admirers of Shakespeare, in all their
emulation of reverence, boast of much more than of having
diffused and paraphrased this epitome of excellence, of having
changed Dryden's gold for baser metal, of lower value though of
greater bulk[5].

199   In this, and in all his other essays on the same subject, the
criticism of Dryden is the criticism of a poet ; not a dull
collection of theorems, nor a rude detection of faults, which
perhaps the censor was not able to have committed ; but a gay
and vigorous dissertation, where delight is mingled with instruction, and where the author proves his right of judgement by his
power of performance.

200   The different manner and effect with which critical knowledge

compass, I was sailing in a vast
ocean, without other help than the
pole-star of the ancients, and the
rules of the French stage amongst
the moderns.' *Works*, xiii. 3.
    [1] *An Essay of English Poesy*,
ante, DRYDEN, 27.
    [2] *Works*, xv. 345.
    [3] *Ib.* p. 344.
    [4] LONGINUS, *De Sublimi*, xvi ;
DEMOSTHENES, *De Corona*, 263. 11.
    [5] *Post*, POPE, 128.
'Read all the prefaces of Dryden,

For these our critics much confide
  in ;
Though merely writ at first for
  filling,
To raise the volume's price a shilling.'   SWIFT, *Works*, xiv. 308.
Not all the Prefaces were written
' for filling,' to judge by the following
passage in Dryden's letter to Tonson about his *Virgil* :—' The Notes
and Prefaces shall be short ; because
you shall get the more by saving
paper.' *Works*, xviii. 125.

may be conveyed was perhaps never more clearly exemplified than in the performances of Rymer and Dryden. It was said of a dispute between two mathematicians, 'malim cum Scaligero errare, quam cum Clavio recte sapere [1]'; that 'it was more eligible to go wrong with one than right with the other.' A tendency of the same kind every mind must feel at the perusal of Dryden's prefaces and Rymer's discourses. With Dryden we are wandering in quest of Truth, whom we find, if we find her at all, drest in the graces of elegance ; and if we miss her, the labour of the pursuit rewards itself: we are led only through fragrance and flowers. Rymer, without taking a nearer, takes a rougher way ; every step is to be made through thorns and brambles, and Truth, if we meet her, appears repulsive by her mien and ungraceful by her habit. Dryden's criticism has the majesty of a queen ; Rymer's has the ferocity of a tyrant [2].

As he had studied with great diligence the art of poetry, [201] and enlarged or rectified his notions by experience perpetually increasing, he had his mind stored with principles and observations: he poured out his knowledge with little labour [3]; for of labour, notwithstanding the multiplicity of his productions, there is sufficient reason to suspect that he was not a lover. To write *con amore*, with fondness for the employment, with perpetual touches and retouches, with unwillingness to take leave of his own idea, and an unwearied pursuit of unattainable perfection, was, I think, no part of his character [4].

His criticism may be considered as general or occasional. In [202] his general precepts, which depend upon the nature of things and the structure of the human mind, he may doubtless be safely recommended to the confidence of the reader ; but his occasional and particular positions were sometimes interested, sometimes negligent, and sometimes capricious [5]. It is not without reason

---

[1] 'Errare malo cum Platone quam cum istis vera sentire.' CICERO, *Tusc.* i. 17, 39.
It was Clavius who, by order of Gregory XIII, corrected the calendar ; in this he was attacked by Joseph Scaliger. *Penny Cyclo.* vii. 245. Johnson applied the saying also to Bentley's and Jason de Nores' *Comments upon Horace.* 'You will admire Bentley more when wrong than Jason when right.' Boswell's *Johnson,* ii. 444.

[2] See Appendix X.

[3] In the first edition:—'He poured out his knowledge with great liberality, and seldom published any work without a critical dissertation, by which he encreased the book and the price, with little labour to himself; for of labour,' &c.

[4] *Post,* DRYDEN, 341 ; POPE, 298, 304.

[5] *Ante,* BUTLER, 50. 'Dryden

that Trapp [1], speaking of the praises which he bestows on *Palamon and Arcite*, says

'Novimus [quidem Angli] judicium Drydeni [popularis nostri] de poemate quodam Chauceri, pulchro sane illo, et admodum [plurimum] laudando, nimirum quod non modo vere epicum sit, sed *Iliada* etiam atque *Æneida* æquet, imo superet [2]. Sed novimus eodem tempore viri illius maximi non semper accuratissimas esse censuras, nec ad severissimam critices normam exactas: Illo judice id plerumque optimum est, quod nunc [optimum est plerumque quod ille] præ manibus habet, et in quo nunc occupatur [3].'

203   He is therefore by no means constant to himself. His defence and desertion of dramatick rhyme is generally known [4]. Spence, in his remarks on Pope's *Odyssey*, produces what he thinks an unconquerable quotation from Dryden's preface to the *Eneid*, in favour of translating an epick poem into blank verse [5]; but he forgets that when his author attempted the *Iliad*, some years afterwards, he departed from his own decision, and translated into rhyme.

was known to have written most of his critical disquisitions only to recommend the work upon which he then happened to be employed.' *The Rambler*, No. 93.

[1] *Ante*, DRYDEN, 179 ; *post*, 310.

[2] *Post*, DRYDEN, 314.

[3] *Praelectiones Poeticae*, 1722, p. 386.

'We know our countryman Mr. Dryden's judgment about a poem of Chaucer's, truly beautiful indeed and worthy of praise ; namely that it was not only equal, but even superior to the *Iliad* and *Aeneid*. But we know likewise that his opinion was not always the most accurate, nor formed upon the severest rules of criticism. What was in hand was generally most in esteem ; if it was uppermost in his thoughts it was so in his judgment too.' TRAPP, *Lectures on Poetry*. Translated from the Latin, 1742, p. 348.

Dryden says of his translations of Ovid, just finished :—' They appear to me the best of all my endeavours in this kind.' *Works*, xii. 62.

[4] *Ante*, DRYDEN, 20. In the Preface to *The Conquest of Granada* (1672; *ante*, DRYDEN, 48) he writes:—' Whether heroic verse ought to be admitted into serious plays is not now to be disputed; it is already in possession of the stage, and I dare confidently affirm that very few tragedies in this age shall be received without it.' *Works*, iv. 18. In the Preface to *All for Love* (1678; *ante*, DRYDEN, 78) he writes:—'In my style I have professed to imitate the divine Shakespeare, which that I might perform more freely, I have disencumbered myself from rhyme.' *Ib*. v. 339.

[5] Spence, in his *Essay on Mr. Pope's Odyssey* (*post*, POPE, 137), ed. 1737, p. 121, quotes Dryden where he writes (*Works*, xiv. 211):—' Hannibal Caro is a great name amongst the Italians ; yet his translation of the *Aeneis* is most scandalously mean, though he has taken the advantage of writing in blank verse. . . . I will only say that he who can write well in rhyme may write better in blank verse.' See also *ante*, MILTON, 273.

For Algarotti's criticism of Caro and Dryden see his *Lettere di Polianzio al Ermogene*, &c. Venice, 1745.

When he has any objection to obviate, or any license to defend, 204 he is not very scrupulous about what he asserts, nor very cautious, if the present purpose be served, not to entangle himself in his own sophistries. But when all arts are exhausted, like other hunted animals, he sometimes stands at bay; when he cannot disown the grossness of one of his plays, he declares that he knows not any law that prescribes morality to a comick poet [1].

His remarks on ancient or modern writers are not always to 205 be trusted. His parallel of the versification of Ovid with that of Claudian has been very justly censured by Sewel [2]. His comparison of the first line of Virgil with the first of Statius is not happier. Virgil, he says, is soft and gentle, and would have thought Statius mad if he had heard him thundering out

'Quæ superimposito moles geminata colosso [3].'

Statius perhaps heats himself, as he proceeds, to exaggerations 206 somewhat hyperbolical; but undoubtedly Virgil would have been too hasty if he had condemned him to straw [4] for one sounding line. Dryden wanted an instance, and the first that occurred was imprest into the service.

What he wishes to say, he says at hazard; he cited *Gorbuduc*, 207 which he had never seen [5]; gives a false account of Chapman's

---

[1] 'It is charged upon me that I make debauched persons happy at the conclusion of my play, against the law of comedy, which is to reward virtue and punish vice. I answer first, that I know no such law to have been constantly observed in comedy, either by the ancient or modern poets.' *Works*, iii. 246; *ante*, DRYDEN, 44.

[2] Preface to Ovid's *Metamorphoses*. JOHNSON. Dryden's 'parallel' is in the Preface to *Dryden's Second Miscellany*, *Works*, xii. 286. For Sewell see *post*, ADDISON, 68, and Campbell's *British Poets*, p. 345, for some pretty verses by him.

[3] *Works*, xvii. 330. This comparison is with the first line of the *Aeneid* and the first of the *Sylvae*. He also compares Statius's line with the first of the *Eclogues*. *Ib.* vi. 407. Dryden speaks of 'the soberness of Virgil,' but does not say 'he is soft and gentle.' For Statius see *post*, POPE, 28.

[4] In *The Guardian*, No. 82, in a list of the effects of 'the property-man' at the Theatre, is 'a truss of straw for the madmen. £o os. 8d.' See also Boswell's *Johnson*, ii. 374.

[5] [Thomas Sackville, afterwards Lord Buckhurst and Earl of Dorset (*post*, POPE, 387 *n*.), was the joint author with Thomas Norton of *Gorboduc*, 'first performed at the Xmas revels at the Temple in 1561 and some three weeks afterwards (Jan. 18, 1561–2) by command before her Majesty.' It was not printed till 1565, when it was surreptitiously published by Griffith. *N. & Q.* 2 S. x. 261. Five years later an authorized edition appeared with the title *The Tragedie of Ferrex and Porrex*. In 1590 it was reprinted as an appendix to Lydgate's *Serpent of Division*, under the title of *Gorboduc*.] In the Dedication of *The Rival Ladies* (*Works*, ii. 135) Dryden cites 'the tragedy of *Queen Gorboduc* in English verse. . . . Shakespeare was the first who invented blank verse.' Langbaine

versification [1]; and discovers in the preface to his *Fables* that he translated the first book of the *Iliad* without knowing what was in the second [2].

208   It will be difficult to prove that Dryden ever made any great advances in literature. As having distinguished himself at Westminster under the tuition of Busby [3], who advanced his scholars to a height of knowledge very rarely attained in grammar-schools, he resided afterwards at Cambridge, it is not to be supposed that his skill in the ancient languages was deficient compared with that of common students; but his scholastick acquisitions seem not proportionate to his opportunities and abilities. He could not, like Milton or Cowley, have made his name illustrious merely by his learning. He mentions but few books, and those such as lie in the beaten track of regular study; from which, if ever he departs, he is in danger of losing himself in unknown regions [4].

209   In his *Dialogue on the Drama* he pronounces with great confidence that the Latin tragedy of *Medea* is not Ovid's, because it is not sufficiently interesting and pathetick [5]. He might have determined the question upon surer evidence, for it is quoted by Quintilian as the work of Seneca [6]; and the only line which remains of Ovid's play, for one line is left us, is not there to be found [7]. There was therefore no need of the gravity of con-

---

points out that Gorboduc was a king, and that ' the play was in blank verse; so that Mr. Shakespeare was not the first beginner of that way of writing.' *Dram. Poets*, p. 168.

[1] Dryden says that Chapman's *Homer* is written ' in Alexandrines, or verses of six feet.' *Works*, ix. 93. On this Malone remarks :—' It is not in verses of twelve syllables, or six feet, but in lines of fourteen syllables.' Malone's *Dryden*, ii. 257. See also *post*, DRYDEN, 344; POPE, 85.

[2] ' You never cool while you read Homer, even not in the second book; but he hastens from the ships, and concludes not that book till he has made you amends by the violent playing of a new machine.' *Works*, xi. 217. *Machine* Johnson defines as ' supernatural agency in poems.' See *post*, POPE, 59.

[3] *Ante*, DRYDEN, 4.

[4] In 1683 he wrote :—' I must con-

fess it to my shame that I never read anything but for pleasure.' *Works*, xvii. 56. He had one taste not common in that age. He was, says Addison, very fond of old English ballads. *The Spectator*, No. 85.
' Our course by Milton's light was sped,
And Shakespeare shining overhead:
Chatting on deck was Dryden too,
The Bacon of the rhyming crew;
None ever crost our mystic sea
More richly stored with thought than he.'
                LANDOR, *Poems*, ii. 179.
See *post*, POPE, 308.

[5] *Works*, xv. 312. ' Ovid wrote a tragedy; but, notwithstanding the judgment of Quintilian, I cannot much regret its loss.' GIBBON, *Misc. Works*, iv. 356. Gibbon goes on to show why he does not regret it.

[6] *Inst.* ix. 2. 8.

[7] ' Nam, cum sit rectum " nocere

jecture, or the discussion of plot or sentiment, to find what was already known upon higher authority than such discussions can ever reach.

His literature, though not always free from ostentation, will 210 be commonly found either obvious, and made his own by the art of dressing it; or superficial, which by what he gives shews what he wanted; or erroneous, hastily collected, and negligently scattered.

Yet it cannot be said that his genius is ever unprovided of 211 matter, or that his fancy languishes in penury of ideas. His works abound with knowledge, and sparkle with illustrations. There is scarcely any science or faculty that does not supply him with occasional images and lucky similitudes; every page discovers a mind very widely acquainted both with art and nature, and in full possession of great stores of intellectual wealth. Of him that knows much it is natural to suppose that he has read with diligence; yet I rather believe that the knowledge of Dryden was gleaned from accidental intelligence and various conversation; by a quick apprehension, a judicious selection, and a happy memory, a keen appetite of knowledge, and a powerful digestion; by vigilance that permitted nothing to pass without notice, and a habit of reflection that suffered nothing useful to be lost. A mind like Dryden's, always curious, always active, to which every understanding was proud to be associated, and of which every one solicited the regard by an ambitious display of himself, had a more pleasant, perhaps a nearer, way to knowledge than by the silent progress of solitary reading. I do not suppose that he despised books or intentionally neglected them; but that he was carried out by the impetuosity of his genius to more vivid and speedy instructors, and that his studies were rather desultory and fortuitous than constant and systematical[1].

It must be confessed that he scarcely ever appears to want 212 book-learning but when he mentions books; and to him may be transferred the praise which he gives his master Charles[2]:

'His conversation, wit, and parts,
His knowledge in the noblest useful arts,

facile est, prodesse difficile," vehementius apud Ovidium Medea dicit:— "Servare potui; perdere an possim rogas?"' *Inst.* viii. 5. 6.

[1] Johnson here describes himself. See *post*, DRYDEN, 321 *n*.; POPE, 291.
[2] In the *Threnodia Augustalis*, l. 337. *Post*, DRYDEN, 275.

Were such, dead authors could not give,
But habitudes of those that [who] live ;
Who, lighting him, did greater lights receive:
He drain'd from all, and all they knew,
His apprehension quick, his judgement true:
That the most learn'd with shame confess
His knowledge more, his reading only less.'

213   Of all this however if the proof be demanded I will not undertake to give it ; the atoms of probability, of which my opinion
has been formed, lie scattered over all his works : and by him
who thinks the question worth his notice his works must be
perused with very close attention.

214   Criticism, either didactick or defensive, occupies almost all his
prose, except those pages which he has devoted to his patrons ;
but none of his prefaces were ever thought tedious. They have
not the formality of a settled style, in which the first half of the
sentence betrays the other. The clauses are never balanced, nor
the periods modelled ; every word seems to drop by chance,
though it falls into its proper place. Nothing is cold or languid ;
the whole is airy, animated, and vigorous: what is little is gay ;
what is great is splendid. He may be thought to mention
himself too frequently ; but while he forces himself upon our
esteem, we cannot refuse him to stand high in his own [1]. Every
thing is excused by the play of images and the spriteliness of
expression. Though all is easy, nothing is feeble ; though all
seems careless, there is nothing harsh ; and though since his
earlier works more than a century has passed they have nothing
yet uncouth or obsolete.

215   He who writes much will not easily escape a manner, such
a recurrence of particular modes as may be easily noted. Dryden
is always 'another and the same [2]'; he does not exhibit a second
time the same elegances in the same form, nor appears to have
any art other than that of expressing with clearness what he
thinks with vigour. His style could not easily be imitated [3],
either seriously or ludicrously ; for, being always equable and
always varied, it has no prominent or discriminative characters.
The beauty who [4] is totally free from disproportion of parts and
features cannot be ridiculed by an overcharged resemblance [5].

---

[1] *Ante*, DRYDEN, 162.
[2] 'Another, yet the same.' *The Dunciad*, iii. 40.
[3] *Post*, POPE, 309.

[4] The editions give *who* : ? read *which*.
[5] 'I have heard Dryden frequently own with pleasure that if he had any

From his prose however Dryden derives only his accidental 216
and secondary praise; the veneration with which his name is
pronounced by every cultivator of English literature is paid to
him as he refined the language[1], improved the sentiments, and
tuned the numbers of English Poetry[2].

After about half a century of forced thoughts and rugged 217
metre some advances towards nature and harmony had been
already made by Waller and Denham[3]; they had shewn that
long discourses in rhyme grew more pleasing when they were
broken into couplets[4], and that verse consisted not only in the
number but the arrangement of syllables.

But though they did much, who can deny that they left much 218
to do? Their works were not many, nor were their minds of

talent for English prose, it was owing
to his having often read the writings
of Tillotson.' CONGREVE, Dryden's
Works, ii. 19. See *post*, ADDISON, 91.
The earliest single sermon of Tillotson's in the *Brit. Mus. Cata.*, entitled
The Wisdom of being Religious, was
published in 1664, four years before
Dryden's *Essay of Dramatic Poesy*.
Gray, who 'thought Dryden's prose
almost equal to his poetry,' was surprised at his attributing his style to
Tillotson. Mitford's *Gray*, v. 38.

Lord Macartney pointed out to
Malone that Burke's characters of
Chatham, Grenville, C. Townshend,
&c., are modelled on the paragraphs
in *The Essay of Dramatic Poesy*,
beginning with 'Shakespeare was the
man who' and proceeding to Beaumont, Fletcher, and Jonson (*Works*,
xv. 344). Malone replied:—'In
the Advertisement prefixed to Dryden's *Critical Works* I have mentioned that Burke's style was formed
on Dryden's.' *N. & Q.* 7 S. ix. 203.

'Dryden's prose,' said Fox, 'was
Burke's great favourite. He seems
to copy him more than he does any
other writer.' *Memoirs of F. Horner*,
1843, i. 324.

'The model writers, Addison, Johnson, &c., have had their day. Dryden
holds, I think; he did not set up for
a model prose man. . . . I think that
to me, Dryden's prose, *quoad* prose,
is the finest style of all.' E. FITZ-
GERALD, *Letters*, ii. 106, 228. See
also *ib.* i. 347 for 'the homely strength

of Shakespeare, Dryden, South, and
Swift.'

'Barrow,' said Coleridge, 'must be
considered as closing the first great
period of the English language.
Dryden began the second.' *Table
Talk*, 1884, p. 269. Coleridge mentions William Taylor as recommending to Klopstock 'the prose
works of Dryden as models of pure
and native English.' *Biog. Lit.* 1847,
ii. 249.

[1] 'I have refined his language,'
Dryden wrote of Shakespeare in the
Preface to *Troilus and Cressida*,
Works, vi. 256.

[2] *Post*, DRYDEN, 356. Johnson
says of Pope's *Homer*:—'It may be
said to have tuned the English
tongue.' *Post*, POPE, 348. According to Swift, the poets from the
Restoration greatly spoilt the English
tongue ' by abbreviating words to fit
them to the measure of their verses.'
He instances the 'jarring sound' in
drudg'd, rebuk'd, and *fledg'd*. Swift's
Works, ix. 143. Addison, in *The
Spectator*, No. 135, after writing to
the same purport, says:—' This reflection on the words that end in *ed*
I have heard in conversation from
one of the greatest geniuses this age
has produced'—Swift, no doubt.
Dryden was much given to these
abbreviations.

[3] *Ante*, DENHAM, 35; WALLER,
142; *post*, DRYDEN, 342.

[4] *Ante*, DENHAM, 37; *post*, DRY-
DEN, 290.

very ample comprehension. More examples of more modes of composition were necessary for the establishment of regularity, and the introduction of propriety in word and thought.

219 Every language of a learned nation necessarily divides itself into diction scholastick and popular, grave and familiar, elegant and gross; and from a nice distinction of these different parts arises a great part of the beauty of style. But if we except a few minds, the favourites of nature, to whom their own original rectitude was in the place of rules, this delicacy of selection was little known to our authors: our speech lay before them in a heap of confusion, and every man took for every purpose what chance might offer him.

220 There was therefore before the time of Dryden no poetical diction [1]: no system of words at once refined from the grossness of domestick use and free from the harshness of terms appropriated to particular arts. Words too familiar or too remote defeat the purpose of a poet [2]. From those sounds which we hear on small or on coarse occasions, we do not easily receive strong impressions or delightful images; and words to which we are nearly strangers, whenever they occur, draw that attention on themselves which they should transmit to things.

221 Those happy combinations of words which distinguish poetry from prose had been rarely attempted; we had few elegances or flowers of speech: the roses had not yet been plucked from the bramble or different colours had not been joined to enliven one another.

---

[1] 'The language of the age is never the language of poetry; except among the French, whose verse, where the thought or image does not support it, differs in nothing from prose. Our poetry, on the contrary, has a language peculiar to itself.' GRAY, *Letters*, i. 97.

[2] In the *Dedication of the Aeneis*, speaking of '*mollis amaracus* on which Venus lays Cupid [Ascanius] in the first *Aeneid*.' Dryden says:— 'If I should translate it *sweet-marjoram*, as the word signifies, the reader would think I had mistaken Virgil; for those village words, as I may call them, give us a mean idea of the thing.' *Works*, xiv. 226. He translates the words 'a flowery bed.'

Ib. p. 264. Lord Bowen gets over the difficulty by using the Latin word—'a yielding amaracus.' *Virgil in English Verse*, 1887, p. 103. See also *post*, POPE, 350.

'Dryden always uses proper language; lively, natural, and fitted to the subject. It is scarce ever too high or too low; never, perhaps, except in his plays.' POPE, Spence's *Anec.* p. 281.

'A fastidious delicacy and a false refinement, in order to avoid meanness, have deterred our writers from the introduction of common words; but Dryden often hazarded it, and it gave a secret charm and a natural air to his verses.' J. WARTON, *Essay on Pope*, ii. 233.

It may be doubted whether Waller and Denham could have 222 over-borne the prejudices which had long prevailed, and which even then were sheltered by the protection of Cowley [1]. The new versification, as it was called, may be considered as owing its establishment to Dryden [2]; from whose time it is apparent that English poetry has had no tendency to relapse to its former savageness.

The affluence and comprehension of our language is very 223 illustriously displayed in our poetical translations of ancient writers: a work which the French seem to relinquish in despair [3], and which we were long unable to perform with dexterity [4]. Ben Jonson thought it necessary to copy Horace almost word by word [5]; Feltham, his contemporary and adversary [6], considers it as indispensably requisite in a translation to give line for line. It is said that Sandys, whom Dryden calls the best versifier of the last age [7], has struggled hard to comprise every book of his

---

[1] *Ante*, DRYDEN, 5.

[2] *Post*, DRYDEN, 343. In the *Postscript to Virgil*, speaking of the English language and poetry, Dryden says:—'Somewhat (give me leave to say) I have added to both of them in the choice of words and harmony of numbers, which were wanting (especially the last) in all our poets.' *Works*, xv. 187.

'Dryden first gave the English tongue regular harmony. . . . It was his pen that formed the Congreves, the Priors, and the Addisons who succeeded him.' GOLDSMITH, *Works*, iii. 127.

'To Dryden and Pope the honour of having perfected our versification is commonly attributed; it is true only with respect to the couplet, the best example of which is assuredly to be found in Dryden.' SOUTHEY, *Specimens*, &c., Preface, p. 29.

'Milton's character of Dryden was, that he was a good rhymist, but no poet.' *Ante*, MILTON, 164.

[3] 'Let the French and Italians value themselves on their regularity; strength and elevation are our standard. I said before, and I repeat it, that the affected purity of the French has unsinewed their heroic verse. The language of an epic poem is almost wholly figurative; yet they

are so fearful of a metaphor that no example of Virgil can encourage them to be bold with safety.' DRYDEN, *Works*, xiv. 221.

For Swift's avoidance of metaphors see *post*, SWIFT, 112.

[4] *Ante*, DRYDEN, 107; *post*, POPE, 347.

[5] He thus translates *Ars Poetica*, ll. 138-40:—

'What doth this promiser such gaping worth
Afford? The mountains travail'd, and brought forth
A scorned mouse! O, how much better his
Who nought assays unaptly or amiss!'

Jonson's *Works*, 1756, vii. 175.

See also Dryden's *Works*, xii. 16, and *ante*, DENHAM, 32; DRYDEN, 107.

[6] Owen Felltham wrote *An Answer to the Ode of 'Come leave the Loathed Stage'* by Jonson. It begins:—

'Come leave this saucy way
Of baiting those that pay
Dear for the sight of your declining wit.'

Felltham's *Lusoria*, 1661, p. 17.

[7] *Works*, xi. 209. Dryden wrote in 1693 that the literal translator 'leaves his author prose where he found him verse; and no better than

English *Metamorphoses* in the same number of verses with the original. Holyday had nothing in view but to shew that he understood his author, with so little regard to the grandeur of his diction, or the volubility of his numbers, that his metres can hardly be called verses ; they cannot be read without reluctance, nor will the labour always be rewarded by understanding them [1]. Cowley saw that such 'copyers' were a 'servile race [2]'; he asserted his liberty, and spread his wings so boldly that he left his authors. It was reserved for Dryden to fix the limits of poetical liberty, and give us just rules and examples of translation [3].

224 When languages are formed upon different principles, it is impossible that the same modes of expression should always be elegant in both. While they run on together the closest translation may be considered as the best ; but when they divaricate [4] each must take its natural course. Where correspondence cannot be obtained it is necessary to be content with something equivalent. 'Translation therefore,' says Dryden, 'is not so loose as paraphrase, nor so close as metaphrase [5].'

225 All polished languages have different styles : the concise, the diffuse, the lofty, and the humble. In the proper choice of style

---

thus has Ovid been served by the so-much-admired Sandys. This is at least the idea which I have remaining of his translation, for I have never read him since I was a boy.' *Works*, xii. 63. See also *ante*, COWLEY, 197 ; DENHAM, 32 ; DRYDEN, 107 ; *post*, POPE, 5.

[1] *Ante*, DRYDEN, 107 ; *post*, 299. 'By the help of Holyday's learned notes and illustrations not only Juvenal and Persius, but, what is yet more obscure, his own verses might be understood.' DRYDEN, *Works*, xiii. 119. See also *ib*. p. 102. For 'his poetry and sublime fancy' see *Ath. Oxon.* iii. 521.

[2] Cowley in the Preface to his *Pindaric Odes*, after speaking of the defects of translations, continues :— 'The like happens too in pictures, from the same root of exact imitation ; which, being a vile and unworthy kind of servitude, is incapable of producing anything good or noble.' *Eng. Poets*, viii. 110. See *ante*,

COWLEY, 125. 'The copier is that servile imitator to whom Horace gives no better a name than that of animal.' DRYDEN, *Works*, xiv. 187. 'O imitatores, servum pecus ! ' HORACE, *Epis.* i. 19. 19.

[3] *Works*, xii. 16, 284 ; xiii. 119 ; xiv. 218 ; *post*, DRYDEN, 356.

[4] Boswell wrote of his father :— 'We divaricate so much, as Dr. Johnson said.' Boswell's *Johnson*, ii. 382 *n*.

[5] 'The way I have taken is not so strait as metaphrase nor so loose as paraphrase.' *Works*, xiv. 219. *Metaphrase* he defines as 'turning an author word by word, and line by line, from one language into another'; and *paraphrase* as 'translation with latitude, where the author is kept in view by the translator, so as never to be lost, but his words are not so strictly followed as his sense ; and that too is admitted to be amplified, but not altered.' *Ib*. xii. 16.

consists the resemblance which Dryden principally exacts from the translator. He is to exhibit his author's thoughts in such a dress of diction as the author would have given them, had his language been English[1]: rugged magnificence is not to be softened; hyperbolical ostentation is not to be repressed, nor sententious affectation to have its points blunted. A translator is to be like his author: it is not his business to excel him.

The reasonableness of these rules seems sufficient for their vindication; and the effects produced by observing them were so happy that I know not whether they were ever opposed but by Sir Edward Sherburne[2], a man whose learning was greater than his powers of poetry, and who, being better qualified to give the meaning than the spirit of Seneca, has introduced his version of three tragedies by a defence of close translation. The authority of Horace[3], which the new translators cited in defence of their practice, he has, by a judicious explanation, taken fairly from them; but reason wants not Horace to support it.

It seldom happens that all the necessary causes concur to any great effect: will is wanting to power, or power to will, or both are impeded by external obstructions. The exigences in which Dryden was condemned to pass his life are reasonably supposed to have blasted his genius, to have driven out his works in a state of immaturity, and to have intercepted the full-blown elegance which longer growth would have supplied[4].

Poverty, like other rigid powers, is sometimes too hastily accused. If the excellence of Dryden's works was lessened by his indigence, their number was increased; and I know not how it will be proved that if he had written less he would have written better[5]; or that indeed he would have undergone the toil

---

[1] 'I have endeavoured to make Virgil speak such English as he would himself have spoken, if he had been born in England and in this present age.' *Ib.* xiv. 220. He says the same of his *Juvenal*. *Ib.* xiii. 122.

[2] Aubrey describes him and his brother as 'both excellent scholars and excellent poets.' *Brief Lives*, ii. 228. Sherburne thus ends his attack on the new school of translators:—'And this may be enough to manifest the groundless prejudice of these *Fastidious Brisks*.' Sherburne's *Seneca*, 1701, Preface, p. 38.

[3] *Ars Poetica*, l. 133.

[4] Pope says of Dryden's 'extreme haste in writing' that it 'never ought to be imputed as a fault to him, but to those who suffered so noble a genius to lie under the necessity of it.' *Iliad*, 1760, i. 13. See also Dryden's *Works*, xiv. 206.

Macaulay describes Scott as 'writing with the slovenly haste of Dryden in order to satisfy wants which were not, like those of Dryden, caused by circumstances beyond his control.' *Macvey Napier Corres.* p. 258.

[5] 'Dryden seems to me greater

of an author, if he had not been solicited by something more pressing than the love of praise[1].

229   But as is said by his Sebastian,

'What had been, is unknown; what is, appears[2].'

We know that Dryden's several productions were so many successive expedients for his support: his plays were therefore often borrowed[3], and his poems were almost all occasional.

230   In an occasional performance no height of excellence can be expected from any mind, however fertile in itself, and however stored with acquisitions[4]. He whose work is general and arbitrary has the choice of his matter, and takes that which his inclination and his studies have best qualified him to display and decorate. He is at liberty to delay his publication, till he has satisfied his friends and himself; till he has reformed his first thoughts by subsequent examination, and polished away those faults which the precipitance of ardent composition is likely to leave behind it[5]. Virgil is related to have poured out a great number of lines in the morning, and to have passed the day in reducing them to fewer[6].

231   The occasional poet is circumscribed by the narrowness of his subject: whatever can happen to man has happened so often that little remains for fancy or invention[7]. We have been all born; we have most of us been married; and so many have died before us that our deaths can supply but few materials for a poet. In the fate of princes the publick has an interest; and what happens to them of good or evil the poets have always considered as

than anything he has written.' E. FITZGERALD, *More Letters*, p. 127.

[1] *Post*, POPE, 296, 304. For Johnson's dislike of writing see Boswell's *Johnson*, iii. 19; iv. 219.

[2] *Works*, vii. 440.

[3] *Ante*, DRYDEN, 103.

[4] *Post*, POPE, 301.

[5] 'Ev'n copious Dryden wanted, or forgot,
   The last and greatest art, the art to blot.'
POPE, *Imit. Hor. Epis.* ii. 1. 280; *post*, POPE, 120.

[6] 'Quum *Georgica* scriberet, traditur quotidie meditatos mane plurimos versus dictare solitus, ac per

totum diem retractando ad paucissimos redigere.' *Life*, attributed to Donatus, *Del. Virgil*, Preface, p. 7.

[7] 'Caetera, quae vacuas tenuissent carmine mentes,
   Omnia iam vulgata.'
   VIRGIL, *Georg.* iii. 3.

Dryden says of the earlier dramatists :—'We acknowledge them our fathers in wit, but they have ruined their estates themselves, before they came to their children's hands. There is scarce a humour, a character, or any kind of plot, which they have not used.' *Works*, xv. 367.

For Goldsmith's complaint 'that he had come too late into the world,' see Boswell's *Johnson*, ii. 358.

business for the Muse. But after so many inauguratory gratulations, nuptial hymns, and funeral dirges, he must be highly favoured by nature or by fortune who says any thing not said before. Even war and conquest, however splendid, suggest no new images; the triumphal chariot of a victorious monarch can be decked only with those ornaments that have graced his predecessors.

Not only matter but time is wanting. The poem must not be 232 delayed till the occasion is forgotten. The lucky moments of animated imagination cannot be attended; elegances and illustrations cannot be multiplied by gradual accumulation: the composition must be dispatched while conversation is yet busy and admiration fresh; and haste is to be made lest some other event should lay hold upon mankind.

Occasional compositions may however secure to a writer the 233 praise both of learning and facility; for they cannot be the effect of long study, and must be furnished immediately from the treasures of the mind.

The death of Cromwell was the first publick event which called 234 forth Dryden's poetical powers[1]. His heroick stanzas have beauties and defects; the thoughts are vigorous, and though not always proper shew a mind replete with ideas; the numbers are smooth, and the diction, if not altogether correct, is elegant and easy.

Davenant was perhaps at this time his favourite author[2], though 235 *Gondibert* never appears to have been popular[3]; and from Davenant he learned to please his ear with the stanza of four lines alternately rhymed[4].

[1] *Ante*, DRYDEN, 7; *post*, 338.
[2] *Ante*, DRYDEN, 24. Dryden, in his *Essay of Heroic Plays* (1672), says of Davenant's dramas:—'We are bound, with all veneration to his memory, to acknowledge what advantage we received from that excellent ground-work which he laid.' *Works*, iv. 20.
[3] [It is styled *An Heroick Poem*, and fills 165 folio pages. It was praised by Cowley, Waller, and Hobbes, but 'Four eminent wits of that age (two of which were Sʳ John Denham and Mr. Donne) published several copies of verses to Sir William's discredit under this title,

Certain Verses Written by Several of the Author's Friends, to be reprinted with the Second edition of Gondibert. London, 1653.' Langbaine's *Dram. Poets*, p. 112. See also *Ath. Oxon.* iii. 808, where the 'wits' are given as 'Sir John Denham, Jo. Donne, Sir Allen Broderick, &c.' Donne would be the son of the Dean of St. Paul's (1604–62), who published 'several frivolous trifles under his own name.' *Fasti*, i. 503. He was the author of *Donne's Satyr*, a ribald production.]
[4] *Gondibert* begins :—
'Of all the Lombards by their trophies known,

236 Dryden very early formed his versification[1] : there are in this early production no traces of Donne's or Jonson's ruggedness[2]; but he did not so soon free his mind from the ambition of forced conceits[3]. In his verses on the Restoration he says of the King's exile :

> ' He, toss'd by Fate . . .
> Could taste no sweets of youth's desired age,
> But found his life too true a pilgrimage[4].'

And afterwards, to shew how virtue and wisdom are increased by adversity, he makes this remark :

> 'Well might the ancient poets then confer
> On Night the honour'd name of *counsellor*,
> Since, struck with rays of prosperous fortune blind,
> We light alone in dark afflictions find[5].'

237 His praise of Monk's dexterity comprises such a cluster of thoughts unallied to one another as will not elsewhere be easily found :

> ' 'Twas Monk, whom providence design'd to loose
> Those real bonds false freedom did impose.
> The blessed saints that watch'd this turning scene
> Did from their stars with joyful wonder lean
> To see small clues draw vastest weights along,
> Not in their bulk, but in their order strong.
> Thus pencils can by one slight touch restore
> Smiles to that changed face that wept before.
> With ease such fond chimæras we pursue,
> As fancy frames for fancy to subdue:
> But, when ourselves to action we betake,
> It shuns the mint, like gold that chymists make:
> How hard was then his task, at once to be
> What in the body natural we see !
> Man's Architect distinctly did ordain
> The charge of muscles, nerves, and of the brain,
> Through viewless conduits spirits to dispense,
> The springs of motion from the seat of sense.

Who sought fame soon, and had her favour long,
King Aribert best seem'd to fill the throne,
And bred most bus'ness for heroick song.'

[1] ' In the meantime, that I may arrogate nothing to myself, I must acknowledge that Virgil in Latin, and Spenser in English, have been my masters.' *Works*, xiv. 208.

[2] See *post*, POPE, 304, for 'Dryden's rejection of unnatural thoughts and rugged numbers.'

[3] *Ante*, DRYDEN, 5.

[4] *Astraea Redux*, l. 51. *Works*, ix. 35 ; *ante*, DRYDEN, 8.

[5] l. 93.

'Twas not the hasty product of a day,
But the well-ripen'd fruit of wise delay.
He, like a patient angler, ere he strook,
Would let them play a-while upon the hook.
Our healthful food the stomach labours thus,
At first embracing what it straight doth crush.
Wise leaches will not vain receipts obtrude,
While growing pains pronounce the humours crude ;
Deaf to complaints, they wait upon the ill,
Till some safe crisis authorize their skill [1].'

He had not yet learned, indeed he never learned well, to 238
forbear the improper use of mythology [2]. After having rewarded
the heathen deities for their care,

'With *alga* who the sacred altar strows ?
To all the sea-gods Charles an offering owes ;
A bull to thee, Portunus, shall be slain,
A ram [lamb] to you, ye [the] Tempests of the Main [3] '—

he tells us, in the language of religion,

'Prayer storm'd the skies, and ravish'd Charles from thence,
As heaven itself is took by violence [4] '—

and afterwards mentions one of the awful passages of
Sacred History [5].

Other conceits there are, too curious to be quite omitted, as

'For by example most we sinn'd before,
And, glass-like, clearness mix'd with frailty bore [6].'

How far he was yet from thinking it necessary to found his 239
sentiments on Nature appears from the extravagance of his
fictions and hyperboles :

'The winds, that never moderation knew,
Afraid to blow too much, too faintly blew ;
Or, out of breath with joy, could not enlarge
Their straiten'd lungs [7].'

---

[1] l. 151.
[2] *Ante*, BUTLER, 41 ; *post*, DRYDEN, 335.
[3] l. 119. Scott, in defence of this passage, says :—' In a poem of which elegance of expression and ingenuity of device are the principal attributes, an allusion to the customs of Greece or of Rome, while it gives a classic air to the composition, seems as little misplaced as an apt quotation from the authors in which they are recorded.' *Works*, ix. 31.
[4] l. 143.
[5] l. 262 ; *Exodus*, xxxiii. 18–end ; xxxiv. 1–6.
[6] l. 207.
[7] l. 242.

'It is no longer motion cheats your view;
As you meet it, the land approacheth you;
The land returns, and in the white it wears
The marks of penitence and sorrow bears[1].'

I know not whether this fancy, however little be its value, was not borrowed. A French poet read to Malherbe some verses, in which he represents France as moving out of its place to receive the king. 'Though this,' said Malherbe[2], 'was in my time, I do not remember it.'

240 His poem on the *Coronation* has a more even tenour of thought. Some lines deserve to be quoted :

'You have already quench'd sedition's brand,
And zeal, that [which] burnt it, only warms the land ;
The jealous sects that durst [dare] not trust their cause
So far from their own will as to the laws,
Him [You] for their umpire and their synod take,
And their appeal alone to Cæsar make[3].'

241 Here may be found one particle of that old versification, of which, I believe, in all his works there is not another :

'Nor is it duty, or our hope [hopes] alone,
Creates [Create] that joy, but full *fruition*[4].'

242 In the verses to the lord chancellor Clarendon two years afterwards is a conceit so hopeless at the first view that few would have attempted it, and so successfully laboured that though at last it gives the reader more perplexity than pleasure, and seems hardly worth the study that it costs, yet it must be valued as a proof of a mind at once subtle and comprehensive :

'In open prospect nothing bounds our eye,
Until the earth seems join'd unto the sky:
So in this hemisphere our outmost view
Is only bounded by our king and you:
Our sight is limited where you are join'd,
And beyond that no farther heaven can find.
So well your virtues do with his agree,
That, though your orbs of different greatness be,

---

[1] *Astraea Redux*, l. 252.
[2] 'Les nombreuses anecdotes que chacun sait par cœur sur Malherbe, et dont plus d'une fait sourire,' &c. SAINTE-BEUVE, *Causeries*, viii. 68.
[3] l. 79. *Works*, ix. 57 *n.*
[4] l. 69. In the unfulfilled forecasts of this poem none is more ridiculous than the following, where he describes the king's wife as :—
'A queen, near whose chaste womb, ordained by fate,
The souls of kings unborn for bodies wait.'   l. 119.

> Yet both are for each other's use dispos'd,
> His to enclose, and yours to be enclos'd:
> Nor could another in your room have been,
> Except an emptiness had come between¹.'

The comparison of the Chancellor to the Indies leaves all 243 resemblance too far behind it:

> ' And as the Indies were not found before
> Those rich perfumes which from the happy shore
> The winds upon their balmy wings convey'd,
> Whose guilty sweetness first their world betray'd ;
> So by your counsels we are brought to view
> A new and undiscover'd world in you².'

There is another comparison, for there is little else in the 244 poem, of which, though perhaps it cannot be explained into plain prosaick meaning, the mind perceives enough to be delighted, and readily forgives its obscurity for its magnificence:

> ' How strangely active are the arts of peace,
> Whose restless motions less than wars do cease !
> Peace is not freed from labour, but from noise,
> And war more force, but not more pains employs :
> Such is the mighty swiftness of your mind
> That, like the earth's, it leaves our sense behind,
> While you so smoothly turn and rowl our sphere,
> That rapid motion does but rest appear.
> For as in nature's swiftness, with the throng
> Of flying orbs while ours is borne along,
> All seems at rest to the deluded eye,
> Mov'd by the soul of the same harmony :
> So carry'd on by your unweary'd care,
> We rest in peace, and yet in motion share³.'

To this succeed four lines, which perhaps afford Dryden's first 245 attempt at those penetrating remarks on human nature, for which he seems to have been peculiarly formed :

> ' Let envy then those crimes within you see,
> From which the happy never must be free ;
> Envy that does with misery reside,
> The joy and the revenge of ruin'd pride⁴.'

Into this poem he seems to have collected all his powers, and 246 after this he did not often bring upon his anvil such stubborn and unmalleable thoughts ; but, as a specimen of his abilities to

---

¹ l. 31. *Works*, ix. 64 *n*.　　² l. 73.　　³ l. 105.　　⁴ l. 119.

unite the most unsociable matter, he has concluded with lines, of which I think not myself obliged to tell the meaning:

> 'Yet, unimpair'd with labours, or with time,
> Your age but seems to a new youth to climb.
> Thus heavenly bodies do our time beget,
> And measure change, but share no part of it:
> And still it shall without a weight increase,
> Like this new year, whose motions never cease.
> For since the glorious course you have begun
> Is led by Charles, as that is by the sun,
> It must both weightless and immortal prove,
> Because the centre of it is above [1].'

247   In the *Annus Mirabilis* [2] he returned to the quatrain, which from that time he totally quitted, perhaps from this experience of its inconvenience, for he complains of its difficulty [3]. This is one of his greatest attempts. He had subjects equal to his abilities, a great naval war, and the Fire of London. Battles have always been described in heroick poetry; but a sea-fight and artillery had yet something of novelty. New arts are long in the world before poets describe them; for they borrow every thing from their predecessors, and commonly derive very little from nature or from life. Boileau was the first French writer that had ever hazarded in verse the mention of modern war, or the effects of gunpowder [4]. We, who are less afraid of novelty, had already possession of those dreadful images: Waller had described a sea-fight [5]. Milton had not yet transferred the invention of fire-arms to the rebellious angels [6].

248   This poem is written with great diligence, yet does not fully

---

[1] l. 147.

[2] *Works*, ix. 79. Pepys recorded on Feb. 2, 1666-7:—'I am very well pleased this night with reading a poem of Dryden's upon the present war; a very good poem.' *Diary*, iii. 390.

[3] The last six words in the sentence are not in the first edition. *Ante*, DRYDEN, 24 *n*. He introduced some quatrains into *The Indian Emperor* (*Works*, ii. 340), which was brought out some months later than *Annus Mirabilis*.

[4] In his *Épître* iv. (written in 1672) l. 119, as well as in other poems, Boileau made this boast:—'Avant moi, les Poètes ne pouvant mettre la poudre à canon en vers, mettaient à leurs héros des traits et des flèches à la main; ce qui était bon pour les Grecs et les Romains, mais qui ne caractérise point du tout notre nation.' In a note the editor quotes the mention of gunpowder by earlier French poets. *Œuvres de Boileau*, v. 52.

[5] [In *On a War with Spain*, written probably in 1656 (Fenton's *Waller: Observations*, p. 116), and first printed in Carrington's *Cromwell*, 1659, p. 195.]

[6] The Preface to *Annus Mirabilis* is dated Nov. 10, 1666. *Works*, ix. 102. *Paradise Lost* was published in 1667. *Ante*, MILTON, 130.

answer the expectation raised by such subjects and such a writer. With the stanza of Davenant he has sometimes his vein of parenthesis and incidental disquisition, and stops his narrative for a wise remark[1].

The general fault is that he affords more sentiment than **249** description, and does not so much impress scenes upon the fancy as deduce consequences and make comparisons.

The initial stanzas have rather too much resemblance to the **250** first lines of Waller's poem on the war with Spain; perhaps such a beginning is natural, and could not be avoided without affectation[2]. Both Waller and Dryden might take their hint from the poem on the civil war of Rome, 'Orbem jam totum[3],' &c.

Of the king collecting his navy, he says: **251**

> 'It seems as every ship their sovereign knows,
>   His awful summons they so soon obey;
> So hear the scaly herds when Proteus blows,
>   And so to pasture follow through the sea[4].'

It would not be hard to believe that Dryden had written the two first lines seriously, and that some wag had added the two latter in burlesque. Who would expect the lines that immediately follow, which are indeed perhaps indecently hyperbolical, but certainly in a mode totally different?

> 'To see this fleet upon the ocean move,
>   Angels drew wide the curtains of the skies;
> And heaven, as if there wanted lights above,
>   For tapers made two glaring comets rise.'

The description of the attempt at Bergen will afford a very **252** compleat specimen of the descriptions in this poem:

> 'And now approach'd their fleet from India, fraught
>   With all the riches of the rising sun:
> And precious sand from southern climates brought,
>   The fatal regions where the war begun.

---

[1] For examples see stanzas 32, 35, 36, 38.

[2] 'Now for some ages had the pride of Spain
Made the sun shine on half the world in vain;
While she bid war to all that durst supply
The place of those her cruelty made die.'
WALLER, *Eng. Poets*, xvi. 143; *ante*,

WALLER, 129.
'In thriving arts long time had Holland grown,
Crouching at home and cruel when abroad;
Scarce leaving us the means to claim our own;
Our King they courted, and our merchants aw'd.' DRYDEN.

[3] PETRONIUS, *Sat.* c. 119, l. 1.

[4] Stanza 15.

'Like hunted castors, conscious of their store,
  Their way-laid wealth to Norway's coast they bring:
Then first the North's cold bosom spices bore,
  And winter brooded on the eastern spring.

'By the rich scent we found our perfum'd prey,
  Which, flank'd with rocks, did close in covert lie:
And round about their murdering cannon lay,
  At once to threaten and invite the eye.

'Fiercer than cannon, and than rocks more hard,
  The English undertake th' unequal war:
Seven ships alone, by which the port is barr'd,
  Besiege the Indies, and all Denmark dare.

'These fight like husbands, but like lovers those:
  These fain would keep, and those more fain enjoy:
And to such height their frantic passion grows,
  That what both love, both hazard to destroy:

'Amidst whole heaps of spices lights a ball,
  And now their odours arm'd against them fly:
Some preciously by shatter'd porcelain fall,
  And some by aromatic splinters die.

'And though by tempests of the prize bereft,
  In heaven's inclemency some ease we find;
Our foes we vanquish'd by our valour left,
  And only yielded to the seas and wind [1].'

253   In this manner is the sublime too often mingled with the
ridiculous. The Dutch seek a shelter for a wealthy fleet: this
surely needed no illustration; yet they must fly, not like all
the rest of mankind on the same occasion, but 'like hunted
castors'; and they might with strict propriety be hunted, for
we winded them by our noses—their 'perfumes' betrayed them.
The 'Husband' and the 'Lover,' though of more dignity than
the 'Castor,' are images too domestick to mingle properly with
the horrors of war. The two quatrains that follow are worthy
of the author.

254   The account of the different sensations with which the two
fleets retired when the night parted them is one of the fairest
flowers of English poetry:

'The night comes on, we eager to pursue
  The combat still, and they asham'd to leave:
'Till the last streaks of dying day withdrew,
  And doubtful moon-light did our rage deceive.

[1] Stanzas 24-30.

'In th' English fleet each ship resounds with joy,
  And loud applause of their great leader's fame;
In fiery dreams the Dutch they still destroy,
  And, slumbering, smile at the imagin'd flame.

'Not so the Holland fleet, who, tir'd and done,
  Stretch'd on their decks like weary oxen lie;
Faint sweats all down their mighty members run
  (Vast bulks, which little souls but ill supply).

'In dreams they fearful precipices tread,
  Or, shipwreck'd, labour to some distant shore,
Or, in dark churches, walk among the dead:
  They wake with horror, and dare sleep no more[1].'

It is a general rule in poetry that all appropriated terms of art 255
should be sunk in general expressions, because poetry is to speak
an universal language[2]. This rule is still stronger with regard
to arts not liberal or confined to few, and therefore far removed
from common knowledge; and of this kind certainly is technical
navigation[3]. Yet Dryden was of opinion that a sea-fight ought
to be described in the nautical language[4]; 'and certainly,' says
he, 'as those who in a logical disputation [dispute] keep to [in]
general terms would hide a fallacy, so those who do it in any
poetical description would veil their ignorance[5].'

Let us then appeal to experience; for by experience at last we 256
learn as well what will please as what will profit. In the battle
his terms seem to have been blown away; but he deals them
liberally in the dock:

'So here some pick out bullets from the side,
  Some drive old *okum* thro' each *seam* and rift:
Their left-hand does the *calking-iron* guide,
  The rattling *mallet* with the right they lift.

'With boiling pitch another near at hand
  (From friendly Sweden brought) the *seams instops*:
Which, well laid [paid] o'er, the salt-sea waves withstand,
  And shake them from the rising beak in drops.

---

[1] Stanzas 68–71.

[2] 'I will not give the reasons why [in translating Virgil] I writ not always in the proper terms of navigation, land-service, or in the cant of any profession. I will only say that Virgil has avoided those proprieties, because he writ not to mariners, soldiers, astronomers, gardeners, peasants, &c., but to all in general.' DRYDEN, *Works*, xiv. 229.

[3] *Ante*, MILTON, 234, 263; *post*, DRYDEN, 336.

[4] 'In general I will only say, I have never yet seen the description of any naval fight in the proper terms which are used at sea. ... For my own part, if I had little knowledge of the sea, yet I have thought it no shame to learn.' *Works*, ix. 93.

[5] *Ib.* ix. 94.

'Some the *gall'd* ropes with dawby *marling* bind,
   Or sear-cloth masts with strong *tarpawling* coats:
To try new *shrouds* one mounts into the wind,
   And one below, their ease or stiffness notes[1].'

I suppose here is not one term which every reader does not wish away[2].

257 His digression to the original and progress of navigation, with his prospect of the advancement which it shall receive from the Royal Society, then newly instituted, may be considered as an example seldom equalled of seasonable excursion and artful return[3].

258 One line, however, leaves me discontented; he says, that by the help of the philosophers,

'Instructed ships shall sail to quick commerce,
   By which remotest regions are allied.'

Which he is constrained to explain in a note, 'By a more exact measure of longitude[4].' It had better become Dryden's learning and genius to have laboured science into poetry, and have shewn, by explaining longitude, that verse did not refuse the ideas of philosophy.

259 His description of the Fire[5] is painted by resolute meditation, out of a mind better formed to reason than to feel. The conflagration of a city, with all its tumults of concomitant distress, is one of the most dreadful spectacles which this world can offer to human eyes; yet it seems to raise little emotion in the breast of the poet: he watches the flame coolly from street to street, with now a reflection and now a simile, till at last he meets the king, for whom he makes a speech, rather tedious in a time so busy[6], and then follows again the progress of the fire.

---

[1] Stanzas 146-48.

[2] 'I agree with you in your censure of the use of sea-terms in Mr. Dryden's *Virgil*, . . . because no terms of art, or cant-words, suit with the majesty and dignity of style which epic poetry requires.' POPE, *Works* (Elwin and Courthope), vi. 107.

Dante, in the *Inferno*, canto xxi, 'deals his terms liberally in the dock.' Who would wish that in Cowper's *Loss of the Royal George* were omitted—
'A land-breeze shook the shrouds'?

[3] Stanzas 161-66. He was elected a member on Nov. 19, 1662. Malone's *Dryden*, i. 50. See *ante*, COWLEY, 31, and *post*, DRYDEN, 330, for a quatrain in this digression ridiculed by Johnson for its absurdities.

[4] In the original, 'longitudes.' *Works*, ix. 150. For 'ascertaining the longitude' see Boswell's *Johnson*, i. 301; *John. Misc.* i. 402.

[5] Stanzas 212-91.

[6] Stanzas 262-70.

There are, however, in this part some passages that deserve 260
attention, as in the beginning:

> 'The diligence of trades, and noiseful gain,
>   And luxury, more late asleep were laid;
> All was the night's, and in her silent reign
>   No sound the rest of Nature did invade.

> 'In this deep quiet—[1]'

The expression 'All was the night's' is taken from Seneca, who
remarks on Virgil's line

> 'Omnia noctis erant placida composta quiete,'

that he might have concluded better,

> 'Omnia noctis erant[2].'

The following quatrain is vigorous and animated: 261

> 'The ghosts of traytors from the bridge descend
>   With bold fanatick spectres to rejoice;
> About the fire into a dance they bend,
>   And sing their sabbath notes with feeble voice[3].'

His prediction of the improvements which shall be made in 262
the new city is elegant and poetical[4], and, with an event which
Poets cannot always boast, has been happily verified. The poem
concludes with a simile that might have better been omitted[5].

Dryden, when he wrote this poem, seems not yet fully to have 263
formed his versification, or settled his system of propriety.

From this time he addicted himself almost wholly to the stage, 264
'to which,' says he, 'my genius never much inclined me[6],' merely
as the most profitable market for poetry. By writing tragedies

---

[1] Stanzas 216, 217.

[2] M. Annaeus Seneca (*Opera*, 1783, p. 215), after quoting Varro's (not Virgil's) lines:—
'Desierant latrare canes, urbesque silebant,
Omnia noctis erant placida composta quiete,'
continues:—'Solebat Ovidius de his versibus dicere, potuisse fieri longe meliores si secundi versus ultima pars abscinderetur, et sic desineret:
    "Omnia noctis erant."'

[3] Stanza 223. The top of the tower on London Bridge 'used to be covered with heads or quarters of unfortunate partizans.' PENNANT, *London*, 1790, p. 297.
'The Sabbath notes are the infernal hymns chanted at the witches' Sabbath.' SCOTT, Dryden's *Works*, ix. 171 *n*.

[4] Stanzas 292–end.

[5] 'Thus to the eastern wealth through storms we go,
    But now, the Cape once doubled, fear no more;
    A constant trade-wind will securely blow,
    And gently lay us on the spicy shore.'

[6] *Works*, xiii. 30; *ante*, DRYDEN, 12, 91; *post*, 329.

in rhyme he continued to improve his diction and his numbers. According to the opinion of Harte[1], who had studied his works with great attention, he settled his principles of versification in 1676, when he produced the play of *Aureng Zebe*[2]; and, according to his own account of the short time in which he wrote *Tyrannick Love*[3] and *The State of Innocence*[4], he soon obtained the full effect of diligence, and added facility to exactness[5].

265   Rhyme has been so long banished from the theatre[6] that we know not its effect upon the passions of an audience; but it has this convenience, that sentences stand more independent on each other, and striking passages are therefore easily selected and retained. Thus the description of Night in *The Indian Emperor*[7] and the rise and fall of empire in *The Conquest of Granada*[8] are more frequently repeated than any lines in *All for Love* or *Don Sebastian*[9].

266   To search his plays for vigorous sallies and sententious elegances, or to fix the dates of any little pieces which he wrote by chance or by solicitation, were labour too tedious and minute.

267   His dramatic labours did not so wholly absorb his thoughts, but that he promulgated the laws of translation in a preface to the English *Epistles of Ovid*[10]; one of which he translated himself, and another in conjunction with the Earl of Mulgrave.

268   *Absalom and Achitophel*[11] is a work so well known that particular criticism is superfluous. If it be considered as a poem political and controversial it will be found to comprise all the excellences of which the subject is susceptible: acrimony of censure, elegance of praise, artful delineation of characters, variety and vigour of sentiment, happy turns of language, and pleasing harmony of numbers; and all these raised to such a height as can scarcely be found in any other English composition.

269   It is not however without faults; some lines are inelegant or improper, and too many are irreligiously licentious. The original structure of the poem was defective: allegories drawn to great

---

[1] Johnson, perhaps, had this opinion from Walter Harte's lips, for he knew him. Boswell's *Johnson*, ii. 120.

[2] *Ante*, DRYDEN, 75.

[3] *Ante*, DRYDEN, 46.

[4] *Ante*, DRYDEN, 71.

[5] Both these plays were written before *Aureng Zebe*. For facility got by diligence see *ante*, MILTON, 178.

[6] *Ante*, DRYDEN, 20.

[7] *Ante*, DRYDEN, 19.

[8] Part ii. act i. sc. 1. *Works*, iv. 123.

[9] His two best plays. *Ante*, DRYDEN, 78, 82.

[10] *Ante*, DRYDEN, 107.

[11] *Ante*, DRYDEN, 108.

length will always break; Charles could not run continually parallel with David.

The subject had likewise another inconvenience: it admitted 270 little imagery or description, and a long poem of mere sentiments easily becomes tedious; though all the parts are forcible and every line kindles new rapture, the reader, if not relieved by the interposition of something that sooths the fancy, grows weary of admiration, and defers the rest [1].

As an approach to historical truth was necessary the action 271 and catastrophe were not in the poet's power; there is therefore an unpleasing disproportion between the beginning and the end. We are alarmed by a faction formed out of many sects various in their principles, but agreeing in their purpose of mischief, formidable for their numbers, and strong by their supports, while the king's friends are few and weak. The chiefs on either part are set forth to view; but when expectation is at the height the king makes a speech, and

'Henceforth a series of new times [time] began [2].'

Who can forbear to think of an enchanted castle, with a wide 272 moat and lofty battlements, walls of marble and gates of brass, which vanishes at once into air when the destined knight blows his horn before it [3]?

In the second part, written by Tate [4], there is a long insertion [5], 273 which for poignancy of satire exceeds any part of the former. Personal resentment, though no laudable motive to satire, can add great force to general principles. Self-love is a busy prompter [6].

The Medal [7], written upon the same principles with *Absalom* 274

---

[1] *Ante*, BUTLER, 35.

[2] 'Henceforth a series of new time began,
The mighty years in long procession ran.'
Absalom and Achitophel, l. 1028.
Twenty-one years earlier he had written :—
'And now Time's whiter series is begun,
Which in soft centuries shall smoothly run.'
Astraea Redux, l. 292.

[3] 'The conclusion of the story I purposely forbore to prosecute, because I could not obtain from myself to show Absalom unfortunate. The frame of it was cut out but for a picture to the waist, and if the draught be so far true it is as much as I designed.' *Works*, ix. 213.

[4] 'She saw slow Philips creep like Tate's poor page.'
The Dunciad, i. 105. See also *post*, ROWE, 21.

[5] Lines 310–509: they were contributed by Dryden.

[6] It was Settle (*ante*, DRYDEN, 32, 115) and Shadwell (*ante*, 136) whom he attacked.

[7] *Ante*, DRYDEN, 114.

and Achitophel, but upon a narrower plan, gives less pleasure, though it discovers equal abilities in the writer. The superstructure cannot extend beyond the foundation; a single character or incident cannot furnish as many ideas as a series of events or multiplicity of agents. This poem therefore, since time has left it to itself, is not much read, nor perhaps generally understood, yet it abounds with touches both of humorous and serious satire. The picture of a man whose propensions to mischief are such that his best actions are but inability of wickedness, is very skilfully delineated and strongly coloured.

> 'Power was his aim : but, thrown from that pretence, ⎫
> The wretch turn'd loyal in his own defence,   ⎬
> And malice reconcil'd him to his Prince.   ⎭
> Him, in the anguish of his soul, he serv'd ;
> Rewarded faster still than he deserv'd.
> Behold him now exalted into trust ;
> His counsels oft convenient, seldom just.
> Ev'n in the most sincere advice he gave,
> He had a grudging still to be a knave.
> The frauds he learnt in his fanatic years
> Made him uneasy in his lawful gears.
> At least [best] as little honest as he cou'd :
> And, like white witches, mischievously good.
> To his first bias, longingly, he leans ;
> And rather would be great by wicked means[1].'

275   The *Threnodia*, which, by a term I am afraid neither authorized nor analogical, he calls *Augustalis*, is not among his happiest productions[2]. Its first and obvious defect is the irregularity of its metre[3], to which the ears of that age however were accustomed. What is worse, it has neither tenderness nor dignity, it is neither magnificent nor pathetick. He seems to look round him for images which he cannot find, and what he has he distorts by endeavouring to enlarge them. He is, he says, 'petrified with grief[4]'; but the marble sometimes relents, and trickles in a joke.

> 'The sons of art all med'cines try'd,
> And every noble remedy apply'd[5];

---

[1] l. 50. *Works*, ix. 442.
[2] *Ante*, DRYDEN, 212. The king died on Feb. 6, 1684–5. 'The British Museum copy has March 9 written on the title-page.' *Works*, x. 62. Scott publishes 'a defence of Dryden's phrase,' by Dr. Adam. *Ib.* p. 61. Professor Robinson Ellis, whom

I have consulted, agrees with Johnson.
[3] Dryden describes it as *A Funeral Pindaric Poem*, x. 55. See *ante*, COWLEY, 141.
[4] 'Like Niobe we marble grow ;
    And petrify with grief.' l. 7.
[5] 'The patient was bled largely. Hot iron was applied to his head.

With emulation each essay'd
His utmost skill; *nay more they pray'd*:
Was never [Never was] losing game with better conduct play'd [1].'

He had been a little inclined to merriment before upon the 276
prayers of a nation for their dying sovereign, nor was he serious
enough to keep heathen fables out of his religion.

'With him th' innumerable crowd
        Of armed prayers
Knock'd at the gates of heaven, and knock'd aloud ;
The first well-meaning rude petitioners.
All for his life assail'd the throne,
All would have brib'd the skies by offering up their own.
So great a throng not heaven itself could bar ;
'Twas almost borne by force *as in the giants' war.*
The prayers, at least, for his reprieve were heard ;
His death, like Hezekiah's, was deferr'd [2].'

There is throughout the composition a desire of splendor 277
without wealth. In the conclusion he seems too much pleased
with the prospect of the new reign to have lamented his old
master with much sincerity [3].

He did not miscarry in this attempt for want of skill either in 278
lyrick or elegiack poetry. His poem *On the death of Mrs. Killigrew* is undoubtedly the noblest ode that our language ever has
produced [4]. The first part flows with a torrent of enthusiasm [5].
'Fervet immensusque ruit [6].' All the stanzas indeed are not
equal. An imperial crown cannot be one continued diamond:
the gems must be held together by some less valuable matter.

In his first *Ode for Cecilia's Day* [7], which is lost in the splendor 279
of the second [8], there are passages which would have dignified

---

A loathsome volatile salt, extracted
from human skulls, was forced into
his mouth.' MACAULAY, *History*,
ii. 6.
    [1] l. 160.   [2] l. 97.
    [3] He hints at the king's shabbiness
towards poets:—
'Though little was their hire, and
    light their gain,
Yet somewhat to their share he
    threw.
        .   .   .   .   .
Oh never let their lays his name
    forget !
The pension of a prince's praise is
    great.'   l. 377.

[4] *Works*, xi. 105. Johnson says
(*post*, DRYDEN, 318) that the *Ode on
St. Cecilia's Day* 'may be pronounced
perhaps superior in the whole.'
    [5] 'The first stanza,' writes Dr.
Warton, 'is full of absurd bombast,
and nearly approaching the realm
of nonsense.' Pope's *Works*, i.
213.
    [6] HORACE, *Odes*, iv. 2. 7.
    [7] *Works*, xi. 171.
    [8] *Alexander's Feast; or the Power
of Music, Ib.* xi. 186. *Ante*, DRY-
DEN, 150; *post*, 318, 406.
    The first Ode was so much 'lost'
that in 1756 Dr. Warton wrote:—

any other poet. The first stanza is vigorous and elegant, though the word *diapason* is too technical [1], and the rhymes are too remote from one another.

> 'From harmony, from heavenly harmony,
> This universal frame began:
> When nature underneath a heap
> Of jarring atoms lay,
> And could not heave her head,
> The tuneful voice was heard from high,
> Arise ye more than dead.
> Then cold and hot, and moist and dry,
> In order to their stations leap,
> And musick's power obey.
> From harmony, from heavenly harmony,
> This universal frame began:
> From harmony to harmony
> Through all the compass of the notes it ran,
> The diapason closing full in man.'

280 The conclusion is likewise striking, but it includes an image so awful in itself that it can owe little to poetry ; and I could wish the antithesis of *musick untuning* had found some other place [2].

> 'As from the power of sacred lays
> The spheres began to move,
> And sung the great Creator's praise
> To all the bless'd above;
> So when the last and dreadful hour
> This crumbling pageant shall devour,
> The trumpet shall be heard on high,
> The dead shall live, the living die,
> And musick shall untune the sky.'

281 Of his skill in Elegy he has given a specimen in his *Eleonora*, of which the following lines discover their author:

> 'Though all these rare endowments of the mind
> Were in a narrow space of life confin'd,

'We have in Tonson's *Miscellanies* preserved an earlier Ode of Dryden on St. Cecilia, one stanza of which [the second] I cannot forbear inserting in this note.' *Essay on Pope,* i. 53 *n.*

[1] Dryden had Milton's authority for the word.

'disproportion'd sin

Jarr'd against nature's chime, and with harsh din
Broke the fair music that all creatures made
To their great Lord, whose love their motion sway'd
In perfect diapason.'
    At a Solemn Music, ll. 19-23.
[2] *Post,* DRYDEN, 320 ; POPE, 326.

The figure was with full perfection crown'd;
Though not so large an orb, as truly round.
As when in glory, through the public place,
The spoils of conquer'd nations were to pass,
And but one day for triumph was allow'd,
The consul was constrain'd his pomp to crowd;
And so the swift procession hurry'd on,
That all, though not distinctly, might be shown:
So, in the straiten'd bounds of life confin'd,
She gave but glimpses of her glorious mind:
And multitudes of virtues pass'd along,
Each pressing foremost in the mighty throng,
Ambitious to be seen, and then make room
For greater multitudes that were to come.
Yet unemploy'd no minute slipp'd away;
Moments were precious in so short a stay.
The haste of heaven to have her was so great,
That some were single acts, though each compleat;
And every act stood ready to repeat [1].'

This piece however is not without its faults; there is so much 282
likeness in the initial comparison that there is no illustration.
As a king would be lamented, Eleonora was lamented.

'As when some great and gracious monarch dies,
Soft whispers first and mournful murmurs rise
Among the sad attendants; then the sound
Soon gathers voice, and spreads the news around,
Through town and country, till the dreadful blast
Is blown to distant colonies at last;
Who then, perhaps, were offering vows in vain,
For his long life and for his happy reign:
So slowly by degrees, unwilling fame
Did matchless Eleonora's fate proclaim,
Till publick as the loss the news became [2].'

This is little better than to say in praise of a shrub that it is as
green as a tree, or of a brook, that it waters a garden as a river
waters a country.

Dryden confesses that he did not know the lady whom he 283
celebrates [3]; the praise being therefore inevitably general fixes

---

[1] l. 270. *Works*, xi. 136.
[2] l. 1. *Ib.* xi. 128.
[3] He defends himself by the
example of Dr. Donne, 'who acknowledges that he had never seen Mrs.
Drury, whom he has made immortal

in his admirable *Anniversaries.*' *Ib.*
xi. 123. 'Eleonora' was the Countess
of Abingdon. 'She died very suddenly at a ball in her own house.'
Prior's *Malone*, p. 447.

no impression on the reader nor excites any tendency to love, nor much desire of imitation[1]. Knowledge of the subject is to the poet what durable materials are to the architect.

284 The *Religio Laici*[2], which borrows its title from the *Religio Medici* of Browne[3], is almost the only work of Dryden which can be considered as a voluntary effusion[4]; in this, therefore, it might be hoped that the full effulgence of his genius would be found. But unhappily the subject is rather argumentative than poetical: he intended only a specimen of metrical disputation.

> ' And this unpolish'd rugged verse I chose,
> As fittest for discourse, and nearest prose[5].'

285 This however is a composition of great excellence in its kind, in which the familiar is very properly diversified with the solemn, and the grave with the humorous; in which metre has neither weakened the force nor clouded the perspicuity of argument: nor will it be easy to find another example equally happy of this middle kind of writing, which, though prosaick in some parts, rises to high poetry in others, and neither towers to the skies nor creeps along the ground[6].

286 Of the same kind, or not far distant from it, is *The Hind and Panther*[7], the longest of all Dryden's original poems; an allegory intended to comprise and to decide the controversy between the Romanists and Protestants. The scheme of the work is injudicious and incommodious: for what can be more absurd than that one beast should counsel another to rest her faith upon a pope and council[8]? He seems well enough skilled in the usual topicks of argument, endeavours to shew the necessity of an infallible judge, and reproaches the Reformers with want of

---

[1] *Post*, POPE, 415.

[2] *Religio Laici, or A Layman's Faith*, 1682, *Works*, x. 1.

[3] For Johnson's account of the *Religio Medici* see his *Works*, vi. 477.

[4] This is not stated in the Preface. In the Preface of *The Hind and the Panther*, Dryden says:—' It was neither imposed on me, nor so much as the subject given me by any man.' *Works*, x. 113.

[5] *Religio Laici*, l. 453.

[6] ' Nothing,' said Landor, ' was ever written in hymn equal to the be-

ginning of the *Religio Laici*,—the first eleven lines.' H. C. Robinson's *Diary*, iii. 194.

[7] *Ante*, DRYDEN, 126.

[8] ' *The Hind and Panther*. This is the masterpiece of a famous writer now living, intended for a complete abstract of sixteen thousand schoolmen, from Scotus to Bellarmin. *Tommy Pots*. Another piece, supposed by the same hand, by way of supplement to the former.' SWIFT, *A Tale of a Tub*, *Works*, x. 73. Swift wrote this in 1697. *Tommy Pots* was a popular ballad. *Ib. n.*

unity; but is weak enough to ask, why since we see without knowing how, we may not have an infallible judge without knowing where [1].

The Hind at one time is afraid to drink at the common brook, 287 because she may be worried [2]; but walking home with the Panther talks by the way of the Nicene Fathers [3], and at last declares herself to be the Catholic Church [4].

This absurdity was very properly ridiculed in *The City Mouse* 288 *and Country Mouse* of Montague and Prior [5]; and in the detection and censure of the incongruity of the fiction chiefly consists the value of their performance [6], which, whatever reputation it might obtain by the help of temporary passions, seems to readers almost a century distant not very forcible or animated.

Pope, whose judgement was perhaps a little bribed by the sub- 289 ject [7], used to mention this poem as the most correct specimen of Dryden's versification. It was indeed written when he had completely formed his manner, and may be supposed to exhibit, negligence excepted, his deliberate and ultimate scheme of metre.

We may therefore reasonably infer that he did not approve 290 the perpetual uniformity which confines the sense to couplets [8], since he has broken his lines in the initial paragraph :

> A milk-white Hind, immortal and unchang'd,
> Fed on the lawns, and in the forest rang'd ;

[1] For 'that wondrous wight, Infallibility,' as the Panther calls it, see Part ii. l. 65.

[2] Part i. l. 528.

[3] Part ii. l. 156.

[4] Part ii. ll. 394–662.

[5] *Ante*, DRYDEN, 127.

[6] 'Is it not as easy to imagine two Mice bilking coachmen and supping at the Devil, as to suppose a Hind entertaining the Panther at a hermit's cell, discussing the greatest mysteries of religion? ... What relation has the Hind to our Saviour? or what notion have we of a panther's Bible? If you say he means the Church, how does the Church feed on lawns and range in the forest? Let it be always a Church, or always the cloven-footed beast, for we cannot bear his shifting the scene every line.' Halifax's *Works*, pp. 33, 35.

[7] Pope was a Roman Catholic.

[8] Dryden, in his *Essay of Dramatic Poesy*, says:—'Though most commonly the sense is to be confined to the couplet, yet nothing that does *perpetuo tenore fluere*, run in the same channel, can please always. 'Tis like the murmuring of a stream, which, not varying in the fall, causes at first attention, at last drowsiness.' *Works*, xv. 363. See *ante*, DENHAM, 37 ; DRYDEN, 217.

'Enfin Malherbe vint, et le premier en France
Fit sentir dans les vers une juste cadence.

   .   .   .   .

Les stances avec grâce apprirent à tomber ;
Et le vers sur le vers n'osa plus enjamber.'

BOILEAU, *L'Art Poétique*, i. 131.

Without unspotted, innocent within,
She fear'd no danger, for she knew no sin [1].
Yet had she oft been chac'd with horns and hounds
And Scythian shafts, and many winged wounds
Aim'd at her heart; was often forc'd to fly,
And doom'd to death, though fated not to die [2].'

291   These lines are lofty, elegant, and musical, notwithstanding the interruption of the pause, of which the effect is rather increase of pleasure by variety than offence by ruggedness.

292   To the first part it was his intention, he says, ' to give the majestick turn of heroick poesy [3] '; and perhaps he might have executed his design not unsuccessfully had not an opportunity of satire, which he cannot forbear, fallen sometimes in his way. The character of a Presbyterian, whose emblem is the Wolf, is not very heroically majestick :

' More haughty than the rest, the wolfish race ⎫
Appear with belly gaunt and famish'd face: ⎬
Never was so deform'd a beast of grace. ⎭
His ragged tail betwixt his legs he wears, ⎫
Close clapp'd for shame; but his rough crest he rears, ⎬
And pricks up his predestinating ears [4].' ⎭

293   His general character of the other sorts of beasts that never go to church, though spritely and keen, has however not much of heroick poesy.

' These are the chief; to number o'er the rest,
And stand like Adam naming every beast,
Were weary work ; nor will the Muse describe
A slimy-born and sun-begotten tribe,
Who, far from steeples and their sacred sound,
In fields their sullen conventicles found.
These gross, half-animated lumps I leave ;
Nor can I think what thoughts they can conceive.
But if they think at all, 'tis sure no higher
Than matter, put in motion, may aspire ;

---

[1] Thus parodied by Montague and Prior:—
' A milk-white mouse, immortal and unchang'd,   [dairy rang'd ;
Fed on soft cheese, and o'er the
Without unspotted, innocent within,
She fear'd no danger, for she knew no gin.'
Halifax's *Works*, 1715, p. 44.

[2] *Works*, x. 119.
[3] ' The first part, consisting most in general characters and narration, I have endeavoured to raise, and give it the majestic turn of heroic poesy.' *Ib.* x. 117. For *majestic* see *ante*, DENHAM, 34 *n*.
[4] Part i. l. 160.

Souls that can scarce ferment their mass of clay; ⎞
So drossy, so divisible are they,   ⎬
As would but serve pure bodies for allay :   ⎠
Such souls as shards produce, such beetle things
As only buz to heaven with evening wings,
Strike in the dark, offending but by chance ;
Such are the blindfold blows of ignorance.
They know not beings, and but hate a name ;
To them the Hind and Panther are the same [1].'

One more instance, and that taken from the narrative part, **294**
where style was more in his choice, will shew how steadily he
kept his resolution of heroick dignity.

' For when the herd, suffic'd, did late repair
To ferny heaths, and to their forest lair,
She made a mannerly excuse to stay,
Proffering the Hind to wait her half the way :
That, since the sky was clear, an hour of talk
Might help her to beguile the tedious walk.
With much good-will the motion was embrac'd,
To chat awhile on their adventures past :
Nor had the grateful Hind so soon forgot
Her friend and fellow-sufferer in the Plot.
Yet wondering how of late she grew estrang'd,
Her forehead cloudy and her count'nance chang'd,
She thought this hour th' occasion would present
To learn her secret cause of discontent,
Which well she hop'd, might be with ease redress'd, ⎞
Considering her a well-bred civil beast,   ⎬
And more a gentlewoman than the rest.   ⎠
After some common talk what rumours ran,
The lady of the spotted muff began [2].'

The second and third parts he professes to have reduced to **295**
diction more familiar and more suitable to dispute and conversation [3]; the difference is not, however, very easily perceived : the
first has familiar, and the two others have sonorous, lines. The
original incongruity runs through the whole : the king is now
Cæsar [4], and now the Lyon [5]; and the name Pan is given to
the Supreme Being [6].

[1] Part i. l. 308.   [2] Part i. l. 554.
[3] ' The Second Part, being matter
of dispute, and chiefly concerning
Church authority, I was obliged to
make as plain and perspicuous as
possibly I could. . . . The Third,
which has more of the nature of
domestic conversation, is, or ought
to be, more free and familiar than
the two former.' *Works*, x. 117.
[4] Part iii. l. 60.   [5] Part i. l. 531.
[6] ' This mean retreat did mighty Pan
    contain.'
Part ii. l. 711. See *ante*, MILTON, 183.

296 But when this constitutional absurdity is forgiven the poem must be confessed to be written with great smoothness of metre, a wide extent of knowledge, and an abundant multiplicity of images ; the controversy is embellished with pointed sentences, diversified by illustrations, and enlivened by sallies of invective. Some of the facts to which allusions are made are now become obscure, and perhaps there may be many satirical passages little understood.

297 As it was by its nature a work of defiance, a composition which would naturally be examined with the utmost acrimony of criticism, it was probably laboured with uncommon attention ; and there are, indeed, few negligences in the subordinate parts. The original impropriety and the subsequent unpopularity of the subject, added to the ridiculousness of its first elements, has sunk it into neglect ; but it may be usefully studied as an example of poetical ratiocination, in which the argument suffers little from the metre.

298 In the poem on *The Birth of the Prince of Wales* [1] nothing is very remarkable but the exorbitant adulation, and that insensibility of the precipice on which the king was then standing, which the laureate apparently shared with the rest of the courtiers [2]. A few months cured him of controversy, dismissed him from court, and made him again a play-wright and translator [3].

299 Of Juvenal there had been a translation by Stapylton, and another by Holiday ; neither of them is very poetical. Stapylton is more smooth, and Holiday's is more esteemed for the learning of his notes [4]. A new version was proposed to the poets of that time, and undertaken by them in conjunction [5]. The main design

---

[1] *Britannia Rediviva, Works*, x. 287.

[2] 'See on his future subjects how he smiles,
Nor meanly flatters, nor with craft beguiles ;
But with an open face, as on his throne,
Assures our birthrights, and assumes his own.'
Brit. Redi., l. 114. See also *ante*, DRYDEN, 123.

[3] *Ante*, DRYDEN, 136, 139, 140.

[4] Sir Robert Stapylton's complete *Juvenal* appeared in 1647, and Holi-day's posthumously in 1673. 'In Holyday and Stapylton my ears are mortally offended.' DRYDEN, *Works*, xiii. 121. 'The learned Holyday, who has made us amends for his bad poetry with his excellent illustrations,' &c. *Ib.* p. 247. See also *ib.* p. 119. For Stapylton see also *ib.* xvii. 325, and for Holyday, *ante*, DRYDEN, 107, 223.

[5] *Ante*, STEPNEY, 4 ; DRYDEN, 140. In the title-page it is described as done 'by Mr. Dryden and several other Eminent Hands.' *Works*, xiii. 1.

was conducted by Dryden, whose reputation was such that no man was unwilling to serve the Muses under him.

The general character of this translation will be given when 300 it is said to preserve the wit, but to want the dignity of the original. The peculiarity of Juvenal is a mixture of gaiety and stateliness, of pointed sentences, and declamatory grandeur [1]. His points have not been neglected; but his grandeur none of the band seemed to consider as necessary to be imitated, except Creech [2], who undertook the thirteenth *Satire*. It is therefore perhaps possible to give a better representation of that great satirist, even in those parts which Dryden himself has translated, some passages excepted, which will never be excelled [3].

With Juvenal was published Persius, translated wholly by 301 Dryden [4]. This work, though like all the other productions of Dryden it may have shining parts, seems to have been written merely for wages, in an uniform mediocrity, without any eager endeavour after excellence or laborious effort of the mind.

There wanders an opinion among the readers of poetry that 302 one of these satires is an exercise of the school. Dryden says that he once translated it at school; but not that he preserved or published the juvenile performance [5].

Not long afterwards he undertook perhaps the most arduous 303 work of its kind, a translation of Virgil, for which he had shewn how well he was qualified by his version of the *Pollio* [6], and two episodes, one of Nisus and Euryalus, the other of Mezentius and Lausus [7].

In the comparison of Homer and Virgil the discriminative 304 excellence of Homer is elevation and comprehension of thought,

---

[1] 'His words are suitable to his thoughts, sublime and lofty.' *Works*, xiii. 88.

[2] *Ante*, DRYDEN, 163.
'Plain truth, dear Murray, needs no
  flowers of speech, [Creech.'
So take it in the very words of
  POPE, *Imit. Hor.*, *Epis.* i. 6. 3.
'Creech's translation of Juvenal, *Sat.* xiii, is equal to any Dryden has given us of that author.' J. WARTON, Warton's *Pope*, iv. 126.

[3] Johnson spoke with authority, having in his *London* and *Vanity of Human Wishes* imitated *Satires* iii and x.

[4] *Ante*, DRYDEN, 140.

[5] 'I remember I translated this *Satire* [the third] when I was a King's scholar at Westminster School, for a Thursday-night's exercise; and believe that it, and many other of my exercises of this nature in English verse, are still in the hands of my learned master, the Rev. Dr. Busby.' *Works*, xiii. 232.

[6] In Dryden's *First Miscellany*, 1684.

[7] In the *Second Miscellany*, 1685. [In translating these passages again for his complete *Virgil* Dryden made not a few changes.]

and that of Virgil is grace and splendor of diction [1]. The beauties of Homer are therefore difficult to be lost, and those of Virgil difficult to be retained [2]. The massy trunk of sentiment is safe by its solidity, but the blossoms of elocution easily drop away. The author, having the choice of his own images, selects those which he can best adorn ; the translator must at all hazards follow his original, and express thoughts which perhaps he would not have chosen [3]. When to this primary difficulty is added the inconvenience of a language so much inferior in harmony to the Latin, it cannot be expected that they who read the *Georgick* and the *Eneid* should be much delighted with any version [4].

305 All these obstacles Dryden saw, and all these he determined to encounter [5]. The expectation of his work was undoubtedly great ; the nation considered its honour as interested in the event [6].

---

[1] 'Of the two ancient epic poets the invention and design were the particular talents of Homer. Virgil must yield to him in both ; ... but the *dictio Virgiliana*, the expression of Virgil, his colouring, was incomparably the better.' *Works*, xvii. 329. See also *ib*. xiii. 89. *Diction* was an unfamiliar word. In 1685 Dryden, after using the phrase, ' in every part of his diction,' continues ' or (to speak English) in all his expressions.' *Ib*. xii. 299.
'What Virgil says of the Sibyl's prophecies may be as properly applied to every word of his ; they must be read in order as they lie ; the least breath discomposes them, and somewhat of their divinity is lost.' *Ib*. xiv. 204.
Addison says of Homer, Virgil, and Ovid :—' The first strikes the imagination wonderfully with what is great, the second with what is beautiful, and the last with what is strange.' *The Spectator*, No. 417.
' In speaking of comparisons upon an unnatural footing Pope mentioned Virgil and Homer ; Corneille and Racine ; the little ivory statue of Polycletus and the Colossus. " Magis pares quam similes ? " " Ay, that 's it in one word." ' Spence's *Anec*. p. 9. See also *post*, POPE, 383, and Boswell's *Johnson*, iii. 193.
' Nam mihi egregie dixisse videtur Servilius Novianus, pares eos magis

quam similes.' QUINCTILIAN, *Inst. Orat*. x. 1. 102.
[2] ' They who have called Virgil the torture of grammarians might also have called him the plague of translators ; for he seems to have studied not to be translated.' *Works*, xii. 288.
[3] ' He who invents is master of his thoughts and words ; he can turn and vary them as he pleases, till he renders them harmonious ; but the wretched translator has no such privilege ; for, being tied to the thoughts, he must make what music he can in the expression.' *Ib*. xiv. 225.
[4] ' If I undertake the translation of Virgil, the little which I can perform will shew at least that no man is fit to write after him in a barbarous modern tongue.' *Ib*. xviii. 116.
[5] He had other obstacles besides these. ' What Virgil wrote in the vigour of his age, in plenty and at ease, I have undertaken to translate in my declining years ; struggling with wants, oppressed with sickness, curbed in my genius, liable to be misconstrued in all I write.' *Ib*. xv. 187.
[6] ' What I have done, imperfect as it is for want of health and leisure to correct it, will be judged in after ages, and possibly in the present, to be no dishonour to my native country.' *Ib*. xv. 187.

One gave him the different editions of his author [1], and another helped him in the subordinate parts. The arguments of the several books were given him by Addison [2].

The hopes of the publick were not disappointed. He produced, 306 says Pope, 'the most noble and spirited translation that I know in any language [3].' It certainly excelled whatever had appeared in English, and appears to have satisfied his friends, and, for the most part, to have silenced his enemies. Milbourne, indeed, a clergyman, attacked it; but his outrages seem to be the ebullitions of a mind agitated by stronger resentment than bad poetry can excite, and previously resolved not to be pleased [4].

His criticism extends only to the *Preface, Pastorals*, and 307 *Georgicks*; and, as he professes, to give his antagonist an opportunity of reprisal he has added his own version of the first and fourth *Pastorals*, and the first *Georgick*. The world has forgotten his book; but since his attempt has given him a place in literary

---

[1] Gilbert Dolben, son of the late Archbishop of York, 'enriched me,' Dryden writes, 'with all the several editions of Virgil, and all the commentaries of those editions in Latin.' *Works*, xv. 190.

[2] Addison wrote also the *Essay on the Georgicks. Post*, ADDISON, 13; *Works*, xiv. 12, 229. Dr. Knightley Chetwood gave Dryden the *Life of Virgil* (*ib.* xiii. 292), and probably the *Preface to the Pastorals. Ib.* xiii. 328; *ante*, WALSH, 4 *n*.

[3] *Preface to the Iliad*, 1760, p. 51. Johnson calls Pope's *Iliad* 'the noblest version of poetry which the world has ever seen.' *Post*, POPE, 93, 245.

Swift, in *The Battle of the Books*, tells how Virgil consented to exchange armour with Dryden, 'though his was of gold, the other's but of rusty iron. However this glittering armour became the modern yet worse than his own.' Swift's *Works*, x. 236. For Swift's 'perpetual malevolence to Dryden' see *post*, SWIFT, 18.

'There is not a single image from nature in the whole body of Dryden's works. In his translation from Virgil, wherever Virgil can be fairly said to have his *eye* upon his object Dryden always spoils the passage.'

WORDSWORTH, Lockhart's *Scott*, ii. 288.

'Dryden's paraphrase of Virgil is stronger than any of the translations.' TENNYSON, *Life*, ii. 385. It is 'enduring and original,' wrote E. FITZGERALD, *More Letters*, p. 104.

Lord Bowen, himself the author of a fine version of parts of Virgil, after describing it as 'the noblest and most masculine of all versions,' continues: —'The silver trumpet has disappeared, and a manly strain is breathed through bronze.' *Virgil in English Verse*, Preface, p. 6.

[4] *Ante*, DRYDEN, 148, 175. A few years earlier Milbourne had sent Tonson some verses in praise of Dryden—'a sacrifice to his genius.' Malone's *Dryden*, i. 315.

'Pride, malice, folly against Dryden rose,
In various shapes of parsons, critics, beaus.

. . . . .

Might he return, and bless once more our eyes,
New Blackmores and new Milbournes must arise.'
POPE, *Essay on Criticism*, l. 458. See also *The Dunciad*, ii. 349; and Pope's *Works* (E. & C.), iv. 238, for a summary of Milbourne's abuse.

history, I will preserve a specimen of his criticism by inserting his remarks on the invocation before the first *Georgick*, and of his poetry, by annexing his own version.

'Ver. 1. "What makes a plenteous harvest, when to turn
The fruitful soil, and when to sow the corn [1]."

It 's unlucky, they say, "to stumble at the threshold," but what has a " plenteous harvest " to do here ? Virgil would not pretend to prescribe *rules* for *that* which depends not on the *husbandman's* care, but the *disposition of Heaven* altogether. Indeed, the *plenteous crop* depends somewhat on the *good method of tillage*, and where the *land*'s ill manur'd the *corn* without a miracle can be but *indifferent*; but the *harvest* may be *good*, which is its *properest* epithet, tho' the *husbandman's skill* were never so *indifferent.* The next *sentence* is *too literal*, and *when to plough* had been Virgil's meaning, and intelligible to every body ; "and when to sow the corn " is a needless *addition.*

'Ver. 3. "The care of sheep, of oxen, and of kine;
And when to geld the lambs, and sheer the swine [2] "

would as well have fallen under the "cura boum, qui cultus habendo sit pecori [3]," as Mr. D.'s *deduction* of particulars.

'Ver. 5. " The birth and genius of the frugal bee
I sing, Mæcenas, and I sing to thee."—

But where did *experientia* [4] ever signify *birth and genius?* or what ground was there for such a *figure* in this place ? How much more manly is Mr. Ogylby's version [5] !

"What makes rich grounds, in what celestial signs,
'Tis good to plough, and marry elms with vines.
What best fits cattle, what with sheep agrees,
And several arts improving frugal bees,
I sing, Mæcenas."

[1] *Works*, xiv. 21.
[2] In Dryden the second line of the couplet runs :—
' And how to raise on elms the teeming vine.'
[3] *Geor.* i. 3.
[4] '. . . apibus quanta experientia parcis.' *Ib.* i. 4.
[5] Dryden replied:—'His own translations of Virgil have answered his criticisms on mine. If, as they say, he has declared in print, he prefers the version of Ogilby to mine, the world has made him the same compliment; for it is agreed on all hands that he writes even below Ogilby; that you will say is not easily to be done ; but what cannot Milbourn bring about ? ' *Works*, xi. 240. See also *ib.* xii. 283.
Pope describes Ogilby's version as 'too mean for criticism.' *Preface to Iliad*, p. 51. He brings him into *The Dunciad*, i. 141 :—
' Here swells the shelf with Ogilby the great.'
See also Conington's *Misc. Writings*, i. 151.
[Ogilby translated Virgil twice, first in 1649, and again in 1654. Milbourne quoted from the 1654 version, which differs considerably from that of 1649.]

'Which four lines, tho' faulty enough, are yet much more to the purpose than Mr. D.'s six.

'Ver. 22. "From fields and mountains to my song repair."

For *patrium linquens nemus, saltusque Lycæi*[1]—Very well explained!'

'Ver. 23, 24. "Inventor Pallas, of the fattening oil,
Thou founder of the plough, and ploughman's toil!"

Written as if *these* had been *Pallas's invention*. *The ploughman's toil*'s impertinent.

'Ver. 25.   " —The shroud-like cypress"—

Why "shroud-like?" Is a *cypress* pulled up by the *roots*, which the *sculpture*[2] in the *last Eclogue* fills *Silvanus's* hand with, so very like a *shroud*? Or did not Mr. D. think of that kind of *cypress* us'd often for *scarves and hatbands* at funerals formerly[3], or for *widow's vails*, &c.? if so, 'twas a *deep good thought*.

'Ver. 26.   ". . . that wear
The royal [rural] honours, and increase the year."

What's meant by *increasing the year*? Did the *gods* or *goddesses* add more *months*, or *days*, or *hours* to it? Or how can "arva tueri" signify to "wear rural honours"? Is this to *translate*, or *abuse* an *author*? The next *couplet* are [*sic*] borrow'd from Ogylby I suppose, because *less to the purpose* than ordinary[4]."

'Ver. 33. "The patron of the world, and Rome's peculiar guard."

Idle, and none of Virgil's, no more than the sense of the *precedent couplet*; so again, he *interpolates* Virgil with that

"And the round circle [circuit] of the year to guide;
Powerful of blessings, which thou strew'st around."

A ridiculous *Latinism*, and an *impertinent addition*; indeed the whole *period* is but one piece of *absurdity* and *nonsense*, as those who lay it with the *original* must find.

---

[1] 'Ipse nemus linquens patrium,' &c.
        Geor. i. 16.
[2] The first edition, as the title-page proclaims, is 'Adorn'd with a Hundred Sculptures.' *Works*, xiii. 274.
[3] Johnson, in his *Dictionary*, spells it *cyprus* :—'*Cyprus* (I suppose from the place where it was made; or corruptly from *cypress* as being used in mourning). A thin transparent black stuff.'

[4] 'You who supply the ground with seeds of grain
And you who swell those seeds with kindly rain.'
        DRYDEN, *Georgics*, i. 28.
'And all you Pow'rs protectors of the field,
Whose kindly influence chears the sprouting grain,
Or send from heav'n on corn large show'rs of rain.' OGILBY, ed. 1654.

'Ver. 42, 43. "And Neptune shall resign the fasces of the sea."
Was he *consul* or *dictator* there?

"And watry virgins for thy bed shall strive."
Both absurd *interpolations.*

'Ver. 47, 48. "Where in the void of heaven a place is free.
Ah, happy D—n, were that place for thee[1]!"

But where is *that void*? Or what does our *translator* mean by
it? He knows what Ovid says *God* did, to prevent such a *void*
in heaven[2]; perhaps, this was then forgotten: but Virgil talks
more sensibly.

'Ver. 49. "The scorpion ready to receive thy laws."
No, he would not then have *gotten out of his way* so fast.

'Ver. 56. "The [Though] Proserpine affects her silent seat."
What made *her* then so *angry* with Ascalaphus, for preventing
her return[3]? She was now mus'd to *Patience* under the *determinations of Fate*, rather than *fond* of her *residence.*

'Ver. 61, 2, 3.

"Pity the poet's and the ploughman's cares,
Interest thy greatness in our mean affairs,
And use thyself betimes to hear [and grant] our prayers."

Which is such a wretched *perversion* of Virgil's *noble thought*[4]
as Vicars would have blush'd at[5]; but Mr. Ogylby makes us
some amends, by his better lines:

"O wheresoe'er thou art, from thence incline,
And grant assistance to my bold design!
Pity, with me, poor husbandmen's affairs,
And now, as if translated, hear our prayers."

This is *sense*, and *to the purpose*: the other, poor *mistaken stuff.*'

---

[1] The couplet ends:—
'Betwixt the Scorpion and the Maid
for thee.'
[2] 'Then, every void of nature to
supply,
With forms of gods he fills the
vacant sky.'
DRYDEN, *Ovid's Metam.* i. 92,
Works, xii. 72.
[3] See OVID, *Metam.* v. 539.
[4] 'Ignarosque viae mecum miseratus
agrestes,
Ingredere, et votis iam nunc as-
suesce vocari.' *Geor.* i. 41.

[5] 'Thou that with ale, or viler li-
quors,
Didst inspire Withers, Pryn and
Vickars,
And force them, tho' it was in
spite
Of nature and their stars, to write.'
Hudibras, i. 1. 645.
Dr. Grey says in a note that
'Vickars translated Virgil's *Aeneids*
into as horrible travestie in earnest
as the French Scarron did in bur-
lesque.'

Such were the strictures of Milbourne, who found few abettors; 308 and of whom it may be reasonably imagined that many who favoured his design were ashamed of his insolence.

When admiration had subsided the translation was more 309 coolly examined, and found like all others to be sometimes erroneous and sometimes licentious. Those who could find faults thought they could avoid them; and Dr. Brady attempted in blank verse a translation of the *Eneid*[1], which, when dragged into the world, did not live long enough to cry. I have never seen it; but that such a version there is, or has been, perhaps some old catalogue informed me.

With not much better success Trapp, when his Tragedy and 310 his *Prelections* had given him reputation, attempted another blank version of the *Eneid*; to which, notwithstanding the slight regard with which it was treated, he had afterwards perseverance enough to add the *Eclogues* and *Georgicks*. His book may continue its existence as long as it is the clandestine refuge of schoolboys[2].

Since the English ear has been accustomed to the mellifluence 311 of Pope's numbers[3], and the diction of poetry has become more splendid, new attempts have been made to translate Virgil; and all his works have been attempted by men better qualified

---

[1] 'Dr. Nicholas Brady's *Aeneids* were published by subscription in 4 vols. 8vo, the last of which appeared in 1726.' *Biog. Brit.* p. 961. The first vol. appeared in 1716.

[2] *Ante*, DRYDEN, 179, 202. Joseph Trapp, 'a most ingenious, honest gentleman,' in 1708 was chosen the first Professor of Poetry in Oxford. Hearne's *Remains*, i. 141. His *Prelections — Praelectiones Poeticae—* were his lectures, delivered in Latin in accordance with the statutes. Lowth's 'incomparable *Praelectiones* on the poetry of the Hebrews' (Gibbon's *Memoirs*, p. 55) were delivered on the same foundation. Trapp's tragedy *Abramule, or Love and Empire*, was acted in 1704. Cibber's *Lives*, v. 158.

Swift describes him as 'a sort of pretender to wit, a second-rate pamphleteer.' Swift's *Works*, ii. 140. 'I will own he has taught me, and, I believe, some other gentlemen who

had lost their Latin, the true grammatical construction of Virgil, and deserves, not our acknowledgments only, but those of Eton and Westminster.' *Ib.* vi. 321.

The following epigram was made on his *Virgil*: —

'Keep to thy preaching, Trapp; translate no further; Is it not written, "Thou shalt do no murder"?'

  Biog. Brit., Suppl., p. 174.
For another version of this epigram see Hearne's *Remains*, ii. 140. In the original MS. of *The Dunciad* was the following couplet:—

'To him who nodding steals a transient nap We give Tate's *Ovid*, and thy *Virgil*, Trapp.'

Pope's *Works* (E. & C.), iv. 287.
For 'the famous epigram' attributed to him see *John. Misc.* i. 171.

[3] *Post*, POPE, 348.

to contend with Dryden[1]. I will not engage myself in an invidious comparison by opposing one passage to another: a work of which there would be no end, and which might be often offensive without use.

312   It is not by comparing line with line that the merit of great works is to be estimated, but by their general effects and ultimate result. It is easy to note a weak line, and write one more vigorous in its place; to find a happiness of expression in the original, and transplant it by force into the version: but what is given to the parts may be subducted from the whole, and the reader may be weary though the critick may commend. Works of imagination excel by their allurement and delight; by their power of attracting and detaining the attention. That book is good in vain which the reader throws away. He only is the master who keeps the mind in pleasing captivity; whose pages are perused with eagerness, and in hope of new pleasure are perused again; and whose conclusion is perceived with an eye of sorrow, such as the traveller casts upon departing day.

313   By his proportion of this predomination I will consent that Dryden should be tried[2]: of this, which, in opposition to reason, makes Ariosto the darling and the pride of Italy; of this, which, in defiance of criticism, continues Shakespeare the sovereign of the drama.

314   His last work was his *Fables*[3], in which he gave us the first example of a mode of writing which the Italians call *refacimento*, a renovation of ancient writers, by modernizing their language. Thus the old poem of Boiardo[4] has been new-dressed by

---

[1] Of these Pitt's *Aeneid* is included in *Eng. Poets. Post*, PITT, 8. Joseph Warton translated the *Eclogues* and *Georgics*. The *Aeneid* was translated in blank verse by Alexander Strahan, 1739–67, and by William Hawkins in 1764. Lowndes's *Bibl. Man.* p. 2784. For a criticism of these translations see Conington's *Misc. Writings*, 1872, i. 159.

[2] Swift wrote in *A Tale of a Tub*, in the *Epistle dedicatory to Posterity*, dated Dec. 1697:—'I do therefore affirm, upon the word of a sincere man, that there is now actually in being a certain poet, called John Dryden, whose translation of Virgil was lately printed in a large folio,

well bound, and, if diligent search were made, for aught I know, is yet to be seen.' Swift's *Works*, x. 47. 'Compare Dryden with other translators, and it will be seen that while none of them have anything of Virgil's individuality, he alone has an individuality of his own of sufficient mark to interest and impress the reader. ... It is a splendid English epic, in which most of the thoughts are Virgil's and most of the language Dryden's.' CONINGTON, *Misc. Writings*, i. 169, 181.

[3] *Ante*, DRYDEN, 149.

[4] Dryden, writing of 'the file of heroic poets,' says that 'Pulci, Boiardo, and Ariosto would cry out,

Domenichi [1] and Berni [2]. The works of Chaucer, upon which this kind of rejuvenescence has been bestowed by Dryden, require little criticism. The tale of *The Cock* seems hardly worth revival [3]; and the story of *Palamon and Arcite*, containing an action unsuitable to the times in which it is placed, can hardly be suffered to pass without censure of the hyperbolical commendation which Dryden has given it in the general Preface [4], and in a poetical Dedication, a piece where his original fondness of remote conceits seems to have revived [5].

Of the three pieces borrowed from Boccace [6] *Sigismunda* [7] may 315 be defended by the celebrity of the story. *Theodore and Honoria* [8], though it contains not much moral, yet afforded opportunities of striking description. And *Cymon* [9] was formerly a tale of such reputation that, at the revival of letters, it was translated into Latin by one of the Beroalds [10].

Whatever subjects employed his pen he was still improving 316 our measures and embellishing our language [11].

" Make room for the Italian poets, the descendants of Virgil in a right line." ' *Works*, xiv. 143.

' " Away," said the priest, " with *The Twelve Peers*, with the faithful historiographer, Turpin. However, I am only for condemning them to perpetual banishment, because they contain some part of the invention of the renowned Mateo Boyardo ; from whom the Christian poet, Ludovico Ariosto, spun his web." ' *Don Quixote*, bk. i. ch. 6.

Macaulay, in 1834, thought of writing an article on ' the romantic poetry of Italy, for which there is an excellent opportunity, Panizzi's reprint of Boiardo.' *Macvey Napier Corres.* p. 155. On Nov. 4, 1838, he wrote from Florence :—' I have not been able to read one-half of Boiardo's poem ; and, in order to do what I propose, I must read Berni's *rifacimento* too.' *Ib.* p. 282.

[1] *Orlando Innamorato* nuovamente riformato per L. D. [Lodovico Domenichi]. 1545. *Brit. Mus. Cata.*

[2] *Orlando Innamorato* nuovamente composto da F. B. [Francesco Berni]. 1541. *Ib.*

' If Berni's *Rifacimento* was not stained with many immoralities it would be the most pleasing poetical thing in our language.' BARETTI, *The Italian Library*, 1757, p. 58. See also Spence's *Anec.* p. 121.

[3] *The Cock and the Fox*, *Works*, xi. 337. Horace Walpole (*Letters*, viii. 524) describes Dryden's poem as ' the standard of good sense, poetry, nature and ease.'

[4] ' The story is more pleasing than either the *Ilias* or the *Aeneis*, the manners as perfect, the diction as poetical, the learning as deep and various, and the disposition full as artful, only it includes a greater length of time.' *Works*, xi. 239 ; *ante*, DRYDEN, 202.

[5] *Ib.* xi. 248. For his ' conceits ' see *ante*, DRYDEN, 5, 236.

[6] ' I think Dryden's translations from Boccace are the best, at least the most poetical, of his poems.' WORDSWORTH, Lockhart's *Scott*, ii. 289.

[7] *Sigismonda and Guiscardo*, *Works*, xi. 425. Wordsworth, after pointing out its defects, continues :— ' With all these defects, and they are very gross ones, it is a noble poem.' Lockhart's *Scott*, ii. 289.

[8] *Works*, xi. 459.

[9] *Cymon and Iphigenia*, *Ib.* xi. 483.

[10] About the year 1495, by Philip Beroald the elder. *Brit. Mus. Cata.*

[11] ' *Absalom and Achitophel* and

317   In this volume are interspersed some short original poems[1], which, with his prologues, epilogues, and songs, may be comprised in Congreve's remark, that even those, if he had written nothing else, would have entitled him to the praise of excellence in his kind[2].

318   One composition must however be distinguished. The ode for *St. Cecilia's Day*[3], perhaps the last effort of his poetry, has been always considered as exhibiting the highest flight of fancy and the exactest nicety of art. This is allowed to stand without a rival. If indeed there is any excellence beyond it in some other of Dryden's works that excellence must be found[4]. Compared with the *Ode on Killigrew*[5] it may be pronounced perhaps superior in the whole; but without any single part equal to the first stanza of the other.

319   It is said to have cost Dryden a fortnight's labour[6]; but it does not want its negligences: some of the lines are without corre-

Theodore and Honoria stood in the first rank of poems in Gray's estimation; and Dryden's plays, not as dramatic compositions but as poetry.' Gray's *Works*, 1835-43, v. 35.

[1] Among them the *Epistle to John Driden, Works*, xi. 69.

[2] 'What he has done in any one species [of writting] would have been sufficient to have acquired him a great name. If he had written nothing but his prefaces, or nothing but his songs, or his prologues, each of them would have entitled him to the preference and distinction of excelling in his kind.' CONGREVE, Dryden's *Works*, ii. 20. For his prologues see Boswell's *Johnson*, ii. 325.

[3] The second ode—*Alexander's Feast*. It was not 'the last effort of Dryden's poetry,' for it was written nearly three years before his death. *Ante*, DRYDEN, 150 n. His last efforts were the Prologue and Epilogue to Vanbrugh's revised version of Fletcher's comedy, *The Pilgrim*. These were written, according to Malone (i. 335), 'not above three weeks before his death.' To it also he supplied a song and a *Secular Masque. Works*, viii. 481, 489, 502.

[4] 'I am glad to hear from all hands,' wrote Dryden, 'that my Ode is esteemed the best of all my poetry by all the town. I thought so myself when I writ it; but being old, I mistrusted my own judgment.' *Works*, xviii. 139.

The Irish Chief Justice Marlay (father of Bishop Marlay, Boswell's *Johnson*, iv. 73), frequenting Will's as a Templar, 'congratulated Dryden on having produced the noblest Ode that had ever been written in any language. "You are right, young gentleman," he replied; "a nobler Ode never was produced, nor ever will."' Malone's *Dryden*, i. 476.

'This Ode has been more applauded perhaps than it has been felt.' GOLDSMITH, *Works*, iii. 436. 'It is said that he wrote it with a view to its being set by Purcell, but that Purcell declined the task, as thinking it beyond the power of music.' Purcell had died nearly two years earlier. Hawkins's *Hist. of Music*, iv. 522. Hawkins adds that 'Dryden knew little about music.' *Ib*. i. 167 n. Perhaps his authority was the line of a ballad addressed to Bayes, quoted by Malone (i. 517):—
'Though thy dull ear be to music untrue.'
Malone says that 'in 1736 Handel set the Ode anew.' *Ib*. i. 307.

[5] *Ante*, DRYDEN, 278.

[6] *Ante*, DRYDEN, 150.

spondent rhymes [1] : a defect, which I never detected but after an acquaintance of many years, and which the enthusiasm of the writer might hinder him from perceiving.

His last stanza has less emotion than the former ; but is not 320 less elegant in the diction. The conclusion is vicious ; the musick of Timotheus, which ' raised a mortal to the skies,' had only a metaphorical power ; that of Cecilia, which ' drew an angel down,' had a real effect ; the crown therefore could not reasonably be divided [2].

IN a general survey of Dryden's labours [3] he appears to have 321 had a mind very comprehensive by nature, and much enriched with acquired knowledge. His compositions are the effects of a vigorous genius operating upon large materials.

The power that predominated in his intellectual operations was 322 rather strong reason than quick sensibility. Upon all occasions that were presented he studied rather than felt, and produced sentiments not such as Nature enforces, but meditation supplies. With the simple and elemental passions, as they spring separate in the mind, he seems not much acquainted, and seldom describes them but as they are complicated by the various relations of society and confused in the tumults and agitations of life [4].

---

[1] Johnson refers to such lines as (ll. 12–19)
' Happy, happy, happy pair !
  None but the brave,
  None but the brave,
None but the brave deserves the fair.'
See also ll. 75-9, 116-20.
A writer in *N. & Q.* 4 S. i. 239 maintains that in these cases, ' though the words are repeated thrice, they are in reality only the first half of the line. Just as well might the members of a congregation complain that in the well-known
  " Oh my poor pol,
  Oh my poor pol,
  Oh my poor polluted soul ! "
there was no rhyme to " pol." '
There are too many faulty rhymes, —' son ' and ' throne,' ' Jove ' and ' above,' ' God ' and ' rode,' ' good ' and blood,' ' need ' and ' fed,' ' move ' and ' love,' ' rear ' and ' hair,' ' high ' and ' joy,' ' abodes ' and ' gods.'

[2] *Ante*, DRYDEN, 280. Johnson finds the same fault in Pope's *Ode*. *Post*, POPE, 326. In reviewing Warton's *Essay on Pope*, he writes :—
' The author observes very justly that the Odes, both of Dryden and Pope, conclude unsuitably and unnaturally with epigram.' Johnson's *Works*, vi. 41. See Warton's *Essay*, i. 60.
' St. Cecilia's music-book is interlined with epigrams, and *Alexander's Feast* smells of gin at second-hand, with true Briton fiddlers full of native *talent* in the orchestra.' LANDOR, *Imag. Conv.* iv. 275.
[3] ' In drawing Dryden's character, Johnson has given, though I suppose unintentionally, some touches of his own.' Boswell's *Johnson*, iv. 45. See also *ante*, DRYDEN, 211 ; *post*, POPE, 310.
[4] ' Ses ouvrages sont pleins de détails naturels à la fois, et brillans, animés, vigoureux, hardis, passionnés, mérite qu'aucun poète de sa nation

323   What he says of love may contribute to the explanation of his
      character :

> 'Love various minds does variously inspire ;
> It stirs in gentle bosoms [natures] gentle fire,
> Like that of incense on the altar [altars] laid ;
> But raging flames tempestuous souls invade,
> A fire which every windy passion blows ;
> With pride it mounts, or [and] with revenge it glows [1].'

324   Dryden's was not one of the 'gentle bosoms': Love, as it subsists
      in itself, with no tendency but to the person loved and wishing
      only for correspondent kindness, such love as shuts out all other
      interest, the Love of the Golden Age, was too soft and subtle to
      put his faculties in motion.   He hardly conceived it but in its
      turbulent effervescence with some other desires : when it was
      inflamed by rivalry or obstructed by difficulties ; when it invigo-
      rated ambition or exasperated revenge.

325   He is therefore, with all his variety of excellence, not often
      pathetick [2] ; and had so little sensibility of the power of effusions
      purely natural that he did not esteem them in others.   Simplicity
      gave him no pleasure ; and for the first part of his life he looked
      on Otway with contempt [3], though at last, indeed very late, he
      confessed that in his play 'there was Nature, which is the chief
      beauty [4].'

326   We do not always know our own motives.   I am not certain
      whether it was not rather the difficulty which he found in exhibit-
      ing the genuine operations of the heart than a servile submission
      to an injudicious audience that filled his plays with false magni-
      ficence [5].   It was necessary to fix attention ; and the mind can be

n'égale, et qu'aucun ancien n'a sur-
passé.' VOLTAIRE, Œuvres, xviii. 273.
   [1] From   Tyrannic Love, act ii.
sc. 3.   Works, iii. 407.
   [2] Landor wrote of him :—
'Tho' never tender nor sublime,
   He wrestles with and conquers
      Time.' Poems, &c. ii. 180.
   'He never aimed at any high mark.
His good sense prevented him from
overvaluing himself, and aspiring to
become eminent either as a sublime
or a pathetic poet.' SOUTHEY, Cowper's Works, ii. 138.
   [3] 'Dryden commonly expressed
a very mean, if not contemptible
opinion, of Otway.' GILDON, The

Laws of Poetry, 1721, p. 211.
   [4] 'Nature is there, which is the
greatest beauty.'   A Parallel of
Poetry and Painting (1695), Works,
xvii. 326; ante, OTWAY, 15.
   [5] In the Dedication of The Spanish
Friar (1681, ante, DRYDEN, 66) he
writes :—'I scorn as much to take it
[reputation] from half-witted judges as
I should to raise an estate by cheating
of bubbles.   Neither do I discommend
the lofty style in tragedy, which is
naturally pompous and magnificent ;
but nothing is truly sublime that is
not just and proper.' Works, vi. 407.
See ante, DRYDEN, 45; post, 334.

captivated only by recollection or by curiosity; by reviving natural sentiments or impressing new appearances of things: sentences were readier at his call than images; he could more easily fill the ear with some splendid novelty than awaken those ideas that slumber in the heart.

The favourite exercise of his mind was ratiocination[1]; and, 327 that argument might not be too soon at an end, he delighted to talk of liberty and necessity, destiny and contingence; these he discusses in the language of the school with so much profundity that the terms which he uses are not always understood. It is indeed learning, but learning out of place.

When once he had engaged himself in disputation, thoughts 328 flowed in on either side: he was now no longer at a loss; he had always objections and solutions at command: 'verbaque provisam rem[2]'—give him matter for his verse, and he finds without difficulty verse for his matter[3].

In comedy, for which he professes himself not naturally quali- 329 fied[4], the mirth which he excites will perhaps not be found so much to arise from any original humour or peculiarity of character nicely distinguished and diligently pursued, as from incidents and circumstances, artifices and surprises; from jests of action rather than of sentiment[5]. What he had of humorous or

---

[1] *Ante*, DRYDEN, 125; *post*, 356; BLACKMORE, 46.

A friend of Scott's, urging him not to neglect the law, wrote:—'The reasoning talents visible in Dryden's verses assure me that he would have ruled in Westminster Hall as easily as he did at Button's [Will's].' Lockhart's *Scott*, ii. 41.

[2] 'Verbaque provisam rem non invita sequentur.'
HORACE, *Ars Poet.* l. 311.

[3] 'Whatever he does, whether he reasons, relates or describes, he is never, to use his own phrase, "cursedly confined" [*Absalom and Achitophel*, l. 4]; never loiters about a single thought or image, or seems to labour about the turn of a phrase. . . . His thoughts, his language, his versification, have all a certain animation and elasticity which no one else has ever equally possessed.' HALLAM, *Edin. Review*, vol. xiii. p. 132.

[4] *Ante*, DRYDEN, 12, 91, 264.

'I never thought myself very fit for an employment, where many of my predecessors have excelled me in all kinds [of plays]; and some of my contemporaries, even in my own partial judgment, have out-done me in comedy.' *Works*, v. 195.

'If Shadwell was preferred to Dryden, it was not for his rhymes but his comedies; and perhaps the public were not wrong.' HALLAM, *Edin. Review*, vol. xiii. p. 135.

'I am not at all happy when I peruse some of Dryden's comedies: they are very stupid as well as indelicate; sometimes, however, there is a considerable vein of liveliness and humour, and all of them present extraordinary pictures of the age in which he lived.' SCOTT, Lockhart's *Scott*, ii. 283.

[5] 'PARTHENOPE. Give you good ev'n, Sir. *Exit.*
VOLSCIUS. O inauspicious stars! that I was born

passionate, he seems to have had not from nature, but from other poets ; if not always as a plagiary, at least as an imitator [1].

330 Next to argument, his delight was in wild and daring sallies of sentiment, in the irregular and excentrick violence of wit [2]. He delighted to tread upon the brink of meaning, where light and darkness begin to mingle ; to approach the precipice of absurdity, and hover over the abyss of unideal vacancy [3]. This inclination sometimes produced nonsense, which he knew, as

' Move swiftly, sun, and fly a lover's pace,
Leave weeks and months behind thee in thy race [4].'

' Amariel flies . . .
To guard thee from the demons of the air ;
My flaming sword above them to display,
All keen, and ground upon the edge of day [5].'

And sometimes it issued in absurdities, of which perhaps he was not conscious :

' Then we upon our orb's last verge shall go,
And see the ocean leaning on the sky ;
From thence our rolling neighbours we shall know,
And on the lunar world securely pry [6].'

To sudden love, and to more sudden scorn !
AMARILLIS, CLORIS. How ! Prince Volscius in love ! Ha ! ha ! ha !
Exeunt, laughing.
SMITH. Sure, Mr. Bayes, we have lost some jest here that they laugh at so.
BAYES. Why did you not observe ? He first resolves to go out of town ; and then, as he is pulling on his boots, falls in love. Ha ! ha ! ha !
SMITH. O, I did not observe ; that, indeed, is a very good jest.'
The Rehearsal, p. 85.
[1] *Ante,* DRYDEN, 103, 229.
[2] ' Indeed wit is so much the *Diana* of this age that he who goes about to set any bounds to it must expect an *uproar, Acts,* 19. 28.' *The Government of the Tongue,* 1674, p. 115.
[3] Dryden writes in the Prologue to *Tyrannic Love :*—
' Poets, like lovers, should be bold and dare,
They spoil their business with an over-care ;

And he who servilely creeps after sense
Is safe, but ne'er will reach an excellence.'
In the Preface he explains this as meaning :—' He who creeps after plain, dull, common sense is safe from committing absurdities ; but can never reach any height or excellence of wit ; and sure I could not mean that any excellence were to be found in nonsense.' *Works,* iii. 381, 383.
' Very near that precipitous border line [of the sublime and the ridiculous] there is a charmed region, where, if the statelier growths of philosophy die out and disappear, the flowers of poetry next the very edge of the chasm have a peculiar and mysterious beauty.' O. W. HOLMES, *Life of Emerson,* 1885, p. 398.
[4] *Ante,* DRYDEN, 58.
[5] *Tyrannic Love,* iv. 1, *Works,* iii. 425.
[6] *Annus Mirabilis,* stanza 164, *Works,* ix. 151. *Ante,* DRYDEN, 257 n.

These lines have no meaning; but may we not say, in imitation of Cowley on another book,

'''Tis so like *sense* 'twill serve the turn as well[1]'?

This endeavour after the grand and the new produced many 331 sentiments either great or bulky, and many images either just or splendid :

'I am as free as Nature first made man, ⎫
Ere the base laws of servitude began, ⎬
When wild in woods the noble savage ran[2].' ⎭

''Tis but because the Living death ne'er knew,
They fear to prove it as a thing that's new :
Let me th' experiment before you try,
I'll show you first how easy 'tis to die[3].'

'There with a forest of their darts he strove,
And stood like Capaneus defying Jove;
With his broad sword the boldest beating down,
While Fate grew pale lest he should win the town,
And turn'd the iron leaves of his [its] dark book
To make new dooms, or mend what it mistook[4].'

'I beg no pity for this mouldering clay ;
For if you give it burial, there it takes
Possession of your earth ;
If burnt, and scatter'd in the air, the winds
That strew my dust diffuse my royalty,
And spread me o'er your clime; for where one atom
Of mine shall light, know there Sebastian reigns[5].'

Of these quotations the two first may be allowed to be great, the two latter only tumid[6].

Of such selection there is no end.   I will add only a few more 332 passages ; of which the first, though it may perhaps not be

---

[1] '''Tis so like truth, 'twill serve our turn as well.'
Ode to Mr. Hobbes, Eng. Poets, viii. 134.
When 'Goldsmith produced some very absurd verses which had been publicly recited to an audience for money,' Johnson said, 'I can match this nonsense,' and quoted these lines. Boswell's *Johnson*, ii. 240.
[2] *Conquest of Granada*, Pt. I. i. 1, *Works*, iv. 43.
[3] *Tyrannic Love*, v. 1, *Works*, iii. 452.
[4] *Ib.* i. 1, *Works*, iii. 394.

[5] *Don Sebastian*, i. 1, *Wks*. vii. 336.
[6] Scott says of the third quotation:—'Such passages, pronounced with due emphasis on the stage, will always meet with popular applause. They are like the fanciful shapes into which a mist is often wreathed ; it requires a near approach, and an attentive consideration, to discover their emptiness and vanity.' *Works*, iii. 372.
'Dryden knew that on the stage bombast might pass for poetry as tinsel served for gold.' SOUTHEY, Cowper's *Works*, ii. 139.

quite clear in prose, is not too obscure for poetry, as the meaning
that it has is noble:

'No, there is a necessity in Fate,
Why still the brave bold man is fortunate;
He keeps his object ever full in sight,
And that assurance holds him firm and right;
True, 'tis a narrow way that leads to bliss,
But right before there is no precipice;
Fear makes men look aside, and so [then] their footing miss [1].'

333   Of the images which the two following citations afford the
first is elegant, the second magnificent; whether either be just,
let the reader judge:

'What precious drops are these [those],
Which silently each other's track pursue,
Bright as young diamonds in their infant dew [2]?'

'Resign your castle.'
'Enter, brave Sir; for when you speak the word,
The [These] gates shall [will] open of their own accord;
The genius of the place its Lord shall [will] meet,
And bow its towery forehead at [to] your feet [3].'

334   These bursts of extravagance Dryden calls the 'Dalilahs of
the Theatre,' and owns that many noisy lines of Maximin and
Almanzor call out for vengeance upon him; but 'I knew,' says
he, 'that they were bad enough to please, even when I wrote
them [4].' There is surely reason to suspect that he pleased himself as well as his audience; and that these, like the harlots of
other men, had his love, though not his approbation.

335   He had sometimes faults of a less generous and splendid kind.
He makes, like almost all other poets, very frequent use of
mythology, and sometimes connects religion and fable too
closely without distinction [5].

336   He descends to display his knowledge with pedantick ostentation; as when, in translating Virgil, he says, 'tack to the larboard'—and 'veer starboard [6]'; and talks, in another work, of

[1] *Conquest of Granada*, Pt. I. iv. 2;
Works, iv. 97.
[2] *Ib.* Pt. II. iii. 1; *Works*, iv. 157.
[3] *Ib.* Pt. II. iii. 3; *Works*, iv. 171.
[4] He continues:—' But I repent of
them amongst my sins, and if any
of their fellows intrude by chance
into my present writings I draw a
stroke over all those Delilahs of the
theatre, and am resolved I will settle
myself no reputation by the applause
of fools.' *Ib.* vi. 406; *ante*, DRYDEN,
45, 48, 52, 326. Scott says, 'This
celebrated apology was certainly invented to justify the fact after it was
committed.' Lockhart's *Scott*, iii. 389.
[5] *Ante*, DRYDEN, 238, 276, 295.
[6] *Ante*, MILTON, 234 *n.*; *Aeneis*
iii. 525.

'virtue spooming before the wind [1].' His vanity now and then betrays his ignorance:

'They [And] Nature's king through Nature's opticks view'd;
Revers'd they view'd him lessen'd to their eyes [eye] [2].'

He had heard of reversing a telescope, and unluckily reverses the object [3].

He is sometimes unexpectedly mean. When he describes the 337 Supreme Being as moved by prayer to stop the Fire of London, what is his expression?

A [An] hollow crystal pyramid he takes,
  In firmamental waters dipp'd above,
Of this [it] a broad *extinguisher* he makes,
  And *hoods* the flames that to their quarry strove [4].'

When he describes the Last Day, and the decisive tribunal, he intermingles this image:

'When rattling bones together fly,
  From the four quarters [corners] of the sky [5].'

It was indeed never in his power to resist the temptation of 338 a jest [6]. In his Elegy on Cromwell:

'No sooner was the Frenchman's cause embrac'd,
  Than the *light Monsieur* the *grave Don* outweigh'd;
His fortune turn'd the scale [7].'

He had a vanity, unworthy of his abilities, to show, as may be 339 suspected, the rank of the company with whom he lived, by the use of French words, which had then crept into conversation [8];

[1] 'When virtue spooms before a prosperous gale
My heaving wishes help to fill the sail.'
The Hind and the Panther, iii. 96.
[2] *Ib.* i. 57.
[3] He reverses the telescope in the following lines:—
'A play, which, like a prospective set right,
Presents our vast expenses close to sight;
But turn the tube, and there we sadly view
Our distant gains, and those uncertain too.'
Prologue to the Prophetess, Works, x. 408.
[4] *Annus Mirabilis*, stanza 281,
Works, ix. 185.
[5] *The Ode on Mrs. Killigrew*, l. 184, *Ib.* xi. 113.
[6] *Ante*, DRYDEN, 276. 'A quibble was to Shakespeare the fatal Cleopatra for which he lost the world, and was content to lose it.' JOHNSON, *Works*, v. 118.
[7] *On the Death of Oliver Cromwell*, stanza 23, *Works*, ix. 21. *Ante*, DRYDEN, 234.
[8] This is taken off in *The Rehearsal*:—
'BAYES. Mark that; I makes 'em both speak French, to shew their breeding' (p. 53).
'Ay, I gad, but is not that *tuant*, now, ha? is it not *tuant*?' (p. 99).

such as *fraicheur* [1] for *coolness*, *fougue* [2] for *turbulence*, and a few
more, none of which the language has incorporated or retained [3].
They continue only where they stood first, perpetual warnings to
future innovators [4].

340   These are his faults of affectation ; his faults of negligence are
beyond recital.   Such is the unevenness of his compositions that
ten lines are seldom found together without something of which
the reader is ashamed [5].   Dryden was no rigid judge of his own
pages ; he seldom struggled after supreme excellence, but snatched
in haste what was within his reach ; and when he could content others, was himself contented [6].   He did not keep present
to his mind an idea of pure perfection ; nor compare his
works, such as they were, with what they might be made.   He
knew to whom he should be opposed.   He had more musick

[1] 'Hither in summer evenings you
    repair,
        To taste the fraischeur of the purer
        air.'
On the Coronation, l. 101, *Wks.*, ix. 58.
[2] 'Henceforth their fougue must
        spend at lesser rate
        Than in its flames to wrap a na-
        tion's fate.'
                    Astraea Redux, l. 203.
Fougue was used by Mrs. Hutchin-
son and Temple. *New Eng. Dict.*
[3] 'I cannot approve of their way
of refining who corrupt our English
idiom by mixing it too much with
French.' *Works*, iv. 234. He says
of the earlier English Poets :—'I
cannot find that any of them had
been conversant in courts, except
Ben Jonson.   Greatness was not
then so easy of access, nor conversation so free as now it is. . . . Now if
they ask me, whence it is that our
conversation is so much refined, I
must freely and without flattery
ascribe it to the Court ; and in it
particularly to the King, whose example gives a law to it.' *Ib.* pp. 240–1.
[4] In the Preface to *Don Sebastian*
he boasts of 'some newnesses of
English, translated from the beauties
of modern tongues, as well as from the
elegancies of the Latin.' *Ib.* vii. 308.
In the Dedication to the *Aeneis* he
writes :—' I trade both with the living
and the dead for the enrichment
of our native language.   We have

enough in England to supply our
necessity ; but if we will have things
of magnificence and splendour we
must get them by commerce.' *Ib.*
xiv. 227.   'Words are not so easily
coined as money.' *Ib.* p. 224.   See
ante, MILTON, 270.
    Johnson attacks translators 'whose
idleness and ignorance, if it be suffered to proceed, will reduce us to
babble a dialect of France.' *Works*,
v. 49.
[5] 'When Garrick was extolling
Dryden in a rapture that I suppose
disgusted his friend, Mr. Johnson
suddenly challenged him to produce
twenty lines in a series that would
not disgrace the poet and his admirer.'
MRS. PIOZZI, *John. Misc.* i. 185.
    See also Boswell's *Johnson*, ii. 96,
where Johnson says :—' Shakespeare
never has six lines together without
a fault.'
    'Dryden has succeeded by mere
dint of genius, and in spite of a laziness and carelessness almost peculiar
to himself.   His faults are number-
less ; but so are his beauties.' COW-
PER, Southey's *Cowper*, iv. 169.
[6] 'A severe critic is the greatest
help to a good wit ; he does the
office of a friend while he designs
that of an enemy ; and his malice
keeps a poet within those bounds
which the luxuriancy of his fancy
would tempt him to overleap.'
Works, iv. 230.

than Waller, more vigour than Denham, and more nature than Cowley ; and from his contemporaries he was in no danger. Standing therefore in the highest place [1] he had no care to rise by contending with himself ; but while there was no name above his own was willing to enjoy fame on the easiest terms.

He was no lover of labour. What he thought sufficient he 341 did not stop to make better, and allowed himself to leave many parts unfinished, in confidence that the good lines would over-balance the bad. What he had once written he dismissed from his thoughts ; and, I believe, there is no example to be found of any correction or improvement made by him after publication [2]. The hastiness of his productions might be the effect of necessity [3] ; but his subsequent neglect could hardly have any other cause than impatience of study.

What can be said of his versification will be little more than 342 a dilatation of the praise given it by Pope :

> 'Waller was smooth ; but Dryden taught to join
> The varying verse, the full-resounding line,
> The long majestick march, and energy divine [4].'

[1] 'Where then was Milton ? ' asks Dr. Warton. Warton's *Pope's Works,* iv. 37. Dryden was born in 1631 ; Milton died in 1674. Johnson had either forgotten Milton, or had in mind the writers of the heroic couplet.

[2] *Ante,* DRYDEN, 201, 228. Dryden, after saying that he had freed *The Indian Emperor* from 'some faults which had escaped the printer,' continues :—'As for the more material faults of writing, which are properly mine, though I see many of them, I want leisure to amend them.' *Works,* ii. 291. He said that he was correcting his Virgil for a second edition. He wrote to Tonson :—' I have broken off my studies ... to review Virgil, and bestowed nine entire days upon him. . . . You cannot take too great care of the printing this edition exactly after my amendments.' *Ib.* xviii. 138–9. I have compared *Aeneid* i. 1–300 in the two editions without discovering a single amendment. The second edition of his *Essay of Dramatic Poesie* he revised with some care, as is shown by the list of emendations given by Malone (i. 2. 2. 135). In

Absalom and Achitophel 'he made some verbal alterations, and introduced sixteen new lines.' For these see *ib.* i. 144, 150. In *Mac Flecknoe* he made 'a few slight alterations.' *Ib.* i. 170. Johnson's statement is substantially correct. Dryden in this differed from Pope, whose 'parental attention never abandoned his works.' *Post,* POPE, 307.

[3] 'Dryden was poor, and in great haste to finish his plays, because by them he chiefly supported his family, and this made him so very incorrect.' SWIFT, *Works,* xviii. 269.

[4] *Imit. Hor. Epis.* ii. 1. 267 ; *post,* POPE, 333.

'Behold, where Dryden's less pre-sumptuous car
Wide o'er the fields of glory bear
Two coursers of ethereal race,
With necks in thunder cloth'd, and long-resounding pace.'
GRAY, *Progress of Poesy,* l. 103.
Gray adds in a note on l. 106 :—
' This verse and the foregoing are meant to express the stately march and sounding energy of Dryden's rhymes.'

' The majestick march of Dryden,' wrote Canning, ' is to my ear the per-

343 Some improvements had been already made in English numbers [1], but the full force of our language was not yet felt: the verse that was smooth was commonly feeble [2].' If Cowley had sometimes a finished line he had it by chance [3]. Dryden knew how to chuse the flowing and the sonorous words; to vary the pauses and adjust the accents; to diversify the cadence, and yet preserve the smoothness of his metre.

344 Of triplets and alexandrines, though he did not introduce the use, he established it. The triplet has long subsisted among us. Dryden seems not to have traced it higher than to Chapman's *Homer* [4]; but it is to be found in Phaer's *Virgil* [5], written in the reign of Mary, and in Hall's *Satires* [6], published five years before the death of Elizabeth.

345 The alexandrine was, I believe, first used by Spenser, for the sake of closing his stanza with a fuller sound [7]. We had a longer measure of fourteen syllables, into which the *Eneid* was translated by Phaer, and other works of the ancients by other writers; of which Chapman's *Iliad* was, I believe, the last.

346 The two first lines of Phaer's third *Eneid* will exemplify this measure:

'When Asia's [Asia] state was overthrown, and Priam's kingdom stout,
All guiltless, by the power of gods above was rooted out.'

fection of harmony.' Lockhart's *Scott*, iii. 321.

'The only qualities,' wrote Wordsworth, 'I can find in Dryden that are *essentially* poetical are a certain ardour and impetuosity of mind, with an excellent ear.' *Ib.* ii. 287.

See *ante*, DENHAM, 34, for Denham's strength and majesty, and *ante*, WALLER, 144, for Waller's smoothness.

[1] *Ante*, DENHAM, 21, 35; ROSCOMMON, 24; WALLER, 153; DRYDEN, 222.

[2] For 'the feeble care of Waller' see *ante*, COWLEY, 185.

[3] *Ante*, COWLEY, 185.

[4] 'Spenser is my example for both these privileges of English verses, and Chapman has followed him. ... Mr. Cowley has given in to them after both. .... I regard them now as the *Magna Charta* of heroic poetry.' *Works*, xiv. 221. For his 'false

account of Chapman's versification' see *ante*, DRYDEN, 207, and for triplets and Alexandrines see *ante*, COWLEY, 196, 199; *post*, POPE, 376.

[5] For Thomas Phaer or Phayer see *Ath. Oxon.* i. 316.

[6] *Ante*, MILTON, 46; *post*, POPE, 380. For a triplet in him and Phaer see extracts from them in Campbell's *British Poets*, pp. lxviii, 70.

'Have you seen Bishop Hall's *Satires*, called *Virgidemiae*? They are full of spirit and poetry.' GRAY, *Letters*, i. 226.

[7] 'Spenser has given me the boldness to make use sometimes of his Alexandrine line, which we call, though improperly, the Pindaric, because Mr. Cowley has often employed it in his Odes. It adds a certain majesty to the verse, when it is used with judgment, and stops the sense from overflowing into another line.' DRYDEN, *Works*, xiv. 208.

As these lines had their break or *cæsura* always at the 347
eighth syllable it was thought in time commodious to divide
them; and quatrains of lines alternately consisting of eight and
six syllables make the most soft and pleasing of our lyrick
measures, as

> 'Relentless Time, destroying power,
> Which [Whom] stone and brass obey,
> Who giv'st to every flying hour
> To work some new decay [1].'

In the alexandrine, when its power was once felt, some poems, 348
as Drayton's *Polyolbion* [2], were wholly written; and sometimes
the measures of twelve and fourteen syllables were interchanged
with one another. Cowley was the first that inserted the alexandrine at pleasure among the heroick lines of ten syllables [3],
and from him Dryden professes to have adopted it [4].

The triplet and alexandrine are not universally approved. 349
Swift always censured them, and wrote some lines to ridicule
them [5]. In examining their propriety it is to be considered that
the essence of verse is regularity, and its ornament is variety [6].
To write verse is to dispose syllables and sounds harmonically
by some known and settled rule—a rule however lax enough to
substitute similitude for identity, to admit change without breach
of order, and to relieve the ear without disappointing it. Thus
a Latin hexameter is formed from dactyls and spondees differently

---

[1] From *An Imitation of some
French Verses*, by Parnell, *Eng.
Poets*, xxvii. 73.
[2] [Part I of the *Polyolbion*, consisting
of eighteen songs, appeared in 1612.
A second part, containing Songs xix-
xxx, was written later, and the complete poem was published in 1622.
D. N. B.]
[3] 'This is an error. The Alexandrine inserted among heroic lines
of ten syllables is found in many of
the writers of Queen Elizabeth's reign.
For instance,
" As tho' the staring world hang'd on
     his sleeve,
  When once he smiles to laugh, and
     when he sighs to grieve."
              Hall's *Sat.* bk. 1. sat. 7.'
J. BOSWELL, JUN., Johnson's *Works*,
vii. 346 *n.*
[4] *Ante*, COWLEY, 196; DRYDEN,
344 *n.* 4.

[5] 'A triplet was a vicious way of
rhyming, wherewith Dryden abounded, and was imitated by all the bad
versifiers in Charles II's reign. . . .
He likewise brought in the Alexandrine verse at the end of his triplets. I was so angry at these cor-
ruptions that about 24 years ago
[1710] I banished them all by one
triplet, with the Alexandrine, upon
a very ridiculous subject.' SWIFT,
Works, xviii. 269. This triplet ends
A Description of a City Shower (*ib.*
xiv. 93) :—
' Sweepings from butchers' stalls,
     dung, guts and blood,
  Drown'd puppies, stinking sprats,
     all drench'd in mud,
  Dead cats and turnip-tops come
     tumbling down the flood.'
See also *post*, POPE, 376.
[6] *Ante*, COWLEY, 141.

combined ; the English heroick admits of acute or grave syllables variously disposed. The Latin never deviates into seven feet, or exceeds the number of seventeen syllables ; but the English alexandrine breaks the lawful bounds, and surprises the reader with two syllables more than he expected.

350   The effect of the triplet is the same: the ear has been accustomed to expect a new rhyme in every couplet; but is on a sudden surprised with three rhymes together, to which the reader could not accommodate his voice did he not obtain notice of the change from the braces of the margins. Surely there is something unskilful in the necessity of such mechanical direction.

351   Considering the metrical art simply as a science, and consequently excluding all casualty, we must allow that triplets and alexandrines inserted by caprice are interruptions of that constancy to which science aspires. And though the variety which they produce may very justly be desired, yet to make our poetry exact there ought to be some stated mode of admitting them.

352   But till some such regulation can be formed, I wish them still to be retained in their present state. They are sometimes grateful to the reader, and sometimes convenient to the poet. Fenton was of opinion that Dryden was too liberal and Pope too sparing in their use [1].

353   The rhymes of Dryden are commonly just, and he valued himself for his readiness in finding them [2]; but he is sometimes open to objection.

354   It is the common practice of our poets to end the second line with a weak or grave syllable:

> ' Together o'er the Alps methinks we fly,
>   Fill'd [Fired] with ideas of fair *Italy* [3].'

Dryden sometimes puts the weak rhyme in the first:

' Laugh [Laughed] all the powers that [who] favour *tyranny*,
   And all the standing army of the sky [4].'

---

[1] *Post*, POPE, 376.

[2] ' Rhyme is certainly a constraint even to the best poets, and those who make it with most ease ; though perhaps I have as little reason to complain of that hardship as any man, excepting Quarles and Withers.' *Works*, xiv. 211. ' Milton's character of Dryden was that he was a good rhymist, but no poet.' *Ante*, MILTON, 164.

[3] POPE, *Epistle to Mr. Jervas*, l. 25.

[4] *Palamon and Arcite*, iii. 671. For other examples see *Absalom and Achitophel*, ll. 159-60, 230-1, 341-2, 481-2.

Sometimes he concludes a period or paragraph with the first line of a couplet [1], which, though the French seem to do it without irregularity [2], always displeases in English poetry.

The alexandrine, though much his favourite, is not always 355 very diligently fabricated by him. It invariably requires a break at the sixth syllable; a rule which the modern French poets never violate, but which Dryden sometimes neglected:

'And with paternal thunder vindicates his throne [3].'

Of Dryden's works it was said by Pope that 'he could select 356 from them better specimens of every mode of poetry than any other English writer could supply [4].' Perhaps no nation ever produced a writer that enriched his language with such variety of models. To him we owe the improvement, perhaps the completion of our metre, the refinement of our language, and much of the correctness of our sentiments [5]. By him we were taught 'sapere et fari [6],' to think naturally and express forcibly. Though Davies has reasoned in rhyme before him, it may be perhaps maintained that he was the first who joined argument with poetry [7]. He shewed us the true bounds of a translator's liberty [8]. What was said of Rome, adorned by Augustus, may be applied by an easy metaphor to English poetry embellished by Dryden, 'lateritiam invenit, marmoream reliquit [9],' he found it brick, and he left it marble [10].

[1] The following is an instance:—
'I did not only view, but will invade.
Could you shed venom from your reverend shade,
Like trees, beneath whose arms 'tis death to sleep,' &c. *Works*, v. 270.
[2] It is not uncommon in Boileau.
[3] 'Still when the giant-brood invades her throne
She stoops from heaven, and meets them half-way down,
And with paternal thunder vindicates her crown.'
The Hind and the Panther, ii. 535.
[4] 'No man hath written in our language so much, and so various matter, and in so various manners so well.' CONGREVE, Dryden's *Works*, ii. 18. I cannot give the reference to Pope.
[5] *Ante*, DRYDEN, 216.
[6] HORACE, *Epis*. i. 4. 9.
[7] In the first edition this sentence stood:—'He taught us that it was possible to reason in rhyme.' See *ante*, DRYDEN, 125, 327.
Sir John Davies (1570–1626) 'carried abstract reasoning into verse with an acuteness and felicity which have seldom been equalled.' CAMPBELL, *British Poets*, Preface, p. 70.
[8] *Ante*, DRYDEN, 223.
[9] SUETONIUS, *Aug*. c. 29.
[10] Atterbury proposed the following epitaph on Dryden:—'Iohanni Drydeno, cui poesis Anglicana vim suam ac veneres debet; si qua in posterum augebitur laude, est adhuc debitura.' Pope's *Works* (E. & C.), ix. 22.
'Here let me bend, great Dryden, at thy shrine,
Thou dearest name to all the tuneful nine.'
CHURCHILL, *The Apology*, *Works*, 1766, i. 72.
Gray wrote to Beattie:—'Remember Dryden, and be blind to all his

357 THE invocation before the *Georgicks* is here inserted from
Mr. Milbourne's version, that, according to his own proposal, his
verses may be compared with those which he censures [1].

> 'What makes the richest *tilth*, beneath what signs
> To *plough*, and when to match your *elms* and *vines*;
> What care with *flocks* and what with *herds* agrees,
> And all the management of frugal *bees*,
> I sing, *Mæcenas!* Ye immensely clear,
> Vast orbs of light which guide the rolling year;
> *Bacchus* and mother *Ceres*, if by you,
> We fat'ning *corn* for hungry *mast* pursue,
> If, taught by you, we first the *cluster* prest,
> And *thin cold streams* with *spritely juice* refresht.
> Ye *fawns* the present *numens* of the field,
> *Wood nymphs* and *fawns*, your kind assistance yield,
> Your gifts I sing! and thou, at whose fear'd stroke
> From rending earth the fiery *courser* broke,
> Great *Neptune*, O assist my artful song!
> And thou to whom the woods and groves belong,
> Whose snowy heifers on her flow'ry plains
> In mighty herds the *Cæan Isle* maintains!
> *Pan*, happy shepherd, if thy cares divine
> E'er to improve thy *Mænalus* incline,
> Leave thy *Lycæan wood* and *native grove*,
> And with thy lucky smiles our work approve!
> Be *Pallas* too, sweet oil's inventor, kind;
> And he, who first the crooked *plough* design'd!
> *Sylvanus*, god of all the woods appear,
> Whose hands a new-drawn tender *cypress* bear!
> Ye *gods* and *goddesses* who e'er with love
> Would guard our pastures, and our fields improve!
> You, who new plants from unsown lands supply;
> And with condensing clouds obscure the sky,
> And drop 'em softly thence in fruitful showers,
> Assist my enterprize, ye gentler powers!
>
> And thou, great *Cæsar!* though we know not yet
> Among what gods thou'lt fix thy lofty seat,
> Whether thou'lt be the kind *tutelar god*
> Of thy own *Rome*; or with thy awful nod,
> Guide the vast world, while thy great hand shall bear ⎫
> The fruits and seasons of the turning year, ⎬
> And thy bright brows thy mother's myrtles wear: ⎭

faults.' Mason adds in a note that
Gray told Beattie 'that if there was
any excellence in his own numbers,
he had learnt it wholly from Dryden.'
Mason's *Gray*, ii. 215.

Tennyson told W. Allingham that
'old Hallam used to say that the
longer one lived the higher one rated
Dryden as a poet.' *Allingham MSS.*
[1] *Ante*, DRYDEN, 148.

Whether thou'lt all the boundless ocean sway,
And sea-men only to thyself shall pray,
Thule, the farthest island, kneel to thee,
And, that thou may'st her son by marriage be,
Tethys will for the happy purchase yield
To make a *dowry* of her watry field;
Whether thou'lt add to heaven a *brighter sign*,
And o'er the *summer months* serenely shine;
Where between *Cancer* and *Erigone*,
There yet remains a spacious *room* for thee.
Where the hot *Scorpion* too his arms declines,
And more to thee than half his *arch* resigns;
Whate'er thou'lt be; for sure the realms below
No just pretence to thy command can show:
No such ambition sways thy vast desires,
Though *Greece* her own *Elysian fields* admires.
And now, at last, contented *Proserpine*
Can all her mother's earnest prayers decline.
Whate'er thou'lt be, O guide our gentle course,
And with thy smiles our bold attempts enforce;
With me th' unknowing *rustics'* wants relieve,
And, though on earth, our sacred vows receive!'

MR. DRYDEN, having received from Rymer his *Remarks on* 358
the Tragedies of the last Age, wrote observations on the blank
leaves [1], which, having been in the possession of Mr. Garrick, are
by his favour [2] communicated to the publick that no particle of
Dryden may be lost:

'That we may the less wonder why pity and terror are not 359
now the only springs on which our tragedies move [3], and that
Shakespeare may be more excused, Rapin confesses that the
French tragedies now all run on the *tendre* [4]; and gives the

[1] It seems likely that Dryden had before him not only Rymer's *Tragedies of the Last Age*, but also his *Short View of Tragedy* (*ante*, DRYDEN, 200 *n.* 2), and his translation of Rapin's *Reflections*.

[2] Garrick died a few weeks before the publication of the first four volumes of the *Lives*. See *post*, SMITH, 76. Johnson altered the arrangement of Dryden's *Observations*. It is restored by Mr. Saintsbury, who also corrects the text, from a MS. copy of the original, in *Works*, xv. 379.

[3] 'Tragedy, as it was anciently composed, hath been ever held the gravest, moralest, and most profitable of all other poems; therefore said by Aristotle to be of power, by raising pity and fear or terror, to purge the mind of those and such like passions.' MILTON, Preface to *Samson Agonistes*. See Aristotle's *Poetics*, c. 13.

[4] Rymer, in 1674, translated (anonymously) R. Rapin's *Reflections on Aristotle's Treatise of Poesie*, and added to it a long preface. For 'the love and *tenderness* to which the French poets bend all their subjects' see *ib.* p. 111; where Rapin adds:—
'The English, our neighbours, love blood in their sports by the quality

reason, because love is the passion which most predominates in our souls, and that therefore the passions represented become insipid, unless they are conformable to the thoughts of the audience. But it is to be concluded that this passion works not now amongst the French so strongly as the other two did amongst the ancients. Amongst us, who have a stronger genius for writing, the operations from the writing are much stronger : for the raising of Shakespeare's passions is more from the excellency of the words and thoughts, than the justness of the occasion ; and if he has been able to pick single occasions he has never founded the whole reasonably, yet, by the genius of poetry in writing, he has succeeded.

360 'Rapin attributes more to the *dictio*, that is, to the words and discourse of a tragedy, than Aristotle [1] has done, who places them in the last rank of beauties, perhaps, only last in order, because they are the last product of the design, of the disposition or connection of its parts ; of the characters, of the manners of those characters, and of the thoughts proceeding from those manners. Rapin's words are remarkable : 'Tis not the admirable intrigue the surprising events, and extraordinary incidents that make the beauty of a tragedy ; 'tis the discourses, when they are natural and passionate [2] : so are Shakespeare's.

361 'The parts of a poem, tragick or heroick, are
' 1. The fable itself.
' 2. The order or manner of its contrivance in relation of the parts to the whole.

of their temperament ; these are *Insulaires*, separated from the rest of men ; we are more humane.' On p. 122 he writes :—'The English have more of genius for tragedy than any other people, as well by the spirit of their nation, which delights in cruelty, as also by the character of their language, which is proper for great expressions.'

Addison, who saw Boileau in 1700, records him as saying :—'Aristotle proposes two passions that are proper to be raised by tragedy, terror and pity, but Corneille endeavours at a new one, which is admiration. He instanced in his *Pompey*, where, in the first scene, the King of Egypt runs into a very pompous and long description of the Battle of Pharsalia, though he was then in a great hurry of affairs, and had not himself been present at it.' Addison's *Works*, v. 333.

[1] *Poetics*, ch. xx. 'Dryden scarce ever mentions Aristotle without discovering that he had looked only at the wrong side of the tapestry.' TWINING, *Aristotle's Poetics*, 1812, i. 281.
'Translating out of one language into another . . . is like presenting to view the wrong side of a piece of tapestry.' Jervas's *Don Quixote*, 1820, iv. 316.

[2] Rapin's *Reflections*, p. 116. His words about Dante are no less remarkable. 'Ariosto,' he writes, 'has too much flame; Dante has none at all.' *Ib.* p. 2. The last defect to be discovered in the *Inferno* is a want of flame. Remarkable too is his criticism of Aeschylus. 'He had scarce any principle for manners and for the decencies ; his fables are too simple, the contrivance wretched, the expression obscure and blundered. . . . In effect he never speaks in cold blood, and says the most indifferent things in a tragic huff.' *Ib.* p. 117.

' 3. The manners or decency of the characters, in speaking or acting what is proper for them, and proper to be shewn by the poet.

' 4. The thoughts which express the manners.

' 5. The words which express those thoughts.

'In the last of these Homer excels Virgil, Virgil all other 362 ancient poets, and Shakespeare all modern poets.

'For the second of these, the order: the meaning is, that 363 a fable ought to have a beginning, middle, and an end, all just and natural [1], so that that part, *e.g.* which is the middle, could not naturally be the beginning or end, and so of the rest: all depend on one another, like the links of a curious chain. If terror and pity are only to be raised, certainly this author follows Aristotle's rules, and Sophocles' and Euripides's example ; but joy may be raised too, and that doubly, either by seeing a wicked man punished, or a good man at last fortunate ; or perhaps indignation, to see wickedness prosperous and goodness depressed : both these may be profitable to the end of tragedy, reformation of manners ; but the last improperly, only as it begets pity in the audience : though Aristotle, I confess, places tragedies of this kind in the second form [2].

'He who undertakes to answer this excellent critique of 364 Mr. Rymer, in behalf of our English poets against the Greek, ought to do it in this manner. Either by yielding to him the greatest part of what he contends for, which consists in this, that the $\mu \hat{v} \theta o s$, *i. e.* the design and conduct of it, is more conducing in the Greeks to those ends of tragedy which Aristotle and he propose, namely, to cause terror and pity [3]; yet the granting this does not set the Greeks above the English poets [4].

'But the answerer ought to prove two things: first, that the 365 fable is not the greatest master-piece of a tragedy, though it be the foundation of it.

'Secondly, That other ends as suitable to the nature of tragedy may be found in the English, which were not in the Greek.

'Aristotle places the fable first [5]; not "quoad dignitatem, sed 366 quoad fundamentum ": for a fable, never so movingly contrived to those ends of his, pity and terror, will operate nothing on our affections, except the characters, manners, thoughts, and words are suitable.

'So that it remains to Mr. Rymer to prove that in all those, 367 or the greatest part of them, we are inferior to Sophocles and

[1] *Ante*, MILTON, 224.
[2] *Poetics*, xi.
[3] *Ib.* vi. 12.
[4] ' I have chiefly consider'd the fable or plot, which all conclude to be the soul of a tragedy ; which with the ancients is always found to be a reasonable soul, but with us, for the most part, a brutish, and often worse than brutish.' Rymer's *Tragedies*, &c., p. 4.
[5] *Poetics*, vi. 12.

Euripides; and this he has offered at in some measure, but, I think, a little partially to the ancients.

368 'For the fable itself: 'tis in the English more adorned with episodes, and larger than in the Greek poets; consequently more diverting. For, if the action be but one, and that plain, without any counter-turn of design or episode, *i. e.* under-plot, how can it be so pleasing as the English, which have both under-plot and a turned design, which keeps the audience in expectation of the catastrophe? whereas in the Greek poets we see through the whole design at first.

369 'For the characters, they are neither so many nor so various in Sophocles and Euripides as in Shakespeare and Fletcher; only they are more adapted to those ends of tragedy which Aristotle commends to us, pity and terror [1].

370 'The manners flow from the characters, and consequently must partake of their advantages and disadvantages.

371 'The thoughts and words, which are the fourth and fifth beauties of tragedy, are certainly more noble and more poetical in the English than in the Greek, which must be proved by comparing them, somewhat more equitably than Mr. Rymer has done.

372 'After all, we need not yield that the English way is less conducing to move pity and terror, because they often shew virtue oppressed and vice punished: where they do not both, or either, they are not to be defended.

373 'And if we should grant that the Greeks performed this better, perhaps it may admit of dispute whether pity and terror are either the prime, or at least the only ends of tragedy.

374 ''Tis not enough that Aristotle has said so, for Aristotle drew his models of tragedy from Sophocles and Euripides; and, if he had seen ours, might have changed his mind [2]. And chiefly we have to say (what I hinted on pity and terror, in the last paragraph save one) that the punishment of vice and reward of virtue are the most adequate ends of tragedy, because most conducing to good example of life. Now pity is not so easily raised for a criminal, and the ancient tragedy always represents its chief person such, as it is for an innocent man; and the

---

[1] 'Aristot. *Poet.* vi. 2. Τραγῳδία μίμησις πράξεως σπουδαίας, &c. Tragoedia est imitatio actionis seriae, &c., per misericordiam et metum perficiens talium affectuum lustrationem.' Motto to *Samson Agonistes.*

[2] Dryden, defending the plot of his *Love Triumphant*, writes:— 'Aristotle has declared that the catastrophe which is made from the change of will is not of the first order of beauty; but it may reasonably be alleged in defence of this play, as well as of Corneille's *Cinna*, that the philosopher who made the rule copied all the laws which he gave for the theatre from the authorities and examples of the Greek poets which he had read. . . . Had it been possible for Aristotle to have seen the *Cinna*, I am confident he would have altered his opinion.' *Works*, viii. 374.

suffering of innocence and punishment of the offender is of the nature of English tragedy: contrarily, in the Greek, innocence is unhappy often, and the offender escapes. Then we are not touched with the sufferings of any sort of men so much as of lovers ; and this was almost unknown to the ancients: so that they neither administered poetical justice, of which Mr. Rymer boasts[1], so well as we ; neither knew they the best common-place of pity, which is love.

'He therefore unjustly blames us for not building on what [375] the ancients left us[2] ; for it seems, upon consideration of the premises, that we have wholly finished what they began.

'My judgement on this piece is this, that it is extremely [376] learned ; but that the author of it is better read in the Greek than in the English poets ; that all writers ought to study this critique, as the best account I have ever seen of the ancients ; that the model of tragedy he has here given is excellent and extreme correct ; but that it is not the only model of all tragedy, because it is too much circumscribed in plot, characters, &c. ; and lastly, that we may be taught here justly to admire and imitate the ancients, without giving them the preference with this author in prejudice to our own country.

'Want of method in this excellent treatise makes the thoughts [377] of the author sometimes obscure.

'His meaning, that pity and terror are to be moved, is, that [378] they are to be moved as the means conducing to the ends of tragedy, which are pleasure and instruction[3].

'And these two ends may be thus distinguished. The chief [379] end of the poet is to please ; for his immediate reputation depends on it.

'The great end of the poem is to instruct, which is performed [380] by making pleasure the vehicle of that instruction ; for poesy is an art, and all arts are made to profit. *Rapin*[4].

'The pity, which the poet is to labour for, is for the criminal, [381] not for those or him whom he has murdered, or who have been the occasion of the tragedy. The terror is likewise in the punishment of the same criminal ; who, if he be represented too great an

---

[1] ' In former times poetry was another thing than history ; or than the law of the land. Poetry discover'd crimes the law could never find out, and punish'd those the law had acquitted.' *The Tragedies of the Last Age*, p. 25.

[2] *Ib.* p. 11.

[3] Rymer criticizing *Rollo* says :— ' Nothing certainly is designed in this fable of *Rollo* either to move pity or terror, either to delight or instruct.' *Tragedies*, &c., p. 19.

[4] ' 'Tis true delight is the end poetry aims at, but not the principal end, as others pretend. In effect, poetry being an art ought to be profitable by the quality of its own nature, and by the essential subordination that all arts should have to polity, whose end in general is the public good.' Rapin's *Reflections*, p. 9.

See *post*, GRAY, 41, where Johnson writes :—' I do not see that *The Bard* promotes any truth, moral or political.'

offender, will not be pitied ; if altogether innocent, his punishment will be unjust [1].

382 'Another obscurity is, where he says Sophocles perfected tragedy by introducing the third actor ; that is, he meant, three kinds of action : one company singing, or another playing on the musick ; a third dancing [2].

383 'To make a true judgement in this competition betwixt the Greek poets and the English, in tragedy :

'Consider, first, how Aristotle has defined a tragedy. Secondly, what he assigns the end of it to be. Thirdly, what he thinks the beauties of it. Fourthly, the means to attain the end proposed.

384 'Compare the Greek and English tragick poets justly and without partiality, according to those rules.

385 'Then secondly, consider whether Aristotle has made a just definition of tragedy ; of its parts, of its ends, and of its beauties ; and whether he, having not seen any others but those of Sophocles, Euripides, &c., had or truly could determine what all the excellences of tragedy are, and wherein they consist.

386 'Next shew in what ancient tragedy was deficient : for example, in the narrowness of its plots, and fewness of persons, and try whether that be not a fault in the Greek poets ; and whether their excellency was so great when the variety was visibly so little ; or whether what they did was not very easy to do.

387 'Then make a judgement on what the English have added to their beauties : as, for example, not only more plot, but also new passions ; as, namely, that of love, scarce touched on by the ancients, except in this one example of Phædra, cited by Mr. Rymer ; and in that how short they were of Fletcher [3] !

388 'Prove also that love, being an heroick passion, is fit for tragedy, which cannot be denied, because of the example alledged of Phædra ; and how far Shakespeare has outdone them in friendship, &c.

389 'To return to the beginning of this enquiry ; consider if pity

---

[1] 'The poets were obliged to have a strict eye on their malefactor, that he transgrest not too far ; that he committed not two crimes, when but responsible for *one* ; nor indeed be so far guilty as to deserve death. . . . The truth is, the poets were to move pity, and this pity was to be moved for the living who remained, and not for the dead.' Rymer's *Tragedies*, &c., pp. 26, 28.

[2] Dryden seems to refer to the following passages in Rymer :—
'Sophocles, adding a third actor and painted scenes, gave (in Aristotle's opinion) the utmost perfection to tragedy.' *The Tragedies*, &c., p. 13. 'When it [tragedy] was brought to the utmost perfection by Sophocles, the chorus continued a necessary part of the tragedy ; but that musick and the dancing which came along with the chorus were mere religion, were no part of the tragedy, nor had anything of philosophy or instruction in them.' *A Short View of Tragedy*, p. 19.

[3] Rymer compares Phaedra in Euripides with Panthea in Beaumont and Fletcher's *King and No King. The Tragedies of the Last Age*, p. 79.

and terror be enough for tragedy to move: and I believe, upon a true definition of tragedy, it will be found that its work extends farther, and that it is to reform manners, by a delightful representation of human life in great persons, by way of dialogue. If this be true, then not only pity and terror are to be moved as the only means to bring us to virtue, but generally love to virtue and hatred to vice; by shewing the rewards of one, and punishments of the other; at least, by rendering virtue always amiable, tho' it be shewn unfortunate; and vice detestable, though it be shewn triumphant.

'If, then, the encouragement of virtue and discouragement of **390** vice be the proper ends of poetry in tragedy, pity and terror, though good means, are not the only. For all the passions, in their turns, are to be set in a ferment: as joy, anger, love, fear are to be used as the poet's common-places; and a general concernment for the principal actors is to be raised, by making them appear such in their characters, their words, and actions, as will interest the audience in their fortunes.

'And if, after all, in a larger sense pity comprehends this **391** concernment for the good, and terror includes detestation for the bad, then let us consider whether the English have not answered this end of tragedy as well as the ancients, or perhaps better.

'And here Mr. Rymer's objections against these plays are to **392** be impartially weighed, that we may see whether they are of weight enough to turn the balance against our countrymen.

''Tis evident those plays which he arraigns [1] have moved both **393** those passions in a high degree upon the stage.'

'To give the glory of this away from the poet, and to place it **394** upon the actors, seems unjust [2].

'One reason is, because whatever actors they have found, the **395** event has been the same, that is, the same passions have been always moved; which shews that there is something of force and merit in the plays themselves, conducing to the design of raising these two passions: and suppose them ever to have been excellently acted, yet action only adds grace, vigour, and more life upon the stage; but cannot give it wholly where it is not first. But secondly, I dare appeal to those who have never seen them acted, if they have not found these two passions moved within

---

[1] *Rollo, Duke of Normandy, A King and No King* and *The Maid's Tragedy* by Beaumont and Fletcher, in *The Tragedies*, &c., pp. 16, 56, 104; *Othello* and *Julius Caesar* by Shakespeare, *Catiline* by Ben Jonson, in *A Short View*, &c., pp. 86, 148, 159.

[2] 'They say (for instance) *A King and No King* pleases. I say the comical part pleases. I say that Mr. Hart pleases; most of the business falls to his share, and what he delivers, every one takes upon content; their eyes are prepossest and charmed by his action, before ought of the poets can approach their ears.' *Tragedies of the Last Age*, p. 5. See also *ib.* p. 138.

them : and if the general voice will carry it Mr. Rymer's prejudice will take off his single testimony.

396 'This, being matter of fact, is reasonably to be established by this appeal ; as if one man says 'tis night, the rest of the world conclude it to be day ; there needs no farther argument against him that it is so.

397 'If he urge that the general taste is depraved his arguments to prove this can at best but evince that our poets took not the best way to raise those passions ; but experience proves against him, that these means, which they have used, have been successful, and have produced them.

398 'And one reason of that success is, in my opinion, this, that Shakespeare and Fletcher have written to the genius of the age and nation in which they lived ; for though nature, as he objects, is the same in all places, and reason too the same, yet the climate, the age, the disposition of the people, to whom a poet writes, may be so different that what pleased the Greeks would not satisfy an English audience.

399 'And if they proceeded upon a foundation of truer reason to please the Athenians than Shakespeare and Fletcher to please the English, it only shews that the Athenians were a more judicious people ; but the poet's business is certainly to please the audience.

400 'Whether our English audience have been pleased hitherto with acorns, as he calls it, or with bread, is the next question [1] ; that is, whether the means which Shakespeare and Fletcher have used in their plays to raise those passions before named, be better applied to the ends by the Greek poets than by them. And perhaps we shall not grant him this wholly : let it be granted that a writer is not to run down with the stream, or to please the people by their own usual methods, but rather to reform their judgements, it still remains to prove that our theatre needs this total reformation.

401 'The faults, which he has found in their designs, are rather wittily aggravated in many places than reasonably urged ; and as much may be returned on the Greeks, by one who were as witty as himself.

402 'They destroy not, if they are granted, the foundation of the fabrick ; only take away from the beauty of the symmetry : for example, the faults in the character of the *King and No-King* [2] are not as he makes them, such as render him detestable, but only imperfections which accompany human nature, and are for the most part excused by the violence of his love ; so that they

---

[1] 'Lastly (though tragedy is a poem chiefly for men of sense) yet I cannot be persuaded that the people are so very mad of acorns but that they could be well content to eat the bread of civil persons.' *The Tragedies of the Last Age*, p. 7.

[2] By Beaumont and Fletcher. *Ib.* p. 56.

destroy not our pity or concernment for him : this answer may be applied to most of his objections of that kind.'

'And Rollo committing many murders, when he is answerable [403] but for one, is too severely arraigned by him[1]; for it adds to our horror and detestation of the criminal: and poetick justice is not neglected neither ; for we stab him in our minds for every offence which he commits; and the point, which the poet is to gain on the audience, is not so much in the death of an offender as the raising an horror of his crimes.

'That the criminal should neither be wholly guilty nor wholly [404] innocent, but so participating of both as to move both pity and terror, is certainly a good rule[2], but not perpetually to be observed ; for that were to make all tragedies too much alike, which objection he foresaw, but has not fully answered.

'To conclude, therefore ; if the plays of the ancients are more [405] correctly plotted, ours are more beautifully written.   And if we can raise passions as high on worse foundations it shews our genius in tragedy is greater; for, in all other parts of it, the English have manifestly excelled them[3].'

THE original of the following letter is preserved in the Library [406] at Lambeth, and was kindly imparted to the publick by the reverend Dr. Vyse[4].

Copy of an original Letter from John Dryden, Esq., to his sons in Italy, from a MS. in the Lambeth Library, marked N° 933. p. 56.

(*Superscribed*)

'Al Illustrissimo Sig[re]
Carlo Dryden Camariere
d' Honore A. S. S.[5]

In Roma.

'Franca per Mantoua.

'Sept. the 3d, our style[6] [1697].

'Dear Sons,

'Being now at Sir William Bowyer's[7] in the country I cannot write at large, because I find myself somewhat indisposed with

---

[1] *Rollo, Duke of Normandy*, by Beaumont and Fletcher. 'When Rollo has murdered his brother he stands condemned by the laws of poetry ; and nothing remains but that the poet see him executed, and the poet is to answer for all the mischief committed afterwards.' *The Tragedies of the Last Age*, p. 37.

[2] *Ante*, DRYDEN, 381.

[3] In the *Preface to Troilus and Cressida* Dryden examines 'the Grounds of Criticism in Tragedy,' quoting both Rymer and Rapin. *Works*, vi. 260.

[4] A friend of Johnson's. Boswell's *Johnson*, iii. 124.

[5] *Ante*, DRYDEN, 157.

[6] By the Roman style it was ten days later.

[7] At Denham Court, near Uxbridge.   Bowyer married a kinswoman of Dryden's wife. Malone's *Dryden*, i. 2. 54.

a cold, and am thick of hearing, rather worse than I was in town. I am glad to find, by your letter of July 26th, your style, that you are both in health; but wonder you should think me so negligent as to forget to give you an account of the ship in which your parcel is to come. I have written to you two or three letters concerning it, which I have sent by safe hands, as I told you, and doubt not but you have them before this can arrive to you. Being out of town, I have forgotten the ship's name, which your mother will enquire, and put it into her letter, which is joined with mine. But the master's name I remember: he is called Mr. Ralph Thorp; the ship is bound to Leghorn, consigned to Mr. Peter and Mr. Tho. Ball, merchants. I am of your opinion, that by Tonson's means almost all our letters have miscarried for this last year[1]. But, however, he has missed of his design in the Dedication, though he had prepared the book for it; for in every figure of Eneas he has caused him to be drawn like King William, with a hooked nose[2]. After my return to town I intend to alter a play of Sir Robert Howard's, written long since, and lately put by him into my hands: 'tis called *The Conquest of China by the Tartars*. It will cost me six weeks' study, with the probable benefit of an hundred pounds. In the mean time I am writing a song for St. Cecilia's Feast, who, you know, is the patroness of musick[3]. This is troublesome, and no way beneficial; but I could not deny the Stewards of the Feast, who came in a body to me to desire that kindness, one of them being Mr. Bridgman, whose parents are your mother's friends. I hope to send you thirty guineas between Michaelmas and Christmas, of which I will give you an account when I come to town. I remember the counsel you give me in your letter; but dissembling, though lawful in some cases, is not my talent; yet, for your sake, I will struggle with the plain openness of my nature, and keep in my just resentments against that degenerate order. In the mean time, I flatter not myself with any manner of hopes, but do my duty, and suffer for God's sake[4]; being

---

[1] Dryden sent letters to his sons through Tonson, as a later one shows. *Works*, xviii. 140. The bookseller, it seems clear, had wished him to dedicate the *Aeneid* to King William. It is most probably to the loss of profits by his refusal to do this that he refers in the end of the present letter. His continuing to use Tonson's agency in corresponding with his sons proves that his suspicion was groundless.

[2] 'He had a Roman eagle nose, bright and sparkling eyes.' Burnet's *Hist*. iii. 335.

Malone quotes the following from the

MS. *Harl*. p. 35 :—' To be published in the next edition of Dryden's *Virgil*.

Old Jacob by deep judgment sway'd
  To please the wise beholders,
Has placed old Nassau's hook-nosed head
  On poor Aeneas' shoulders.
To make the parallel hold tack,
  Methinks there 's little lacking;
One took his father pick-a-pack,
  And t'other sent his packing.'
Malone's *Dryden*, i. 2. 55. See also *ante*, DRYDEN, 147 *n*. 6.

[3] *Ante*, DRYDEN, 150, 318.

[4] *Ante*, DRYDEN, 136. In 1699 a law against Papists was passed.

assured, beforehand, never to be rewarded, though the times should alter.   Towards the latter end of this month, September, Charles will begin to recover his perfect health, according to his nativity, which, casting it myself, I am sure is true, and all things hitherto have happened accordingly to the very time that I predicted them[1]; I hope at the same time to recover more health, according to my age.   Remember me to poor Harry, whose prayers I earnestly desire.   My *Virgil* succeeds in the world beyond its desert or my expectation[2].   You know the profits might have been more; but neither my conscience nor my honour would suffer me to take them : but I never can repent of my constancy, since I am thoroughly persuaded of the justice of the cause for which I suffer.   It has pleased God to raise up many friends to me amongst my enemies, though they who ought to have been my friends are negligent of me.   I am called to dinner, and cannot go on with this letter, which I desire you to excuse ; and am

'Your most affectionate father,

'JOHN DRYDEN.'

APPENDIX Q (PAGE 340)

For Davenant, who succeeded Ben Jonson, and who died on April 7, 1668, see *ante*, DENHAM, 22 ; MILTON, 102 ; DRYDEN, 30, 97, 235 ; and Aubrey's *Brief Lives*, i. 204.

'Dryden did not obtain the laurel till Aug. 18, 1670,' when he was also made Historiographer Royal.   'The patent had a retrospect, and the salary [for the two offices], which was £200 a year, was made payable from the midsummer after Davenant's death.'   Malone's *Dryden*, i. 87. See also *post*, SHEFFIELD, 9.

Dryden and Rowe (*post*, ROWE, 21) are the only laureates among the poets in Johnson's *Lives*.   Gray, who 'had the honour of refusing the laurel' (*post*, GRAY, 15), wrote of Dryden that 'he was as disgraceful to the office from his character as the poorest scribbler could have been from his verses.'   *Letters*, i. 374.   See also *post*, SAVAGE, 172 *n*.

'The title of poet laureate, which custom, rather than vanity, perpetuates in the English Court, was first invented by the Caesars of Germany.'   GIBBON, *Decline and Fall*, vii. 256.   Gibbon, in a note, after telling how the laureate 'is bound to furnish twice a year a measure of praise and verse,' continues :—'The best time for abolishing this ridiculous custom is while the prince is a man of virtue [George III],

Burnet's *Hist.* iii. 253.   Dryden wrote to one of his cousins on Nov. 7 of that year :—'I can neither take the oaths nor forsake my religion ; because I know not what church to go to, if I leave the Catholic. . . . May God be pleased to open your eyes, as he has opened mine !   Truth is but one ; and they who have once heard of it can plead no excuse if they do not embrace it.'   *Works*, xviii. 161.   For the loss which Pope suffered as a Papist see *post*, POPE, 71.

[1] *Ante*, DRYDEN, 191.
[2] *Ante*, DRYDEN, 146.

and the poet a man of genius [Thomas Warton].' This custom 'seems to have commenced soon after Dryden was deprived of the laurel.' Malone's *Dryden*, i. 209.

For the office see Malone's *Dryden*, i. 78, 209. Scott, who declined the laureateship in 1813, writes :—' A sort of ridicule has always attached to the character.' *Familiar Letters*, i. 307. See also Lockhart's *Scott*, iv. 103, and Warton's *Pope's Works*, iv. 149; vi. 309.

The grant of ' one terse of Canary Spanish wine yearly ' was made in 1630. Jonson's *Works*, 1756, Preface, pp. 46, 60. A terse or tierce is a third of a pipe. James II, in renewing Dryden's patent, cut off the wine. Macaulay's *Hist. of Eng.* ii. 455.

Southey wrote, on being made Poet Laureate in 1813 :—' The tierce is now wickedly commuted for £26; which said sum, unlike the canary, is subject to income-tax, land-tax, and heaven knows what taxes beside. The whole income is little more or less than £90. It comes to me as a Godsend.' Southey's *Life*, &c. 1850, iv. 49.

In Messrs. Sotheby's Catalogue for July 22, 1901, is a document (No. 34) dated April 6, 1720, ordering that ' £30, in lieu of a Pipe of Sack, be paid to Laurence Eusden, Esq. Poet Laureat to his Maj[tie].'

APPENDIX R (PAGE 369)

' There had always been allowed such ludicrous liberties of observation upon anything new or remarkable in the state of the stage as Mr. Bayes might think proper to take.' CIBBER, *Letter to Mr. Pope*, 1742, p. 17; *post*, POPE, 233.

In the Key prefixed to *The Rehearsal*, 1710, it is said that the play was ready for acting in 1665, when the Plague broke out. The poet was Bilboa, by which name the Town generally understood Howard. It was not acted till 1671. 'Mr. Dryden, a new Laureate, appeared on the stage, which moved the Duke to change the name to Bayes.' For a list of the plays ridiculed see *ib.* and the notes on the text. For Howard see DRYDEN, 17, 21, 23, 25.

Evelyn describes him as 'a gentleman pretending to all manner of arts and sciences, for which he had been the subject of comedy, under the name of Sir Positive [in Shadwell's *Sullen Lovers*]; not ill-natured, but insufferably boasting.' *Diary*, ii. 221. His brothers, Edward Howard (Boswell's *Johnson*, ii. 108) and J. Howard, were taken off in *The Rehearsal*, ed. Arber, pp. 28, 82.

' Assuredly the original hero was not Howard, but Davenant.' When Dryden was made the hero ' the piece became a kind of patchwork.' Malone's *Dryden*, i. 97.

' I knew,' wrote Dryden, ' that my betters were more concerned than I was in that satire.' *Works*, xiii. 9.

Langbaine was afraid to explain the allusions. ' There are some,' he wrote, ' who pretend to furnish a *Clavis* to it ; my talent not lying to politics, I know no more of it than that the author lashes several plays of Mr. Dryden.' *Dram. Poets*, p. 546.

' Tonson,' said Lockier, ' has a good key to it, but refuses to print it, because he had been so much obliged to Dryden.' Spence's *Anec.* p. 63.

APPENDIX S (Page 378)

Dryden published the translation of Maimbourg's *History of the League* in 1684, before his conversion. In the Dedication to Charles II, at whose command he translated it, he says :—'Never was there a plainer parallel than of the troubles of France and of Great Britain ; of their leagues, covenants, associations, and ours.' *Works*, xvii. 89 ; DRYDEN, 69. He is cruel in urging the king to fresh judicial murders. *Works*, xvii. 84. He was proud of his work. ' 'Tis the best translation of any history in English,' he wrote to his bookseller. *Ib.* xviii. 105. He had found it a tiresome task. He says of 'the disease of translation ' :—' The cold prose fits of it, which are always the most tedious with me, were spent in the *History of the League.*' *Ib.* xii. 281.

Mme de Sévigné wrote of Maimbourg on Sept. 14, 1675 :—'Le style du P. Maimbourg me déplaît fort : il sent l'auteur qui a ramassé le délicat des mauvaises ruelles.'

Evelyn recorded on Oct. 2, 1685, that Pepys had lately been shown by James 'two papers in the late King's own hand, containing several arguments opposite to the doctrine of the Church of England.' James gave Pepys copies, which Evelyn read. *Diary*, ii. 247. 'Tenison,' says Burnet (*Hist.* ii. 235), 'saw the original in Pepys's hand.' He adds that Charles could never have composed them, 'for he never read the Scriptures, nor laid things together, further than to turn them to a jest, or for some lively expression.' See also Macaulay's *England*, ii. 297.

These papers James published, together with one by his first wife, justifying her conversion. To these papers Stillingfleet wrote *An Answer*. To the third part, dealing with her conversion, Dryden rejoined. Stillingfleet replied in *A Vindication of the Answer*. Malone's *Dryden*, i. 192 ; *Works*, i. 271 ; xvii. 189, 196, 210, 255.

APPENDIX T (Page 394)

' He was of a nature exceedingly humane and compassionate ; easily forgiving injuries, and capable of a prompt and sincere reconciliation with them who had offended him. . . .

'His friendship, where he professed it, went much beyond his professions.

'As his reading had been very extensive, so was he very happy in a memory tenacious of every thing that he had read. He was not more possessed of knowledge than he was communicative of it. But then his communication of it was by no means pedantic, or imposed upon the conversation, but just such, and went so far as, by the natural turns of the discourse in which he was engaged, it was necessarily promoted or required. He was extreme ready and gentle in his correction of the errors of any writer who thought fit to consult him, and full as ready and patient to admit of the reprehension of others in respect of his own oversight or mistakes. He was of very easy, I may say of very pleasing access ; but something slow, and as it were diffident in his advances to others. He had something in his nature that abhorred intrusion into any society whatsoever. . . . By that means he was personally less known, and consequently his character might become liable both to misapprehensions and misrepresentations.

'He was, of all the men that ever I knew, one of the most modest, and the most easily to be discountenanced in his approaches either to his superiors or his equals.' Dryden's *Works*, ii. 17, 18.

APPENDIX U (PAGE 405)

Malone shows that, taking the value of money in Dryden's time as three times greater than it was at the end of the eighteenth century, his income was by no means small. In 1654 he inherited an estate of £40 a year, increased to £60 on his mother's death in 1671. His wife's settlement 'was probably not less than £60 a year.' From 1668 to 1685, as Poet Laureate and Historiographer, he received £200 a year; increased to £300 from 1685 to 1689. From 1665 to 1670 (with the omission of eighteen months when the theatres were closed on account of the Plague and Fire, but when he gained something by his poems) he made from the theatre £100 a year. In the next five or six years this rose to £200, but fell to £100 from 1676 to 1685, when it ceased for a time. It was with the loss of his office in 1689 that he began to be distressed; 'his certain income being reduced to £120 a year.' With what he made by his pen, added to the presents he received, 'his annual income, even during this distressful period, was above £400.' Malone's *Dryden*, i. 436–59. Cunningham (*Lives of the Poets*, i. 334) shows that in 1683 he was appointed Collector of Customs. His salaries were not, however, regularly paid. About that same year he wrote to Lord Treasurer Rochester :—'I know not whether my Lord Sunderland has interceded with your Lordship for half a year of my salary; but I have two other advocates, my extreme wants, even almost to arresting, and my ill health. . . . I only think I merit not to starve. . . . 'Tis enough for one age to have neglected Mr. Cowley and starved Mr. Butler.' *Works*, xviii. 103; *ante*, COWLEY, 35; BUTLER, 18. See also *Works*, viii. 217; DRYDEN, 189.

A few months before his death he wrote of the Court :—'If they will consider me as a man who has done my best to improve the language, and especially the poetry, and will be content with my acquiescence under the present government, and forbearing satire on it, that I can promise, because I can perform it; but I can neither take the oaths, nor forsake my religion.' *Works*, xviii. 161. All this time Titus Oates enjoyed a pension of £300 a year. Malone's *Dryden*, i. 460.

APPENDIX X (PAGE 413)

Johnson should rather have said, 'the insolence of a pedantic fool.' In *A Short View of Tragedy, It's Original, Excellency and Corruption, with some Reflections on Shakespeare and other Practitioners for the Stage* Rymer has such reflections as the following :—'Should the poet have provided such a husband [as Othello] for an only daughter of any noble peer in England, the blackamoor must have changed his skin to look our House of Lords in the face,' p. 102. 'The Italian painters are noted for drawing the Madonnas by their own wives or mistresses; one might wonder what sort of Betty Mackerel Shakespeare found in his days to sit for his Portia and Desdemona,' p. 157.

Dryden wrote of him :—'For my own part I reverence Mr. Rymer's learning, but I detest his ill nature and his arrogance. I indeed, and such as I, have reason to be afraid of him, but Shakespeare has not.' *Works*, xviii. 117. See also the *Epistle to Mr. Congreve*, l. 48, where he scornfully calls him 'Tom the second,' Shadwell being 'Tom the first.' *Ib.* xi. 58.

Rymer's 'Heroic Tragedy called *Edgar*' is ridiculed by Addison in *The Spectator*, No. 592.

'Rymer is generally right, though rather too severe in his opinion of the particular plays he speaks of, and is, on the whole, one of the best critics we ever had.' POPE, Spence's *Anec.* p. 172.

'Rymer, after making remarks on what he calls our three epic poets, Spenser, Davenant, and Cowley, mentions not one syllable of Milton.' J. WARTON, Warton's *Pope*, v. 173. See DRYDEN, 19, 358.

Rymer's folly as a critic cannot depress his merit as the editor of the *Foedera*.

ADDITIONAL APPENDIX A* (PAGE 141)

[SCRIVENER'S COPY OF 'PARADISE LOST,' BOOK I.

The following note has been kindly supplied by Mr. G. K. Fortescue, Keeper of Printed Books in the British Museum.

On Jan. 25, 1904, a Manuscript relating to Milton was offered for sale by Messrs. Sotheby, Wilkinson, & Hodge, but was withdrawn, the reserved price of £5,000 not having been reached. Shortly afterwards the Manuscript was sold to an American collector for a price the amount of which has not been disclosed. The Manuscript consists of thirty-five quarto pages, containing on the first leaf the Imprimatur signed by Thomas Tomkyns, Chaplain to the Archbishop of Canterbury (Gilbert Sheldon), and by Richard Royston, Warden of the Stationers' Company, curiously enough the publisher of *Eikon Basilike* and the *Works of Charles I.* The licence is followed by the first book of *Paradise Lost* in the formal handwriting of a professional scrivener.

There can be little or no doubt that this Manuscript was the copy sent to the Licencers and afterwards used for printing the book. Its interest lies in the strong probability that it was read to Milton and verbally corrected by him. Besides many alterations in the spelling there are several emendations of the text, which one may almost say must necessarily have been dictated by the author.

The most important are—Book I. line 156, the Manuscript of this line originally read 'The Fiend replied,' which has been corrected to 'Th' Archfiend replied.' Book I. line 709,—the original words are 'To many a hundred pipes,' but these have been twice corrected. First, the word *hundred* has been rewritten *hunderd*; then *hunderd* has been struck out and the line altered to the form in which it was printed, 'To many a row of pipes.'

The Manuscript is accompanied by an interesting letter written in 1731 by Jacob Tonson, which helps to authenticate its history. It originally belonged to Samuel Simmons, the first printer of the book; from him it passed through the hands of his assignee Brabazon Aylmer to Jacob Tonson the elder, who purchased Aylmer's rights in *Paradise Lost* in 1683 and 1690. It remained in the possession of the Tonson family until 1772, when it was inherited by William Baker, a grandson of the younger Tonson. Until its recent sale it was in the possession of William Baker's great-great-grandson, Henry Clinton Baker, Esq., of Bayfordbury. The remainder of the Manuscript is unfortunately lost.]

ADDITIONAL APPENDIX B* (PAGES 389–92)

[DRYDEN'S FUNERAL.

It seems certain that preceding the public funeral in the Abbey, Dryden's corpse had been privately buried in his parish church of St. Anne, Soho. The story may be followed in three letters which have lately appeared in the *Athenaeum*—the first from the Rev. Ramsay W. Couper, Curate of St. Anne's, Soho, communicated to the *Athenaeum* on July 30, 1904, the others from Mr. William J. Harvey, to the issues of Aug. 27 and Oct. 22, 1904. Thanks to these letters and to the series of extracts collected by Mr. Harvey from contemporary newspapers, Malone's account of the fate of Dryden's corpse (DRYDEN, 153, 154 *n.*) may be supplemented. Dryden died on Wednesday, May 1, 1700, at three o'clock in the morning. In the case of death by gangrene rapid burial is necessary. Accordingly on May 2, the day after his death, the body was taken to St. Anne's, Soho, which is not five minutes' walk from Dryden's house in Gerrard Street, and privately buried. The Rev. Ramsay W. Couper states that on that day only two names appear in the burial Register. The entry is as follows: '2 May. John Dryden. Sarah Perkins, C.' 'Several Persons of Quality and others' appear to have intervened at this point and prevailed on the relations to have the body embalmed, and on the College of Physicians to have it deposited at the College in Warwick Lane, where it was to lie in state, with a view to a public funeral. Accordingly on

Thursday or Friday the corpse was embalmed and brought to the College of Physicians. By May 7 the arrangements were completed, as is shown by the announcement in *The Post Boy* of that date, which states that 'the Corps of John Dryden, Esq; is to lye in State for some time in the Colledge of Physicians and on Monday next [May 13] he is to be Conveyed from thence in a Hearse in great Splendor to Westminster Abby, where he is to be Interred with Chaucer, Cowley and the rest of the renowned Poets.' Tickets of invitation were issued, desiring those attending the funeral to accompany the corpse from the College of Physicians in Warwick Lane to Westminster Abbey. The funeral took place on May 13, as announced, and was preceded by the strange ceremony at the College [DRYDEN, 153, 154 *n.*]. In *The Post Man* and *The Post Boy* under May 14, 1700, accounts appeared describing how 'the Corps was carried in great state to Westminster Abbey from the Colledge of Physicians . . . attended by above one hundred Coaches of the Chief of our Nobility and Gentry.' Both papers describe the ceremony at the College preceding the removal of the corpse, when Dr. Garth made his 'eloquent oration in Latin in praise of the Deceased, and the Ode of Horace beginning *Monumentum exegi aere perennius*, set to Mournful Musick was sung, with a Consort of Trumpets, Hautboys and other Instruments.' There were present 'a world of People—abundance of the Nobility and Gentry.' Even the little Duke of Gloucester was 'pleased to send one of his Coaches to attend the Funeral.' When the procession set forth on its way to the Abbey, 'the Corps was preceded by several Mourners on Horseback; before the Hearse went the Musick on Foot which made a very Harmonious Noise; the Hearse was followed by 20 Coaches drawn by 6 Horses and 24 drawn by 2 Horses each, most of them in Mourning.'

In spite of all the splendour of the funeral, twenty years were to pass by before Dryden had a monument in the Abbey. 'Last Monday [Jan. 23, 1721] was first expos'd to publick View the Curious Marble Tomb of Mr. Dryden . . . erected to his Memory by his Grace the Duke of Buckingham.' *Weekly Journal*, Jan. 28, 1720-1.]

END OF VOLUME I